FINANCIAL MARKETS

Instruments and Concepts

EDITED BY

John R. Brick

Michigan State University

ROBERT F. DAME, INC.
1905 Huguenot Road
Richmond, Virginia 23235

To Martha, Kerry, Bridget and Jeffrey

© Robert F. Dame, Inc. 1981
Second Printing, 1982

ISBN 0-936-328-08-8
Library of Congress Catalog No. 81-66816

PRINTED IN THE UNITED STATES OF AMERICA

Designed and typeset by Publications Development Co. of
Crockett, Texas, Developmental Editor: Nancy Marcus Land,
Production Editor: Bessie Graham

Preface

One of the distinguishing aspects of the United States economy relative to those of other countries is its well-developed system of financial markets. In recent years these markets have been subjected to unusual stresses resulting from historically high interest rates and unparalleled volatility in both interest rates and the values of financial assets. The effects of such conditions are pervasive and potentially destructive. Many corporate borrowers find it difficult or even impossible to obtain the capital necessary to expand and create jobs. Even those firms with continual access to the capital markets are often forced to accept less-than-optimal financial arrangements. Mortgage loans for homebuyers become restricted and expensive, thus limiting the benefits of homeownership. The solvency of many businesses, banks, credit unions, savings and loan associations, pension funds, and other organizations becomes jeopardized. The primary culprit, of course, is inflation.

In response to these inflation-induced conditions, technological advances, and a "de-regulation" environment, the pace of financial innovation in the market has accelerated. The result has been a broad range of changes in market instruments and procedures and the development of entirely new financing mechanisms. Among the new mechanisms are *variable rate CDs, Eurodollar CDs, short-term investment pools, variable rate mortgages, graduated payment mortgages, shared appreciation mortgages, pass-through securities, mortgage-backed bonds, money market funds, interest rate futures*, and *exchange-traded options*. In addition, market participation has opened to more firms in recent years. For example, it was once necessary for an issuer of *commercial paper* to be a large, well-known, and prime borrower. However, the availability of commercial paper backed by bank letters of credit, or *documented discount notes*, has allowed smaller and less well-known firms to tap this market. With the passage of the *Depository Institutions Deregulation and Monetary Control Act of 1980*, nonbank depository institutions were allowed access to the *discount window*. Similarly, in 1981 credit unions were permitted to engage in *federal funds* transactions for the first time. The purpose of these and the many other structural changes that have occurred was to enable businesses, financial institutions, governments, individuals, and other market participants to cope with a volatile and uncertain financial environment. As a result, the financial markets of the 1980s bear scant resemblance to those that existed in the 1960s and throughout much of the 1970s.

Notwithstanding these changes, certain analytical and conceptual aspects of the financial markets remain intact. However, the high degree of volatility of interest rates and asset prices has increased the overall riskiness of all segments of the financial markets. As a result, it has become increasingly important from a decision-making standpoint to understand analytical relationships and conceptual issues that relate to absolute and relative pricing, risk and return, forecasting, and equilibrium relationships.

Against this background, the objectives of this book are twofold. The first is to provide an overview of the contemporary financial markets with particular emphasis on the instruments, their markets, and the innovations and changes that have occurred in recent years. The second objective is to improve the financial decision-making process by focusing on applications, concepts, and relationships. In order to accomplish these objectives, the readings in this book were selected on the basis of several criteria. In addition to readability, it was essential that each article focus on an important aspect of the financial markets or related conceptual issues. In order to reflect the changes that have occurred, it was also essential that most of the articles be current. Twenty-four of the thirty-five articles have original publication dates of 1979 or later. Thirteen of the articles were published for the first time in 1981. Several of the articles were written specifically for this book.

The book is designed for use in courses that deal with *financial markets*. Because of the nature of the subject matter and the range of topics covered in the readings, the book is also an appropriate supplement in courses dealing with *bank management* and the *management of financial institutions*. On the practitioner level, the book may be used as an educational vehicle by the managers of financial institutions, cash managers, portfolio managers, and individual investors.

The book is divided into four parts as follows:

Part   I   Money Market Instruments
Part II   Capital Market Instruments
Part III   Market Relationships and Concepts
Part IV   Regulation and Financial Innovations

In addition to covering the instruments, Part I focuses on their individual markets and the money market as a whole. Part II covers *capital market instruments* and is further divided into four sections—*the bond market, the equity market, mortgage-related instruments*, and *interest rate futures*. The articles in Part III focus on analytical concepts that explain market behavior and link the various instruments and markets together. Some of the more prominent effects of both regulation and de-regulation are examined in the articles contained in Part IV. *Money market funds, short-term investment pools*, and *innovations as they affect the nation's payments system* are among the topics covered.

As is the case with most other books, a number of acknowledgments are in order. First, we are deeply indebted to the authors and their respective organizations, as well as the copyright holders for granting permission to reprint these articles. The editor would also like to acknowledge the able assistance of Bruce S. Berlin and Bruce T. Colasanti, graduate assistants at Michigan State University, Nancy Marcus Land of Publications Development Company of Texas, Helen A. Church of Michigan State University, and Diane Lashua of Robert F. Dame, Inc. Also, the editor is especially grateful to the publisher, Robert F. Dame, for his help and cooperation. In addition, John M. Finkelstein of the University of Florida, Timothy Q. Cook of the Federal Reserve Bank of Richmond, and Kelly Price of Wayne State University were particularly helpful in the development of this book and deserve special mention.

John R. Brick

Michigan State University
East Lansing, Michigan
June, 1981

Contents

Part I

Money
Market Instruments

The readings in Part I of this book focus on the money market and the various instruments that make up this market. These instruments are characterized by their short-term, high quality, marketability, and liquidity. Because of these characteristics, money market instruments play a key role in the management of financial institutions, non-financial corporations, trust funds, state and local governments, universities, and mutual funds. Such instruments often constitute a large proportion of assets of financial institutions. By their very nature, financial institutions have considerable uncertainty associated with their cash flows. The availability of a broad spectrum of money market instruments facilitates the management of short-term funds. Furthermore, when held as assets in financial institutions, many of these instruments may be used to satisfy legal reserve requirements and liquidity requirements imposed by management. In addition to being an asset, or outlet for funds, certain instruments may be issued by financial institu-

tions as liabilities and, as such, they constitute an on-going source of funds. For example, a commercial bank may both buy and sell federal funds, certificates of deposit, and bankers' acceptances. In this way, banks may operate on both sides of the money market.

Some non-financial corporations issue money market instruments such as commercial paper or obtain "acceptance" financing. However, in non-financial corporations, trust funds, universities, or other organizations with large cash flows, the primary interest in money market instruments is as short-term investments. The double-digit interest rates that have prevailed in recent years has resulted in considerable emphasis on the *cash management* process by these market participants. By collecting funds as quickly as possible and investing the proceeds in money market instruments, cash managers have been contributing significantly to the overall profitability of many firms and organizations. The investment of "lumpy" cash flows that result from tuition payments to universi-

1

ties and property tax collections by municipalities are other examples of how these instruments are used and their significance. The enormous growth of money market funds and other short-term investment pools that specialize in money market instruments is further testimony to the significance of these instruments in the financial system. (These specialized mutual funds and short-term investment pools are covered in the last section of the book.)

Like so many other aspects of the financial market system, most of the money market instruments and their individual markets have undergone dramatic changes or modifications in recent years. These changes are reflected in the articles in this section.

The first article, by James Parthemos and Timothy Q. Cook, provides a brief description of the *money market* and how it functions. The article by Charles Lucas, Marcos Jones, and Thom Thurston is a thorough discussion of two of the most important and yet obscure money market instruments—*federal funds* and *repurchase agreements*. The interest rates on these instruments are the most volatile and among the most closely watched in the financial markets. The article on *Treasury bills* by Timothy Q. Cook summarizes the characteristics of the best known of all money market instruments. The character-

istics of *Federally sponsored agency securities* are examined in Donna Howell's article. With the passage of the *Depository Institutions Deregulation and Monetary Control Act of 1980*, the operations of the *discount window* of the Federal Reserve System were changed dramatically. For example, non-bank depository institutions such as credit unions, savings and loan associations, and mutual savings banks were allowed access to window borrowing. This and other aspects of the discount window are discussed in the article by James Parthemos and Walter Varvel. Although they are one of the safest of the private-sector money market instruments, *bankers' acceptances* are relatively unknown outside the banking community. In his definitive article, Jack L. Hervey provides a thorough explanation of this instrument and its function as both a source and use of funds.

Negotiable certificates of deposit (CDs) are, like Treasury bills, well-known. Unlike Treasury bills, however, this instrument and its market have undergone significant changes in recent years in response to the needs of market participants. The market is no longer limited to fixed-rate CDs issued by domestic commercial banks, as explained in Bruce J. Summers' article. Terms such as *Yankee CDs, variable rate CDs, thrift institution CDs,* and *Eurodollar CDs* are now integral parts of market terminology.

Like CDs, the *commercial paper* market has changed in recent years. In addition to such topics as tax-exempt paper, foreign issuers, and basic market characteristics, the relationship between the commercial paper market and bank lending is explained in Peter Abken's article.

In the last article in this section, Marvin Goodfriend discusses the *Eurodollar* market. The characteristics of this market, the various types of instruments, and the risks involved in Eurodollar transactions are among the topics covered.

THE MONEY MARKET*

James Parthemos

1

Economic units, such as financial institutions, other business firms, governmental units, and even individuals, find, as a rule, that their inflow of cash receipts does not coincide exactly with their cash disbursements. The typical economic unit finds that on some days its cash holdings build up because receipts exceed outlays. On other days, it might experience a sharp reduction in cash balances because spending outstrips cash inflow.

One of the most important reasons for holding cash reserves is to bridge the gap between receipts and outlays and to insure that a planned stream of expenditures can be maintained somewhat independently of cash inflow. There are, of course, other reasons for holding reserves. In particular, depository institutions must meet legal reserve requirements.[1]

Maintenance of cash reserves involves cost, either in the form of interest paid on borrowed balances, or in the form of interest foregone on non-borrowed balances which have not been lent out. For many economic units, especially large firms, these costs can be significant, particularly in periods of high interest rates. To minimize such costs, economic units usually seek

*Reprinted, with deletions, from *Instruments of the Money Market*, 5th edition, edited by Timothy Q. Cook and Bruce T. Summers, 1981, with permission from the Federal Reserve Bank of Richmond.

[1] As a result of the Depository Institutions Deregulation and Monetary Control Act of 1980, all depository institutions must meet Federal reserve requirements on reservable liabilities, i. e., transactions accounts and nonpersonal time deposits. These requirements are prescribed in Regulation D of the Federal Reserve System.

to keep their cash holdings at a minimum consistent with their working capital needs and, in the case of depository institutions, with their reserve requirements. This may be done by holding low risk and highly marketable income bearing assets instead of cash and by maintaining access to the market for short-term credit. The *money market* has evolved to meet the needs of such economic units.

THE MONEY MARKET

The term "money market" applies not to one but rather to a group of markets. In the early part of the United States' financial history, the term was frequently used in a narrow sense to denote the market for call loans to securities brokers and dealers. At other times in the past, it has been employed broadly to embrace some long-term as well as short-term markets. In current usage, the term "money market" generally refers to the markets for short term credit instruments such as Treasury bills, commercial paper, bankers' acceptances, negotiable certificates of deposit (CDs), loans to security dealers repurchase agreements, and Federal funds.

In general, money market instruments are issued by obligors of the highest credit rating, and are characterized by a high degree of safety of principal Maturities may be as long as one year but usually are of 90 days or less, and sometimes span only a few days or even one day. The market for money market instruments is extremely broad and on a given day it can absorb a large volume of transactions with relatively little effect on yields. The market is also highly efficient and allows quick, convenient, and low cost trading in virtually any volume. Unlike organized securities or commodities markets, the money market has no specific location. Like other important financial markets in this country, its center is in New York, but it is primarily a 'telephone" market and is easily accessible from all parts of the nation as well as foreign financial centers. No economic unit is ever more than a telephone call away from the money market.

At the center of the money market are numerous "money market banks," including the large banks in New York and other important financial centers; about 34 Government securities dealers, some of which are large banks; a dozen odd commercial paper dealers; a few bankers' acceptance dealers; and a number of money brokers who specialize in finding short-term funds for money market borrowers and placing such funds for money market lenders. The most important money market brokers are the major Federal funds brokers in New York.

MARKET PARTICIPANTS

Apart from the groups that provide the basic trading machinery, money market participants usually enter the market either to raise short-term funds or to convert cash surpluses into highly liquid interest-bearing investments. Funds may be raised by borrowing outright, by selling holdings of money market instruments, or by issuing new instruments. The issue and sale of new money market instruments is, of course, a form of borrowing.

Generally, money market rates are below the prime lending rates of the large money market banks. Consequently, borrowers who have the ability to do so find it advantageous to tap the money market directly rather than obtaining funds through banking intermediaries. The U. S. Treasury, many commercial banks, large sales finance companies, and well-known nonfinancial corporations of the highest credit standing borrow regularly in the money market by issuing their own short-term debt obligations. Short-term loans to Government securities dealers, loans of reserves among depository institutions and Federal Reserve discount window loans to depository institutions are also money market instruments although they do not give rise to negotiable paper.

Suppliers of funds in the market are those who buy money market instruments or make very short-term loans. Potentially, these include all those economic units that can realize a significant gain through arranging to meet future cash requirements by holding interest-bearing liquid assets in place of nonbearing cash balances. The major participants on this side of the market are commercial banks, state and local governments, large nonfinancial businesses, nonbank financial institutions, and foreign bank and nonbank businesses. In recent years individuals have also become a significant supplier of funds to the money market both indirectly through investment in short-term investment pools such as money market mutual funds and directly through the purchase of Treasury bills and short-term Federal agency securities.

By far the most important market participant is the Federal Reserve System. Through the Open Market Trading Desk at the New York Federal Reserve Bank, which executes the directives of the Federal Open Market Committee. the System is in the market on a virtually continuous basis, either as a buyer or as a seller, depending on financial conditions and monetary policy objectives. The System's purpose in entering the market is quite different from that of other participants, however. As noted in greater detail below, the Federal Reserve buys and sells in certain parts of the money market not with the objective of managing its own cash position more efficiently but rather to supply or withdraw bank reserves in order to achieve its monetary policy objectives. In addition, the Federal Reserve enters the market as an agent, sometimes as a buyer and sometimes as a seller, for the accounts of foreign official institutions and for the U. S. Treasury. Overall, the operations of the Federal Reserve dwarf those of any other money market participant.

INTERRELATION AND SIZE OF THE VARIOUS MARKET SECTORS

While the various money market instruments have their individual differences, they nonetheless are close substitutes for each other in many investment portfolios. For this reason the rates of return on the various instruments tend to fluctuate closely together. For short periods of time, the rate of return on a particular instrument may diverge from the rest or "get out of line," but this sets in motion forces which tend to pull the rates back together. For example, a large supply of new commercial paper may produce a rapid run-up of commercial paper rates, resulting in a relatively large spread between these rates and rates on CDs. Sophisticated traders note the abnormal differential and shift funds from CDs into commercial paper, causing CD rates to rise and commercial paper rates to fall. In this way, a more "normal" or usual rate relation is restored. This process, known as interest arbitrage, insures general conformity of all money market rates to major interest rate movements.

THE MARKET'S SIGNIFICANCE

The money market provides an important source of short-term funds for many borrowers. In addition, since there is a continuous flow of loan funds through the market, it is possible for borrowers, through successive "roll-overs," or renewals of loans, to raise funds on a more or less continuous basis and in this fashion to finance not only their immediate cash requirements but also working capital and some long-term capital needs as well. By bringing together quickly and conveniently those units with cash surpluses and those with cash deficits, the market promotes a more intensive use of the cash balances held in the economy.

The market is especially important to commercial banks in managing their money positions. Banks in the aggregate are large-scale buyers and sellers of most money market instruments, especially Federal funds. The money market permits a more intensive use of bank reserves and enhances the ability of the commercial banking system to allocate funds efficiently. By allowing banks to operate with lower excess reserves, it also makes the banking system more sensitive to central bank policy actions.[2]

Finally, conditions in the money market provide an important guide for monetary policy. The money market is an eminently free and competitive market, and the yields on money market instruments react instantaneously to changes in supply and demand. As a result, the behavior of the market provides the most immediate indication of the current relationship between credit supplies and credit demands.

THE FEDERAL RESERVE AND THE MONEY MARKET

The Federal Reserve System influences the money market not only through open market operations but also through the discount windows of the 12 Federal Reserve Banks. Commercial banks may borrow short-term from the Federal Reserve to meet temporary liquidity needs and to cover reserve deficiencies as an alternative to selling money market securities or borrowing Federal funds. Similarly, banks with cash or reserve surpluses can repay outstanding borrowings at the Federal Reserve rather than invest the surpluses in money market instruments.

Reserve adjustments made by individual institutions using the discount window differ in one important respect from alternative adjustment techniques. Trading in such instruments as Federal funds, negotiable certificates of deposit, and Treasury bills among commercial banks or between banks and their customers involves no net creation of new bank reserves. Rather, existing reserves are simply shifted about within the banking system. On the other hand, net borrowings or repayments at the discount window result in a net change in Federal Reserve credit outstanding and, consequently, they affect the volume of bank reserves. Thus, the choice by individual institutions between using the discount window or alternative means of reserve adjustment may influence the supply of money and credit in the economy. Decisions to use the discount window or raise funds elsewhere in the money market depend importantly upon the relation of the Federal Reserve's discount rate to yields on money market investments and on the legal and administrative arrangements surrounding use of the discount window. Both sets of factors are determined primarily by Federal Reserve actions.

The daily operations of the Federal Open Market Trading Desk occupy

[2] As the phase-in of required reserves for nonbank depository institutions, mandated by the Monetary Control Act of 1980, progresses, it is likely that these institutions will also become active in the market for reserve funds.

a central role in the money market. For many years the Desk has conducted transactions in U. S. Government securities and in bankers' acceptances, and in December 1966 it was authorized to conduct operations in Federal Agency issues also. The Federal Reserve enters the market frequently either to provide new depository institution reserves through purchases or to withdraw reserves through sales. To a large extent, Federal Reserve operations are undertaken to compensate for changes in other factors that affect the volume of reserves, such as float, Treasury balances, and currency in circulation. Such operations are undertaken primarily to insure the smooth technical functioning of the market mechanism. But the operations of the greatest importance from the standpoint of the economy are those undertaken by the Federal Reserve to achieve its policy objectives. Since the early 1970s these objectives have centered on achieving targeted growth rates of the money supply. Thus, in addition to its other functions, the money market serves as the mechanism for implementing the Federal Reserve's objectives.

FEDERAL FUNDS AND REPURCHASE AGREEMENTS*

Charles M. Lucas, Marcos T. Jones, and Thom Thurston

2

The markets for Federal funds and repurchase agreements (RPs) are among the most important financial markets in the United States. Using these instruments, many banks, large corporations, and nonbank financial firms trade large amounts of liquid funds with one another for periods as short as one day. Such institutions provide and use much of the credit made available in the United States and typically manage their financial positions carefully and aggressively. The interest rate on overnight (one day) Federal funds measures the return on the most liquid of all financial assets, and for this reason is critical to investment decisions.

The Federal funds market is also important because it is related to the conduct of Federal Reserve monetary policy. The interest rate on Federal funds is highly sensitive to Federal Reserve actions that supply reserves to member commercial banks, and the rate influences commercial bank decisions concerning loans to business, individual, and other borrowers. Moreover, interest rates paid on other short-term financial assets—commercial paper and Treasury bills, for example—usually move up or down roughly in parallel with the Federal funds rate. Thus the rate also influences the cost of credit obtained from sources other than commercial banks.

Frequently, the Federal funds market is described as one in which commercial banks borrow and lend excess reserve balances held at the Federal Reserve, hence the name Federal funds. While banks often use the Federal

---

*Reprinted, with deletions, from the *Quarterly Review*, Summer 1977, pp. 33-48, with permission, from the Federal Reserve Bank of New York and the authors.

funds market for this purpose, growth and change in the market have made this description highly oversimplified. Many active market participants do not hold balances at the Federal Reserve. These include commercial banks that are not members of the Federal Reserve System, thrift institutions, certain agencies of the United States Government, and branches and agencies of foreign banks operating on United States soil. Moreover, this broad set of market participants borrows and lends amounts far beyond the modest total of excess reserve balances.

A closely related market for short-term funds is the market for RPs involving United States Government and Federal agency securities.[1] This market includes many of the same participants that trade Federal funds, but it also includes large nonfinancial corporations, state and local governments, and dealers in United States Government and Federal agency securities. The RP market has expanded rapidly of late, and its workings are perhaps less widely known than those of the Federal funds market.

Although the Federal funds and RP markets are distinct, they share many common features. Both, for example, primarily involve transactions for one business day, although transactions with maturities of up to several weeks are not uncommon. In both markets, commercial banks that are members of the Federal Reserve System can acquire funds not subject to reserve requirements. A lesser known but nevertheless very important common element is the fact that transactions in both markets are settled in what are known as "immediately available funds". Indeed, some observers see the two markets as so closely related that they might appropriately be grouped together under a broader designation—"the markets for short-term immediately available funds". For an elaboration of the nature and uses of immediately available funds, see Box.

The main purpose of this article is to review major recent developments in the markets for Federal funds and RPs. The most significant changes are the dramatic growth of the volume of transactions and of the number and type of institutions active in these markets. At the same time, the language of the market has been changing, mostly because of the evolution in market practices. It is, therefore, necessary to begin with definitions of some terms most frequently used by market participants.

FEDERAL FUNDS

Federal funds transactions are frequently described as the borrowing and

---

[1] The term "Federal agency" is used here in its popular meaning, which refers both to Federal agencies, such as the Commodity Credit Corporation, and to Federally sponsored quasi-public corporations, such as the Federal National Mortgage Association.

lending of "excess reserve" balances among commercial banks.[2] This description of Federal funds was accurate years ago but is now seriously deficient, even though it still appears in the financial press. While such commercial bank use of the market persists in substantial volume, Federal funds transactions are no longer confined to the borrowing and lending of excess reserve balances. Moreover—and this is a key point—a Federal funds transaction does not necessarily involve transfer of a reserve balance, even though such a transfer usually does occur. For example, a commercial bank can borrow the "correspondent balances" held with it by other banks. The execution of such a transaction involves only accounting entries on the books of both the borrower and lender.

The most useful description of Federal funds has several elements, some based on regulations, others simply on market convention. In practice, Federal funds are overnight loans that are settled in immediately available funds. Only a limited group of institutions are in a position to borrow in this fashion, mostly commercial banks and some other financial institutions such as agencies of foreign banks. If a member bank borrows Federal funds, Federal Reserve regulations do not require it to hold reserves against the borrowing, as it must for funds acquired in the form of demand or time deposits. But, under Federal Reserve regulations, member banks are permitted to borrow reserve-free funds only from a certain group of institutions. This group includes other commercial banks, Federal agencies, savings and loan associations, mutual savings banks, domestic agencies and branches of foreign banks, and, to a limited degree, Government securities dealers. Market convention has adjusted to these regulatory restrictions, and a Federal funds borrowing has come to mean an overnight loan not just between two commercial banks but between any two of the group of institutions from which member banks may borrow free of reserve requirements. A savings and loan association, for example, can lend Federal funds to an agency of a foreign bank.

This description makes it easy to see that the Federal funds market is by no means limited to the lending of excess reserves. Many of the institutions that participate in the market are not members of the Federal Reserve System and, therefore, do not have reserve accounts. Moreover, the excess reserves of individual member banks are normally very small in relation to their total reserves. The excess reserves characterization of Federal funds borrowing suggests that total activity in the market is likewise rather modest. While this was once true, it no longer is. In recent years,

---

[2] A fundamental difficulty with this notion of Federal funds borrowing is that the use of the term "excess reserves" is very imprecise. No distinction is made between the actual excess reserves held in a bank's reserve account and what might be called "potential" excess reserves. Clearly, an individual bank can control the amount of excess reserves it has available to sell in the Federal funds market most easily by selling assets and converting the proceeds into balances at a Federal Reserve Bank. In this sense, the potential excess reserves of an individual bank are nearly as large as its total earning asset portfolio.

IMMEDIATELY AVAILABLE FUNDS

The Means of Settlement for Transactions in Federal Funds and RPs

An essential feature of both Federal funds and RPs is that transactions are settled in "immediately available funds". Therefore it is necessary to specify precisely what such funds are. Immediately available funds are two related but distinct types of financial claims: (1) deposit liabilities of Federal Reserve Banks and (2) certain "collected" liabilities of commercial banks that may be transferred or withdrawn during a business day on the order of account holders.

Federal Reserve Banks, of course, are "banks for banks", and deposits are held there mainly by commercial banks that are members of the Federal Reserve System in order to satisfy the reserve requirements imposed on members. These deposits have special features, however. Along with currency and coin, they are the only form of money created directly by a Federal authority. This reflects the fact that these deposits are the direct liabilities of the Federal Reserve Banks. In addition, the Federal Reserve operates a nationwide electronic communications network over which these deposits can be transferred anywhere in the country within a business day. Deposits at Federal Reserve Banks are therefore termed immediately available funds, since they can be converted to cash or transferred anywhere in the United States within a single day on demand.

Immediately available funds also consist of certain collected liabilities of commercial banks. This group of liabilities include a portion of a bank's demand and time deposits, as well as certain other liabilities which are used very much like deposits but which are classed separately for accounting or regulatory reasons. These liabilities are termed immediately available funds because commercial banks permit them to be withdrawn in cash or used for payment without question within a single day. The immediate and unquestioned use of these bank liabilities for payment depends on the fact that they are collected, a feature which can be illustrated by describing how an individual's checking deposit with a bank becomes collected.

Typically, an individual increases his bank balance by depositing checks payable to him drawn on the same or some other bank. When the check is drawn on some other bank, the individual is normally unable to withdraw or otherwise use the funds on the same day that the deposit is made. Frequently, several days elapse, during which time the credit to the depositor's account is only provisional and the check is in the process of being collected. That is, it is cleared and then payment is received by the depositor's bank from the bank on which the check is drawn. Payment may be received in any one of several forms: a deposit at a Federal Reserve Bank, a collected deposit at another commercial bank, or conceivably in currency or coin. Whatever the case, once collected, the individual's balance can be transferred on his order.

Alternatively, a depositor may receive payment to his account in immediately available funds. In this case, the funds can be withdrawn in cash or otherwise used on the day of receipt with no intervening period for collection. For credit to be received immediately, the deposit must be made in some form other than the common check. The most obvious alternative is cash, used frequently for small deposits but only rarely for sizable transactions because of the risk of loss.

More commonly, when the depositor wishes to receive immediately available funds, the transfer is accomplished through the Federal Reserve electronic communications network. This network is used either within or between Federal Reserve Districts. Any member bank may send or receive immediately available funds—in the form of reserve deposits—to or from any other member bank, and the entire transfer takes place within one business day. The use of the Federal Reserve network can be accomplished indirectly by individuals or institutions other than member banks. This requires the transfer of a depositor's collected balance from one member bank to another, in effect using a reserve balance at the Federal Reserve as a means of payment between banks. If the transaction results in a transfer of funds from one account to another within a single bank, only balance-sheet entries are affected since there need be no actual movement of funds over the Federal Reserve network.

Immediately available funds can be used by a customer of a commercial bank to make payment in any sort of transaction. Among the principal users are sizable financial, business, and government institutions. In practice, such funds are used only for large transactions including, for example, payment for purchase of a financial asset, for raw materials, or for a construction contract. In all these cases, immediately available funds are used as a means of payment because the parties to the transactions wish to use them. Thus, not all transactions involving the use of immediately available funds are related to either the Federal funds or the repurchase agreement markets.

daily outstanding borrowings by member banks in the Federal funds market have approached $50 billion, or about 40 percent more than the *total* reserves they hold. Some individual banks continually borrow as much as four times their required reserves in the Federal funds market.

Fairly recently, banks have begun to borrow immediately available funds for periods longer than a single business day. This form of borrowing was developed by agencies of Canadian banks located in the United States. The transactions are arranged among the same institutions which participate in the overnight market and are similar in all respects except maturity. For these reasons, the transactions have come to be called "term Federal funds" transactions.

The Federal funds and term Federal funds transactions described above are normally "unsecured". This means that the lending institutions have no guarantee of repayment other than the promise of the borrower. For this reason, unsecured Federal funds transactions are done only by institutions that enjoy a very high degree of mutual confidence. At times, however, a lender of Federal funds will ask that the transaction be "secured". This means that the borrower must pledge an asset, usually a Government or Federal agency security, as "collateral" against the loan. The borrower may either set aside the collateral in a custody account or actually deliver it to the lender. However, secured Federal funds transactions are not very common.[3]

REPURCHASE AGREEMENTS

A repurchase agreement (RP) is an acquisition of immediately available funds through the sale of securities, together with a simultaneous agreement to repurchase them at a later date. RPs are most commonly made for one business day, though longer maturities are also frequent. The funds that a member bank acquires in this manner are free of reserve requirements so long as the securities involved are those of the United States Government or Federal agencies. When an RP is arranged, the acquirer of funds agrees to sell to the provider of funds United States Government or Federal agency securities in exchange for immediately available funds. At the maturity of the agreement, the transaction is reversed, again using immediately available funds. Market insiders use different terms to describe the RP, including "repo" and "buy back".

Those who supply or acquire funds view RPs as involving little risk. Transactions are usually arranged only among institutions enjoying a high degree

---

[3] Banks chartered in certain states face regulations that require collateral to be provided for the portion of an individual Federal funds transaction in excess of some proportion of the lender's combined capital and surplus.

of confidence in one another. In addition, contracts are usually of very short maturity. Protection against any residual risk can be incorporated in an RP contract by establishing a differential—called a margin—between the quantity of funds supplied and the market value of the securities involved. The margin can protect either party to the transaction, but not both. It protects the supplier of funds if the value of the securities exceeds the quantity of funds supplied. It protects the taker of funds if the securities are of less value than the amount of funds supplied. The supplier of funds generally considers the consequences of default by the other party to be minor, because the securities acquired are obligations either issued or guaranteed by the Federal Government. Another element of risk arises from the possibility that the price of the securities may fall between the time the RP is arranged and the time of any default. For this reason, the margin is most often set to protect the supplier of funds.

This article is concerned with RPs involving only United States Government and Federal agency securities, but it should be noted in passing that an RP can involve any sort of asset which the supplier of funds is willing to accept. RPs involving other assets are executed to a limited degree, for example using certificates of deposit of large banks.

Transactions are executed in several ways, but two approaches are most common. One approach is for the securities to be both sold and repurchased at the same price, with charges representing the agreed-upon rate of return added to the principal at the maturity of the contract. The second approach involves setting a higher price for repayment than for selling.

The term "reverse repurchase agreement" is sometimes thought to be quite different from an RP. In fact, it refers to exactly the same transaction viewed from the perspective of the supplier of funds rather than the recipient. Compare the two views of the transaction: The recipient of funds sells a security to obtain funds, and "repurchases" it at maturity by redelivery of funds. In a reverse RP, the supplier of funds buys a security by delivering funds when the agreement is made and "resells" the security for immediately available funds on maturity of the contract. From the perspective of the party acquiring funds, the term "repurchase agreement" seems apt, and from that of the supplier of funds, the transaction is exactly the "reverse". However, whether funds are acquired or supplied, the transaction is usually referred to in the marketplace simply as an RP.

THE MARKETS FOR FEDERAL FUNDS AND RPs

There is no central physical marketplace for Federal funds; the market consists of a loosely structured telephone network connecting the major participants. These participants, as already mentioned, include commercial banks and those other financial institutions from which, under Federal Reserve regulations, member banks can buy reserve-free Federal funds. The market also includes a small group of firms that act as brokers for Federal funds. These firms neither lend nor borrow but arrange transactions between borrowers and lenders in exchange for a very small percentage commission.

All major participants employ traders. These individuals make the actual telephone contact on behalf of lending or borrowing institutions, making offers to borrow or lend at specific interest rates. They also negotiate any differences between the rate bid by a borrower and that offered by a lender. Transactions are usually executed in lots of $1 million or more. Frequently, but not always, settlement of the transaction requires transfer of funds over the Federal Reserve wire transfer network, first when the agreement is reached and again the next day when repayment is made.

Many banks, particularly medium-sized and large ones, frequently borrow and lend Federal funds on the same day, thereby performing an intermediary function in the Federal funds market. Such banks channel funds from banks with lesser need for funds to banks with greater need for them, frequently borrowing from smaller banks and lending to larger ones. Over the past decade, more medium-sized regional banks have begun to act as intermediaries. In addition, many more banks during this period have come to borrow significantly more than they lend, that is, they have become continual net borrowers.

In recent years a growing portion of the market has consisted of large banks' borrowing of correspondent balances from small banks. Historically, these correspondent balances earned no interest. But both large and small banks have come to regard correspondent relationships as convenient bases for arranging Federal funds transactions. Small banks now intentionally accumulate large balances selling off daily the excess not needed for the clearing of checks or for other purposes. In such cases, it is not necessary to transfer funds over the Federal Reserve wire transfer network, and reserve balances need not change ownership. Rather, bookkeeping entries are posted by both the borrower and lender to reflect the fact that a non-interest-bearing correspondent demand balance has been converted into a Federal funds borrowing.

No central physical marketplace for repurchase agreements exists either. Transactions are arranged by telephone, largely on a direct basis between the parties supplying and acquiring funds but increasingly through a small group of market specialists. These specialists, mostly Government securities dealers, arrange a repurchase agreement with one party to acquire funds and a reverse repurchase agreement with another party to supply funds. They earn a profit by acquiring funds more cheaply than they supply them.

Large banks and Government securities dealers are the primary seekers of funds in the RP market. Banks use the market as one among many sources of funds, but have a distinct advantage over other institutions as acquirers of funds because they hold large portfolios of United States Government and Federal agency securities. Moreover, because the supplier of funds receives securities, and because member banks acquiring funds need not hold reserves against RPs regardless of the source of funds, the RP market attracts a wider array of participants than does the Federal funds market. Government securities dealers use the market as a source of funds to finance their holdings of Government and agency securities. Many types of institutions supply immediately available funds in this market, but large non-financial corporations and state and local governments dominate.

Typically, participants on both sides of the RP market have lists of customers with whom they routinely do business. Each of the largest participants uses an "RP trader", an individual whose job it is to contact other traders and to negotiate the best arrangements possible. A trader begins the day with information on the amount of funds he must supply or acquire. His objective is to arrange transactions at the maximum return obtainable if he is to provide funds and at the minimum cost possible if he is to acquire funds.

With these definitions and descriptions in mind, it is possible to discuss in some detail the roles of the major institutional participants in the markets for immediately available funds. It is appropriate to begin with an examination of the role played by commercial banks, who are currently the most important of those who obtain funds in these markets. Moreover, the reserve position adjustments that banks make in the markets for immediately available funds are important links in transmitting the effects of monetary policy throughout the financial system.

COMMERCIAL BANKS AND IMMEDIATELY AVAILABLE FUNDS

Commercial banks are the largest and most active participants in the markets for immediately available funds. Banks use these markets for several purposes, among which is the day-to-day adjustment of reserve positions. Large banks have made such adjustments in the Federal funds market for over fifty years and continue to do so in substantial volume. But commercial bank use of both the Federal funds and the RP markets is best understood in the much broader context of how banks obtain and use funds. In addition, bank operations in the Federal funds and RP markets have been heavily influenced by changes in the regulations that govern bank activities.

The traditional view of banks has been that they accept deposit liabilities from customers and use the funds to lend or invest. In the process, they make a profit by earning more in interest on loans and investments than their cost of operations, including interest they pay on deposits. This approach has undergone significant modification over the past decade at least, particularly at large banks. In place of a passive stance, banks have become active solicitors of funds in the open markets. Moreover, they have developed liabilities in addition to standard demand and savings accounts. Fifteen years ago, for example, banks developed and began to exploit the negotiable certificate of deposit (CD). More recently, Euro-dollars, commercial paper issued by bank holding companies, and other instruments have been developed and used as sources of funds. Large banks set a target for the total amount of liabilities they will attempt to secure, basing that target on the total of loans and investments thought to be profitable. The overall approach, summarized here in its barest outlines, is generally known as "liability management".

The spread of the practice of liability management has had two related effects on commercial bank activity in the Federal funds market. First, instead of just engaging in relatively small trades for the purpose of making daily reserve adjustments, today banks may rely on this market to meet a desired proportion of liabilities. Thus, they at times borrow amounts that are large relative to their total assets or liabilities. Second, instead of individual banks lending as often as they borrow, some banks are continual net borrowers, while others are continual lenders. The borrowers use the market both to offset the impact on their reserve holdings of day-to-day inflows and outflows of deposits and as an ongoing source of funds to finance loans and investments. The lenders, usually smaller banks, treat Federal funds as a highly liquid interest-earning short-term asset.

RECENT DEVELOPMENTS IN THE BANKING SECTOR

Some rather dramatic events occurred in the markets for immediately available funds beginning in 1973. Monetary policy was tightened that year in response to rapid inflation and a booming economy. The tightening placed severe pressure on the banking system—which had a limited supply of funds and faced strong demand for loans, particularly from businesses. Under these circumstances, banks with a strong liability management orientation turned to any and all potential sources of funds. In early 1973, large banks began to borrow heavily in the CD market. This borrowing was facilitated by the suspension in May 1973 of interest rate ceilings on all maturities of large denomination CDs. From early 1973 through mid-1974, CD borrowing jumped by about $38 billion. Large banks sought short-term open market funds to meet loan demands much more heavily than before, taking in about $18 billion of additional Federal funds and RPs during the same period.

The United States economy went through a sharp recession between late 1973 and early 1975. Demand for credit from commercial banks as well as other lenders remained strong for a time, but progressively weakened through the later stages of the downslide and into the recovery which began in mid-1975. With loans contracting, large banks gradually reduced their lending rates and also sought liabilities with lessened intensity. Their CDs dropped sharply, falling by $28 billion between early 1975 and late 1976. Commercial bank acquisition of Federal funds and RPs, however, did not follow the pattern set in the CD market. Holdings of these funds declined by only about $4 billion in late 1974 and 1975, then grew by about $17 billion in 1976. This reflected a continuing basic growth of the markets for Federal funds and RPs.

The basic growth also was manifest in the continuing entry of banks into the markets for immediately available funds. Call reports of member banks of the Federal Reserve System show that in 1969 about 55 percent of all member banks either bought or sold Federal funds. By 1976, the proportion of member banks that was in the market had climbed to 88 percent. Most of the new entrants to the market were small banks.

Thus, even in the early 1970s many commercial banks were newcomers to the markets for immediately available funds. These markets broadened and deepened in stages which typically occurred in periods of high interest rates. The concentration of entry in such periods is due at least partially to sizable start-up expenditures for trading in immediately available funds. Start-up costs are incurred mostly by borrowers, and mainly involve expenses of finding and establishing a trading relationship with potential suppliers of funds. The expenditures are more easily justified when interest rates (and potential earnings) are high. Once established, trading relationships tend to remain active even after interest rates fall.

Other developments also contributed to the greater acquisition of Federal funds and RPs by banks during 1975 and 1976. In 1974, the Treasury changed the way it handled its deposits at commercial banks (Tax and Loan Accounts). Such accounts had been held at banks for decades. Beginning in August 1974, however, most of these balances were transferred to the twelve Federal Reserve Banks. This reduced the volume of Government and agency securities that commercial banks were required to hold as pledged collateral against Treasury deposits. Once free from this purpose, these securities were available for use in the market for repurchase agreements.

With loan demand light in 1975, commercial banks began to accumulate large amounts of additional Government and agency securities. The process was significantly aided by the large amounts of new Government securities the Treasury sold in order to finance the sizable deficits the Federal Government was running. These securities were heavily used by large banks to acquire funds in repurchase agreements since they could be financed in this way at a cost below their interest yield. At about the same time, the effects of the recession led corporations to reduce inventories and expenditures for fixed plant and equipment. This enabled corporations to begin to rebuild their liquidity, partly through the purchase of Government securities and also by supplying funds to the RP market. The use of RPs grew rapidly as corporations increasingly came to view repurchase agreements as income-generating substitutes for demand deposits at commercial banks.

Quite separately, small banks and nonbank financial institutions were also increasing their offerings of immediately available funds. Both types of institutions experienced a decline in loan demand from corporate and other borrowers with the onset of the recession. But individuals stepped up their savings in the form of deposits with small banks and with nonbank thrift institutions. With increasing deposit inflows and declining demand for loans, these institutions looked for alternative investments and became active suppliers of immediately available funds.

THE ROLE OF GOVERNMENT SECURITIES DEALERS

Government securities dealers are the second major group of participants active in the markets for immediately available funds. Dealers are in the markets primarily to acquire funds, but they also supply funds under some circumstances. In some ways dealers act as financial intermediaries, but their operations also have speculative features. Dealers earn income in two ways: "carry income" and "trading profits". Carry income (or loss) refers to the difference between the interest yield of a dealer's portfolio and the cost of the funds which support that portfolio. Trading profits refer to the gain (or loss) a dealer earns by selling securities for more (or less) than the dealer paid for them.

Government securities dealers often hold sizable positions in United States Government and Federal agency securities. These positions are highly leveraged in that the dealers borrow a very high percentage of the cost of purchasing securities. The search for low cost money to finance his position is a central part of the operations of any successful Government securities dealer. This search led the dealer community to promote the use of the repurchase agreement shortly after World War II. RPs were offered mainly to large corporations, which found them attractive because the short maturities of the RP contracts made them much like demand deposits, with the added advantage of earning income. The use of RPs by dealers has expanded ever since, in part because more corporations and others have come to accept the repurchase agreement as a reliable short-term money market instrument. Dealers have also come to vary the size of their positions much more than before, in response to the greater variability of interest rates and securities prices in recent years.

Because of greater interest rate variability, and in an effort to broaden their activities, Government securities dealers have developed new trading techniques and expanded the use of others. One of the greatly expanded techniques enables dealers to act essentially as brokers in the RP markets.

They obtain funds in exchange for securities in one transaction and simultaneously release funds in exchange for securities in a separate transaction. When the maturities of the two transactions—one a repurchase agreement and the other a reverse repurchase agreement—are identical, the two are said to be "matched". The dealer profits by obtaining funds at a cost slightly lower than the return received for the funds supplied. After arranging such a pair of transactions, a dealer is exposed to credit risk (the possibility of default), but not to market risk (changes in the value of the portfolio due to changes in market prices).

A commonly used variant of the "matched" agreement gives the dealer greater opportunity to try to take advantage of movements in interest rates. A dealer may deliberately not "match" the maturity of an RP with the maturity of a reverse RP. Usually the RP is for a period shorter than the reverse RP, establishing what is called a "tail". The "tail" refers to the difference in the maturities of the two transactions. If during this period the dealer is able to refinance the reverse RP with an RP at a lower cost, he makes a profit; if not, he loses money.

Another use of the reverse RP has been developed more recently. Reverse RPs are now used frequently to facilitate "short sales" of Government and Federal agency securities.[4] In the past, dealers wishing to establish such positions had to borrow securities from commercial banks, usually at an interest fee of 50 basis points (½ percent). Now dealers often acquire securities elsewhere under reverse RPs and frequently through this device reduce the cost of obtaining securities for the purpose of short sales.

Use of the reverse RP to facilitate the short sale has led to the appearance of a new subsector of the repurchase agreement market, known as the "specific issue market". The subsector has developed because, for purposes of a short sale, a dealer tries to obtain the exact issue whose price he expects to fall. In a usual reverse RP, the specific securities to be exchanged are rarely discussed (though their maturity should exceed that of the reverse RP), since the parties to the agreement are primarily concerned with the cost of the money involved. The placement of securities in the specific issue market is advantageous for both principals to the transaction. Since it is apparent that the dealer is interested in a particular issue, the holder of the securities is able to negotiate with the dealer and can often get funds at a slightly lower cost than if he were to place the securities in the overall RP market.

---

[4] The dealer does not own the securities that it promises to deliver in a short sale. It "covers" the short by buying in the open market the particular security it has promised to deliver. Trading profits can be earned during periods of falling securities prices if the securities that were sold short become available at below-contract prices prior to the agreed-upon delivery date.

CORPORATIONS AND THE RP MARKET

Up to this point, the analysis has concentrated on the major demanders of Federal funds and RPs. The discussion of major nonbank suppliers begins with non-financial corporations. They have been supplying funds through RPs against Government and agency securities for about thirty years.

The principal reason corporations hold cash and other short-term liquid assets is to bridge timing gaps between receipts and expenditures. Large quantities of funds are accumulated in anticipation of payments for dividends, corporate taxes, payrolls, and other regular expenses. In addition, corporations also accumulate short-term liquid assets in anticipation of expenditures for plant and equipment. In general, corporate liquidity is related to economic conditions and expectations about the future course of the economy and interest rates. Liquidity is often low—i.e., corporations have small amounts of liquid assets and large amounts of short-term borrowing—in periods of rapid economic expansion. Liquidity is rebuilt by reducing short-term borrowings and acquiring liquid assets during an economic slowdown or the early stages of an expansion.

Corporations have traditionally held significant amounts of their liquid assets in the form of demand deposits at commercial banks. Such balances have not earned interest since 1933, but this was not of great significance during the low interest rate periods of the depression and just after World War II. Interest rates began to climb in the late 1950s, and the higher rates have had a significant impact on how corporations handle their liquidity positions. They constituted an inducement to develop "cash management" techniques in some ways parallel to the "liability management" techniques adopted by banks during the same period. Cash management consists of a variety of procedures designed to achieve four goals: to speed up the receipt of payments due; to slow down the disbursement of payments owed; to keep a corporation's demand deposits to a minimum because they earn no interest; and to earn the maximum return on liquid asset holdings.

Repurchase agreements are particularly useful as tools for cash management. They generate income for the supplier of funds and are generally regarded as secure. Their key advantage is flexibility, primarily because they can be arranged for periods as short as one day. Few if any other income-generating assets have this feature. Regulations prevent banks from issuing CDs with maturities of less than thirty days; commercial paper and bankers' acceptances can be obtained for shorter periods, but as a practical matter not for one day. None of these instruments are viewed as being quite as secure as repurchase agreements, where there is a margin between the amount of funds supplied and the value of the securities. Corporations can buy Government securities or other financial assets and hold them for short periods, but the transaction costs can be relatively high and the possibility of capital loss reduces the attractiveness of such alternatives. The overnight feature of RPs means that corporations treat them as if they are income-earning demand deposits.

Corporations make heavy use of a particular form of RP known as the "continuing contract". Under such a contract, a corporation will agree to provide a specific volume of funds to a bank or a dealer for a certain period of time. However, during the life of the contract the repurchase agreement is treated almost as if it were reestablished each day. That is, earnings are calculated daily often related to the prevailing overnight RP rate. Either party has the right to withdraw at any time, although this right is seldom used. The principal advantage of the continuing contract over the daily renewals of an RP is that securities and funds are exchanged only at the beginning and at the end of the contract. The continuing contract therefore significantly reduces transactions costs, compared with daily RPs. An additional feature of the continuing contract RP is the seller's right of substitution, under which securities of equal value may be used to replace those originally involved in the RP. This option does not appear in all continuing contracts but, where it does appear, it is frequently exercised.

Another RP arrangement rather similar to the continuing contract specifies neither a definite period nor a fixed amount. Arrangements are made by banks chiefly for their corporate customers. The corporation concentrates all its demand balances in a single account at that bank daily. Before the bank closes its books each day, the corporation's balance in this account is determined, and any excess over a specified minimum is automatically converted into an RP. The following morning the funds are moved from the RP back to the corporation's demand balance for use during the day. Such automatic arrangements for the conversion of demand deposits to RPs are often included in packages of services offered by banks to their corporate customers. Among the services in such packages are lines of credit, payroll administration, and the use of safekeeping facilities. Payment for such service packages is usually not made on the basis of a stated fee. Instead, average or minimum demand deposit balances—called compensating balances—are usually required.

RPs also can be used to provide liquidity for somewhat longer periods, for example, to allow the accumulation of funds for a tax or dividend payment. This option is particularly attractive to corporations if the income that can be earned on a longer RP exceeds that available on an overnight RP. One or several RPs can be written, as liquidity is accumulated over the period prior to a payment date, with the contracts maturing on the day disbursements must be made. The RP has less commanding advantages over other money market assets for longer periods, however. Commercial paper can frequently be tailored to mature on a specific day, and Treasury bills that mature very close to the desired date can often be purchased. RPs are nevertheless used very frequently for such purposes, primarily because they can be arranged easily and quickly once a corporation has established a routine trading relationship with market participants.

State and local government units have entered the RP market only in recent years but have quickly become major suppliers of funds. The RP is particularly well suited to their needs. These governments usually are required by law to hold their assets in the most secure form, generally in bank deposits or Government and Federal agency securities. The RP provides a way of meeting these requirements while earning income on short-term investments.

Tax receipts of state and local governments never match exactly the timing pattern of their expenditures, thereby creating the need for them either to borrow or to invest for short periods at various times of the year. Until recently their major investment alternative to deposits has been Treasury bills. As the advantages of the RP have become more widely recognized, these governments have switched more of their liquid investments into RPs.

THE ROLE OF NONBANK FINANCIAL INSTITUTIONS

Several types of nonbank financial institutions are active in the markets for immediately available funds. These include mutual savings banks, savings and loan associations, branches and agencies of foreign banks that operate on United States soil, and Edge Act corporations. (The latter are affiliates of United States commercial banks empowered to engage in international or foreign banking in the United States or abroad.) All of these institutions are active primarily in the market for Federal funds, and generally do not enter into repurchase agreements in volume. They generally lend Federal funds to commercial banks, although under certain circumstances agencies and branches of foreign banks will borrow from banks or other nonbank lenders.

The appearance of all these institutions in the Federal funds market has occurred relatively recently. Their entry has dramatically changed the function of the Federal funds market, allowing the banking system to draw funds from a wide array of institutions, instead of just reallocating reserves. The expanded borrowing ability of banks serves to integrate more closely the United States financial structure, and to help break down the barriers which have traditionally existed among various types of financial institutions.

The agencies and branches of foreign banks have also become active participants in the Federal funds market. These institutions deal with or represent foreign commercial banks, which trade in both the money markets of their home countries and in the Euro-currency markets. Through the Federal funds market, the agencies and branches of foreign banks provide a link between the various markets abroad and the United States commercial banking system.

The participation of these institutions in United States financial markets mirrors the activities of United States commercial banks overseas. In the last three decades, overseas branch networks of United States banks have grown significantly in both the scale and range of their operations, and these networks have provided United States banks with easy access to foreign and international financial markets. Entry into the Federal funds market by agencies and branches of foreign banks, therefore, has contributed to the continuing integration of credit markets and banking in the United States and abroad.

THE ROLE OF THE FEDERAL RESERVE

The Federal Reserve is important to the markets for Federal funds and RPs for two quite different reasons. One is that Federal Reserve regulations play a very important role in the markets by limiting the type and terms of transactions member banks may undertake. A second is that actions taken by the Federal Reserve in the normal conduct of monetary policy have a major influence on the levels of interest rates in general and on the Federal funds rate in particular. Federal Reserve monetary policy is oriented toward achieving steady and sustained growth of the economy, along with reasonably stable prices. Such a sound economy depends on a multiplicity of factors, one of which is the capacity of the commercial banking system to extend loans and create deposits. These capacities, in turn, are strongly influenced by the interest rate on Federal funds and the supply of reserves to member banks.

The Federal Reserve controls the supply of reserves through open market operations, mainly via outright purchases and sales of Government and Federal agency securities. An outright purchase of securities provides reserves permanently, while a sale permanently reduces the total supply of reserves. But the Federal Reserve also needs to provide and absorb reserves for short periods, mainly to accommodate the seasonal needs of banks for reserves and to offset the effects on reserves of day-to-day changes in currency in circulation, in the Treasury's balance at Federal Reserve Banks, and in Federal Reserve float. Reserves can be supplied temporarily by use of repurchase agreements, and absorbed temporarily through "matched sale-purchase transactions", which most market participants call reverse RPs.

Federal Reserve use of RPs and matched sale-purchase transactions for temporary reserve adjustment has grown sharply in the past few years, but for generally different reasons than those which explain the increase in the use of RPs by banks and others. The increase has arisen in large part from a change in Treasury procedures for handling its cash balances. Prior to August 1974, the Treasury received payments into accounts at commercial banks, and generally moved funds into its balance at the Federal Reserve only as funds were needed to make payments on behalf of the Federal Government. Under this scheme, Treasury balances in commercial banks fluctuated widely, but the Treasury balance at the Federal Reserve was reasonably stable. In August 1974, the Treasury began to move its balances more quickly into its accounts at the Federal Reserve Banks, which climbed by several billion dollars over a period of several months. This policy has led to much wider fluctuation in these accounts. This in turn has created greater variability in the supply of reserves available to the banking system which the Federal Reserve usually offsets by temporary adjustments to reserves through RPs or matched sale-purchase transactions.

SOME MAJOR IMPLICATIONS

The Federal funds and RP markets have grown dramatically in the past few years. This growth is due in part to changes in the regulations which govern the operations of commercial banks, but is more basically due to the changing practices and behavior of all participants in these markets. The circumstances influencing each group of market participants have differed in detail, but for all, the quite high interest rates since the mid-1960s have provided the major motivation.

The growth in the Federal funds and RP markets has several implications. Most importantly, the markets have expanded to include a broader range of domestic and international financial institutions and corporations. They use the markets as a link in a worldwide network that transfers interest-sensitive dollar balances to wherever they are in great demand. To be sure, mechanisms to move funds to high-demand uses have existed for some time, but the Federal funds and RP markets help make the task easier and more efficient by bringing interest-sensitive funds into a central marketplace from a broader arena. For example, most individuals who hold deposits at thrift institutions do not move their funds quickly from one investment to another in response to small interest rate changes. But thrift institutions can lend in the Federal funds market, in effect allowing the small deposits of individuals to be combined and placed directly in the national markets for short-term credit. Similar considerations apply with respect to international credit flows.

These developments have some implications for the conduct of Federal Reserve monetary policy. Policy actions significantly influence the Federal funds and RP markets, which commercial banks now use as sources of funds more extensively than ever before. Hence any change in the availability of funds in these markets probably has a more direct impact than before on the cost to banks of making loans and on the rates they charge. Moreover, many more small banks and nonbank financial institutions have become quite active in the markets. Through this mechanism, Federal Reserve monetary policy is felt more quickly and directly by a broader range of the financial institutions, including those that provide a major portion of the total credit available in the United States economy.

United States and international financial markets have also become more closely integrated in recent years. There are multiple linkages among the various markets, but they center on the activities in this country and abroad of multinational corporations and of United States and foreign commercial banks. These institutions borrow and lend sizable amounts in both the United States and international markets, and are sensitive to the margins between borrowing and lending rates in different countries. For example, if short-term interest rates in the United States were higher than abroad, the differential would quickly draw funds from other uses abroad and channel liquidity into the United States financial markets. These flows would tend to reduce the differential between interest rates abroad and in this country.

But the flows of credit induced by such interest rate differentials may not be in keeping with Federal Reserve policy objectives at the time. For example, a restrictive monetary policy works to reduce spending by individuals and businesses, partly because it makes borrowing more expensive and difficult to obtain. The effects of such policies on the domestic economy could be dampened if large corporations and financial institutions can readily obtain credit elsewhere.

While high interest rates and inflation have encouraged growth of the Federal funds and RP markets, the evolution of technology, particularly the use of computer facilities, has also played an important part. The new and changing technology speeds the transfer of funds, reduces the cost of record keeping, and increases the availability of information concerning investment opportunities. It seems certain that technological change will continue at a rapid rate, thereby reducing further the costs of arranging and executing financial transactions and reinforcing the already strong trend toward aggressive financial management.

The rapid growth of the markets for Federal funds and RPs in recent years can be viewed as part of a pervasive trend in all United States financial markets toward more aggressive portfolio management by holders of financial assets. This trend will clearly continue to be a strong influence on the markets. Participants will no doubt devise new trading techniques, refine existing ones, and attract others into the marketplace. But the Federal funds and RP markets are only two of many markets for short-term financial claims, and their growth relative to others will be heavily influenced by the regulatory and legal framework in which they operate.

TREASURY BILLS*

*Timothy Q. Cook and
Jimmie R. Monhollon*

3

A Treasury bill is a short-term obligation of the United States Government.
Treasury bills are perhaps the single most important type of money market
instrument. They are a widely held liquid investment and an important
tool in Federal debt management and in the execution of monetary policy.
Before World War II the amount of Treasury bills outstanding rarely exceeded
$2.5 billion. By 1945, however, the total had risen to over $17 billion,
and by December 1980 the outstanding volume was $216.1 billion.

TREASURY BILL OFFERINGS

The Treasury sells bills at a discount through competitive biddings; the
return to the investor is the difference between the purchase price of the
bill and its face or par value. Treasury bills are currently sold in minimum
amounts of $20,000 and multiples of $5,000 above the minimum, although
at times they have been issued in smaller denominations. Treasury bills are
issued only in book-entry form. Under this arrangement ownership is
recorded in a book-entry account established at the Treasury and investors
receive only a receipt as evidence of purchase.

*Reprinted from *Instruments of the Money Market*, 5th edition, edited by Timothy Q. Cook and
Bruce J. Summers, 1981, with permission from the Federal Reserve Bank of Richmond.

Regularly scheduled offerings of 91- and 182-day bills are currently made on a weekly basis and regularly scheduled offerings of 52-week bills are made on a monthly basis. These regularly scheduled offerings are to refinance maturing issues and, if necessary, to help finance current Federal deficits. The Treasury also sells bills on an irregular basis to smooth out the uneven flow of revenues from corporate and individual tax receipts.

Regularly Scheduled Issues

Treasury bills were first offered in their modern form in December 1929. From then until 1934, 30-, 60-, and 90-day maturities were offered. Between February 1934 and October 1937, the Treasury experimented with maturities of 182 days to 273 days in order to reduce the frequency with which bills had to be rolled over. In 1937, largely at the insistence of commercial banks, the Treasury reverted to exclusive issue of 91-day bills. Then in December 1958 these were supplemented with six-month bills in the regular weekly auctions.

In 1959 the Treasury began to auction one-year bills on a quarterly basis. The quarterly auction of one-year bills was replaced by a monthly auction in August 1963. The Treasury added a nine-month maturity to the monthly auction in September 1966 but the sale of this maturity was discontinued in late 1972. Since then, the only regular bill cycles have been for maturities of 91 days, 6 months, and a year. The Treasury has increased the size of its weekly and monthly bill auctions as new money is needed to meet Federal borrowing requirements. In 1980 monthly sales of 52-week bills were for $4.0 billion, while the weekly auctions of 13- and 26-week bills ranged from $6.5 to $8.6 billion.

Irregularly Scheduled Issues

Prior to the mid-1970s the Treasury sold bills on an irregular basis through the use of tax anticipation bills.[1] Introduced in October 1951, tax anticipation bills were designed specifically to help smooth out the Treasury's uneven flow of tax receipts while providing corporations with an investment vehicle for funds accumulated for tax payments. These bills were accepted at par on the tax date in payment for taxes due—hence the name, tax anticipation bills. They actually matured a week later, usually on the 22nd of the month. Tax anticipation bills did not have to be used in lieu of tax payments, and some investors chose to hold them to maturity.

Tax anticipation bills were sold in periods of low Treasury revenues and scheduled to mature in periods of heavy tax receipts. Since two of the five

---

[1] Tax anticipation bills are described in more detail in [5].

major tax payment dates fall in the April-June quarter of the year, that quarter generally registers a budget surplus that either completely or partially offsets budget deficits in the other three quarters. Because of this pattern the great majority of the $159.4 billion of tax anticipation bills issued from 1951 through 1974 were sold in the period from July through March and were scheduled to mature in March, April, and June. Of the 83 tax bill auctions carried out through 1974, 19 were scheduled to mature in March, 17 in April, and 36 in June; only 9 were scheduled to mature in September and 2 in December.

No tax anticipation bills have been issued since 1974. In their place the Treasury has raised money on an irregular basis through the sale of *cash management bills*, which are usually "reopenings" or sales of additional amounts of outstanding maturities of Treasury bills. Cash management bills usually have maturities that fall after one of the five major tax dates and, like tax anticipation bills, are designed to help finance the Treasury's requirements until tax payments are received. Thirty-eight issues of cash management bills were sold in the 1975-1980 period. The maturities of these 38 issues ranged from 2 to 167 days and averaged 51 days. Annual sales of cash management bills varied from $4 billion in 1976 to $45 billion in 1980. Very short-term cash management bills are sometimes referred to as "short-dated" bills.

Auctioning New Bills

New offerings of three- and six-month bills are made each week by the Treasury. Ordinarily, an offering is announced on Tuesday and the amount of the offering is set at that time. The auction is usually conducted on the following Monday, with delivery and payment on the following Thursday.

Bids, or tenders, in the weekly auctions must be presented at Federal Reserve Banks or their branches, which act as agents for the Treasury, by 1:30 P. M., New York time, on the day of the auction. Bids may be made on a competitive or a noncompetitive basis. In making a competitive bid the investor states the quantity of bills desired and the price. A subscriber may enter more than one bid indicating the various quantities willing to be taken at different prices. Competitive bids, which are usually made by large investors who are in close contact with the market, comprise the largest portion of subscriptions on a dollar basis. In making a noncompetitive bid the investor indicates the quantity of bills desired and agrees to pay the average price of accepted competitive bids. Individuals and other small investors usually enter noncompetitive bids, which are awarded in full up to $500,000 on both the 91-day and the 182-day bills. By bidding noncompetitively, small investors avoid the risks inherent in competitive bidding. In the first place, they do not risk losing their chance to buy as a result of bidding too low. Nor do they run the risk of bidding too high and paying a price near the top. The dollar amount of non-competitive awards as a percent of total awards is generally quite small, usually less than 15 percent of the total auction amount, although it typically rises substantially in periods of high interest rates.

Subscription books at the various Federal Reserve Banks and branches close promptly at 1:30 P. M., after which the bids are tabulated and submitted to the Treasury for allocation. Allocations are first made for foreign official institutions and the Federal Reserve to roll over maturing issues. Then the Treasury allocates whatever part of the total offering is needed to make all noncompetitive awards. The remainder is then allocated to those competitive bidders submitting the highest offers, ranging downward from the highest bid until the total amount offered is allocated. The "stop-out price" is the lowest price, or highest yield, at which bills are awarded. Usually only a portion of the total bids made at this price is accepted. The average issuing price, which is usually closer to the lowest accepted price than to the highest is then computed on the basis of the competitive bids accepted.

In the weekly auction of February 2, 1981, for example, accepted bids for the three-month bills ranged from a high of $96.319 per $100 of face amount (equivalent to an annual discount rate of 14.562 percent) to a stop-out price of $96.279 (14.729 percent). A total of $4.3 billion of bids was accepted, $859 million of which was for noncompetitive tenders accepted at the average issuing price of $96.295 (14.657 percent). The relatively high proportion (20 percent) of bills purchased on a non-competitive basis was not unusual, given the high level of interest rates prevailing at the time of the auction.

In addition to the regular weekly auctions, 52-week bills are auctioned every fourth Thursday for issue the following Thursday and special auctions are held for cash management bills. The procedure for these auctions is similar to the weekly auctions.

Advantages of Auctions

Treasury bills are marketed by the Treasury solely through the auction technique. Treasury notes and bonds, however, can be sold either through auctions or through subscriptions. Under the subscription method the Treasury sets both the coupon and price (typically par) of a new issue, thereby determining the issue's yield prior to sale. Subscriptions may be allotted completely or may be allotted in part if aggregate subscriptions are greater than the amount of notes or bonds the Treasury wishes to sell.

In general, the auction method is simpler and less time-consuming than the subscription method. In auctions the market establishes a yield, making it unnecessary for the Treasury to second-guess market conditions, and thereby eliminating the problems associated with over-subscriptions or under-subscriptions. The Treasury merely chooses the amount of the offering and the market does the rest. For these reasons the Treasury in recent years has used the auction method exclusively not only for bills but also for notes and bonds. The last time the subscription method was used was in the Treasury's quarterly refunding operation of August 1976.

The auction technique is especially suited to the market for Treasury bills, which is enormous and can absorb billions of dollars of new bills with only minimal impact on yields. Bill auctions also provide the Treasury with a very flexible debt financing tool, since relatively small increases or decreases in the Treasury debt can be engineered simply by changing the supply of bills in the weekly auction.

INVESTMENT CHARACTERISTICS

There are four investment characteristics of Treasury bills that distinguish them from other money market securities and that consequently influence investor decisions to purchase bills. These characteristics of bills include (1) lack of default risk, (2) liquidity, (3) favorable tax status, and (4) a low minimum denomination.

Lack of Default Risk

Because Treasury bills are an obligation of the U. S. Treasury, they are considered to be free of default risk. In contrast, even the highest grade of other money market instruments, such as commercial paper or CDs, is perceived to have some degree of default risk. Concern over default risk typically increases in times of weak economic conditions. In such periods the risk-free feature of bills increases their attractiveness to some investors.

The absence of default risk for Treasury bills not only directly but also indirectly affects the demand for bills because various laws and regulations have given Treasury bills a special role in the portfolio of some investors, especially commercial banks and state and local governments.[2] Treasury bills serve a number of purposes for commercial banks that often cannot be served by private money market instruments such as commercial paper or bankers' acceptances. For example, banks use bills to make repurchase agreements with businesses and state and local governments and banks use bills to satisfy pledging requirements on state, local and Federal government deposits. Many state and local governments invest in bills to satisfy requirements that limit the types of financial assets they can hold. Bills are always a permissible investment for state and local governments, while many other types of money market instruments frequently are not.

[2] These regulations are described in more detail in [1].

Liquidity

A second characteristic of bills is their high degree of liquidity. Liquidity refers to assets that may be converted to cash quickly with low transactions costs and a low degree of price risk resulting from changes in the level of interest rates. Treasury bills have this characteristic because they are a short-term and homogeneous instrument traded in a highly organized, efficient and competitive market.

Of course if an investor desires cash, the choice of whether to sell a bill or raise money through an alternative means will depend heavily on the length of time the funds are expected to be needed. The turnaround costs involved in selling bills one day and buying them back at a later date may make such sales a relatively unattractive way to cover very short-term cash need. These turnaround costs include incidental transaction costs such as phone calls and paper work and costs which arise due to the spread between bid and asked prices. Government securities dealers buy bills at a price (the bid price) slightly lower than the price at which they sell (the asked price). Thus, if interest rates do not change, an investor seeking to raise funds for only one day would sell bills at a given price and buy them back the following day at a slightly higher price. In 1980 the typical bid-asked spread on actively traded Treasury bills, such as the current three- and six-month bills, was 4 to 8 basis points. Four basis points is equivalent to about $0.01 on each $100 par value of three-month bills. Thus, for example, a bank would lose one cent per $100 by selling bills to cover a one-day reserve need. An alternative means of covering the one-day reserve need, such as borrowing Federal funds or doing repurchase agreements against the bills, would be far less costly.

Minimum Denomination

A third important investment characteristic of Treasury bills is the low minimum denomination compared to the minimum denomination of other money market instruments. Prior to 1970, the minimum denomination of bills was $1,000. In early 1970 the minimum denomination of bills was raised from $1,000 to $10,000. The stated purposes of this change were to discourage noncompetitive bids by small investors in order to retain the Treasury bill as an instrument for attracting large quantities of funds primarily from institutional investors, to reduce the costs of processing many small subscriptions yielding only a small volume of funds, and to discourage the exodus of funds from financial intermediaries and the mortgage market. As will be shown below, the increase in the minimum denomination of bills was not very successful as a deterent to increased purchases of bills by small investors in periods of high interest rates.

Even at $10,000 the minimum denomination of Treasury bills is far below the minimum denomination required to purchase all other short-term securities, with the exception of some Federal agency securities. Typically, it takes at least $100,000 to purchase other money market instruments such as CDs or commercial paper. Consequently, for many small investors, bills have been the only security available for purchase directly in the money market.

Taxes

Unlike other money market instruments, the income earned on Treasury bills is exempt from state and local income taxes. Given a state income tax rate (t), the relationship between, say, the commercial paper rate (or some other discount-type rate) and the bill rate that leaves an investor indifferent between the two other considerations aside[3], is given by

$$R_{cp}(1 - t) = R_{tb}.$$

From this formula it can be seen that the advantage of the tax-exempt feature for a particular investor depends on (1) the investor's state and local tax rate and (2) the current level of interest rates. For a given before-tax yield differential between bill rates and commercial paper rates, the higher the rate of state and local taxes, the more attractive bills become. Similarly, the higher the level of market interest rates, the more attractive bills become. For example, the interest rate differential at which an investor subject to a marginal state income tax rate of 6 percent is indifferent between bills and commercial paper rises from 32 basis points when the Treasury bill rate is 5 percent to 64 basis points when the Treasury bill rate is 10 percent.

This investment characteristic of bills is relevant only to those investors that pay state and local income taxes. Some investors, such as state and local governments, are not subject to state income taxes. Other investors, such as commercial banks in most states, pay a "franchise" or "excise" tax that in fact requires them to pay state taxes on interest income from Treasury bills.

---

[3] Since the yields on Treasury bills, commercial paper, bankers' acceptances, and some Federal agency issues are quoted on a discounted basis using a 360-day year, the yields are on the same basis and thus may be directly compared. However, when analyzing Treasury bill yields relative to interest-bearing instruments such as CDs, the yields must be converted to an equivalent yield basis. Since the discounting approach and the use of a 360-day year results in an understatement of the actual yield, a procedure is presented later in this article to find the "true" yield. This yield may then be compared with the true yield on interest-bearing CDs, which is obtained by multiplying the quoted CD rate by 365/360. In 1981, some banks began issuing discounted CDs. As a result, the quoted yields on CDs may have to be converted to their true yield in order to be compared.

INVESTORS

While comprehensive data on Treasury bill holdings does not exist, the Federal Reserve System's "Flow of Funds Accounts" uses available information to construct estimates of the amounts of marketable U. S. debt with a maturity of one year or less held by various investors.[4] These estimates are shown in Table 1 for the 1960 to 1980 period. The table shows that as of 1980, the largest investors in bills were individuals, commercial banks, foreigners, and the Federal Reserve.[5]

Individuals

Individuals, especially since the mid-1960s, have become substantial investors in Treasury bills. Prior to developments in the late 1970s, the relatively small minimum denomination of bills made them the only feasible money market investment for many individual investors. The volume of investment by individuals has varied greatly depending on the level of bill rates relative to the rates paid on time and savings deposits at depository institutions. Until 1978 all deposit rates at Federally-insured institutions were subject to fixed ceilings that did not vary with market interest rates. Consequently, when market rates rose above the deposit rates ceilings, many individuals reacted by shifting funds from depository institutions into the bill market. As a result, investment by individuals in the bill market has risen sharply in periods of high interest rates, such as 1969, 1973, and 1974.

Two developments in the late 1970s greatly expanded the short-term investment options available to small investors. First, Regulation Q of the Federal Reserve Act was altered to allow depository institutions to offer six-month "money market certificates" bearing rates tied to the six-month Treasury bill rate prevailing at the time of purchase. Second, the proliferation of money market mutual funds offered investors indirect access to current money market yields. Money market funds typically require a minimum investment of only $1,000 to $5,000.

By offering small investors two additional means of earning a market yield, the availability of money market certificates and money market funds would be expected to decrease the demand for bills by individuals in high interest rate periods relative to what it would have been without these alternatives. The Flow of Funds estimates indicate that when short-term rates rose to record levels in the late 1970s, individuals again purchased

---

[4] The short-term marketable debt series in the Flow of Funds Accounts does not correspond exactly to Treasury bills because the series includes other marketable debt with a remaining maturity of less than one year. However, movement in the series is dominated by Treasury bills.

[5] The term "individuals" is used in the text to refer to the "households" sector of the Flow of Funds. The households sector also includes personal trusts and nonprofit organizations.

Table 1

Holdings of Short-Term Marketable U.S. Securities (end-of-year Flow of Funds estimates in billions)

	Foreigners		Federal Reserve		Households		Commercial Banks		State and Local Governments		Private Nonbank Financial Institutions		Nonfinancial Corporate Business	
	$	%	$	%	$	%	$	%	$	%	$	%	$	%
1960	7.7	8.8	19.2	22.1	10.6	12.1	22.9	26.3	7.6	8.8	5.8	6.6	13.3	15.2
1961	7.1	7.2	18.3	18.7	10.8	11.0	33.5	34.3	8.0	8.2	7.6	7.8	12.5	12.8
1962	9.2	9.4	20.7	21.1	12.6	12.8	27.8	28.3	9.0	9.1	8.4	8.5	10.7	10.8
1963	8.7	8.7	25.6	25.7	16.3	16.4	24.2	24.3	9.2	9.2	7.2	7.2	8.5	8.5
1964	8.5	8.1	28.2	27.0	15.8	15.1	28.3	27.1	8.4	8.0	7.7	7.4	7.5	7.2
1965	7.6	7.1	31.9	29.6	18.0	16.8	26.2	24.4	10.5	9.7	7.3	6.8	6.0	5.6
1966	6.7	6.2	36.5	33.5	19.3	17.7	21.5	20.0	11.5	10.6	8.5	7.8	4.7	4.3
1967	7.6	6.5	39.2	33.6	18.9	16.2	27.0	23.2	12.2	10.5	8.6	7.4	3.1	2.6
1968	5.9	5.0	32.6	27.8	25.7	21.9	28.6	24.4	11.5	9.8	10.0	8.5	3.0	2.5
1969	3.7	2.9	37.6	29.6	34.7	27.3	24.3	19.1	14.1	11.1	9.0	7.1	3.8	3.0
1970	11.5	8.8	38.5	29.3	21.0	16.0	30.1	22.9	14.8	11.3	10.8	8.2	4.7	3.6
1971	25.4	19.8	39.5	30.8	8.5	6.6	25.2	19.6	13.5	10.5	7.8	6.1	8.4	6.6
1972	26.7	18.7	41.2	28.8	9.7	6.8	30.8	21.6	18.1	12.7	10.4	7.3	5.8	4.0
1973	21.0	13.8	50.6	33.3	25.7	16.9	28.3	18.6	16.2	10.6	9.7	6.3	0.9	0.6
1974	28.6	17.7	50.5	31.2	36.2	22.3	26.9	16.6	9.0	5.5	10.1	6.2	0.6	0.4
1975	35.3	16.3	52.4	24.3	41.0	19.0	48.8	22.6	12.7	5.9	15.9	7.3	10.0	4.6
1976	38.6	16.2	58.6	24.6	31.6	13.3	56.5	23.8	16.7	7.0	23.4	9.9	12.4	5.2
1977	46.7	18.0	61.7	23.8	48.4	18.7	52.0	20.0	19.6	7.6	24.3	9.4	6.7	2.6
1978	60.6	22.3	62.1	22.8	59.1	21.7	41.7	15.3	24.4	9.0	23.7	8.7	0.5	0.2
1979	38.5	13.6	55.8	19.7	64.6	22.8	56.6	20.0	24.3	8.5	29.8	10.5	13.8	4.9

very large amounts of bills. However, as a percentage of total bills outstanding, individual holdings were no greater in 1979 and 1980 than in 1974 when Treasury bill rates peaked at 9 percent. Given the extremely high level of bill rates in the 1979-1980 period, it is likely that the individual purchases of bills in that period would have been far greater were money market certificates and money market funds unavailable as investment alternatives.

Commercial Banks

The commercial banking system's holdings of total bills outstanding has trended down somewhat over the last 20 years. The Treasury bill holdings of commercial banks varies cyclically, but in the opposite direction of the holdings of individuals. In periods of strong economic activity and rising interest rates, bank investment in bills generally declines, while in periods of slack economic activity banks typically add substantially to their bill holdings.

This pattern of bank investment in bills has generally been attributed to the role of bills as "secondary reserves" for banks. According to this view, banks purchase bills to convert excess reserves into earnings assets quickly with little loss of liquidity and sell bills to acquire additional funds promptly for lending or meeting legal reserve requirements. Consequently, when loan demand is slack, banks turn to Treasury bills as a temporary investment outlet. Conversely, when loan demand is increasing, banks reduce their bill holdings in order to expand loans. Of course, banks finance increases in business loans not only through the sale of securities but also through the issue of liabilities such as CDs. Also, as discussed above, banks hold Treasury bills for other reasons in addition to their use as a buffer source of funds to finance loan expansion.

Foreign Investors

Foreign investors held about $50 billion of short-term marketable U. S. securities at the end of 1980. Bill holdings of foreigners grew sharply in the 1970s primarily due to substantial acquisitions by oil-exporting countries and foreign central bank investment of dollars obtained in exchange rate operations.

Federal Reserve System and Others

The Federal Reserve System's holdings of short-term marketable U. S. debt has generally ranged from 20 to 30 percent of the total outstanding over the last 20 years. Other investors in Treasury bills are state and local governments, nonbank financial institutions, and nonfinancial corporations. The relative holdings of both state and local governments and corporations fell in the latter half of the 1970s compared to earlier years. The decline in the share of state and local governments probably reflects the increased investment flexibility available to many of these governments.

YIELDS

Treasury bill yields are generally quoted on a discount basis using a 360-day year. Under this procedure the stated rate of return on a bill of a given maturity is calculated by dividing the discount by par and expressing this percentage at an annual rate, using a 360-day year. For example, in the weekly auction of February 2, 1981 discussed above, a price of $96.295 per $100 of face amount for a 91-day bill produced an annual rate of return on a discount basis of

$$\frac{100\text{-}96.295}{100} \times \frac{360}{91} = 14.657\%.$$

The True Yield

To calculate the true yield of a Treasury bill for comparison with other yields, the discount must be divided by the *price* and a 365-day year used. In the above example, the true yield is

$$\frac{100 - 96.295}{96.295} \times \frac{365}{91} = 15.432\%.$$

As this example demonstrates, the yield calculated on a discount basis can seriously understate the true yield of a Treasury bill. The difference between the true yield of a bill and the discount yield is greater the longer the maturity of the bill and the higher the level of interest rates.

Yield Spreads

Most money market rates move together closely over time. Perhaps more than any other money market rate, however, the rate on Treasury bills has at times diverged substantially from other short-term rates. Figure 1 shows the differential between the three-month prime CD rate and the three-month Treasury bill rates. The chart shows that this differential varies greatly over

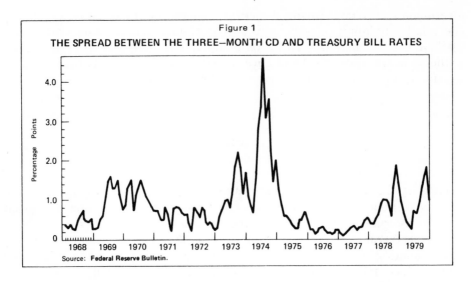

Figure 1

THE SPREAD BETWEEN THE THREE—MONTH CD AND TREASURY BILL RATES

Source: Federal Reserve Bulletin.

time, typically rising in high interest rate periods and falling to low levels in low interest rate periods. The spread widened to over 400 basis points in the middle of 1974. Not only does the spread vary over years but it also has a tendency to move on a seasonal basis, reaching its widest levels in the middle of the calendar year and its narrowest in February.[6]

In attempting to understand the highly variable spread between bill rates and other money market rates, it is useful to focus on the investment characteristic of bills discussed above to investigate if the effects of these characteristics on short-term yield spreads might change over time. Three characteristics that may provide insight into the behavior of the spread are default risk, taxes, and minimum denomination.

The most common explanation of the movement in the spreads between Treasury bill and other money market rates focuses on default risk. According to this explanation, the spreads between other short-term rates and bill rates vary over time due to a cyclical risk premium pushing up the yields on private sector money market instruments relative to the yields on Treasury bills in periods of weak economic activity. In fact, throughout the money and capital markets yields spreads between debt instruments of different investment quality do tend to widen in periods of economic weakness. However, yields spreads that isolate the influence of cyclical risk premiums generally do not rise much until the onset of a recession and typically peak near the end of a recession. In contrast, the spreads between private sector

[6] This is analyzed in [2].

money market rates and bill rates have risen well before the beginning of recessions and have generally fallen sharply prior to the end of recessions. This strongly suggests that cyclically varying risk premiums do not provide a complete explanation of the movement in the spreads between private money market and Treasury bill rates.

Another possible factor influencing the spread between the bill rate and other short-term rates is the exemption of Treasury bills from state and local income tax. As shown above, the higher the level of interest rates the wider the spread between bill rates and other short-term rates that is necessary to leave an investor with a given state income tax rate indifferent between bills and other money market instruments. Consequently, as interest rates rise, this tax feature of bills will induce some investors to increase their purchases of bills, thereby putting pressure on the spread between bill rates and other rates to widen.

Of course this is not to say that the tax-exempt feature of bills will necessarily cause the spread to rise with the level of interest rates. As noted above, many investors in the bill market are not subject to state and local income taxes. A widening spread between bill and CD rates could induce these investors to sell bills and buy CDs. In any case, even if investors subject to state income taxes dominated the bill market, this aspect of bills could only explain a relatively small part of the movement in the spread observed in such periods as 1969, 1973, and 1974, when the spread reached such high levels.

A third explanation for the spread focuses on the minimum denomination of bills and the behavior of individual investors in periods of disintermediation. This explanation is that massive purchases of Treasury bills by individuals that occur in periods of disintermediation have driven bill rates down relative to the rates on other money market instruments. According to this view, the inability of most individuals to meet the minimum purchase requirements necessary to acquire private-sector money market instruments prevented them from reducing the differential between bill rates and other money market rates by switching their purchases from bills to these other instruments.[7]

To the extent that this third explanation is a valid one, the spreads between bill rates and CD rates should be smaller, at a given level of interest rates, than in the past. This is because the availability of money market funds and other short-term investment polling arrangements have effectively broken down the minimum investment barriers that have prevented many individuals from acquiring money market instruments other than Treasury bills.

---

[7] This explanation is given in more detail in [1].

RELATION TO MONETARY POLICY

Treasury bills perform an important role in the implementation of monetary policy. Under its current operating procedures the Federal Reserve System manipulates the level of commercial bank reserves in order to achieve desired growth rates of the money supply. The Federal Reserve influences the reserve positions of commercial banks primarily through the purchase and sale of bills, either outright in the bill cash market or on a temporary basis in the market for repurchase agreements (RPs). Most Federal Reserve operations are RPs, which are the purchase or sale of bills under an agreement to reverse the transaction one or more days later. Essentially, these RPs are loans collateralized by Treasury bills. RPs have a temporary effect on the supply of bank reserves and are typically used to offset temporary fluctuations in reserves arising from other sources, such as changes in Treasury deposits at the Federal Reserve Banks.

REFERENCES

1. Cook, Timothy Q. "Determinants of the Spread Between Treasury Bill and Private Sector Money Market Rates," *Journal of Economics and Business* (Spring, 1981).

2. Lawler, T. A. "Seasonal Movements in Short-Term Yield Spreads," *Economic Review*, Federal Reserve Bank of Richmond, 64 (July/August 1978): 10-17.

3. McCurdy, Christopher J. "The Dealer Market for United States Government Securities," *Quarterly Review*, Federal Reserve Bank of New York (Winter 1977-78): 35-47.

4. Monhollon, Jimmie R. "Treasury Bills," *Instruments of the Money Market*, 4th ed. Federal Reserve Bank of Richmond, 1977.

5. Nelson, Jane F. "Tax Anticipation Bills," *Instruments of the Money Market*, 4th ed. Federal Reserve Bank of Richmond, 1977.

6. Tucker, James F. "Buying Treasury Securities at Federal Reserve Banks," Federal Reserve Bank of Richmond, 1980.

FEDERALLY SPONSORED CREDIT AGENCY SECURITIES[*]

Donna Howell

4

The Federally sponsored credit agencies have been one of the fastest growing components of the nation's financial system.[1] As a result, the stock of Federally sponsored agency securities outstanding grew from $13.8 billion in 1965 to $38.9 billion in 1970 and then to $78.8 billion in 1975. After a lull in growth in 1976 and 1977, agency debt exploded in the last three years of the decade to a level of $159.9 billion at the end of 1980. Over the whole period from 1965 to 1980 the outstanding debt of the Federally sponsored credit agencies grew at an annual rate of 17.7 percent.

THE ISSUING AGENCIES

Federally sponsored credit agencies are financial intermediaries established by the Federal Government to supply credit for certain economic purposes, e.g., housing and agriculture. To carry out their function, the agencies sell debt obligations in the financial markets and channel the proceeds to agricultural and mortgage lending institutions either through direct loans or through the purchase of loans originated by these institutions.

*Reprinted from *Instruments of the Money Market*, 5th Edition, edited by Timothy Q. Cook and Bruce J. Summers, 1981, with permission from the Federal Reserve Bank of Richmond.
[1] This article deals with direct debt issues of the Federally sponsored agencies. Mortgage pools are excluded from the discussion and from all numbers. Figures on total agency debt are from the Flow of Funds. Figures on short-term debt were collected by the author.

The five Federally sponsored credit agencies are the *Federal National Mortgage Association* (FNMA), *Federal Land Banks, Federal Intermediate Credit Banks, Banks for Cooperatives*, and *Federal Home Loan Banks* (FHLB). Included with the last agency is the *Federal Home Loan Mortgage Corporation* (FHLMC), all of whose capital stock is owned by the Federal Home Loan Banks. The primary function of the FHLB, the FHLMC, and FNMA is to provide funds to the mortgage and home construction markets. The other three corporations—collectively referred to as the *Federal Farm Credit Banks*—are part of the *Farm Credit System*, which provides credit primarily to farmers.

Most of the capital stock of the Federally sponsored credit agencies was originally owned by the Treasury. All of the agencies have repaid initial Government capital and are now operated as private corporations, wholly-owned by the financial institutions and the ultimate borrowers to which they lend. The capital stock of the Federal Home Loan Banks has been owned entirely by member savings and loan associations since 1951, and the other four agencies completed the transition to private ownership following the passage of enabling legislation in the fall of 1968. Despite their independent status, the Federally sponsored credit agencies remain subject to some Congressional control.

The Farm Credit Agencies

The Federal Intermediate Credit Banks, the Banks for Cooperatives, and the Federal Land Banks are similarly organized and operated. Each agency consists of a system composed of twelve regional banks which operate in twelve farm credit districts. The Banks for Cooperatives also have a Central Bank for Cooperatives, so all together there are thirty-seven banks in the Farm Credit System. These banks are owned by the private intermediaries through which they operate. The intermediaries, in turn, are owned by the ultimate users of the Farm Credit System, the nation's farmers and ranchers. Indirect Government supervision is maintained over the Farm Credit Banks through the Farm Credit Administration, an independent agency in the Executive Branch of the U. S. Government.

The twelve Federal Land Banks, established in 1917, are the oldest of the Federally sponsored agencies. Through Federal Land Bank Associations, Federal Land Banks make long-term loans to farmers for a variety of purposes, including the purchase of farms, machinery, and livestock, and for the refinancing of existing debts. The loans are made with maturities ranging from 5 to 40 years and are financed primarily through the sale of long-term debt obligations.

The Federal Intermediate Credit Banks provide short- and intermediate-term loans to and discount the paper of Production Credit Associations and other agriculture financing institutions which in turn lend to farmers, commercial fishermen and other farm-related businesses. These loans are made to meet seasonal credit requirements such as production and marketing expenses. They usually mature in one year but may be extended for up to seven years.

The Banks for Cooperatives are the smallest of the Farm Credit Banks. They extend credit to agricultural and aquatic marketing, supply, and business service cooperatives to meet marketing and operating capital needs. The main function of the Central Bank for Cooperatives is to participate with the districts banks in large loans that exceed their individual lending capacities.

The Housing Credit Agencies

Established in response to the financial plight of mortgage lending institutions during the depression years, the Federal Home Loan Bank System serves primarily as a source of secondary liquidity to member institutions. These institutions include Federally chartered savings and loan associations, which are required by law to belong to the system, and other eligible mortgage lending institutions such as state chartered savings and loan associations and mutual savings banks. The System is composed of twelve regional banks and a supervisory body, the Federal Home Loan Bank Board, which is an independent agency of the Executive Branch of the U. S. Government.

In performing their function, the FHLBs make loans, called advances, to member institutions. The demand for these advances is especially large during periods of disintermediation, which occur when open market interest rates are high relative to the regulatory interest rate ceilings placed on time and saving deposits. Consequently, the amount of funds raised by the FHLBs in the money and capital markets rises sharply in high interest rate periods. Advances are also made to meet seasonal mortgage demand as well as to expand overall mortgage lending consistent with the FHLBs' goal of fostering home ownership. Most of the FHLBs make advances with maturities of up to five years and some banks offer maturities of up to ten years.

The Federal National Mortgage Association, popularly known as "Fannie Mae," is the largest of the Federally sponsored agencies. Since its inception in 1938 under the original name of National Mortgage Association of Washington, FNMA has undergone several reorganizations on the way to its present status as a private corporation. The Federal Government maintains limited control over FNMA through the Department of Housing and Urban Development.

Under its current charter, the function of FNMA is " . . . to provide supplementary assistance to the secondary market for home mortgages by providing a degree of liquidity to mortgage investments thereby improving the distribution of investment capital for home mortgage financing. . ."

To accomplish this function, FNMA has been authorized to purchase and sell FHA, VA, and conventional loans from banks, savings and loan associations, mortgage bankers, and other organizations that meet its specified requirements. In general, FNMA increases its purchases of mortgages when the supply of funds to the mortgage market from other sources is declining. As a result, like the FHLBs, its demand for funds in the financial markets typically rises sharply in periods of high interest rates and disintermediation at the thrift institutions.

Federally Owned Agencies and the Federal Financing Bank

In addition to the Federally sponsored credit agencies, more than fifteen agencies *owned* by the Federal Government also used to borrow directly in the financial markets by placing their own individual securities. Consequently, the financial markets were faced with a wide variety of agency debt issues, with differing terms and guarantees. The *Federal Financing Bank* was established in 1974 to consolidate and streamline the borrowing activity of these Federally owned agencies and thereby lower the cost of raising agency funds.

Since the establishment of the Federal Financing Bank, all Federally owned agencies have raised funds through it rather than directly in the financial markets. Hence, there have not been any new issues of Federally owned agency debt since the mid-1970s. The Federal Financing Bank can acquire the funds it supplies to the Federally owned agencies either by borrowing in the financial markets itself or by borrowing from the Treasury. With the exception of one issue of $1.5 billion of eight-month notes sold in July 1974, the Federal Financing Bank has acquired all of its funds from the Treasury.

SHORT–TERM ISSUES

As of the end of 1979 there was $31.6 billion of Federally sponsored agency debt outstanding that had an original maturity of one year or less. This was 23.5 percent of the total outstanding, which represented a substantial decline from ten years earlier because of the more rapid growth of intermediate- and long-term agency debt during the 1970s. Compared to most other sectors of the money market, the agency market remains small.

Two types of short-term debt issues are sold by the Federally sponsored credit agencies: (1) bonds which carry a coupon and (2) discount notes that are sold at a discount from par and redeemed at their face value at maturity. As will be explained below, these two types of issues differ in the way they are marketed. Bonds are sold periodically through a selling group assembled by the agency's Fiscal Agent, whereas discount notes can be sold continuously on a daily basis through a small number of dealers associated with the agency. Currently, the Farm Credit Banks sell both short-term bonds and discount notes, while the FHLBs and FNMA sell only discount notes.

The Federal Intermediate Credit Banks, the Banks for Cooperatives and the Federal Land Banks sell their debt jointly through the use of "consolidated" issues backed by the assets of all 37 banks. The Farm Credit Banks have sold consolidated systemwide bonds since 1977 and consolidated systemwide discount notes since 1975.

Consolidated systemwide bonds are sold by the Farm Credit Banks each month with maturities of six and nine months in minimum denominations of $5,000. These securities are issued in *book-entry form*, meaning that an investor does not receive a physical certificate as evidence of purchase. Instead, computerized records are maintained at Federal Reserve Banks in the name of the purchasing institution. In turn, the purchasing institution maintains separate records of those securities they own and those maintained for other investors. Investors may choose as custodian any bank or other financial institution that maintains book-entry accounts with the Federal Reserve System.[2]

The discount notes of the Farm Credit Banks are issued daily over a maturity range of 5 to 270 days. The specific maturity date is designated by the investor at the time of purchase subject to the limitations of the issuing agency. Unlike bonds, discount notes of the Farm Credit Banks are currently sold only in certificate form.

Beginning in 1974 the FHLBs also began to sell short-term discount notes. These have maturities from 30 to 270 days and are issued in certificate form with a minimum denomination of $100,000. This high minimum denomination serves to deter small savers from withdrawing their deposits from member institutions to invest in FHLB securities.

FNMA has been selling short-term discount notes since 1960. Unlike the obligations of the other agencies, income earned on FNMA securities is subject to state and local taxes. While FNMA discount notes are issued in a relatively low minimum denomination of $5,000, FNMA has restricted minimum purchases to $50,000 in an attempt to avoid contributing to disintermediation at thrift institutions during periods of high interest rates. FNMA does not post competitive rates on its discount notes on a regular basis. It may stay out of the market for several weeks at a time but will enter aggressively when it needs to raise money. The maturity of FNMA discount notes ranges from 30 to 270 days.[3] The characteristics of the short-term Federally sponsored agency issues are summarized in Table 1.

---

[2] Beginning in October 1981, all depository institutions will be able to have these book-entry accounts.

[3] FNMA discount notes are also available in interest-bearing form. However, only a relative small amount of these are issued at any one time due to limited demand.

Table I Characteristics of Short-Term Agency Securities

Issuer	Type	Maturities	Form	Offering Schedule	Minimum Denomination	Tax Exemption
FCB	Consolidated system-wide bonds	6- and 9-month	Book-entry	Monthly	$ 5,000	state, local
	Consolidated system-wide discount notes	5-270 days	Certificate	Daily	$ 50,000	state, local
FHLB	Consolidated discount notes	30-270 days	Certificate	Daily	$100,000	state, local
FNMA	Discount notes	30-270 days	Certificate	Daily	$ 5,000*	none

*Minimum purchase of $50,000.

The greater use of discount notes in recent years by the Federally sponsored credit agencies reflects certain advantages these notes offer compared to short-term bonds. The use of discount notes increases the ability of agencies to exercise close control over their cash balances. Unlike bond sales, which require advance announcements, discount notes can be sold as the need for funds arises. An agency wishing to sell additional notes needs only to raise its rates to be more competitive with rates on other money market instruments. Similarly, an agency wishing to use idle funds to retire debt can simply post unattractive rates on its discount notes.

Discount notes also allow the agencies greater control over the maturity structure of their short-term debt. Through selective pricing policies, the agencies can more or less confine investor demand to a desired maturity area. Rates can quickly be adjusted as necessary to obtain the desired amount of funds at the desired maturities. It is not unusual, for example, for FNMA to change rates several times within a given day.

PRIMARY MARKET

The Federally sponsored credit agencies generally sell their new debt through a Fiscal Agent in New York City. When an interest-bearing note or bond offering is to be made, the Fiscal Agent assembles the selling group of securities dealers, brokerage houses, and dealer banks. Unlike syndicates formed for the sale of a specific stock or bond issue, members of the Agent's selling group do not bid against each other. Rather, each agency offering is made through only one selling group. To establish the price or price range of the new issues, the Fiscal Agent consults with the members of the selling group, the Treasury, the Trading Desk of the Federal Reserve Bank of New York, and the issuing agency regarding maturity, amount, coupon, and price. When the sale date arrives, the price is telegraphed by the Agent to the members of the group, who then make subscriptions through the Agent. The Agent determines the allotments, which are usually a fraction of total subscriptions.

The procedure for marketing discount notes is simpler. Discount notes are typically offered on a continuous basis through a small number of dealers who, as noted above, regularly adjust their rates to meet the borrowing desires of the agencies at various maturities.

SECONDARY MARKET

Short-term obligations of the Farm Credit Banks, the Federal Home Loan Banks, and the Federal National Mortgage Associations have well-established secondary markets. Dealers' inventories usually include large amounts of these securities. The spread between the bid and offered prices is narrow in short-term issues of these agencies, and trades of several million dollars can generally be made without upsetting the market. Generally, the primary selling group of dealers for a particular agency's discount notes or short-term bonds maintains a secondary market for those instruments, as do other dealers.

In December 1966 the Federal Open Market Committee, pursuant to an Act of Congress, authorized the use of repurchase agreements involving agency obligations in its open market operations. In August 1971 the Committee voted to conduct outright transactions in Federal agency securities. These developments not only increased the means available to the System for supplying and absorbing reserves but also tended to strengthen and broaden the secondary market for agency securities.

Secondary market activity in agency issues has kept pace with the growth in the outstanding supply of agency debt. Daily average gross dealer transactions in agency securities grew steadily from $140 million in 1965 to $2.72 billion in 1979. About 29 percent of the 1979 dealer transactions were accounted for by issues maturing within one year. Daily average dealer positions in agency securities rose over the same period, although more erratically, from $337 million in 1965 to $1.472 billion in 1979. The percentage of dealer positions represented by issues maturing in less than a year declined from 69 percent in 1965 to 43 percent in 1979, reflecting the relatively greater growth of longer-term issues.

INVESTMENT CHARACTERISTICS

Although Federally sponsored credit obligations are not obligations of, or guaranteed by, the U. S. Government, the issuing agencies are considered to be instrumentalities of the U. S. Government. As such, their securities are issued under the authority of Congress and subject to the same general regulations as those governing U. S. Treasury securities. As a result, investors generally perceive agency securities as carrying almost as low a degree of default risk as Treasury securities. Another attractive feature of short-term agency securities is their well-developed secondary market, which insures liquidity and low transactions costs.

Federal agency securities have a number of other characteristics, many of which are not common to other money market instruments, with the exception of Treasury bills. Among these characteristics are: (1) they are eligible as collateral for borrowing at the Federal Reserve Banks; (2) they are public securities and eligible to be held without limit by national banks; (3) they are supported, or "backstopped" by a limited authority to borrow from the United States Treasury; (4) they are eligible as collateral for tax and loan accounts; (5) they are eligible for purchase by the Federal Open Market Committee; and (6) they are issuable and payable through the facilities of the Federal Reserve Banks.

Yield

As a result of the low perception of default risk on agency issues, and perhaps also in part due to their relatively high degree of liquidity, the yield on short-term agency issues is generally below that of most private sector money market instruments of comparable maturity, and only moderately above Treasury bill rates.

Over the 20-year period from 1961 through 1980 the three- and six-month agency rates averaged 24 and 19 basis points, respectively, above Treasury bill rates of comparable maturity.[4] The spread between short-term agency and Treasury bill rates exhibits no trend over this 20-year period, although it does have a cyclical movement that is positively correlated to the level of interest rates. In particular, in 1974 the average spread between the three-month Federal agency and Treasury bill rates rose to a record level of 78 basis points. Perhaps the most common explanation for this relationship points to the relative supply of bills and short-term agency issues in high interest periods, at least prior to the late 1970s. High short-term interest rates typically have occurred in the latter phases of an expanding economy. In such periods the Treasury's demand for funds is generally small, which decreases the supply of Treasury bills coming to the market. In contrast, the supply of short-term agency securities rises sharply in such periods because of the increased activity of the housing-related agencies. In the 1978-80 period the spread between the three-month Federal agency and Treasury bill rates averaged only 34 basis points despite a rise in short-term rates to record levels. However, unlike earlier periods of high short-term

---

[4] The rates in this comparison are calculated on a bond equivalent basis and are from Salomon Brothers' *An Analytical Record of Yields and Yield Spreads.*

interest rates, there was a large supply of Treasury bills throughout this period.

INVESTORS

Federally sponsored credit agency securities are close substitutes for U. S. Government securities and, like U. S. securities, are held by virtually all sectors of the economy. A precise breakdown of relative shares is difficult, since in the Treasury's Survey of Ownership over half of the total outstanding are included in the residual "all other" category, which includes individuals, commercial bank trust departments, and all other institutions not covered by the Survey. Undoubtedly individuals hold a significant share. Among the reporting categories, the largest holder of agency issues throughout the history of the Survey has been commercial banks, which held 18.6 percent of the total as of December 1980.[5] Next in line at that time were state and local governments (including general and pension funds) with 6.7 percent and U. S. Government accounts and Federal Reserve Banks with 5.5 percent.

In recent years the residual "other" category in the Treasury survey has grown considerably to 61.0 percent in December 1980. The growth in this category partially reflects the growing percentage of outstanding short-term agency issues purchased by short-term investment pooling arrangements, such as money market mutual funds. These funds have enabled even small investors to indirectly invest in money market instruments. As a result, the large minimum purchase requirements placed on the short-term issues of FNMA and the FHLBs have become largely ineffective as a barrier to disintermediation.

REFERENCES

1. Craigie Incorporated. "Pertinent Facts for the Potential Investor in United States Federal Agency Securities," Richmond, Virginia.
2. Federal Home Loan Bank System "Consolidated Discount Notes," Washington, D. C.
3. Federal National Mortgage Association, *Background and History*, 1973, Washington, D. C.: Federal National Mortgage Association, November 1973.
4. ———— "Debentures" Washington, D. C.
5. Fiscal Agency for the Farm Credit Banks "An Investors Guide to Farm Credit Securities," New York.
6. ———— Farm Credit Banks Report to Investors, 1979, *New York: Fiscal Agency for the Farm Credit Banks, 1979.*
7. Nelson, Jane F. "Federal Agency Securities," *Instruments of the Money Market*, 4th ed. Edited by Timothy Q. Cook, Richmond: Federal Reserve Bank of Richmond, 1977.

[5] Mortgage-backed bonds and certificates are excluded from these calculations.

THE DISCOUNT WINDOW*

James Parthemos and
Walter Varvel

5

Adjustments in bank reserve positions are accomplished through purchase and sales of financial instruments in the money market. In addition to reliance on money market instruments, member banks have long had the "privilege" of acquiring reserves by borrowing at the discount window of their regional Federal Reserve Bank. By arranging an advance at the Federal Reserve, a bank suffering an unexpected reserve loss can bring its reserve position back to the desired or required level. Similarly, an institution experiencing a temporary buildup of reserves beyond desired levels may, before placing funds in the money market, pay off any borrowings it may owe at the window. In any event, the discount window affords an additional recourse in working out reserve adjustments and may be properly viewed as an operational part of the money market.

Following passage of the *Depository Institutions Deregulation and Monetary Control Act of 1980*, or *Monetary Control Act* as it is often called, nonmember banks and thrift institutions can also choose to adjust reserve positions through the discount window. The new legislation requires nonmembers to maintain reserve balances against transaction and nonpersonal time deposits. In addition, all institutions issuing reservable deposit liabilities are authorized access to the discount window.

Reserve adjustments made by individual institutions using the discount window differ in one important respect from alternative adjustment tech-

*Reprinted, with deletions, from *Instruments of the Money Market*, 5th edition, edited by Timothy Q. Cook and Bruce J. Summers, 1981, with permission from the Federal Reserve Bank of Richmond.

niques. Trading in such instruments as Federal funds, negotiable certificates of deposit, and Treasury bills among commercial banks or between banks and their customers involves no net creation of new bank reserves. Rather, existing reserves are simply shifted about within the banking system. On the other hand, net borrowings or repayments at the discount window result in a net change in Federal Reserve credit outstanding and, consequently, affect the volume of bank reserves. Thus, the choice by individual institutions between using the discount window or alternative means of reserve adjustment may influence the availability of money and credit in the economy. Policy decisions of the Federal Reserve affecting discount window borrowing, therefore, have ramifications for the conduct of monetary policy.

Decisions to use the discount window relative to other segments of the money market for making reserve adjustments depend importantly upon the relation of the Federal Reserve's discount rate to yields on money market investments and on legal and administrative arrangements regarding use of the discount window. Neither of these factors are determined by the competitive interaction of market forces, but rather by administrative decision. Adjustments in interest rates on window borrowings are recommended by the Boards of Directors of the regional Reserve Banks in accord with current economic and money market conditions, with final approval required by the Board of Governors. In addition, the legal requirements and administrative guidelines for extensions of credit through the window are embodied in Federal Reserve Regulation A.

EARLY DISCOUNTING PRINCIPLES

An important principle underlying creation of the Federal Reserve System was providing a pool of funds which could be drawn on by banks experiencing reserve shortages. The ability of banks to draw on this pool, however, was not envisaged as an absolute right. Rather, it was linked to a widely held theory of commercial banking which is known as the commercial loan or "real bills" doctrine. According to this doctrine, commercial banks should borrow only against short-term, self-liquidating paper arising from the normal conduct of production and trade. Member banks were initially permitted to borrow from the Federal Reserve Banks only by rediscounting customer loans which met certain carefully specified conditions based on the commercial loan theory. Promissory notes and other credit instruments meeting these specifications were defined as "eligible paper," that is, paper eligible for rediscount at the Federal Reserve. By and large, the real bills doctrine dominated member bank use of the discount window until the banking crisis of 1933.

During the 1920s, trading in such money market instruments as short-term government debt and Federal funds was not nearly so well developed as at present. Consequently, the discount window was a primary tool of adjustment for member banks. While banks made extensive use of bankers' acceptances, commercial paper, and call loans against stock exchange collateral for reserve adjustment purposes, they also relied heavily on the discount window. Many bankers made it a regular practice to hold a supply of eligible paper which would be readily available for reserve adjustment through the discount window. Throughout the 1920s, average daily borrowings at the discount window usually exceeded $500 million and at times amounted to more than twice that figure.

FROM THE 1930s TO THE ACCORD

The banking reforms of the 1930s incorporated features designed to encourage use of the discount window by banks. In some measure, these features were related to a growing conviction that the real bills doctrine and discount window eligibility requirements unduly restricted banks seeking central bank assistance in times of stress. The effect of the reforms was to sweep away the real bills basis for discounting, although the concept of eligible paper was retained in the language of Federal Reserve discount regulations.

At an early stage in Federal Reserve history, member banks were allowed to borrow on their own notes, secured by eligible paper or government securities, instead of by rediscounting customer paper. Since 1933 direct advances against government securities have accounted for most Federal Reserve lending. In addition, banking legislation of the 1930s incorporated a new section, 10(b), into the Federal Reserve Act authorizing loans to member banks against any collateral satisfactory to the lending Reserve Bank.

Despite the encouragement of these changes and low discount rates, banks used the discount window sparingly between 1933 and 1951. From 1935 to 1940 daily borrowings generally averaged below $10 million. For the most part, banks held large amounts of excess reserves and were under little pressure to borrow. Even after the business recovery of the early 1940s, borrowing remained at low levels. By that time, banks held large quantities of government securities and the Federal Reserve's practice of pegging the market for these securities, instituted in 1942, eliminated the market risk of adjusting reserve positions through sales of governments. The Treasury-Federal Reserve Accord of 1951, however, ended the pegged market for government securities and began a new chapter in the history of the discount window.

DISCOUNTING SINCE THE ACCORD

Prices of government securities fluctuated over a broader range after the Accord, and it became riskier for banks to rely on these securities as a source of reserves when adjustments were necessary. Consequently, banks began to reassess the relative attractiveness of the discount window. Partly for this reason, borrowings jumped sharply, reaching the $1 billion level in mid-1952 for the first time in more than 20 years. For most of the 1950s borrowings were at levels comparable in absolute terms (although smaller relative to required reserves) with those of the 1920s.

The renewed importance of the discount window, coming in an overall economic and credit environment quite different from that prevailing in the 1920s, suggested the need for a general review of the principles on which the discount privilege was based. In 1955, after an extended inquiry, the Board of Governors promulgated a major revision in its Regulation A. As embodied in Regulation A, administrative restrictions on use of the discount window relate to the broader aspects of the Federal Reserve's operations rather than to any particular banking theory. For example, Regulation A recognizes that discount borrowing creates new reserves and, unless subject to some restraint, could conflict with policy goals such as economic and price stability. It also recognizes the necessity for insuring that the public resources administered by the Federal Reserve are not used to support questionable banking practices, but rather to insure the continuity of banking services provided to the public.

Generally, Regulation A envisages use of the discount window primarily as a temporary expedient open to institutions requiring reserve adjustments resulting from unanticipated shortages of funds. Indeed, short term adjustment credit represents the great bulk of window borrowings. In addition, two other categories of borrowing have been considered "appropriate." Reserve needs of smaller institutions occasioned by seasonal swings in credit demand and in deposits may give rise to appropriate borrowing. Similarly, reserve problems associated with emergency situations affecting a community or a region, or with local or regional secular change, provide appropriate reasons for borrowing. Within the constraints embodied in Regulation A, the discount window is open to depository institutions in a variety of situations that may be considered more or less normal commercial banking operations. As long as an institution demonstrates in its overall performance its intention to operate within the limits of its own resources, it can usually arrange temporary accommodation to cover a variety of needs.

Continuous borrowing at the discount window is considered "inappropriate" whatever its cause since it implies that the borrowing bank has permanent reserve difficulties that should be corrected through basic portfolio adjustments. Extended use of central bank funds would supplement an institution's capital resources as a permanent base for investment in bank assets. The Federal Reserve has enumerated specific purposes for which use of the discount window is deemed inappropriate. These include borrowing to profit from interest rate differentials, to substitute Federal Reserve credit for normal sources of short-term interest-sensitive funds, and to support increases in loan or investment portfolios [2].

In April 1973, Regulation A was revised to permit greater use of the discount window for seasonal borrowing. Short-term access to the discount window had previously been available to member banks experiencing unusually strong seasonal reserve needs. The revision in Regulation A was designed explicitly to assist those member banks, especially small institutions, that lacked access to the national money markets in meeting seasonal needs arising out of predictable patterns in deposits and loans.

Under the 1973 revision, a member bank could obtain Federal Reserve credit to meet seasonal needs exceeding 5 percent of its average annual deposits. In order to qualify for the seasonal borrowing privilege, the bank had to provide the Federal Reserve with advance evidence indicating that the seasonal need would persist for at least eight consecutive weeks. The seasonal borrowing program initiated in 1973 was available only to banks with deposits of less than $250 million. Furthermore, member banks were not permitted to use the seasonal borrowing privilege and at the same time be net sellers of Federal funds.

In August 1976, Regulation A was further revised to liberalize the seasonal borrowing privilege. Under the revised regulations member banks could use the seasonal borrowing privilege to meet that part of their seasonal need for funds exceeding 4 percent of the first $100 million of the previous years average deposits; 7 percent of the second $100 million; and 10 percent of any deposits over $200 million. The period over which the seasonal need must persist was lowered from eight weeks to four weeks, and banks with deposits up to $500 million were made eligible for the seasonal borrowing privilege. In practice, however, the increasing deductible makes it unlikely that institutions with deposits in excess of $250 million will qualify for seasonal credit. In addition, the revision permits net sales of Federal funds while banks are engaged in seasonal borrowing from the Federal Reserve, as long as the sales represent the institution's normal operating pattern of Federal funds sales—including its usual seasonal and cyclical variation in sales and allowance for growth. This change was made in recognition of the growing number of small banks that were continuous net sellers of Federal funds. Since the initiation of the seasonal borrowing program in 1973, seasonal borrowing has generally been heaviest in the period from July through October. The magnitude of average monthly seasonal borrowing has varied over subsequent years from a low of $18 million in 1974 to a high of $145 million in 1979.

Emergency credit assistance at the discount window has been infrequently extended to institutions facing liquidity crises. Such assistance is sometimes necessary to minimize potentially serious adverse impacts of failure on financial flows in the economy and to provide federal banking agencies sufficient time to work out a satisfactory permanent solution. In the case of Franklin National Bank in 1974, deteriorating earnings and massive withdrawals of deposits induced the Federal Reserve, in its role as "lender of last resort,"[1] to advance funds to Franklin, peaking at $1.75 billion just prior to takeover of the bulk of the bank's assets and deposits by the European American Bank. More recently, large discount window borrowings played a key role in alleviating liquidity problems at First Pennsylvania Bank. Regulation A permits emergency credit extensions to nondepository institutions when alternative sources of credit are not available and failure to obtain such credit would adversely affect the economy. Such credit, however, will be at a higher rate of interest than that applicable to depository institutions.

THE MONETARY CONTROL ACT: A NEW ERA

The *Monetary Control Act*, enacted in March 1980, gives all nonmember banks, savings and loan associations, savings banks, and credit unions holding transaction accounts or nonpersonal time deposits the same discount and borrowing privileges as member banks. The Act directs the Federal Reserve to administer the window taking into consideration "the special needs of savings and other depository institutions for access to discount and borrowing facilities consistent with their long-term asset portfolios and the sensitivity of such institutions to trends in the national money markets." The impact of this legislation on the administration of the discount window is far-reaching.

In September 1980, the Federal Reserve revised Regulation A to implement the provisions of the Act. The revision establishes an additional lending category to provide credit for an extended period for other than seasonal needs. "Other extended credit" can now be arranged for individual depository institutions experiencing financial strains due to exceptional circumstances such as sustained deposit drains, impaired access to money market funds, or sudden deterioration in loan repayment performance. Depository institutions with investment portfolios composed of primarily longer-term assets and experiencing difficulties adjusting to changing money market conditions, particularly during periods of deposit disintermediation, may also borrow under the other extended credit provision.

The revised lending provisions do not, however, alter the Federal Reserve's expectation that depository institutions are to rely primarily on their usual

---

[1] For a discussion of the classical concept of the role of the central bank as lender of last resort, see [5].

sources of funds before turning to the discount window for assistance. Discount window credit will generally be made available only after alternative sources have been exhausted. In the case of thrift institutions, alternative sources of funds include special industry lenders such as the Federal Home Loan Banks, the National Credit Union Administration's Central Liquidity Facility, and corporate central credit unions. Before extending credit, the Reserve Banks will consult with the borrowing institution's supervising agency to determine why funds are not available from other sources.

The September 1980 revision in Regulation A made discretionary use of a discount rate surcharge a permanent addition to the Federal Reserve's discount lending policy. Such a surcharge can be made applicable to both adjustments and extended credit. In March 1980, as part of the special credit restraint program, the System briefly instituted a 3 percent surcharge on adjustment credit of member banks with over $500 million in deposits when such borrowings occurred successively in two reserve statement weeks or more, or when the borrowing occurred in more than four weeks in a calendar quarter. The surcharge which did not apply to seasonal borrowings or emergency loans, was designed to discourage frequent use of the discount window. The surcharge was eliminated in May but was reinstated on adjustment credit extended to frequent borrowings of large depository institutions in late 1980.

ADMINISTRATION OF THE WINDOW

Currently, most Federal Reserve loans are made under the provisions of Section 13 of the Federal Reserve Act and are in the form of direct advances secured by U. S. Government securities. Advances under Section 13 can also be made against Federal agency securities. Loans under Section 10(b) may be secured by any collateral satisfactory to the lending Reserve Bank, including State and local government securities, mortgage notes covering 1-4 family residences, and business and other customer notes. The use of these additional types of collateral has been relatively unimportant in recent discount activity, in part, because the rate charged on 10(b) loans was ½ of one percentage point higher than on Section 13 loans. Moreover, depending on the collateral offered, 10(b) loans may involve some delay before funds are made available. Banks borrowing under this Section usually offered municipal securities as collateral. The *Monetary Control Act* authorized the Federal Reserve to eliminate the ½ of one percentage point differential required on 10(b) loans, a change that became effective in September 1980. With the removal of the penalty rate, institutions may choose to increase use of municipals and residential mortgages as collateral for window borrowings.

Maturities of up to 90 days are authorized on Section 13 loans, while the statutory limit on 10(b) maturities is four months. In practice, however, Reserve Banks encourage borrowers to limit maturities to shorter periods. Large institutions with broad access to money market funds are expected to make necessary adjustments in their portfolios faster than smaller banks. Consequently, adjustment credit extended to money market banks will normally be only to the next business day. Smaller institutions may borrow with somewhat longer maturities.

Adjustment credit is available on a short-term basis to assist depository institutions "in meeting temporary requirements for funds, or to cushion more persistent outflows of funds pending an orderly adjustment of the institution's assets and liabilities."[2] It is the responsibility of the Reserve Bank discount officer to ensure that adjustment borrowing is for appropriate purposes and not simply a substitute for regular sources of funds. Borrowing requests from institutions that are not presently in the window or that have not in the recent past relied heavily on the window are normally accommodated immediately. When the size or frequency of borrowing increases, however, an institution may be asked to provide information justifying continued use of discount credit. If the borrowing is judged to be inappropriate, the borrower is asked to discontinue use of the window. Such administrative pressure represents nonprice rationing of discount credit.

To assist in the determination of the appropriateness of window borrowing, heavy reliance is placed on analysis of balance sheet trends, especially flows in loans and deposits, net positions in Federal funds, and changes in liquid assets. Balance sheets are examined to determine the extent of liquidity pressures and to see if appropriate adjustments are taking place.

An extensive review of discount window policy conducted by the Federal Reserve in the late 1960s [2] reported that some differences existed among Regional Banks in the determination of what constituted appropriate borrowing. To help achieve uniformity in discount administration, numerical guidelines for the size and frequency of borrowing by an individual institution have been established. Such guidelines, used as a secondary measure by the discount officer, provide a norm for the amount of borrowing a typical bank is likely to require, the amount of time usually needed to adjust the bank's position, and a measure of how frequently a bank is likely to need adjustment credit. Borrowing that exceeds the guidelines does not necessarily mean that the borrowing will be considered inappropriate.

Since large institutions generally have greater access to alternative sources of funds than smaller institutions, the guidelines are more stringent for large borrowers. Borrowings as a percentage of domestic deposits are generally expected to be lower than for smaller institutions, and less frequent. Some variation in the size classifications included in the guidelines exists among the regional Reserve Banks.

[2] Regulation A, Section 201.3(a).

MECHANICS OF BORROWING

In order to borrow, an institution must furnish the Federal Reserve Bank a resolution adopted by its Board of Directors specifying which of its officers are authorized to borrow on its behalf. A *Continuing Lending Agreement* is normally executed facilitating prompt extension of discount credit upon telephone requests from borrowing institutions.

Advances secured by government obligations can be made up to the face amount of the collateral. The collateral must be held by the Federal Reserve Bank unless prior arrangements have been made permitting another institution to hold the securities under a custody receipt arrangement. Under such an arrangement, the securities may be held by a "custody" bank which in the usual course of business performs correspondent bank services, including the holding in custody of government securities, for the borrower. While institutions may also borrow on their promissory note secured by eligible paper, this procedure can be more time-consuming since the Reserve Bank must verify the eligibility of the collateral, then analyze and value it. Institutions, therefore, often submit collateral in advance of the date of the borrowing. Applications processing is prompt when municipal securities are offered as collateral, but delays may result when customer notes are offered. In addition, 10(b) collateral may be valued at less than the face amount.

Once an application for Federal Reserve credit is approved by the Reserve Bank, borrowings are normally credited directly to the institution's reserve account. Unless the Federal Reserve is notified to the contrary, the principal plus interest due on the note is automatically charged against the borrower's reserve account on the maturity date. Notes may, of course, be paid in part or in full before maturity. Nonmember institutions may (a) decide not to hold reserves directly with the Federal Reserve but hold them with a correspondent institution on a "pass-through" basis or (b) have reserve liabilities that can be met with vault cash. In these instances, three-party arrangements may be made among the Federal Reserve, borrower, and a correspondent institution providing for credits and debits to be charged against the correspondent's reserve account.

BORROWING LEVELS

The volume of borrowings at the discount window fluctuates over a wide range. Borrowings generally increase in periods of high or rising market interest rates and decline in periods of low or falling rates. To a large extent, this is because changes in the discount rate lag behind movements in money market rates. Consequently, in periods of rising rates, the cost of borrowing at the discount window frequently becomes relatively more attractive compared to the cost of raising funds in the money market.

There is a strong relationship between total member bank borrowing and the differential between the Federal funds rate and the discount rate. The 1950s and early 1960s were generally characterized by periods of relatively stable interest rates. Throughout this period, the discount rate was usually maintained at or above market rates, providing little financial incentive for discount borrowing. The latter 1960s and much of the 1970s, however, saw large swings in the interest differential. Borrowing averaged well over $1 billion throughout most of 1969 and early 1970 when the Federal funds rate exceeded the discount rate, at times, by over 3 percentage points. Throughout 1973 and 1974 member bank borrowings averaged nearly $2 billion and exceeded $3 billion in June through September 1974 when the interest differential approached 5 percent. Borrowings fell rapidly with the onset of the recession and the related drop-off in loan demand in late 1974 and early 1975. Market rates fell dramatically and were generally below the discount rate from early 1975 through mid-1977, when window borrowing was minimal.

From 1977 through most of 1979, the Federal Reserve demonstrated a desire to keep the discount rate more closely in line with increasing market rates. Discount rate increases were more frequent but still lagged behind market rates resulting in a general increase in borrowing levels. Borrowing grew rapidly, approaching a level of $3 billion following the Federal Reserve's shift to a reserve targeting procedure (described below) in October 1979 which resulted in large differentials between the funds rate and the discount rate. The imposition of the credit restraint program with its temporary three percentage point surcharge on large bank borrowings and the reduced economic activity beginning in early 1980, contributed to the subsequent sharp drop in market rates (relative to the discount rate) and the lower level of discount borrowing. Considering the low level of the discount rate relative to the cost of alternative sources of reserve adjustment funds during periods of high interest rates, the volume of borrowings would undoubtedly have been much greater without the use of discount administration as a rationing device.

During periods of high interest rates, the discount rate has usually remained below market rates and, in effect, subsidized member bank borrowing from the Federal Reserve. In such times, reduced interest expenses from borrowing at below market rates provided a partial offset to the opportunity costs associated with maintaining non-earning reserve balances with the Federal Reserve [1].

Both small and large banks use the discount window, but in most years large banks have accounted for the greater dollar volume of borrowings. Banks that manage their reserve positions closely usually meet short-run reserve deficiencies either by borrowing from the Federal Reserve or by buying Federal funds. Large banks tend to incur reserve deficiencies more frequently than small banks. Thus, they tend to rely more heavily on borrowed funds. The tendency to use both the discount window and Federal funds increases with bank size.

Since large banks are more frequent users of discount window credit than small banks, most savings on interest expenses resulting from borrowing at below-market discount rates would seem to accrue to large banks. A study analyzing member bank borrowing in the Eighth Federal Reserve District from 1974 to 1977 confirms that the dollar amounts of such benefits are disproportionately concentrated among the largest banks. Measures of the interest savings per dollar borrowed and interest savings as a percentage of average reserve balances held at the Federal Reserve, however, show that relatively small banks which borrowed heavily "benefited as much or more than the large banks" when market rates were substantially above the discount rate [4].

ROLE OF THE DISCOUNT WINDOW IN MONETARY POLICY

The role of discount rate administration in the making of monetary policy has changed somewhat since the October 1979 shift in Federal Reserve operating strategy. Prior to October 1979, the Federal Reserve attempted to achieve its money supply objectives by manipulating the Federal funds rate. Because in that policy setting the Federal Reserve chose to fix the Federal funds rate in the short-run, increases in the discount rate reduced the differential between the Federal funds rate and the discount rate, and decreased the demand for borrowed reserves. To keep the Federal funds rate steady following an increase in the discount rate, the Federal Reserve had to increase the supply of nonborrowed reserves. Consequently, increases in the discount rate did not directly affect the level of short-run interest rates; they simply changed the mix of nonborrowed and borrowed reserves. At most, under the old regime, discount rate changes were used by the monetary authorities to signal changes in policy through what was referred to as the "announcement effect."

The importance of discount window policy has been enhanced under the reserve targeting strategy adopted by the Federal Open Market Committee in October 1979. Under this strategy, the Federal Reserve attempts to achieve its money supply objectives by setting targets for nonborrowed and borrowed reserves. The demand for borrowed reserves is largely dependent on the spread between the Federal funds rate and the discount rate. Consequently, a given borrowed reserve objective will, roughly speaking, produce a particular spread between the funds rate and the discount rate. The more the Federal Reserve makes the banking system borrow, the higher the funds rate will be in relation to the discount rate. Under the new operating procedure, then, given a specific borrowed reserves objective, a rise in the discount rate is immediately transmitted to the Federal funds rate and to other short-term interest rates. For this reason in all instances from October 1979 through the end of 1980, increases in the discount rate resulted in increases in the Federal funds rate of at least equal magnitude.

The change in the effect of discount rate movements on short-term interest rates since the October 1979 change in operating strategy illustrates an important point, namely, that the effect of discount rate movements on market interest rates depends on the operating strategy of the Federal Reserve.

REFERENCES

1.   George J. Benston, *Federal Reserve Membership: Consequences, Costs, Benefits, and Alternatives*, Association of Reserve City Bankers, 1978, p. 34.

2.   Board of Governors of the Federal Reserve System, "Operation of the Federal Reserve Discount Window Under the Monetary Control Act of 1980," September 1980.

3.   Board of Governors of the Federal Reserve System, *Reappraisal of the Federal Reserve Discount Mechanism: Volume I*, August 1971.

4.   R. Alton Gilbert, "Benefits of Borrowing From the Federal Reserve When the Discount Rate is Below Market Interest Rates," *Review*, Federal Reserve Bank of St. Louis, March 1979, pp. 25.32.

5.   Thomas M. Humphrey, "The Classical Concept of the Lender of Last Resort," *Economic Review*, Federal Reserve Bank of Richmond, January/February 1975, pp. 2-9.

BANKERS' ACCEPTANCES*

Jack L. Hervey

6

Perhaps no other financial instrument—apart from money itself—has been as important to the development of international commerce as the bill of exchange and its more refined form, the banker's acceptance. By providing an efficient means of facilitating the shipment of goods through the extension of trade credit, these instruments have made it possible for two traders virtually unknown to each other and located in different parts of the world to enter into commercial transactions.

Economic historians trace the origin of early forms of these instruments to the twelfth century and attribute to their development the onset of the "commercial revolution." Over time, other instruments and means of settling international transactions were developed by banks, and consequently, bankers' acceptances have lost the unique place in international trade and finance they once enjoyed. Nevertheless, they continue to play in important role as modern financial instruments.

WHAT IS A BANKER'S ACCEPTANCE?

A banker's acceptance is a time draft, essentially an "order to pay" a specified sum of money at a specified date, drawn on and "accepted" by a bank.

*Reprinted from *Business Conditions*, May 1976, pp. 3-11, with permission from the Federal Reserve Bank of Chicago and the author.

By accepting the draft, a bank assumes the responsibility to make payment at maturity of the draft. Acceptance of a time draft by a bank serves to make the draft, already a negotiable instrument, more readily salable (marketable) because by its acceptance the bank lends its integrity and credit rating to the instrument. The drawing of the draft is frequently preauthorized by a "letter of credit" issued by either the bank on which the order is drawn or by that bank's correspondent bank in the country of the buyer. However, the major dollar volume of acceptances created takes the form of "outright" acceptances—that is, the instrument arises out of a contractual arrangement less formal than a letter of credit and is later supported by the appropriate documentation.

Bankers' acceptances possess several attributes that make them desirable financial instruments from the point of view of traders (exporters and importers), bankers, and investors. To the seller of goods the major advantage

The Life of An Acceptance

To illustrate the process by which an acceptance may be created, consider an example where a firm in Brussels contracts for the purchase of office equipment from a firm in Rockford, Illinois. (See flow chart for the sequence of events described below.) Following inquiries and an exchange of correspondence between the two firms, it is agreed that the Brussels firm will arrange for the issuance of a letter of credit in favor of the Rockford supplier. The Brussels firm sends a "purchase order" to the Rockford firm (1), and also makes application to its local bank for a letter of credit (2), under a line of credit extended by the bank to the firm. The Brussels firm foresees a need for financing the office equipment for a period of 90 days from the time of shipment. Therefore, it stipulates in the letter of credit application that the draft is to be drawn at 90 days sight and further that it agrees to bear the charges for discounting of the draft in the United States by the Rockford firm. (The burden of who bears the cost of the discount varies with the relative bargaining power of the exporting and importing firms and may, as a result, rest with the exporter.) The Brussels bank issues a letter of credit available by draft at 90 days sight on its Chicago correspondent and mails it to the correspondent for delivery to the Rockford firm (3). Upon receipt of the letter of credit the Chicago bank verifies the authenticity of the signatures on the credit and mails it to the Rockford firm (4). The Rockford firm inspects the terms of the letter of credit and being satisfied with them, makes the shipment. It then collects the bill of lading and other documents called for under the letter of credit, draws a draft at 90 days sight on the Chicago bank and presents them to the bank along with the letter of credit (5). The Chicago bank satisfies itself that the documents are in compliance with the terms of the credit. It then accepts the 90 days draft, thereby creating a banker's acceptance (9), discounts it—charging discount and other charges to the account

in extending credit to the buyer through an acceptance lies in the fact that the instrument provides him with a bank's assurance of repayment. This feature has been particularly important in international trade, where the parties to the transaction may not be well known to each other or where the seller cannot readily ascertain the credit rating of the buyer. By using acceptance credit, the seller of goods in effect shifts the burden of guaranteeing the integrity of credit to the accepting bank.

The acceptance form of financing may be used to cover the shipment stage, which may amount to a substantial period—for example, an ocean shipment. The finance period may, however, extend into the period prior to shipment by the seller as well as into the marketing stage after receipt of the shipment by the buyer. To the trading party bearing the cost of the credit, bankers' acceptances also offer certain advantages over other forms of credit. A banker's acceptance usually compares favorably in cost with a conven-

---

of the Brussels bank—and pays the face amount of the draft to the Rockford firm (6). The shipping documents, the advice of debit covering the acceptance fee and other charges, and notification of the due date of the acceptance are mailed to the Brussels bank (7), which makes appropriate entries on its books. The documents are then forwarded to the Brussels firm, which will use them to clear the merchandise when it arrives (8).

The Chicago bank subsequently finds that it needs funds for its banking business. It sells the acceptance to an acceptance dealer (9) and receives the face amount of the acceptance less discount at the going bankers' acceptance rate for the number of days remaining to maturity (10). The Chicago bank has thus been able to replenish its reserves, earn some income arising from the difference in the rates at which it discounted the draft and sold it to the dealer, and earn interest for the period during which it held the draft. The dealer in turn sells the acceptance to an investor (11) and receives the net proceeds (12), after deduction of a discount, which should be slightly less than what he charged to the bank.

At maturity of the acceptance the investor presents it for payment to the Chicago bank (13) and receives the face amount of the draft in payment (14). The Chicago bank in the meantime will have received payment from the Brussels bank (15), which in turn has received payment from the Brussels firm (16).

Bankers' acceptances arise out of the financing of a U.S. import in a similar manner. The major difference is that if the foreign exporter submits the draft for acceptance, it does so to a U.S. bank that is a correspondent to its home bank. The reason the acceptance is not created by its home bank is that the U.S. acceptance market is the only one of consequence among the various national financial markets.

The procedure for a third-country acceptance may follow a similar procedure with the major difference being that the trading participants are outside the United States.

A banker's acceptance is created, discounted, sold, and paid at maturity

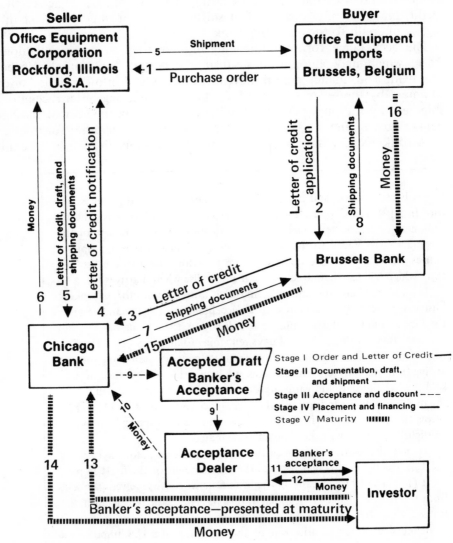

Note: This section was developed with the cooperation of Naran J. Patel, Operations Officer, The Northern Trust Company, Chicago, Illinois.

tional bank loan despite the fact that the rate of interest charged (technically a discount on the face value of the acceptance) on credit extended through bankers' acceptances is often higher than the "prime rate" charged on conventional loans. In part this is because banks usually require conventional borrowers to maintain "compensating balances"—that is, the lending bank requires that a portion of the loan proceeds be maintained as a noninterest-bearing deposit. Because of this requirement, the effective cost of conventional credit is typically higher than the nominal quoted rate. Also, acceptance credit is typically more attractive for firms that are less than "prime" borrowers.

The attractiveness of an acceptance, as far as a bank is concerned, is that a bank earns a fee (usually 1½ percent per annum of the amount of the acceptance) for merely lending its name and credit rating by accepting a draft, without tying up any of its funds. The actual credit extension is, under these circumstances, undertaken by the seller of the goods. Only when the acceptance-creating bank purchases (discounts) the acceptance, from the seller of goods, for its own account does the bank tie up funds, earning not only the acceptance fee but also the discount charge on the acceptance credit. Even when the acceptance-creating bank purchases the acceptance (and thus, in effect extends the credit), the acceptance form of credit offers the bank certain advantages over a conventional loan. Unlike a conventional loan an acceptance is marketable and may be sold to an acceptance dealer, who in turn sells it to an investor that becomes the party financing the original transaction. As such, the acceptance when purchased by the bank serves as a form of secondary liquidity reserve. Finally, in the case of certain types of domestic shipment or storage drafts, acceptances are secured by title to the goods or a warehouse receipt (at the time the acceptance is created) and offer the accepting bank the advantage of good collateral. (See table for an outline of the applicable conditions.)

From the viewpoint of the investor bankers' acceptances hold two primary advantages. First, an acceptance is a relatively secure investment. By definition, an accepting bank assumes the primary obligation for payment of the face value of the acceptance at maturity. An acceptance is based on specific goods in transit or storage and, as noted above, in the case of domestic acceptances is in some cases secured by title or warehouse receipt. Further, an obligation for payment also rests with the drawer of the acceptance who assumes a liability contingent to that of the primary liability of the accepting bank (such an acceptance is sometimes referred to as "two-name paper"). While it is conceivable that these "lines of security" could break down, an acceptance is viewed by many as one of the safest forms of short-term investment. Second, acceptances are a relatively liquid investment. While the acceptance market is "thin" in comparison with the government securities market and concentrated with the relatively few New York acceptance dealers, quality acceptances are nevertheless readily marketable instruments.[1]

---

[1] The quality of an acceptance depends largely upon the familiarity of the accepting bank in the acceptance market, the financial soundness of the accepting bank, and the "eligibility" category of the acceptance itself. This is discussed in detail later.

Bankers' Acceptances—Conditions and Characteristics Governing
Eligibility, Reserve Requirements, and Acceptance Limits

	Federal Reserve System treatment			
Bankers' acceptance categories	Eligible for discount[1]	Eligible for purchase[2]	Reserve require-ments[3]	Aggregate acceptance limits[4]
1. To cover specific international transactions				
a. U.S. exports or imports.				
Maturity-6 months or less	yes[5]	yes	no	yes
6 months to 9 months.	no	yes	yes	no
more than 9 months	no	no	yes	no
b. Shipment of goods *between* foreign countries.				
Maturity-6 months or less	yes[5]	yes	no	yes
6 months to 9 months.	no	yes	yes	no
more than 9 months	no	no	yes	no
c. Shipment of goods *within* a foreign country.				
Maturity-any term	no	no	yes	no
d. Storage of goods within a foreign country (readily marketable staples secured by warehouse receipt).				
Maturity-6 months or less	yes[5]	no	no	yes
6 months to 9 months.	no	no	yes	no
more than 9 months	no	no	yes	no
e. Dollar exchange—required by usages of trade in approved countries only.				
Maturity-3 months or less	yes	no	no	yes
more than 3 months	no	no	yes	no
2. To cover specific domestic transactions (i.e., within the U.S.)				
a. Domestic shipment of goods—*with* documents conveying title attached at time of acceptance.				
Maturity-6 months or less	yes[5]	yes	no	yes
6 months to 9 months.	no	yes	yes	no
more than 9 months	no	no	yes	no
b. Domestic shipment of goods—*without* documents conveying title.				
Maturity-6 months or less	no	yes	yes	no
6 months to 9 months.	no	yes	yes	no
more than 9 months	no	no	yes	no

ACCEPTANCES BY TYPE OF TRANSACTION

Traditionally, the most typical use of bankers' acceptances has been in financing imports and exports. The rapid expansion in the volume of acceptances in this category during the past decade (1966-75) by and large paralleled

Bankers' Acceptances–Conditions and Characteristics Governing
Eligibility, Reserve Requirements, and Acceptance Limits

	Federal Reserve System treatment			
Bankers' acceptance categories	Eligible for discount[1]	Eligible for purchase[2]	Reserve require-ments[3]	Aggregate acceptance limits[4]
c. Domestic storage *-readily marketable staples* secured by warehouse receipt.				
Maturity-6 months or less	yes[5]	yes	no	yes
6 months to 9 months.	no	yes	yes	no
more than 9 months	no	no	yes	no
d. Domestic storage–*any goods* in the U.S. under contract of sale or going into channels of trade and secured through-out their life by warehouse receipts.				
Maturity-6 months or less	no	yes	yes	no
6 months to 9 months.	no	yes	yes	no
more than 9 months	no	no	yes	no
3. Marketable time deposits (finance bills or working capital acceptances) not related to any specific transaction.				
Maturity-any term	no	no	yes	no

NOTE: This table is based, in part, on an unpublished paper from the 7th Annual CIB Conference at New Orleans, October 13, 1975, by A. Bardenhagen, Vice President, Irving Trust Company, New York.

[1] In accordance with Regulation A of the Board of Governors as provided by the Federal Reserve Act.

[2] Authorizations for the purchase of acceptances as announced by the Federal Open Market Committee on April 1, 1974.*

[3] In accordance with Regulation D of the Board of Governors as provided by the Federal Reserve Act.

[4] Member banks may accept bills in an amount not exceeding at any time 50 percent (or 100 percent if approved by the Board of Governors of the Federal Reserve System) of unimpaired capital stock and surplus (as defined in FRB, Chicago Circular No. 2156 of April 2, 1971). Acceptances growing out of domestic transactions are not to exceed 50 percent of the unimpaired capital stock and surplus. The aggregate limit for a bank accepting dollar exchange bills is 50 percent of unimpaired capital stock and surplus over and above the aforementioned 100 percent limitation. (Section 13(7) and (12) of the Federal Reserve Act.)

[5] The maturity of nonagricultural bills may not exceed 90 days at the time of discount.

*On March 15, 1977, following the original publication of this article, the Federal Open Market Committee issued a directive indicating ". . . that the system should permit its existing holdings of bankers' acceptances to mature and that it should no longer purchase these instruments outright under ordinary circumstances." (Editor's footnote.)

the boom in U.S. and world trade. The value of U.S. exports and imports expanded by 3.7 times, while acceptances financing that trade increased 4.2 times. However, during the last five years the rate of expansion in trade substantially outstripped the growth in acceptances. While both exports and imports increased about 2.5 times, acceptances financing export and import trade were up 1.9 times. This recent lag in growth in acceptance financing of

U.S. trade is attributable to a relatively slower growth in acceptances financing imports, which were up only 1.4 times from December 1970 to December 1975. Over the same period export acceptances increased 2.6 times. By the end of 1975 there were $4 billion of export acceptances and $3.7 billion of import acceptances outstanding.

The most dramatic increase in acceptance financing in recent years took place in bills created to finance trade between foreign countries and goods stored abroad—the so-called "third-country" bills. At the end of 1975 over $10.3 billion, or 55 percent, of all bankers' acceptances outstanding were third-country bills. This amount was 3.9 times larger than at the end of 1970. The surge in third-country bills has been primarily due to increased utilization of the U.S. acceptance market by the Japanese. A large proportion of Japan's foreign trade—even with non-U.S. trade—has been denominated and settled in U.S. dollars, thus leading Japanese traders to utilize the U.S. acceptance market rather intensively.[2]

Domestic shipment and storage acceptances have accounted for a minor portion of total acceptances outstanding during most of the post-World War II period. At the end of 1975 just over 3 percent of outstanding acceptances were domestic—about $600 million. The lack of popularity for the domestic acceptance derives in part, from the requirement that to be *eligible for discount* by the Federal Reserve, the instrument must be secured by attached documents conveying title at the time of acceptance, or a warehouse receipt or other documents securing title to readily marketable staples (see table).

Another category of acceptances is the "dollar exchange" bill. The nominal purpose of "dollar exchange" acceptances is the short-term creation of dollar exchange for a foreign country. They may be utilized to alleviate temporary or seasonal shortages of dollar exchange, "as required by usages of trade." As such, dollar exchange acceptances are unique, among bankers' acceptances, in that they are not based on specific merchandise trade or storage transactions.

The creation of dollar-exchange acceptances has been restricted by the Federal Reserve Act. Member banks may accept dollar exchange bills only from certain countries that are eligible for this form of credit. Further, since April 1974 such acceptances cannot be purchased by the Federal Reserve (see table covering eligibility conditions). These restrictions—plus the availability of alternative, more flexible sources of credit—have made these acceptances rather unpopular. At the end of 1975 they accounted for less than 1 percent of total U.S. acceptances outstanding.

ACCEPTANCES AND THE FEDERAL RESERVE

The Federal Reserve Act of 1913, Sections 13 and 14, broadly outlined the authority of the Federal Reserve System with respect to regulation of

---

[2] It has been estimated that less than 15 percent of Japan's exports and 3 percent of its imports are settled in the Japanese yen.

the purchase and sale of bankers' acceptances. This authority, along with that contained in Sections 9 and 19 of the Act, was used to promulgate the detailed Regulations A, D, and H of the Board of Governors of the Federal Reserve System and the regulations relating to open market operations of the Federal Reserve System. The following highlights the nature of these regulations.

The Federal Reserve may "acquire" acceptances under three sets of conditions. First, it may initiate purchases (and sales) of bankers' acceptances in open market operations. Second, a bank that is a member of the Federal Reserve System may submit acceptances to its district Federal Reserve Bank for discount (technically rediscount) at the "discount window"; if the Fed discounts the acceptance, the proceeds are credited to the member bank's reserve account. Third, a member bank may pledge acceptances as security against an advance or loan requested from the Federal Reserve.

Ongoing involvement of the Federal Reserve in the acceptance market has been largely confined to open market dealings. Buying and selling activity in the open market is carried out for two primary reasons. First, as a part of the System's implementation of monetary policy, it may acquire acceptances from dealers to hold for its own account (outright purchases). Alternatively, the Fed may enter into repurchase agreements with acceptance dealers whereby the Fed acquires acceptances for a short period of time—typically a week or less. These purchases, or repurchase agreements, allow the Fed to temporarily increase the amount of reserves in the banking system in the same way as if it were to purchase, sell, or enter into repurchase agreements covering U.S. Treasury securities.

The second reason for which the Fed periodically enters the acceptance market is to function as an "agent" for foreign customers, primarily foreign central banks, who wish to acquire the instruments for investment purposes. Until recently, the Federal Reserve added its own endorsement (i.e., "guarantee" of payment), thus enhancing the security of the investment. This practice was discontinued in November 1974.

Acceptances that are purchased by the Federal Reserve, used as collateral against a loan to a member bank by the Federal Reserve, or discounted at the Federal Reserve must meet certain requirements (see table). In creating acceptances banks try to adhere to these requirements, even though they may have no intention of selling or discounting them with the Fed. This is for two major reasons. First, acceptances meeting the conditions for *eligibility for discount* or *eligibility for purchase* are more readily salable in the market than are acceptances that do not meet these conditions—*ineligible* acceptances. As such, they provide a greater degree of liquidity for the accepting bank. Second, as will be explained later, acceptances that are *eligible for discount* are not subject to reserve requirements.

The distinction between *eligible for discount* and *eligible for purchase* by the Federal Reserve is important for two reasons: one reason derives from certain restrictions imposed by the Federal Reserve Act.[3] Section 13(7) and

[3]The market's reaction to the technical distinction between acceptances *eligible for discount*, acceptances *eligible for purchase*, and *ineligible* acceptances does not appear to follow this clear differ-

(12) of the Act limits the amount of acceptances that a bank can create for any individual, and have eligible for discount by the Federal Reserve, to 10 percent of that bank's paidup and unimpaired capital and surplus (unless the acceptance is "adequately secured"). Further, the Act limits the aggregate amount of acceptances, *eligible for discount* with the Federal Reserve, created by a bank to 50 percent (100 percent with approval of the Board of Governors of the Federal Reserve System) of that bank's capital and surplus. Acceptances that are *eligible for purchase* or are *ineligible* for either discount or purchase by the Federal Reserve *are not* subject to Section 13 quantity limitations.

Second, as noted above, the applicability of reserve requirements to acceptances outstanding varies according to the "eligibility" category of the acceptance. According to Regulation D, Section 204.1 (f) 5, of the Federal Reserve Board a banker's acceptance that meets the conditions that make it *eligible for discount* may be sold by the creating and discounting bank without subjecting the proceeds of the sale to reserve requirements. Thus, a member bank that sells an acceptance that meets such eligibility requirements is free from the obligation to set aside a certain portion of its funds in non-interest-bearing balances with the Federal Reserve. Conversely, a member bank must maintain reserves against the proceeds of the sale of acceptances "undertaken . . . as a means to obtaining funds to be used in the banking business . . ." that do not meet the *eligibility for discount* conditions of Section 13 of the Federal Reserve Act.

Purchase of acceptances by the Federal Reserve is governed not only by the *eligibility* requirements, but also by the underlying "quality" of the instrument. The Federal Reserve purchases only "prime" acceptances. A prime classification is based upon a number of factors including the marketability of the instrument (which is importantly dependent upon the view held by the acceptance dealers), the financial condition of the banks accepting the paper, the volume of transactions in the acceptance market carried out by the accepting bank (bank size itself is not a determining factor), and a set of physical standards and forms of documentation that are to be adhered to in the instrument itself. Even the designation of an acceptance as prime does not guarantee that at any given time an acceptance created by a particular bank will be purchased by the Federal Reserve because of restrictions on the proportions of acceptances from any one source that the Federal Reserve will acquire.

---

entiation. As reflected by the terminology of bankers involved with acceptances and as reflected by rates quoted by acceptance dealers, *eligible* acceptances are those technically *eligible for discount*. *Ineligible* acceptances include the rest: *eligible for purchase* and *ineligible*. The relative willingness of acceptance dealers to deal in acceptances *eligible for purchase* as compared with *ineligible* acceptances appears to be the major distinction between these categories—a nonprice differentiation.

REGIONAL DISTRIBUTION OF ACCEPTANCES

Historically, the majority of bankers' acceptances outstanding have been acceptances of banks located in New York and San Francisco. At the end of 1975 nearly 84 percent of acceptances outstanding were from banks located in these two Federal Reserve districts. This stems from East and West Coast banks having been traditionally more heavily involved in international transactions and in financing international trade than the inland banks. Moreover, New York has been the traditional financial center of the United States, hosting the most active domestic money market where acceptances can be readily traded. It is also the home base for the relatively few dealers that are active in the acceptance market.

Chicago ranks as a distant third in the value of acceptances outstanding from banks in that Federal Reserve District—about 4.5 percent of the national total at the end of 1975. During the post-World War II period Chicago's share of acceptances outstanding has ranged from about 2.5 percent at the end of 1950 to 6 percent at the end of 1971. Of course, as noted earlier, the volume of acceptances outstanding nationwide increased markedly over the postwar period—more than 47 times from 1950 through 1975. The volume of acceptances outstanding from Chicago district banks increased more than 80 times over the same period. It has been over the last five years, however, that the bulk of the dollar volume surge has occurred. Chicago district acceptances outstanding increased from $353 million at the end of 1970 to $837 million at the end of 1975. Over the same five-year period bankers' acceptances outstanding nationwide increased from $7.1 billion to $18.7 billion.

CONCLUSION

For many years bankers' acceptances have been an important element in the financing of international trade. Over time, improved lines of communication between parties involved in international transactions and the development of other financial instruments and modes of settlement of international transactions have reduced the overall importance of the acceptance. Only a relatively small portion of world trade is financed by means of bankers' acceptances. For example, estimates based on the average amount of export and import acceptances outstanding during 1975, assuming a 90-day maturity, suggest that only about 15 percent of U.S. merchandise trade was financed by acceptances. Nevertheless, acceptances continue to play an important role as a highly specialized financial instrument for facilitating international commerce, a role for which they are ideally suited.

NEGOTIABLE CERTIFICATES OF DEPOSIT*

Bruce J. Summers

7

Negotiable certificates of deposit (negotiable CDs) are the most important source of purchased funds to U. S. banks that are practitioners of liability management. Moreover, they have become one of the major types of liquid assets in the portfolios of many investors. Recent financial market developments, including increased competition among financial institutions, high and sometimes volatile patterns of interest rates, and regulatory changes have all led to significant changes in the money markets generally, and in the market for negotiable CDs in particular. This article describes the market for negotiable CDs, placing particular emphasis on developments that have occurred over the past decade or so.

TYPES OF ISSUERS

It is possible to distinguish between four general classes of negotiable CDs based on the type of issuer, because the characteristics of these four types of CDs, including rates paid, risk, and depth of market, can vary considerably. The most important, and the oldest of the four groups, consists of negotiable CDs, called domestic CDs, issued by U. S. banks domestically. Dollar denominated negotiable CDs issued by banks abroad are called

*Reprinted, with deletions, from the *Economic Review,* July/August 1980, pp. 8-19, with permission from the Federal Reserve Bank of Richmond.

Eurodollar CDs or Euro CDs,[1] while negotiable CDs issued by the U. S. branches of foreign banks are known as Yankee CDs; Finally, some nonbank depository institutions, particularly savings and loan associations, have begun to issue negotiable CDs. These are referred to as thrift CDs.

DOMESTIC CDs

Negotiable CDs issued by U. S. banks domestically are large denomination (greater than $100,000) time deposit liabilities evidenced by a written instrument or certificate. The certificate specifies the amount of the deposit, the maturity date, the rate of interest, and the terms under which interest is calculated. While banks are free to offer market determined interest rates on time deposits in amounts above $100,000, negotiable CDs included, the minimum denomination acceptable for secondary market trading in domestic CDs is $1 million. The term to maturity on newly issued domestic CDs is the outcome of negotiation between a bank and its customers, the individual instrument usually tailored to fit the liquidity requirements of the purchaser. Regulations limit the minimum maturity on deposits of U. S. banks to 14 days.[2] Newly issued domestic CDs typically have maturities that run from 30 days to 12 months. The average maturity of outstanding negotiable CDs is about three months.

Interest rates on newly issued negotiable CDs, called primary market rates, are determined by market forces and sometimes are directly negotiated between the issuer and the depositor. Domestic CD rates are quoted on an interest-bearing basis; rates on most other money market instruments, such as Treasury bills, bankers acceptances, and commercial paper are calculated on a discount basis. Interest is computed for the actual number of days to maturity on a 360-day year basis and can be either fixed for the term of the instrument or variable. Interest on fixed-rate negotiable CDs with original terms to maturity of up to one year is normally paid at maturity; on longer-dated instruments, interest is normally paid semiannually. If variable, the rate usually changes every month or three months and is tied to the secondary market rate on domestic CDs having maturities equal to the variable term of the contract.

Domestic CDs may be issued in either registered or bearer form. The great majority of negotiable CDs, however, are bearer instruments. In fact, most banks automatically classify bearer CDs as negotiable instruments and classi-

---

[1] Some dollar denominated CDs are issued in foreign locations other than Europe. For example, banks in Hong Kong have issued Asian CDs, while the branches of at least two U. S. banks have issued Nassau CDs. Markets for these instruments are just developing, however.

[2] Prior to mid-1980 the minimum maturity was 30 days. (Ed. footnote.)

fy registered CDs along with large time deposits open account as nonnegotiable instruments.

Domestic CDs are paid for in immediately available funds on the day of purchase. They are redeemed for immediately available funds on the maturity date. Many investors in domestic CDs prefer to purchase and settle in New York. For this reason, regional banks that are active in the CD market issue and redeem their CDs sold to national customers through a New York correspondent bank acting as a clearing agent.

The Importance of Regulation

Unlike most other participants in the domestic money market, commercial banks are heavily regulated. Government regulation has had an important influence on the development of the market for negotiable CDs since its inception. Two Federal Reserve regulations in particular have had an influence on the negotiable CD market, namely Regulation Q, which governs interest paid on deposits by member banks, and Regulation D, which prescribes reserve requirements that must be held against deposits.

Both Regulations D and Q require that time deposits have a minimum maturity of fourteen days. Moreover, Regulation Q prohibits commercial banks from purchasing their own outstanding negotiable CDs, an action that would be interpreted under the regulation as payment of a deposit before maturity. Some investors have horizons much shorter than 14 days and might prefer to avoid having to routinely enter the secondary market to raise cash by selling negotiable CDs. Consequently, banks have had an incentive to develop alternative instruments to negotiable CDs to meet these investors' demands. The minimum maturity requirement on negotiable CDs is likely an important factor explaining the rapid growth in bank repurchase agreements, which are considered nondeposit liabilities and are therefore not subject to the 14-day minimum maturity requirement on interest-bearing deposits.

Member banks of the Federal Reserve System, a group that accounts for the largest share of negotiable CDs outstanding, have always been required to hold noninterest-bearing reserves against deposits as prescribed by Regulation D. Beginning September 1, 1980, all depository institutions having either transactions accounts or nonpersonal time deposits (which include virtually all negotiable CDs) will be required to hold reserves as specified in Regulation D. Reserve requirements increase the cost of funds to depository institutions since a portion of total assets must be set aside in noninterest-earning reserve accounts. Reserve requirements against negotiable CDs have varied over the years and have at times been graduated by both the maturity of the deposit and the amount of total balances held. The Federal Reserve varies reserve requirements primarily as an aid in achieving the objectives of monetary and credit policy. In the case of CDs, however, Regulation D has also been used to achieve a bank regulatory goal, namely the lengthening of the maturity structure of the commercial banking system's liabilities. Thus, the size of reserve requirements on CDs has at times been inversely related to maturity.

Money Center versus Regional

About one-third of domestic CDs are issued by a handful of large money center banks in New York City, while the remainder are issued by about two hundred large regional banks located around the U. S. Although both the money center and regional institutions sell their newly issued instruments primarily to large national and multinational investors, the former group of banks is much more heavily involved in this market. Banks issuing negotiable CDs usually post a list of base rates, with spreads expressed in increments of five basis points, for the various maturities they are writing. These rates are adjusted upward or downward depending on the particular bank's need for funds and on market conditions. Regional banks located in cities that serve as headquarters for major corporations are often able to book a large portion of their CDs directly through the main office, without having to work through a New York correspondent. The regional issuers that are most active in the CD market, however, keep a supply of blank but signed certificates in New York so that investors not located in their area and wishing to purchase their CDs can do so conveniently. Regional banks that issue large amounts of domestic CDs but that depend heavily on purchases by investors located outside their geographic area typically employ a sales force to actively market their certificates.

Although almost all banks on occasion sell their newly issued certificates to securities dealers, most prefer to sell directly to investors. The advantages of selling directly to retail include paying a lower rate on the new issues, since the dealer intermediary is eliminated, and having more information over where certificates are ending up. Banks would prefer that their CDs be held as investments and not sold before maturity, since secondary market sales could compete with attempts to market new offerings in the future. Although dealers sometimes hold CDs for investment purposes, most of their purchases are passed through to retail investors in the secondary or resale market. Regional banks that are attempting to build a name in the domestic CD market, or that are trying to reestablish a name after a period of inactivity, generally must operate through dealers. In these cases, the dealers accept marketing responsibility for the newly issued certificates. When particularly large offerings come to market most banks, even the money center institutions, rely on dealers to help distribute the issue. A new offering of several hundred million dollars, for example, may be difficult to place directly even for a bank with a large base of regular customers.

Over the years, investors have developed preferences for the CDs of certain issuers, or groups of issuers, that are reflected in the rate structure on CDs. The rate required on the CD of a top name bank may be 5 to 25 basis points lower than that required on the CD of a lesser known institution. Historically, the rate spread on domestic CDs of the top and lesser name issuers has fluctuated with the level of interest rates, the spread widening in high interest rate periods. Prior to 1974, investors distinguished roughly between two groups of issuing banks in the domestic CD market, prime and non-prime. The prime banks included the large and well-known major money-center institutions, while the nonprime category included the smaller, lesser known regional banks. In 1974, as concerns about the liquidity of the banking system were aroused by problems at Franklin National Bank and Herstatt Bank of West Germany, investor tiering of domestic CDs by issuer became more flexible and complicated. Size remained important, but investors' perceptions of financial strength began to be formed more specifically, so that the top tier of preferred banks dropped in number and tended to vary over time. Nonetheless, investors still place the greatest emphasis in assessing risk on bank size, so that New York City banks continue to dominate the top tier. The more conventional factors used to assess risk, for example, capital ratios, asset growth rates, and earnings variability, remain of secondary importance in determining which banks are classified in the top tier. An implication of this is that portfolio managers have the opportunity to improve yield, without taking a commensurate increase in risk, by investing in the domestic CDs of regional banks that meet the traditional tests of financial soundness but that do not fall within the top tier.

EURODOLLAR CDs

Like a domestic CD, a Eurodollar CD is a dollar denominated instrument evidencing a time deposit placed with a bank at an agreed upon rate of interest for a specific period of time. Unlike a domestic CD, however, a Euro CD is issued abroad, either by the foreign branch of a U. S. bank or by a foreign bank. The market for Euro CDs is centered in London and is therefore frequently called the London dollar CD market.

This market originated in 1966 with a Eurodollar CD issue by the London branch of Citibank. The incentive to U. S. banks to start issuing CDs abroad was provided by regulations restricting their ability to raise funds in the domestic money market, especially Regulation Q. Since it is free of interest rate regulation, the Eurodollar market provides banks the opportunity to raise funds for domestic lending even when their ability to issue domestic CDs is restricted. The Euro CD market has grown rapidly since 1966. Euro CD outstandings at London banks totaled over $43 billion at year-end

1979. The foreign branches of U. S. banks dominate the London dollar CD market, accounting for about 60 percent of all CDs issued by banks located in London. Japanese banks rank second in importance, their share of the market having increased from 9 percent in 1976 to 17 percent in 1979.

Euro CD maturities run from 30 days out to 5 years, but shorter terms ranging from one month to one year are most common. By and large, the customer base is the same as that for domestic CDs, i.e., most Euro CDs are placed with the same large corporations that are active purchasers of domestic CDs in the U. S. In fact, some of the largest CD dealers in the U. S. are represented in London, where they make an active market in Euro CDs. These dealers, and many large investors as well, view their investment activity as essentially one worldwide position and manage their Euro CD and domestic CD portfolios in an integrated fashion.

Inasmuch as there is a five-hour time zone difference between London and New York, perfect synchronization of delivery and payment on Euro CDs is very difficult. Therefore, settlement for Euro CDs is normally two working days forward, which is the value date, and payment is made in clearing house funds. Dollar settlement is made in New York, even though the certificates themselves are issued and held in safekeeping in London. The First National Bank of Chicago has set up a Euro CD clearing center in London to smooth payment and delivery on these instruments. The clearing center, which is open to banks, dealers, and investors, operates on the clearing-house concept, where debits and credits are cancelled by computer and only net settlement is made.

YANKEE CDs

Yankee CDs are negotiable CDs issued and payable in dollars to bearer in the U. S. (more specifically, in New York) by the branch offices of major foreign banks. They are sometimes referred to as foreign-domestic CDs. The foreign issuers of Yankee CDs are well-known international banks headquartered primarily in Western Europe, England and Japan. Investors in Yankee CDs look to the creditworthiness of the parent organization in assessing their risk, since the obligation of a branch of a foreign bank is in actuality an obligation of the parent bank. The Yankee CD market is primarily a shorter term market; most newly issued instruments have maturities of three months or less.

Foreign banks have operated branches in the U. S. for many years, most being located in New York City. These banks were initially established to provide credit services to their parent banks' multi-national business customers. Their number increased greatly during the 1970s, and the U. S. branches became more aggressive competitors for the loan business of U. S.

corporations. Their major sources of funds have included borrowings from foreign parent organizations, purchases in the Federal funds market, and more recently the issuance of large time deposits to U. S. investors. At year-end 1979 the time deposits of U. S. branches of foreign banks due to private investors and public bodies totaled about $25 billion. It is estimated that about $20 billion of this amount was in the form of negotiable CDs. Some individual foreign branches have Yankee CDs outstanding well in excess of $1 billion.

The U. S. branches of foreign banks at first placed most of their Yankee CDs directly with their established loan customers, who through experience were familiar with the reputations of the issuers. Since their names were not well known outside this small group, the U. S. branches of foreign banks were forced to rely on dealers to market their CDs as reliance on this source of funds grew. The largest part of their offerings have until recently been placed through dealers, several of which are now active market makers for Yankee CDs. Foreign bank names have become much better known and acceptable in the U. S., however, so that today it is much more commonplace for foreign branches to sell their negotiable CDs directly at retail. Secondary market trading in Yankee CDs has increased greatly in just the last several years so that the liquidity of such instruments now rivals that of better rated domestic CDs.

An important institutional feature of foreign banking operations in the U. S. is that, until recently, foreign branches have been state-licensed and not subject to Federal Reserve regulations. Thus, until recently Yankee CDs have not been subject to reserve requirements under Regulation D. This exemption from regulation probably helped establish the market for Yankee CDs, because the U. S. branches of foreign banks could pay higher rates on their certificates than could domestic banks but still not incur higher costs than their U. S. banking competitors as a result of savings on reserve requirements. *The International Banking Act of 1978* provides that large foreign banks doing business in the U. S. should be subject to the same Federal Reserve regulations as domestic banks. The U. S. branches of large foreign banks become subject to Regulations D and Q as of September 4, 1980.

Yankee CDs, along with certain other managed liabilities of the U. S. branches of foreign banks, became subject to reserve requirements for the first time in October 1979. This change subjected certain managed liabilities above a base amount to an 8 percent reserve requirement, which was subsequently increased to 10 percent in March 1980, and then reduced to 5 percent in May 1980. The imposition of marginal reserve requirements on the managed liabilities of the U. S. branches of foreign banks may have had the effect of slowing the growth of Yankee CDs. This is because the market is still young, with new issuing banks entering regularly. These new banks entering the Yankee CD market typically market their negotiable CDs aggressively in an attempt to build volume and goodwill quickly. Starting from a low or zero reserve exempt base, however, the newly entering banks bear a reserve cost on all of their negotiable CDs, not just a fractional amount like established issuers. This higher cost has likely discouraged new entries into the Yankee CD market.

THRIFT INSTITUTION CDs

Thrift institutions, particularly savings and loan associations (SLAs), have become active competitors for large time deposits not subject to Regulation Q ceilings. Most of their large domestic time deposits are practically if not legally nonnegotiable, i.e., there is very little secondary market activity in thrift CDs. The large denomination CDs of FSLIC insured SLAs totaled nearly $30 billion at year-end 1979.

Recent changes in Federal Home Loan Bank Board regulations grant Federally insured savings and loans considerable broadened authority to market Euro CDs. At least one large California SLA has placed a $10 million package of unsecured CDs in the Eurodollar market. The success of such placements depends on the size and financial strength of the issuing thrift. Other thrifts have taken steps to place Euro CDs that are backed by mortgage loan collateral. Part of this process involves obtaining a credit rating from Standard & Poor's Corporation, which is now making such ratings. So far, these mortgage-backed offerings have been for longer terms, i.e., five years.

NONNEGOTIABLE CDs

Nonnegotiable CDs are an important part of total large time deposits issued by commercial banks. In fact, nonnegotiable CDs of U. S. banks have grown faster than domestic negotiable CDs in recent years and now are more important than domestic negotiable CDs as a source of funds. It is important to understand what nonnegotiable CDs are, because many investors active in the market for negotiable CDs are willing to substitute between the two types of instruments.

Nonnegotiable CDs are not considered money market instruments because they lack the liquidity of negotiable certificates. Some nonnegotiable instruments, such as time deposits open account, are legally nonnegotiable. Others, such as registered CDs, are technically negotiable but are in practice nonnegotiable because of the administrative difficulty involved in changing ownership. Some banks have ceased issuing certificates and have instead instituted book entry accounting procedures for registered CDs. This practice seems to confirm that liquidity is a secondary consideration to investors purchasing such instruments.

Among the largest investors in nonnegotiable CDs are public bodies, e.g., state and municipal governments. Often, state law requires that public bodies invest their funds locally, that all investments be registered in the name of the governmental unit, and that investments be secured. A large share of banks' total large time deposits are secured CDs issued in registered form to state and local governments. As might be expected, regional banks are more heavily dependent upon such funds than are the money center banks.

It is not just public bodies that invest in nonnegotiable certificates, however. Some corporate investors are willing to sacrifice the liquidity provided by an instrument that can be traded in the secondary market for a small increase in yield. Also, some banks have gentleman's agreements with customers who take their registered or book-entry CDs which provide that, in the event cash is needed on an emergency basis, the bank will exchange the registered CD for a bearer CD. In addition to nonfinancial corporations, some money market funds have invested in nonnegotiable CDs.

RISK AND RETURN

Negotiable CDs subject investors to two major types of risk, credit risk and marketability risk. Credit risk is the risk of default on the part of the bank issuing the CD. This is relevant even for U. S. banks which are insured by the FDIC, since domestic CDs are issued in large denominations and deposit insurance only covers up to $100,000 of a depositor's funds. Marketability risk reflects the fact that a ready buyer for a CD might not be available when the owner is ready to sell. Although the secondary market in CDs is well developed, it does not possess the depth of the U. S. Government securities market. These risks are reflected in the yields on negotiable CDs. It should be noted, however, that yields on money market instruments may vary for reasons other than differences in risk,e.g., due to changes in their relative supplies.

Chart 1 plots the spread between the secondary market yields on two types of 3-month CDs, domestic and Euro, and the secondary market rate on 3-month Treasury bills. The spread is positive and tends to widen in periods of high interest rates. For example, the domestic CD-Treasury bill spread was generally below 100 basis points for the periods 1971-72 and 1976-78, but widened greatly in 1973-74. The spread peaked at 458 basis points in August 1974. The chart shows that rates on Euro CDs are almost always above those on domestic CDs, typically by about 20-30 basis points,

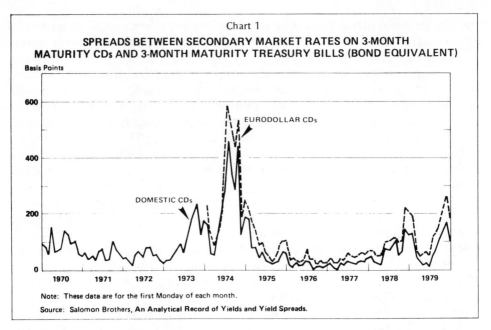

Chart 1

**SPREADS BETWEEN SECONDARY MARKET RATES ON 3-MONTH
MATURITY CDs AND 3-MONTH MATURITY TREASURY BILLS (BOND EQUIVALENT)**

Note: These data are for the first Monday of each month.

Source: Salomon Brothers, An Analytical Record of Yields and Yield Spreads.

and that the Euro-domestic CD rate spread tends to widen in periods of high interest rates. The higher rate on Euro CDs in part reflects the credit risk premium required by investors in these instruments; this premium tends to increase in periods of stress in the financial markets. There is no reserve requirement against such deposits, and therefore the total cost to the issuing institution is not necessarily greater than the total cost to a domestic bank issuing a CD. In fact, the reserve adjusted costs of domestic and Euro CDs tend to be very close in times of financial market normalcy.

There is no published rate series for Yankee CDs. Dealers indicate, however, that Yankee CD rates move very closely, within plus or minus 10 basis points, of Euro CD rates. These two types of CDs are good substitutes and their rates should be expected to move close together except due to technical factors, such as relative supply. On average, though, Yankee CD rates average somewhat lower than Euro CD rates. There are two reasons for this. First, Yankee CDs, unlike Euro CDs are subject to U. S. laws and regulations and therefore do not bear sovereign or foreign country risk. Second, it is easier and less costly for dealers to engage in Yankee CD transactions than in Euro CD transactions. Yankee CDs are purchased in the U. S. and positions are financed with RPs or Federal funds, while Euro CDs are purchased abroad and entail international money transfers.

Quality Ratings

One major rating firm, Moody's Investors Service, Inc., has begun to rate the CDs of banks. So far, only a small number of regional U. S. banks have received ratings and a handful of applications are in process. Foreign banks issuing Yankee CDs, however, have more actively sought formal ratings than have U. S. banks. This is understandable, since they are still attempting to establish their names with U. S. investors. The rating process used by Moody's for CDs is virtually identical to that used for rating commercial paper. It is not the particular issue that is rated but rather the issuing organization itself. The CD ratings, like those for commercial paper, are designated P-1, P-2, and P-3. Because of the closeness of the rating processes, one should never expect to see a divergence between a bank's CD rating and its commercial paper rating. It is possible, however, for a bank's CD rating to differ somewhat from the commercial paper rating of its parent holding company.

Standard & Poor's Corporation has begun rating the CDs of SLAs. Like Moody's, S&P has experience rating commercial paper issued by SLAs, but has so far applied bond rating methods to thrift CDs because of their longer terms. If asked to rate short-term thrift CDs, S&P will likely apply a variant of its commercial paper rating system.

RATES AND MATURITIES

During the first decade of their existence, negotiable CDs were written exclusively under fixed interest coupon contracts. Certificates were written specifying a particular rate of interest that would be paid for a given term to maturity. This pricing arrangement suited investors quite well, at least during the relatively stable interest rate environment of the 1960s. Those seeking a compromise between return and liquidity could invest in short-dated negotiable CDs, while those seeking extra yield could extend the maturity of their investments out to six months or perhaps even longer. So long as the upward sloping yield curve remained the norm, banks and investors had a reasonable basis for trading off higher yield against longer term.

In the latter part of the 1960s interest rate conditions changed dramatically. Interest rate fluctuations increased, and the general level of rates began to trend upward. Under such circumstances, investors can be expected to shift their preferences to shorter term instruments, and this happened in the CD market. by 1974 the average maturity of outstanding domestic CDs fell dramatically to about two months from the three-and-one-half-month length more common in the 1960s. In September 1974 the Federal Reserve provided banks an incentive to lengthen their negotiable CD maturities by restructuring reserve requirements in such a way as to raise the reserve cost of shorter term certificates. This incentive was reinforced in December 1974 when reserve requirements were set at 6 percent for negotiable CDs with an original maturity of less than six months and at 3 percent for negotiable CDs with an original maturity of six months or more. In

October 1975 the reserve requirement was further lowered to 1 percent for CDs with original maturities of four years or more, and finally in January 1976 the requirement was lowered to 2½ percent on certificates with original maturities of from six months to four years. In keeping with this pattern, the marginal reserve program introduced in October 1979 exempts CDs with original maturities of one year and greater. In addition to these changes in reserve requirements, domestic banks had an incentive to increase CD maturities as a result of the deteriorating liquidity positions of their balance sheets. By the mid-1970s, therefore, the time was ripe for a fundamental change in the terms under which negotiable CDs had traditionally been offered.

Fixed-Rate Rollover CDs

Early in 1977 a large New York bank, Morgan Guaranty Trust Company, introduced to its customers on a selective basis fixed-rate rollover CDs, or "roly poly" CDs, in minimum amounts of $5 million. These instruments had full terms to maturity of from two to five years, but consisted of a series of 6-month maturity instruments. Investors would sign a contract to leave a deposit with the bank for, say, four years, but instead of receiving a CD maturing in four years would receive a 6-month CD. The contract obligated the investor to renew, or roll over, the 6-month instrument eight consecutive times at the rate negotiated at the inception of the contract. Although the bank hoped to qualify for the four year CD reserve requirement with these deposits, a ruling by the Federal Reserve made the rollover CDs reservable at the higher 6-month maturity reserve requirement.

These instruments bore rates somewhat above the rate on Treasury notes of equal maturity, but below the rate offered on a straight two to five year CD. The feeling was that an investor would earn the long-term rate but get enhanced liquidity since a single 6-month issue in the series could be sold in the secondary market. This fixed-rate type of instrument proved more attractive to the issuing banks than to the investing public during a period of rising interest rates. Consequently, a sizable market in fixed-rate rollover CDs never developed.

Variable Rate CDs

Variable rate or variable coupon CDs (VRCDs or VCCDs) have the rollover feature described above but also entail periodic resettings of the coupon rate and periodic payment of interest. Interest on each component or "leg" of a VRCD is calculated according to the same rules as on conventional CDs.

The dated date is the original dated date for the first leg, and for subsequent legs it is the date of the interest payment on the preceding leg. VRCDs were first offered in the Euro CD market, where floating rate instruments were an accepted method of doing business long before they were in the U. S. The VRCD was initially introduced in the domestic and Yankee CD markets by those large banks having Euro CD experience, but the new method of writing certificates was quickly adopted by the major regional banks as well. VRCDs were introduced domestically in 1975, grew in popularity in the latter 1970s, and have now become a major innovation in the market for negotiable CDs.

VRCDs range in full maturity from six months to four years, the most common full maturities being six months and one year. The rollover period for these instruments varies. For example, from 1975 to 1977, three- and six-month rollovers were common. The higher short-term interest rates of 1979 and 1980, however, have resulted in the three-month and one-month rollovers becoming standard. Investor preferences for full maturity and roll-over frequency are directly related to expected interest rate patterns, periods of stable or declining rates leading to preferences for longer full maturities and longer rolls, and periods of rising rates and upward sloping yield curves leading to preferences for shorter maturities and shorter rolls. The four VRCD issues having the greatest popularity at present are (1) six-month (full maturity)/three-month (roll), (2) six-month/one-month, (3) one-year/three-month, and (4) one-year/one-month.

Coupon rates set on each new leg of VRCDs are based on the preceding day's secondary market CD rates reported daily by the Federal Reserve Bank of New York. These are averages of offered rates quoted by major dealers. Collection of interest payments, and of principal at final maturity, is made by presenting the VRCD to the issuing bank or the issuing bank's agent. When presented for collection of interest, the certificate is stamped with the amount of the previous period's interest and the new coupon rate. Payment of interest and principal is made in immediately available funds. VRCDs normally carry an interest premium over the rate one would expect to receive on a conventional CD. This premium has usually been about 15 basis points for six-month full maturities, 20 basis points for one-year full maturities, and 25 basis points for eighteen-month full maturities. As in the case of conventional CDs, VRCDs issued by the top tier banks carry some-what lower rates than those issued by the lesser name institutions.

The typical size of a VRCD issue ranges from $50-$200 million for large banks and $25-$100 million for smaller banks, but issues as large as $400 million are not uncommon. The largest portion of VRCD issues is under-written by dealers, who usually charge the issuing bank a small commission for underwriting and distribution services. Dealers have been willing to take larger positions in VRCDs than in longer term conventional CDs since there is less market risk involved and because retail demand has proved quite strong. So far, retail demand has been so strong that dealers have placed a major portion of newly issued VRCDs on an order basis.

Investors treat VRCDs as a conventional CD once the coupon has been set for the last time and the certificate is on its last leg. Since VRCDs carry an interest premium over the rate paid on a conventional CD, a VRCD on its last leg offers the potential for trading profits.

Estimates by market participants place the total amount of VRCDs outstanding in early 1980 at $12 billion, about double the amount outstanding only six months earlier. Most of these are domestic CDs. Thus, in the short time since they have become popular, VRCDs have grown to equal over 10 percent of the total volume of domestic CDs outstanding. To date, money market funds have been the most active investors in VRCDs.

DEALERS

There are currently about 25 dealers in CDs, all of which are active in the domestic CDs of top tier banks and some of which specialize in regional names or Yankee CDs. The center of the dealer market is New York City but the larger dealers have branches in major U. S. cities and in London. Two main functions of the CD dealers are to distribute CDs at retail, either after first taking new issues into their own positions or by acting as brokers, and to support a secondary market in negotiable CDs. In accomplishing the latter, dealers must stand ready to make a market, i.e., buy and sell CDs. Bid and offering prices are constantly maintained and the typical spread is between 5 and 10 basis points, but narrower spreads on good names with short remaining terms to maturity are common.

The normal round-lot trade in negotiable CDs between dealers and retail customers is $1 million, but increases to $5 million for interdealer trades. There is, of course, a great deal of variety among the CDs being traded at any given time with respect to issuer, maturity, and other contractual terms. Consequently, dealers post bid and asked prices for certificates issued by a particular tier bank, with maturity identified as early or late in a particular month. For example, the bid and ask price for a top trading name might be for "early December" or "late January."

Financing of dealer CD positions is largely done using RPs. Since CD collateral is more risky than U. S. Government security collateral, RPs against CDs are usually slightly more expensive than RPs against, say, Treasury bills. For the same reason, it is more difficult to get term RP financing for CDs. Normal practice in the RP market is to finance the face value of a money market instrument. Since CDs bear interest, dealers must finance any accrued interest on CDs held in position from some source other than RP, e.g., from capital.

Growth in dealer activity has paralleled growth in the market for negotiable CDs. As the market expanded in the 1960s daily average dealer transactions were in the $50-$60 million range, and the daily average dealer positions ranged from $200-$300 million. As mentioned, the secondary market nearly dried up in 1969, daily average dealer transactions falling to only $9 million and daily average positions falling to only $27 million during that year. Dealer activity burgeoned in the 1970s, when trading opportunities increased due to the more aggressive marketing of negotiable CDs by regional banks and with the development of the Yankee CD. By 1975, for example, daily average dealer positions increased about five-fold to $1.4 billion and transactions increased sixteen times to $800 million. By 1979, positions further expanded to $2.7 billion and transactions to $1.7 billion.

SUMMARY

The market for negotiable CDs issued domestically by U. S. banks grew rapidly but, due to the effects of interest rate regulation, unevenly during the 1960s. Regulation Q restrictions on rates that could be paid on domestic CDs led to the introduction of the Euro CD in 1966. After interest rate ceilings on domestic CDs were removed in the early 1970s the market grew dramatically. Regional banks became particularly active issuers during this period, and the U. S. branches of foreign banks began issuing Yankee CDs. Most recently, savings and loan associations have also begun issuing CDs. Investors can now choose among a number of issuers in selecting CDs, i.e., domestic, Euro, Yankee, and thrift.

Not only have the types of issuers multiplied, but the character of CD contracts has changed as well, The conventional fixed-rate CD, which is primarily a short-term instrument, has been modified to extend the term and float the rate. The resulting instrument, the variable rate CD, has quickly gained popularity among investors. The terms under which VRCDs are offered, however, change constantly in response to investor preferences.

The rate of change in the market for negotiable CDs has been particularly rapid in recent years. This change is the outcome of competitive forces working to redesign a financial market to better suit the needs of its major participants.

REFERENCES

1. Crane, Dwight B. "A Study of Interest Rate Spreads in the 1974 CD Market." *Journal of Bank Research* (Autumn 1976), pp. 213-224.

2. Giddy, Ian H. "Why Eurodollars Grow." *Columbia Journal of World Business* (Fall 1979), pp. 54-60.

3. Melton, William C. "The Market for Large Negotiable CDs." *Quarterly Review*, Federal Reserve Bank of New York (Winter 1977-78), pp. 22-34.

4. Slovin, Myron B., and Sushka, Marie Elizabeth. "An Econometric Model of the Market for Negotiable Certificates of Deposits." *Journal of Monetary Economics* (October 1979), pp. 551-568.

5. Stigum, Marcia. *The Money Market: Myth, Reality, and Practice*. Homewood, Illinois: Dow-Jones-Irwin, 1978.

COMMERCIAL PAPER*

Peter A. Abken

8

Commercial paper is a short-term unsecured promissory note that is generally sold by large corporations on a discount basis to institutional investors and to other corporations. Since commercial paper is unsecured and bears only the name of the issuer, the market has generally been dominated by large corporations with the highest credit ratings. In recent years commercial paper has attracted much attention because of its rapid growth and its use as an alternative to short-term bank loans. The number of firms issuing commercial paper rose from slightly over 300 in 1965 to about 1,000 in 1980. Moreover, the outstanding volume of commercial paper increased at an annual rate of 12.4 percent during the 1970s to a level of $123 billion in June 1980. This article describes the commercial paper market.

MARKET CHARACTERISTICS

The principal issuers of commercial paper include finance companies, nonfinancial companies, and bank holding companies. These issuers participate in the market for different reasons and in different ways. Finance companies raise funds on a more-or-less continuous basis in the commercial paper mar-

*Reprinted, with deletions, from the *Economic Review*, March/April 1981, pp. 11-22, with permission from the Federal Reserve Bank of Richmond.

ket to support their consumer and business lending. These commercial paper sales in part provide interim financing between issues of long-term debentures. Nonfinancial companies issue commercial paper at less frequent intervals than do finance companies. These firms issue paper to meet their funding requirements for short-term or seasonal expenditures such as inventories, payrolls, and tax liabilities. Bank holding companies use the commercial paper market to finance primarily banking-related activities such as leasing, mortgage banking, and consumer finance.

Denominations and Maturities

Like other instruments of the money market, commercial paper is sold to raise large sums of money quickly and for short periods of time. Although sometimes issued in denominations as small as $25,000 or $50,000, most commercial paper offerings are in multiples of $100,000. The average purchase size of commercial paper is about $2 million. The average issuer has $120 million in outstanding commercial paper; some of the largest issuers individually have several billion dollars in outstanding paper.

Exemption from registration requirements with the Securities and Exchange Commission reduces the time and expense of readying an issue of commercial paper for sale. Almost all outstanding commercial paper meets the conditions for exemption, namely: (1) that it have an original maturity of no greater than 270 days and (2) that the proceeds be used to finance current transactions. The average maturity of outstanding commercial paper is under 30 days, with most paper falling within the 20- to 45-day range.

Placement

Issuers place commercial paper with investors either directly using their own sales force or indirectly using commercial paper dealers. The method of placement depends primarily on the transaction costs of these alternatives. Dealers generally charge a one-eighth of one percent (annualized) commission on face value for placing paper. For example, if a firm places $100 million of 45-day commercial paper using the intermediary services of a dealer, commissions would be $100 million $\times$ .00125 $\times$ (45/360) = $15,625. The annualized cost would be $125,000. There are six major commercial paper dealers.

Firms with an average amount of outstanding commercial paper of several hundred million dollars or more generally find it less costly to maintain a sales force and market their commercial paper directly. Almost all direct issuers are large finance companies. The short-term credit demands of nonfinancial companies are usually seasonal or cyclical in nature, which lessens the attractiveness of establishing a permanent commercial paper sales staff.

Consequently, almost all nonfinancial companies, including large ones, rely on dealers to distribute their paper.

There is no active secondary market in commercial paper. Dealers and direct issuers may redeem commercial paper before maturity if an investor has an urgent demand for funds. However, dealers and direct issuers discourage this practice. Early redemptions of commercial paper rarely occur primarily because the average maturity of commercial paper is so short. One major commercial paper dealer estimates that only about two percent of their outstanding commercial paper is redeemed prior to maturity.

Quality Ratings

The one thousand or so firms issuing paper obtain ratings from at least one of three services, and most obtain two ratings. The three rating companies that grade commercial paper borrowers are Moody's Investors Service, Standard & Poor's Corporation, and Fitch Investor Service. Table I shows the number of companies rated by Moody's, classified by industry. This table, covering 881 issuers, gives a good indication of the industry grouping of issuers. Moody's describes its ratings procedure as follows:

> Moody's evaluates the salient features that affect a commercial paper issuer's financial and competitive position. Our appraisal includes, but is not limited to the review of factors such as: quality of management, industry strengths

Table I

INDUSTRY GROUPING OF COMMERCIAL PAPER
ISSUERS RATED BY MOODY'S

November 3, 1980

Industry Grouping	Number of Firms Rated	Percentage of Total Firms Rated
Industrial	370	42.0
Public Utilities	193	21.9
Finance	155	17.6
Bank Holding	119	13.6
Mortgage Finance	9	1.0
Insurance	25	2.8
Transportation	10	1.1
Total	881	100.0

Source: **Moody's Bond Survey**, Annual Review.

and risks, vulnerability to business cycles, competitive position, liquidity mea-
surements, debt structure, operating trends, and access to capital markets.
Differing weights are applied to these factors as deemed appropriate for individual situations.[1]

The other rating services use similar criteria in evaluating issuers. From highest to lowest quality, paper ratings run: P-1, P-2, P-3 for Moody's; A-1, A-2,
A-3 for Standard & Poor's; and F-1, F-2, F-3 for Fitch. For all rating services
as of mid-1980, the average distribution of outstanding commercial paper for
the three quality gradations was about 75 percent for grade 1, 24 percent for
grade 2, and 1 percent for grade 3. As will be discussed below, the difference
in ratings can translate into considerable differences in rates, particularly
during periods of financial stress.

The multifaceted rating system used by Moody's reflects the heteroge-
neous financial characteristics of commercial paper. Paper of different issuers,
even with the same quality rating, is not readily substitutable. Consequently,
commercial paper tends to be difficult to trade, and bid-asked spreads on paper of a particular grade and maturity run a wide 1/8 of a percentage point.

Backup Lines of Credit

In most cases, issuers back their paper 100 percent with lines of credit
from commercial banks. Even though its average maturity is very short, com-
merical paper still poses the risk that an issuer might not be able to pay off
or roll over maturing paper. Consequently, issuers use a variety of backup
lines as insurance against periods of financial stress or tight money. These
credit lines are contractual agreements that are tailored to issuers' needs.
Standard credit line agreements allow commercial paper issuers to borrow
under a 90-day note. So-called *swing lines* provide funds over very short
periods, often to cover a shortfall in the actual proceeds of paper issued on a
particular day. Revolving lines of credit establish credit sources that are available over longer periods of time, usually several years.

Noninterest Costs of Issuing Commercial Paper

There are three major noninterest costs associated with commercial paper:
(1) backup lines of credit, (2) fees to commercial banks, and (3) rating services fees. Payment for backup lines is usually made in the form of compensating balances, which generally equal about 10 percent of total credit lines
extended plus 20 percent of credit lines activated. Instead of compensating

---

[1] Sumner N. Levin, ed., *The 1979 Dow Jones-Irwin Business Almanac* (Homewood, Ill.: Dow Jones-
Irwin, 1979), pp. 256-57.

balances, issuers sometimes pay straight fees ranging from 3/8 to 3/4 of one percent of the line of credit; this explicit pricing procedure has been gaining acceptance in recent years. Another cost associated with issuing commercial paper is fees paid to the large commercial banks that act as issuing and paying agents for the paper issuers. These commercial banks handle the paper work involved in issuing commercial paper and collect the proceeds from an issue to pay off or roll over a maturing issue. Finally, rating services charge fees ranging from $5,000 to $25,000 per year to provide ratings for issuers. Foreign issuers pay from $3,500 to $10,000 per year more for ratings, depending on the rating service.

Investors

Investors in commercial paper include money center banks, nonfinancial firms, investment firms, state and local governments, private pension funds, foundations, and individuals. In addition, savings and loan associations and mutual savings banks have recently been granted authority to invest up to 20 percent of their assets in commercial paper. These groups may buy commercial paper from dealers or directly from issuers, or they may buy shares in short-term investment pools that include commercial paper. Except for scattered statistics, the distribution of commercial paper held by the various investor groups is not precisely known. At year-end 1979 all manufacturing, mining, and trade corporations held outright over $11 billion in commercial paper. A substantial but undocumented amount is held by utilities, communications, and service companies. Commercial banks held approximately $5 billion in their loan portfolios, while insurance companies had about $9 billion. Much commercial paper, about one-third of the total amount outstanding or $40 billion, is held indirectly through short-term investment pools, such as money market funds and short-term investment funds operated by bank trust departments. At year-end 1979, short-term investment pools held 32.5 percent of all outstanding commercial paper.

DEVELOPMENTS SINCE THE MID-1960s

Two events stimulated growth in commercial paper in the 1960s. First, during the last three quarters of 1966, interest rates rose above Regulation Q ceilings on bank negotiable certificates of deposit (CDs), making it difficult for banks to raise funds to meet the strong corporate loan demand existing at that time. Without sufficient funds to lend, banks encouraged their financially strongest customers to issue commercial paper and offered back-up lines of credit. Many potential commercial paper borrowers who formerly relied exclusively on bank short-term credit now turned to the commercial paper market. Consequently, the percentage increase in total outstanding commercial paper rose from 7.8 percent in 1965 to 46.6 percent in 1966.

Second, credit market tightness recurred in 1969 as open market interest rates rose above Regulation Q ceilings, again boosting growth in commercial paper. Financial innovation by banks contributed to this growth. The banking system sold commercial paper through bank holding companies, which used the funds to purchase part of their subsidiary banks' loan portfolios. This method of financing new loans resulted in rapid growth in bank-related commercial paper during late 1969 and early 1970, as is seen in Chart 1. The annual growth rate of total outstanding commercial paper more than doubled to 54.7 percent in 1969. In August 1970, the Federal Reserve System imposed a reserve requirement on funds raised in the commercial paper market and channeled to a member bank by a bank holding company, or any of its affiliates or subsidiaries.[2] As a result, bank related commercial paper outstanding plummeted late in 1970 and early in 1971. This episode, however, marked only the beginning of bank use of commercial paper, which would regain prominence by the mid-1970s.

The Penn Central Crisis

The commercial paper market grew steadily during the 1960s. Only five defaults occurred during this decade, the largest of which amounted to $35 million. In 1970, however, the commercial paper market was rocked by Penn Central's default on $82 million of its outstanding commercial paper. The default caused investors to become wary of commercial paper issuers and more concerned about their creditworthiness. In the aftermath of the Penn Central default, many corporations experienced difficulty refinancing their maturing commercial paper. Financial disruption was lessened due to a Federal Reserve action which removed Regulation Q interest rate ceilings on 30- to 89-day CDs and temporarily liberalized the discount policy for member banks. These actions insured that funds were available from commercial banks to provide alternative financing for corporations having difficulty rolling over commercial paper.

After the Penn Central episode, investors became more conscious of creditworthiness and more selective in their commercial paper purchases. During this period, the heightened concern over credit worthiness was evidenced by a widening rate spread between the financially strongest and weakest paper issuers. Although some paper had been rated long before the Penn Central crisis, paper was now rated on a widespread basis.

---

[2] See footnote 3.

Chart 1

OUTSTANDING COMMERCIAL PAPER

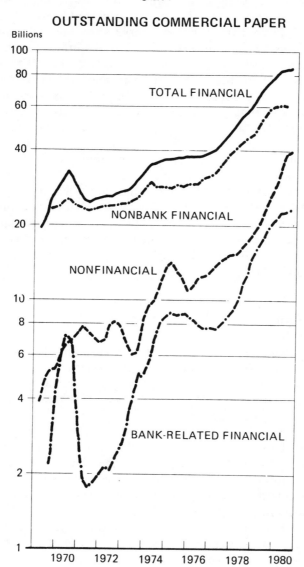

Source: Board of Governors of the Federal Reserve System.

Interest Rate Controls

Wage and price controls imposed during the early 1970s dampened the growth of the commercial paper market. On October 15, 1971, the Committee on Interest and Dividends (CID) established voluntary restraints on "administered" rates, such as the prime rate. No restraints were placed on open market rates, however. This policy triggered flows of funds between controlled and uncontrolled credit markets as the relationship between administered rates and market rates changed. As interest rates rose in 1972, banks came under pressure from the CID to moderate their prime rate increases. By early 1973, the prime rate was held artificially below the commercial paper rate as a consequence of CID policy. Nonfinancial firms substituted short-term bank credit for funds raised through commercial paper issues. Consequently the volume of nonfinancial commercial paper outstanding fell sharply during the first and second quarters of 1973, as is seen in Chart 1. In April of 1973, the CID tried to stem the exodus from the commercial paper market by establishing a dual prime rate. One rate for large firms moved with open market rates, while the other for smaller firms was controlled. Despite these measures, the spread between commercial paper rates and the prime rate persisted and substitution out of paper continued. In the fourth quarter of 1973 CID controls were removed and the commercial paper rate dropped below the prime rate, causing substantial growth in commercial paper. This growth continued throughout 1975.

The 1973-75 Period

The recession of 1973-75 strained the paper market as investors became increasingly concerned about the financial strength of commercial paper issuers. Reflecting this concern, the quality rate spread (the difference between the interest rates on highest quality paper and medium quality paper) rose from about 12 basis points in January 1974 to 200 basis points in November of that year. Chart 2 shows movements in the quality spread from 1974 to 1980. Utility companies experienced problems selling commercial paper as their ratings were downgraded. Real Estate Investments Trusts (REITs) were another group to encounter problems in the commercial paper market. Loan defaults and foreclosure proceedings early in the recession led to financial difficulties and resulted in a downgrading of REIT paper. As a result, many REITs and utilities were forced to turn to bank credit.

Bank holding companies also experienced difficulty issuing commercial paper in the spring of 1974. The failure of Franklin National Bank caused widespread concern about the strength of other banking organizations. As a consequence, smaller bank holding companies in particular found it hard to place their paper. Nonetheless, the aggregate volume of outstanding bank-related commercial paper remained relatively unchanged during this period of uncertainty. In general, the strongest paper issuers with prime ratings sold their paper without problems during the 1973-75 recession, although less financially sound issuers had to pay a premium to acquire funds in the commercial paper market.

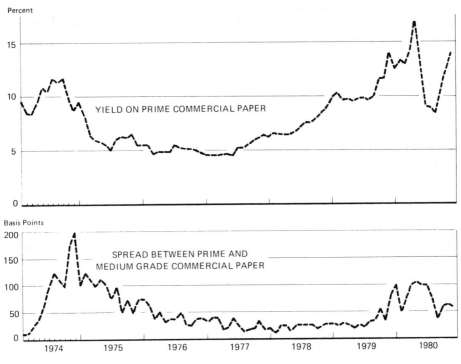

Chart 2

YIELDS AND SPREADS ON 30–DAY COMMERCIAL PAPER

Percent

YIELD ON PRIME COMMERCIAL PAPER

Basis Points

SPREAD BETWEEN PRIME AND
MEDIUM GRADE COMMERCIAL PAPER

1974   1975   1976   1977   1978   1979   1980

Source: Salomon Brothers.

The Late 1970s

After the 1973-75 recession the commercial paper market grew rapidly. The volume of outstanding nonfinancial commercial paper expanded at a 31.9 percent compound annual rate from the first quarter of 1976 to the first quarter of 1980. Over the same period, nonbank financial paper grew at a 20.1 percent compound annual rate and bank-related paper at a 27.9 percent annual rate. The number of commercial paper issuers increased substantially as well. For example, issuers rated by Moody's Investor Service increased from 516 at year-end 1975 to 881 at year-end 1980.

The recent rapid growth in the commercial paper market owes much to the secular substitution of short-term for long-term debt, which accelerated because of the high rate of inflation in the late 1970s. Volatile interest rates due to uncertainty about the future rate of inflation make firms hesitant to structure their balance sheets with long-term, fixed rate assets and liabilities. In addition, because of inflation's debilitating effects on equity markets, debt has grown more than twice as fast as equity during the past decade. On the demand side, investors also have become wary of long-term fixed rate securities because of the uncertainty about the real rate of return on such commitments of funds. Therefore, funds have tended to flow away from the capital markets and into the money markets. A large share of these funds have been channeled into the commercial paper market.

Nonfinancial Paper

As nonfinancial firms acquired familiarity with open market finance during the 1970s, they gradually reduced their reliance on short-term bank loans. This is understandable since use of open market funds offers the potential for substantial savings to corporate borrowers compared to the cost of bank credit. Large commercial banks' primary source of funds for financing loans is the CD market, where interest rates are roughly equal to commercial paper rates. In addition, the cost of funds to commercial banks includes reserve requirements.[3] Noninterest expenses associated with lending also add to the cost of bank operations. These various costs drive a wedge between open market and bank lending rates, and the spread between the prime rate and the commercial paper rate is a good proxy for the difference in financing costs facing companies that need funds.

Large, financially sound nonfinancial firms, therefore, have relied to an increasing extent on the commercial paper market for short-term credit. The ratio of nonfinancial commercial paper to commercial and industrial (C&I) loans at large commercial banks, rose from about 11 percent in the mid-1970s to almost 25 percent in 1980. Chart 3 shows the movements in the ratio of paper to loans from 1972 to 1980.

Banks reacted to this loss of market share by becoming more aggressive in pricing loans. Since 1979, for example, some banks have begun making loans below the prime rate. In a Federal Reserve Board survey of 48 large banks, the percentage of below prime loans rose from about 20 percent of all commercial loan extensions in the fourth quarter of 1978 to about 60 percent by the second quarter of 1980. Most of these loans were extended at rates determined by cost of funds formulas. In addition, the average maturity of loans over $1 billion, which make up almost half of all C&I loans in volume, fell from about 3 months in 1977 to a low of 1.2 months in August 1980. Loans below prime had an average maturity of well under one month. These below prime loans were in the same maturity range as the average maturity for commercial paper.

---

[3] The following example illustrates how reserve requirements on CDs increases the cost of funds to banks. Suppose the reserve requirement against CDs is 3 percent and a bank's CD offers a 12 percent yield. Then for every dollar obtained through the CD, only 97 cents are available to lend. The funds idled as reserves increase the effective cost of funds raised by issuing a CD. In this example, the additional cost imposed by the reserve requirement is 37 basis points, i.e., $12 \div .97 = 12.37$.

Chart 3

RATIO OF NONFINANCIAL
CP*TO C&I LOANS OF LARGE WEEKLY
REPORTING COMMERCIAL BANKS

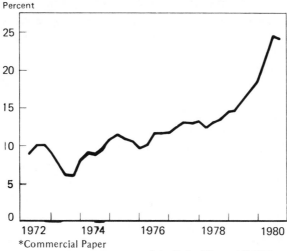

*Commercial Paper

Source: Board of Governors of the Federal Reserve System.

Aside from becoming more competitive with the commercial paper market, banks have tried at the same time to provide services to support their customers' commercial paper issues. Some banks have offered customers more flexible short-term borrowing arrangements to allow commercial paper issuers to adjust the timing of their paper sales. Morgan Guaranty Trust Company, which originated this service, calls its open line of credit a "Commercial Paper Adjustment Facility" and prices the service below the prime rate. Commercial banks also provide back-up lines of credit and act as issuing agents, as discussed above.

In summary, competition with the commercial paper market is changing the lending practices of commercial banks. Although banks still extend a large volume of short-term business loans, the profitability of loans to their largest customers has been reduced partly because of competition with the commercial paper market, and some commercial bank activity now focuses on supporting the issuance of their customers' commercial paper.

Financial Paper

Since the 1920s, finance companies have been important participants in the commercial paper market. They provide much of the credit used to finance consumer purchases. Historically, around 20 percent of outstanding consumer credit has come from finance companies. Finance companies also supply a large and growing amount of business credit such as wholesale and retail financing of inventory, receivables financing, and commercial and leasing financing. About half of all the credit extended by finance companies goes to businesses, predominantly to small- and medium-sized firms.

The primary source of short-term funds for finance companies is sales of commercial paper. In fact, the outstanding commercial paper liabilities of finance companies were about five times as large as their bank loans in the late 1970s. Like nonfinancial companies, finance companies since the mid-1960s gradually increased the proportion of borrowing in the commercial paper market compared to short-term borrowing from commercial banks.

As seen in Chart 1, nonbank financial paper constitutes the largest proportion of outstanding commercial paper. Sixty percent of all commercial paper is directly placed and the greatest proportion of this is finance company paper. Finance company paper, however, is issued by only a small fraction of the total number of finance companies. According to the Federal Reserve Board's *Survey of Finance Companies, 1975*, 88 of the largest finance companies out of a total of about 3,400 such firms issued 97 percent of all finance company paper and extended 90 percent of total finance company credit.

The outstanding volume of bank-related financial paper has been extremely volatile compared to nonbank financial paper. As mentioned above, this market received a major jolt when the Federal Reserve imposed reserve requirements on bank-related commercial paper issues in August 1970. Growth in outstanding bank-related commercial paper resumed by mid-1971, however. This growth corresponded with record acquisitions of nonbank firms by bank holding companies, which peaked at 332 nonbank firms acquired in 1973 and 264 firms in 1974. Some of the primary activities of these newly acquired subsidiaries are commercial finance, factoring, and leasing. The 1973-75 recession curtailed the growth in bank paper, but growth resumed its upward trend by 1976 and has continued strongly since.

NEW DIRECTIONS FOR THE COMMERCIAL PAPER MARKET

Recently several new groups of issuers have entered the commercial paper market. These include foreign banks, multinational corporations, and public utilities; thrift institutions; second tier issuers relying on guarantees from supporting entities; and tax-exempt issuers. These issuers have found the commercial paper market to be a flexible and attractive way to borrow short-term funds.

Foreign Issuers

Foreign participation in the commercial paper market has been growing and will probably continue to be an important source of new growth. As of year-end 1980, Moody's rated 70 foreign issuers, which collectively had about $7 billion in outstanding commercial paper. These issuers fall into three general categories: foreign-based multinational corporations, nationalized utilities, and banks. Some large foreign multinational corporations issue paper to finance their operations in the United States. Others borrow to support a variety of activities that require dollar payments for goods and services. Nationalized utilities have been major borrowers in the commercial paper market largely because their purchases of oil require payment in dollars. Finally, foreign banks raise funds for their banking activity or act as guarantors for the commercial paper of their clients by issuing letters of credit. These banks have been among the most recent entrants into the market.

The commercial paper market is often the cheapest source of dollars for foreign issuers. A major alternative source of dollar borrowing is the Eurodollar market, where rates are generally linked to the London Interbank Offered Rate (LIBOR). Many foreign banks, for example, obtain funds in the commercial paper market for ¼ of one percent or more below LIBOR. Aside from cost considerations, another important motivation behind foreign participation in the commercial paper market is foreign issuers' interest in obtaining ratings and gaining acceptance with the American financial community. The exposure from selling paper helps to broaden a foreign issuer's investor base and prepares the way for entering the bond and equity markets.

Two obstacles to foreign participation in the commercial paper market are obtaining prime credit ratings and coping with foreign withholding taxes on interest paid to investors outside the country. Ratings below top quality wipe out the cost advantage of raising short-term funds in the commercial paper market. To date, for example, no foreign banks have issued paper with less than top ratings.

Withholding taxes on interest paid to investors outside the country also may eliminate commercial paper's cost advantage over the Eurodollar market. These taxes are intended to curtail short-term capital outflows and are used in France, Belgium, Australia, Canada, and other countries. For foreign issuers' commercial paper to be marketable, the issuer must bear the cost of the withholding tax. The tax therefore raises the cost of acquiring funds using commercial paper.

By taking advantage of loopholes and technicalities in the withholding tax laws, foreign issuers often circumvent these laws. For example, the nationalized French electric company, Electricite de France, one of the largest foreign or domestic paper issuers, has its commercial paper classified as long-term debt, which is not subject to France's 15 percent withholding tax on interest. The reason for this classification is that the utility backs its paper with a 10-year revolving credit facility from its banks that establishes the commercial paper borrowing as long-term debt. French banks use a different approach to take advantage of a withholding tax exemption on short-term time deposits like CDs. They set up U. S. subsidiaries to sell commercial paper and then transfer the proceeds to the French parent banks by issuing CDs to their U. S. subsidiaries.

In general, foreign issuers pay more to borrow in the commercial paper market than domestic issuers for two reasons. First, almost all foreign commercial paper issues have a sovereign risk associated with the issuer that results from additional uncertainty in the investor's mind about the probability of default on commercial paper because of government intervention, political turmoil, economic disruption, etc. This uncertainty creates a risk premium which increases the interest rate on foreign issues relative to domestic issues. The size of the premium depends on the issuer, the country, and the level of interest rates. A second source of additional costs arises when foreign issuers pay to establish and operate U.S. subsidiaries to issue paper and, in the case of foreign banks, incur reserve requirement costs on commercial paper issues. In addition, rating service fees are higher for foreign issuers than for domestic issuers, as mentioned earlier. Nevertheless, the commercial paper market is proving to be the least expensive source of short-term dollar funds for an increasing number of foreign borrowers.

Thrift Commercial Paper

Both savings and loan associations and mutual savings banks have recently been allowed to borrow funds in the commercial paper market. Mutual savings banks (MSBs) had the authority to issue commercial paper, but faced restrictions on advertising, interest payments, and minimum maturity that effectively prevented them from issuing commercial paper. On March 3, 1980 the Federal Deposit Insurance Corporation (FDIC) removed the restrictions and thereby cleared the way for MSB participation in the commercial paper market. The FDIC ruled that MSB commercial paper must be unsecured, have a maximum maturity of nine months, sell at a minimum price of $100,000, state that it is uninsured by FDIC, and bear a notice that the instrument will pay no interest after maturity. Despite the relaxation of restrictions, as of early 1981 no MSBs have issued paper. The failure of MSBs to issue commercial paper has been largely due to impaired MSB earnings, which make it difficult to obtain the high credit ratings necessary to realize the cost advantage in borrowing in the commercial paper market.

Savings and loan associations have had access to the commercial paper market since January 1979, when the Federal Home Loan Bank Board approved the first applications for S&Ls to issue commercial paper and short-term notes secured by mortgage loans. S&Ls use commercial paper principally to finance seasonal surges in loan demand and to finance secondary mortgage market operations. Commercial paper allows greater flexibility for S&Ls in managing liquidity because they can borrow large amounts of cash quickly and for periods as short as five days. Relatively few S&Ls carry commercial paper ratings. Of the 60 or so large S&Ls expected to participate in the market after the FHLBB approved the first applications, only 12 had ratings from Moody's as of mid-1980, though all were P-1. These S&Ls collectively had $327 million in outstanding commercial paper as of mid-1980.

The attractiveness of commercial paper for S&Ls and MSBs has been sharply diminished as a result of the *Depository Institutions Deregulation and Monetary Control Act of 1980*. Under the Act, commercial paper is considered a reservable liability, except when issued to certain exempt investors such as depository institutions. S&Ls and MSBs have to hold reserves in the ratio of 3 percent against outstanding commercial paper, which is classified as a nonpersonal time deposit. Reserve requirements increase the cost of funds raised through commercial paper and consequently reduce the incentive for S&Ls and MSBs to issue paper.

Support Arrangements

Many lesser known firms gain access to the commercial paper market through financial support arrangements obtained from firms with the highest credit ratings. Second tier issuers frequently issue paper by obtaining a letter of credit from a commercial bank. This procedure substitutes the credit of a bank for that of the issuer and thereby reduces the cost of issuing commercial paper. This kind of support arrangement is known as "commercial paper supported by letter of credit" and resembles bankers' acceptance financing except that the issuance of commercial paper is not associated with the shipment of goods. Because the letter of credit is appended to the commercial paper note, commercial paper supported by letter of credit is alternatively referred to as a "documented discount note." Typically, letters of credit are valid for a specific term or are subject to termination upon written notice by either party. To have a commercial bank stand ready to back up an issue of paper, an issuer must pay a fee that ranges from one-quarter to three-quarters of a percentage point.

Although commercial paper with letter of credit support reached an outstanding volume of about $2 billion by mid-1980, this segment of the market is still comparatively small. Many issuers of letter of credit commercial paper are subsidiaries of larger corporate entities. These second tier issuers include firms involved in pipeline construction, vehicle leasing, nuclear fuel supply, and power plant construction. Other commercial paper issuers also have acquired letter of credit support from commercial banks, particularly during the period of restricted credit growth in early 1980. Issuers whose ratings were downgraded faced difficulty selling their paper and paid substantial premiums over high grade paper. Buying a letter of credit from a commercial bank reduced their borrowing costs in the commercial paper market and still offered a cheaper alternative to short-term bank loans.

Other supporting entities that provide guarantees or endorsements are insurance companies, governments for government-owned companies, and parent companies for their subsidiaries. For example, the commercial paper of the nationalized French utilities, such as Electricite de France, carries the guarantee of the Republic of France. Guarantees or endorsements by parent companies for their subsidiaries are the most prevalent form of support arrangement.

Tax-Exempt Paper

One of the most recent innovations in the commercial paper market is tax-exempt paper. Except for its tax-exempt feature, this paper differs little from other commercial paper. To qualify for tax-exempt status the paper must be issued by state or municipal governments, or by qualified nonprofit organizations. Like taxable commercial paper, tax-exempt paper is also exempt from Securities and Exchange Commission registration provided the paper matures within 270 days. Most tax-exempt paper matures within 15 to 90 days. These short-term debt obligations are alternatively known as *short-term revenue bonds* or *short-term interim certificates*.

The outstanding volume of tax-exempt paper has grown rapidly, rising from an insignificant amount in 1979 to about $500 million in 1980. It will probably exceed $1 billion in 1981. Much of the demand for tax-exempt paper comes from short-term tax-exempt funds, which had assets of $1.5 billion in mid-1980, and from bank trust departments. Many mutual fund groups are setting up tax-exempt money market funds in response to the apparent increasing demands for this type of investment. A current shortage of tax-exempt commercial paper has depressed the yields on outstanding issues, making this instrument especially attractive to tax-exempt issuers. However, constraints on public agency use of short-term debt in some states may continue to limit the supply of tax-exempt commercial paper.

CONCLUSION

The commercial paper market has served the short-term financing needs of several groups of borrowers to an increasing degree in recent years. Many nonfinancial companies, especially large firms, have substituted commercial paper for short-term bank loans to satisfy their working capital requirements. Commercial paper has generally been a less costly financing alternative than bank short-term credit for these firms. Finance companies have relied to a greater extent on commercial paper than nonfinancial companies for short-term financing and have issued the greatest proportion of outstanding commercial paper. Most large finance companies realize economies of scale by placing commercial paper directly with investors. Bank holding companies also have depended on the paper market to finance their banking-related activities, which increased in size and scope during the 1970s.

Other types of issuers have been recently attracted to the commercial paper market because of the potential saving in interest costs over alternative ways of borrowing short-term funds. Foreign issuers have sold a substantial amount of commercial paper since entering the market in the mid-1970s. Foreign and domestic issuers who lack sufficient financial strength to offer commercial paper on their own have gained access to the market via support arrangements with stronger financial or corporate entities. Tax-exempt issuers are expected to increase in number and generate larger supplies of tax-exempt paper. Thrift institutions, on the other hand, probably will not make much use of the market in the future because recently imposed reserve requirements on commercial paper have reduced its cost-advantage over other sources of short-term credit.

Many investors find commercial paper to be an attractive short-term financial instrument. Although corporations and other institutional investors held most outstanding commercial paper in the past, financial intermediation by money market funds and other short-term investment pooling arrangements has given many new investors, especially individuals, indirect access to commercial paper.

REFERENCES

1. Board of Governors of the Federal Reserve System. "Short-Term Business Lending at Rates Below the Prime Rate." *Federal Monetary Policy and Its Effect on Small Business, Part 3. Hearings before a Subcommittee on Access to Equity Capital and Business Opportunities of the House Committee on Small Business.* U. S. Congress, House. Committee on Small Business, 96th Cong., 2nd sess., 1980, pp. 318-327.

2. Chell, Gretchen. "Tax-Exempt Commercial Paper Beginning to Catch on as an Investment Medium." *The Money Manager*, July 21, 1980.

3. Hurley, Evelyn M. "Survey of Finance Companies, 1975." *Federal Reserve Bulletin* (March 1976).

4. ——. "The Commercial Paper Market." *Federal Reserve Bulletin* (June 1977).

5. Judd, John P. "Competition Between the Commercial Paper Market and Commercial Banks." *Economic Review*, Federal Reserve Bank of San Francisco (Winter 1979).

6. Levin, Sumner N., ed. *The 1979 Dow Jones-Irwin Business Almanac.* Homewood, Illinois: Dow Jones-Irwin, 1979.

7. McKenzie, Joseph A. "Commercial Paper: Plugging into a New and Stable Source of Financing." *Federal Home Loan Bank Board Journal* (March 1979), pp. 2-5.

8. Puglisi, Donald J. "Commercial Paper: A Primer." *Federal Home Loan Bank Board Journal*, 13 (December 1980): 4-10.

9. Stigum, Marcia. *The Money Market: Myth, Reality, and Practice*. Homewood, Illinois: Dow Jones-Irwin, 1978.

EURODOLLARS*

Marvin Goodfriend[†]

9

Eurodollars are deposit liabilities, denominated in United States dollars, of banks located outside the United States.[1] Eurodollar deposits may be owned by individuals, corporations, or governments from anywhere in the world. The term Eurodollar dates from an earlier period when the market was located primarily in Europe. Although the bulk of Eurodollar deposits are still held in Europe, today dollar-denominated deposits are held in such places as the Bahamas, Bahrain, Canada, the Cayman Islands, Hong Kong, Japan, Panama, and Singapore, as well as in major European financial centers.[2] Nevertheless, dollar-denominated deposits located anywhere in the world outside the United States are still referred to as Eurodollars.

Banks in the Eurodollar market and banks located in the United States compete to attract dollar-denominated funds worldwide. Since the Eurodollar market is relatively free of regulation, banks in the Eurodollar market can operate on narrower margins or spreads between dollar borrowing and lending rates than banks in the United States. This allows Eurodollar deposits to compete effectively with deposits issued by banks located in the

---

*Reprinted from *Instruments of the Money Market*, 5th edition, edited by Timothy Q. Cook and Bruce J. Summers, 1981, with permission from the Federal Reserve Bank of Richmond.

†Dr. Goodfriend is Research officer at the Federal Reserve Bank of Richmond.

[1] Dollar-denominated deposits at a bank located outside the U.S. are Eurodollars, even if the bank is affiliated with a bank whose home office is in the United States.

[2] See Ashby (1978) and (1979) for discussions of Europe's declining share of the global Euro-currency market. The Euro-currency market includes, along with Eurodollars, foreign currency-denominated deposits held at banks located outside a currency's home country.

United States. In short, the Eurodollar market has grown up largely as a means of separating the currency of denomination of a financial instrument (the United States dollar) from the country of jurisdiction or responsibility for that currency (the United States), in order to reduce the regulatory costs involved in dollar-denominated financial intermediation.

THE SIZE OF THE EURODOLLAR MARKET

Measuring the size of the Eurodollar market involves looking at the volume of dollar-denominated loans and deposits on the books of banks located outside the United States. However, dollar-denominated loans and deposits may not match. Consequently, a decision must be made whether to measure the volume of Eurodollars from the asset or liability side of the balance sheet.

A liability side measure may be too broad, since it may include foreign currency liabilities incurred to fund loans to domestic residents denominated in domestic currency. Strictly speaking, this is a traditional type of international financial intermediation. Measuring Eurodollar market volume from dollar-denominated assets, however, may also overstate the size of Eurodollar volume since these assets may reflect nothing more than traditional foreign lending funded with domestic currency-denominated deposits supplied by domestic residents.

In practice, Eurodollar volume is measured as the dollar-denominated deposit liabilities of banks located outside the United States. For example, the Bank for International Settlements (BIS) defines and measures Eurodollars as dollars that have "been acquired by a bank outside the United States and used directly or after conversion into another currency for lending to a non-bank customer, perhaps after one or more redeposits from one bank to another."[3]

Under a liability side measure such as the one used by the BIS, the sum of all dollar-denominated liabilities of banks outside the United States measures the gross size of the Eurodollar market. For some purposes, it is useful to net part of interbank deposits out of the gross to arrive at an estimate of Eurodollar deposits held by original suppliers to the Eurodollar market. Roughly speaking, to construct the net size measure, deposits owned by banks in the Eurodollar market are netted out. But deposits owned by banks located outside of the Eurodollar market area are not netted out because banks located outside the Eurodollar market area are considered to be original suppliers of funds to the Eurodollar market. For still other purposes, such as comparing the volume of deposits created in the Eurodollar market

---

[3] Bank for International Settlements, *1964 Annual Report*, p. 127.

with the United States monetary aggregates, it is useful to further net out all bank-owned Eurodollar deposits. Doing so leaves only the non-bank portion of the net size measure, or what might be called the net-net size of the Eurodollar market.

The most readily accessible estimates of the size of the Eurodollar market are compiled by Morgan Guaranty Trust Company of New York and reported in the monthly bank letter *World Financial Markets.*[4] Morgan's estimates are based on a liability side measure and include data compiled by the BIS. However, Morgan's estimates are somewhat more comprehensive. Morgan reports estimates of the size of the entire Euro-currency market based roughly on all foreign-currency liabilities and claims of banks in major European countries and eight other market areas.

As of mid-1980 Morgan estimated the gross size of the Euro-currency market at $1,310 billion.[5] The net size was put at $670 billion.[6] Morgan also reports that Eurodollars made up 72 percent of gross Euro-currency liabilities, putting the gross size of the Eurodollar market at roughly $940 billion.[7] No net Eurodollar market size is given. However, 72 percent of the net size of the Euro-currency market yields $480 billion as an approximate measure of the net size of the Eurodollar market. Finally, Morgan reports Eurodollar deposits to non-banks at $200 billion, and those held by United States non-bank residents as less than $50 billion.[8]

M2 is the narrowest United States monetary aggregate that includes Eurodollar deposits. M2 includes overnight Eurodollar deposits held by United States non-bank residents at Caribbean branches of United States member banks. As of June 1980, M2 measured $1,587 billion; its Eurodollar component was $2.9 billion.[9]

Even though it is conceptually appropriate to include term Eurodollar deposits held by United States non-bank residents in M3, they are only included in L, the broadest measure of money and liquid assets reported by the Federal Reserve, because the data used to estimate their volume is available with a long lag relative to other data in M3. M3 was approximately $1,846 billion in June 1980, the Eurodollar component of L was $51.8

[4] See Morgan Guaranty Trust Company of New York, *World Financial Markets* (January 1979, pp. 9-13, for a discussion of Morgan's method of measuring the size of the Eurodollar market. Other useful discussions of issues involved in measuring the Eurodollar market's size are found in Dufey and Giddy (1978), pp. 21-34, and Mayer (1976).

[5] Morgan Guaranty (December 1980), p. 15. Most of the growth of the Euro-currency market has occurred in the last two decades. Morgan reported the net size of the Euro-currency market as only $21 billion in 1966. See Dufey and Giddy (1978), Chapter III, for a discussion of the growth of the Euro-currency market.

[6] Morgan Guaranty (December 1980), p. 15.

[7] Ibid.

[8] Ibid., p. 4.

[9] Board of Governors of the Federal Reserve System, H.6 statistical release, "Money Stock Measures and Liquid Assets" (February 20, 1981), pp. 1 and 4.

billion.[10] Eurodollar deposits owned by United States non-bank residents continue to grow rapidly, but these comparisons show clearly that such Eurodollar deposits still account for a relatively small portion of the United States non-bank resident holdings of money and liquid assets.

INCENTIVES FOR DEVELOPMENT
OF THE EURODOLLAR MARKET[11]

By accepting deposits and making loans denominated in United States dollars outside the United States, banks can avoid United States banking regulations. In particular, banks located outside the United States are not required to keep non-interest bearing reserves against Eurodollar deposits. These foreign banks hold reserves with United States banks for clearing purposes only. Moreover, there is no required Federal Deposit Insurance Corporation insurance assessment associated with Eurodollar deposits. Virtually no restrictions exist for interest rates payable on Eurodollar deposits or charged on Eurodollar loans; nor are there any restrictions on the types of assets allowed in portfolio.

In most Eurodollar financial centers, entry into Eurodollar banking is virtually free of regulatory impediments. In addition, banks intending to do Eurodollar business can set up in locations where tax rates are low. For example, Eurodollar deposits and loans negotiated in London or elsewhere are often booked in locations such as Nassau and the Cayman Islands to obtain more favorable tax treatment.

Foreign monetary authorities are generally reluctant to regulate Eurodollar business because to do so would drive the business away, denying the host country income, tax revenue, and jobs. Moreover, host countries are not responsible for the United States dollar and so are relatively indifferent to what happens in dollar-denominated money markets. Even if the United States monetary authorities could induce a group of foreign countries to

---

[10] Ibid., pp. 1 and 5.

   L includes Eurodollar deposits held by U. S. non-bank residents at all banks in the U.K., Canada, and at branches of U. S. banks in other countries. These account for nearly all Eurodollar holdings of non-bank U. S. residents. Some overnight Eurodollar deposits issued to U. S. non-bank residents by banks other than Caribbean branches of member banks are only included in L because current data do not separate these overnight Eurodollars from term Eurodollars. See Board of Governors of the Federal Reserve Bulletin (February 1980), p. 98.

   At present, Eurodollars held by non-U.S. residents are not included in any of the U. S. monetary aggregates. As improved data sources become available, the possible inclusion of Eurodollars held by non-U.S. residents other than banks and official insitutions could be reviewed. *Federal Reserve Bulletin* (February 1980), p. 98.

[11] See Dufey and Giddy (1978), pp. 110-12, for more discussion of the conditions that made large-scale Eurodollar market growth possible.

participate in a plan to regulate their Euromarkets, such a plan would be ineffective unless every country agreed not to host unregulated Eurodollar business. In practice, competition for this business has been fierce, so even if a consensus should develop in the United States to regulate Eurodollar business, it would be extremely difficult to impose regulations on the entire Eurodollar market.

The worldwide competition for Eurodollar business together with lack of foreign government interference have combined to produce low cost, efficient dollar-denominated financial intermediation outside the United States.

INSTRUMENTS OF THE EURODOLLAR MARKET [12]

The overwhelming majority of money in the Eurodollar market is held in fixed-rate time deposits (TDs). The maturities of Eurodollar TDs range from overnight to several years, with most of the money held in the one-week to six-month maturity range. Eurodollar time deposits are intrinsically different from dollar deposits held at banks in the United States only in that the former are liabilities of financial institutions located outside the United States. The bulk of Eurodollar time deposits are interbank liabilities. They pay a rate of return which, although fixed for the term of the deposit, is initially competitively determined.[13]

From their introduction in 1966, the volume of negotiable Eurodollar certificates of deposit (CDs) outstanding reached roughly $50 billion at the beginning of 1980.[14] Essentially, a Eurodollar CD is a negotiable receipt for a dollar deposit at a bank located outside the United States.

On average over the past seven years, fixed-rate three-month Eurodollar CDs have yielded approximately 30 basis points below the three-month time deposit London interbank offer rate (LIBOR).[15] LIBOR is the rate at which major international banks are willing to offer term Eurodollar deposits to each other.

An active secondary market allows investors to sell Eurodollar CDs before

---

[12] Dobbs-Higginson (1980), pp. 55-61; Dufey and Giddy (1978), pp. 228-32; and Stigum (1978), Chapters 15 and 16, contain useful surveys of Eurodollar instruments.

[13] Eurodollar deposit rates are tiered according to maturity as well as according to the perceived creditworthiness of individual issuing banks. See Stigum (1978), p. 433, and Dufey and Giddy (1978), p. 227.

[14] Bank of England, Financial Statistics Division, International Banking Group. This data only includes London dollar CDs. But until recently, virtually all Eurodollar CDs have been issued in London. See "Out-of-Towners," *The Economist* (July 12, 1980), p. 89.

[15] This spread was calculated from data in Salomon Brothers, *An Analytical Record of Yields and Yield Spreads* (1980).

the deposits mature. Secondary market makers' spreads for short-term fixed-rate CDs are usually 5 or 10 basis points.[16]

Eurodollar CDs are issued by banks to "tap" the market for funds. Consequently, they have come to be called *Tap CDs*. Such Tap CDs are commonly issued in denominations of from $250,000 to $5 million. Some large Eurodollar CD issues are marketed in several portions in order to satisfy investors with preferences for smaller instruments. These are known as *Tranche CDs*. Tranche CDs are issued in aggregate amounts of $10 to $30 million and offered to individual investors in $10,000 certificates with each certificate having the same interest rate, issue date, interest payment dates, and maturity.

In recent years *Eurodollar Floating Rate CDs* (FRCDs) and *Eurodollar Floating Rate Notes* (FRNs) have come into use as a means of protecting both borrower and lender against interest rate risk. Specifically, these "floaters" shift the burden of risk from the principal value of the paper to its coupon.

Eurodollar FRCDs and FRNs are both negotiable bearer paper. The coupon or interest rate on these instruments is reset periodically, typically every three or six months, at a small spread above the corresponding LIBOR. Eurodollar FRCDs yield, depending on maturity, between 1/8 and 1/4 of one percentage point over the six-month LIBOR.[17] They are an attractive alternative to placing six-month time deposits at the London interbank bid rate. Eurodollar FRN issues have usually been brought to market with a margin of 1/8 to 1/4 of one percentage point over either the three- or six-month LIBOR or the mean of the London interbank bid and offered rates.[18] To determine LIBOR for Eurodollar FRNs, "the issuer chooses an agent bank who in turn polls three or four Reference Banks—generally, the London offices of major international banks. Rates are those prevailing at 11:00 a.m. London time two business days prior to the commencement of the next coupon period."[19]

Eurodollar FRCDs have been issued in maturities from 1-1/2 to 5 years and are employed as an alternative to short-term money market instruments. Eurodollar FRNs have been issued in maturities from 4 to 20 years, with the majority of issues concentrated in the 5- to 7-year range. Eurodollar FRNs tend to be seen as an alternative to straight fixed interest bonds, but they can in principle be used like FRCDs. Eurodollar FRNs have been issued primarily, but not exclusively, by banks.

---

[16] Dobbs-Higginson (1980), p. 59.

[17] Credit Suisse First Boston Limited, "A Description of the London Dollar Negotiable Certificate of Deposit Market" (January 1980), p. 3.

[18] Salomon Brothers, *Eurodollar Floating Rate Notes: A Guide to the Market* (1980), p. 3. The spread between interbank bid and offer rates is normally 1/8 percent, so an issue priced at 1/4 percent over the mean of the bid and offer rates would return 3/16 percent over LIBOR.

[19] Ibid., p. 7.

A secondary market exists in Eurodollar FRCDs and FRNs, although dealer spreads are quite large. Secondary market makers' spreads for FRCDs are normally 1/4 of one percent of the principal value.[20] The spread quoted on FRNs in the secondary market is generally 1/2 of one percent of the principal value.[21]

INTEREST RATE RELATIONSHIPS BETWEEN EURODOLLAR DEPOSITS AND DEPOSITS AT BANKS IN THE UNITED STATES

Arbitrage keeps interest rates closely aligned between Eurodollar deposits and deposits with roughly comparable characteristics at banks located in the United States. This is illustrated in Charts 1 and 2. Chart 1 shows yields

Chart 1

YIELDS ON FEDERAL FUNDS AND OVERNIGHT EURODOLLAR DEPOSITS
(monthly average)

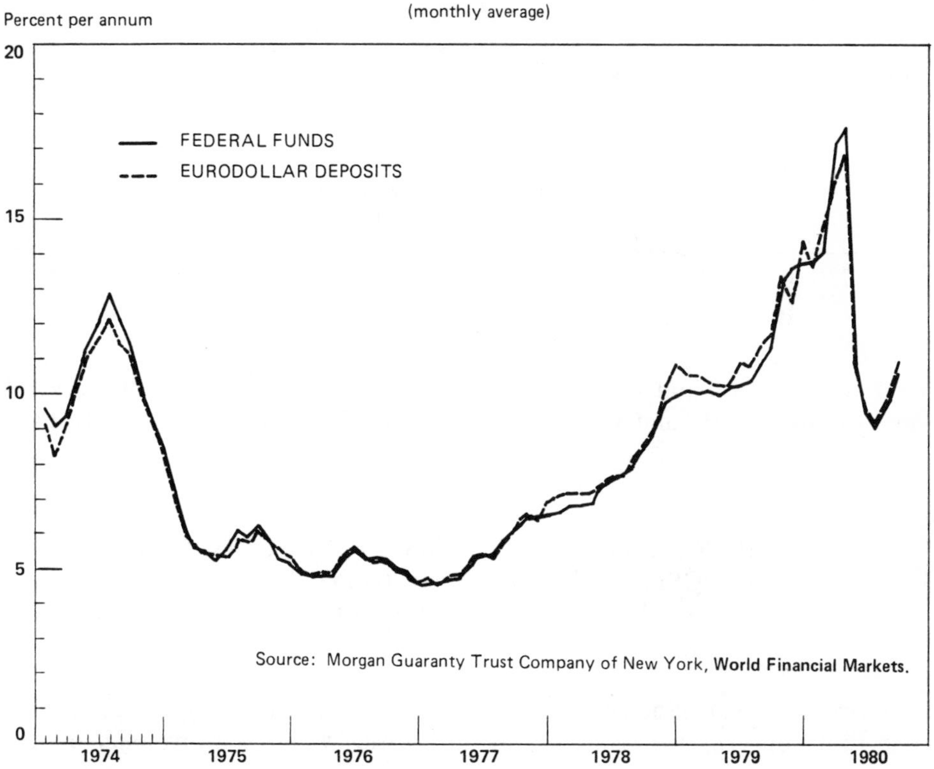
Percent per annum
20
15
10
5
0
FEDERAL FUNDS
EURODOLLAR DEPOSITS
Source: Morgan Guaranty Trust Company of New York, World Financial Markets.
1974
1975
1976
1977
1978
1979
1980

[20] Dobbs-Higginson (1980), p. 59.
[21] Ibid., p. 56.

Chart 2

YIELDS ON UNITED STATES AND EURODOLLAR
THREE-MONTH CERTIFICATES OF DEPOSIT

Percent per annum   (at or near the first of the month)

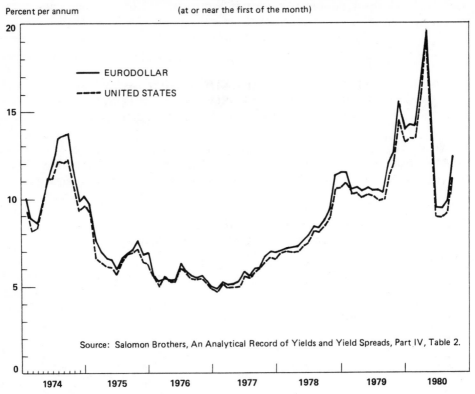

Source: Salomon Brothers, An Analytical Record of Yields and Yield Spreads, Part IV, Table 2.

on Federal funds and overnight Eurodollar deposits. Chart 2 shows yields on Eurodollar CDs and CDs issued by banks located in the United States.

THE RELATIVE RISKINESS OF EURODOLLAR DEPOSITS AND DOLLAR DEPOSITS HELD IN THE UNITED STATES [22]

There are three basic sources of risk associated with holding Eurodollars. The first concerns the chance that authorities where a Eurodollar deposit

---

[22] See Dufey and Giddy (1978), pp. 187-90, and Tyson (July 1980) for more discussion of the riskiness of Eurodollars.

is held may interfere in the movement or repatriation of interest or principal of the deposit. But this risk factor does not necessarily imply that Eurodollar deposits are riskier than dollar deposits held in the United States. The riskiness of a Eurodollar deposit relative to a dollar deposit held in the United States can depend on the deposit holder's residence. For United States residents, Eurodollars may appear riskier than domestic deposits because of the possibility that authorities in the foreign country where the deposit is located may interfere in the movement or repatriation of the interest or principal of the deposit. Foreign residents, Iranians for example, may feel that the United States Government is more likely to block their deposits than the British Government. Consequently, Iranians may perceive greater risk from potential government interference by holding dollar deposits in the United States than by holding Eurodollar deposits in London.

A second element of risk associated with Eurodollars concerns the potential for international jurisdictional legal disputes. For example, uncertainty surrounding interaction between United States and foreign legal systems compounds the difficulty in assessing the likelihood and timing of Eurodollar deposit payment in the event of a Eurodollar issuing bank's failure.

A third type of risk associated with holding Eurodollars concerns. the relative soundness *per se* of foreign banks compared to banks located in the United States. Specifically, it has been argued that Eurodollars are absolutely riskier than deposits held in the United States because deposits held in the United States generally carry deposit insurance of some kind while Eurodollar deposits generally do not. In addition, it has been argued that in event of a financial crisis banks located in the United States are more likely to be supported by the Federal Reserve System, whereas neither Federal Reserve support nor the support of foreign central banks for Eurodollar banking activities in their jurisdiction is certain.

A related factor compounding the three basic risk factors identified above is the greater cost of evaluating foreign investments compared with domestic investments. Acquiring information on the soundness of foreign banks is generally more costly than assessing the soundness of more well-known domestic banks. This means that for a given level of expenditure on information acquisition, investors must generally accept more ignorance about the soundness of a foreign bank than a domestic bank.

Two comments on this argument are relevant here. First, the fact that it is more costly to evaluate foreign than domestic investments does not imply that Eurodollar deposits are inherently riskier than deposits held in the United States. If a depositor resides in the United States the argument implies that a given expenditure on research will generally yield more information about the safety of deposits located in the United States than in the Eurodollar market. But if the depositor resides outside the United States, the reverse may be true.

Having said this, it must be pointed out that the amount of financial disclosure required by regulatory authorities abroad is generally not as great as in the United States. This fact may make it more difficult to evaluate the soundness of non-U.S. banks than U.S. banks for any depositor, regardless of his residence.

Second, to a large extent assessing the safety of Eurodollar deposits relative to deposits in banks located in the United States is made easier by the fact that many banks in the Eurodollar market are affiliated with and bear the name of a bank whose home office is in the United States. For example, a London branch of a United States bank is as closely associated with its home office as a branch located in the United States.

However, foreign offices bearing the name of a United States bank, usually in a slightly altered form, have been set up as subsidiaries. Under most legal systems, a branch can not fail unless its head office fails; but a subsidiary can fail even if its parent institution remains in business. Technically, a foreign office can bear the name of a United States bank in some form, and yet the parent institution may not be legally bound to stand fully behind the obligations of its foreign office. This suggests that a foreign office named after a parent United States bank may not be as sound as its namesake, although the parent bank, unquestionably, has great incentive to aid the foreign office in meeting its obligations in order to preserve confidence in the bank's name.

On the whole, it is difficult to assess the relative riskiness of Eurodollar deposits and dollar deposits held in the United States. Some factors affecting relative risk can be identified, but their importance is difficult to measure. What is more, perceived relative riskiness can depend on the residence of the investor. The extent to which risk-related factors affect the interest rate relationship between Eurodollar deposits and comparable deposits at banks in the United States remains unclear.

SUMMARY

From the depositor's point of view, Eurodollar deposits are relatively close substitutes for dollar deposits at banks located in the United States. Eurodollar deposits are able to compete effectively with deposits offered by banks located in the United States because Eurodollar deposits are free of reserve requirements and other regulatory burdens imposed by the United States monetary authorities on banks located in the United States. In fact, the tremendous growth of the Eurodollar market in the last two decades has largely been the result of efforts to move dollar financial intermediation outside the regulatory jurisdiction of the United States monetary authorities.

Host countries have competed eagerly for Eurodollar business by promising relatively few regulations, low taxes, and other incentives to attract a portion of the Eurodollar banking industry. Financial intermediation in United States dollars is likely to continue to move abroad as long as incentives exist for it to do so. Since these incentives are not likely to disappear soon, the Eurodollar market's share of world dollar financial intermediation is likely to continue growing.

REFERENCES

Ashby, David F. V. "Challenge from the New Euro-Centres." *The Banker*, January 1978, pp. 53-61.
———. "Changing Patterns in the $800 Billion Super-Dollar Market." *The Banker*, March 1979, pp. 21-23.
Bank of England. Personal correspondence, Financial Statistics Division, International Banking Group.
Bank for International Settlements. *1964 Annual Report*. Basle, Switzerland.
Board of Governors of the Federal Reserve System.*Federal Reserve Bulletin*, February 1980.
———. H.6 statistical release, "Money Stock Measures and Liquid Assets," February 20, 1981.
Credit Suisse First Boston Limited. "A Description of the London Dollar Negotiable Certificate of Deposit Market," January 1980.
Dobbs-Higginson, M.S. *Investment Manual for Fixed Income Securities in the International and Major Domestic Capital Markets*. London: Credit Suisse First Boston Limited, 1980.
Dufey, Gunter, and Giddy, Ian H. *The International Money Market*. Englewood Cliffs, New Jersey: Prentice-Hall, 1978.
"The London Dollar Certificate of Deposit." Bank of England *Quarterly Bulletin* 13, no. 4 (December 1973): 446-52.
Mayer, Helmut W. "The BIS Concept of the Eurocurrency Market." *Euromoney*, May 1976, pp.60-66.
Morgan Guaranty Trust Company of New York. *World Financial Markets*. Various issues.
"Out-of-Towners." *The Economist*, July 12, 1980, p. 89.
Salomon Brothers. *An Analytical Record of Yields and Yield Spreads*. New York: Salomon Brothers, 1980.
———. *Eurodollar Floating Rate Notes: A Guide to the Market*. New York: Salomon Brothers, 1980.
Stigum, Marcia. *The Money Market: Myth, Reality, and Practice*. Homewood, Illinois: Dow Jones-Irwin, 1978.
Tyson, David O. "Fund Managers Wary of Risks in Non-Domestic CDs." *The Money Manager*, July 14, 1980, pp. 3-4.

Part II

Capital
Market Instruments

A. THE BOND MARKET

Part II of this book relates to topics collectively referred to as *capital market instruments*. In contrast to their money market counterparts, most of these instruments are characterized as having greater price risk, less liquidity, and, with the exception of U.S. Treasury and agency issues, a higher degree of default risk. Not surprisingly, the expected returns on most of these instruments are higher than the expected returns on money market instruments. Because of the risks associated with these instruments, the higher expected returns are not always realized. Some of these instruments such as interest rate futures and options may be used in a speculative manner or in a risk-reducing capacity. The higher expected earnings on capital market instruments result in their use as the primary class of earning assets in the investment portfolios of most non-bank financial institutions, individuals, endowments, and other long-term investors.

Part II is divided into four sections: *the bond market, the equity market, mortgage-related instruments*, and *interest rate futures*. In the first section dealing with the bond market, the lead article by Christopher J. McCurdy provides an overview of the market for *U.S. Government securities* with particular emphasis on the role of dealers and their activities. The basic structure of the *corporate bond market* and the dramatic changes in that market in recent years are discussed in the following article by Burton Zwick. Although not well known outside investment banking and institutional investors' circles, the *private placement market* is an extremely important conduit for capital in the financial markets. Approximately one-third of the total long-term capital raised in the financial markets may be traced to the private placement sector. The nature of this market, the participants, and the investors are examined in an article condensed from a Federal Reserve Board Staff Study. A noteworthy aspect of the study is the rapid emergence of commercial banks as agents of borrowers and, of course, as competitors of investment bankers. The final article in this section is by Richard H. Rosenbloom who reviews the *municipal bond market*. Because this market is comprised of securities that are tax-exempt, it is important to understand the linkage between this market and the markets for taxable securities. As shown in the article, the nature of the linkage changes dramatically at times because of the unusual stresses imposed on the municipal market.

THE DEALER MARKET FOR U.S. GOVERNMENT SECURITIES*

Christopher J. McCurdy

10

The market for United States Government securities occupies a central position in the nation's financial system. The market helps the Treasury finance the Government debt and provides the Federal Reserve with an effective means of implementing monetary policy. While the safety of Government securities is a fundamental feature, perhaps their most vital quality to investors is their liquidity—the ability to transform them into cash quickly and at low cost. The market is an over-the-telephone one in which dealer firms stand ready to buy and sell from a wide range of public and private participants. The dynamic interaction of all participants enhances the attractiveness of Treasury securities and the importance of the market itself.

The dealer market is an effective conduit for the distribution of new Government securities to investors. Treasury financing requirements have grown significantly in recent years, owing to a series of increased Government deficits and to the need for refinancing a heavy schedule of maturities. Since 1974, dealers have initially bought slightly more than 40 percent of the securities competitively auctioned to the public by the Treasury. Moreover, the active role that the dealers have taken in making a secondary market, *i.e.*, buying and selling outstanding issues, has enabled investors to use Government securities more readily in carrying out their portfolio strategies.

Federal Reserve open market operations are undertaken with dealers in the market to implement monetary policy. The Manager of the System Open

*Reprinted, with deletions, from the *Quarterly Review*, Winter 1977-78, pp. 35-47, with permission from the Federal Reserve Bank of New York.

Market Account buys and sells securities on a temporary or outright basis either to augment (through purchases) or to reduce (through sales) the reserves available to member banks. These operations, conducted at the Trading Desk of the Federal Reserve Bank of New York (FRBNY), have an important bearing on overall economic activity. They help to determine the growth of monetary aggregates and the availability of credit, and they influence the trend of interest rates.

Open market operations are also used to counter sharp fluctuations in bank reserves, which arise from such factors as changes in the public's demand for currency or in the size of Treasury cash balances held at Federal Reserve Banks. The Federal Reserve serves as the fiscal agent for the Treasury and as agent for Government and foreign official institutions in the market, buying and selling Treasury securities for them. Activity at the Trading Desk has grown significantly in recent years, mainly in reflection of greater fluctuations in other factors affecting reserves and the increased participation of foreign central banks in the market. The expansion of this activity has also contributed to the growth and liquidity of the secondary market.

The Treasury and the Federal Reserve closely monitor developments in the market. The Trading Desk at the FRBNY conducts regular meetings with representatives of dealer firms and throughout the day remains in telephone contact with their trading rooms, receiving price quotations and assessments of the state of the market. Officials of the Treasury are also in frequent contact with these firms and often solicit their views on debt management. The FRBNY has recently stepped up its surveillance of dealer firms. In addition to obtaining statistical reports from them, it visits the individual firms to gain further insight into market practices and to evaluate the activities of the firms themselves.

The market has expanded sharply in the past few years, both in overall trading activity and in the number of dealer firms. The growth of trading, outright buying and selling, reflects the greater short-run variation in interest rates in the 1970's as well as the large increase in Treasury debt. The Treasury's debt management policies, especially efforts to extend the maturity of the Government debt while meeting enlarged borrowing needs, have also contributed to the market's development. There has also been a growing willingness on the part of portfolio managers to seek to anticipate interest rate movements and thus to trade more actively in the short run.

The entry of a number of new dealer firms into the market has substantially reduced the concentration of trading activity—*i.e.*, the share of trading activity accounted for by the largest firms—and has to some extent altered the trading relationships among the dealer firms. A more impersonal and even more competitive market atmosphere has developed. At times, participants, in seeking greater returns, may also have overreacted to events that could affect interest rates. This, combined with the active trading, could have contributed to short-run volatility in interest rates.

STOCK IN TRADE: UNITED STATES TREASURY DEBT

The Treasury increased its borrowing sharply following the onset of the 1973-75 recession. This mainly reflected the large increases in spending during the most severe business downturn in the post-World War II era.

The Treasury was able to float the bulk of the sizable increases in its debt without major disruptions to the financial markets, partly because the expansion of private credit demands and inflationary expectations both abated amid a more moderate pace of economic growth. At the same time, the Treasury adopted new techniques to aid its sales efforts. Initially, it concentrated debt offerings in the most liquid areas of the market, raising a substantial amount of new cash in bills during 1975. (For a discussion of the types and characteristics of Treasury debt, see Box.) It then turned heavily to the coupon sector, particularly the two- to five-year area, and also issued long-term bonds as the Congress acted to ease existing interest rate constraints on new issues of these securities. The greater reliance on the coupon sector helped make these securities more liquid by increasing the size and number of securities available for trading.

To facilitate its financing operations, the Treasury increased the amount of information provided to the public on the expected amount and characteristics of its financing each quarter. The Treasury began to expand the schedule of routine coupon offerings so that by 1976 it was holding monthly sales of two-year notes and quarterly sales of four- and five-year notes. Mid-quarter refundings of maturing coupon securities generally contained offerings of a three-year note, an intermediate-term note, and a long-term bond. This evolving pattern helped to extend the maturity of the debt. Starting in 1970, the Treasury came to rely increasingly on auctions to sell its coupon issues, thus letting the market set the rate competitively. This technique makes pricing easier, because it allows market participants to adjust their bidding to incorporate evaluations of last-minute developments in the credit markets. Notable exceptions to this policy occurred in 1976, when on three occasions the Treasury used a fixed price and coupon subscription method that led to successful sales of very large amounts of seven- and ten-year notes.

INVESTORS

The largest investors in Government securities are financial institutions who prefer to have very liquid and high-quality assets in their portfolios. Domestic commercial banks owned over $100 billion of Government securities in mid-1977 (Table 1). Banks shape their portfolio decisions in response

---

Characteristics of Treasury Securities

The Treasury sells two different kinds of marketable obligations: coupon-bearing securities and bills. The investor's return on a coupon-bearing security comes from semiannual interest payments plus any gain or loss in the price of the security from the time of purchase to maturity or sale if it is sold before it matures. Coupon-bearing securities are either notes or bonds. By law, notes have an original maturity of from one to ten years. Securities designated as bonds are permitted to have any maturity, but the Congress has restricted to $27 billion the amount of bonds in the hands of the public that may bear coupons exceeding 4¼ percent. As of June 30, 1977, only $13½ billion of bonds with coupons over 4¼ percent was in private hands, *i.e.*, outside the Federal Reserve System and official United States Government accounts. There is no comparable restriction on notes. In recent years, most coupon securities have been issued in minimum denominations of $1,000 except for two- and three-year notes for which $5,000 has been the minimum.

Coupon securities are usually sold through auctions in which bidders submit competitive bids expressed as annual yields to two decimal places— 7.31 percent, for example. Noncompetitive bidders may submit tenders of up to $1 million. The Treasury allots to the noncompetitive bidders first and then allots competitive bids, beginning with those at the lowest yield. When the issue has been fully allotted, the Treasury calculates the weighted average of the yields it has accepted and then establishes a fixed coupon to the nearest eighth percent, so that the average price is usually at par or slightly below par. For example, a security sold with an average issuing yield of 7.31 percent would have a 7¼ percent coupon and an average price slightly below par. A security is sold at par when the average yield is exactly equal to the coupon. All noncompetitive bidders pay the average

---

to pronounced seasonal and cyclical flows of funds. For example, bank holdings of Government securities increased substantially in 1975 and 1976 as an offset to cyclically weak demand for loans caused by a restructuring of balance sheets on the part of bank customers in the aftermath of the 1973-75 recession. The expansion in holdings of Government securities followed many years of little or no growth while customer loan demand was heavy. Other private financial institutions—such as thrift institutions, insurance companies, and pension funds—hold somewhat less than half the amount of Government securities held by commercial banks. While they keep Treasury issues in their securities portfolios, their needs for funds are generally more predictable than those of commercial banks. They typically hold a larger

issuing price, and competitive bidders pay the price associated with the bids accepted by the Treasury.

Price quotations in the secondary market are expressed in points with par value equal to 100 points. Fractions of a point are expressed in 32nds. Thus, the price of a coupon security when it is below par might be expressed as 99 10/32 *i.e.*, $993.12 for a $1,000 bond. (When the price is above par, the quote might be 102 3/32, *i.e.*, $1,020.94 for a $1,000 bond.) The quoted price does not include any interest that has accrued on the security after the previous semiannual coupon payment date. The accrued interest is added to the quoted price the buyer agrees to pay the seller.

Bills do not carry coupons. They are initially sold and subsequently trade at a discount from par value. The investor's return is derived from the increase in value from the original discounted price at purchase to the par value at maturity. The Treasury auctions three- and six-month bills every week and 52-week bills every four weeks. Bills in the secondary market are quoted in terms of bank discount rates: the dollar discount is expressed as a percentage of par value computed at an annual rate until maturity (based on a 360-day year). The minimum denomination for a bill is $10,000, and noncompetitive tenders are allotted in full up to $500,000 each at the average auction price.

Another characteristic of Treasury securities is their marketability or nonmarketability. Marketable securities may be resold after issue, while nonmarketable securities are sold to designated purchasers who may not sell them to others. Official United States Government accounts hold slightly more than half the Treasury's nonmarketable securities. Among the most important accounts are the Federal employee retirement funds and the Federal old-age and survivors insurance trust fund. Savings bonds held by individuals constitute slightly less than one third of the nonmarketable debt. Other important holders of nonmarketable debt are foreign governments and state and local governments.

proportion of mortgages and other securities that offer higher yields but are less liquid than Treasury issues.

The Federal Reserve System's holdings of Government securities rival the amount held by the commercial banks. These issues constitute the great bulk of the System's assets and they support its liabilities, primarily Federal Reserve notes which constitute most of the nation's currency in circulation, member bank reserves, and Treasury deposits. The principal reason for the growth of Federal Reserve holdings of Government securities has been the expansion of Federal Reserve notes and, to a lesser extent, the increases in average Treasury cash balances at the Reserve Banks. Member bank reserves have expanded little in recent years, since the growth of member bank liabil-

Table 1 United States Treasury Debt
In billions of dollars

	Amounts outstanding on				
Public debt	December 31, 1960	December 31, 1965	December 31, 1970	December 31, 1975	June 30, 1977
Gross public debt	290	321	389	577	674
Nonmarketable debt	101	106	140	213	242
Marketable debt	189*	215	248	363	431
Marketable by type of security:					
Bills	39	60	88	157	155
Notes	51	50	101	167	233
Bonds	80	104	59	39	43
Marketable by type of holder:†					
United States Government accounts	6	12	17	19	15
Federal Reserve System	27	41	62	88	102
Commercial banks	62	61	63	85	102
Mutual savings banks	6	5	3	5	6
Insurance companies	10	10	7	9	14
Other corporations	19	16	7	20	24
State and local governments	19	23	28	33	39
Individuals	20	22	29	24	28
Foreign and international	10	11	13	44	65
Other investors	7	16	22	36	35

Discrepancies in totals due to rounding.
*Includes $18 billion of certificates of indebtedness.
†Partially estimated.
Source: *Treasury Bulletin.*

ities subject to reserve requirements has been offset by reductions in average requirements.

Other governmental units, both domestic and foreign, hold substantial amounts of United States Government securities because they are bound either by law or custom to hold the safest and most liquid securities available. Foreign and international investors, primarily official institutions, held about $65 billion of marketable Treasury issues in mid-1977.[1] The growth of foreign holdings of Treasury securities mainly reflected foreign central bank investments of dollars obtained in exchange market operations as well as substantial acquisitions by oil-exporting nations. State and local governments invest in short-term Treasury securities to bridge the gap between the timing of periodic tax receipts and Federal grants-in-aid and the more continuous flow of payments for goods and services.

Individuals hold a considerable volume of marketable Treasury issues even though there are several factors tending to inhibit purchases by small investors. The transaction costs for small purchases and sales, the cost of custody, and large minimum denominations for shorter term issues have tended to restrain purchases by individuals except in periods when market yields on Treasury securities moved substantially above those on alternative liquid investments, mainly thrift and savings deposits. (The major portion of the Treasury debt held by individuals consists of savings bonds with small denominations. They are not marketable, but they are redeemable prior to maturity.)

THE DEALER MARKET

The market for United States Government securities centers on the dealers who report activity daily to the FRBNY. The dealers buy and sell securities for their own account, arrange transactions with both their customers and other dealers, and also purchase debt directly from the Treasury for resale to investors. In the normal course of these activities, they hold a substantial amount of securities. In addition to the dealer firms, there are brokers that specialize in matching buyers and sellers among the dealers in the Government securities market.

The dealer firms include dealer departments of commercial banks (bank dealers) and all others (nonbank dealers). Bank dealers call upon the custodial and other facilities of the bank and frequently obtain a portion of the financing of their securities holdings from the bank. The bank dealer often acts to meet the needs of the correspondent banks of the parent. In addition to trading in Government securities, bank dealers are generally active in other

---

[1] Foreign investors also held about $22 billion of nonmarketable Treasury securities in mid-1977.

money market instruments and in the market for tax-exempt general obligation securities of state and local governments. They are, however, proscribed by the Banking Act of 1933 (Glass-Steagall) from trading corporate equities and bonds, as well as tax-exempt revenue issues. The Glass-Steagall Act was intended to create a legal distinction between commercial banking and investment banking. Nonbank dealers face no such proscription, and most of them trade in these other markets, although a few firms concentrate their energies on Government securities and money market instruments such as bankers' acceptances, commercial paper, and large negotiable bank certificates of deposit.

At the end of 1977, there were thirty-six securities dealers that reported their transactions, financing, and inventories to the FRBNY daily; twelve were commercial banks and twenty-four were nonbank dealers. A firm is added to the reporting list when it demonstrates that it conducts a significant amount of business with customers as well as with other dealers, that it operates in size in the major maturity areas of the market, and that it is adequately capitalized and managed by responsible personnel. If a firm's performance meets high standards in these respects for some period of time, the Manager of the System Open Market Account will generally establish a trading relationship with it. Thus, not all firms on the FRBNY reporting list necessarily trade with the System Open Market Account.

Dealers trade actively among themselves as well as with customers. Brokers facilitate this interdealer trading because they bring buyers and sellers together; the interdealer brokers themselves do not make markets or hold securities for their own account. They charge a commission on each transaction, amounting to roughly $78 per $1 million of Treasury coupon issues sold. The commission on Treasury bill transactions is generally calculated in basis points: for example, the commission on three-month bills frequently is half of 1 basis point, approximately $62 on a $5 million trade. (A basis point is 1/100 of 1 percentage point in interest rate terms.) In many cases, brokers provide their services by displaying participating dealers' bids and offers on closed circuit television screens located in the dealers' trading rooms. Other dealers then may contact the broker, respond to the quoted price, and complete the transaction. Some brokers operate completely by telephone, contacting dealers to pass along bids and offers.

In the dealer market, practically all trading is transacted over the telephone. There is no formal centralized marketplace such as an exchange; instead, the market consists of a decentralized group of firms, each willing to quote prices for purchase or sale of Treasury securities. Each firm's traders quote prices and buy from, and sell to, their counterparts at other dealer firms directly or with brokers. The firm's sales personnel use the telephone to contact customers to learn their investment needs and to arrange trades with them. The price for each block of securities traded is negotiated, and many customers will typically canvass the market to find the dealer with the best price.

The over-the-telephone organization of the Government securities market parallels that of other fixed-income securities markets. In contrast, stock exchanges largely rely on brokers to funnel orders from customers to the floor of an exchange. There, brokers called specialists attempt to match orders with designated prices from buyers and sellers in an auction market. At times, the specialists are required to act as principals and to buy and sell securities, especially when there is an imbalance of buy and sell orders.

For the most part, the delivery of Treasury bills takes place on the same business day (called "cash" delivery) while coupon issues are generally delivered on the following business day (called "regular" delivery). Delivery and safekeeping of securities is in large part handled by a book entry system provided by the Federal Reserve Banks. At the beginning of 1977, four fifths of the Treasury's marketable debt was in the form of bookkeeping entries on computers at the Federal Reserve Banks; the remainder was in paper certificates. The computerized system eliminates physical handling of certificates, since the securities can be transferred electronically from sellers to buyers through entries on the safekeeping accounts of commercial banks that are members of the Federal Reserve System and who act as agent for these transactions. When transactions are arranged between participants in different Reserve Districts, the securities transfer is carried over the Federal Reserve wire-transfer network. Book entries and wire transfers facilitate rapid and low cost transfers of securities, especially among dealers and customers who are separated geographically.

THE ROLE OF THE DEALER

The dealer firm makes markets by purchasing and selling securities for its own account. Dealers do not typically charge commissions on their trades. Rather they hope to sell securities at prices above the ones at which they were bought. Dealers also seek to have a positive "carry" on the securities they have in position, *i.e.*, they try to earn more interest on their inventory than they must pay on the funds raised to finance that inventory.

Dealers attempt to establish positions in the various maturities of Treasury securities in light of their expectations about interest rates and then trade around that position. But the initiative often rests with customers trying to undertake specific transactions, and the dealer must be willing to bid or offer at competitive prices to retain his customer base. When traders quote prices to customers and to other dealers, they continuously make small adjustments in relation to perceived prices elsewhere in order to maintain the firm's position, its inventories of securities, within the limits laid down by the firm's management. The management relies heavily on the traders' skills to enable the firm to change its position in various maturities whenever the outlook changes. A good trader is also expected to make money from the spread between bid and offered prices in a steady market.

The spread between bid and offered prices in general depends on a variety of factors. Two basic determinants are the current state of market activity and the outlook for interest rates. Spreads are narrower for actively traded issues, because the dealer is fairly certain about the price at which the issue can be purchased or sold. Spreads are narrowest of all on Treasury bills, because they are both actively traded and involve less risk of price loss than longer term securities. Spreads for three-month bills are often as small as 2 basis points on recent issues, *i.e.*, $50 per $1 million. The spread on an actively traded coupon issue might be 2/32 to 4/32, or $625 to $1,250 per $1 million of securities. The spread is wider the longer the term to maturity and the smaller the size of a requested transaction. Spreads also widen—sometimes dramatically—when new developments generate caution or uncertainty in the market.

A substantial increase in the short-run volatility of interest rates—and thus securities prices—in the 1970's has caused dealer firms to place great emphasis on position management. Sharp, unexpected price movements can lead to profits or losses on their net position, gross long positions minus gross short positions, that can easily outweigh the gains or losses arising from other sources.[2] Consequently, they manage their positions actively, frequently altering them in response to changing economic news, the perceived supply and demand conditions for Government securities, and other factors affecting the outlook for the securities markets. In the past, when rates were reasonably steady in the short run, dealers placed somewhat more emphasis on structuring their inventories to meet customer needs.

Dealer inventories are highly leveraged. More than 95 percent of the value of their holdings is typically financed with borrowed money; the dealer's own capital furnishes the remainder. Thus, the cost and availability of funds is an important consideration in a dealer's willingness to hold securities. When interest rates on the securities themselves are higher than the cost of the funds needed to finance the position, there is a "positive" carry. A dealer will tend to hold a higher inventory than in the opposite case when "negative" carry prevails. In all but a few periods in the last several years, interest rates have generally been higher on longer maturities—*i.e.*, the yield curve, the market yield at a specific time for each available maturity outstanding, is usually upward sloping. Thus, the cost of day-to-day funds is usually below the yield on all but the shortest term securities in the dealer's inventory. However, the full risk of any rise in interest rates falls on the dealer. Carry

---

[2] A dealer firm has a long position in a security when the firm is an owner of the security. The firm stands to gain if the price of the security rises. A firm establishes a short position by selling a security it does not own; it makes delivery to the buyer by obtaining temporary possession of the security, for example, by borrowing it from a third party. In this case, the firm stands to gain if the price falls because the firm can then purchase the security to return it to the lender at a price lower than the price at which it sold the security.

profits can quickly vanish.[3] The amount of risk a dealer is willing to take by holding a longer term portfolio is one of the distinguishing characteristics of management style.

Searching out and obtaining financing at the lowest cost is a vital ingredient in making markets and the pursuit of profit. In doing so, the dealers provide temporary investment outlets for market participants with idle cash. In addition, dealers take in funds to provide them to others who are temporarily short of cash, in effect acting as intermediaries between short-term lenders and borrowers. (See section on dealer financing and the growth of intermediation later in this article.)

Dealers also provide a service to their customers by giving their views about and advice on the market. Many dealer firms distribute market letters about recent and prospective market developments. The letters often contain assessments of Treasury financing needs, Federal Reserve actions, and prospects for the economy and interest rates. Salesmen discuss these subjects directly with participants and also seek to develop a familiarity with customers' investment objectives so that the firm's traders can provide the customers with buying and selling opportunities that mesh with their plans.

THE GROWTH OF TRADING ACTIVITY

Trading activity has grown sharply in the last few years after many years of more modest expansion. Outright trading, the total of purchases and sales, amounted to nearly $10½ billion on a daily average basis in 1976, roughly three times the level in 1974. In part, the growth of activity reflected the substantial outpouring of Treasury debt. But the efforts of all market participants in seeking superior returns on their portfolios have also been an important factor. Many investors, disenchanted by falling stock prices, have sought to obtain higher returns in the securities market by buying and selling more frequently in response to anticipated short-run movements in interest rates. Inter-dealer activity has expanded as well, particularly in the brokers' market.

While trading in bills has continued to dominate activity in the dealer market, trading in coupon securities has grown in relative importance. As recently as 1974, coupon trading accounted for 29 percent of total activity, but by 1976 it had reached 36 percent. The growing share of coupons resulted from

---

[3] Profits earned from positive carry can be rather small, compared with those resulting from buying and selling on the bid-asked spread or the profits and losses stemming from price changes. For example, a change of 1 basis point in the discount rate on a bill due in slightly more than three months is equivalent to the carry profits earned in one day if the financing cost of carrying the bill is 100 basis points (1 percentage point) lower than the rate on the bill itself. Moreover, positive carry rarely reaches magnitudes of 1 percentage point while a daily change of at least 1 basis point in bill rates is quite common.

the more rapid growth of coupon debt outstanding, and this growth in turn led to a more active secondary market for these issues. When measured by activity per dollar of debt outstanding in the hands of the public, the expansion of trading in longer term securities from 1974 to 1976 exceeded that for shorter term securities.

The growing importance of the coupon sector also stems from the increased liquidity of these issues. For several reasons, participants can make desired portfolio changes more easily than in the past. The number of coupon securities outstanding has expanded sharply, and by mid-1977 there were nearly 100 different coupon issues, over 50 percent more than in 1974. Several maturity gaps were filled in, especially in the under-five-area, thus facilitating adjustments to the maturity distribution of portfolios. Secondary market activity has been encouraged by an increase in the average size of coupon offerings from about $1.5 billion in 1974 to about $2.8 billion in 1977. Thus, dealers and other participants now have a greater variety of fairly sizable issues available with which to engage in hedge or arbitrage operations. A dealer, for example, may hedge to avoid market risk by matching a short sale in one issue with a purchase of a similar issue whose price is expected to move by about the same amount as that on the security sold short. In an arbitrage operation, a participant would attempt to profit from what is expected to be a temporary disparity in the market's pricing of two issues by selling one and buying the other. The dealer would then wait until the disparity is eliminated to reverse the transaction. If it is not eliminated, the dealer might take a loss on the operation.

The dealers' customers, who account for slightly more than half of total dealer trading activity, have expanded their trading substantially. Portfolio managers often seek to anticipate movements in interest rates and to lengthen or shorten the average maturity of their holdings to take advantage of expected rate changes. Changes in the outlook for interest rates over a day, week, or month now play an important role in portfolio decisions. In the past, such decisions were often tied to the investor's expectations of short- and long-run needs for liquidity. The profits generated by falling interest rates, *i.e.*, rising prices, in 1975 and 1976 also acted as an inducement to active trading. The annual growth in trading activity moderated through the first three quarters of 1977, compared with 1976, and trading per dollar of debt declined sharply from the highs posted at the end of 1976, as short-term interest rates rose and longer term rates fluctuated irregularly over a good part of the year.

Commercial banks account for over 40 percent of dealer trading with non-dealer customers. In recent years, banks have come to rely on their securities holdings less as a secondary source of reserves, given their emphasis on liability management, and to use securities trading more as a means of maximizing profits. The more active approach to asset management has also meant greater variability in bank holdings of coupon issues. Banks have not been the only institutions that have adopted a more aggressive approach to portfolio management and trading. In fact, the activity of other customers, including state and local governments and nonfinancial corporations, has grown even more rapidly. As a result, trading activity by dealers with customers other than banks grew from 35 percent to 57 percent of total trading with customers between 1970 and 1976.

Trading within the dealer community itself is conducted either directly between the firms themselves or indirectly through brokers. In the past few years, trading through brokers, who put together trades between dealers, has come to dominate interdealer trading, such brokering now accounts for nearly three quarters of dealer trading with other dealers, compared with about one third in 1972 (the first year for which separate data on trading through brokers are available). Using a broker provides anonymity and allows a dealer to shield information about his activity and position from other dealers and market participants. Another factor contributing to the popularity of trading through brokers is the rapid transmission of quotes to other dealers, reducing the costs of canvassing a large number of dealers to collect that information.

Still, dealers continue to arrange a portion of their trades, slightly more than 10 percent of total activity, directly with other dealers. This activity reflects established interdealer trading relationships. A dealer firm specializing in one area of the market can sometimes meet customer needs by dealing directly with a firm primarily engaged in another area of the market.

The increased emphasis on position management has contributed to a tendency for total interdealer trading to assume a larger share of total activity, since dealers will typically look first to other dealers to find bids or offers for issues they want to sell or buy. Such trading has expanded from about one third of total activity in the early 1960's to about 45 percent recently. To some extent, this reflects an increase in the number of reporting dealers. But over the longer run the expansion of the reporting list has probably not substantially distorted the measurement of the rising trend in activity. Many of the new entrants were not active in the Treasury market for very long before they became reporting dealers, and their trading volume was essentially nonexistent in the 1960's.

On the other hand, many of the newer firms are relatively more active in interdealer trading and have no doubt contributed to its measured rise. They have used trading with other dealers as a way of building up expertise and volume. (To meet the criteria for the reporting list, however, a firm must show a substantial volume of trading with customers.)

DEALERS' POSITIONS

Several important changes in the market have enabled dealers to conduct their operations with a lower level of inventories in relation to trading volume than in the 1960's and early 1970's. While dealers have placed greater emphasis on managing their positions actively, they can meet their customers' needs with inventories that are lower relative to sales than in the past. The wider range of participants in the market, the growth in the activity of brokers, the greater ease in covering short positions (as is discussed below), and possibly more caution in exposing capital have contributed to this trend. Positions were sharply cut back—in the aggregate and in relation to sales— during the 1973-74 period of steep increases in interest rates. When money market pressures later abated and rate expectations changed, inventories expanded threefold to $7½ billion by 1976, about the same as the expansion in trading activity. Even with the enlargement of inventory positions, however, dealer inventories were lower in relation to trading activity in 1976 than they had been during the years before the bear markets in bonds in 1973-74. The ratio of inventories to activity continued to fall over 1977 as a whole, when positions declined while growth of activity was rather modest.

The more performance-oriented approach of customers has generated a higher turnover of their portfolios. Dealers now find it easier to obtain issues to meet demands, especially for coupon issues. Moreover, the expansion of activity by brokers and the price quotations they provide almost continuously have probably bolstered dealers' confidence that particular issues can be found more readily than before.

The growth of the market for repurchase agreements (RPs) and reverse RPs[4] has facilitated short sales—either to meet demands of customers or because of interest rate expectations. The availability of securities in this market has made it easier for a dealer to locate the particular issue he needs to deliver by acquiring the security under a reverse RP. In fact, a market for "specific issues", with the party obtaining the securities specifying the particular issue, has developed in the RP and reverse RP markets and has become an alternative to borrowing securities. The older method of finding a holder willing to lend securities could be more costly and cumbersome. It often meant that a dealer's positioning move became obvious to others and required the borrower to put up other securities as collateral. The growth of RP markets has enabled dealers to take larger short positions than they had before during periods when interest rates were expected to rise. In other periods, dealers on average have not enlarged their long positions by as much as they had previously.

Dealers may also have become more cautious about exposing capital by assuming large short or long positions. Year-end capital relative to positions in

---

[4] See "Federal Funds and Repurchase Agreements", this Review (Summer 1977), pages 33-48. In a repurchase agreement, the owner of a security sells it outright to the provider of funds and agrees to repurchase the issue at a specified future date and price. In a reverse repurchase agreement, the provider of funds purchases a security and agrees to sell it back at a specified future date and price. These terms, RPs and reverse RPs, are sometimes interchanged in market parlance, however, and RPs are often used to describe the usual transactions of an institution in the market—whether it is a provider or user of funds.

Treasury securities at the nonbank dealers has moved somewhat higher in recent years, compared with the 1960's and early 1970's. However, capital which has reached the industry in part through the entry of additional firms did not grow so rapidly as trading volume.

DEALER FINANCING AND THE GROWTH OF INTERMEDIATION

Dealers have broadened their sources of funds significantly in recent years. Their greater participation in the money market has enabled them to reduce their reliance on borrowing from banks in money centers. The growth of the market for RPs reflects the changes in dealer financing patterns and the increasingly sophisticated cash management techniques used by many money market participants. Dealers typically raise more funds than they need to finance their positions in securities and have become important as intermediaries in the money market.

Dealers employ two basic methods of financing inventories: entering into RPs or furnishing securities as collateral for a loan. The rate of return on overnight RPs is related to the Federal funds rate but is typically below it, in part because the agreements are viewed as secured loans by many market participants. The interest rate on collateral loans to dealers by large banks in money centers is usually somewhat above the Federal funds rate since the banks view the latter rate as the cost of funding the loan.

Collateral loans have remained a significant source of dealer financing despite their higher cost. The banks are often residual suppliers of funds when money market conditions are tight and liquidity is scarce. Thus, collateral loans amounted to about one third of nonbank dealers' financings through collateral loans and RPs combined in 1973-74 but that proportion declined substantially in 1975-76. Bank loans can be obtained late in the day—and often are—after dealers have searched out other sources of funds. They can be used when a dealer agrees during the day to take delivery that same day, say, in Treasury bills, or ends up with securities that were expected to be sold but were not. Dealer departments of commercial banks do not use collateral loans. They rely on RPs and on other forms of financing and often obtain funds from their own banks.

Dealers also obtain funds to provide them to others. A dealer may raise funds through use of RPs and provide them to others by arranging a reverse RP. The growth in holdings of Government securities by many institutions over the past few years has enabled them to sell their holdings temporarily through RPs to meet short-term cash needs as an alternative to raising funds in the commercial paper market or at banks. In addition, corporations and financial institutions have also been willing to invest temporary cash surpluses in short-term RPs in preference to holding demand deposits which pay no interest.

Frequently the dealer acts as a middleman in these transactions, obtaining funds from one customer to provide them to another. While the dealers are principals in the transactions, some are essentially acting as brokers because they "match" the maturities of the RP and the reverse RP that they arrange with customers. When the maturities of such transactions are not exactly matched, the dealer shoulders some risk with respect to interest rates. There can also be some risk in that the dealer is dependent on the performance of one customer in order to ensure that he can fulfill his obligation to another customer. Dealers are often willing to finance the placement of funds under reverse RPs through a series of RPs with shorter maturities. The upward slope of the yield curve over the past few years has encouraged this pattern.

CONCLUSIONS

Recent years have witnessed substantial growth in the Government securities market, both in terms of activity and in the number of dealer firms. The market has responded well to sizable increases in Treasury financing requirements and in Federal Reserve open market operations. The liquidity of Government securities, particularly coupon issues—the fact that they can be converted into cash more quickly than other assets of similar maturity—has been enhanced in the process. Consequently, participants can carry out investment decisions readily at competitive prices.

Increased activity has both contributed to and resulted from the greater efficiency and competitiveness of the market. The market's capacity to handle large Treasury financings and Federal Reserve operations smoothly has expanded in recent years. The market is also better able to weather surges in trading activity precipitated by shifts in participants' perceptions of the economic outlook. These expanded capabilities are due in part to the increase in the number of available maturities, the enhanced ability to establish long or short positions, and the wider variety of independent decision makers active in the market. Competition has been strengthened through the large increase in the number of dealers and the resulting reduction in market concentration.

The expansion in the market and in activity has not been an unmixed benefit, however. Trading has taken on speculative overtones at times, which may well have exacerbated the volatility of prices. Participants—in searching for information about the probable course of interest rates—have increased their focus on, and reacted more to, temporary phenomena. The emphasis on trading and performance may not always have been accompanied by adequate appreciation of the increased position and credit risks that derive from this approach. Experience in 1977 seems to have served as a pertinent reminder of these risks. The dealers in the market confront a new challenge to develop and maintain activity in the more cautious but increasingly competitive market environment with which 1978 begins.

THE MARKET FOR CORPORATE BONDS*

Burton Zwick

11

The market for corporate bonds has undergone a number of major changes over the past fifteen years. Perhaps the most striking has been the increased purchase of corporate bonds by households. During the 1950s and early 1960s, households invested heavily in corporate equities. Then, as the bull market in equities ended in the mid-1960s and interest rates began rising sharply, households increased their corporate bond holdings relative to those of equities. Pension funds also began to channel large amounts of funds into the corporate bond market because of the large inflows they were receiving as well as a broadening of the authority of many public pension funds (state and local government retirement funds) to include investments in corporate bonds. The increase in household and pension fund holdings of corporate bonds has meant that these investor groups now rival life insurance companies as major suppliers of funds to the corporate bond market.

On the issuer side of the market, corporations have made large adjustments in their approach to financing. From 1960 through the early 1970s, corporations increased the debt portion of their capital structures. Financial leverage—or the ratio of debt to total financing—of nonfinancial corporations rose by about one fifth, and the ratio of bonds to total financing rose somewhat more moderately. A lower level of uncertainty or expected variability of corporations' income before interest and taxes may have encouraged corporations to increase debt financing during the early and mid-

*Reprinted, with deletions, from the *Quarterly Review*, Autumn 1977, pp. 27-36, with permission from the Federal Reserve Bank of New York.

1960s. From 1968 and into the 1970s, a new factor was at work: higher rates of inflation encouraged firms to issue debt as the real or inflation-adjusted cost of debt financing declined. In 1975, however, financial leverage declined for the first time in fifteen years. The decline occurred in part because of the reduction of short-term debt as inventories were liquidated and may also have reflected the response of corporations to greater economic uncertainty.

Borrowing and lending decisions in the corporate bond market have resulted in an 8½ percent annual growth rate since 1960 in the outstanding stock of corporate bonds. At the end of 1976, the total outstanding amounted to $323 billion, about one third more than that of state and local government securities and about half as much as that of home mortgages and United States Treasury securities. Borrowing and lending decisions—particularly those involving substitution between corporate bonds and other instruments by both issuers and purchasers of corporate bonds—affect not only the size and rate of growth of the corporate bond market but also the effectiveness of selective credit and other public policies designed to alter the price and quantity of particular financial securities, such as home mortgages or state and local government obligations.

PURCHASERS OF CORPORATE BONDS, 1960-76

The major purchasers of corporate bonds are life insurance companies, households, private pension funds, public pension funds, and mutual savings banks. Data on the distribution of holdings among these purchasers are presented in Table 1. The largest and steadiest buyers of corporate bonds have been life insurance companies. The bulk of these companies' investments are confined to bonds and real estate mortgages. Inflows of life insurance premiums create actuarially determined outflows, most of which are expected to occur far in the future, and these inflows must be invested to insure that those distant liabilities are covered. Corporate bonds are attractive instruments, because they insure a specific cash flow over a long period and their yields are higher than on government bonds. Insurance companies can accept the lower marketability of most corporate bonds, compared with government bonds, since they generally expect to hold them until maturity regardless of interim movements in interest rates and bond prices. Not all corporate bonds are acceptable to life insurance companies, however. These companies are extremely averse to the provisions in some corporate bonds calling for redemption and refunding shortly after the issuance date. Such provisions create uncertainty about investment income during the period from the refunding to maturity. (Refunding provisions and other investment characteristics of corporate bonds are described in the Box.)

Table 1
Holdings of Corporate Bonds Outstanding
In billions of dollars

Sector	1950	1960	1970	1976
Households*.	$ 5	$10	$ 36	$ 72
Life insurance companies†.	25	48	74	122
Private pension funds.	3	16	30	39
Public pension funds‡	1	7	35	67
Mutual savings banks	2	4	8	20
Other.	4	5	19	34
Total	$40	$90	$202	$354

While life insurance companies have remained the largest holder of corporate bonds, the amount they held relative to the total outstanding fell from 53 percent in 1960 to 35 percent in 1976. This occurred mainly because growth in the assets of life insurance companies was slower than the growth in the outstanding volume of corporate bonds. However, as revealed in Table 2, where each sector's corporate bond holdings are expressed as a percentage of the purchaser's portfolio of financial assets, a shift in life insurance company assets from corporate bonds to other assets also made a minor contribution to the reduction of their share of the amount outstanding.

Household investment portfolios are more diversified than those of life insurance companies and include large amounts of short-term securities, equities, and municipal bonds, as well as corporate bonds. Since households have greater flexibility in making portfolio choices, their participation in the corporate bond market has varied a great deal over the post-World War II period. Their holdings have shown a marked increase since 1960, both as

Table 2
Importance of Corporate Bonds in Purchasers' Portfolios
Corporate bonds as a percentage of total financial assets of purchasers

Sector	1950	1960	1970	1976
Households*.	1.0%	1.0%	1.9%	2.5%
Life insurance companies†.	40.0	41.0	37.0	39.0
Private pension funds.	40.0	42.0	27.0	22.0
Public pension funds‡	10.0	37.0	58.0	54.0
Mutual savings banks	9.0	9.0	10.0	15.0

Corporate bond holdings include dollar-denominated bonds issued by foreign corporations in the United States market. The volume of these "Yankee bonds" increased from $6 billion in 1960 to $31 billion in 1976.

*"Households" includes funds held by commercial banks in trust accounts and funds held by nonprofit organizations.

†Includes private pension funds managed by life insurance companies.

‡State and local government retirement funds.

Source: Board of Governors of the Federal Reserve System.

THE CHARACTERISTICS OF CORPORATE BONDS

A bond is a debt contract which promises its holder an amount equal to the bond's par value on a stated maturity date as well as specific interest payments at fixed intervals prior to maturity. Holders of corporate bonds that are "unsubordinated" or "senior"debt have a prior claim (relative to holders of equity and "subordinated" or "junior" debt) against the issuer's income, whether generated through normal operations or through liquidation. The payments of some corporate bonds, generally called mortgage bonds, are also secured by liens on particular assets of the issuer. Corporate bonds that are unsecured by specific properties are referred to as debentures. Over the years, investors have lowered their evaluation of mortgage bonds relative to debentures. Many railroad bankruptcies have shown that a mortgage on a property is of little value unless the property produces a good flow of income. Debentures, on the other hand, have come to be very acceptable when issued by companies with good earning power. While many utilities continue to offer mortgage bonds, large and well-regarded industrial firms typically use debenture financing to avoid encumbering fixed property with liens.

Almost all bonds, whether based on a mortgage or on the general earning power of the issuing corporation, have their terms spelled out in a detailed contract called an indenture. This agreement describes the rights and obligations of both parties, mainly the rights of lenders and the obligations of the debtor. The enforcement of this indenture is usually left to a trustee who acts for the bondholders collectively. The terms of the agreement are described in the Trust Indenture Act of 1939.

To insure that bond liabilities do not exceed the value of assets financed by these liabilities, corporate bonds usually are issued with sinking fund provisions. The schedule of sinking fund payments is directly related to the estimated depreciation of the assets financed by the bonds. These provisions also name a trustee, frequently a commercial bank, who insures that funds are set aside by the issuer in a reserve account or sinking fund. The funds placed in the sinking fund generally are used to retire a portion of the outstanding bonds, and that portion of bonds scheduled for retirement can be retired or called by the trustee on behalf of the issuer, at par, even if market yields have fallen and the price of the bonds has risen above par. Some sinking fund arrangements permit the trustee to "double" or to call at par twice as many bonds as are scheduled for retirement in any particular year under the sinking fund provisions. However, this ability to double cannot be carried over and cumulated but applies only on a year-to-year basis.

For most utility bonds, the sinking fund requirement has until recently been met by applying some minimum percentage of revenues to capital improvements or to the maintenance of the assets financed by the bonds. In recent years, however, as the sharp cost increases in energy and raw materials were passed on in price increases and as maintenance expenditures declined as a percentage of total revenues, a part of the sinking fund requirements of utilities, as well as industrials, has been met by the retirement of a portion of outstanding bonds.

In addition to the call of bonds before maturity through sinking fund provisions, special call or "refunding" provisions have been introduced into most corporate bond issues during the past decade. These refunding provisions provide issuers an opportunity, otherwise precluded by the protection of investors against refunding, to retire bonds before maturity with funds obtained by issuing other securities at a lower rate. Refundability generally occurs after five years for utility bonds and after ten years for industrial issues, frequently at a price of 5 to 10 percent above par. Since bonds with refunding provisions will be called only if interest rates decline, the initial investors require a higher yield when purchasing securities that include refunding provisions. Issuers have been increasingly willing to offer the higher yields necessary to obtain these provisions on account of the greater uncertainty about future interest rates and capital costs due to high and variable rates of inflation.

The length of bonds, or the average period that principal is outstanding, is reduced by sinking fund or other provisions to call bonds before the final maturity date. The increased use of refunding provisions, which introduce a probability that the entire principal will be repaid before maturity, has shortened the expected length of most recently issued corporate bonds. The length of bonds may be shortened further if the increased uncertainty about future taxes makes investors as well as issuers more reluctant to commit themselves over a long period. Apart from a shortening of the length of bonds because of either call provisions or earlier final maturity dates, the length of most recently issued bonds—when the average timing of all payments, interest and principal, is taken into account—has been shortened as higher market rates in recent years have resulted in higher coupon rates. The investor recoups a given proportion of the purchase price of recently issued bonds with their higher coupons earlier than on bonds with similar terms to maturity issued, say, in the mid-1960s.

a percentage of total corporate bonds outstanding and of total household assets. The increase in long-term rates and the weak performance of the equity market contributed to this shift.

The corporate bond holdings of private and public pension funds have grown even more in value since the 1960s, almost reaching the level of life insurance company holdings. This development primarily reflects the rapid growth in total assets of pension funds. For public pension funds, corporate bonds also rose as a percentage of their total assets over the period, as the broadening in their investment authority enabled them to buy corporate bonds and so obtain the higher returns available on them in comparison with those on government bonds. By contrast, corporate bonds declined as a percentage of the total assets of private pension funds after 1960 as these funds increased the equity or variable income portion of their portfolios. Still, the corporate bond portion of both public and private pension fund assets greatly exceeds that of households. Pension funds are exempt from taxes on all forms of investment income—interest payments, dividends, and capital gains. Households are taxed at the full personal income tax rate on interest and dividends, while the tax rate on capital gains is, of course, lower. Households are, therefore, sensitive to whether income arises from interest or capital gains, whereas pension funds are not. The differential tax treatment is thus a major reason for the difference in investment choices of the two groups.

Mutual savings banks also purchase sizable amounts of corporate bonds. Their holdings have risen sharply since the 1960s, reflecting both an increase in the corporate bond portion of mutual savings bank assets (Table 2) and growth in the total assets of these banks. The increase in the corporate bond portion was matched by a decrease in mortgage holdings relative to total assets. Savings and loan associations, the other major group of thrift institutions, hold almost all of their assets in home mortgages.

HOW CORPORATE BONDS ARE MARKETED

New corporate bonds are sold in one of two ways. Issues are sold in the public market or they are placed directly with particular lenders. Private placements are often made by less highly regarded or less widely known companies. Over the 1953-64 period, about one half of new corporate bond funds was raised through public offerings. Subsequently, the proportion of funds raised through public offerings rose to about two thirds. The decline in private placements reflects the reduced share of life insurance companies in bond acquisitions, since they do most of the purchasing by this method. Apart from the long-term trend, the ratio of publicly offered to total corporate bond borrowing moves up and down with the business cycle. Public utilities are better able to pass on higher borrowing costs to their customers than are industrial firms. So during periods of high and rising interest rates, the volume of publicly offered utility issues remains fairly high while the volume of industrial issues—particularly those of weaker firms that are generally placed privately—is cut back because of the increase in borrowing costs.

During the 1920s, most public issues were handled by commercial banks. There was much concern that commercial bank underwriting and dealing in corporate securities increased financial instability, concentrated economic power, and led to conflicts of interest for banks. Therefore, bank underwriting of corporate bond issues was terminated in 1933 by passage of the Glass-Steagall Act. This legislation was passed during an era in which several important measures affecting financial markets were enacted, including the bill that created the Securities and Exchange Commission (SEC).

Since Glass-Steagall, investment banking firms have been the major underwriters of corporate bond issues. As underwriters, investment bankers purchase an issue themselves or guarantee the issuer a specific price for the bonds. Investment bankers thus bear the risk of gain or loss when the bonds are sold through competitive bidding to the particular underwriter that offers the issuer the highest price for the bonds, which of course means the lowest interest cost to the issuer. The winning underwriter then sells the bonds to the public at a price calculated to cover all costs and to provide an adequate return on the capital funds tied up in the transaction.

A large issue requires the participation of many investment banking firms, who combine under the leadership of a particular underwriter or group of underwriters to form a syndicate. The syndicate leaders must have good information about the marketability of an issue to bid aggressively for it. This information is difficult and costly to obtain if the leaders do not have close contact with the retail market. Because of the importance of accurate information about retail demand in order to bid successfully for an issue, underwriters have a strong incentive to be involved in the final sale of the bonds to retail customers. Accordingly, some large underwriting firms have recently merged with retail brokerage firms, and a number of large retail firms have increased their underwriting activities.

Many corporations maintain long-term relationships with a single underwriting firm and negotiate all of their offerings with it to encourage the underwriter to make a strong effort to sell the company's issues. The designated underwriter—who may organize a syndicate—will typically advise the corporation about the maturities, coupons, and other terms in order to attract the strongest market interest. The choice between competitive and negotiated public offerings is usually determined by the issuer's assessment of whether the benefits of competition for the issue among several groups would be offset by the increased commitment and advice of a particular underwriter. The decision may depend on how well the borrowing firm is known and how specific its borrowing needs are with regard to maturities and other terms. However, many issuers subject to regulatory authorities, such as public utilities, are required to sell their bonds through competitive bidding. In periods of high and rising rates, such as 1974, these authorities sometimes waive this requirement because of concern that strong bids will not be forthcoming.

For both negotiated and competitive offerings, the underwriter normally seeks to obtain commitments from potential buyers prior to obtaining them from the issuer. The retail purchasers will have had an opportunity to review a prospectus on the issue, prepared according to the regulations of the SEC, as well as a more detailed registration statement that must be filed with the Commission.[1] Since the actual price of the issue is not set by the syndicate until the syndicate takes ownership of the bonds the prospectus is in "red herring" form, i.e. some red printing is substituted for final prices and other details that are not known until receipt from the issuer.

Upon receipt of the bonds from the issuer, the underwriting syndicate announces the sale of bonds by advertisement at a price reached by mutual agreements within the syndicate. Because of the prior arrangements with customers, usually most of the bonds have been sold before this announcement, particularly in the case of negotiated issues. In cases where the price set by the syndicate on the bonds is too high, the syndicate will sometimes be forced to disband. The rest of the unsold bonds will then be sold by individual members of the syndicate at prices determined by the market rather than by the initial agreement of the syndicate.

The underwriter hopes that the price of the bonds will rise by a small amount after the sale so as to satisfy the investors that they have gotten a good buy. However, too large a premium may cause issuers to believe that the interest rates they have agreed to pay are too high. On many high-quality industrial issues, the flotation cost or the spread between the public price of the bonds and the proceeds to the issuer is 7/8 percent. An underwriting commission of .2 percent is shared on a pro rata basis by all members of the underwriting syndicate, while the managers receive an additional fee of .175 percent. The remaining ½ percent, or $5 per $1,000 bond, is typically paid out as a selling "concession" to salesmen. On utility issues, the total spread is usually between .45 percent and .75 percent. The lower underwriting spread on utility issues is due to their greater marketability. In the case of both industrial and utility issues, the total underwriting spread does not include other flotation costs, such as legal, printing, and other costs necessary to satisfy the registration requirement of the SEC, which can run from about 1 percent of total proceeds for issues of under $10 million to about ¼ percent for issues over $100 million.

---

[1] Issues of a number of firms regulated by the Interstate Commerce Commission are exempt from registration with the SEC.

The most consistent purchasers of corporate bonds through private placement are life insurance companies, who frequently purchase the bonds of small, lesser known companies. This method of placement saves the borrowers most of the marketing costs of a public issue, including the costs of registration with the SEC. More importantly, private placement allows these small borrowers, whose financing needs are often unusual or specialized, to sell issues that probably would meet with a poor reception in the public market. In private placements, highly complex indentures or contracts (see Box) can be included to aid the issuer and to protect the investor. Companies unable to enter the public market because the quality of their obligations is inadequate to attract large-scale public interest pay a substantially higher rate than do public offerers, and they typically agree not to redeem their securities prior to maturity. The terms usually allow some prepayment of principal through retained earnings, though often with severe penalties. Prepayment to refinance at lower rates is generally prohibited.

RISK AND CORPORATE BOND YIELDS

The yields on particular bonds are partly determined by default and marketability risk. Default, or business risk, refers to the risk that payments guaranteed in the bond contract will not be made. This is not a measurable quantity, and qualitative factors—such as the quality and experience of management, the competitive position of a firm within its industry and the prospects for the industry as a whole—affect assessments or default risk. A number of quantitative financial variables, including financial leverage (the ratio of fixed to variable operating costs), and the variability of revenues, also affect default risk. Corporations that borrow sizable amounts through public offerings frequently pay one or both of the major rating agencies—Moody's or Standard & Poor's—to rate their bonds with respect to default risk. In the publication of bond ratings, the convention is that a rating by Moody's (Aaa, for example) precedes one by Standard & Poor's (AAA),*viz.*, Aaa/AAA. The agencies' rating categories differ somewhat, but in general the meaning of their ratings is similar. The first four categories—Aaa/AAA through Baa/BBB—are all of "investment grade", meaning that interest and principal are considered secure. The Baa/BBB category is said by Moody's to have some "speculative characteristics", while Standard & Poor's terms such issues as on the "borderline" between sound obligations and speculations. Ba/BB issues are far more speculative and B/Bs are even riskier. Moody's then continues through Caa, Ca and C for highly speculative issues, some of which are in default. Standard & Poor's goes down as far as DDD, DD, and D, all of which are for bonds in default but with differences in relative salvage value.

Variations in the financial condition of companies whose issues are rated by the agencies tend to be related to the ratings they receive, as summarized in Table 3. The rating of issues is also influenced, of course, by a number of qualitative factors affecting the outlook of individual firms. In the postwar period, no industrial or utility issue has gone into default while rated "investment grade." However, several investment-grade railroad issues went into default in the Penn Central and other railroad bankruptcies. During the Depression, 11 percent (in dollar volume) of investment-grade issues went into default.

Almost all newly issued and rated bonds carry ratings of Baa/BBB or above by Moody's, about one third carried their Aaa rating, while about 30 percent were rated Aa, another 30 percent rated A, and about 7 percent rated Baa. About two thirds of the dollar volume of bonds in these four highest rating categories were issued by utilities, and industrial offerings accounted for the rest. In the Aaa category, more than 75 percent of the dollar volume was offered by utilities, and telephone bonds accounted for the bulk.

The marketability risk of an issue concerns the possibility that, if a holder wants to sell that issue, his inability to find a buyer may force him to take a loss unrelated to any deterioration in the corporation's financial position. Marketability (or salability) depends on the breadth of ownership of a corporation's securities—and frequently on how many securities are outstanding. The presence of a large number of potential purchasers and sellers causes dealers to become willing to buy and sell them and thus to make a secondary market. The default risk of a bond also affects marketability, insofar as issues with low ratings do not attract a wide variety of buyers.

The marketability of corporate issues is reflected in the difference—or spread—between the bid and offered prices that dealers quote (for certain

Table 3
Ratings of Corporate Bonds and Selected Financial Ratios

Rating*	Ratio of earnings to interest plus sinking fund obligations	Ratio of cash flow to senior debt (percent)	Ratio of long-term debt to total capitalization (percent)
Aaa/AAA	At least 5	Above 65	Below 25
Aa/AA	At least 4	45 to 65	Below 30
A/A	At least 3	35 to 45	Below 35
Baa/BBB	At least 2½	25 to 35	Below 40

*In the publication of bond ratings, the convention is that the Moody's rating comes first and Standard & Poor's uses capital letters exclusively.

Source: Irwin Ross, "Higher Stakes in the Bond Rating Game," *Fortune* (April 1976), page 136.

minimum amounts of bonds) when they make a market in an issue. The dealer spread in a $500,000 to $1 million transaction for a highly market-able corporate bond is typically about 1/8 point. Spreads for less market-able issues range from about ¼ point to ½ point. (The smallest spreads in the bond market are for actively traded Government securities, and these range from 1/32 point to 1/16 point.)

Since trading is generally more active immediately after new issues are brought to the market, new issues are typically quoted at narrower spreads than issues that are firmly held in investor's portfolios. The amount of un-certainty about future interest rates may also affect spreads. An increase in the degree of uncertainty or in the expected variability of rates will cause spreads to widen.

SUBSTITUTION IN THE CORPORATE BOND MARKET

The amount of corporate bonds on the balance sheets of both issuers and purchasers of corporates reflects a variety of portfolio constraints. For example, because of the pattern of their inflows and outflows, pension funds and life insurance companies are generally limited to long-term invest-ments. On the issuer side, corporations tend to match the maturities of their liabilities with those of their assets. Nevertheless, these constraints typically permit some substitution or alteration in the bond portions of both issuer and purchaser balance sheets in response to changes in relative yields and other factors.

Bonds are issued by corporations to finance the acquisition of assets. It is convenient to look at the corporate financing process, first, as a decision about the distribution of total financing between debt and equity and, second, as a decision about the distribution of debt financing between bonds and short-term debt obligations. A number of factors affect corpora-tions' choice between debt and equity financing, inculding the levels of corporate and personal income tax rates, the rate of inflation, and the level of corporations' asset risk, *i.e.*, the amount of uncertainty or expected vari-ability of their earnings before interest and taxes.

The current tax system favors debt financing by corporations, because interest payments made by corporations are deductible from their taxable income while any dividend payments they make are not. However, the ownership of corporations resides in a collection of individuals, and the tax advantage of debt financing accruing to the owners of corporations because of taxation at the corporate level may be offset in the taxation of the owners' personal incomes. This offset may occur because interest and dividend in-come to the owners is taxed at the ordinary personal income tax rate, while income in the form of capital gains is taxed at half the personal tax rate—up to a maximum rate of 25 percent. The tax benefits to corporations from debt financing exceed those from equity financing except when securities are held by the small number of individuals whose personal tax rates are very high relative to the corporate tax rate. Inflation also encourages corporations to favor debt relative to equity financing if the real or inflation-adjusted cost of borrowing declines.

While the tax structure and inflation encourage firms to use debt rather than equity financing, the greater use of debt increases a firm's fixed commitments. In the case of debt financing—given the amount of asset risk—the resulting rise in fixed commitments increases the risk of bankruptcy, and bankruptcy creates two general categories of costs. The first category—direct costs—includes lawyers' and accountants' fees, other professional fees, and the value of the managerial time spent in administering the bankruptcy. Evidence in the bankruptcies of eleven large railroad firms between 1930 and 1955 suggests that these costs were small relative to the value of the firms. However, the second category—indirect costs—may be larger. These costs include lost sales, lost profits, and possibly the inability of firms to obtain credit or to issue securities except under especially onerous terms. Unless the direct and indirect costs of bankruptcy are negligible, debt financing or any other factor increasing the probability of bankruptcy may be expected to increase a firm's cost of financing or the yield required by holders of the firm's securities. The positive relation of asset risk—and the greater possibility of bankruptcy as more debt is issued—to the cost of debt relative to equity financing explains why public utilities and other firms with low asset risk maintain high debt ratios while firms with higher asset risk limit their use of financial leverage.

The inverse relation between the asset risk of individual firms and the debt ratios of the same firms should also apply over time for the corporate sector as a whole. An increase in asset risk for the corporate sector—because of an increase in the general amount of fluctuation or instability in the economy—should cause firms to reduce their debt ratios and their fixed commitments in order to reduce the risk of bankruptcy.

From 1948 through the 1950s, the debt portion of the financing of non-financial corporations remained stable. Subsequently, from 1960 to 1974, the ratio of debt to total financing or total assets underwent a steady and sizable increase. When the balance sheet is expressed in terms of historical costs, the ratio rose from .47 in 1960 to .50 in 1967 and then to an average of .55 during the 1972-74 period. However, the ratio of debt to assets tends to be overstated during periods of inflation. During inflationary periods, the historical costs of physical assets as reported in balance sheets fall below the current value or replacement costs of these assets. There is no corresponding understatement of debt, because inflation does not increase the value of liabilities which represent dollars not physical units. When the historical costs of physical assets are replaced by the current or replacement costs of assets, the debt ratio rose from .40 in 1960 to .44 in 1967 to an average of .47 over the 1972-74 period. In 1975, the debt ratio experienced its first decline in fifteen years, as firms reduced their short-term debt. Because some of the short-term debt was replaced by bonds as well as equity, the bond proportion of total financing increased slightly during this period.

The rising debt ratios in 1960-74 should be separated into two roughly equal subperiods because of the different factors affecting debt ratios in each. Inflation remained fairly moderate until 1968 except for brief inflation episodes in the late 1940s and during the Korean war. The corporate tax burden declined slightly during the early and mid-1960s because of the investment tax credit. This behavior of inflation and the tax burden suggests that the increase in debt ratios from 1960 through 1967—after fifteen years of little change—occurred because of a decrease in asset risk rather than an increase in taxes or inflation. The decrease in asset risk after 1960—or the perception that it was higher before 1960—may reflect a dimming of early postwar memories of the Great Depression during the 1930s. In contrast to the early and mid-1960s, inflation rates from 1968 on were substantially higher than during most of the 1940s and 1950s. The increase in debt ratios after 1967 seems to have resulted from this increase in inflation and a decline in the inflation-adjusted cost of debt financing.

The decrease in debt ratios during 1975 was related to the decline in short-term debt as inventories were liquidated; the moderation of inflation may also have contributed. The decline also may reflect the perceptions of both issuers and investors that corporation asset risk had increased. An increase in asset risk beginning in the mid-1960s is suggested by the deviations of corporate profits from their long-term trend. Larger deviations from trend occurred in the 1965-75 period than in the 1948-65 period, even if the 1965-75 deviations are divided by the larger values of profits in the later years. The relatively and absolutely larger deviations in the 1965-75 period indicate a higher level of profit variability—a close proxy for asset risk.

Choosing between short- and long-term debt financing is much more closely related to the business cycle and the bahavior of interest rates, including short-term rates, than is the choice between debt and equity financing. During 1960-76, the ratio of long-term debt to total debt maintained a consistent and inverse relation with short-term rates. At least part of the decline in bond financing relative to short-term debt financing during periods of rising short-term rates presumably reflects large increases in inventories, which firms typically finance with short-term debt. However, the relative decline in bond financing during these intervals may also have reflected firms' efforts to substitute between short-term and long-term debt in order to reduce financing costs. This happened despite high short-term rates, both in absolute terms and relative to long term rates. Firms may have used short-term rather than long-term financing because they expected a decline in both short- and long-term rates and they wanted to defer long-term financing until the decline in rates had occurred. Bond financing then increased relative to total debt financing, as inventories were liquidated and firms took advantage of declines in long-term rates to issue long-term debt.

SUBSTITUTION BY INVESTORS

The degree of substitution between corporate bonds and other instruments differs substantially among the major groups of holders. Households substitute freely among corporate bonds, equities, and short-term securities. During the 1920s, households owned about two thirds of the corporate bonds outstanding. After World War II, their holdings dropped sharply while their investments in equities rose substantially. As bond yields increased in the 1960s and the performance of equity investments worsened, households again became large holders of corporate bonds.

Although life insurance companies have in recent years been devoting somewhat less of their investments to obligations with very long maturities, their unique time pattern of inflows and outflows inevitably reduces their ability to substitute between corporate bonds and other instruments, particularly short-term securities. Pension funds also tend to hold most of their assets in long-term investments. The principal difference between pension funds and other corporate bondholders, however, is that all forms of investment income of pension funds are free of Federal income taxes. Since households are taxed more heavily on investment income than on capital gains and income from municipal bonds, household investment as compared with pension fund investment is more heavily concentrated in municipal bonds and growth-oriented equity issues. Pension funds invest more heavily in corporate bonds and income-oriented equity issues.

Although the differences in the tax status of households and pension funds cause their relative holdings of various financial instruments to differ, these differences do not reduce their incentive or ability to substitute between different instruments in order to maximize the aftertax return on their investment portfolio. Both households and pension funds—life insurance companies do so to a lesser degree—substitute between assets on the basis of alternative aftertax yields, and his substitution does not exclude assets that are typically held by others.

There is considerable evidence that suggests such substitution by financial market participants over a wide range of financial assets including corporate bonds. Also indicative of extensive substitution is the broad similarity of interest rate movements over the 1960-76 period. Yields on corporate and government bonds moved very similarly over these years. And, although yields on commercial paper fluctuate much more than those on corporate bonds, the yields on commercial paper and corporate bonds also tended to behave alike. Parallel movements of corporate bond and stock yields also took place, though the parallelism in yield patterns of these yields was somewhat less than in the other comparisons.

Apart from the different cash flow patterns of various financial market participants, the volume and the distribution of corporate bond holdings in the economy reflect a variety of public policies. In the area of taxation, these policies include the differential treatment of interest and dividend payments in the taxation of corporate income, the differential treatment of capital gains and other investment income in the taxation of personal income, and the exemption of pension funds from taxes on all of their investment income. Statutory factors, such as prohibiting commercial banks from underwriting corporate bonds, also affect the pattern of ownership and the marketing of these bonds. However, the extensive substitution between corporate bonds and other financial instruments—by both issuers and purchasers of corporate bonds—tends to offset a part of the effects of these tax and statutory factors on the volume and distribution of corporate bond holdings. As tax and statutory factors alter the supply or the demand for corporate bonds in the market and cause prices on these bonds to change, market participants purchase corporate bonds if the new price is lower and sell them if the new price is higher. Although the substitution between assets does not reverse the desired effect of the policy on the market, the substitution does reduce the size of the effect.

Similarly, substitution between corporate bonds and other investments weakens the effects of public policies designed to alter the demand or supply of securities that are substitutes for corporate bonds. For example, the most comprehensive attempt to alter the supply of securities in a financial market has been the variety of policies designed to increase the supply or availability of mortgages in order to sustain housing expenditures. These policies include interest rate ceilings on deposits to protect mortgage lending institutions from excessive competition for funds and the creation of Federal Government agencies to raise funds in the capital markets for reinvestment in mortgages. The impact of those policies on the mortgage market was partly offset as other mortgage holders have responded to the increased purchase of mortgages by Federal agencies and mortgage lending institutions by selling mortgages and purchasing other assets. The other assets include corporate bonds, since mortgages and corporate bonds are substitutes in the portfolios of mutual savings banks, households, life insurance companies, and other investment groups. Perhaps more importantly, the moderate increase in the supply of mortgage credit that did result from selective credit policies in the mortgage market caused an even smaller reduction in yields on mortgages. Mortgage yields changed very little because the total demand for mortgage credit increased as households substituted mortgage credit for other credit in their financing of both housing and nonhousing expenditures.

This example of substitution illustrates the difficulty policymakers may have in attempting to alter supplies in particular financial markets. Financial assets are fungible, and investors in a relatively free market move their funds from one market to another on the basis of relative yields. Indeed, substitution because of yield or cost differentials—an increase in corporate bond purchases by households and pension funds on the investor side and an increase in debt financing relative to equity financing on the issuer side— has accounted for the major changes in the corporate bond market over the past fifteen years. As investors and issuers of securities shift between securities and markets on the basis of relative yields, policies to steer financing into particular channels will be offset even if elaborate measures are taken to do so.

THE PRIVATE PLACEMENT MARKET*

Federal Reserve Board Staff

12

Since the mid-1960s about one-third of long-term debt and equity offerings sold by domestic businesses and foreign issuers have been placed privately rather than through public offerings. The private placement market has been a major outlet for smaller or riskier issuers. The market also has been attractive when the issuer's financial structure or the proposed transaction is relatively complex, and when factors such as speed, flexibility in financial covenants, and control of sensitive information are important. The institutional investors that purchase most private placements—life insurance companies and, to a lesser degree, pension funds—have the specialized staffs needed to handle the financing of riskier and more complex transactions. The workings of this market—the issuers, the investors, and the role of advisors—are discussed in the following sections.

THE ISSUERS

From 1966 through the mid-1970s the volume of funds raised privately fluctuated considerably, ranging from as low as 15 percent to over 40 per-

*This article is excerpted and adapted from Chapters 3 and 4 of a study entitled *Commercial Bank Private Placement Activities*, by the staff of the Federal Reserve Board, June 1977. The purpose of this study was to examine the role of commercial banks in the private placement market. The study was based on the analysis of extensive publicly available data and a Federal Reserve Board Special Survey. Since the data is now obsolete, the tabular material contained in the original paper has been deleted. For the same reason, many text references to specific statistics were also deleted. The purpose of this edited version is to provide an overview of the private placement market. Readers interested in the tabular material or the conclusion of the study are referred to the original source. (*Ed. note.*)

cent of the total long-term capital raised. As might be expected, domestic corporations have been the main issuers in the market, accounting for over three-fourths of the private placement volume. Most of the securities sold by these firms have been debt issues. Foreigners, mostly Canadians, have tapped the U.S. capital market increasingly since the removal in early 1974 of the interest equalization tax and quantitative restrictions on capital flows. Equity sales by foreigners, though, are rare so that the current offerings of both foreign and domestic issues are mainly debt.

Use of the private placement market varies greatly according to factors such as issuer size, reputation, and special needs. Some firms are required by regulatory commissions to offer debt through public sealed bidding and therefore are precluded from making private placements. A number of larger, more established companies may choose between public offerings and private placements as alternative sources of financing, largely on the basis of relative interest costs. In other instances, issuers may choose to offer securities privately because of the complexity of the company's business or financial structure, or because a transaction makes the standard provisions of contracts used in public offerings unsuitable and securities difficult to market to the general public. The private placement contract can be tailored so that funds can be disbursed at intervals in accord with specific financing requirements, such as for construction projects or equipment purchases, or so that funds, if need be, can be obtained on short notice. Widespread dissemination of sensitive information, moreover, is unnecessary.

In the case of smaller offerings, a private placement has great appeal because flotation costs are frequently lower than for public offerings. Many of the expenses of a public offering, such as SEC fees, listing and trustee fees, printing fees, and state taxes are relatively fixed, and can be quite high as a percent of the proceeds of a small issue. The differences in distribution, preparation, and registration costs partly explain a lower average size of private relative to public offerings.

The smaller size also reflects a market receptivity to less financially secure issues, which tend to be small- and medium-sized firms. Large institutions, which are the dominant investors in private placements, are well equipped to appraise riskier offerings. Since regulatory and legal requirements do not limit discussions of the future and since sensitive information need not be circulated widely, issuers and investors can discuss prospects in a relatively unrestricted fashion.

The covenants of a private placement agreement, moreover, can be tailor-made to suit the special needs of the issuer and to control the issuer's operations and limit risk. For example, it is not uncommon for the private, long-term debt agreement to contain covenants that, among other things, restrict funded debt, dividend payouts, lease obligations, expansion or diversification, and establish a minimum level of working capital. These are, in addition to the fairly standard provisions, also found in a publicly offered debt instrument such as call protection, a sinking fund, and possibly convertibility or the attachment of warrants. Financial and protective covenants subsequently may be renegotiated regularly, in accord with the changing circumstances of the issuer. Repayments or sinking fund payments may be increased or decreased to accommodate events such as unexpectedly large or small earnings, if adjustment is thought appropriate by the lender. Such arrangements permit the lender to control the riskiness of the loan and allow the less well established borrower access to long-term funds at rates not very much greater than those paid by highly-rated companies in the public market. As a result, a major share of funds raised in the private placement market goes for lower-rated securities than typically sold in the public market.

THE INVESTORS

Under Section 4(2) of the *Securities Act of 1933* and SEC Rule 146, a private sale of unregistered securities must be to a limited number of investors. The investor or offeree, under this Rule, should be known to be capable of evaluating the merits and risks of the prospective investment and capable, as well, of bearing the risk.

In practice, by far the largest portion of all directly placed securities are purchased by the 50 largest life insurance companies. Most of the remaining amounts are taken by smaller insurance companies, private and public pension funds, and other investors such as bond funds and mutual savings banks. The larger life insurance companies, which in many cases employ large, specialized staffs, use their expertise to evaluate and finance a substantial portion of the riskier and more complex transactions. Smaller insurance companies and other institutions, though they may participate with the large life insurance companies in many of these transactions, tend to be somewhat more conservative investors.

Because of the heavy reliance of the private placement market on life insurance companies, much depends on the overall availability of funds to these institutions and their allocation of funds to directly placed securities. Except for periods of unusually high interest rates that induced policyholders to borrow against their policies, life insurance companies in recent years have had record cash flows and have increased their proportion of investments in private placements. The surge in cash flows in large part can be traced to the *Employee Retirement Income Security Act of 1974* (ERISA). This legislation, which strengthened fiduciary responsibilities and increased the administrative burdens of pension fund management, led many organizations to turn the management of retirement funds over to insurance companies. Some increase in individual pension accounts at life insurance companies was stimulated by growth in *Keogh* retirement programs, which were made more attractive by ERISA, and in *Individual Retirement Accounts*, which were created by that legislation. Some life insurance companies, in addition, began offering long-term, guaranteed income contracts (or GIC's) as an investment medium for thrift or pension plans. These contracts proved attractive to many financial managers in light of their increased fiduciary responsibilities and the relatively poor performance of the stock market.

As sizable cash flows became available to life insurance companies, private placements provided an especially attractive investment outlet. In the aftermath of the severe deterioration in corporate financial positions which had occurred until around the end of 1974, there were substantial demands by businesses for long-term funds to restructure balance sheets and rebuild liquidity. Also, throughout most of the 1975-76 period, traditional outlets for life insurance companies, other than private placements, were relatively unattractive. The market for commercial and multi-family mortgages was depressed. Equity investments had little appeal, given the earlier poor performance of the stock market and the increased emphasis on meeting fiduciary responsibilities. Therefore, with ample funds available for private placements and strong business demands for long-term financing, the total value of private placements reached a new record in the mid-1970s. In 1976, the total funds raised in the public and private markets was $61.9 billion, of which $19.8 billion was in the form of private placements.[1] In 1975, private placements amounted to $12.6 billion.

ADVISED PRIVATE PLACEMENTS

The work done by an advisor includes making recommendations regarding the terms and timing of the transaction, assisting in the preparation of a financing memorandum which describes the proposed terms of the placement, contacting a limited number of institutional investors for signs of interest in the proposal, gathering together the investors' comments for the prospective issuer, arranging meetings between the client and potential investors, and often assisting in subsequent negotiations.

The issuer has responsibility for providing financial and operating data, the accuracy of which is typically subject to independent review by the investors in analyzing the issuer's financial soundness and future prospects. The final contract is signed by the investors and the issuer, and the proceeds of the sale go directly to the issuer.

[1] In 1979, subsequent to the publication of this study, private placements totaled $22.5 billion. In 1980, high interest rates resulted in a high volume of policy loans and thus sharply reduced the cash flows of life insurance companies. As a result, the volume of private placements fell to $16.3 billion in 1980. (Ed. fn.)

An issuer offering placements for the first time or proposing a relatively complex transaction may find an advisor particularly valuable. When there are large or frequent offerings to be sold and saturation of a small segment of the market could be a problem, an advisor's knowledge of investors also may be highly useful. In other cases, though, a repeat borrower may find it unnecessary to use an intermediary. A small issuer, moreover, may find an advisor's fee high relative to the size of the proposed placement. In addition, outlets for the smaller or riskier placements, particularly the larger life insurance companies, are reasonably well known so that investors for such placements can be readily found without an intermediary. Accordingly, an unassisted offering tends to be much smaller than one that is assisted.

In terms of both value and number of transactions, most private placements are aided by advisors. Typically, over 75 percent of both the number and dollar volume of private placements in a given year are aided by advisors. Investment banking firms have been the main suppliers of private placement advisory services, while commercial banks have enjoyed a modest, although rapidly growing market share. The value of private placements assisted by commercial banks in 1972 was 1.8 percent of all assisted direct placements. By 1975, the commercial bank share had grown to 7.3 percent and it remained at that level in 1976. The dollar volume of business done by commercial banks rose dramatically throughout the entire 1972-76 period, as both their market share and the overall volume of advised placements expanded significantly. Many of the commercial bank advised placements reflect fairly extensive experience in lease financing.

Most of the private placement clients of commercial banks are deposit and/or loan customers. However, the proceeds of bank-assisted placements are usually not used to repay bank loans made by the advisor bank. The advisor bank may be one of the lenders in conjunction with other banks, pension funds and life insurance companies. When acting in this capacity, banks have a preference for the short- to intermediate-term maturities because of their shorter-term liability structure. On the other hand, the major nonbank investors prefer longer-term, fixed-rate loans in order to more closely match the characteristics of these assets with their actuarially based fixed-rate, longer-term liabilities.

A REVIEW OF THE MUNICIPAL BOND MARKET *

Richard H. Rosenbloom

13

Recent developments in the municipal bond market have increased public awareness of the problems state and local governments face in obtaining debt financing.[1] Of special concern to many interested observers is the recent steep rise in the yields on municipal bonds relative to those on corporate bonds with the same credit rating. This article undertakes to assess the significance of this development through an evaluation of recent trends affecting both the supply of and demand for municipal bonds and the resulting effects on the borrowing costs of state and local governments. The discussion focuses on the primary (new issue) market for municipal bonds with emphasis on market participants, market trends over the past fifteen years, recent market developments, and the probable future course of the market.

MEASUREMENT OF MUNICIPAL BOND MARKET CONDITIONS

Municipal bonds have generally the same investment characteristics and attributes as corporate bonds with one fundamental exception. The interest income from municipal bonds is exempt from Federal income taxation.[2] This tax-exempt feature makes municipals sufficiently different from corporates that it is uncommon to find the two types of bonds together in the

---

*Reprinted, with deletions, from the *Economic Review,* March/April 1976, pp. 10-19, with permission from the Federal Reserve Bank of Richmond.

[1] Municipal bonds are any tax-exempt debt security of a state or local government, agency, or special authority.

[2] In many cases, the interest income is also exempt from state and local taxation in the issuing state and/or locality.

same portfolio. The purpose of the tax-exempt feature is to lower the borrowing costs of state and local governments by enabling them to offer investors a lower yield that is competitive with the after-tax yield available on corporate bonds.

The relationship between the yields on equal credit-rated municipal and corporate bonds differs for investors in different income brackets since the value of the tax-exempt feature, given a progressive income tax structure, increases as taxable income moves into brackets for which the tax rate is higher. The investor in tax bracket "t" would be indifferent between investment in corporates and in municipals when:

$$(1) \quad Rm = Rc(1 - t)$$

where Rm = the yield on municipal bonds, Rc = the yield on corporate bonds, and t = the marginal tax rate at which the after-tax yields on municipal and corporate bonds are equal. Given t and Rc, equation (1) determines the minimum municipal yield necessary to induce investors in tax bracket t to buy municipal rather than corporate bonds. When transposed, the equation can be solved for t as follows:

$$(1a) \quad t = 1 - Rm/Rc.$$

This equation says simply that given the relationship between yields on municipals (Rm) and yields on corporates (Rc), the marginal tax rate at which investors are indifferent between the two types of bonds is automati-

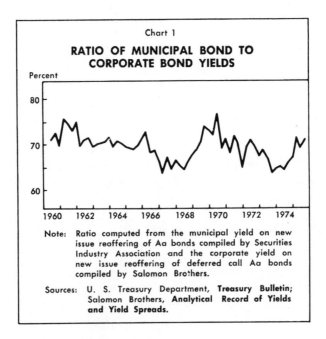

Chart 1

RATIO OF MUNICIPAL BOND TO CORPORATE BOND YIELDS

Note: Ratio computed from the municipal yield on new issue reoffering of Aa bonds compiled by Securities Industry Association and the corporate yield on new issue reoffering of deferred call Aa bonds compiled by Salomon Brothers.

Sources: U. S. Treasury Department, **Treasury Bulletin;** Salomon Brothers, **Analytical Record of Yields and Yield Spreads.**

cally determined. The relationship between Rm and Rc can be affected, of course, by factors other than the value of the tax exemption to investors. Relative risks and call protection, for example, could be major factors. However, the risk factor has been minimized in the discussion by using both Aa-rated corporate and Aa-rated municipal bonds and by assuming the risk relationship between them has remained stable. The call protection factor has been minimized by the use of corporate and municipal bonds with approximately the same call protection.

The relationship Rm/Rc is a widely used measure of conditions in the municipal bond market relative to other capital markets and specifically to the corporate bond market. High levels of Rm/Rc are taken to indicate relatively tight credit conditions in the municipal bond market, while low levels of Rm/Rc indicate comparatively easier credit conditions for municipal borrowers.

The course of Rm/Rc over the past fifteen years is shown in Chart 1. As can be seen, the movements are quite erratic with no long-term trends. There are, however, a number of conspicuous short-term movements that merit examination along with the general volatility of the series.

THE SUPPLY OF MUNICIPAL BONDS

Municipal bonds are issued by state and local governments and their special governmental agencies and authorities primarily to finance capital outlays that are too large to be financed out of current revenue. In many cases a new agency or authority, such as a transportation authority, is created solely to issue bonds for a specific project and, perhaps, to administer the project upon completion.[3]

There are two general types of municipal bonds—general obligation bonds and revenue bonds. General obligation bonds are "full faith and credit" obligations of the issuing body. As such, they are secured by the taxing power of the issuer. These long-term debt obligations are usually issued as serial bonds[4] with maturities from 1 to 30 years. Revenue bonds are issued primarily by governmental authorities that have no taxing power. They are secured solely by the revenue collected from the users of the particular capital project funded by the debt issue. Thus, the credit quality of a revenue bond is directly related to the ability of the issuer to collect revenues from the project involved. In the case of a well established sewer

---

[3] In many cases special authorities are established to provide services "off-budget," thereby by-passing state constitutional requirements for balanced budgets.

[4] Serial bonds are single bond issues comprised of many different maturities, as opposed to a term bond issue in which all the bonds have the same date of maturity.

authority this credit quality is likely to be high, whereas the bonds of a new mass transit authority in a low-density city, for example, might be more speculative. These obligations consist largely of one or two long-term issues with a smaller amount of serial bonds with shorter maturities. One type of revenue bond worth noting is the "moral obligation bond." This type of bond is secured by ear-marked revenue and by a promise from the issuing government to appropriate funds from general revenues to cover debt service if revenues prove insufficient. The credit quality of these bonds is as good as the promise or moral obligation to redeem them.

Occasionally, state and local governments will issue short-term debt in the form of tax, revenue or bond anticipation notes which generally have a maturity of less than one year. As the name implies, tax and revenue antici-pation notes are issued to aid cash flow while waiting for taxes and revenues to come in, at which time the debt is retired. Bond anticipation notes are generally issued to finance a project during periods of tight credit conditions to prevent getting locked into a high rate, long-term debt obligation. When

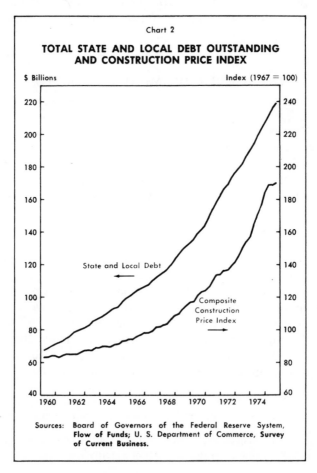

Chart 2

TOTAL STATE AND LOCAL DEBT OUTSTANDING AND CONSTRUCTION PRICE INDEX

Sources: Board of Governors of the Federal Reserve System, Flow of Funds; U. S. Department of Commerce, **Survey of Current Business.**

more favorable credit conditions develop, the short-term debt is refinanced by a bond issue.

The growth in the dollar amount of total state and local debt outstanding is shown in Chart 2. The sharp increases in the supply of municipal bonds might be explained by the acceleration in the pace of inflation in 1968 and again in late 1970, particularly the acceleration of construction costs. This development had two effects. First, as shown in Chart 2, inflation increased the cost of construction, thus requiring a larger bond issue to finance any given project. Second, to the extent inflation impacts on expenditures more rapidly than on revenues, it increased the costs of providing government services, which are payable out of current receipts. This reduced the availability of funds from current receipts to help finance capital projects. Consequently, more bonds were issued to help fill this gap. The growth in state and local debt may also have been affected by the entry of New York City into the long-term market to finance operating expenditures and by sharp increases in short-term debt issuance by New York City and New York State.

The stable and continued growth of the total supply of outstanding municipal securities masks some changes in the composition of the total supply that warrant examination. As shown in Chart 3, the percentage of total municipal debt outstanding accounted for by short-term debt is small but increasing. It is a highly volatile function but seems closely related, with a small lag, to the yield on municipal bonds. When yields are stable, little short-term financing is used. As yields rise, short-term bond anticipation notes are increasingly used while finance officers await lower rates, which sometimes fail to materialize. As yields turn lower, the short-term debt is retired by the issuance of bonds.

Another interesting development concerning the supply of municipal bonds is the increasing use of revenue bonds as opposed to general obligation bonds. In 1960 revenue bonds accounted for approximately 27 percent of total bonds issued. By 1975 this percentage increased to nearly 40 percent.

This increasing use of revenue bond financing reflects two influences. The first is the apparently growing reluctance of taxpayers to pay higher taxes for debt service and, thus, their disinclination to approve new general obligation bond issues. Accordingly, state and local governments have increasingly resorted to revenue bonds, which do not require voter approval. The second influence is the enlarged concept of what constitutes a proper government service and the growing feeling that, as much as possible, the users of particular government services should pay for them. This enlarged concept of government services is particularly evident in the growing use of tax-exempt financing to obtain funds for pollution control and industrial development projects, which are then leased or sold to private businesses. The governmental unit is, in effect, an agent of industrial tax-exempt borrowing. Ostensibly the government service is the attraction of business enterprises to provide employment. More frequently, therefore, government-

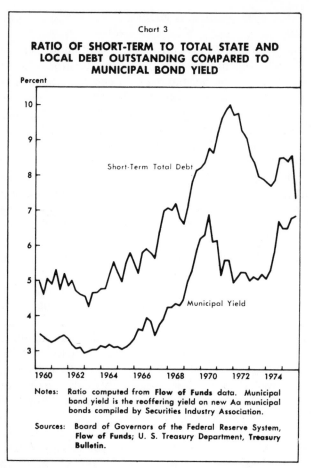

Chart 3

**RATIO OF SHORT-TERM TO TOTAL STATE AND
LOCAL DEBT OUTSTANDING COMPARED TO
MUNICIPAL BOND YIELD**

Notes: Ratio computed from **Flow of Funds** data. Municipal
bond yield is the reoffering yield on new Aa municipal
bonds compiled by Securities Industry Association.

Sources: Board of Governors of the Federal Reserve System,
Flow of Funds; U. S. Treasury Department, **Treasury
Bulletin.**

sponsored corporations or authorities are created to issue bonds, provide
services, and collect the revenues to retire the bonds. Revenue bonds are
likely to continue to be of growing importance in the municipal bond
market.

To sum up, the supply of municipal bonds has grown at a steady pace
with no apparent relationship to the business cycle. While there have been
some structural changes in the component mix of the supply of municipal
bonds, there seems to be no reason to believe that supply phenomena in
the municipal market are responsible for the movements in the ratio of the
yields on like-rated bonds.

THE DEMAND FOR MUNICIPAL BONDS

Due to the tax-exempt nature of municipal bonds, investors are generally
those persons and institutions subject to high marginal income tax rates.

Chief among these are commercial banks, individuals and individual trusts, fire and casualty insurance companies, and to a lesser extent, nonfinancial corporations and life insurance companies. Although not immediately apparent, the market for municipal bonds is rather narrow and has become more so since 1960. While all the previously mentioned groups participate in the market, individual demand and commercial bank demand are of prime importance. In 1960 individual and commercial bank holdings of municipal bonds accounted for 67 percent of the total amount outstanding; by the third quarter of 1975 this percentage had risen to 78 percent.

The nature of the demand for municipal bonds may offer a reasonable explanation for the erratic movements in municipal bond market conditions relative to other capital markets shown in Chart 1. An examination of the patterns of investment behavior by various types of municipal bond investors in recent years may, accordingly, prove instructive.

Commercial Banks

Of fundamental importance to the understanding of developments in the municipal bond market is the fact that the demand for municipal bonds by commercial banks is a residual demand, i.e., banks purchase municipals with any funds remaining after commitments to other borrowers have been met. The primary investment outlet for commercial banks is loans, and much of the variation in commercial bank participation in the municipal bond market can be explained by the variation in loan demand.

Chart 4 shows an index of loan demand pressure expressed as the ratio of commercial loans to time deposits. This ratio is intended to measure the extent to which banks have residual funds available. The relationship between the loan demand pressure and commercial bank participation in the municipal market is quite clear, particularly during the tight credit conditions of 1968-69. Generally as loan demand pressure falls, demand for municipal bonds by banks rises. As loan demand pressure rises, due to either a rise in loans or a runoff of time deposits, municipal bond demand by banks stabilizes or falls. A notable exception to this tendency, however, has developed since the third quarter of 1974. During that period both loan demand pressure and bank demand for municipals have declined. This recent experience suggests the presence of a new influence tending to reduce bank demand for municipal bonds, a development which will be discussed later.

Commercial banks are presently the primary holders of municipal bonds, although this was not always true. To maintain liquidity, banks tend to prefer short- or intermediate-term bonds. Chart 4 shows the municipal bond investment record of commercial banks, both absolutely and relative to the entire market. The dollar amount of bank holdings has trended generally upward, but not without interruption. Prior to 1961 the participation of commercial banks in the market was limited and erratic. From mid-1961 to

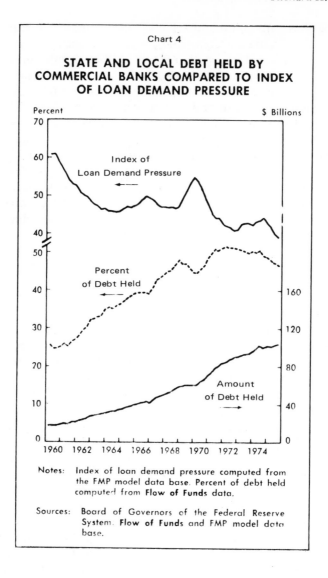

Chart 4

**STATE AND LOCAL DEBT HELD BY
COMMERCIAL BANKS COMPARED TO INDEX
OF LOAN DEMAND PRESSURE**

Notes: Index of loan demand pressure computed from
the FMP model data base. Percent of debt held
computed from **Flow of Funds** data.

Sources: Board of Governors of the Federal Reserve
System. **Flow of Funds** and FMP model data
base.

late 1968 holdings grew steadily with the exception of one quarter of liquidation during the tight credit conditions of 1966. In the latter part of 1968,
due to increasing loan demand pressure, banks sharply curtailed new purchases of municipal bonds and did not resume them until early 1970. As
will be seen, their departure from the market at this point was responsible
for a rise in Rm/Rc much like that experienced from the second quarter
of 1974 through the first quarter of 1975. The growth in holdings then
continued from early 1970 until early 1974, when banks again essentially
pulled out of the new issue market.

Individuals and Individual Trusts

For individual investors the principal investment alternatives to the municipal bond market are the stock and corporate bond markets. The reasons for this are that capital gains are taxed at a lower rate than regular income and corporate bonds can provide an income-producing alternative to municipals, depending, of course, on the individual's tax bracket. While there is probably a hard core of high income, risk-averse individuals who seldom seek investment alternatives to municipal bonds, changes in stock prices and the corresponding changes in opportunities for capital gains may cause other, less risk-averse individuals to alternate between stocks and municipals.

The variation in individual participation in the municipal bond market can be explained to a large degree by variations in stock prices and in the level of municipal bond yields relative to yields on other bonds (Rm/Rc). The data in Chart 5 indicate a pronounced inverse relationship between stock prices and individual holdings of municipals. As stock prices rise,

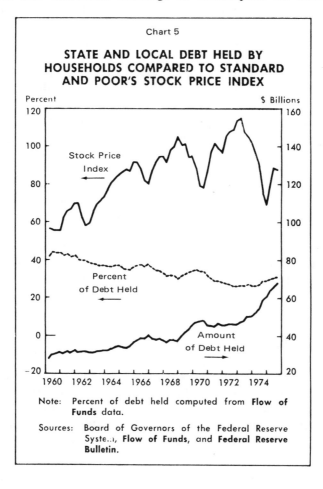

Chart 5

STATE AND LOCAL DEBT HELD BY HOUSEHOLDS COMPARED TO STANDARD AND POOR'S STOCK PRICE INDEX

Note: Percent of debt held computed from **Flow of Funds** data.

Sources: Board of Governors of the Federal Reserve Syste..., **Flow of Funds,** and **Federal Reserve Bulletin.**

bond holdings are increased at a slower rate or are liquidated; the reverse seems to be the case when stock prices fall. This reverse relationship is particularly evident during the periods of generally declining stock market prices from the fourth quarter of 1968 through the second quarter of 1970 and from the first quarter of 1973 through the third quarter of 1974.

The relative level of bond yields (Rm/Rc) is important to individual demand for municipals, because as the yield ratio increases the number of potential individual investors rises. Unlike the institutional investors, most of whom face approximately the same income tax rate, individual investors face different tax rates. As Rm/Rc rises, t (the tax rate of indifference) falls, lowering the marginal tax bracket at which investment in municipals becomes attractive to individuals. For this reason when banks or other institutional investors leave the market, yields rise until t falls sufficiently to encourage enough individuals to fill the gap in the demand for municipal bonds and thereby clear the market.

Individuals and individual trusts are now the second most important source of demand for municipal bonds, having fallen from the dominant position that they held during the first half of the 1960s. These investors tend to hold the longer maturities of an issue. Chart 5 shows the municipal bond demand by individuals in absolute and relative terms. Although there is a general upward trend in the dollar volume of total bonds held by households, its movement is much more erratic than that displayed by bank holdings and shows many periods of liquidation.

In relative terms, household demand for municipal bonds has exhibited a general downward trend since 1960. Individual holdings declined from 43 percent of total outstandings in 1960 to a low of 26 percent in 1972-73. Recently, however, this fraction has increased to 30 percent, largely as a result of the decline in the market share of commercial banks and the introduction of municipal bond funds that facilitate investment by individuals.

Generally speaking, the high rate of inflation in recent years may be expected to have reduced the attractiveness of fixed income securities. But, combined with a progressive tax structure a high inflation rate raises the marginal tax bracket of many individuals, thereby increasing the value of the tax-exempt feature of municipal bonds through a reduction in the effective after-tax yield on taxable securities.

Fire and Casualty Insurance Companies

Fire and casualty insurance companies are ranked third in importance in the municipal bond market. These companies, like commercial banks, are subject to the standard corporate income tax rate and thus desire the tax-exempt income municipal bonds can provide. Unlike life insurance companies, fire and casualty insurance companies cannot accurately predict

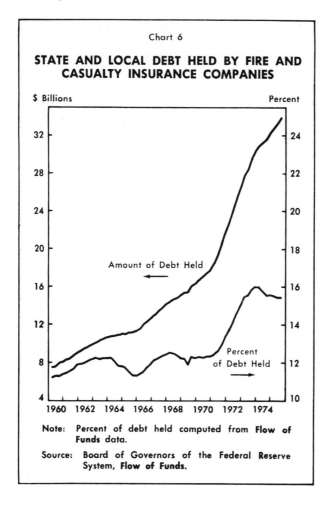

Chart 6

STATE AND LOCAL DEBT HELD BY FIRE AND CASUALTY INSURANCE COMPANIES

Note: Percent of debt held computed from **Flow of Funds** data.

Source: **Board of Governors of the Federal Reserve System, Flow of Funds.**

their probable losses; thus their net taxable income, as well as their cash needs, are highly variable. For these reasons, the demand for municipals of any fire and casualty insurance company is unstable. However, while any particular company may be highly erratic in its purchases, fire and casualty insurance companies as a group are the most stable source of demand in the market. Chart 6 shows a steady upward trend in holdings of this group since 1960, with no periods of liquidation.

The percentage of total municipal outstandings held by fire and casualty insurance companies was remarkably stable from 1960 through 1970 at approximately 12 percent. By 1973, this market share had increased to its present level of 15 percent. Recent reductions in purchases appear to be due to lower industry profits and should prove temporary.

Nonfinancial Corporations and Life Insurance Companies

Both individually and as a group, nonfinancial corporations and life insurance companies are relatively insignificant buyers of municipal bonds. Life insurance companies buy few municipals because they are unable to take full advantage of the tax exemption due to the low effective tax rate on these companies. In 1960, nonfinancial corporations held roughly 3 percent of outstanding municipals, while life insurance companies held 5 percent. The market share of each fell to roughly 2 percent by the first quarter of 1975. The participation of these investors is the most erratic of any in the market. Nonfinancial corporations primarily buy short-term obligations to meet cash management needs. For most of the 1960s, life insurance companies were a supply factor in the secondary market rather than a demand factor in the new issue market, although their purchases of new issues have recently increased. In general, these two investor groups have little impact on the municipal bond market.

PAST EXPERIENCE IN THE MUNICIPAL BOND MARKET

Due to the residual nature of the demand for municipal bonds by the commercial banks, the overall composition of demand is highly sensitive to developments in other capital markets and in the economy generally. The participation of various investor groups changes greatly over short periods as well as over the longer term. This variation in the composition of demand for municipal bonds seems to be a major factor explaining movements in Rm/Rc.

Figure 1 illustrates the mechanism through which changes in demand composition affect Rm/Rc and the municipal market in general. An increase in the level of demand for municipal securities among institutions subject to high marginal tax rates (e.g., an increase in commercial bank demand triggered by a decline in loan demand pressure) causes municipal bond prices to rise, resulting in lower levels of Rm/Rc and thus higher levels of t. At the higher levels of t, the relative attractiveness of municipal bonds declines along with the value of the tax exemption. Individual demand for municipals falls as many individual investors forego purchases of municipal bonds in favor of alternative investments in stocks and corporate bonds. Under these circumstances most investors are in the same tax bracket as the marginal investors, and all receive a yield very near the after-tax yield available on corporate bonds.

When demand for municipal bonds declines among tax-exposed institutional investors, as when loan demand pressure rises, the situation is reversed. Municipal prices fall, causing Rm/Rc to rise and t to fall. This falling level

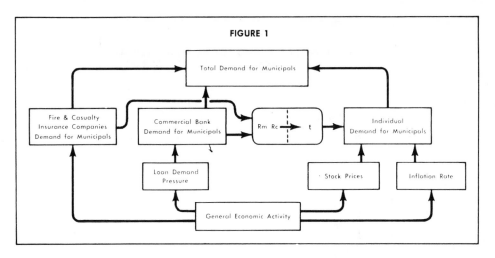

FIGURE 1

of t increases the value of the tax exemption and the demand for municipal bonds among investors in lower tax brackets, thereby inducing individuals and tax-sheltered institutions to enter the market. Due to progressive taxation, a larger number of individual investors will be in tax brackets above the marginal tax bracket (t) of the marginal investors. Thus, in this situation, many more investors receive a tax-exempt yield considerably greater than the after-tax yield available on corporate bonds.

Chart 7 shows the composition of demand for municipal bonds and the ratio of municipal bond to corporate bond yields since 1960. Rm/Rc generally fell from 1961 through the second quarter of 1968. This fall was due to the rising market participation of commercial banks (caused by generally falling or stable loan demand pressure), which also reduced the participation of individual investors. In the second quarter of 1968 Rm/Rc started a steep rise (steeper than the recent one) that lasted, with one interruption, through the second quarter of 1970. This period was one of high loan demand pressure on banks. To accommodate loan customers, commercial banks halted new purchases of municipal bonds. The departure of banks from the municipal market reduced institutional demand for municipals, causing Rm/Rc to rise and t to fall until individual demand for municipals, spurred both by rising Rm/Rc and falling stock prices, rose sufficiently to clear the market.

The rising participation of institutions caused Rm/Rc and the participation of individuals to generally decline from the second quarter of 1970 to the second quarter of 1974. Owing to easier loan demand pressure conditions, bank demand for municipals resumed in the first quarter of 1970 and rose through the first quarter of 1972. At that time a period of relative stability in bank demand for municipals began that lasted until the second quarter of 1974. Municipal bond demand by institutions was aided by the growth in municipal market participation of fire and casualty insurance

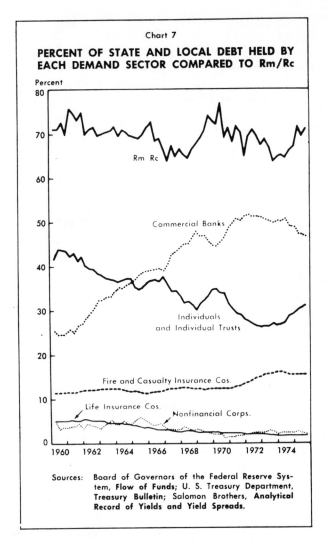

Chart 7

PERCENT OF STATE AND LOCAL DEBT HELD BY EACH DEMAND SECTOR COMPARED TO Rm/Rc

Sources: Board of Governors of the Federal Reserve System, **Flow of Funds;** U. S. Treasury Department, **Treasury Bulletin;** Salomon Brothers, **Analytical Record of Yields and Yield Spreads.**

companies from 1971 to 1973. This institutional demand supplanted a portion of the participation of individuals, whose market share declined from the first quarter of 1970 to the third quarter of 1972, due both to falling Rm/Rc and rising stock prices, and then stabilized until the second quarter of 1974.

SUMMARY AND CONCLUSION

The ratio of municipal bond to corporate bond yields exhibits considerable variability, part of which takes the form of explainable short-term cyclical movements. An analysis of the municipal bond market indicates that while supply is steadily rising at a stable rate, demand is continually changing in composition. These changing demand patterns are primarily due to the influence of other capital markets on municipal bond investors, i.e., to the residual nature of commercial bank demand for municipal bonds and to individuals' changing demand for municipals versus stocks and corporate bonds. The continual change in demand is responsible for the short-term volatility in the movement of Rm/Rc as well as its longer-term movements.

Part II

B.   THE EQUITY MARKET

In this section of Part II, three articles focus on several important aspects of the equity market. The first article, written by Neil G. Berkman, deals with the *random walk model* of stock price behavior. This article is particularly noteworthy because it not only provides a clear explanation of a controversial topic, but it presents an unusually insightful reconciliation of the "fundamental approach" toward equity valuation with the random walk hypothesis. Since the late 1960s, the market performance of equities has raised questions regarding the effectiveness of common stocks as an inflation hedge. The article by Marcelle Arak focuses on this issue by examining *the relationship between equity values, inflation, and taxes*. The last article in this section is by Kenneth D. Garbade and Monica M. Kaicher and deals with *exchange-traded options on common stock*. Although primarily viewed as a speculative activity, the use of options as a risk-reducing instrument is becoming more widely recognized, especially among trust funds and equity-oriented financial institutions such as pension funds and property-liability insurers.

A PRIMER ON RANDOM WALKS IN THE STOCK MARKET[*]

Neil G. Berkman[†]

14

The random walk model of stock prices, often succinctly represented by the phrase "the best prediction of tomorrow's price is today's price," is probably the most controversial yet least understood result produced by economists in recent years. This model has proved to be particularly irksome to professional money managers, apparently because it is believed to undermine the claim, made implicitly or otherwise, that they can consistently pick winners. In response, technical and fundamental analysts alike, normally unable to agree on much of anything, have rallied together in the opinion that the random walk model must somehow be wrong. Faced with abundant empirical evidence in support of the model, some members of the investing public have concluded that it leads to a pure dart-throwing strategy of stock selection, others in their confusion have abandoned the market entirely. But is the random walk model really an insult to the competence of professional security analysts? Does it suggest that one cannot make money in the stock market? Does it imply that stock prices changes are unrelated to events occurring in the outside world? By examining the random walk model, by showing what it does and does not say, this paper explains why the answer to these and similar questions is "no" and shows by means of an example that the model is entirely consistent with traditional approaches to stock valuation.

*Reprinted from the *New England Economic Review*, September/October 1978, pp. 32-50, with permission from the Federal Reserve Bank of Boston.

†Economist, Federal Reserve Bank of Boston. The author wishes to thank Stephen C. Peck for his suggestions on the form of the model in Section IV and Elizabeth Berman for her research assistance.

WHAT IS A RANDOM WALK?

Most of the confusion surrounding the implications of the random walk model of stock prices no doubt stems from a misunderstanding of precisely what is meant by a random walk. This is both unfortunate and unnecessary, since the concept may be easily explained. A convenient way to do so is by means of a simple experiment based on the outcomes of repeated throws of a pair of dice.[1] Such an experiment is particularly useful in explaining the notion of a random walk because of a well-known property of dice games. Assuming the dice are not "loaded" and thus have no "memory," knowledge of the outcome of any particular throw in no way increases one's knowledge of the likely outcome of the next throw, except insofar as it is certain to be between 2 and 12. In other words, each toss of the dice is an independent event, so that the probability of any outcome on any throw is unrelated to the pattern of outcomes on all previous throws.[2] A clear understanding of the independence property is all that is needed to resolve the mystery surrounding a random walk.

The experiment is conducted as follows. Beginning with an arbitrary number of "points," 100, say, the dice are thrown and points are added or subtracted according to a schedule based on the probability of the various possible outcomes. These probabilities are stable, of course; no matter how many times the dice are thrown the chance of rolling a seven is always one in six, the chance of rolling a two is always 1 in 36.[3] Since seven is the most likely outcome, no points are awarded for this roll. A roll of two is awarded minus five points, a roll of three minus four points, a roll of four minus three points, a roll of five minus two points, and a roll of six minus one point. Analogous gains are awarded rolls of 8 through 12. By following these rules and repeatedly adding or subtracting the appropriate numbers of points after each roll, a series such as that displayed in the upper panel of Chart 1, in this case the result of 52 throws, is obtained.

---

[1] H. Roberts was the first to use the "chance model" as a device to explain the meaning of a random walk. See Harry V. Roberts, "Stock Market 'Patterns' and Financial Analysis: Methodoligical Suggestions," *Journal of Finance*, Vol. 14, No. 1 (March 1959), pp. 1-10.

[2] Technically, independence requires that the conditional probability of any outcome equal its corresponding marginal probability.

[3] Let $P(2)$ equal the probability of rolling two on a throw of two unloaded dice. This requires that each die come up one. Since there are six possible outcomes on a throw of a single die, the probability of a one, $P(1)$, equals 1/6. Since the throws are independent, the probability of rolling a second one given that a one has already been thrown (i.e., $P(1/1)$) is also 1/6. Therefore $P(2) = P(1)P(1/1) = 1/6 \times 1/6 = 1/36$. To roll three on a throw of two dice requires a one on the first throw and a two on the second or a two on the first throw and a one on the second. Therefore $P(3) = P(1)P(2/1) + P(2)P(1/2) = (1/6 \times 1/6) + (1/6 \times 1/6) = 2/36$, and so on for the other possible outcomes between 4 and 12.

Chart 1

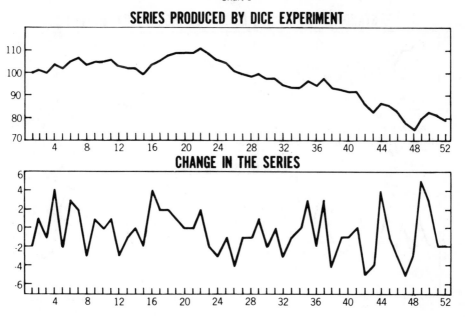

SERIES PRODUCED BY DICE EXPERIMENT

CHANGE IN THE SERIES

The similarities between the series in Chart 1 and any number of economic time series one could name are too striking to require extended comment. Compare, for example, the experimental series to the weekly values of the Standard and Poor's Composite Index for 1977 presented in the upper panel of Chart 2. Both series contain certain apparently repetitive patterns of fluctuation which suggest that it may be possible to predict their future course by careful study of their past behavior. Indeed, this possibility is the foundation of a technical school of stock market analysis.[4] Yet the design of the experiment that produced the series in Chart 1 insures that its next "step" will be determined only by the random outcome of a throw of the dice, and since the outcomes are independent, nothing in the pattern of the past behavior of the series provides any help in forecasting what the next step will turn out to be. The lower panel of Chart 1, which shows the number of points awarded for each of the 52 throws of the dice, illustrates this idea quite clearly. Inspection of the series reveals no discernible patterns that could be exploited to predict its future behavior. Similarly, the lower panel of Chart 2, showing the series of successive changes in the weekly stock price index, displays none of the characteristic regularity normally associated with a series easily forecast from its behavior in the past. The movements of series such as these, where the size and the sign of each change

---

[4] Technical analysis includes all theories of stock price behavior that base forecasts solely on the past history of prices. A prominent example of technical analysis is the Dow Theory.

Chart 2

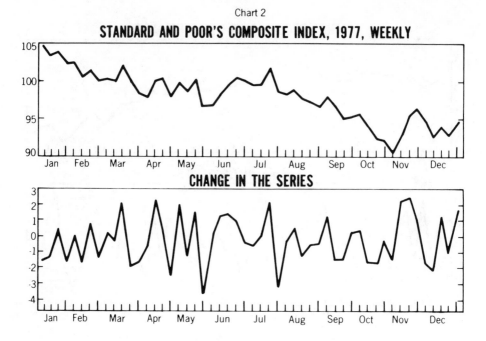

are independent of the pattern of all previous changes, are thus very naturally described as following a random walk.

In the case of the dice experiment, the probability associated with each
outcome was known a priori, as was the fact that each throw of the dice is
an independent event. The latter property insured that the experimental
series had no choice but to follow a random walk, the former property
served only to define its allowable range of step-to-step variation. Obviously,
the frequency distribution of changes of any series, whether stock prices or
some other "real world" series generated by a complex economic process,
may be measured from historical data and used as an estimate of the
probable range of future movements.[5] On the other hand, an examination
of the data evidence will not necessarily show that past changes in a given
series are independent. The quarterly changes in nominal final sales displayed
in the lower panel of Chart 3, for example, follow a clear cyclical pattern,
with large changes tending to be followed by large changes and small changes.
Thus, because successive changes in final sales are apparently related in such

---

[5] While the sample variance of a stock price series may always be computed by the formula

$$1/N \sum_{i=1}^{N} (p_i - \overline{p})^2,$$

where p_i is the i-th price change, p is the average price change and N is the number of observations,
the variance of the true underlying population may not exist (e.g., if the true distribution is stable
Paretian). Further, the variance of the underlying population, if it exists, may change over time, so
that the sample variance must be interpreted with caution.

Chart 3

NOMINAL FINAL SALES, QUARTERLY

CHANGE IN THE SERIES

a way that the pattern of previous changes provides potentially useful information for forecasting the size of future changes, it is doubtful that the changes are independent or that the series follows a random walk.[6] For stock prices, however, abundant empirical research has uncovered precious little evidence of a lack of independence in successive price changes, so the random walk model has become widely accepted as a description of actual stock price behavior.

Empirical analysis of stock prices has of course also been concerned with characterizing the frequency distribution of price changes. This issue has proved surprisingly difficult to resolve, although early work generally favored a "bell-shaped" distribution centered about zero as a reasonable approximation to reality.[7] Assuming this is true, then successive stock price changes may be thought of as the random outcome of independent draws

---

[6] Visual inspection is frequently misleading, hence the caveat "doubtful." The empirical techniques commonly used to test for independence will be described in a subsequent section.

[7] The dispute has revolved around the common assumption that the distribution of price changes is normal. While convenient for statistical work (the techniques used in this area are strictly applicable only if the distribution of price changes is normal), the assumption is inconsistent with observed stock price change distributions that have "fat tails" and a peak centered near zero (i.e., that are "leptokurtic"). In addition, there is no general agreement about the appropriate transformation of the stock price data (i.e., first difference, percentage change, change in logarithm) required to induce stationarity. For some recent evidence on this issue, as well as a bibliography of previous work, see Randolph Westerfield, "The Distribution of Common Stock Price Changes: An Application of Transactions Time and Subordinated Stochastic Models," *Journal of Financial and Quantitative Analysis*, Vol. 12, No. 5 (December 1977), pp. 743-766.

from the bell-shaped distribution, just as each step in the experimental series was the result of the random outcome of independent throws of the dice. Further, just as seven is the most likely outcome of a throw of the dice, making zero points the most likely award on any throw, zero is the most likely draw from the observed frequency distribution, making zero change the most likely movement of stock prices between any two points in time.[8] Thus, since empirical analysis has shown that stock price changes are independent and that the frequency distribution of changes is approximately bell-shaped and centered near zero, the entire process is aptly summarized by the phrase, "the best prediction of tomorrow's price is today's price."

Although the pattern of observed stock price changes may be accurately described as following a random walk, this is not to say that stock prices are actually *determined* in this chance way. The common error of interpreting the random walk model as *causing* stock prices rather than as simply *describing* their behavior is the source of the misconceptions mentioned at the outset. In particular, the random walk model does not imply that stock prices are unrelated to events taking place in the economy that underlies the stock market. The model implies only that changes in the price of a stock cannot be predicted from the behavior of earlier changes in the price of that stock.

WHY DO STOCK PRICES FOLLOW
A RANDOM WALK

Hardly anyone would be surprised to learn that stock prices are a leading indicator of future economic activity, turning down in advance of recessions and turning up in advance of recoveries. Nor would many be surprised to learn the reason for this phenomenon. Stocks represent pro-rata shares to ownership of the real assets used to produce output. The market value of stock is thus intimately related to the value of this underlying capital, whose own value is in turn dependent on the profits it is expected to earn over the course of its useful life.[9] For this reason, stock prices, and the value of the capital they measure, reflect forecasts of the future course of business conditions; hence, their movements anticipate movements in the economy as a whole. Many people would be surprised, however, to learn that it is precisely because stock prices reflect forecasts that their movements follow a random walk.

[8] The relevant unit period may range from transaction-to-transaction to year-to-year or even longer. The dispersion of possible price changes will increase as the measurement interval is lengthened, however.

[9] This is the familiar asset pricing model which holds that in equilibrium the current price of a capital good is equal to the present discounted value of the profits it is expected to earn in the future.

Only two assumptions are required to move from the observation that stock prices reflect forecasts to the conclusion that price changes will follow a random walk. The first assumption, often referred to as the "rational expectations" hypothesis, concerns the quality of the forecasts used by investors in assessing the future course of the economy.[10] Expectations are rational if in the process of their formation, the forecaster uses all the current information he believes to be relevant for predicting the future course of the variable at hand. Naturally, both differences of opinion as to how the economy works and individual constraints on the amount of re-sources devoted to forecasting will influence the nature and quantity of the information incorporated in a given forecast. Idiosyncratic notions concerning the "true" casual links in the system will lead one forecaster to stress one sort of information, while others trying to predict the same variable will prefer information of some other kind.[11] The resulting forecasts may differ—witness the notorious divergence of opinion among professional economic forecasters, for example—but as long as each reflects all the information appropriate to the particular world view underlying the forecast, there is no reason to consider any one of them "irrational." Further, because information is not costless, the assumption of rational expectations requires forecasters to acquire additional data only up to the point where the value of the increase in forecast accuracy due to the marginal unit of information is just equal to the cost of acquiring and incorporating this information into the forecast. Thus, since the value of marginal improvements in forecast accuracy that presumably accompany the acquisition of additional information varies across individuals, as do the costs of acquiring the additional information itself, the amount of information incorporated in a rational forecast may vary across individuals as well.[12] Therefore, subject to the constraints imposed by the costs of acquiring information and by the nature of the information required by the model implicitly or explicitly guiding the forecast, expectations are rational if no information available at the time the forecast is made that would be expected to improve its accuracy is ignored.[13] Under this assumption, the investors' expectations embody all that is knowable from available information about the future behavior of those variables believed relevant in determining the value of stocks.

---

[10] The term "rational expectations" was introduced by Muth. See John F. Muth, "Rational Expectations and the Theory of Price Movements," *Econometrica*, Vol. 29 (July 1961), pp. 315-35.

[11] For example, in an attempt to forecast nominal GNP, a "Keynesian" might prefer information on the components of aggregate demand, while a "monetarist" might want to study money supply data.

[12] As a practical matter, however, there is little evidence that forecast accuracy is a strictly increasing function of the quantity of information used as input to the forecast.

[13] In this view, rational expectations emerge simply as the outcome of constrained utility maximization, where the utility function includes "knowledge of the future" as an argument. The more common statement that a forecast is rational only if it is set equal to the conditional mathematical expectation of the variable, so that rational forecasts are always unbiased, is a special case that arises when utility functions are linear, information is costless, and everyone knows the "true" (linear) model of the economy.

Although this assumption may at first sight seem highly restrictive, it can be shown to be quite a reasonable description of investor behavior. The primary motivation for investing in stocks is to earn profits, of course, and the consistent attainment of this objective involves the early discovery of "undervalued" or "overvalued" issues.[14] The lure of trading profits available to investors who seek out information that will allow them to recognize and exploit such situations is a potent argument for rationality, as is the observation that competition among investors and their advisers has led to the development of ever more sophisticated information gathering and processing capabilities. Technological developments have also significantly reduced the cost of data collection, making the incorporation of large amounts of information into expectations economically feasible for many market participants. The concept of rationality is thus quite general, its appeal resting in the simple notion that greed should induce investors to act in this way.

The second assumption needed to develop a theoretical foundation for the random walk is that the stock market is "efficient" in the sense that available information is rapidly incorporated into current stock prices. Essentially this involves nothing more than assuming that investors attempt to earn profits from their investment in expectations formation by purchasing or selling stocks on the basis of their latest forecasts, in the perhaps mistaken belief that they have better information about the future than is already reflected in market values. This assumption follows quite naturally from the assumption of rational expectations, since investors would not bother to devote resources to processing information if they did not intend to make timely use of the forecasts they produce. In well-organized exchanges such as currently exist in the United States, where millions of investors are frequent participants, the combined effect of their transactions is to insure that stock prices at any point in time reflect all the information that is considered relevant to their value.

The precise mechanism through which available information is reflected in stock prices in efficient markets may perhaps best be illustrated by means of an example. Suppose the rational processing of current information has produced a generally held expectation that corporate profits will increase from current levels over the next few quarters. Faced with this expectation, an individual transactor might justifiably expect stock prices to rise in the near future as well. How could he profit from this expectation? Simply by purchasing stock now and waiting for the ensuing bull market to drive prices up. Clearly, however, other traders with similar expectations will act in the same fashion, and their combined purchases will drive prices up

---

[14] The terminology is loose. As used in the text, the terms refer simply to stocks whose prices, when viewed ex post, were about to exhibit significant increases or decreases.

immediately.[15] Indeed, prices will rise by just enough to eliminate any further extraordinary gains that the expected increase in corporate profits had promised. This mechanism explains why stock prices lead the business cycle and defines the sense in which current prices fully reflect expectations, the profit motive provides the incentive for the stock market to behave in this way.

An important implication of the assumptions of rationality and efficiency is that one cannot consistently earn extraordinary profits by trading on the basis of generally available information, since such information is always rapidly incorporated into current stock prices. Another implication is that stock prices will change only when the arrival of "new" information causes expectations to be revised. For information to be truly new, it must of course have been unpredictable from information available previously, since it would otherwise already be reflected in expectations and stock prices by the time it is announced. The release of quarterly corporate profits data, for example, provides new information and results in an alteration of expectations only if the actual figures differ from the figures that had been expected earlier.[16] Since surprises such as these occur randomly (if they did not, they would not be surprises), the changes in stock prices that result from new information will be random as well. If expectations are rational and if the stock market is efficient, stock prices will follow a random walk.

HOW HAS THE RANDOM WALK
MODEL BEEN TESTED?

The discussion up to this point has been intentionally vague regarding the precise meaning of the word "information." The random walk model defines information to include only the past history of stock prices and nothing more, arguing that information so defined cannot be used to predict future prices.[17] The assumptions of rationality and efficiency that provide the

---

[15] It is not necessary for literally everyone to hold the same expectation, although the logic of the argument suggests that unless some traders disagree with the concensus view, prices will adjust without any trades taking place at all.

[16] Some traders may be surprised by the new information, while for others it may only confirm what was previously expected. The fact that shares change hands on such announcement dates merely confirms that expectations differ across individuals.

[17] Since a pattern in a price series, like an earnings announcement, is information, the efficient market hypothesis requires that it too be continuously reflected in current prices. As an extreme example, suppose that analysis of historical data shows that the price of a particular stock has always doubled two days after it reaches a new yearly low. Assuming that this pattern is widely known, and in view of its potential profitability it certainly would be, then the price will double immediately after a new low is reached, since traders will try to buy in before the anticipated price reaction occurs. This behavior has the effect of eliminating the historical pattern, of course, so that such opportunities, if they ever exist, must be extremely short-lived.

theoretical underpinning for the random walk model implicitly allow a much broader universe of information than just past prices, however. In principle, the logic of the argument suggests that literally every conceivable bit of available information is continuously reflected in stock prices, so that neither past prices nor other information will be of any use for forecasting future prices and hence for earning extraordinary returns on stock market transactions. Whether this is true in fact is an empirical question, one which will probably never be answered completely due to the enormous amount of information that exists in the world today. Undaunted by this consideration, researchers have nevertheless devoted considerable effort to the task of testing both the simple random walk model and the broader efficient market model from which it is derived.

Tests of the Random Walk Model

Empirical analysis of the random walk model has been concerned both with testing for independence in stock price changes and with checking to see if the past history of prices provides information that can be used to predict their movements in the future and thus act as the basis for a profitable trading rule. These issues are closely related, of course; if price changes are random, then it will be impossible to predict future changes from past changes. It is nevertheless worth considering the tests separately, since the basic technique applied in trading rule tests is also widely used in tests of market efficiency generally.

The most straightforward test for independence is the "runs" test. A run is defined as a sequence of one or more price changes of the same sign. For example, replacing the numerical value of price changes by a "+" when the change is positive and by a "−" when the change is negative, the sequence "−−−+−++−" consists of five runs. For given probabilities of a stock price increase or decrease, if positive changes tend to be followed by positive changes and negative changes by further negative changes, then the number of runs in a particular price series will be less than if the changes are independent. Similarly, if there is a tendency for positive changes to be followed by negative changes, then the number of runs will be greater than if the changes are independent. To illustrate, in the case of stock price changes as measured by the last day of the month closing values of the Standard and Poor's Composite Index for the 1928-1964 period, the observed probability of a price increase was .59 and of a price decrease .41.[18] Under the assumptions that these probabilities hold for the period 1965-1977 and that price changes are random, the expected number of runs in

---

[18] Of the 442 price changes observed during this period, 259 were increases and 183 were decreases. Thus, an estimate of the probability of a price increase is 259/442 = .59 and of a price decrease is 183/442 = .41.

the latter period is 76.5.[19] The actual number of runs was 73, well within the expected range for standard levels of statistical significance. Thus, the result of this runs test would not allow one to reject the hypothesis that the sequence of monthly price changes between 1965 and 1977 is random.

Another popular method of analyzing stock prices is to estimate the correlation coefficient between successive price changes over a long period of time.[20] The random walk model argues that the sign and the magnitude of price changes from period to period are unrelated to each other, so that the correlation between them should be zero. Table I shows the estimated correlation coefficients between successive monthly, quarterly, and yearly changes in the Standard and Poor's Composite Index for the 1928-1977 period. As expected, the estimated coefficients are all quite small in absolute value, and none is different from zero in the statistical sense. Further, the percentage of the variability of current price change that is explained by its correlation with the previous change is virtually zero for all three differencing intervals. The correlation between successive price changes in this index therefore provides no information that would be useful for prediction, so the results of the test also support the random walk model.[21]

Table I
Correlation Coefficients for Changes in the Standard and Poor's Composite Index

Interval	Correlation Coefficient	Standard Error of Estimate	t-Ratio	Percentage of Variance of Current Change in Price Index "Explained" by Its Change Last Period[1]
Month	0.0386	.0409	0.942	0.0%
Quarter	0.0964	.0649	1.485	0.6%
Year	−0.00535	.1020	−0.053	0.0%

Note. These estimates were produced by an ordinary least squares regression of current change in stock price against a constant and lagged change in stock price for the period 1928-1977.

[1] These figures are the adjusted R^2s from the regression of current against lagged price change.

[19] This expectation was calculated as follows. There were 156 months in the 1965-1977 period. Assuming the probabilities of an increase and a decrease of .59 and .41, respectively, 92 price increases and 64 price decreases are expected. Under the null hypothesis that the changes are random, the expected number of runs is then computed as:

$$E(R) = \frac{2(92)(64)}{(92 + 64)} + 1 = 76.5$$

with a standard deviation of:

$$\sigma_R = \sqrt{\frac{2(92)(64)(2(92)(64) - 92 - 64)}{(156)^2(155)}} = 6.02$$

[20] The correlation coefficient between successive changes in a series is $(\Sigma (p_i - \bar{p})(p_{i-1} - \bar{p}))/\Sigma (p_i - \bar{p})^2$, where p_i equals the i-th price change and $\bar{p}$ equals the average price change.

[21] Strictly speaking, the absence of correlation is sufficient for independence only if the distribution of price changes is normal. Since the available evidence suggests that the distribution may not be normal (see footnote 7), the test described in the text may be of very low power. Unfortunately, parametric statistical tests of independence for non-normal distributions do not exist.

More sophisticated statistical techniques have been applied to price data both for individual stocks and market indices in a search for significant correlations between successive price changes or departures from randomness in sequences of runs, and price changes measured at intervals as short as transaction-to-transaction and as long as year-to-year have been analyzed, but no strong evidence inconsistent with the random walk model as a good working description of stock price behavior has been discovered. The most common conclusion is that no correlation exists, and when statistically significant correlations are reported, suggesting that the random walk model may not hold precisely, they always turn out to be too small to provide information that can be exploited as a forecasting device.[22] However, while these results indicate that at least provisional acceptance of the model is in order, they do not close the issue of the information content of a stock price series entirely because the possibility that more complex patterns exist in the data is not directly addressed by correlation and runs tests. Firm believers in the efficacy of chartist trading strategies may then justifiably argue that these tests provide unconvincing evidence against the ability of their models to predict stock prices, since chartist forecasts are typically based on intricate patterns of past behavior (the "double bottom," for example) that do not depend crucially on the presence or absence of correlation between successive movements in the price series.[23] Contrary to the implications of the efficient market hypothesis, this argument holds that the stock market does not incorporate all of the information contained in the pattern of past prices into current price. It was in an effort to counter this objection that trading rule tests were orginally devised.

The goal of a trading rule test is to determine if a particular bit of information can be used to earn profits greater than could be earned without the information. The question then is can information about the past history of a stock's price be used to earn profits greater than would be earned if one just bought the stock and held it? An archetypal chartist trading scheme that has been tested in this way is the filter rule.[24] Under this rule, a stock is purchased if its price increases by x percent and held until its price declines by x percent from a subsequent high, at which time the trader simul-

---

[22] Some selected references from the vast literature on this subject are: Eugene F. Fama, "Efficient Capital Markets: A Review of Theory and Empirical Work" *Journal of Finance*, Vol. 25, No. 2 (May 1970), pp. 383-417; Clive W. J. Granger and Oskar Morgenstern, *Predictability of Stock Market Prices*, Lexington: D. C. Heath and Co., 1970; Paul Cootner, editor, *The Random Character of Stock Market Prices*, Cambridge, Ma.: MIT Press, 1964. The interested reader will find extensive bibliographies in each of these selections.

[23] Correlation is a measure of linear dependence. Technical (or chartist) analysis is based on the identification of highly *non-linear* patterns of dependence, so that traditional statistical tests are irrelevant for analyzing the usefulness of these models.

[24] This trading strategy is very similar to the popular Dow Theory, a chartist scheme that is supposed to identify price trends. Detailed analysis of the profitability of such trading rules may be found in Sidney S. Alexander, "Price Movements in Speculative Markets: Trends or Random Walks," *Industrial Management Review*, Vol. 39 (Special Supplement, January 1966), pp. 226-41.

taneously sells and goes short, covering his position when the price increases by x percent from a subsequent low. Price movements of less than x percent are ignored. For filters ranging in size from 0.5 to 1.5 percent this rule has been shown to generate greater profits than are earned if the stock is simply purchased at the beginning of the sample period and sold at the end, but *only* if the transactions costs (commissions, clearinghouse fees and the like) incurred in pursuing the strategy are not taken into account. When these costs are included, and they are substantial due to the frequent trades produced by small filters, the trader always does better under the buy-and-hold alternative. The fact that this chartist strategy can be used to earn "abnormal" returns in the absence of transactions costs is evidence against a strict random walk in stock prices, since it indicates a tendency for positive correlation in successive price changes. On the other hand, the departure from randomness is too slight to be useful as a forecasting device, since the excess profits available as a result of the observed correlation do not cover the costs involved in trying to exploit it. Indeed, although the random walk model thus appears to hold only as a very close approximation to actual price behavior, the stock market is evidently extremely efficient in incorporating the information contained in past price changes into current price. Patterns in a price series are traded upon and hence removed up to the point that any remaining patterns are not worth exploiting because of transactions costs. If transactions costs were zero, one would therefore expect stock prices to follow a random walk precisely.

Numerous runs, correlation, and trading rule tests have been conducted, none yielding results substantially different from those reviewed here. It is of course impossible to analyze every stock, so that skeptics will always have reason to remain unconvinced, but the weight of the data evidence clearly favors acceptance of the random walk model and the presence of market efficiency with respect to the information contained in the history of stock prices.[25] The next step is to determine if stock prices efficiently reflect other kinds of information as well.

Tests of Broader Forms of Market Efficiency

Tests of market efficiency must begin with the selection of an appropriate bit of information from the vast universe of available data to which stock prices might react. The pragmatic approach is to narrow the search initially to a subset of information, such as that appearing in the *Wall Street Journal*, that can be reasonably expected to be available to the public at large. Even this restriction does not narrow the universe very much, of course, so the

---

[25] It is worth noting in this context that it is very unlikely for anyone who has discovered a profitable trading rule to ever make it public, since by doing so the profitability of the system will be quickly eliminated.

choices are ultimately made by heuristic appeal to the theory of the firm. Analyzing the market's reaction to information that on theoretical grounds should obviously be reflected in stock prices, such as earnings announcements, stock splits, or new security issues, will then show whether or not additional tests of price adjustment to more subtle information would be worthwhile.

Given a particular piece of information, for instance the announcement of a stock split, the problem is to determine if this knowledge can be used to earn profits in excess of those that could be earned without the information. In an efficient market, where stock prices continuously reflect available information, the answer is clearly "no," since the new data are impounded in market price before any trades can take place. On the other hand, evidence which reveals a consistent tendency for a slow price response, or a response that is rapid but subsequently reversed, would suggest that profitable trading rules are possible and hence that the market is not efficient. An empirical resolution of these two possibilities requires a measure of the extent and the timing of price changes in response to the arrival of new information.

A technique which has been widely used to assess price responses to new information is based on the so-called "market model."[26] This model posits a stable relationship between the returns (i.e., capital gains plus dividends expressed as a percentage of purchase price) on a stock during a period of time and the returns on the "market portfolio" (generally represented by a broad-based index) during the same time period. The estimated coefficient between the returns on a stock and the returns on the market portfolio—the "beta" coefficient—is then a measure of the "riskiness" of that stock relative to movements in the market as a whole. For example, the returns on a stock with a measured beta of one tend, on average, to move in proportion to general market movements, whereas the returns on another stock with a beta of 1.5 tend to move more than in proportion to movements in the overall market. Investment advisers have found estimated betas to be useful tools for the construction of stock portfolios tailored to the individual risk tolerance of their clients. Efficient market researchers have found the model useful for another reason, however. Given the observed returns on the market portfolio during a particular time period and a set of betas for various stocks estimated from historical data, the market model can be used to estimate the "normal" returns expected to accrue to each stock on the basis of its relationship with the overall market during that period. Because re-

---

[26] See William F. Sharpe, "Capital Asset Prices: A Theory of Market Equilibrium Under Conditions of Risk," *Journal of Finance*, Vol. 20, No. 4 (December 1965), pp. 587-615; and John Lintner, "The Valuation of Risk Assets and the Selection of Risky Investments in Stock Portfolios and Capital Budgets," *Review of Economics and Statistics*, Vol. 47, No. 1 (February 1965), pp. 13-37. The seminal contributions in the development of the risk-return framework of portfolio analysis are by James Tobin, "Liquidity Preference as Behavior Towards Risk," *Review of Economic Studies*, Vol. 25, No. 1 (February 1958), pp. 65-85 and Harry Markowitz, *Portfolio Selection: Efficient Diversification of Investment*, New York: John Wiley and Sons, 1959.

turns on individual stocks are also influenced by many "firm-specific" factors not captured by returns on the market portfolio, deviations of actual returns from those predicted by the model are to be expected. The behavior of these deviations from normal returns in the period surrounding the announcement of new information provides a measure of the extent and the timing of the price reaction required for testing market efficiency.

One famous application of this technique examined the deviations from normal returns for a large sample of firms which had announced a coming stock split.[27] Examination of the cumulative deviations from normal returns for each stock for a period beginning 30 months prior to the announcement of the coming split and ending 30 months after the announcement revealed the following consistent pattern: The cumulative deviations increased *prior* to the announcement of the intended split and became flat on the announcement date and thereafter. Three important conclusions follow from this result. First, the market evidently *anticipates* the split announcement, since returns in excess of those expected from the relationship of each stock to the market are present before the information is made public. Second, the information is completely reflected in price by the time the split is announced, since deviations from normal behavior cease to accumulate on that date. Third, the adjustment of stock prices to the new information is "unbiased." since the cumulative deviations neither increase nor decrease in the 30 months after the announcement. Thus, once a coming split has been publicly announced, the stock's price fully reflects this information and no further "abnormal" returns can be expected.

Efficient market tests such as this have been conducted for many kinds of publicly available information, and rarely has the conclusion that published data cannot be used to earn abnormal returns been refuted.[28] Trends in the cumulative deviations from normal returns after the announcement of new information sufficient to more than cover the transactions costs required to exploit them have occasionally been detected, so that, as in the case of the random walk model, the efficient market hypothesis as applied to published information does not appear to hold absolutely. Such potentially profitable situations cannot be expected to be repeated, however, since their discovery will inevitably lead to their exploitation and hence their

[27] See Eugene F. Fama, Lawrence Fisher, Michael C. Jensen, and Richard Roll, "The Adjustment of Stock Prices to New Information," *International Economic Review* Vol. X, No. 1 (February 1969), pp. 1-21.

[28] These studies are too numerous to cite here in toto. The volumes edited by Cootner, *op. cit.*, and James Lorie and Richard Brealey, *Modern Developments in Investment Management*, New York: Praeger, 1972 contain many early examples. In addition, nearly every issue of *The Journal of Finance, The Journal of Business*, and *The Journal of Financial and Quantitative Analysis* contains a new study of market efficiency. Two recent studies that fail to support the efficient market hypothesis are Stewart L. Brown, "Earnings Changes, Stock Prices, and Market Efficiency," *Journal of Finance*, Vol. 33, No. 1 (March 1978), pp. 17-28 and Peter Lloyd Davies and Michael Canes, "Stock Prices and the Publication of Second Hand Information," *Journal of Business*, Vol. 51, No. 1 (January 1978), pp. 43-56.

disappearance.[29] In any event, the weight of current evidence strongly favors market efficiency with respect to published information as a very close approximation to reality.

The fact that cumulative deviations from the market model show a strong trend prior to the announcement of new information suggests that abnormal returns are being earned by someone during this period. This in turn suggests that the market is probably not efficient with respect to information not generally available, since the transactions of those lucky few who have access to the knowledge, either directly or through forecasts, must be the source of this abnormal return behavior. Indeed, it is this group that causes the market to be efficient with respect to *available* information by impounding it in stock prices before it is made public. On theoretical grounds, price adjustments in an efficient market should be essentially instantaneous, so the observed long and gradual adjustment may be viewed as the combined result of the slow dissemination of "inside" information and the limited financial resources of those who possess it. Still, in the absence of a complete monopoly over inside information, it is unlikely that any individual or group can consistently reap these excess returns. Because reliable data on insider trading is naturally difficult to obtain, only indirect tests of this form of the efficient market hypothesis have been attempted. One study compared the returns on a sample of mutual fund portfolios with those on unmanaged but equally risky (i.e., with the same beta) portfolios for the period 1955-1964.[30] The idea was to determine if portfolios managed by professional investors, who as a group might reasonably be expected to have superior insight into the significance of publicly available information as well as access to information not widely known by the general public, could outperform portfolios "managed" under a naive buy-and-hold strategy. Only 26 of the 115 funds examined earned returns averaged over the entire period in excess of those produced by the naive strategy, and across all the sample funds the average return was well below that earned by the corresponding unmanaged portfolios. Further, none of the funds was consistently able to beat the market, since those which did so in one part of the sample period were unable to do so in another part. This important group of traders therefore did not appear to have continued access to information not already reflected in market prices.[31]

---

[29] This is a testable proposition. Since tests of market efficiency must of necessity be based on historical data (so that price adjustments can be observed both before and after the announcement of new information), those studies which uncover an apparent departure from efficiency can be performed again on more recent information as it becomes available to determine if the profitable situation still exists.

[30] See Michael C. Jensen, "The Performance of Mutual Funds in the Period 1945-64," *Journal of Finance*, Vol. 23, No. 2 (May 1968), pp. 389-416.

[31] It should be noted that these results may be sensitive to the particular definition of returns and to the form of the model used in the test. For a discussion of these issues see Norman E. Mains, "Risk, the Pricing of Capital Assets, and the Evaluation of Investment Portfolios: Comment," *Journal of Business*, Vol. 50, No. 3 (July 1977), pp. 371-384.

To summarize, extensive empirical analysis of stock price data has shown fairly convincingly that price changes follow a random walk and that new information is reflected in prices by the time it is publicly announced. The significant price adjustments that are observed to occur prior to the release of new data suggest that market participants formulate and act on forecasts of coming events, as required by the assumption underlying the efficient market hypothesis, although it is doubtful that any one group is consistently able to earn the extraordinary returns available during this anticipatory period of adjustment. Thus, the stock market is apparently efficient in the narrow sense that it removes exploitable patterns in price series themselves and in the broader sense that current prices fully reflect other publicly available information.

DOES THE RANDOM WALK MODEL REQUIRE REJECTION OF TRADITIONAL STOCK PRICING MODELS?

Despite the evidence in support of the random walk model, in the minds of many its validity remains in doubt. Perhaps this skepticism arises from the apparent anomaly that stock prices follow a random walk in a world where the progression of most economic events through time is so obviously highly correlated. The efficient market hypothesis reconciles these observations by arguing that investors exploit regularities in the data in the process of forming and acting upon their expectations, thereby fully incorporating predictable events into current stock prices and leaving only random "surprises" to produce changes in their values. Although this theory too has been shown to be consistent with available evidence, resistance to the efficient market-cum-random walk models may persist because many fear that they must abandon more traditional models of stock price formation. The example presented in this section is designed to dispel this confusion.

Surely the most traditional of all valuation models is that the price of a stock is equal at any point in time to the present discounted value of the per share profits expected to accrue to the firm underlying the stock. Consider, then, a highly simplified economy in which nominal corporate profits depend only on past profits (a "trend" term) and the current change in nominal GNP (a "stage-of-the-business-cycle" term). Suppose in addition that changes in nominal GNP arise solely because of current and past changes in variables controlled by the government. Specifically, let these variables be the supply of money and Federal Government expenditure.[32] In such a

---

[32] This is simply the famous St. Louis equation. See Leonall C. Andersen and Keith M. Carlson, "A Monetarist Model for Economic Stabilization," Federal Reserve Bank of St. Louis *Review*, Vol. 52, No. 4 (April 1970), pp. 7-25.

world, one could produce "rational" corporate profit forecasts, and infer the "efficient market" level of stock prices implied by the valuation model at a particular point in time, by applying the following scheme: First, forecast the likely course of future change in money and government spending from the behavior of these variables in the past; second, use these forecasts to predict the probable path of GNP by substituting them into the historical GNP relationship; third, plug the GNP forecasts and the value of past profits into the profit relationship to predict the behavior of profits in the future; fourth, using an appropriate discount rate, compute the present value of the expected profit stream to arrive at a figure which represents the current price of stock (a "price index"). As new information becomes available, the forecasts must be updated to reflect the difference, if any, between actual and previously expected profits. If the new data turn out to equal the expected values, then a re-application of the valuation model will produce no change in stock prices. On the other hand, a surprise in the figures will result in a revision of expectations, and therefore a change in stock prices.

A notable feature of this example is that the universe of relevant information has been intentionally restricted to include only past changes in money, government spending, and corporate profits. The example is also based on the assumptions that all investors know the true structure of the economy and that information gathering and processing is costless, thus insuring that everyone's expectations will be the same. These simplifications, by making operational the rather vague notions that "all available information" is included in rational forecasts and that the market "efficiently incorporates" the information into current prices, highlight the essential characteristics of the mechanism of stock price determination hypothesized by efficient market theorists and illustrates how this theory fits into the framework of traditional valuation models. The crucial question, however, is whether or not the stock price series generated by the model follows a random walk.

In an effort to answer this question, a computer simulation of the model was performed using quarterly data for the United States for the 1948-1977 period to estimate the structural relationships involved. These estimated relationships were then used to generate 25-quarter ahead profit forecasts beginning in the first quarter of 1955, updated after each quarter.[33] The discount rate required to compute present value of each of these expected profit streams was represented by the sum of the real discount rate for equity and the expected rate of price inflation, where the expected

---

[33] In theory, expected profits should be discounted over the entire life of the asset. Since the underlying corporation exists "forever," this means that the time horizon should be infinite. For positive discount rates, however, the present value of the marginal profit forecast approaches zero as the forecasting horizon increases. Experimentation revealed that for the data being considered here, the present value of profit forecasts beyond 25 quarters contributed less than 1 percent to the total value of the expected profit stream. Therefore, as a close approximation to the infinite, a 25-quarter forecasting horizon was assumed.

Chart 4

FLOW DIAGRAM OF STOCK PRICE SIMULATION MODEL

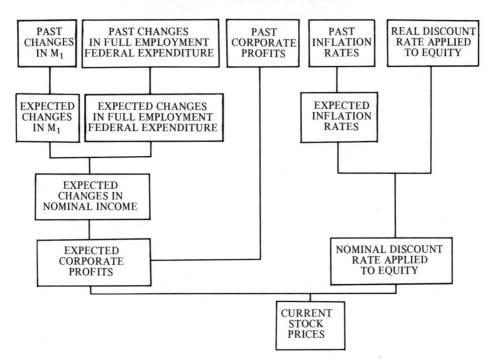

inflation rate was forecast in each quarter on the basis of its past behavior and the real discount rate was taken from a series developed by Kopcke.[34] A flow diagram of the complete model is presented in Chart 4, and the estimated equations themselves are reported in the Technical Appendix. The quarterly "stock price" series produced by the model is displayed in the upper panel of Chart 5, together with the actual quarterly values of the Standard and Poor's Composite Index for purposes of comparison. Finally, the lower panel of Chart 5 shows the quarter-to-quarter change in the simulated stock price series.

Inspection of Chart 5 shows that the model generates a surprisingly realistic-looking stock price series. Indeed, the simulated data track turning points in the actual series quite closely, with the major exception of the dramatic bear market of 1977. Further, no predictable pattern is apparent in the series of successive changes in the simulated data. The estimated correlation coefficient between these changes is only .05, reinforcing the visual impression that changes in the series are independent. In a world

[34] See Richard W. Kopcke, "The Decline in Corporate Profitability," *New England Economic Review*, May/June 1978.

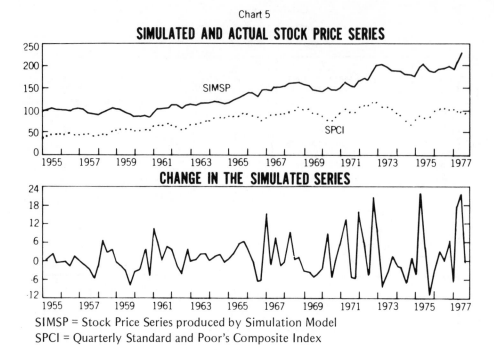

Chart 5
SIMULATED AND ACTUAL STOCK PRICE SERIES

SIMSP = Stock Price Series produced by Simulation Model
SPCI = Quarterly Standard and Poor's Composite Index

where stocks are capitalized at the present discounted value of expected profits, and where all available information is incorporated in profit forecasts, stock price changes evidently follow a random walk.[35]

The efficient market hypothesis thus emerges not as a radical alternative approach to the problem of stock price determination, but rather as a formalization and rationalization of the implicit axioms of asset valuation that have guided stock price models from the beginning. The efficient markets hypothesis makes an assumption about the nature of forecasts, but since it has always been well understood that asset values depend on expectations about events in the future, this assumption is hardly revolutionary. The efficient market hypothesis assumes that stock prices react to changes in forecasts, but this is also implied by models which set prices equal to the present value of expected profits, or to some multiple of earnings, or to a level determined by returns on alternative assets. All that is really new in the efficient market hypothesis is that it extends the logic of these familiar assumptions to reach the unfamiliar conclusion that stock prices follow a random walk.

[35] Samuelson has proved a theorem that supports this assertion. See Paul A. Samuelson, "Proof that Properly Discounted Present Value of Assets Vibrate Randomly," *Bell Journal of Economics and Management Science*, Vol. 4, No. 2 (Autumn 1973), pp. 369-374.

As for the common misconceptions concerning the random walk model mentioned in the introduction, it should now be clear why the fact that stock price changes are independent does not imply that one cannot make money in the stock market, or that prices are unrelated to other economic events, or that professional security analysis is useless. While it is true that *excess* returns will not be consistently available in an efficient market, stock prices do rise in anticipation of favorable developments and fall when the outlook appears less optimistic. Success in the stock market thus involves just the same combination of forecasting skill and luck today as it did before economists began talking about random walks. Nor does the existence of efficient markets imply the superiority of dart-throwing strategies of stock selection, unless the riskiness of the resulting portfolio is considered irrelevant. An investor can make use of the fact that returns on individual stocks are systematically related to overall market movements in the process of designing a portfolio tailored to his willingness to assume a particular degree of risk. Since such information is readily available to professional security analysts, they have an important role to play in a client's stock selection process. Furthermore, it is precisely because so many analysts continually strive to improve their forecasting tools and information processing capabilities, and are willing to trade on the basis of their knowledge, that the stock market is as efficient as it appears to be. The random walk model is not an insult to the competence of professional money managers. On the contrary, it is a compliment.

Technical Appendix
Simulation Model for the "Stock Price" Series
Displayed in Chart 5

Expected changes in the money supply and full employment Federal Expenditures are generated by:

1) $\Delta M_t = \Delta M_{t-1} + .0407 + .465\epsilon_{t-1} + .388\epsilon_{t-2}$
   $\quad\quad\quad\quad\quad\quad (2.81)\quad (5.41)\quad\quad (4.47)$

$\hat{\sigma}_\epsilon = 1.0027 \quad \chi^2_{21\,D.F.} = 17.18$

2) $\Delta FEE_t = 1.0954 + .218\ \Delta FEE_{t-1} +$
   $\quad\quad\quad\quad (2.10)\quad (2.50)$

   $.205\ \Delta FEE_{t-2} + .321\ \Delta FEE_{t-3}$
   $(2.24)\quad\quad\quad\quad (3.47)$

$\hat{\sigma}_\epsilon = 4.178, \chi^2_{20\,D.F.} = 25.42$

The forecasts from these equations are fed into the following two equations to produce forecasts of expected corporate profits:

3) $\Delta Y_t = -.0623 + \sum_{i=0}^{4} m_i\Delta M_{t-i} + \sum_{i=0}^{4} e_i\Delta FEE_{t-i}$
   $\quad\quad\quad (0.05)$

$\bar{R}^2 = .687, S.E. = 8.100, D.W. = 1.521$

Constraints: Fourth degree polynomial; $e_{+1} = m_{+1} = 0 = e_{-5} = m_{-5}$

Lag Weights (t-statistics)

$$m_0 = 2.506 \, (4.57) \qquad e_0 = 0.265 \, (1.61)$$
$$m_1 = 1.704 \, (4.94) \qquad e_1 = 0.271 \, (2.18)$$
$$m_2 = 0.542 \, (1.12) \qquad e_2 = 0.227 \, (1.57)$$
$$m_3 = 0.343 \, (0.97) \qquad e_3 = 0.218 \, (1.72)$$
$$m_4 = 0.805 \, (1.43) \qquad e_4 = 0.199 \, (1.14)$$
$$\Sigma m_i = 5.899 \, (7.97) \qquad \Sigma e_i = 1.18 \, (3.57)$$

4) $\Pi_t = 2.758 + .835\Pi_{t-1} + .226\Delta Y_t$
$\qquad\quad (2.54) \quad\;\; (24.78) \qquad (8.29)$

$\bar{R}^2 = .907$, S.E. = 2.681, D.W. = 1.878

The discount rate applied to the expected profit stream (ρ) was computed by adding to the Kopcke real discount rate figures on expected inflation premium generated by:

5) $(\%\Delta IPD)_t = .405 + \displaystyle\sum_{i=1}^{8} p_i (\%\Delta IPD)_{t-i}$
$\qquad\qquad\quad (4.05)$

$\bar{R}^2 = .352$, S.E. = .588, D.W. = 1.250

Constraints: third degree polynomial; $p_{+1} = 0 = p_{-9}$

Lag Weights (t-statistics)

$$p_1 = .150 \, (7.19) \qquad p_5 = .054 \, (3.04)$$
$$p_2 = .207 \, (7.54) \qquad p_6 = -.024 \, (1.02)$$
$$p_3 = .193 \, (7.94) \qquad p_7 = -.075 \, (2.80)$$
$$p_4 = .134 \, (7.46) \qquad p_8 = -.075 \, (3.65)$$

Finally, the profit and discount rate forecasts were fed into the following equation to produce the simulated stock price series displayed in Chart 5 in the text:

6) $SP_t = \displaystyle\sum_{\tau=1}^{25} \left({}_t\Pi^e_{t+\tau} \Big/ (1 + {}_t\rho^e_{t+1})^\tau \right)$

DEFINITIONS:

ΔM = quarterly change in seasonally adjusted nominal M_1;

ϵ = forecast error;

ΔFEE = quarterly change in seasonally adjusted nominal full employment Federal expenditures;

ΔY = quarterly change in seasonally adjusted nominal GNP;

Π = seasonally adjusted nominal corporate after-tax profits (= corporate profits with capital consumption and inventory valuation adjustments less corporate profits tax liability), quarterly;

$\%\Delta IPD$ = quarterly percentage change in the implicit price deflator for GNP;

SP = simulated stock price series, quarterly;

ρ = discount rate applied to expected profit stream;

${}_t\Pi^e_{t+\tau}, {}_t\rho^e_{t+1}$ = corporate profits (discount rate) expected as of time t to obtain in period $t + \tau \, (t + 1)$.

DATA SOURCES: Data on the real discount rate for equity were taken from Richard W. Kopcke, "The Decline in Corporate Profitability" *New England Economic Review*, July–August 1978. All other data were taken from the NBER data base.

ESTIMATION PROCEDURES: The period of fit for all equations is 1948: II–1977: IV. The numbers in parentheses are t-statistics. Equations (1) and (2) were fit by the maximum likelihood methods of Box and Jenkins; equations (3)–(5) were fit by ordinary least squares.

INFLATION AND STOCK VALUES: Is Our Tax Structure the Villain?*

Marcelle Arak

15

At one time, investors regarded common stocks as a good inflation hedge. Because stocks represented the ownership of real capital, people thought that their value would rise roughly in proportion to the general price level, at least over periods of several years. For the last decade or so, however, stock prices have not kept pace with inflation. The Standard and Poor's index of stock prices, for example, stood at 133 in the fourth quarter of 1980, up only 26 percent from its 1968 fourth-quarter level. Yet, the price level more than doubled in that same period. This meant that the real value of equity fell almost 50 percent.

Why did this tremendous drop in real value of equity occur? Some observers have suggested that inflation itself may account for this phenomenon. One theory is that the tax structure in the United States, particularly that applicable to corporations, becomes more burdensome when the price level rises. As a consequence, a change in inflation can reduce a corporation's real aftertax earnings. This could, in turn, lower the value of owning equity.

This article explores the question of whether the tax system—along with the acceleration in inflation—could account for the poor performance of stock prices. Overall, the analysis indicates that the tax structure may well have played a sizable role in reducing real stock prices. At the same time, the analysis indicates that the tax structure cannot account for the whole decline.

*Reprinted from the *Quarterly Review* Winter 1980-81, pp. 3-13, with permission from the Federal Reserve Bank of New York.

A CLOSER LOOK AT REAL STOCK PRICES

Stock price averages such as the Standard and Poor's index of 500 common stock prices moved up sharply in the early 1960s and then more slowly from 1966 to 1973 (Chart 1). Then, in 1974, prices plunged. Although there was some recovery from 1971 through 1973, real stock prices did not regain their previous peak. Then, in late 1973 and 1974, real stock prices dropped precipitously back to their 1954-55 level. They have not since recovered substantially.

How can one explain this phenomenal drop in real stock values? One simple hypothesis is that stockholders were paid dividends in excess of aftertax corporate earnings. In this case, corporations would not have had sufficient funds to replace equipment or structures as they depreciated unless they borrowed. Whether corporations ran down their stock of fixed capital or borrowed to maintain it, the amount of fixed capital owned free

Chart 1

Standard & Poor's Stock Price Index of 500 Stocks

1941-43=10

Source: Standard & Poor's Corporation.

and clear by stockholders would decline. The data, however, do not support this hypothesis: in every year from 1967 to 1979, corporations paid dividends smaller than their aftertax "true" profits (see glossary). Thus, the stock price per dollar of equity investment, which includes retained earnings, declined even more sharply than the real stock prices shown in Chart 2.

A second hypothesis is that inflation was responsible for the decline in equity values. Here the data do lend support. For example, the acceleration of inflation in the seventies (Chart 3) does coincide roughly with the deterioration of real stock values. Moreover, statistical analyses over long periods of time indicate that stock prices were negatively correlated with the rate of inflation.[1] Other statistical studies show that the returns to equity— which may have been reflected in equity values—were also negatively affected by inflation.[2] All this evidence suggests a negative correlation be-

Chart 2

"Real" Stock Prices

Standard & Poor's index deflated by
the GNP price deflator

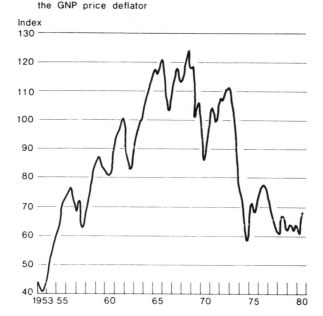

Sources: Standard & Poor's index of 500 stocks:
Standard & Poor's Corporation; gross national product
implicit price deflator: United States Department of
Commerce, Bureau of Economic Analysis.

[1] See Franco Modigliani and Richard A. Cohn, "Inflation, Rational Valuation and the Market,"

in Periods of Inflation," *Journal of Financial and Quantitative Analysis* (March 1973); and John Lintner, "Inflation and Security Returns," *Journal of Finance* (May 1975).

[2] See Eugene F. Fama, "Stock Returns, Real Activity, Inflation and Money," Graduate School of Business, University of Chicago Working Paper (1979).

Chart 3

Growth Rate of GNP Price Deflator

From four quarters earlier

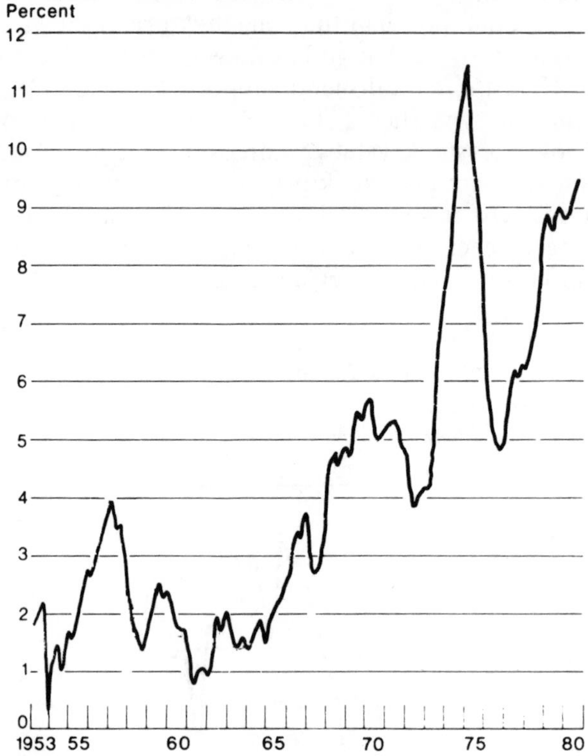

Percent

Source: GNP price deflator from United States
Department of Commerce, Bureau of Economic Analysis.

tween inflation and stock values. However, it does not explain the linkage. One explanation of the linkage is that the structure of the tax system reduces equity returns when inflation accelerates.

TAX NONNEUTRALITY AS AN EXPLANATION
OF STOCK PRICES

A tax is "neutral" with respect to inflation if it collects the same tax monies, in real terms, from a given amount of real income regardless of the price level. That is, the taxation ratio associated with a given real income does not change with inflation. Both the personal income tax and the corporate income tax codes in the United States contain features that are not neutral. For example, the marginal tax rate brackets of the personal income tax are based upon dollar income rather than real income. If tax rates are unchanged, a proportional rise in prices and nominal incomes will put taxpayers in higher marginal tax brackets and their taxes will rise more than in proportion to prices. As a result, a larger percentage of their income will be paid in taxes even though their real income is no higher. Also, the dollar value of realized capital gains is taxed even if the asset did not appreciate in real terms, i.e., no additional purchasing power was achieved.

At the corporate level, the Federal tax code has two main features that cause an increase in the tax burden when prices accelerate: (1) "nominal" inventory profits are taxable[3] and (2) allowable depreciation is based upon the original, rather than the replacement, cost of equipment and structures.

Inventory Profits

Corporations are taxed on total *nominal inventory profits.* Like capital gains, inventory profits are taxed even if the goods do not appreciate in real

---

Glossary

Cash flow is defined as profits before taxes plus capital consumption allowances plus net interest paid.

A *neutral tax* (in an inflationary sense) collects the same monies, in real terms, from a given amount of real income regardless of the price level.

Reported profits (after taxes) are corporate taxable income less corporate tax liability.

Adjusted profits are reported profits minus (a) inventory profits and (b) a correction factor to put depreciation on a replacement-cost basis.

True profits are adjusted profits plus the reduction of the real value of net outstanding financial debt due to inflation.

True profitability is the ratio of true profits to capital, valued at replacement cost, less the market value of net debt.

The *rate of return on total capital* is calculated as the ratio of total adjusted capital income—interest plus aftertax profits, adjusted to eliminate inventory profits and to reflect depreciation on a replacement-cost basis —to the replacement cost of capital.

---

[3] There is no easy way to calculate true inventory profits.

Chart 4

Inventory Profits

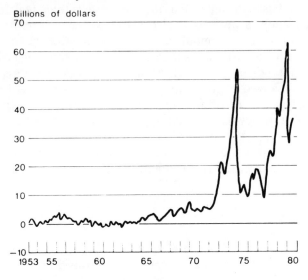

Source: United States Department of Commerce,
Bureau of Economic Analysis.

terms. The value of inventories is typically computed by using one of two accounting methods: "first in–first out" (FIFO) or "last in–first out" (LIFO). For a corporation using FIFO, the oldest item in inventory is assumed to be the first sold. The value of a fixed volume of raw materials, say, will rise as "old" items are taken from inventory and new higher priced ones are added. In contrast, for corporations using the LIFO procedure, the item inventoried most recently is the one assumed to be removed from inventory and replaced with a newly produced item. The inventory profit calculated by this method is typically small, unless a firm liquidates an extensive portion of its inventory. As a consequence, firms have an incentive to switch to LIFO and some of them did switch particularly in 1973-74. Many more, however, were reluctant to do so, perhaps because of costs entailed in making the switch or because they feared that their stock price would decline if they implemented an accounting change which reduced reported profits even though increasing true aftertax profits. On balance, only a small proportion of the inventory profits are computed on a LIFO basis and, in aggregate, inventory profits are therefore substantial in an inflationary period. For example, inventory profits soared in 1973-74 and again in 1979 when inflation accelerated (Chart 4). As a consequence of this link between inventory profits and inflation, the tax burden associated with inventories increases in real terms when inflation accelerates.

Depreciation Allowances

Corporations are permitted to deduct allowances for depreciation of their fixed capital—structures and equipment—in computing their taxable income. These allowances are based upon the "service life" of the capital goods, as specified by the Internal Revenue Service (IRS), and the *original* cost of the capital good. The service lives set out by the IRS are generally shorter than the useful service lives of capital goods. Thus, capital goods can be depreciated faster than they wear out. When prices are rising, however, the depreciation allowances that are permitted, based upon original cost, will understate the true cost of replacing capital goods. And the more rapidly the price level is projected to increase, the smaller is the anticipated

Table 1

The Present Value of Statutory Depreciation Allowances Relative to the Present Value of Price-Level-Adjusted Depreciation Allowances

In percent

| Inflation rate | Ten-year equipment* | | Thirty-year structure* |
	Sum-of-years digits	Straight-line	Straight-line
0	102	108	111
2	95	100	88
4	88	93	73
6	83	87	61
8	77	82	53

* Statutory lifetimes.

Statutory depreciation allowances are based on the sum-of-years digits formula for equipment and the 150 percent declining-balance formula for structures. (For structures, a switch is made to the straight-line formula in the eleventh year, so that the present value of statutory allowances is as large as possible.) The statutory allowances for both equipment and structures use the stated lifetimes. The alternative sum-of-years digits and straight-line allowances for equipment and the straight-line allowances for structures are based on price-level-adjusted depreciation formulas extending over lifetimes 25 percent longer than the statutory lifetimes.

The entries in the table are ratios of the present value of the statutory allowances and their price-level-adjusted alternatives. The real aftertax discount rate is 3 percent.

Source: Taken from Richard Kopcke, "Are Stocks a Bargain?", *New England Economic Review* (May/June 1979).

present value of the depreciation allowances on a new capital good. For example, when the inflation rate is 8 percent, a corporation is permitted to deduct only 53 percent of the "true" depreciation on a thirty-year structure (Table 1).

DEBT

While the Federal code taxes nominal capital gains, which may not represent an increase in the general purchasing power of the asset, some implicit real capital gains are not taxed. Consider, for example, the real value of a corporation's outstanding debt declines and the shareholders' real wealth increases. Yet there is no tax on this real gain. (Unexpected inflation would cause some wealth shift toward debtors even if part of it were taxed.)

Second, a change in the anticipated rate of inflation that affects nominal rates of interest may also benefit shareholders in a firm which has net debt outstanding.[4] Suppose, for example, that the expected rate of inflation rose by 1 percentage point. To earn (or pay) the same real rate of interest, the *aftertax nominal yield* would have to rise by 1 percentage point in order to offset the inflation increase. A creditor in a 25 percent marginal tax bracket would require an interest rate increase of 1 1/3 percentage points to net 1 percent more after taxes $[(1 - .25) (1\ 1/3) = 1]$. The corporation in a 46 percent tax bracket, in contrast, would require a 1.85 percentage point increase in the nominal bond rate to pay 1 percentage point more

---

[4] There are two parts to this argument. The first concerns the tax treatment of interest and the second the difference between the tax rates of the corporation that pays interest and the individual who receives it.

In general, the real cost of borrowing after taxes and inflation is: $r - p - T$, where r is the nominal interest rate, T is the reduction of taxes permitted because of the interest payment, and p is the expected annual percentage decline in the real value of the principal that is owed. A tax which is neutral with respect to the rate of inflation would allow a deduction of the real interest cost $(r - p)$ per dollar of debt. The aftertax cost would therefore be $(1 - t_c) (r - p)$, where t_c is the corporate tax rate on marginal income. One way of looking at this neutral tax system is that it allows all interest to be deducted but counts the reduction of the real value of the debt as taxable corporate income. (That is, the aftertax real cost could be written as: $r - rt_c - p + t_c p$, which is identical to the neutral tax formula shown a few lines above.) In the United States tax system, however, nominal interest payments, rather than real interest payments are tax deductible. The aftertax real cost of a dollar of debt to the corporation is therefore: $(1 - t_c) r - p$. From the viewpoint of the interest recipient, a neutral tax system would apply the marginal tax rate to the real interest earnings. The recipient, under a neutral tax, would therefore be left with $(1 - t_p) (r - p)$ after taxes and inflation, where t_p is the personal tax rate on marginal income. But, under the United States Federal tax code, nominal interest is fully taxed, so that after taxes and inflation the earnings per dollar of principal are: $(1 - t_p) r - p$. If the inflation rate went up by 1 percentage point, the interest recipient would be at least as well off providing the nominal rate of interest increased by more than $1/(1 - t_p)$ while the corporation would be at least as well off providing the interest rate increased by less than $1/(1 - t_c)$.

after taxes [(1 − .46) (1.85) = 1]. Any smaller increase in the nominal rate of interest would improve its real income. Therefore, if the interest rate increased by 1 1/3 percentage points, just enough to maintain the real after-tax cost earnings of the recipient of interest, the corporations real after-tax cost would decline.

To summarize, inflation influences the aftertax real income of stock-holders, reducing it through the generation of taxable nominal capital gains and nominal inventory profits, as well as through the reduction of the real value of depreciation allowances, and increasing it through the tax treatment of debt and debt servicing.

Can we say on balance how large an effect inflation has had on the value of stockownership? First, let us define precisely what we mean by "inflation." For purposes of computing the impacts on real stock values, three different cases must be distinguished:

- the occurrence of inflation that was expected,
- the occurrence of more inflation than was expected, and
- an increase in the rate of inflation expected to prevail in the future.

Each of these events should in principle have a different effect on stock prices. When expected inflation occurs, the real valuation of the first should not be affected; any effect on anticipated real earnings should have altered equity valuation when the anticipation was formulated.[5]

Unexpected inflation, in contrast, can alter the real value of the firm's equity when it occurs since its impact on real tax liability was not anticipated. For example, this inflation would give rise to a once-and-for-all nominal inventory profit on which corporate tax must be paid. In addition, it would cause a loss in the real value of the depreciation allowance on capital purchased prior to the unexpected price rise. Tending to offset these negative effects is the unexpected reduction of the real value of the firm's outstanding debt.

A change in the expected rate of inflation affects real tax liabilities in ways similar to those from unexpected inflation—through the creation of inventory gain and the understatement of depreciation. However, in this case, both of these effects are ongoing. (Note that, in the case of an unexpected price rise, there is a one-time loss on existing fixed capital only. New equipment, purchased at the higher price level, would have a depreciation allowance that is the same percentage of replacement cost as was typical prior to the unexpected price level rise.) In addition, stockholders can anticipate that the accrued nominal capital gain between any two future

---

[5] The real value of equity equals the present discounted value of expected future real earnings. To the extent that actual dividends are less than the permanent level of dividends (where permanent dividends are defined as that constant level which has the same present value as the stream of aftertax corporate profits), the real value of the firm will rise over time. In the case where dividends are equal to permanent aftertax profits, the real value of the firm should remain constant.

points of time will be larger if the price level is expected to rise more rapidly. Should they sell, the realized capital gain and their personal tax liability would be larger in the higher inflation case.

It is possible to obtain a rough idea of the maximum effect of a change in the expected rate of inflation by examining the formula for the rate of return and figuring how much it would be affected by inflation working through each tax feature.[6] For example, the present value of depreciation allowances can be expressed as a function of the rate of inflation. How much a change in the rate of inflation impacts the present value of depreciation allowances can therefore be calculated. The effect on depreciation allowances can then be translated into the effect on taxes and into the effect on aftertax income.

The percentage impact on stockholder returns is an upper limit of the possible percentage impact on real stock prices. If there are other assets whose real returns are unaffected and these assets were available in unlimited supply, then stock prices would have to fall enough to produce the same real return on equity as prevailed before the inflation increase. That is, stock prices would have to fall as much as the real return. Suppose, on the other hand, there were few alternative assets. At the same time, the public wanted to maintain the same stock of accumulated wealth despite the lower returns. In this case, there could be no attempted shift out of equities and the public would simply end up accepting a lower return on stocks. In addition, my estimates overstate the impact because:

(1) The investment tax credit, which has been greatly increased since its inception, is not figured into my calculations. This would offset part of the negative effects on stock values.

(2) Taxes have been reduced on average partly in response to inflation-caused rises in revenues. Therefore, figuring the impact while holding the tax structure constant will overstate the net effect.

(3) There has been a shift away from straight-line depreciation to accelerated depreciation, a reduction of permissible service lives for the calculation of depreciation deductions, and a shift from FIFO and LIFO. All these changes tend to reduce the impact of inflation on stock values.

The results of the calculations for a change in the expected rate of inflation are displayed in Table 2, first column. My estimates show that the prescribed rules for depreciation allowances are the tax element with the largest impact. Indeed, a 4 percentage point rise in the expected rate of inflation could lower stock values by 11 percent through this one tax feature. The taxation of inventory profits and the taxation of capital gains

---

[6] These calculations assume no change in the capital intensity of production and no change in the firm's debt/equity ratio.

Table 2

Inflation's Effect via the Tax System

Component of tax system	Percentage change in equity value due to a 4 percentage point rise in the expected inflation rate*	Percentage change in equity value due to an unexpected once-and-for-all rise in the price level of 4 percent
Tax on inventory profits	− 5.4	−0.6
Tax on understated depreciation allowances	−10.9	−0.9
Effect on nominal debt and debt servicing	4.8†	1.1
Capital gains tax (in personal income tax code)	− 5.3	0
Total	−16.8	−0.4

* Upper limits of the impacts.

† Assumes that real rate of interest earned by bondholders remains constant, the corporation reaping the entire gain from the tax treatment of interest payments. (Refer to discussion in the text.)

Source: Marcelle Arak. "Can the Performance of the Stock Market Be Explained by Inflation Coupled with Our Tax System?", Federal Reserve Bank of New York Research Paper Number 7820.

at the individual level each account for about a 5 percent fall. Working in the opposite direction, the real interest rate effect could raise the return by about 5 percent, offsetting about one quarter of the negative effects of the other three tax features.

The effects of a once-and-for-all bout of unexpected inflation are shown in Table 2, last column. Because unexpected inflation is not reflected in the interest rate, the gain to the firm from the reduction of the real value of outstanding debt is not offset by higher interest payments on that old debt. (In the case of a change in inflationary *expectations,* the interest rates would be higher, limiting the gain to the firm.) This large positive benefit from inflation washes out almost all negative effects of inflation on inventory profits and the understatement of depreciation allowances.

Altogether, a 4 percentage point increase in the expected rate of inflation could lower real stock prices by as much as 17 percent. The expected rate of inflation has probably risen by 6 percent over the past decade. According to my calculations, the increase in the expected rate of inflation coupled with our tax system could account for as much as half. Although this suggests that the tax structure may have had a significant effect on stock values, clearly it is not a full explanation. Indeed, at least half of the decline in stock values, remains to be explained by other factors.

Kopcke and Feldstein, Green, and Sheshinski (FGS) also evaluated the impact of inflation on stockholders' returns.[7] Kopcke calculated the effect of the same four tax elements that I examined, obtaining estimates about 50 percent larger than mine. In a different approach, FGS compared two situations with different rates of inflation. According to their model, a 6 percent inflation differential leads to a 21 percent differential in the rate

[7] Richard Kopcke, "Are Stocks a Bargain," *New England Economic Review* (May/June 1979) Martin Feldstein, Jerry Green, and Eytan Sheshinski, "Inflation and Taxes in a Growing Economy with Debt and Equity Finance," *Journal of Political Economy* (April 1978), Part 2.

of return on equity, a bit less than my calculations indicate. All in all, the different methodologies indicate that the tax system could be an important factor in the performance of the stock market but it cannot explain the entire decline in real stock prices.

CRITICISM OF THE CORPORATE TAXATION ARGUMENT

Although taxes appear to be a plausible explanation of at least part of the stock price decline, several researchers have argued that the historical data are inconsistent with this explanation.

One piece of evidence cited is the ratio of taxes to before-tax cash flow (see glossary). This tax ratio *declined* from the fifties to the sixties to the seventies, whereas the tax structure hypothesis suggests an increase in the ratio of taxes to capital income.[8]

Although the movement of the ratio of taxes to cash flow is suggestive, it is not necessarily an accurate measure of the tax burden on *stockholders*. First, it uses all capital income rather than income earned by stockholders. If a larger fraction of funds is raised through debt, the relative tax burden will fall because interest is deductible in computing taxable corporate income. Second, the ratio of taxes to corporate income reflects *current* taxes. But a change in the expected inflation rate will affect anticipated *future* taxes and their ratio to cash flow. The ratio of current taxes to current cash flow could be affected very little.

Another piece of evidence cited is the rate of return on total capital (see glossary). This rate of return shows no trend in the postwar period as a whole, although it was somewhat lower in the midseventies than in the midsixties, when it was particularly high.

In this case also, it is not accurate to interpret the total return to capital as a measure of the return to stockholders. From the sixties to the seventies, there was a shift toward debt finance which has a more advantageous tax treatment. Because interest payments create a tax deduction for the corporation while dividend payments do not, the increased use of debt will raise total capital income, other things being constant. (Of course, it also raises leverage and riskiness.) For example, a corporation which raised the proportion of capital financed with debt by 10 percentage points could raise its *total* return on capital by about ½ percentage point.[9]

---

[8] According to Fama (1979), the decline in the tax ratio resulted from improved depreciation allowances—shorter service lives and accelerated depreciation—and the deductibility of interest payments. In the seventies, the larger investment tax credit was important.

[9] Let K be the capital stock, D the corporations debt, r the interest rate, and G gross earnings after labor and depreciation costs. Total capital income is aftertax corporate profits $(1 - t) (G - rD)$

Let us look more closely at the income of stockholders and their return on capital. To obtain the income of stockholders, reported aftertax corporate profits (see glossary) must be adjusted to eliminate inventory profits and to reflect depreciation on a replacement-cost basis; both of these adjustments reduce aftertax profits. Then, to this adjusted profits (see glossary) figure must be added the gain to stockholders from the reduction of the real value of their net financial liabilities. Inflation lowers stockholders' real debt to bondholders, banks, etc., so that the corporation could issue more nominal debt without raising the future real burden of its debt; the funds from the new bond issues could be used to increase stockholder dividends without reducing the corporation's ability to maintain the same level of future real dividends. Thus, according to standard economic definitions of "income," such gains on outstanding liabilities should be included in income.

Reported profits and true profits have been very different in recent years (Chart 5). The divergence between the measures in the fifties and early sixties reflected primarily the relatively long service lives specified by the IRS. These kept depreciation allowances below true depreciation. As service lives were liberalized, this situation changed. When inflation accelerated in 1973, however, it became the predominant influence on the relationship between profit measures. True profits began to fall very far short of the standard profits. For example, in the fourth quarter of 1979, true profits were running at a $90 billion annual rate, 23 percent below reported profits.

The adjusted profits measure—used by many analysts—fell even more relative to standard profits. But it is apparent that this measure substantially overstates the effect of inflation on stockholder income. The adjusted profits measure involves subtractions from reported corporate profits for inventory profits and true depreciation but does not add in the gain to stockholders from their reduced bond obligations.

The true profits figures can be used to calculate the tax rate of, and rate of return to, stockholders. The tax burden on stockholders (as measured by taxes relative to before-tax true profits) declined from the fifties to the sixties (Chart 6). Since the 1960s, however, the tax burden on profits increased, in contrast to the tax burden on total capital income cited above.

The rate of return to capital owned by stockholders—the stockholder analogue to the rate of return to total capital—was computed using true profits in the numerator. The denominator was the replacement cost of capital minus the market value of (net) financial debt, as calculated by

plus interest payments rD. If the fraction "b" of capital is financed by debt, income per dollar of capital is

$$\frac{(1-t)(G-rbK)+rbK}{K} \qquad \text{or} \qquad (1-t)\frac{G}{K}+trb.$$

A change in "b" alters the return by tr (Δb). If "t" is 0.46 and r is 0.12, then Δb of 0.1 produces a change in the rate of return of 0.55 percent.

Chart 5

**Alternative Measures of Aftertax Corporate
Profits of Nonfinancial Corporations**

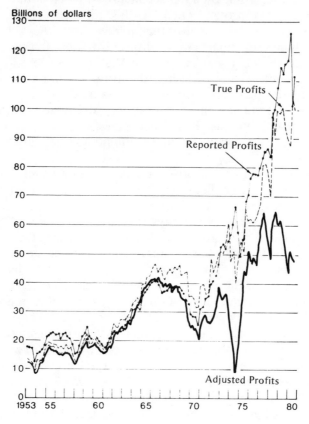

Source: Reported and adjusted profits: United States
Department of Commerce, Bureau of Economic Analysis.
True profits: calculated by the author as described
in the text.

George Von Furstenberg.[10] The decline in the stockholder returns from the
high levels of the sixties to the seventies was enormous (Chart 7), whereas
the total capital return did not decline much.

The data therefore support the view that the tax burden on stockholders
increased since the sixties. The data also suggest that there was a very substantial decline in the aftertax return to equity capital, a decline only partly
attributable to the higher effective tax rate.

[10] George Von Furstenberg, "Corporate Investment: Does Market Valuation Matter in the Aggregate?", *Brookings Papers on Economic Activity* (1972:2).

Chart 6

Taxation of Alternative Measures of Corporate Profits of Nonfinancial Corporations

Four-quarter moving average

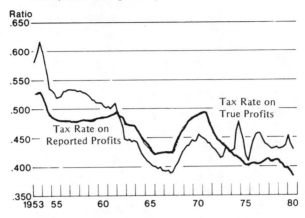

Source: Tax payments and reported profits: United States Department of Commerce, Bureau of Economic Analysis. True profits: calculated by the author as described in the text.

Chart 7

Aftertax Profitability of Corporate Capital

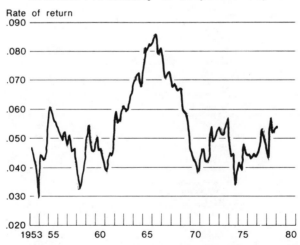

Numerator is true profits; denominator is capital valued at replacement cost less the market value of net financial debt. See text for a description of the calculations and the data sources.

ALTERNATIVE EXPLANATIONS OF THE FALL
IN REAL STOCK PRICES

Economists have put forth several alternative explanations of the decline in real stock prices (Table 3). One cogent argument begins with the observation that our tax system treats owner-occupied dwellings in a special way. In an inflationary environment, homeowners expect the value of their houses to appreciate; at the same time, interest rates will be high, reflecting the expectation of price rise. Homeowners can deduct their interest payments in figuring their taxable income. However, the services rendered by owner-occupied dwellings, that is, the implicit rental value, is not taxed, and the capital gains are taxed only when a home is sold and then only in some circumstances.[11] In effect, if an owner lives in his own house, the "dividends" —the current rental services—are not taxed as they would be if provided by a third party. Also, the capital gains on owner-occupied housing are effectively taxed less heavily than capital gains on other assets because home-sale capital gains taxes often can be postponed by reinvestment or completely avoided by selling after age 55. When inflation accelerates, both interest costs and expected capital gains increase and the asymmetry in tax treatment becomes more valuable. This asymmetry in the tax treatment of owner-occupied housing has caused the user cost of housing to decline substantially. For example, if a person is in a 45 percent tax bracket, the decline has been about 4 percentage points according to Hendershott (1979).[12]

Table 3

Views on Inflation and Stock Values

Author	Major reason why inflation harms stock value	Is the corporate tax structure relevant?	Are other tax elements important?
Arak	Taxation of equity a partial explanation	Yes	Yes, capital gains
Fama	No true connection	No	No
Hendershott	Favored tax treatment of housing	No (Equity values should be helped by inflation)	Yes, treatment of housing
Kopcke	Taxation of equity explains a large portion	Yes	Yes, capital gains
Modigliani-Cohn	Use of a nominal interest rate to discount profit streams, plus error in calculating profits	No	No

Sources: See text.

[11] For those under age 55, gains from sale of a principal residence which are reinvested in a new principal residence are not taxed at the time of receipt. For those over 55, $100,000 of the capital gain may be excluded from taxation, subject to certain conditions.

[12] Patric H. Hendershott, "The Decline in Aggregate Share Values: Inflation, Taxation, Risk and Profitability", Conference on the Taxation of Capital (November 16-18, 1979).

What effect would the reduction of the cost of housing have on stock prices? Lower housing costs will influence people to buy rather than rent and to buy larger and/or higher quality houses. The shift of funds toward housing and away from other investments would tend to push down equity prices. Profits relative to stock prices would then be higher, comparable to the attractive yield on homeownership. This argument is both logical and consistent with most of the facts including the rapid increases in the prices of homes. The one fact that does not quite fit is that bond yields have increased about as much as the rate of inflation, so that the real return on bonds has not risen along with the return on houses and corporate equity.

A different argument is that inflation causes people to make mistakes in evaluating investment opportunities. Modigliani and Cohn, for example, hypothesize that investors use a nominal interest rate in calculations which should be done with a real interest rate. During an inflationary period when the nominal rate is substantially higher than the real rate, this error means that they are discounting future earnings too heavily and therefore undervaluating equity ownership. Suppose, for example, that current dividends per share of a particular corporation are $2, the real return on risky investments is 7 percent, and the expected inflation rate is 8 percent. The nominal return to risky investments is therefore 15 percent (= 7 + 8). With an inflation rate of 8 percent, dividends will probably be 2 (1.08) next year, 2 $(1.08)^2$ the following year, etc. The value of a share of stock is the present discounted value of that flow of dividends. Discounting this stream of nominal earnings by the nominal rate of interest, the value of the share of stock is:

$$\text{(a)} \quad 2 + 2(1.08)/1.15 + 2(1.08)^2/(1.15)^2 + .. + .,$$

or roughly

$$\text{(b)} \quad 2 + 2/1.07 + 2/(1.07)^2 + ... +$$

which amounts to about $30. Note that, according to (b), the current dividend should be discounted at the *real rate of interest*, not the nominal rate of interest. (This is true for other returns and inflation rates as well.) If the current dividends were discounted by the nominal return of 15 percent, the stock would be mistakenly valued at only $13!

In addition, Modigliani and Cohn hypothesize that investors make a second mistake: they fail to include the reduction of the real value of outstanding debt caused by price increases as part of profits.

They test these hypotheses by analyzing the factors that influenced share prices in the past. Specifically, the authors estimate an equation for share prices which includes among other items (a) the nominal rate of interest and (b) a weighted average of past inflation rates that was assumed to represent expected inflation. Since the real rate of interest can be represented as a nominal interest rate *less* the expected rate of inflation, (b) ought to get a coefficient of opposite sign to (a). As it turns out, however, both the interest rate and the inflation rate variable get negative coefficients! The negative coefficient on the price variable is not significantly different from zero in a statistical sense. However, even zero is much too low a coefficient.[13]

The authors interpret this result as evidence that investors are making two valuation errors—misusing a nominal rate as a real rate and failing to include the fall in the real value of outstanding debt as part of equity earnings.

How strong is their argument? Hendershott pointed out that it is difficult to reconcile such a misvaluation with the fact that the nominal bond rates have risen about one for one with the increase in inflation. By his model, investor shifts from stocks into bonds cause the real aftertax returns, adjusted for risk, to be equal. Therefore, if investors did not properly account for inflation, bond returns would have stayed low, in tandem with real returns on stocks.

Moreover, there are other ways to explain the empirical results obtained by Modigliani and Cohn. For example, a weighted average of past inflation rates could be a poor estimate of the inflation rate expected to prevail over the long term. On the other hand, because nominal bond rates incorporate price expectations, changes in bond rates could be a good proxy for changes in expected inflation. Indeed, if variations in the real rate of interest tend to be small, then most of the changes in the bond yield will reflect changes in price expectations. In this case, the bond rate would be proxying for expected inflation and its coefficient would represent the effect of expected inflation on equity values rather than the effect of real interest rates on equity values. By this interpretation, the coefficient of −0.059 obtained in one of their regressions indicates that each 1 percentage point increase in the expected rate of inflation would reduce stock values by 5.9 percent; a 6 percentage point increase in the rate of inflation would therefore reduce real stock prices by about 35 percent. Interestingly enough, this is within the range of the Arak-Kopcke stock price impact calculated from the tax structure.

While many explanations of stock price behavior are related to inflation in some way, others are not. For example, some economists argue that equity prices have declined for the simple reason that corporate profitability before taxes has dropped sharply. Charts 6 and 7 lend support to this view; they show that stockholders' (aftertax) return dropped substantially while the tax rate on stockholders increased only moderately. Another factor may be that the growth prospects during the 1960s were much brighter than during the 1970s. Since stock values are based upon expected dividend growth, the outlook could well be an important element.

---

[13] Expected inflation should have an equal and opposite sign from the nominal rate of interest— to convert the nominal rate to a real rate—plus a coefficient reflecting the anticipated future inflation-produced capital gains on the outstanding debt.

CONCLUSIONS AND IMPLICATIONS

There is no single factor that can plausibly explain the substantial fall in real stock values over the past ten to fifteen years. However, the tax system—the corporate and capital gains tax as well as the tax treatment of housing—probably has played a significant role.

Besides lowering real stock values, the current tax system may impair productivity by lowering desired capital investment and encouraging shorter lived capital than is optimal from an economy-wide vantage point. Moreover, the tax system gives firms a large incentive to leverage themselves. Taken together, there would be important gains from reforming the corporate tax system to get rid of the features which cause nonneutrality with respect to inflation.

Of the features considered above, the depreciation-allowance rules are the single most important in terms of the impact on real stock values. Moreover, the depreciation allowances probably were important in inducing business to build less durable capital than is desirable from society's viewpoint.[14] The ideal solution is to base allowances on replacement cost, rather than on original cost, while using write-off schemes that approximate the true depreciation of each piece of capital. *Ad hoc* schemes to improve depreciation allowances, such as shortening the permissible service lives or widening the scope for use of accelerated depreciation, work imperfectly. Only at one particular inflation rate and with one particular technological mix will they exactly offset the shortfall in the true depreciation generated by the use of original cost. If the inflation rate were to fall, such schemes would lead to higher profits and longer lived equipment than is economically efficient. According to the Bureau of Economic Analysis, Department of Commerce, the understatement of depreciation was about $17 billion in 1979. If this were added to the depreciation write-offs currently allowed, it would have cost the United States Treasury less than $8 billion in 1979, far less than some of the other schemes that have been proposed to improve depreciation write-offs.

Another issue is whether the United States wants to retain tax provisions that allow the full deduction of nominal interest payments by both business and homeowners, and the full taxability of interest receipts. For the corporation, the deduction of nominal interest payments about offsets the taxability of nominal inventory profits. However, for the homeowner there is no similar offset; the homeowner clearly benefits. Although this country wants to encourage homeownership, inflation undoubtedly has widened the encouragement far beyond the original plan. Some tax change that would alter this situation without greatly hurting current homeowners would be desirable.

[14] Patrick Corcoran, "Inflation, Taxes, and the Composition of Business Investment," this *Quarterly Review* (Autumn 1979), pages 13-24.

EXCHANGE-TRADED OPTIONS ON COMMON STOCK[*]

Kenneth D. Garbade and
Monica M. Kaicher

16

No financial instrument has aroused the enthusiasm of speculators, hedgers, and arbitrageurs—and the concern of regulatory authorities—as quickly and completely as exchange-traded stock options following their introduction in 1973 by the Chicago Board Options Exchange (CBOE). Market participants and informed observers have argued variously that options offer opportunities for speculative profits and for hedging or reducing risk, that options provide strong incentives for the manipulation of stock prices and the defrauding of investors, and that options may ultimately be the cause of a collapse comparable in magnitude to the great crash of 1929.

The explosive popularity of stock options is evident from the growth in trading volume from under 6 million call option contracts in 1974 to almost 39 million contracts in the first nine months of 1978.[1] When the CBOE first opened for business, it sponsored trading in call options on sixteen common stock issues. By the fall of 1978, four additional exchanges were sponsoring trading in options, including the American Stock Exchange, the Philadelphia Stock Exchange, the Midwest Stock Exchange, and the Pacific Stock Exchange. The five options exchanges presently sponsor trading in call options on about 220 stock issues and put options on twenty-five of those issues.

---

[*]Reprinted, with deletions, from the *Quarterly Review*, Winter 1978-79, pp. 26-40, with permission from the Federal Reserve Bank of New York.

[1] Exchange-traded options are traded as contracts for the purchase or sale of one round lot of stock which is 100 shares.

The concern of regulatory authorities with this remarkable growth became evident during the summer of 1977, when the Securities and Exchange Commission (SEC) declared an informal moratorium on additions to the list of stocks on which exchange-traded option contracts may be written. In the fall of 1977, the SEC formalized that moratorium and began an extensive study of the options market. Among the major questions being examined in that study are the adequacy of self-regulation by the options exchanges, the financial integrity of the options markets, practices in selling options to individual investors, and the relation between trading in stocks and options on those stocks.

CONTRACTUAL ASPECTS OF STOCK OPTIONS

A stock option is a contract, granting to the holder specified rights which can be exercised against the writer of the contract. There are two basic types of option contracts: puts and calls. Under the most common form of call option, the holder can purchase from the writer of the option some number of shares of a specified stock (called the *underlying stock*) at a designated *strike price* on or before an *expiration date*. Thus, an investor may hold a call option for the purchase of 100 shares of International Business Machines (IBM) stock at a strike price of $260 per share which can be exercised on or before April 21, 1979.[2]

Should the holder of a call option choose to exercise the contract rights, the holder tenders to the option writer funds sufficient to complete the purchase. If an option holder does not exercise the right to purchase on or before the expiration date, all obligations of the writer terminate and the option *expires*.

A put option is a right to sell stock. Under the most common form of put option, a holder can sell a specified number of shares of some underlying stock to the writer of the put contract, on or before an expiration date, at a designated strike price. If an option holder decides to exercise the put op-

---

[2] The concepts discussed in this article are illustrated with options on IBM common stock. IBM stock is widely owned and familiar to many investors, and both the stock and the options are actively traded. On December 19, 1978, IBM announced a four-for-one stock split, to take effect on or after May 10, 1979. Following the effective date of the split, each previously outstanding exchange-traded option contract for 100 shares of IBM stock will become four contracts for 100 shares each, with strike prices equal to one quarter of the original strike prices. For example, the holder of one call option contract for 100 shares at $260 per share will become the holder of four call option contracts for 100 shares each at $65 per share. The stock split will have no impact on the economic position of either writers or holders of IBM options. The stock split will also not affect any of the illustrative examples given below, since all of those examples involve options which expire on or before April 21, 1979.

tion, the underlying shares are tendered to the option writer. The right to sell the stock terminates after the expiration date.

Why An Option Has Value

An option will have value if a holder can profit by exercising immediately the contract rights, or if the holder thinks profits may be obtained by exercising the rights on or before the expiration date of the option.[3] If IBM stock is trading at, say, $293.50 a share, then an option to purchase IBM at a price of $240 per share is clearly a valuable right. An option to purchase IBM at $300 per share is also valuable if there is a possibility that the price of IBM stock will go over $300 before the expiration date of the option.

Tables 1 and 2 show an array of values on twelve different IBM put and call options as reflected in the closing prices on the CBOE on Friday, September 1, 1978. Table 1 shows that the price of a call option decreases as the strike price of the option increases. An option to purchase IBM at a price of $260 per share, for example, is more valuable than a call option with the same expiration date and a strike price of $280. Table 1 also shows that the price of an option increases with the futurity of the option. An option to purchase IBM stock on or before April 21, 1979 confers on the holder more rights than an option which expires on January 20, 1979. It follows that call options with more distant expiration dates will have higher prices, everything else being the same. Table 2 shows that the value of a put option increases with the strike price (since puts are rights to sell, a higher strike price implies a more valuable option) and increases with the futurity of the expiration date of the option.

Table 1

Closing Prices of IBM Call Options on September 1, 1978*

In dollars; per share optioned

		Expiration date	
Strike price	October 21 1978	January 20 1979	April 21 1979
240	56.00	58.75	62.00
260	38.00	41.00	45.75
280	20.63	26.75	32.38
300	8.63	15.13	20.00

* International Business Machines stock closed at $293.50 a share on the New York Stock Exchange on September 1, 1978.

Table 2

Closing Prices of IBM Put Options on September 1, 1978*

In dollars; per share optioned

		Expiration date	
Strike price	October 21 1978	January 20 1979	April 21 1979
240	.07	1.19	2.88
260	.56	3.75	6.50
280	3.63	9.00	11.63
300	11.63	17.00	20.25

* International Business Machines stock closed at $293.50 a share on the New York Stock Exchange on September 1, 1978.

[3] It is noted in an appendix to this article that, under one theory of option pricing, the price of an option is equal to the discounted present value of the price the option is expected to have on its expiration date.

EXCHANGE MARKETS FOR STOCK OPTIONS

Until 1973, stock options were bought and sold in the over-the-counter (OTC) market. In practice, a secondary market sale of an unexpired OTC option was rare. Most of the business consisted of buying options and holding them to expiration, at which time they were either exercised or allowed to expire. The strike price on an OTC option was generally set at the contemporaneous price of the underlying stock, and the expiration date was most often set at one, two, three, or six months in the future. At any point in time there typically existed a wide variety of options on a given stock, with little uniformity of either strike prices or expiration dates among different options.

The innovation in 1973 by the CBOE of an organized market for options revolutionized trading in those securities. Perhaps the single most important CBOE innovation was the standardization of option strike prices and expiration dates.

Looking again at Table 1, note that there were only twelve call option contracts in IBM available for trading on the CBOE on September 1, 1978. There are only four potential expiration dates for IBM options each year: the Saturday following the third Friday in January, April, July, and October.[4] Only the three nearest dates are open for trading at any one time.

Strike prices on exchange-traded options are initially selected to bracket the price of the underlying stock. Strike prices are set in intervals of $5 for stocks priced below $50, in intervals of $10 for stocks priced between $50 and $200, and in intervals of $20 for stocks priced over $200. Trading in a new strike price will be opened if the price of the underlying stock moves at least halfway through the interval bounded by the new strike price. For example, if there are options with strike prices of $80 and $90, the underlying stock must trade at or above $95 a share before trading is opened in options with a $100 strike price.

The standardization of contract terms and the limitation of the number of different contracts available for trading is a deliberate policy decision of the options exchanges. Standardization of the terms of put and call options means that trading is concentrated in a small number of contracts rather than spread out over tens or hundreds of different contracts, as was the case prior to 1973. This has resulted in more liquid markets and has facilitated trading in options.

Purchase and Sale of Exchange-Traded Options

Most investors are familiar with the mechanics of trading stock on an exchange like the New York Stock Exchange (NYSE). Brokers representing the

---

[4] This is called the January-April-July-October expiration cycle. Other options may have the same expiration cycle, or may have a February-May-August-November cycle or a March-June-September-December cycle.

buyer and seller meet on the Exchange's floor and agree to a mutually acceptable transaction price.[5] The seller delivers the stock to the broker, who redelivers the stock to the buyer's broker, who in turn sends it to the ultimate buyer. Payment for the stock follows the reverse path. Transactions in exchange-traded options *do not* occur the same way.

Suppose one investor wants to sell a single IBM April 280 call option contract, *i.e.*, a call option on 100 shares of IBM stock with a strike price of $280 per share and an expiration date of April 21, 1979, and a second investor wants to buy the same option. As in the case of stock trading, brokers representing the two investors will meet on the floor of the CBOE and agree to a mutually acceptable transaction price. The transaction will not, however, be completed by the delivery of a call option contract written by the seller to the buyer.

Transactions in exchange-traded stock options result in the establishment of a series of contractual relationships. Following the agreement of the two brokers in the example to a transaction price on the IBM April 280 calls, the broker representing the *seller* will give a call option contract to an organization known as The Options Clearing Corporation (OCC), agreeing to deliver 100 shares of IBM stock upon payment of $280 per share before the April expiration date. The OCC in turn gives an identical call option contract to the broker representing the *buyer* of the option. The buyer has a right to demand 100 shares of IBM stock from its broker upon payment of the strike price, and the seller's broker has a similar right to demand stock from the seller. Funds from the ultimate buyer reach the ultimate seller through the OCC and the transactors' brokers.

The significance of these contractual relations is that the option contract does not run directly from the seller's broker to the buyer's broker, but rather runs *through* the OCC. The OCC is a contractual intermediary in all exchange-traded stock options.[6]

The importance of the OCC stems from the homogeneity of risk which it imparts to exchange-traded options. In the OTC options market that existed before 1973, an investor had to be careful not to buy an option from a financially unreliable writer. A holder certainly wanted to have confidence that the writer would deliver stock if the call was exercised, or would deliver cash if the put was exercised. A buyer of exchange-traded options does not need to know or pass judgment upon the creditworthiness of either a seller or a seller's broker, since no contract exists with either one. The contract is with the OCC, and the integrity of that contract rests solely on the creditworthiness of the OCC.

---

[5] The mechanics of trading stock on an exchange is discussed more completely in William Melton, "Corporate Equities and the National Market System," this *Review*, box on pages 14-15.

[6] The OCC deals only with brokers who are members of one of the five options exchanges and who have sufficient financial resources. Such brokers are called "clearing members" of the OCC. Any participant in the options market who is not a clearing member of the OCC must have purchases and sales booked through a clearing member. This includes other brokers and traders active on the floors of the options exchanges.

The Options Clearing Corporation

The OCC is a corporation owned by the five exchanges that sponsor trading in options. Legally, it is an *issuer* of option contracts to brokerage firms. It does not, however, act like an ordinary corporation selling securities. The OCC issues an option only when a buyer and seller have agreed, through brokers on an exchange floor, to a transaction in that option. The OCC then issues an option contract to the buyer's broker and acquires an option contract from the seller's broker. In this way, the OCC maintains a balanced book in option contracts: it writes exactly the same type and number of contracts that it holds. The number of contracts in a particular option which the OCC has written is called the *open interest* in that option.

The holder of an OCC option can sell the option by locating, through a broker, an agreeable buyer on an exchange floor. Technically, however, the sale of an option contract by an existing holder is actually a repurchase by the OCC of one of its outstanding contracts and, unless the buyer had previously written an identical contract to the OCC, the reissuance of that contract to the new buyer. Had the buyer previously written an identical contract to the OCC, a purchase would close out that earlier position. That is, a purchase would eliminate any contractual obligation to the OCC. The difference between the two sales is that in the first case the open interest in the option is unchanged while in the second case the open interest is reduced by one contract.

Exercising OCC Options

When a holder decides to exercise a call option the broker is informed, which in turn informs the OCC that it is exercising an option which it holds on that corporation. To complete the exercise, the OCC randomly selects a broker on whom it holds an identical option. That broker will then select one of its customers who has written call options to deliver stock according to his or her contract. The broker can select the customer randomly, or by any other reasonable method. The stock obtained from the exercise of a call option moves from the ultimate writer to the ultimate holder through their respective brokers. Put options are exercised in a similar way.

A broker who has written an option to the OCC is contractually obligated to make good on the option regardless of whether or not its customers can deliver stock (on calls) or cash (on puts). To ensure that brokers can meet their obligations, the OCC requires brokers representing option writers to maintain deposits of cash, United States Government securities, or bank letters of credit or, in the case of writers of call options, deposits of the underlying stock. In practice, the bulk of the deposits held by the OCC is in the form of letters of credit, which amounted to over $780 million on June 30,

1978. The OCC, of course, remains liable for the options that it has written to brokerage firms representing option holders.

If the price per share of some stock is greater than the strike price of a call option on that stock, the option clearly has positive value. When such an option approaches expiration, a holder will usually either sell or exercise the option, since its value will fall to zero following the expiration date. Experience with exchange-traded options has shown that most (but not all) holders of such valuable option contracts never exercise those contracts. Instead, they close out their positions by selling to other investors who are short to the OCC. If the strike price of a call option exceeds the price of the underlying stock, a holder may allow his option simply to expire.

HOW MUCH IS A CALL OPTION WORTH?

Call options have positive value because they impose obligations only on the writer and not on the holder. As Table 1 shows, however, the value of an option depends on its strike price and expiration date. The characteristics of this dependence illuminate the nature of a call option.[7]

The Intrinsic Value of a Call Option

Consider, in Table 1, the October 280 call option in IBM. Since IBM was trading at $293.50 a share at the close of the markets on September 1, 1978, an investor holding that option could profitably exercise his right to buy IBM stock at a price of $280 a share. The net revenue would be the difference between the market price of the stock and the strike price of the call option, or $13.50 per share. This price difference is called the *intrinsic value* of the option.

The intrinsic value of a call option measures the value of the option to an investor who would buy and exercise the option immediately. If the stock price is greater than the option strike price, an option exercise, followed by a sale of the stock, produces a profit. Hence, the option has a positive intrinsic value, and is said to be *in-the-money*. If the stock price is less than the strike price, an exercise would not generate any revenues (it would, in fact, cause a loss), so the option has zero intrinsic value and is *out-of-the money*. The

---

[7] Because trading in call options is far more important at present than trading in put options, this section on option valuation, and the two following sections on hedging and speculating, discuss only the former.

IBM October 300 call option shown in Table 1 was out-of-the-money and had zero intrinsic value on September 1, 1978.

The price of an unexpired option must always be greater than, or equal to, its intrinsic value. If the option price is less than intrinsic value, arbitrageurs will buy and exercise the option and simultaneously sell the underlying stock at a price greater than the cost of the option and its strike price. They will use the shares obtained from the exercise to deliver against the stock sale. Such riskless arbitrage will keep the option price from falling below the intrinsic value of the option. Table 3 shows the intrinsic values of the twelve call option contracts exhibited in Table 1. All of the option prices exceed the corresponding intrinsic values.

The Time Value of a Call Option

Market participants will value an option at a premium over the revenue they can get from an immediate exercise if they believe they may be able to make even more money by exercising the option at some future date. When the price of an option exceeds its intrinsic value, the option is said to have a positive *time value*.

That options should have a positive time value is most easily seen by considering out-of-the-money options with zero intrinsic value. Such options are clearly not worthless because there is always the chance that the stock price will move above the option strike price before the expiration date. In Table 1, an IBM October 300 call option was worth $8.63 on September 1, 1978, even though the underlying stock was then trading at less than $300 a share. Investors knew it was not impossible that the stock price could exceed $300 some time during the fifty days before the October 21 expiration date.

Table 4 shows the time values of the twelve IBM call options contracts. Observe that the time values of options with a common strike price increase as the futurity of the expiration date increases. This shows that "time" really is a valuable aspect of an option.

Table 3

Intrinsic Values of IBM Call Options on September 1, 1978*

In dollars; per share optioned

Strike price	Expiration date		
	October 21 1978	January 20 1979	April 21 1979
240	53.50	53.50	53.50
260	33.50	33.50	33.50
280	13.50	13.50	13.50
300	0	0	0

* Computed as the greater of (a) zero and (b) the difference between the closing stock price of $293.50 and the strike price of the option.

Table 4

Time Values of IBM Call Options on September 1, 1978*

In dollars; per share optioned

Strike price	Expiration date		
	October 21 1978	January 20 1979	April 21 1979
240	2.50	5.25	8.50
260	4.50	7.50	12.25
280	7.13	13.25	18.88
300	8.63	15.13	20.00

* Computed as the difference between the closing option price in Table 1 and the intrinsic value of the option in Table 3.

The Total Value of a Call Option

Chart 1 shows the relation between call option prices and stock prices (both expressed as a percentage of the option strike price) for IBM options with three different expiration dates. On its expiration date, an option will have a price which lies on one of the two intrinsic value line segments. Prior to that date, the value of an option will vary with the price of the underlying stock approximately as shown in the chart. The option/stock price curve will shift closer to the intrinsic value line segments as the expiration date approaches. This downward shifting shows why market participants sometimes refer to an option as a *wasting asset*. As the time remaining to expiration declines, so does the value of an option when the price of the underlying stock remains unchanged.

The option/stock price curves shown in Chart 1 were computed from a theoretical model of option pricing derived by Fischer Black and Myron Scholes. (Their model is described in the appendix.) That model has come into general use among participants in the options markets and is available through several electronic information systems.

Chart 1

**Estimated Values of IBM Call Options
as a Function of the Stock Price on
September 1, 1978***

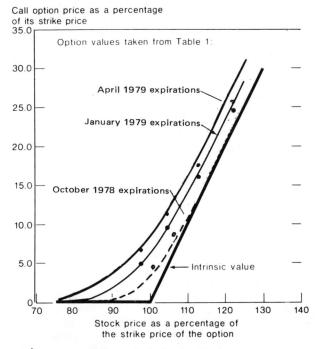

*See appendix for method of estimation.

How Option/Stock Price Relationships are Maintained

Chart 1 also locates the values of the twelve IBM call option contracts shown in Table 1. Although the option/stock price curves exhibited in Chart 1 are based on a theoretical model, the proximity of the actual IBM option prices to their predicted value suggests the model is reasonably accurate. This is the result of arbitrage activity by market participants.

Suppose, for example, that the price of IBM common stock increases in trading on the NYSE but that IBM option prices remain unchanged on the CBOE. The option/stock price curves imply that the options have become "undervalued," i.e., priced below their theoretical values derived from the now higher price of the underlying stock. This may lead some market participants to buy the options and, if they want to hedge their risk, sell the stock. (Exactly how they hedge their risk is explained in the next section.) Their transactions drive up the price of the options relative to the stock price. Such arbitrage activity will continue until the predicted option/stock price relationships are reestablished.[8]

Information on the price at which an underlying stock is trading is a critically important piece of information to the market in options on that stock. Under normal circumstances, stock price information reaches the options exchanges via ticker tapes and price interrogation systems. Although these systems usually report the price of a stock trade within a minute or two after it has occurred, market participants have a substantial incentive to get even faster information. In the summer of 1976, the NYSE found some of its members were relaying information on IBM stock price changes to colleagues at the CBOE over open telephone lines. Their colleagues then bought or sold IBM options in arbitrage activities like that described above. This practice, known as *tape racing*, ended when the NYSE upgraded the speed of reporting transactions in IBM. The incident is noteworthy because it illustrates the value to the options markets of information on stock transactions and the lengths to which market participants will go to obtain and use such valuable information.[9]

It should not be assumed that causality runs only in the direction of stock price changes affecting option prices. The converse, whereby changes in option prices are reflected in subsequent stock price changes, can also occur. Indeed, since call options give an investor substantial leverage of his capital, it may sometimes make more sense to buy options instead of stock, especial-

---

[8] Since clearing charges and other transactions costs are incurred in trading both stock and options, an option/stock price discrepancy must be large enough to permit an arbitrageur to make a profit net of those costs. Thus, there is a region around the "equilibrium" option value within which the actual option price can fluctuate freely without inducing arbitrage activity.

[9] A related, but different, type of activity, called *front running*, involves the purchase or sale of options on the basis of *future* stock transactions. For example, if a market participant learns of the impending sale of a large block of stock, he may anticipate a price decline and hasten to sell options on that stock. Tape racing involves the use of information on transactions which occurred in the *past*, but which have not yet been reported to the options markets.

ly if the buyer has access to favorable information about a stock issuer which has not yet been fully reflected in securities prices. Any resulting increase in option prices relative to stock prices would lead arbitrageurs to sell options and, as a hedge, buy the underlying stock. Their efforts to restore equilibrium between the stock and options markets will push up the stock price, an increase which would appear as a sympathetic response of stock prices to the original increase in option prices.

The option/stock price curves of Chart 1 illustrate a price *level* equilibrium between the stock and options markets. That chart does not, however, give any hint as to whether price *changes* will first appear in the stock market or in the options market.

Spreading

Arbitrage keeps stock prices and option prices approximately at their relative equilibrium values. A similar activity, called *spreading*, maintains the relative values of different option contracts. Suppose, for example, an influx of retail purchase orders on the floor of the CBOE was to drive up the price of IBM January 280 call options. Market professionals would quickly observe that those options had become overpriced relative to other IBM option contracts. They would then sell January 280 calls at what they perceive as a premium price and, to hedge their exposure to risk, buy other IBM call options.

Spreading, or the simultaneous purchase and sale of different option contracts, is an arbitrage of relative values between two options rather than between an option and the underlying stock. It is usually undertaken by floor traders on an options exchange, because their access to trading in options is quicker than the access of off-floor arbitrageurs.

Spreading is important to options markets, because it increases the liquidity of contracts which trade infrequently. In the absence of spreading, a relatively small public purchase or sale order in a thinly traded option could cause a large price change in that contract. Because of the opportunity to spread, however, market professionals are willing to take the other side of a public trade, thereby dampening price fluctuations, since they know they can hedge their risk in more actively traded contracts. Even though they may have to hold a position in the infrequently traded option for some time, their spread hedging removes much of their exposure to market risk.

HEDGING RISK BY WRITING CALL OPTIONS

When an investor owns common stock, there is exposure to the risk of unanticipated changes in the value of the stock. One way to avoid that risk is, of course, to sell the stock. Another, and increasingly popular, way to reduce or to eliminate risk on equity investments is to write call options.

Chart 1 shows that call option prices move in the same direction as stock prices. If the price of a stock declines, an investor who earlier wrote call options on his stock can recover part of the losses on that stock by buying back the same options at their new, lower, price. This method of hedging risk depends on the relation between changes in option prices and changes in stock prices, a relation known as the *hedge ratio.*

The Hedge Ratio

The hedge ratio of an option is defined as the dollar change in option value which accompanies a one-dollar change in the price of the underlying stock.[10] This ratio must lie somewhere in the interval between zero and unity. It will be zero if the option is far out-of-the-money, so that changes in the stock price hardly affect the value of the option. The hedge ratio will be unity if the option is deep-in-the-money, for the option is then tantamount to a commitment to buy the underlying stock. In that case, the stock and the option change in value dollar for dollar. In general, the hedge ratio will depend on the strike price and time to expiration of the option and on the price of the underlying stock. Table 5 shows estimated hedge ratios for twelve different call options on IBM common stock at the close of the markets on September 1, 1978. Note that deep-in-the-money contracts, like the April 240s, have hedge ratios near unity regardless of their expiration dates, while out-of-the-money contracts which are close to expiration (the October 300 contract) have lower hedge ratios.

Hedge Ratios and Small Price Changes

To illustrate how writing call options can reduce the risk on a stock position, consider writing January 280 calls against a position in IBM stock. As

Table 5

Estimated Hedge Ratios for IBM Call Options on September 1, 1978*

Change in dollar price of an option on one share per $1.00 change in the stock price

Strike price	October 21 1978	Expiration date January 20 1979	April 21 1979
240	1.00	.98	.96
260	.97	.91	.88
280	.81	.77	.77
300	.46	.56	.61

* See appendix for method of estimation.

Table 6

Estimated Elasticities of IBM Call Options on September 1, 1978*

Percentage change in dollar price of an option per 1 percent change in the stock price.

Strike price	October 21 1978	Expiration date January 20 1979	April 21 1979
240	5.21	4.66	4.21
260	7.76	6.16	5.24
280	12.37	8.14	6.48
300	19.24	10.54	7.91

* See appendix for method of estimation.

[10] The hedge ratio of an option is also called the option delta, a reflection of its definition as the *change* in option value associated with a small change in the stock price.

shown in Table 5, on September 1, 1978 a $1.00 increase (or decrease) in the price of IBM stock would have been accompanied by approximately a $0.77 increase (or decrease) in the price of the January 280 call option. Suppose an investor owned 10,000 shares of IBM stock and wrote calls on 13,000 shares of the stock. If the stock decreased in value by $1.00 per share, the options would decrease in value by $0.77 per share optioned. The investor could then repurchase the previously written options at a cost $10,000 less than the revenues received when the contracts were written ($10,000 = 13,000 shares optioned × $0.77 per share optioned). This gain just balances the decline in the value of this stock. Conversely, had the price of IBM stock increased by $1.00 a share, the investor would have gained $10,000 on the stock position and lost $10,000 on the option position. For this reason, the short position in options is a hedge against the risk of small changes in the price of the underlying stock. The decision to write calls on 13,000 shares, rather than on 14,000 shares or 12,000 shares, is based on this balancing or hedging, i.e., 13,000 = 10,000/0.77.

Among the most active writers of call options for hedging purposes are securities firms which provide block positioning services to their customers. When an investor wants to sell more stock than its broker can readily find buyers for, the broker may offer to purchase the remaining unsold stock for

Chart 2

Estimated Hedge Ratios of IBM Call Options as a Function of the Stock Price on September 1, 1978 *

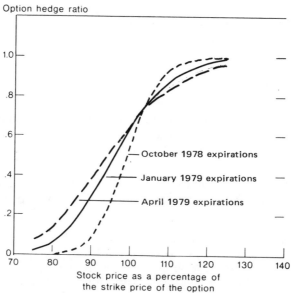

Option hedge ratio

October 1978 expirations

January 1979 expirations

April 1979 expirations

Stock price as a percentage of the strike price of the option

* See appendix for method of estimation.

its own inventory, or to "position" the excess shares. As long as the stock remains in inventory, the broker has capital at risk. Until 1973, this risk could be eliminated only by selling the positioned stock. Because the markets in exchange-traded options have become so active, however, it is now sometimes more efficient for a broker to hedge this risk by writing call options rather than by selling the underlying stock.

It should not be assumed that simply because an investor has hedged a long stock position by writing call options, all risk has been shifted. The value of the portfolio may be insulated against small stock price changes, but it is not immune to losses which can result from sudden, large stock price changes. Moreover, the investor must monitor continually the price of the stock, because hedge ratios change with stock prices. The number of options written against the stock may have to be increased or decreased from time to time to maintain the hedge. The implications of large stock price changes for hedged positions and the consequences of changes in the hedge ratio are discussed in the box.

SPECULATING WITH CALL OPTIONS

When it is felt that there is an unusually strong likelihood of a security appreciating rapidly in price, an investor may be willing to expose capital to substantial risk by making a leveraged investment in that security. Options provide a remarkably efficient vehicle for leveraged speculation, because their values are extraordinarily sensitive to underlying stock prices. Where a stock price might increase by 5 or 10 percent on favorable news, an option can appreciate by 30 or 60 percent on the same news.

The Elasticity of Option Prices

The elasticity of an option is defined as the *percentage* change in the value of the option which accompanies a 1 percent change in the value of the underlying stock.[11] Thus, elasticity is a measure of the relative price sensitivity of an option contract.

The elasticity of an option depends on the strike price and time to expiration of the option and on the price of the underlying stock. Table 6 shows

---

[11] If a call option changes in value from C_0 to C_1 while the price of the underlying stock changes from S_0 to S_1, then the elasticity of the option is $e = ([C_1 - C_0]/C_0)/([S_1 - S_0]/S_0)$. $[C_1 - C_0]/C_0$ measures the relative change in price of the option contract and $[S_1 - S_0]/S_0$ measures the relative change in the stock price. Note that the hedge ratio is $h = [C_1 - C_0]/[S_1 - S_0]$, so the elasticity may also be defined as $e = h S_0/C_0$.

the estimated elasticities of twelve call options on IBM stock at the close of the markets on September 1, 1978. Taking, as an example, the October 240 option, if IBM had closed on that day at a price of 1 percent higher (at $296.44 = 1.01 × 293.50), then an October 240 call option would have closed approximately 5.21 percent higher (at $58.92 = 1.0521 × 56.00).

As shown in Table 6, for a given strike price, option contracts close to expiration are more elastic than contracts with relatively distant expiration dates. For contracts with a common expiration date, an out-of-the-money option will be more elastic than an in-the-money option.

The foregoing comments illustrate why out-of-the-money options close to expiration are considered volatile securities: they are extremely sensitive to movements in the underlying stock price. This sensitivity is well illustrated by the behavior of IBM options during the April 1978 market rally. Table 7 gives the prices of IBM stock and the April 240 call option on that stock at the close of the markets each day for the two weeks preceding the April 22 expiration date of the options. On April 12, the April 240 options were out-of-the-money because IBM stock was then trading at $236.75 a share. Over the next nine days, however, the stock market enjoyed a substantial rally. The price of IBM stock rose to $253.25 a share by April 21, and the April 240 calls expired in-the-money. Between April 12 and April 21, the April 240 calls appreciated from $1.06 to $15.25 per share optioned, an increase of 1,339 percent. Over the same interval, the price of IBM common stock showed a gain of 7 percent. The April 240 options clearly provided enormous leverage for an investor prescient enought to have predicted the mid-April rally. Of course, had the market fallen during April, those same options

Table 7

Closing IBM Stock and Option Prices in April 1978

Date	Stock price (dollars)	April 240 options Price (dollars)	April 240 options Hedge ratio
April 10	241.25	2.94	.60
April 11	239.88	2.56	.53
April 12	236.75	1.06	.34
April 13	238.00	1.44	.41
April 14	243.50	4.75	.75
April 17	251.13	11.75	.99
April 18	251.63	11.88	1.00
April 19	253.00	13.25	1.00
April 20	253.25	13.25	1.00
April 21*	253.25	15.25	1.00

*Trading in options on the CBOE terminates at 3:00 p.m. Eastern time on the day prior to their expiration (April 22 in the above table). The underlying stock trades on the NYSE until 4:00 p.m. Thus, the $2.00 time value of the option on April 21 may be an artifact of closing stock and option prices recorded at different times.

EFFECT OF CHANGES IN THE HEDGE RATIO
ON A "HEDGED" POSITION

An investor can lose money on a supposedly "hedged" position because the hedge ratio of an option changes with the price of the underlying stock. The variation in the hedge ratio which follows a stock price change is illustrated in Chart 2. Note that the hedge ratio becomes larger when the stock price rises, and grows smaller when the stock price falls. One consequence of this behavior is that a long position in stock and a short position in call options may be hedged but it is not riskless.

As was demonstrated in the text, on September 1, 1978, an investor who was long 10,000 shares of IBM stock and short January 280 call options on 13,000 shares was hedged against the risk of small changes in the price of the stock. If the stock price began to fall, however, the hedge ratio on the options would also decrease. Were the hedge ratio to fall from 0.77 (its value on September 1) to, say, 0.72, the investor hedging 10,000 shares of stock would need to increase the short option position to call options on 13,900 shares of IBM (13,900 = 10,000/0.72). In the event of failure to sell options on an additional 900 shares, then for every additional $1.00 decrease in the stock price the loss will be $640 (−$640 = 0.72 × 13,000 − 10,000). Were the stock price to continue to fall, the risk exposure to further price declines would become progressively larger.

A similar argument applies in the case of increases in the stock price. If the stock price increased, the hedge ratio on the January 280 options would also increase. Were the hedge ratio to increase from 0.77 to, say, 0.80, the investor hedging 10,000 shares of stock would need to maintain a short position in January 280 calls on only 12,500 shares of IBM (12,500 = 10,000/0.80). Unless the investor buys back calls on 500 shares of stock, for every additional $1.00 increase in the stock price the loss will be $400 (−$400 = −0.80 × 13,000 + 10,000). This happens because the short position in calls on 13,000 shares now hedge 10,400 shares of IBM, yet the investor owns only 10,000 shares.

HEDGE RATIOS AND LARGE PRICE CHANGES

The loss on a hedged position which can result when stock prices change by a large amount in a short interval of time provides an extreme example of the consequences of failing to maintain the correct number of short calls against long stock. Suppose again that an investor hedged on September 1, 1978 a position in 10,000 shares of IBM stock by writing January 280 call options on 13,000 shares. The portfolio would then be insulated from small positive or negative changes in the price of IBM stock. Suppose, however, another corporation announced on Tuesday, September 5, a cash tender offer for any and all shares of IBM common stock at a price of $400 per share, *i.e.*, at a premium of 36 percent over the market price of $293.50.[1] The value of a January 280 call would rise *immediately* to about $120 a share. This implies a gain of $106.50 per share on the stock ($106.50 = $400.00 new stock price − $293.50 old stock price) and a loss of $93.25 per share optioned ($93.25 = $120.00 new option price − $26.75 old option price). The investor would incur a loss of $147,250 ($147,250 = 13,000 shares optioned × $93.25 per share optioned, minus 10,000 shares owned × $106.50 per share owned). These losses are un-avoidable because the investor will be unable to repurchase the calls while the price of IBM stock is rising; the stock price will move to about $400 a share in a single, large jump as soon as the tender offer is announced.

NAKED OPTIONS AND COVERED OPTIONS

Because the hedge ratio of a call option cannot exceed unity, an inves-tor hedging a long stock position by selling calls can be protected against unlimited losses due to stock price increases by writing calls on only as many shares of the underlying stock as is actually owned. This is called "covered" writing.

Covered option writing limits an investor's losses.[2] In the "worst case," where a stock price increase pushes the option hedge ratio almost to unity, any further losses on the short option position will be balanced by gains on the stock held long. Looked at another way, a covered option writer has just enough stock to deliver in the event his options are exercised, so he will never have to draw on any cash reserves to unwind the stock and option positions.

To hedge fully a long stock position against small stock price changes the investor must write options on more stock than is owned. In the exam-ple of an investor hedging 10,000 shares of IBM by selling January 280 calls, the investor had to write options on 13,000 shares. Call options on 3,000 shares are not covered and are called *naked* options. It is the sale of these naked options which gives rise to the investor's risk exposure on *large* price increases, even though they must be written to complete the hedge against *small* price changes.

---

[1] While an "any and all" tender offer for IBM is unlikely in view of the amount of cash which would be required, tender offer premiums of 40 percent over the market price of the target stock are hardly unusual any more, and as there is trading in op-tions on many companies much smaller than IBM, the example is not without merit.

[2] The maximum loss the investor can experience is the original value of his stock at the time he wrote the calls, less the proceeds from writing the calls. This loss will occur if the stock price falls to zero. Because his options are fully covered, he has *no* risk exposure to stock price increases, although his gains are limited to the strike price of the options plus the proceeds from writing the calls.

would have expired out-of-the-money and a holder would have lost his investment.

Writing Naked Options

Investors can speculate against declines in securities prices by writing call options without owning the underlying stock, or by writing *naked* options (see Box). If an investor is primarily concerned with small price fluctuations, such naked writing will put the investor in a position comparable to that of a short seller. For example, an investor who wrote on September 1, 1978, January 280 call options on 13,000 shares of IBM would have had a position similar to that of an investor who sold short 10,000 shares of IBM stock on the same day. A $1.00 decrease in the price of the stock would increase the wealth of both the short seller and the option writer by about $10,000. (This is obviously true for the short seller. It is true for the option writer because the hedge ratio of the January 280 calls was 0.77 on September 1, 1978, as shown in Table 5.)

Should the price of an underlying stock rise instead of fall, the losses incurred by a writer of naked options will accumulate more rapidly than those of a short seller. This follows because the hedge ratio of an option increases with the price of the underlying stock. (The variation of the hedge ratio of an option with respect to stock price changes is described in the Box.) January 280 calls on 13,000 shares of IBM were equivalent to 10,000 shares of stock on September 1, 1978, when IBM was trading at $293.50 a share. However, if the stock price subsequently rose, the hedge ratio would begin to increase. If it reached, say 0.80, then every additional $1.00 increase in the price of the stock would cost the naked option writer $10,400 ($10,400 = 0.80 × 13,000 shares optioned.) A short seller of 10,000 shares would still be losing $10,000 for every $1.00 increase in the stock.

An extreme example of this type of risk from writing naked options occurs when an out-of-the money option is close to expiration. Hedge ratios on such options are small. If, however, the stock price rises and the option goes in-the-money, the hedge ratio of the option will change very rapidly to almost unity and the price of the option will increase to more than its now positive intrinsic value. A writer of naked options would then face the risk of catastrophic losses from further increases in the stock price (because the hedge ratio is almost unity), and the risk can be avoided only by buying back the options at a substantial loss.

The April 1978 experience in IBM options illustrates this point. As shown in Table 7, on April 12, 1978, the April 240 calls on IBM had a hedge ratio of 0.34 and a price of $1.06 per share optioned. By Wednesday, April 19, the April 240 calls had gone in-the-money as a result of increases in the price of IBM stock. The price of the calls rose to $13.25 per share optioned and the hedge ratio had jumped to unity. Speculators who wrote naked calls on

April 12 suffered substantial paper losses by April 19. They then faced the choice of taking those losses immediately by buying back their much appreciated options or remaining exposed to the risk of additional stock price increases.

Another difference between short selling and writing naked options is that, while a short seller eventually has to cover his borrowing of the stock sold short, a short position in options which expire out-of-the-money never has to be covered. To a writer of options who looks toward the expiration date, if there is only a small probability of an option having positive intrinsic value on its expiration date, then there is a large probability that he will be able to keep the proceeds of his option sales. Of course, as the April 1978 experience showed, there is always some finite probability that a rally will lead, unexpectedly, to options going in-the-money. The losses borne by those who wrote naked options can then become catastrophic.

DOES THE EXISTENCE OF AN OPTIONS MARKET AFFECT THE MARKETS FOR UNDERLYING STOCK ISSUES?

One of the principal concerns expressed by the SEC when it imposed its moratorium on new options was whether options affect the market for underlying stocks. This issue is important because corporations raise equity capital by selling stock, not by selling options. If options somehow reduce the willingness of investors, in the aggregate, to hold stock, regulatory authorities might conclude that restrictions on option trading may be in the public interest.

It appears that options could affect the prices of underlying stocks in three ways: (1) by affecting the *level* of stock prices; (2) by affecting the *volatility* of stock prices, and (3) by inducing *fraudulent manipulation* of stock prices.

Effects on the Level of Stock Prices

As pointed out in the previous section, call options provide a convenient vehicle for optimistic investors who want to make highly leveraged investments in a particular stock. Because they believe the stock is undervalued, optimistic investors necessarily also believe that call options on that stock are undervalued.[12] In buying options for their leverage, optimistic investors

---

[12] That is, even though option prices may be in equilibrium with respect to the *existing* price of the underlying stock, optimistic investors believe that the stock price is "too low" and likely to appreciate substantially in the future. They would expect options to appreciate in value even more substantially as a consequence of the leverage of those securities.

may bid option prices to a premium *relative* to the price of the stock. As the options rise to a premium, arbitrageurs will enter the markets to sell what they perceive as relatively overvalued options and to buy the underlying stock to hedge their option sales. They will continue to sell options and to buy stock as long as they continue to perceive the options as relatively overvalued. Eventually, the buying activities of arbitrageurs will push up stock prices. Thus, the purchase of call options by a group of optimistic speculators may find expression in rising stock prices through the perfectly normal activities of arbitrageurs.

The foregoing scenario suggests that call options, and especially highly elastic call options with substantial leverage, may facilitate the formation of speculative bubbles in stock prices. such bubbles could collapse when the optimistic holders of options liquidate their positions, depressing the relative values of the options. Arbitrageurs would then reverse their former activities by buying back the options which they had previously sold and by selling the stock which they had previously bought. These stock sales may have a depressing effect on stock prices.

Effects on Stock Price Volatility

The existence of an options market may increase the short-term volatility of stock prices, especially when a particular option series is close to expiration.

When a call option is close to expiration, it will have negligible time value and its price will be only slightly greater than its intrinsic value, where the latter is defined as the excess, if any, of the stock price over the strike price of the option. If the price of an in-the-money option which is close to expiration moves significantly above its intrinsic value, arbitrageurs will sell the option and buy stock in anticipation of an imminent exercise of the option. If the price of an option falls significantly below its intrinsic value, arbitrageurs will buy the option and sell the stock. The stock needed to deliver against the sale is obtained by exercising the option.

While arbitrage plays the important role of keeping stock prices and option prices at their "correct" relative values, it also leads to purchase and sale orders for stock, which would not have appeared in the absence of an options market. An in-the-money option close to expiration is a virtually perfect substitute for the underlying stock.[13] The existence of geographically separated trading in stock and options thus gives rise to a type of market

---

[13] That is, an investor can buy the stock or he can buy an in-the-money option which is close to expiration, knowing that it is almost certain that he will want to exercise the latter on the expiration date. Conversely, a holder of the stock can either sell stock or write an in-the-money call option which is virtually certain to result in an exercise. The idea of stock and in-the-money options being close substitutes is therefore quite similar to the more familiar observation that the purchase of stock in one market is a perfect substitute for the purchase of the same stock in some other market.

fragmentation not much different from the more familiar fragmentation associated with multiple markets trading identical securities.

When trading in options and underlying stocks is fragmented, arbitrageurs will send purchase and sale orders to one or both markets as they seek to take advantage of transient price discrepancies. Indeed, the very existence of arbitrage orders is evidence that the markets were not previously well integrated. While this induced order flow is beneficial to both the options market and the stock market because it keeps prices on close substitutes in line with each other, it may also have the effect of inducing transient fluctuations in stock prices which would not have been present had the options and stock markets been better integrated. In particular, market makers may not realize that the sudden appearance of selling interest in a stock is the result of an option trading below its intrinsic value and may lower their bid and offer quotations for the stock too rapidly, only to induce countervailing purchase orders from arbitrageurs. Such surges in order flow between market centers could be anticipated whenever securities trade actively in multiple, fragmented, markets, but they may be especially important in the present context in view of the now substantial size of the options markets.

Observers have generally agreed that the deleterious consequences of market fragmentation can be mitigated by enhancing the integration of competing market centers. With respect to stock and options markets, such enhancement could be obtained either by geographic concentration of trading in both stock and options on the same exchange floor or by improved communications between exchanges trading in options and exchanges trading in stocks.

Fraudulent Manipulation of Stock Prices

A third way an options market can affect the prices of underlying securities is the unusually strong incentive options give for the fraudulent manipulation of stock prices. *Capping* is a frequently cited example of such manipulation.

Suppose a market participant has a naked short position on soon-to-expire call options with a strike price only a few dollars above the contemporaneous price of the underlying stock. If the options expire out-of-the-money, the investor can keep the price received originally for writing the options. If, however, the stock price moves above the option strike price prior to expiration, the investor's losses from covering his short option position could be substantial. The investor may, therefore, try to "place a cap" on the stock price by short selling the stock whenever its price approaches the strike price of his options. If the investor can defer what may be an ultimately irresistible stock price increase until after the options expire, the total loss incurred may be less than the loss if the options were to expire in-the-money.

Manipulative stock transactions can also push stock prices above the strike price of an option. If an investor has a long position in options which are only slightly out-of-the-money, an attempt may be made to push up the stock prices through the strike price by purchasing the stock and then selling the in-the-money options rather than simply allowing the options to expire out-of-the-money.

It appears that the incentives which options provide for the manipulation of stock prices are unlikely to be important except immediately before option expiration dates. Near those dates, there may be substantial rewards to a manipulator who can defer or accelerate a stock price change by a few days. At other times, the capital required to effect and maintain a prolonged change in the level of stock prices will be beyond the resources of almost all market participants. The SEC and self-regulatory organizations like the NYSE, the American Stock Exchange, and the CBOE have substantially enhanced their market surveillance programs and improved their ability to detect manipulative activities. These efforts are important for creating public confidence that the stock and options markets are fair and equitable for all participants.

CONCLUSIONS

The last five years have witnessed a remarkable growth in investor interest in options. This growth can be attributed to the much enhanced liquidity of exchange-traded option contracts. The limitation of contract terms to a modest number of expiration dates and strike prices resolved the problem of trading interest in OTC options being spread too thinly over too many different contracts to permit a viable secondary market. The creation of the OCC as a contractual intermediary eliminated the need for holders of options to evaluate the creditworthiness of ultimate writers. Greater homogeneity of both credit risks and contract terms reduced the "investigation" costs of trading in options and led to greater investor interest in those securities.

Exchange-traded options have now become important as both hedging and speculative devices. The ability to write call options against stock positions has given investors an important new way to reduce their risk exposure to price fluctuations on specific securities. On the other hand, because call option prices are extremely sensitive to the prices of underlying stocks, optimistic investors can obtain substantially leveraged returns from small capital commitments in options.

The growth of interest in option trading has also created new problems for regulators and for the securities industry in general. More frequent occurrences of manipulative practices like capping might be expected in view of the greater stake which more investors now have in options. The SEC and the self-regulatory organizations have recognized the need for much more careful scrutiny of markets and trading practices in an environment of active options markets.

Because the experience with exchange-traded options is still relatively limited, there exist additional problems whose importance is difficult to assess at present. Call options could provide a vehicle for the formation of speculative bubbles in stock prices. The collapse of such bubbles would bring losses not only to options traders but also to investors in the underlying stocks. Nor is it entirely obvious that there is adequate preparation for the possibility of catastrophic losses by writers of naked call options. History suggests, however, that, as the interests of participants in the options markets become more entrenched, the chances for an orderly appraisal of these potential problems will diminish. Moreover, any reform which follows in reaction to catastrophic losses by writers of naked options will likely be excessive. The current SEC review of the options markets is thus both timely and important.

APPENDIX: THE BLACK-SCHOLES OPTION PRICING MODEL

In 1973, Fischer Black and Myron Scholes advanced a model for valuing call options on securities such as common stock.[1] Their model has since become widely accepted and used by financial market participants. The authors showed that the value of a call option depends on five parameters: (1) the price of the underlying stock, denoted S, (2) the strike price of the option, denoted E, (3) the time remaining to the expiration of the option, denoted t, (4) the level of interest rates, denoted r, and (5) the volatility of the price of the underlying stock, denoted v. The stock price S and the option strike price E are measured in dollars per share and the time t remaining to expiration is measured in years or fractions thereof. The interest rate r is usually taken as the rate on high-quality commercial paper having a maturity comparable to the expiration date of the option. The stock price volatility v is measured as the variance per year of the natural logarithm of the stock price.

The Black-Scholes model for the dollar value C of a call option is:

$$C = S \cdot N[d_1] - E \cdot N[d_2] \cdot e^{-rt}$$

where:

$$d_1 = \left(\ln[S/E] + (r + V/2)t \right) / \left\{ vt \right\}^{1/2}$$

$$d_2 = d_1 - \left\{ vt \right\}^{1/2}$$

$$N[x] = (2\Pi)^{-1/2} \int_{-\infty}^{x} e^{-u^2} \, du$$

Chart 1 shows the predicted values of call options on IBM stock computed from the Black-Scholes model for three different values of t. In that chart, option values are expressed as a percentage of the strike price of the option, *i.e.*, as the ratio C/E. The stock price is also expressed as a percentage of the strike price, or as the ratio S/E. The interest rate was set at 8.5 percent per annum, or r = 0.085. This is approximately the rate on high-quality commercial paper that prevailed at the beginning of September 1978.

The only unobservable variable in the Black-Scholes model is the stock price volatility, v. This variable can be estimated by computing the value of v which leads to a predicted option price equal to the actual market price of the option.[2] When this was done for the twelve call options on IBM on September 1, 1978, the average v came out to be .0372. This implies that there was about a 66 percent chance that the price of IBM stock would vary in one day by less than 1 percent of its previous closing price.[3] The value of v = .0372 was used to compute the option values shown in Chart 1. The volatility parameter can also be estimated from the historical price volatility of a stock if one is willing to assume that the future price volatility will be like the historical volatility.

Clifford Smith has pointed out that the Black-Scholes option pricing model may be interpreted as the *expected intrinsic* value of an option, on its expiration date, times a discount factor which converts that future value to a present value.[4] The expected future intrinsic value depends on the probability that the option will expire in-the-money, and hence depends on the volatility of the underlying stock. Other things being equal, options on more volatile stocks have a higher probability of expiring with a greater in-the-money value than options on more stable stocks. Thus, the value of an option increases with stock volatility.

The Black-Scholes pricing model is frequently used by market participants to estimate the hedge ratio and the elasticity of an option. The hedge ratio is defined as the ratio of simultaneous *dollar* changes in option and stock prices. It can be shown that the hedge ratio of an option is $N[d_1]$. This result was used to compute the entries of Tables 5 and 7 and the curves of Chart 2. The elasticity of an option is defined as the ratio of simultaneous *percentage* changes in option and stock values. From the Black-Scholes model, this ratio is $S \cdot N[d_1]/C$. This result was used to compute the entries of Table 6. The values of the hedge ratio and elasticity of an option both depend on the volatility parameter. Because that parameter cannot be estimated without error and because a particular estimate depends on the method of estimation, the computed hedge ratio and elasticity can only be viewed as imperfect estimates of the true values.

---

[1] Fischer Black and Myron Scholes, "The Pricing of Options and Corporate Liabilities," *Journal of Political Economy*, 81 (May/June 1973), pages 637-54.

[2] This method of obtaining the volatility parameter is discussed by Richard Schmalensee and Robert Trippi, "Common Stock Volatility Expectations Implied by Option Premia," *Journal of Finance*, 33 (March 1978) pages 129-47.

[3] The variance of the log of the price of IBM stock is 0.0372 per year, or .000102 per day (.000102 = 0.0372/365). The standard deviation of the change in the log of the stock price over a one-day interval is therefore .0101 (.0101 = $(.000102)^{1/2}$), or about 1 percent. The probability that a normally distributed variable will be less than one standard deviation from its mean is about 66 percent, so the probability that the price of IBM will change by less than 1 percent in value in one day is about 66 percent.

[4] Clifford Smith, Jr., "Option Pricing: A Review," *Journal of Financial Economics*, 3 (January/March 1976) pages 3-51, at footnote 22.

Part II

C. MORTGAGE RELATED
INSTRUMENTS

Some of the most dramatic innovations in the financial markets have occurred in the residential mortgage sector. The first article in this section is by William C. Melton and Diane L. Heidt and focuses on two of these innovations—the *variable rate mortgage* loan and the *rollover mortgage* loan. The economic rationale, consumer safeguards, pricing, and mechanics are among the topics covered. Another mortgage lending innovation is covered in William C. Melton's article on the *graduated payment mortgage*. This instrument was designed to assist first-time homebuyers overcome the high cost of homeownership. By "tilting" the payment stream to more closely match mortgage payments with the borrower's present and expected future income, housing may be made more affordable for the younger, first-

time homebuyers. Another type of mortgage loan designed primarily for the first-time homebuyer is the *shared appreciation mortgage*. The article by Thomas J. Parliment and James S. Kaden provides an overview of this instrument and a framework for decision-making by both the lender and the borrower. In addition to these new types of mortgage loans, the development of *mortgage-backed securities* has enabled mortgage lenders to tap alternative sources of funds by selling mortgage loans in the form of *pass-through certificates* or issuing *mortgage-backed bonds*. These topics are discussed in the article by Charles M. Sivesind.

VARIABLE RATE MORTGAGES *

William C. Melton and
Diane L. Heidt

17

Recently, Federally chartered savings and loan associations were authorized to offer variable rate mortgages. Prior to that authorization, various forms of variable rate mortgage instruments were being offered in a number of states, and several states currently are considering introducing some form of them. This interest in variable rate mortgages is due to the difficulties which the standard fixed payment mortgage has created for many lenders in periods of volatile interest rates as well as the prospect that, as restrictions on deposit interest rates are relaxed, lenders' exposure to interest rate volatility is likely to increase.

As its name suggests, a variable rate mortgage (VRM) is a mortgage loan which provides for adjustment of its interest rate as market interest rates change. Often adjustments of VRM interest rates are linked to the movement of some reference market interest rate or index. As a result, the current interest rate on a VRM may differ from its origination rate, *i.e.,* the rate when the loan was made. This is the major difference between a VRM and the standard fixed payment mortgage (FPM), on which the interest rate and the monthly payment are constant throughout the term. Because VRM rates can increase over the term of the loan, VRM borrowers share with lenders the risk of rising interest rates.

*Reprinted from the *Quarterly Review*, Summer 1979, pp. 23-31, with permission from the Federal Reserve Bank of New York and the authors.

INTEREST RATE RISK

The major mortgage lenders obtain funds primarily from relatively short-term deposits. The FPM, which generally has a term of twenty-five to thirty years, has significant interest rate risk for them because the maturity imbalance between lenders' liabilities and their mortgage assets exposes them to the risk of short-term rates paid on deposits and borrowings rising above yields on outstanding mortgages.[1] In such a situation, the interest expense of lenders approaches their interest income, causing losses which, if great enough, could threaten their viability. As a result of the FPM's interest rate risk, lenders make mortgage credit available on less favorable terms than they otherwise would, and their large holdings of seasoned mortgages paying below-market interest rates have limited their ability to obtain funds by paying market rates on deposits.

During the 1950's and early 1960's, when the variability of interest rates was relatively mild and long-term rates consistently exceeded short-term rates, the maturity imbalance of the major mortgage lenders was of little importance. However, with the acceleration of inflation in the mid-1960's, the average level and variability of short-term interest rates rose much more than long-term rates. This increased the risk of borrowing short to lend long, and thrift institutions sought to reduce this risk by lengthening the maturities of their deposits. For example, in the period from 1969 to 1978, savings and loan associations (S&Ls) reduced the share of their total deposits accounted for by passbook accounts, which are effectively payable on demand, from 69 percent to 32 percent. Mutual savings banks reduced their passbook share from 99 percent to 51 percent. Nevertheless, the average maturity of thrift institutions' assets still far exceeds that of their liabilities.

The constant interest rate on an FPM protects borrowers from increases in mortgage interest costs.[2] Borrowers can also prepay their mortgages in advance of maturity, although penalties typically must be paid if the loan is repaid within three years of its origination, and there generally will be other, possibly substantial, costs involved in originating a new mortgage, such as fees for appraisal, title search, etc. Prepayment may be attractive to the borrower if the original loan can be replaced by a new loan bearing a significantly lower interest rate. These advantages for borrowers are mirrored by disadvantages for lenders, whose return on a mortgage may decline but will not increase.[3]

---

[1] Nondepository mortgage investors, such as life insurance companies and pension funds, typically have long-term liabilities, so that they are less exposed to interest rate risk through mortgage investments.

[2] Moreover, if the loan is assumable—*i.e.,* if it can be transferred from the original borrower to a buyer of the house without the terms of the loan being altered—then the borrower may realize a capital gain in the form of a higher price for his house if current rates rise above the original rate.

[3] However, the lender still has an opportunity for returns on a *portfolio* of mortgages to increase to some extent at times of rising interest rates, even if the rates on the individual FPMs which comprise the portfolio are constant. One reason is that, in a market with substantial housing turnover, many loans will be prepaid well before maturity, so that they can be replaced with loans bearing current yields. Also, as outstanding loans are amortized, new loans can be made at current yields.

The VRM changes the distribution of interest rate risk by allowing interest rates on outstanding loans to increase if current market rates rise. Should market rates decline, downward adjustment of VRM rates saves the borrower the transactions costs involved in prepayment of an FPM and refinancing. VRM contracts almost never provide for a minimum rate—which would be difficult to enforce when borrowers can prepay their loans without penalty.

VRM TERMS AND RATES

VRMs differ greatly in the extent to which they protect borrowers against increases in interest costs. For example, some VRMs provide a rate ceiling, while others do not. Obviously, the rate "cap" is advantageous to the borrower, since it places an upper bound on interest costs. However, it is important to realize that the major protection against interest rate increases may be current mortgage rates, not the rate cap. If lenders attempted to increase rates on outstanding VRMs above the current market rate, borrowers could prepay their VRMs and refinance the loans at current market rates. Thus, depending on the level of prepayment penalties and costs of originating a new mortgage, the current mortgage rate provides an effective ceiling on VRM rate increases. In practice, when lenders in California and other states have been allowed to raise VRM rates, many have not done so in cases where the new rate would have been higher than, or close to, the prevailing rate on new mortgages.

Like FPM rates, VRM origination rates are affected by expected future interest rates. However, the expected pattern of interest rates in the near future may cause origination rates on FPMs and VRMs to diverge. If rates are expected to rise, the VRM rate should be lower than the FPM rate. But, if interest rates are relatively high and expected to decline in the near future, a lender might well feel that, other things being equal, VRM rate reductions could be more costly to him than the possible prepayment of an FPM, especially if subject to prepayment penalties. In such a case, the lender would require a higher origination rate on a VRM than on an FPM.

Other features of VRM contracts which affect their origination rates are prepayment and assumability provisions. For reasons explained earlier, the absence of prepayment penalties significantly increases the borrower's ability to take advantage of rate declines and avoid rate increases. Similarly, assumability is valuable in that it may allow the borrower to sell a house more easily or to realize a capital gain if the loan rate is below current rates and is not subject to adjustment when the loan is assumed. Other things being equal, a mortgage loan which incorporates liberal prepayment and assumability provisions will carry a higher rate than one which does not.

In addition, VRM origination rates are affected by the index (if any) used for adjusting the rate and the magnitude and frequency or permissible adjustments. If the index does not reflect movements in current market rates—or if index changes may be incorporated into rate adjustments only infrequently—

Canadian Rollover Mortgages

Rollover mortgages (ROMs) incorporate interest rate adjustments by structuring the loan as a series of relatively short-term loans, each one of which carries a constant interest rate. At the end of the term of the preceding loan, a new loan is originated at the current interest rate.[1] Since amortization is scheduled over a long period of years, a borrower may "roll over" a series of successively smaller loans before the debt is paid off.

ROMs currently account for almost all Canadian single-family residential mortgages. Although they were first introduced in Canada in the 1930's, ROMs have been widely used only since the 1960's. ROMs exist both as conventional mortgage loans and as government-guaranteed loans authorized under the Canadian National Housing Act (NHA). Both types typically have five-year terms.[2] Amortization is scheduled over a twenty- to thirty-year period for conventional ROMs and twenty-five to forty years for NHA ROMs. At the end of the term, the loan is renewed at the current mortgage market rate.

The government first began to guarantee five-year ROMs in 1969 and last year allowed three-year ROMs to be included in the NHA program. The interest rate on a government-guaranteed ROM is usually lower than the rate on a conventional loan, and the amortization period is longer. Borrowers have the option to extend the maturity of NHA loans to a maximum of forty years to avoid higher monthly payments if the rate is increased when the loan is refinanced. Borrowers generally do not have this option with conventional ROMs.

During the first two years of the term, up to 10 percent of the principal balance of a NHA ROM may be prepaid with a three-month interest fee. Any amount may be prepaid after the two years with a fee equal to three months' interest. At the end of the term, the borrower may make a prepayment without incurring a fee simply by taking out a smaller loan. Prepayment penalties on conventional ROMs vary with the lender. Generally there is a charge of three months' interest for prepayment during the term, but any amount of the loan may be prepaid without penalty at the end of the term.

[1] Canadian law does not require the lender to guarantee to originate a new loan at the maturity of the preceding loan, but such commitments are the standard practice among mortgage lenders.

[2] ROMs with terms of from one to four years do exist but are less common.

VRMs may have little advantage to lenders over FPMs. If current mortgage rates decline to a level below the VRM rate, borrowers have an incentive to refinance their loans, just as if they had FPMs. Alternatively, VRM borrowers benefit if the loan carries a lower than market rate. Also, if restrictions on

VRM rate increases reduce the likelihood of borrowers being unable to meet their payments, VRM default risk will be little different from that on FPMs, and VRM origination rates will not have to incorporate a special risk premium.

Default risk may also be reduced if borrowers have the option of keeping their monthly payments constant by extending the maturities of their loans to offset VRM rate increases. However, if borrowers use the option, lenders may find that the reduction of VRM amortization payments largely offsets the favorable effect on their cash flow of increases in VRM rates. The small increase in cash flow would then do little to assist lenders to meet their rising cost of funds.[4]

VRM ACTIVITY IN THE UNITED STATES

In different forms variable rate lending has been for years a central feature of housing finance in many European countries.[5] In addition, rollover mortgages (ROMs) have been the major mortgage instrument in Canada since the 1960's (see box). In contrast, VRM activity in the United States is of more recent origin. Substantial numbers of VRMs have been made in a number of states in the last several years, and the recent authorization of VRMs for Federally chartered S&Ls should spur such activity further. To date, the bulk of VRM activity has been concentrated in California, and California's VRM regulations served as a model for the VRM regulations recently issued by the Federal Home Loan Bank Board (FHLBB).[6] As a result, there is a tendency in popular discussion to identify VRMs with the specific version employed in California. As the accompanying box on pages 114-117 makes clear, the California VRM regulations are different for S&Ls and commercial banks and also differ in important ways from the FHLBB's regulations. Currently the most common kind of VRM originated by state-chartered S&Ls in California must incorporate a 2½ percentage point cap on cumulative rate increases, and rate adjustments are indexed to the average cost of funds index for California S&Ls published by the San Francisco Federal Home Loan Bank. Rate increases are at the option of the lender, while rate decreases are mandatory.

In contrast to the widespread usage of VRMs in California, VRM activity elsewhere in the country has been uneven. While few states have legislation which specifically forbids VRMs, the law in most states is silent on the matter, and the uncertain legal authority in these states probably has discouraged their introduction. Also usury ceilings in many states preclude meaningful

[4]The seriousness of this possibility is illustrated by the response of California VRM borrowers to the August 1978 rate increase. About two thirds of the affected borrowers exercised their option to extend the maturities of their loans rather than allow their monthly payments to increase.

[5]For example, variable rate mortgages of various types are used extensively in the United Kingdom, France, and Germany. In addition, rollover mortgages are common in Switzerland and the Netherlands.

[6]Title 12, Code of Federal Regulations, Parts 545 and 555.

CALIFORNIA VARIABLE RATE MORTGAGES

VRM Regulations

Regulations governing California VRMs are the product of legislation and of regulation by the California Commissioner of Savings and Loan. In addition, Federally chartered savings and loan associations (S&Ls) in California are subject to the VRM regulations of the Federal Home Loan Bank Board.

Prior to November 23, 1970, VRM lending in California was unregulated. On that date, legislation became effective which allows lenders the option of increasing the VRM interest rate only if the index to which it is tied increases, but a decrease in the rate is mandatory if the index decreases. The index itself is not specified. Semiannual adjustments of VRM rates are provided, with a maximum adjustment of ¼ percentage point. Prepayment without penalty is permitted up to ninety days following notification of a rate increase. Also, the terms of the variable interest rate provision are required to be fully disclosed to the borrower before closing the loan and to be described in both the mortgage (or trust deed) and the note. The legislation was amended in 1976 to provide additional protection to borrowers by requiring a 2½ percentage point ceiling on the cumulative increase in the VRM interest rate. In addition, in the event of a rate increase, borrowers were given the option of extending the maturity of their loans to a maximum of forty years in order to keep monthly payments stable. In January 1978, lenders were also allowed to offer a VRM with rate adjustments every five years and a maximum rate increase of 2½ percentage points.[1] These regulations apply to all lenders in California.

In addition, California S&Ls are subject to the more restrictive regulations of the State Commissioner of Savings and Loan.[2] VRMs providing for semiannual interest rate adjustments must be indexed to the weighted average cost-of-funds index for all California S&Ls published by the Federal Home Loan Bank of San Francisco.[3] Effective June 23, 1979, VRMs

---

[1] To date this new variant does not seem to have attracted much attention.

[2] In practice, California commercial banks offering VRMs in most cases voluntarily adhere to the rulings and regulations of the Savings and Loan Commissioner.

[3] Between June 24, 1971 and January 1, 1976, S&Ls were required to use an index of the cost of funds of all S&Ls in the Eleventh Federal Home Loan Bank District, which includes Arizona, California, and Nevada.

The index now used with California VRMs is calculated by dividing California S&Ls' total annualized funds cost by their average total funds:

$$2 \times \frac{\begin{bmatrix} \text{total interest or dividends paid on:} \\ \text{savings capital, FHLB advances, debentures, and} \\ \text{other borrowings} \end{bmatrix}}{\begin{bmatrix} \text{averages of:} \\ \text{savings capital, advances, debentures, and other} \\ \text{borrowings outstanding} \end{bmatrix}}$$

The index is released semiannually, usually in February and August, for the six-month periods ended December 31 and June 30.

providing for interest rate adjustments every five years must be indexed to the average yield on accepted bids for commitments to sell conventional mortgages to the Federal Home Loan Mortgage Corporation. Also, the minimum rate increase which can be implemented is 1/10 percentage point, except that, for VRMs with semiannual rate adjustments, smaller increases may be implemented if the ¼ percentage point maximum prevented rates from being adjusted fully in the previous semiannual period. Index increases of less than 1/10 percentage point may be accumulated until they total at least 1/10 percentage point. Borrowers are also required to be notified at least thirty days in advance of any rate adjustments.

Effective January 1, 1979, the Federal Home Loan Bank Board (FHLBB) authorized VRM lending by Federally chartered S&Ls in areas where Federally chartered associations had faced a competitive disadvantage in the market. At the time, California was the only state which the FHLBB felt met this requirement. Most of the FHLBB's VRM regulations for Federally chartered S&Ls are essentially identical to those currently applicable to state-chartered S&Ls in California. However, Federally chartered S&Ls may make only annual rate adjustments no greater than ½ percentage point. Also, in the event of a rate decrease, Federal associations must decrease the maturity of the loan first—but not to less than the original maturity of the loan—and then adjust the monthly payments. Other FHLBB regulations are significantly more restrictive. Federally chartered S&Ls must offer fixed payment mortgages (FPMs) as well as VRMs and must provide detailed information to facilitate the borrower's intelligent choice between them. To force Federally chartered S&Ls to continue to offer FPMs on reasonable terms, VRM acquisitions are restricted to 50 percent of their total mortgage originations and purchases. Also, effective July 1, Federally chartered S&Ls must index their VRMs to the national cost-of-funds index published by the FHLBB.

Growth of VRMs

VRMs had a very slow start in California. In the mid-1960's, one state-chartered savings and loan association attempted to incorporate provisions for variable interest rates in its mortgage loan contracts, but strongly negative consumer response discouraged the effort. Two S&Ls tried to promote VRMs in 1970 but met with only modest success. In 1971 another S&L began offering VRMs more successfully. In 1975 VRM activity finally picked up, as a significant number of large lenders began to offer them. Currently there are about twenty-seven state-chartered S&Ls, two national banks, and two state-chartered banks offering VRMs in California. Federally chartered S&Ls are beginning to offer them as well.

From mid-1975 through 1977, the volume of VRMs increased rapidly, as large California VRM lenders had about 60 to 80 percent of their new loan originations in VRMs (chart). However, during 1978, as mortgage interest rates rose sharply, the VRM percentage declined to about 40 to 50 percent, and VRM growth has slowed. The reason apparently is that lenders are offering VRMs on less attractive terms relative to RPMs in anticipation

(Box continued)

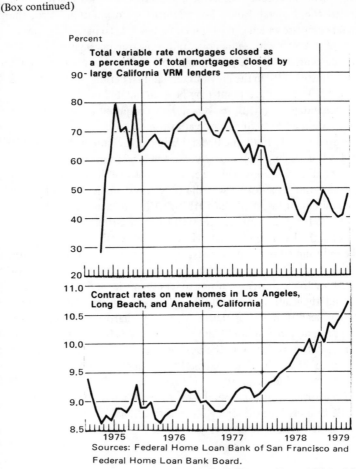

Percent

Total variable rate mortgages closed as a percentage of total mortgages closed by large California VRM lenders

Contract rates on new homes in Los Angeles, Long Beach, and Anaheim, California

Sources: Federal Home Loan Bank of San Francisco and Federal Home Loan Bank Board.

of declining interest rates. Other things being equal, an FPM with prepayment penalties is more attractive to the lender in these circumstances since it locks in high interest rates.

After September 1978 the VRM percentage increased sharply, though it has resumed its decline since the beginning of this year. The resurgence was probably stimulated in part by the California Supreme Court's August 1978 decision in *Wellenkamp vs. Bank of America* that "due-on-sale"

VRM lending activity. Finally, until recently, Federally chartered S&Ls outside California were not authorized to offer VRMs.

Two states with considerable VRM activity are Ohio and Wisconsin. VRMs offered in Ohio are essentially similar to California VRMs, but the dominant form of VRM in Wisconsin differs from most others in that its rate is not tied to an index. Called the "escalator clause mortgage", it provides for a constant rate for three years, after which the rate may be adjusted once a year. The borrower is protected by restrictions on rate increases. The maximum initial rate increase is 1 percentage point, and a 0.5 percentage point maximum ap-

clauses in mortgage contracts cannot be exercised by lenders in order to increase interest rates on mortgages to current market levels.[4] The decision severely reduces lenders' ability to increase interest rates on FPMs in the active California housing market. Unless the law is changed or the Court reserves itself, VRMs should be even more attractive to California lenders in the future than they were in the past.

VRM Rate Changes

Interest rates on VRMs have decreased only once since 1970 but have increased several times. Following a rate decrease of 15 basis points in October 1972, the only S&L actively lending through VRMs implemented 25 basis point rate increases in April and October 1974 and in April 1975. The first rate increase implemented by a significant number of large lenders occurred following the August 1978 announcement that the cost-of-funds index increased in the first half of 1978 by 12.9 basis points. This increase in the cost of funds, plus earlier small accumulated increases, allowed about a 20 to 22 basis point rise in VRM rates, and twenty S&Ls out of twenty-one implemented it for most of their VRMs. There was very little consumer reaction to the increases. According to a survey conducted by the California Commissioner of Savings and Loan, only 4 percent of the borrowers who received notice that their rates were being raised wrote inquiries to lenders, and only 5 percent of the inquiries were complaints. A large majority of VRM borrowers—67 percent—decided to extend the maturity of their loans to avoid any increase in monthly payments. Most recently, the San Francisco FHLB announced in February of this year that, in the second half of 1978, the cost-of-funds index increased 30.1 basis points. This increase allowed lenders to raise their rates on most VRMs by the maximum increase of 25 basis points, with a further 5 basis point increase possible six months later.

---

[4] A due-on-sale clause is a device commonly used in real property security transactions to provide, at the lender's option, for acceleration of the maturity of the loan upon the sale of the real property security.

plies to successive increases. Borrowers are also protected to some extent by the option to prepay their loans without penalty within four months following a rate increase or anytime the rate is 2 percentage points or more above the original contract rate. For this kind of VRM, then, the current mortgage rate serves as an effective "index", since the virtual absence of prepayment penalties insures that lenders will not increase rates on outstanding VRMs above current mortgage rates.

Wisconsin lenders may offer a California-type VRM as well as the escalator clause mortgage. However, lenders strongly prefer the "escalator", and virtually all state-chartered S&Ls offer it, as do a number of Federally chartered S&Ls.[7] In contrast, activity in the California-type VRM is negligible. Though there were some complaints from borrowers who had their interest rates increased in 1974, following 1975 legislation governing the frequency and size of increases, rate adjustments seem generally to have been accepted by borrowers.

There has also been substantial VRM activity in several New England states, most notably Massachusetts.[8] VRMs in New England differ in a number of respects from those in California. Typically there is no cap on cumulative upward adjustments of VRM rates, and borrowers have either very limited options to extend maturities to offset rate increases or none at all. Indexes used also vary. In Maine and New Hampshire, VRM lenders generally have used as an index some measure of the cost of funds to lending institutions. In Massachusetts and Connecticut the norm is an index of current interest rates on new mortgages. Absence of a cap on rate increases and a maturity-extension option, together with indexation to mortgage rates, means that VRM borrowers in New England share more interest rate risk than their California counterparts. As a result, VRM lenders in New England must offer more attractive "discounts" off the FPM lending rate than do California VRM lenders. In New England the norm seems to be about a ½ percentage point reduction of the VRM rate relative to the FPM rate—considerably greater than the typical reductions of ¼ percentage point or less in California.

VRMs AS SHORT-TERM MORTGAGES

Borrowers seem to have responded to the substantial rate discounts offered in New England by favoring VRMs over FPMs when they expected to move, to sell their homes, and to prepay their mortgages in the near future. Although it is still too early to say so definitely, it appears that substantially lower initial rates on VRMs may lead to selection of borrowers preferring lower current interest rates in anticipation of prepaying their loans well before any substantial rate increases will have occurred. If this proves to be generally true, then VRMs, instead of functioning solely as a long-term variable-rate lending instrument, in effect would also be a device for making short-term mortgage loans. Indeed, at least one New England mortgage lender has specifically designed and marketed its VRM to appeal to "transient" homeowners who expect to move within a few years after originating their mortgages.

---

[7] There is some uncertainty as to whether an escalator clause mortgage complies with FHLBB regulations, which in general prohibit loans with an increasing sequence of monthly payments. Some Federally chartered S&Ls avoid the appearance of a conflict by extending the term of the mortgage to offset the effect of a rate increase on monthly payments. Others have interpreted the regulation as allowing them to increase monthly payments.

[8] A number of lenders in New England also offer ROMs similar to those used in Canada.

The major advantage to such a use of the VRM is that, under certain circumstances, it allows individuals who expect to be short-term borrowers to reduce their borrowing costs. In addition, borrowers avoid both the expense of writing a new loan upon maturity of a short-term loan and the risk that new finance might not be available then. Moreover, borrowers have flexibility in determining when to prepay or transfer their loans (if the loans are assumable). Thus, VRMs may provide a mechanism through which lenders, without attempting to screen short-term borrowers from long-term borrowers, may offer what are in effect short-term mortgage loans while retaining for borrowers many of the advantages of long-term financing.

CONSUMER PROTECTION

Consumer protection figures prominently in most discussions of VRMs. At the heart of the issue is disclosure of the terms of the mortgage contract. The FHLBB and a number of states have promulgated comprehensive regulations designed to insure that a borrower understands his potential mortgage costs with a VRM. By encouraging consumers to evaluate their borrowing options carefully and by insuring that lenders disclose to borrowers all information relevant for an intelligent choice between different mortgage instruments, these regulations facilitate the sound development of VRMs.

In addition to disclosure regulations, consumer protection measures have taken several other forms. For example, for many lenders the FPM is, for all practical purposes, the only mortgage design permitted. As a means for implementing consumer protection, such a draconian approach has obvious drawbacks.

Another approach to consumer protection is incorporated in the regulations issued by the FHLBB in December of last year, which required that any Federally chartered S&L offering VRMs also offer FPMs to prospective borrowers to assure them "the freedom to choose". While there are some mortgage lenders which lend only through VRMs, the great majority of VRM lenders also offer FPMs. There are two main reasons. First, since many individuals continue to prefer fixed monthly payments, it can still be profitable for lenders to offer FPMs. Second, for reasons developed more fully below, the VRM is likely to gain less acceptance in the secondary mortgage market than the FPM, so that lenders desiring to originate and sell mortgages have a strong incentive to offer FPMs. In light of these factors, the FHLBB's regulation will probably have little overall effect, though it may constrain some individual lenders.

Another, more important, way in which regulators and legislators occasionally have sought to protect the interest of borrowers is through placing restrictions on the form of the mortgage contract. For example, California VRMs have a 2½ percentage point cap on cumulative rate increases, and lenders must permit borrowers to extend the maturity of their loans (subject to certain limitations) to prevent rate increases from adding to their monthly payments. Since these features make VRMs more similar to FPMs and thus lessen their attractiveness to lenders, they contribute to limiting the rate discounts offered on California VRMs.

Also contributing to the smallness of the discounts is the linkage of most VRM rates to a statewide S&L cost-of-funds index. The California requirement resulted from a view that VRMs should enable lenders only to recoup variations in their average cost of funds and should not reflect movements in mortgage rates unrelated to movements in the cost of funds. While this view has an intuitive appeal as a means of insulating lenders' profits from fluctuations in the cost of funds, the insulation provided is only partial. In a period of rising interest rates, lenders' average returns on VRMs will rise about in tandem with their average funds costs, and their profit rates will be relatively stable. However, in a period of declining interest rates, yields on new mortgages will probably fall more than average funds costs, causing downward adjustments of VRM rates to lag behind the declining mortgage rates. Such a situation might lead to some consumer resentment until mortgage rates declined sufficiently to make it attractive for borrowers to prepay the VRMs and refinance them. As a result, returns on VRMs indexed to lenders' average cost of funds should rise roughly in tandem with average funds costs as rates rise, but probably will fall disproportionately as rates decline. This prospect clearly limits the magnitude of rate discounts which lenders can offer on VRMs.

Indexing VRM rates to funds costs also contributes to concerns that the progressive removal of deposit interest ceilings may raise funds costs and thus increase VRM rates, at least until the cap rates are encountered. The actual situation is more complex—and less threatening to borrowers—since they may prepay and refinance VRMs if their rates get out of line with market mortgage rates. No doubt some increases of mortgage rates will result from removal of deposit interest ceilings, but these will probably be substantially less than the increases in deposit interest rates.[9] The probable result, then, is that current mortgage rates will constrain increases in VRM rates resulting from indexing the rates to lenders' funds costs.

Since California VRMs are less attractive to lenders than those indexed to mortgage rates without rate caps and maturity extension options, it is not surprising that VRM rate discounts in California are relatively small. Ironically, though California VRMs do incorporate protections for consumers, they may also prevent individuals who expect to remain in their homes for relatively short periods of time from obtaining more favorable mortgage rates than long-term borrowers. In a housing market with turnover as high as that in California, the generally small rate discounts available to short-term borrowers may represent a considerable cost to consumers.

---

[9]Part of the reason is that as deposit interest ceilings are removed, lenders may initiate explicit charges for services heretofore provided free as a form of noninterest renumeration. In addition, many investors in the mortgage market—such as insurance companies and pension funds—are unaffected by deposit interest ceilings, and their demand for mortgages will dampen upward movements in mortgage rates relative to rates on alternative investments.

VRMs IN THE SECONDARY MORTGAGE MARKET

Because VRMs are a new mortgage instrument, sales of VRMs in the secondary mortgage market are a relatively new phenomenon. They are almost always arranged through negotiation between the originator and the investor—either directly or through a broker. However, in March 1978, the first public offering of VRM pass-through securities was made by the Home Savings and Loan Association of Los Angeles, the largest S&L in the country. The issue was well received by primarily institutional investors. A second issue in October met a somewhat poorer reception, and there have been no further public offerings of VRM pass-through securities since then. At this time, two main factors account for the relative unattractiveness of California VRMs in the secondary market. The California usury law limits the interest rate increases which out-of-state investors may expect.[10] Also, prevailing expectations of future declines in interest rates make fixed-rate investments more attractive to investors. Should rates decline significantly, public offerings of VRM pass-through securities could become attractive once again.

Nevertheless, a number of obstacles currently prevent VRMs from becoming a standard fixture of the secondary market. Since some states prohibit VRMs, lenders in such states may not buy them—either as whole loans or as participation certificates in pools of VRMs—for inclusion in their portfolios.[11] Moreover, even in states where VRMs are legal, Federally chartered S&Ls cannot purchase VRMs originated, for example, by California lenders with terms different from those authorized by the FHLBB. Also, Federal housing agencies such as the Federal National Mortgage Association and the Federal Home Loan Mortgage Corporation currently do not purchase VRMs.

The fundamental obstacle to purchases by the housing agencies as well as to trading VRMs in the secondary market is their lack of uniformity. Non-homogeneous mortgage pass-through securities can be traded only after some detailed examination of the underlying mortgages. While newly issued Government National Mortgage Association pass-through securities bearing a given contract interest rate are uniform as to the contract rate and the original term, VRM pass-through securities, even if they have the same origination rate, may have different rate caps and different rate indexes. Moreover, although the indexes could be formally identical, different regional conditions affecting funds costs or current mortgage rates—especially state usury ceilings—might lead to variations in the pattern of implementation of VRM rate adjustments. Thus, with regional differences in deposit and mortgage markets, the origination rates as well as the course of rate adjustments will differ from one region to another. As a result, it will be difficult to trade VRM pass-

---

[10] Out-of-state lenders are subject to a 10 percent usury ceiling which does not apply to California S&Ls and commercial banks.

[11] However, since FHLBB regulations authorizing VRMs take precedence over such state laws, Federally chartered S&Ls in such states may offer VRMs.

through securities without some inspection of the underlying mortgages. This situation clearly favors determination of the terms of secondary market transactions in VRMs through negotiation between the buyer and seller, either directly or through a broker. Where the offering is large enough and the seller is sufficiently well-known to investors, it may be feasible to arrange a public offering. But, due to the lack of uniformity of VRMs, it will be difficult for securities dealers to "make markets" for them by posting the prices at which they stand ready to buy and sell.

To avoid such "fragmentation" of the secondary market for VRMs, a single, nationwide index has been suggested in place of the various local or regional indexes currently being used. The FHLBB lent support to this view in its recent regulations which required that all Federally chartered S&Ls offering VRMs after July 1 use the same nationwide cost-of-funds index. While widespread adoption of a uniform index clearly would reduce the variety of VRMs, several problems would remain. First, not all lenders would be attracted to the uniform index. For example, lenders in California might prefer to continue to index their VRMs to their average cost of funds. The California average cost of funds generally has tracked the national average very closely —the simple correlation coefficient between the two indexes is 0.99—but discrepancies have emerged, especially during periods of rising interest rates. Another reason why lenders might prefer to avoid using the nationwide index is that they might want to use VRMs to make short-term mortgage loans as described earlier, in which case they probably would want to index them to current mortgage rates. Moreover, even if all VRMs were tied to the nationwide index, local mortgage market conditions, including usury ceilings, would affect the ability of lenders to implement the VRM rate adjustments allowed by the national index. As a result, some heterogeneity would remain. Thus, use of a national index, though it will increase the uniformity of VRMs, does not appear likely to eliminate the fragmentation of the secondary market for VRMs.

OUTLOOK FOR VRMs

While it is difficult to predict the future growth and impact of VRMs, experience in California and elsewhere suggests that they should enjoy a ready market in states where they have not yet been introduced. In the near future VRMs are likely to spread more widely throughout the country. Effective July 1, the FHLBB authorized Federally chartered S&Ls in all states to offer VRMs and, as pressure grows to raise or eliminate deposit interest ceilings, interest in expanding lending through VRMs should increase. As more lenders are able to use VRMs to reduce the risk of lending long and borrowing short, VRMs should have a favorable impact on the supply of mortgage credit throughout the business cycle.

Experience to date illustrates the variety of feasible VRM designs, including nonindexed VRMs like the Canadian ROM and the "escalator clause" mortgage popular in Wisconsin, VRMs indexed to current mortgage rates as in New England, and VRMs indexed to a measure of lenders' funds costs as in California. Some of these VRMs provide borrowers considerable protection against future rate increases, though not so much as an FPM. But such protection is generally obtained only at the cost of higher origination rates, which may prevent short-term borrowers from reducing their borrowing costs with a VRM. Thus, in the future development of VRMs, the cost of imposing restrictions on the form of VRMs should be weighed carefully against the expected benefits.

GRADUATED PAYMENT MORTGAGES*

William C. Melton

18

In the space of a few years graduated payment mortgages have achieved fairly widespread acceptance. They presently are the most rapidly growing category of Federal Housing Administration (FHA)-insured mortgages, and legislation has recently been enacted which could expand their use still further. Moreover, the private sector has begun to offer a novel form of mortgage loan which allows the lender to receive a stream of constant payments while the borrower makes graduated payments.

The need to come to grips with the problems which high rates of inflation create for the standard fixed payment mortgage (FPM) has provided the impetus for two basic modifications of the FPM. Variable rate mortgages provide for interest rate adjustments to share the risk of interest rate changes between borrower and lender, but otherwise employ the same schedule of constant monthly payments of interest and principal as the FPM.[1] In contrast, the graduated payment mortgage (GPM) retains the constant interest rate of the FPM, but lowers the monthly payments in the early years of the loan and increases them according to a predetermined schedule.

This article would not have been possible without the assistance of Henry J. Cassidy, Chester C. Foster, Diane L. Heidt, and Warren Lasko, none of whom bear any responsibility for the views expressed herein.

*Reprinted from the *Quarterly Review*, Spring 1980, pp. 21-28, with permission from the Federal Reserve Bank of New York.

[1] See William C. Melton and Diane L. Heidt, "Variable Rate Mortgages", this *Review* (Summer 1979), pages 23-31.

FIXED PAYMENT MORTGAGES

The adoption of the fully amortizing, fixed rate, level-payment mortgage as the standard mortgage design owes a great deal to its ability to reduce mortgage defaults. Prior to the 1930s the fully amortizing loan contract—though apparently the most common form of mortgage loan—was nowhere nearly so prevalent as it is now.[2] Contracts often provided for no amortization or for only partial amortization of the principal amount prior to the maturity date. As a result, a "balloon" payment of principal often became due on maturity. Terms to maturity were frequently short, often only about five years. Common practice was for such loans to be renegotiated at maturity, with a new loan being made to refinance the part of the principal which the borrower did not pay down at that time.

This procedure entailed a number of risks, as became apparent during the depression of the 1930s. First, the short term to maturity, together with the balloon payment feature, meant that, if the borrower had not accumulated sufficient funds to repay the loan at maturity, he might be subject to foreclosure on his property unless he was able to negotiate a new loan for the unpaid balance of principal. Second, since a relatively small amount of amortization—or perhaps none at all—was required, the borrower's equity in the property did not necessarily increase significantly as time went by. As a result, in the event of a loss of income to the borrower or erosion of the value of the property, the temptation to default on the loan might be strong.

With the onset of the depression, loan defaults mushroomed, and many lenders were unable to roll over maturing loans, so that foreclosures surged to a massive rate. In response, the Congress took a variety of measures to reduce the short-term threat of foreclosures as well as to restructure the procedures of housing finance to avoid a recurrence.

Among these measures was Government mortgage insurance administered by the FHA. FHA insurance, begun in 1934, required that loans be long term and fully amortizing, with constant monthly payments. Similarly, Federally chartered savings and loan associations, first created in the 1930s, were limited almost exclusively to making mortgages with those characteristics, and many states passed legislation applying similar restrictions to mortgage lending institutions under their jurisdiction.[3] In addition, the Federal National Mortgage Association (FNMA), organized in 1938, restricted its secondary

---

[2] Almost all mortgages held by savings and loan associations during the 1920s and early 1930s were fully amortizing, but other lenders held primarily partially amortizing or nonamortizing mortgages. Available data indicate that a variety of short-term mortgages, partially amortizing or nonamortizing, constituted slightly more than half of all mortgages in lending institutions' portfolios before the depression. For more details, see Henry J. Cassidy, "The Changing Home Mortgage instrument in the United States", Federal Home Loan Bank Board *Journal* (December 1978), pages 11-17.

[3] With the exception of the recently authorized reverse annuity mortgages, Federally chartered savings and loan associations may make balloon residential mortgages with a maximum term of five years, but the value of the loan may not exceed 50 percent of the security (Federal Home Loan Bank Board, *Annotated Manual of Statutes and Regulations*, section 545.6-1). This regulation restricts balloon mortgages to the relatively few individuals capable of making a 50 percent downpayment on a home.

market mortgage purchases to Government-insured mortgages, thus giving still further impetus to the adoption of the FPM as the standard mortgage instrument.[4] As a result of these measures, by the early postwar period the FPM was by far the dominant residential mortgage loan contract.

The adoption of the FPM as the standard form of mortgage contract was successful in overcoming the major problems of the residential mortgage market which existed during the 1920s and the 1930s. Its weaknesses began to become apparent only during the 1960s and 1970s—a period of rapid inflation and historically high and variable interest rates.

One of the FPM's most severe problems is the burden it creates for young families acquiring a home for the first time. Such families require housing services to accommodate their growing households, yet their current income —which is of major importance for determining the monthly mortgage payments they can afford—is often substantially less than their expected future income. Unfortunately, the FPM, by keeping monthly payments constant, does not allow such families to tailor their payments to their expected income growth. This "life cycle" problem exists even in an environment of stable prices.

Inflation causes an additional problem by making the burden of real mortgage costs in the early years of the loan term even greater relative to borrowers' current income than it would have been with no inflation. As inflation comes to be expected, nominal interest rates adjust upward to compensate lenders, at least in part, for the loss of purchasing power expected to occur during the term of the loan. Thus, if the rate of interest on mortgages were 3 percent in an environment of stable prices, it might rise to about 11 percent if an 8 percent rate of inflation is expected over the term of the loan. If the term to maturity of an FPM is not altered, this increased nominal interest rate raises the monthly payment. However, if the expected rate of inflation actually turns out to be correct, the increased rate of interest is approximately offset by the progressive reduction in the purchasing power of the interest and principal payments, so that the real cost of the loan remains essentially unchanged at about 3 percent per annum.[5]

Though the real cost—*i.e.*, the value of the monthly payments adjusted for price changes—is almost unchanged, its distribution through the term of the loan changes dramatically. Since inflation erodes the value of the higher nominal payments only gradually, the real cost is significantly higher in the early years of the term and is lower during the later years. For example, an increase in the expected rate of inflation from zero to 8 percent, reflected in an increase in the mortgage interest rate from 3 percent to 11 percent, causes the real cost of the first year's monthly payments on a $60,000 mortgage with a thirty-year term to rise from $253 per month to about $550 (Chart 1). By the eleventh year of the term, the real cost of the 11 percent mortgage

---

[4] In February 1972, FNMA broadened its mortgage purchase program to include conventional mortgages as well.

[5] This statement abstracts from considerations such as the tax treatment of interest expense which would reduce the real cost of the 11 percent mortgage relative to that of the 3 percent mortgage.

Chart 1

**Real Payments of Interest and Principal
on Mortgages under Different
Inflationary Conditions**

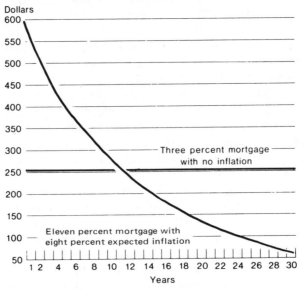

Both mortgages are assumed to have a thirty-year term
and a $60,000 original principal amount.

has declined almost to the real cost of the 3 percent mortgage; afterward it is less.

Most individuals are highly sensitive to the timing of real payments during the term of their mortgages, because they must make mortgage payments out of their current incomes and still have sufficient income remaining to meet other expenses. Hence the "front-end load" created by the concentration of the real payments in the early years can be a major burden. While the level of monthly payments can be reduced by decreasing the size of the loan (and increasing the down-payment), this alternative is generally impractical for young, first-time home buyers. In addition, the burden of other expenses relative to income is also likely to be substantial in the early years of homeownership, when many younger persons are starting their families.

FHA-INSURED GRADUATED PAYMENT MORTGAGES

The development of GPMs was the outgrowth of the Experimental Finance Program of the United States Department of Housing and Urban Development (HUD), authorized by the Congress in 1974.[6] Section 245 of the National Housing Act as amended that year authorized HUD to initiate an experimental program to insure mortgages with "provisions of varying rates of amortization corresponding to anticipated variations in family income". The program was an effort to determine whether the problems of first-time home buyers could be alleviated within the framework of accepted mortgage lending practices. In 1977 the Housing and Community Development Act made the program permanent.

As their name suggests, FHA-insured GPMs have monthly payments which are low at first and rise gradually for a period of years before leveling off. Since they have a constant interest rate and a fixed term, the graduated payment feature means that the early monthly payments are insufficient to cover accrued interest. As the unpaid accrued interest is added to the principal balance of the loan, the outstanding loan principal increases; in other words, there is negative amortization in the early years of its term.

Like other FHA-insured loans, Section 245 GPMs are fully insured and intended to be made on an actuarially sound basis—*i.e.,* insurance premium payments are expected to be adequate to cover any losses. Originally, FHA-insured GPMs were subject to the same maximum loan-to-value ratio as FHA Section 203(b) FPMs and, since a GPM's principal increased in the early years, the minimum initial downpayment had to be greater than for an FPM. The Housing and Community Development Act of 1977 relaxed the requirement somewhat by allowing the principal amount of GPM loans to increase as high as 97 percent of the original estimated value.

Since the GPM program was new, HUD restricted it to five alternatives which differ according to the pattern of graduation of the initial payments. Three plans permit payments to increase at 2½, 5, and 7½ percent annually for five years, and two plans allow payments to increase at 2 and 3 percent annually for ten years. Monthly payments during each year are level; increases occur annually. After the final annual increase, the payments become constant for the remaining term of the loan. Payment schedules for an FPM and for Plan III and Plan V GPMs are illustrated in Chart 2. All the mortgages are assumed to have a thirty-year term and a $60,000 initial principal amount. The GPM payments are significantly less in the early years than those of the FPM. Indeed, during the first four years of the Plan III GPM, the total payments are $4,058 less than those for the FPM. Over the first six years of the Plan V GPM, total payments are $3,790 less than for the FPM. This early cost advantage is offset in two main respects. First, as noted earlier, the GPM plans require somewhat higher downpayments than the FPM. Second, when the GPM payments flatten out, they do so at a higher level than the FPM,

---

[6]The first kind of GPM authorized nationally was the "flexible payment mortgage" authorized by the Federal Home Loan Bank Board in February 1974. The idea behind it was to reduce the early monthly payments by omitting amortization in the early years of the term. However, since amortization constitutes only a small portion of the early payments for an FPM, the payment schedule for a flexible payment mortgage was not greatly different from that for an FPM, and the innovation never attracted much interest.

Chart 2

Monthly Payments of Interest and Principal for a Fixed Payment Mortgage and Two Graduated Payment Mortgages

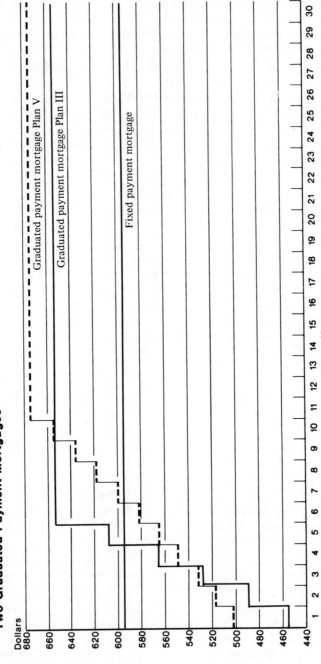

A term of thirty-years and a contract rate of 11½ percent are assumed. Payments for mortgage insurance are not included.

owing to the negative amortization in the early years of term.[7] The result is that, while payments of interest and principal total $213,905 over the thirty-year term of the FPM, they are $14,155 (6.6 percent) more for the Plan III GPM and $17,217 (8.0 percent) more for the Plan V GPM.

The GPM program got off to a slow start. Regulations in some states against collecting compound interest on residential mortgage loans prevented many lenders from offering them. This problem was resolved by the Housing and Community Development Act of 1977, which exempted FHA-insured GPMs from such restrictions. Another problem which has yet to be resolved is that GPMs with negative amortization like those in the Section 245 program can increase the tax liability of taxpayers who calculate their income on an accrual basis—which includes most financial institutions. The reason is that, while the unpaid interest on such a GPM is added to the loan principal and not received by the lender in the year it was earned (accrued), it does increase the lender's tax liability for that year. Other things equal, this feature makes GPMs a less attractive investment than a standard FPM.

Expansion of the program was also slowed by the relative unattractiveness of the GPMs for the thrift institutions which originate most single-family mortgages. Since the low early payments of the FHA-insured GPMs initially produce less cash flow for lenders than do FPMs, they are not attractive to thrift institutions which rely largely on short-term sources of funds. The lack of enthusiasm on the part of thrift institutions, together with mortgage banks' traditional dominance of FHA originations, meant that mortgage banks accounted for almost all GPM originations. The statutory restriction of FHA single-family loans to $45,000—raised to $60,000 in 1977 and to $67,500 in 1979—also reduced the attractiveness of FHA financing in areas where housing prices are relatively high.

Since the GPM program was new, lenders also needed time to become familiar with the alternative designs, to make adjustments in their loan processing procedures, and then to market GPMs to potential borrowers. The result was that, out of a total of 321,118 FHA single-family mortgage insurance endorsements in 1977, only 331 were for GPMs. However, following the increase in the maximum FHA loan size, the Federal override of state laws barring collection of compound interest on residential mortgages, and the establishment of the Section 245 program on a permanent basis in late 1977, the situation changed dramatically. By December 1978, over 25 percent of total new single-family endorsements were GPMs. During 1979, about 27 percent of the total were GPMs.

The regional distribution of GPMs is highly uneven, with most activity taking place on the West Coast and in the southeastern part of the country. Indeed, by the end of 1979, California alone accounted for about a third of all GPMs in the country. This uneven pattern of introduction of GPMs is probably attributable to regional differences in the composition and strength of housing demand as well as state usury laws and other restrictions on the ability of lenders to offer them.

---

[7]There is a third small offset due to the insurance premium being larger for the increasing principal balance of the GPM than for the FPM.

Two provisions of the Housing and Community Development Amendments of 1979, signed into law on January 4, 1980, may expand the GPM program significantly. First, the maximum loan size for single-family mortgages insured by the FHA was increased from $60,000 to $67,500. Second, the GPM program was modified to increase the permissible GPM loan size when the initial home value is below or slightly above the maximum loan size. The new GPM authorized in Section 245(b)—the previous Section 245 is now renamed Section 245(a)—is similar to the earlier GPM and, for both programs, the loan balance at no time can exceed 97 percent of the value of the house. However, for the earlier program this was the initial appraised value; in the new Section 245(b) program the value of the home is assumed to increase over time, thus relaxing the 97 percent limitation. In projecting the future home value, HUD is authorized to employ a maximum 2½ percent annual rate of price appreciation—a rate well below that observed in recent years.

Depending on how the new program is implemented, the Section 245(b) GPMs may allow GPM borrowers to increase substantially their initial loan size and thus to reduce their downpayments.[8] The smaller downpayment would increase the attractiveness of GPMs for many people. However, the Congress placed a number of restrictions on the program. First, to concentrate the Section 245(b) program on first-time home buyers, applicants must not have owned a home in the preceding three years. Second, the number of mortgages insured in any fiscal year is limited to 10 percent of the aggregate initial principal amount of all one- to four-family mortgages insured under Section 245(b) during the preceding fiscal year or 50,000 mortgages, whichever is greater. Nevertheless, there appears to be ample scope for the new program to expand.

CONVENTIONAL GRADUATED PAYMENT MORTGAGES

The HUD program has given impetus to the development by the private sector of conventional—*i.e.,* nonFHA-insured—GPMs. First, the relatively low maximum FHA loan size, together with the rather demanding FHA construction standards and paperwork requirements, makes FHA loans of whatever form unattractive for many borrowers and lenders. Second, as noted earlier, the negative amortization in the early years of an FHA-insured GPM can create an increased tax liability and a cash flow pattern unattractive to many lenders. The former problem can be avoided through conventional financing. The latter problem has been alleviated through the development of a novel form of mortgage loan which allows the lender to receive a stream of constant monthly payments while the borrower makes graduated payments.

---

[8] As of this writing, HUD has not yet determined whether the new program would operate in the same Plans I-V as the Section 245(a) GPMs or whether new graduation periods and rates would be created.

WHO BORROWS THROUGH FHA-INSURED GRADUATED PAYMENT MORTGAGES?

Data collected in a special survey conducted by the United States Department of Housing and Urban Development indicate that the GPM (Section 245) borrower is on average 29-30 years old—one to two years younger than the average FPM (Section 203(b)) borrower. Most borrowers in both programs are married, but there is substantial singles participation as well. As one would expect, considering their lower average age, GPM borrowers generally have slightly fewer dependents than do FPM borrowers. A large majority—three quarters or more—of borrowers under both programs are first-time home buyers. However, GPM borrowers are somewhat more likely to own a home which is being sold to finance the purchase of a new home. The income of GPM borrowers is on the whole not very different from that of FPM borrowers—though in some individual markets GPM borrowers have markedly lower average incomes.

Though nationwide comparisons of FPM and GPM borrower characteristics are complicated by the fact that California has accounted for a disproportionate share of GPM volume, it appears that GPM borrowers buy significantly more expensive homes which they finance with larger mortgages. Because of the low early monthly payments of the GPM, this results in only a slightly greater burden of first-year housing expense relative to income for GPM borrowers, compared with FPM borrowers. GPM borrowers also put down significantly larger downpayments—in part because the most popular Plan III GPM requires a larger downpayment, but also because in many cases the maximum FHA loan size is a constraint. As a consequence, GPM borrowers generally have a lower loan-to-value ratio than FPM borrowers.

Average Characteristics of FPM and GPM Borrowers

Characteristic	FPM borrowers	GPM borrowers
Sales price	$36,130	$48,996
Mortgage amount	$34,427	$44,557
Total annual family income	$22,167	$22,128
Loan-to-value ratio	92.6%	89.8%
Total housing expense/ net effective income	30.9%	32.3%
Total fixed payments/ net effective income	51.7%	50.9%

Data are for loans on existing single-family structures endorsed during the first quarter of 1979. Fixed payment mortgage loans (FPMs) are those endorsed under Section 203(b); graduated payment mortgage loans (GPMs) are those endorsed under Section 245.

Source: United States Department of Housing and Urban Development.

The loan is structured so that part of its proceeds is placed with the lending institution in a pledged savings account from which withdrawals are gradually made to supplement the borrower's early payments. The result is a loan with constant payments to the lender and graduated payments by the borrower. This means that the loan does not have the FHA-insured GPM's tax and cash flow disadvantages for lenders, who in addition acquire funds through the pledged account. Moreover, the pledged-account GPM circumvents many states' prohibitions against increasing monthly mortgage payments and the charging of interest on accrued interest—an important consideration, since the Housing and Community Development Act of 1977 overrode such state laws only for FHA-insured GPMs.

Finally, even though lenders typically pay only the passbook savings account interest rate on the pledged account, generally a tax saving will be realized which offsets or exceeds the loss of income created by borrowing funds at the mortgage rate and investing them at the passbook rate. The reason is that the borrower may deduct the withdrawals from the pledged account from his taxable income, since they are used to pay part of the mortgage interest. As a result, his deductible interest expense exceeds his actual out-of-pocket outlay for mortgage interest during the early years of the loan.

It is difficult to estimate the volume of originations of pledged-account GPMs. Since the loan is essentially an FPM from the standpoint of lenders, available data do not separate out the pledged-account GPMs from other mortgages. However, judging by the vigor with which they have been promoted, the volume of pledged-account GPMs may well be substantial.

GPMs IN THE SECONDARY MARKET

Additional impetus to GPM lending has been provided by the opening-up of the secondary mortgage market to FHA-insured GPMs. Initially, almost the only part of the secondary market in which FHA-insured GPMs were sold was the FNMA purchase program. Early in 1979, the Government National Mortgage Association (GNMA) expanded its pass-through certificate program to allow FHA-insured GPMs to be included in mortgage pools underlying the certificates.[9]

The GPM-GNMA certificates—familiarly referred to as "Jeeps"—provide an ownership interest in a pool containing mortgages with five-year graduation periods (Plans I-III). In practice, since the vast majority of GPM borrowers prefer Plan III, which has the steepest graduation schedule, the pools consist overwhelmingly of mortgages of this type. Because of the graduation feature, GPM-GNMAs have a slightly longer average maturity, or "duration", than do standard GNMAs. This is true both of the contracted term to matur-

---

[9]For a description of the GNMA certificate program, see Charles M. Sivesind, "Mortgage-Backed Securities: The Revolution in Real Estate Finance", this *Review* (Autumn 1979), pages 1-10.

ity and also of the average maturity calculated on the basis of prior experience with prepayments of FHA mortgages. As a result, the price of a GPM-GNMA security should be slightly more volatile than that of a standard GNMA security.

Yields of GNMA securities—including GPM-GNMAs—currently are quoted on the basis of a twelve-year prepayment assumption.[10] This is convenient for standard GNMA securities, since in most cases the yield distortions are not large. However, the assumption is less firmly grounded in the case of GPM-GNMAs, since there is no prior experience on which to base an evaluation of the accuracy of the approximation. On the one hand, if GPM borrowers are more likely to consider their homes as permanent investments and are less inclined to move than other borrowers, the GPM prepayment experience will be slower than prior FHA experience. On the other hand, if GPMs are especially attractive to upwardly mobile families inclined to move to a better house after a few years, then the GPM-GNMA prepayment rate could be faster than prior experience. In these circumstances, GNMA, for want of any better alternative, has applied the standard twelve-year prepayment assumption to yield calculations for GPM-GNMAs.

Trading in GPM-GNMAs has reflected the fact that the instrument is new, with few pools existing compared with standard GNMA securities. As a result of their less liquid market and their longer expected average term, GPM-GNMAs have traded at a discount of one to two points relative to level-payment GNMAs with the same coupon interest rate.

The number of GPM-GNMA pools has increased substantially—to 1,102 pools with an unpaid principal balance aggregating to $2.3 billion at the end of February 1980—and GNMA anticipates that the volume will expand in tandem with the growth of GPM originations. The liquidity of the market should improve in the future as the number of pools increases further.

Secondary market activity in pledged-account GPMs has been more modest. A number of sales of packages of GPMs carrying mortgage insurance provided by private mortgage insurance firms have occurred. Activity should be stimulated, however, when the Federal Home Loan Mortgage Corporation initiates its planned pilot purchase program.

EVALUATION OF GRADUATED PAYMENT MORTGAGES

As noted earlier, FHA-insured GPMs have expanded rapidly in the few years the program has existed. Though it is too early to make a definitive judgment, indications are that to some extent the expansion of Section 245 GPMs has been at the expense of Section 203(b) FPMs. If this pattern continues and also holds for conventionally financed GPMs, then the impact of continued growth of GPMs would not be primarily to expand the mortgage

---

[10] For a description of the calculation of yields on GNMA securities, see Sivesind, *loc. cit.*

market, though some increase would occur, but rather to allow borrowers to arrange their housing finance more conveniently than at present.

The major unanswered question concerning the growth and development of GPMs is not, however, a matter of relative rates of expansion; it is the implications of GPMs for loan defaults in the years ahead. As noted earlier, a key benefit obtained from adoption of the FPM as the standard mortgage design was to avoid any recurrence of the enormous volume of mortgage defaults which was precipitated by the depression of the 1930s. To the extent that the FPM is modified, defaults might once again become a source of concern.

In the past, the most important determinant of mortgage defaults has been the amount of equity which the borrower has in his house. Since equity is lowest in the early years of the mortgage term, the incentive to default—and its observed incidence—is greatest then. To the extent that a GPM with negative amortization—such as the FHA-insured GPM—increases the balance of the loan in the early years of the term, the owner's equity relative to the original purchase price declines. Other things equal, this should increase his incentive to default. This effect could be offset, however, if the rate of appreciation of the home's value exceeds the rate at which the loan balance increases. The requisite rate of increase in value depends on the level of the interest rate but is generally quite modest, on the order of 1 percent or so per year during the first five years of the thirty-year term of a Plan III GPM. The loan balance of pledged-account GPMs decreases continuously, but the larger initial loan size means that an additional default incentive is created, compared with both an FPM and an FHA-insured GPM. Both kinds of GPMs reduce the front-end load in the time pattern of the real payments on the mortgage, and this will probably reduce defaults in the early years, though they might be increased later on.

While the short period of time during which the FHA GPM program has been in operation precludes firm generalizations about default rates, there have been some indications that Section 245 GPMs have default rates which are either the same as, or lower than, Section 203(b) FPMs. However, more than ordinary caution is needed in interpreting this performance. First, downpayments on FHA-insured GPMs frequently have been greater than required under the program, and this should reduce defaults. The most likely reason for the larger downpayments is that the FHA's loan size limitation required buyers of more expensive homes to increase their downpayments to qualify for FHA insurance. In addition, since FHA-insured GPMs have a slower cash flow than FPMs of equal maturity and interest rate, persons financing through GPMs should expect to pay more points than with an FPM.[11] This also would tend to restrict the availability of GPM financing to borrowers capable of making larger downpayments. Finally, some GPM borrowers may have a

---

[11] A point is 1 percent of the principal value of a mortgage note. Since the maximum FHA mortgage rate is generally held well below market levels, points are charged to raise to market levels the yield on the funds actually advanced. While sellers are legally obligated to pay any points charged on an FHA mortgage, they generally attempt to shift this cost to the buyer by increasing the sale price and thus the downpayment required of the buyer.

preference for low monthly payments—to such an extent that they would be willing to reduce their liquid assets in order to lower the loan size and thus the monthly payments. This approach can make sense when the mortgage interest rate is substantially higher than the savings account interest rate, as has been the case during the FHA program's existence.

The absence of hard evidence concerning the default experience with FHA-insured GPMs raises the issue of precisely what an "actuarially sound" GPM is. The designers of the FHA program had in mind a mortgage contract in which the degree of graduation did not exceed the prospective rise in income of the borrower during the early years of the loan term. In fact, however, the available evidence suggests that income projections are not taken very seriously by GPM originators, with the result that Plan III—which has the steepest graduation rate—dominates all FHA's other GPM options. Now that the Congress has authorized the Section 245(b) GPM, in which an assumption is made concerning the future rate of price appreciation of the house, the evaluation of the soundness of GPMs has still less to do with actuarial methodology as usually understood. In the near future, continued inflation may ratify any such assumption and prevent the emergence of problems in the GPM program but, as inflation is brought under control, the validity of the assumption could be eroded. In such a case, as both inflation and mortgage interest rates declined, GPM borrowers—because of their larger loan sizes—would have an especially strong incentive to refinance their loans at lower interest rates. In addition, defaults and delinquencies might increase.

OUTLOOK FOR GRADUATED PAYMENT MORTGAGES

In the long run, the best way to deal with the front-end load induced in the real payments of an FPM is to reduce the rate of inflation. In the near-term, however, the GPM—whether FHA-insured or conventional—clearly has an important role to play in alleviating some of the problems created for many borrowers, especially young families, by exclusive reliance on the FPM as the standard mortgage design. GPMs will likely continue to expand at a brisk rate in the near future. Perhaps the principal obstacle to their doing so is the recent advent of single-family mortgages financed through issues of tax-exempt bonds. In areas where such programs have been actively employed, GPM activity has been very slight, for GPMs obviously are less attractive to house buyers than mortgages offered at below-market interest rates. Thus, the outlook for growth of GPMs will be influenced by the outcome of pending legislation to restrict issues of single-family mortgage revenue bonds.

In the longer term, even after inflation is brought under control, graduated payment mortgages are likely to remain an important innovation in the mortgage market, by virtue of providing greater flexibility in tailoring mortgage payments to anticipated income growth than does the fixed payment mortgage.

THE SHARED APPRECIATION CONCEPT IN RESIDENTIAL FINANCING*

Thomas J. Parliment and
James S. Kaden†

19

Real estate partnerships based on a sharing of the capital gains accruing from price appreciation is a relatively common financing technique. Equity splitting, or sharing, has been most commonly seen in commercial real estate transactions. However, as inflation has caused an increasing number of households to be short of the capital necessary for home purchase, various equity sharing arrangements have been surfacing in the area of residential real estate. These arrangements can take the form of a mortgage instrument known as the *shared appreciation mortgage* (SAM). Alternatively, they can take the form of a co-ownership arrangement between non-occupant investor(s) and an owner-occupant.

Home financing mechanisms which involve sharing anticipated price appreciation have raised a particularly virulent brand of criticism. This criticism emanates as much from general frustration concerning inflation as from the financing mechanism itself. Inflation and the related economic conditions that it fosters have forced a tremendous rate of innovation in the financial markets. The pace of this innovation has also been amplified by the substantial deregulation that depository institutions have been undergoing. As a result, the number and complexity of both savings and mortgage instruments coming to market is bewildering to both consumers and lenders.

The criticism involves the traditional issues attendant to the introduction of all alternative mortgage instruments. How is the home buyer affected? What additional costs will a new mortgage instrument impose on the home-

*Reprinted, with deletions, from *United States League of Savings Associations Economics Working Paper*. Copyright 1981, United States League of Savings Associations. Reprinted with permission.
†The authors are in the Economics Department of the United States League of Savings Associations.

owner that were not imposed with the fixed-rate mortgage? Are the mechanics of the new mortgage too complex to be readily understood by the borrower? A similar range of concerns relate to the lender's perspective. What are the effects of a new instrument on a lender's portfolio? Yield, underwriting risk, interest rate risk, and projected cash flows represent variables that must be evaluated by the lender before the mortgage concept can be sold to the prospective borrower.

The purpose of this paper is to provide a framework within which the controversy surrounding the shared appreciation concept in residential finance can be evaluated.

THE CONTEXT OF INNOVATION
IN MORTGAGE MARKETS

Perhaps it is most important to view shared appreciation financing mechanisms as a part of a wave of change sweeping the nation's financial intermediaries. It was inevitable that the onset of intense competition for capital would cause substantial innovation in financial market instruments. To some extent, inflation has acted as the mother of financial innovation. In addition, the pace of competition brought on by inflation has certainly been spurred by interest rate deregulation of the nation's depository-type financial institutions. Competing for savings in the presence of these fundamental changes has required the payment of higher interest rates to savers and the proliferation of savings instruments with shorter maturities. Such instruments as money market certificates, money market funds, and variable rate bonds reflect this development. Of course, the exposure of thrifts to increased levels of interest rate risk and the increased costs that characterize these new instruments had to be passed through to the purchasers of mortgage money—the homebuyers.

Since most mortgage capital is intermediated, the increased cost of competition for funds is necessarily transferred to mortgage borrowers. If savers are to be paid market rates, then mortgage borrowers must pay more for funds as well as accept adjustable rate arrangements which, in effect, turn the purchase of mortgage money into a shorter-term transaction.

It must be clear that the mortgage borrower has to be able to tap all resources in order to compete for mortgage money as a result of the fundamental changes taking place in the capital markets. In this respect, the borrower can:

1. Stretch present income, devoting a greater share of the budget to service mortgage indebtedness. Innovations in mortgage insurance first by the government and then in the private sector have facilitated this development through spreading the increased underwriting risk;

2. Convert present wealth by devoting a larger share of personal assets to real estate;

3. Transfer a portion of the cash flow burden to future income. Graduated payment mortgages and variable rate mortgages with adjustable payment features allow the borrower to rely on increases in future income to absorb part of the present costs of acquiring mortgage capital; and

4. Transfer a portion of the cash flow burden such that it is absorbed by expected future wealth which includes the expected appreciation of real estate assets. Shared appreciation mechanisms and variable rate mortgages which allow negative amortization (increasing loan balances) allow borrowers to utilize expected increases in future wealth to absorb part of the present costs of acquiring mortgage capital.

It is important to understand that the impetus behind innovation in mortgage instruments is the necessity to compete for capital in a deregulated, inflationary economic environment. No single mortgage instrument can be claimed to represent a panacea for all borrowers, all lender/investors, in all markets. In this perspective, shared appreciation mechanisms represent only one of a range of tools necessary to enable the mortgage borrower to compete in an increasingly complex capital market.

THE BASIC STRUCTURE OF SHARED APPRECIATION FINANCING AS APPLIED TO RESIDENTIAL FINANCE

Though many different plans have been suggested for this shared appreciation concept, most can be analyzed utilizing a relatively simple cash-flow format. A lender or (investor) makes an offer to the borrower for a price. The offer is either a lump-sum payment made up front or is a "supplemental annuity" in the form of reduced payments for a given period. The price is a contracted percentage of the price appreciation which has accumulated over the specified period. Whatever offer-price combination is agreed upon directly determines the rate of return for both the lender and the borrower.

Two general cases arise when looking at the investors relevant cash flows. Concerning the first case, consider an example of the shared appreciation mortgage as it is commonly known. In this case the investor is also the mortgage lender. The borrower applies for an $80,000 loan at 15 percent for 30 years. The fixed monthly payment is $1,011.55 and is a bit too steep for the borrower's ability to finance. The lender responds by offering to drop the 15 percent rate on the loan to 10 percent in return for a 30 percent share of the borrower's accumulated appreciation after five years. The monthly payments are reduced to $702.05. The loan balance that is to be paid after five years is $77,259.46. Finally, the lender will require 30 percent of the difference between the final selling price of the home and the initial selling price of the home. Assuming that the initial selling price is $100,000 and the final selling price is $200,000 this amount is $30,000.

In this example of the shared appreciation concept, the reduced monthly payment is $1,011.55 − $702.05 = $309.50. It is important to understand that this reduction in the payment constitutes an "annuity" paid to the borrower for the right to share in the appreciation of the property. For these "payments," the lender receives $30,000 which is 24.4 percent of the borrower's ending equity [$30,000/($200,000 − $72,259.46)].

The cash flow diagram for this example is illustrated in Figure 1. Present value analysis of these cash flows shows that the lender can make a return of 15.13 percent on the shared appreciation mortgage. This return to the lender essentially represents a weighted combination of the 10 percent return on the mortgage and the 18.51 percent rate on the "equity investment."

The second general case arises when the investor participating is someone other than the lender originating the mortgage and is buying in solely by means of an "annuity." As an illustration of this case consider the following example.

The borrower makes a loan of $80,000 at 15 percent for 30 years. The fixed monthly payment required is $1,011.55. The borrower is unable to finance this monthly payment and seeks help from an outside investor. An investor agrees to supplement the borrower's financing with a fixed monthly payment of $310 for the entire participation period of five years.

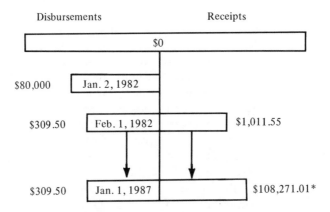

*The final "payment" received by the investor is the sum of the remaining loan balance, the share of appreciation, and the unadjusted monthly payment of $1,011.55. The unadjusted payment is offset by the "annuity" payment of $309.50.

Figure 1   Investor cash flows for a shared appreciation mortage.

In return for this service the borrower agrees to pay the investor one lump-sum amount equal to 25 percent of the total equity at the end of the participation term. Assuming that the home being purchased appreciates from $100,000 to $200,000 during the five year participation term, the borrower's total equity will be $200,000 − $78,976.50 = $121,023.50. (Unlike the preceding example in which the loan was written on the basis of a 10 percent rate, this loan is written at the 15 percent rate and thus the loan balance after five years is higher.) Consequently, the payoff to the investor will amount to $121,023.50 × .25 = $30,255.87. The cash flow diagram for this example is shown in Figure 2. Future value analysis of this cash flow shows that the investor can make a rate of return of 18.51 percent on the investment. Also, unlike the preceding example, the lender shares in the total equity at the end of the period and not just the appreciation.

The second general case, discussed above involved a borrower, lender, and an outside investor who acquired a participation by means of annuity payments. A special case of this general approach would arise if the investor paid for its participation with an initial lump-sum payment. Whatever its specific form, the three-party arrangement is not usual structure underlying the SAM as it is presently known in residential mortgage finance. The main purpose of this example was to demonstrate the flexibility of the equity sharing concept so that it may be more widely understood and, where appropriate, applied. In the balance of this paper, the focus will be on the two-party arrangement in which the lender is also the investor. As pointed out, this structure characterizes the shared appreciation mortgage as it is commonly known.

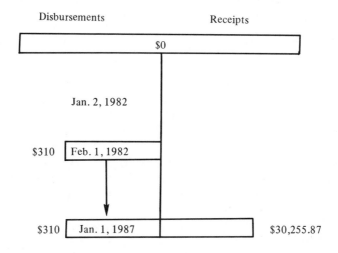

Figure 2   Cash flow pattern with outside investor.

EVALUATING THE SHARED
APPRECIATION MORTGAGE

Issues Relevant to the Lender

A variety of factors confront the investor considering a shared appreciation instrument. Pricing, cash flows, interest rate risk, underwriting risk, and the expected appreciation rate on the home are among the most prominent of these variables.

Shared appreciation financing places both the borrower and the investor in a complex bargaining situation, with uncertainty regarding pricing becoming their paramount concern. We can learn something about the nature of this pricing decision by focusing on a lender's breakeven analysis with respect to the shared appreciation mortgage. Competitive pricing of the SAM will require an understanding of three key variables: (1) the estimated rate of the home's appreciation; (2) the lender's share of home appreciation—the appreciation "kicker," and (3) the downpayment.

Table 1 shows how these factors impact the breakeven rates that the lender may offer the homebuyer under several alternative market rates. For example, assuming that a savings and loan association (S&L) offers a five-year loan term and that the local mortgage rate is 14.5 percent, what is the rate that the lender can offer to a homebuyer by using a shared appreciation mortgage and still achieve a 14.5 percent return? If we further assume that the home will appreciate at a rate of 10 percent per year, the homebuyer puts 20 percent down and the lender's share of the home's appreciation is 30 percent, then the lender's breakeven return will be 11.91 percent. The breakeven rates of return shown in Table 1 and discussed in the remainder of this paper reflect the deduction of selling costs equal to 7 percent of the home's value at the end of the participation period of five years. The property, of course, need not be sold at the end of the period. Although the five-year participation term is somewhat arbitrary, it is consistent with several of the shared appreciation plans presently being offered by lenders. The term could, of course, be something other than five years, such as three, seven or ten years.

In the example given above, if the lender offers a SAM for a rate above 11.91 percent, then it is likely that the return will exceed 14.5 percent. On the other hand, if the SAM is offered at a rate below 11.91 percent, the lender would have been better off simply making a straight mortgage loan at 14.5 percent.

One would expect the lender to design the contractual arrangements of the SAM to at least reach the breakeven point. After all, the source of the contingent interest is estimated appreciation; the lender cannot be expected to supply risk capital for a lower return than would be obtained for supplying debt capital at a fixed and known return. In fact, if capital is to be attracted into the mortgage markets via the SAM, lenders must price their mortgages to do better than simply break even. Secondary markets for these mortgages will demand a risk premium. However, estimating the size of this risk premium is outside of the scope of the present paper, and we have simply specified breakeven discounts for illustrative purposes.

The Appreciation Rate. It is readily apparent from Table 1 that the greater the estimated rate of home appreciation, the lower the breakeven mortgage rate that can be offered to the homebuyer. This simply reflects the larger ending equity base from which it is estimated the lender will draw its contingent interest. In our previous example, which involved a 20 percent down payment and a market rate of 14.5 percent, the lender would only be able to offer the homebuyer a mortgage loan rate of 12.60 percent if the rate of appreciation is 8 percent. Similarly, if the lender actually anticipated a 12 percent rate, the breakeven rate would be 11.17 percent.

The lender is clearly not indifferent to the estimates of home appreciation upon which the mortgage rate offer is made to the homebuyer. It will suit the lender's purpose to hedge downside risks by basing the extent of the rate discount on as low an estimated rate of home price appreciation as is practical. This procedure will decrease the probability that the actual rate of appreciation will fall below the estimated rate of appreciation and therefore fail to yield a breakeven return. The lender's rate of return is directly related to the positive difference between the actual and the expected rate of appreciation. For illustrative purposes, consider the following example.

Suppose the homebuyer wants to purchase a $100,000 home and applies for an $80,000 mortgage at 14.5 percent for 30 years. The lender offers the borrower a reduction of $162.29 in the monthly payment, which is equivalent to a discounted rate of 11.91 percent. The lender's expected return is 14.5 percent and is based on a participation term of five years, a 30 percent share of the appreciation and the expectation that the home will appreciate in value at a rate of 10 percent per year. The relevant cash flow to the lender in this case is illustrated in Figure 3. If all goes as expected, the lender will make a 14.5 percent rate of return on the investment.

Now suppose that the actual appreciation rate of the home turns out to be only 8 percent—less than the lender expected. In this case, the share of the borrower's appreciation will decrease from $14,933.23 to $10,994.25. This will reduce the final cash flow from $94,010.31 to $90,071.33 and reduce the lender's rate of return to 13.85 percent. This realized return would be below the desired return of 14.50 percent.

Next, suppose that the actual appreciation rate of the home turns out to be 12 percent per year—higher than the lender expected. In this case, the lender's share of the appreciation will increase from $14,933.23 to

Table 1   Breakeven Rates of Return for

Rate of Apprec.	Share of Apprec.	10.50% Downpayment			11.50% Downpayment		
		.10	.20	.30	.10	.20	.30
0	.10	10.62	10.64	10.65	11.62	11.63	11.65
0	.20	10.74	10.77	10.81	11.73	11.76	11.80
0	.30	10.86	10.91	10.96	11.85	11.89	11.95
0	.40	10.98	11.04	11.12	11.97	12.03	12.10
.02	.10	10.45	10.45	10.44	11.46	11.45	11.44
.02	.20	10.41	10.40	10.38	11.41	11.40	11.38
.02	.30	10.36	10.34	10.32	11.37	11.35	11.33
.02	.40	10.32	10.29	10.26	11.32	11.30	11.27
.04	.10	10.27	10.25	10.21	11.28	11.25	11.22
.04	.20	10.05	9.99	9.92	11.06	11.00	10.93
.04	.30	9.82	9.73	9.63	10.84	10.76	10.65
.04	.40	9.59	9.48	9.33	10.62	10.51	10.37
.06	.10	10.08	10.03	9.96	11.09	11.04	10.97
.06	.20	9.66	9.55	9.41	10.68	10.58	10.45
.06	.30	9.23	9.07	8.87	10.27	10.12	9.92
.06	.40	8.81	8.60	8.32	9.86	9.65	9.39
.08	.10	9.87	9.79	9.69	10.89	10.81	10.71
.08	.20	9.23	9.08	8.87	10.27	10.12	9.92
.08	.30	8.60	8.36	8.05	9.65	9.42	9.12
.08	.40	7.96	7.63	7.22	9.03	8.72	8.32
.10	.10	9.64	9.53	9.40	10.67	10.56	10.43
.10	.20	8.78	8.56	8.28	9.83	9.62	9.35
.10	.30	7.91	7.58	7.16	8.99	8.67	8.26
.10	.40	7.03	6.59	6.02	8.14	7.71	7.16
.12	.10	9.40	9.26	9.08	10.43	10.29	10.12
.12	.20	8.29	8.01	7.65	9.35	9.08	8.73
.12	.30	7.16	6.74	6.19	8.27	7.86	7.33
.12	.40	6.03	5.45	4.70	7.17	6.61	5.90
.14	.10	9.13	8.96	8.74	10.17	10.01	9.79
.14	.20	7.75	7.41	6.96	8.84	8.50	8.07
.14	.30	6.36	5.82	5.13	7.49	6.97	6.31
.14	.40	4.93	4.20	3.25	6.11	5.42	4.51
.16	.10	8.85	8.64	8.38	9.90	9.70	9.44
.16	.20	7.18	6.76	6.21	8.28	7.88	7.35
.16	.30	5.48	4.83	3.98	6.64	6.02	5.21
.16	.40	3.73	2.83	1.64	4.96	4.10	2.98

[a]The breakeven rates are calculated based on the assumption that selling expenses equal to 7 percent of the property value are incurred. These expenses

$19,169.33, causing receipts to increase while disbursements remain fixed. The rate of return implied by this cash flow is 15.17 percent, which is above the lender's desired rate of return.

It is instructive to note that the SAM provides the lender with an ability to partially hedge against unanticipated inflation. Although the hedge is not perfect, the contingent interest feature of the SAM represents an important inflation adjustment feature. Moreover, since changes in interest rates over the long run reflect changes in the inflation rate, the SAM provides a partial interest rate hedge that is useful for secular increases in interest rates.

Alternative SAM Proposals with 5-Year Participation Term[a]

Market Rate 12.50%			13.50%			14.50%		
Downpayment			Downpayment			Downpayment		
.10	.20	.30	.10	.20	.30	.10	.20	.30
12.61	12.63	12.65	13.61	13.62	13.64	14.61	14.62	14.64
12.73	12.76	12.79	13.72	13.75	13.78	14.71	14.74	14.78
12.84	12.88	12.94	13.83	13.87	13.93	14.82	14.86	14.91
12.95	13.01	13.08	13.94	14.00	14.07	14.93	14.98	15.05
12.46	12.45	12.44	13.46	13.45	13.45	14.46	14.45	14.45
12.41	12.40	12.39	13.42	13.40	13.39	14.42	14.41	14.39
12.37	12.35	12.33	13.37	13.36	13.34	14.38	14.36	14.34
12.33	12.30	12.28	13.33	13.31	13.28	14.34	14.31	14.29
12.29	12.26	12.23	13.29	13.27	13.23	14.30	14.27	14.24
12.07	12.02	11.95	13.08	13.03	12.97	14.10	14.05	13.98
11.86	11.78	11.67	12.88	12.80	12.70	13.89	13.82	13.72
11.64	11.54	11.40	12.67	12.56	12.43	13.69	13.59	13.46
12.10	12.05	11.99	13.11	13.07	13.00	14.12	14.08	14.02
11.70	11.60	11.48	12.73	12.63	12.51	13.75	13.65	13.53
11.31	11.16	10.96	12.34	12.19	12.01	13.37	13.23	13.05
10.91	10.71	10.45	11.95	11.76	11.51	13.00	12.81	12.57
11.90	11.83	11.73	12.92	12.85	12.76	13.94	13.87	13.78
11.31	11.16	10.96	12.34	12.20	12.01	13.37	13.23	13.05
10.71	10.48	10.19	11.76	11.54	11.26	12.81	12.60	12.32
10.11	9.81	9.42	11.18	10.88	10.51	12.24	11.96	11.60
11.69	11.59	11.46	12.71	12.61	12.49	13.74	13.64	13.52
10.88	10.67	10.41	11.92	11.73	11.47	12.97	12.78	12.53
10.06	9.75	9.36	11.13	10.84	10.45	12.20	11.91	11.54
9.24	8.83	8.30	10.34	9.97	9.42	11.43	11.04	10.55
11.46	11.33	11.16	12.49	12.36	12.20	13.52	13.40	13.24
10.42	10.15	9.82	11.48	11.22	10.89	12.53	12.29	11.97
9.36	8.97	8.46	10.46	10.07	9.58	11.55	11.17	10.69
8.30	7.77	7.08	9.43	8.91	8.25	10.55	10.05	9.41
11.21	11.05	10.84	12.25	12.09	11.89	13.29	13.13	12.94
9.92	9.59	9.17	10.99	10.68	10.27	12.07	11.76	11.37
8.61	8.12	7.48	9.73	9.25	8.63	10.84	10.38	9.78
7.29	6.62	5.75	8.45	7.80	6.97	9.60	8.98	8.17
10.95	10.75	10.50	11.99	11.80	11.56	13.03	12.85	12.61
9.38	8.99	8.48	10.47	10.09	9.60	11.56	11.19	10.72
7.79	7.19	6.41	8.94	8.36	7.61	10.08	9.52	8.79
6.18	5.36	4.28	7.38	6.60	5.57	8.58	7.82	6.83

are deducted from the assumed sale of the house at the end of the participation period. Monthly payments are on a 30-year amortization basis.

The Appreciation "Kicker."

The percentage share of appreciation, or equity "kicker" contracted for by the lender will have the most significant impact upon the rate offer the lender can make to the homebuyer and still reach the breakeven point. It is easy to understand that the greater the lender's appreciation kicker, the deeper the mortgage rate discount that can be offered. For instance, in our example which assumed a 14.5 percent market rate, 20 percent downpayment and 10 percent estimated annual rate of appreciation, the breakeven mortgage rate offer could vary from 13.64 percent on a 10 percent kicker to 11.04 percent on a 40 percent kicker—a spread of 260 basis points. Of course, this spread, representing the

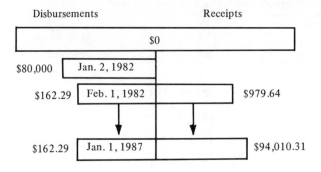

Figure 3   Lender's expected cash flow pattern.

importance of the lender's share of appreciation, grows as the estimated annual rate of home appreciation increases.

It is very important to recognize that a substantial appreciation kicker is the lender's best hedge against risk. For example, turning to Table 1 we see that a 12.81 percent mortgage made to a homebuyer with a 20 percent downpayment and a 40 percent appreciation kicker in a 14.5 percent market requires a mere 6 percent annual home price appreciation to break even. The same mortgage with only a 10 percent kicker will require an appreciation rate of 16 percent to break even.

Several interesting tradeoffs present themselves. How does the lender balance the loss of cash flow with gains in the share of appreciation? Assume a 14.50 percent market. Does the lender make a 12.81 percent mortgage with a 40 percent appreciation kicker or a higher rate 13.40 percent mortgage with a smaller 10 percent appreciation kicker? The former 12.81 percent offer breaks even if only a 6 percent annual rate of appreciation is realized. The latter 13.40 percent offer only breaks even if a 12 percent annual rate of appreciation is realized. A high probability exists that the 6 percent rate of appreciation will be exceeded, and if so, the lender's 40 percent share of appreciation will easily produce a better-than-break-even yield. The mortgage with a 10 percent appreciation kicker is less likely to produce a better-than-break-even yield since the annual rate of appreciation would have to exceed 12 percent for it to do so.

One additional consideration presents an impact on the lender's tradeoff decision between loss of cash flow with gains from the share of appreciation. That is, if the lender is experiencing a period of depressed earnings along with a declining level of excess net worth, the lender may lean toward the higher rate 13.40 percent mortgage to accommodate its current cost of funds and operations costs. Table 1 provides a means for the lender to make this important decision.

The Downpayment. The impact of the downpayment size on breakeven rates is straightforward. The phenomenon for reverse leverage works to the lender's advantage. The less the lender has to loan the homebuyer, other factors being equal, the greater will be the potential return to the lender. In other words, given a larger downpayment, the lender will be able to offer to the borrower a greater rate discount while still breaking even. For example, in a 14.5 percent market in which a 10 percent annual rate of home appreciation is being assumed and a 30 percent appreciation kicker is being asked, a lender could break even by offering a 12.20 percent mortgage with a 10 percent downpayment, a 11.91 percent mortgage with a 20 percent downpayment, and a 11.54 percent mortgage with a 30 percent downpayment.

The above effect can be seen more clearly if we consider the impact of the downpayment size on the lender's rate of return. Suppose a homebuyer is seeking a mortgage loan to finance the purchase of a home valued at $100,000. The buyer has a 20 percent downpayment, or $20,000, so the amount of the loan would be $80,000. The terms of the SAM call for a five-year participation term, a 30 percent share of the appreciation. Based on these terms, a market rate of 14.5 percent, and an expected appreciation rate of 10 percent per year, the lender is able to offer a loan rate of 11.91 percent and thus lower the borrower's monthly payment from $979.65 to $817.36, a reduction of $162.29. (The payments are based on a 30-year amortization schedule.) The lender's return is 14.5 percent, as mentioned above. However, if the borrower makes a 30 percent downpayment and borrows $70,000 on the same terms, including the loan rate of 11.91 percent, the mortgage payment is reduced fro $857.19 to $715.18, a reduction of $142.01. The investor's cash flow structure is shown in Figure 4. The rate of return implied by this cash flow is 14.84 percent, an increase of 34 basis points over the return on a loan involving a 20 percent downpayment. Thus, as the downpayment increases, the lender's return increases. Alternatively, the offering rate on the SAM may be lowered.

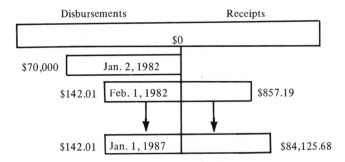

Figure 4   Lender cash flow with 30% downpayment.

Costs and Benefits.   We have seen up to this point how three key variables—the appreciation rate, the equity share, and the downpayment—affect the lender's pricing decision. In addition to these, the lender must be aware of the benefits and costs of offering a SAM. One benefit has already been mentioned—that of being able to partially hedge against inflation and interest rate risk. Another way in which the SAM provides a hedge against interest rate risk is in the potential shorter-term nature of the instrument. If the lender chooses, the outstanding balance on the SAM can be brought to market after a short period of time such as three years. This is a step toward matching asset maturities to liability maturities. Furthermore, there is the possibility of integrating a variable rate interest feature and a shared appreciation mechanism.

The costs to the lender involve some underwriting problems and the problem of default risk incurred by a possible large payment jump at the time of refinancing. One problem encountered in the underwriting is that there is no place for the expectation of an increase in property value. Current loan underwriting standards on 1-4 family properties include an analysis of expected property price *depreciation*. This may only be considered to the extent that a decline in the value of the property may result in a negative equity position and default on the loan. If the underwriter has no factual basis for an expectation of property price declines, then property price expectations have no legitimate role in the underwriting process.

A second underwriting problem deals with possible discrimination charges. For example, if the lender issues the same SAM to two different customers—each from a different neighborhood where price appreciation may differ drastically—the lender may be charged with issuing too high an interest rate to one of the customers.

The problem of possible default due to a large increase in the mortgage payment at the time of refinancing also presents itself. Suppose the borrower obtains a $50,000 SAM at 9.5 percent on a $60,000 home. Suppose further that price appreciation is 10 percent, the participation term is eight years, and the appreciation kicker is 40 percent. After eight years, the contingent interest and outstanding balance amount to $73,929.83. If this sum is refinanced at 14 percent for 20 years the payment skyrockets from $420.42 to $919.33. Even when the new term is 30 years, the payment is a burdensome $875.97. The borrower's income may not increase at the pace required to cover this large monthly payment.

Issues Relevant to the Borrower

The primary attraction of SAMs to borrowers is the reduced interest rate. First-time homebuyers who have a meager downpayment do not have to worry about supporting a high monthly mortgage payment as in the case of the fixed-rate mortgage. Depending upon the three key variables mentioned in the lender section, the borrower can negotiate for a fixed monthly payment based on an interest rate that is well below the market rate.

It is important for the borrower to understand how the expected appreciation rate, appreciation share, and size of the downpayment affect the borrower's return. Although the first-time home-buyer is probably more concerned about acquiring the ownership of a home than about calculating the internal rate of return, it is still wise for the borrower to analyze this transaction from an investment standpoint.

The borrower's cash flow can be analyzed in the same manner as the lender's flows. Disbursements consist of monthly payments during the participation period which are equal to the difference between the original mortgage payment based on the market rate and the investor "annuity," the downpayment at the beginning of the period, and a lump-sum at the end of the participation period. This lump-sum consists of two components—the mortgage balance and the appreciation kicker. The borrower's receipts consist of one lump-sum payment, the final selling price of the home at the end of the participation term. Figure 5 illustrates the structure of this cash flow pattern.

As stated earlier, one of the key variables decided upon in the negotiation period is the expected appreciation rate. It was shown that it was in the lender's interest to negotiate a lower expected appreciation rate. The opposite is true for the borrower; it is in the borrower's best interest to negotiate the highest expected appreciation rate possible. In doing so, the borrower receives a larger discount on the mortgage rate as Table 1 shows.

The borrower's rate of return is directly related to the positive difference between the expected and the actual rate of appreciation. That is, the more the expected appreciation rate exceeds the actual appreciation rate, the better off is the borrower. An example illustrates this point. Consider the SAM that was discussed earlier with the lender's cash flows shown in Figure 3.

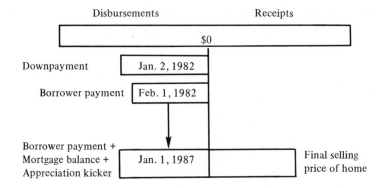

Figure 5   Borrower's expected cash flow pattern.

In this example, the borrower was acquiring a home for $100,000 with a downpayment of $20,000 and a mortgage loan of $80,000. The lender offers the borrower a discounted interest rate of 11.91 percent based on the lender's desired rate of return of 14.5 percent, an appreciation kicker of 30 percent, and an expected appreciation rate of 10 percent per year. The participation term is five years. The payments are calculated assuming a 30-year amortization period. The borrower's disbursements amount to a downpayment of $20,000, sixty monthly payments of $817.35, and at the end of 5 years, a lump-sum payment of the mortgage loan balance and the appreciation kicker. In this instance, the loan balance is $78,097.44. Assuming that the actual appreciation rate is also 10 percent per year, the home would be sold for $100,000 $(1.10)^5$ = $161,051. Further assuming selling costs of 7 percent, the net proceeds would amount to $161,051 $\times$ .93 = $149,777.43. The net appreciation, therefore, would be $49,777.43 of which 30 percent or $14,933.23 goes to the lender. Thus, the lump-sum payment to the lender is $78,097.44 + $14,933.23 = $93,030.67. In return for these outlays, the borrower receives 93 percent of the sales price or $149,777.43. These cash flows result in a rate of return of -6.30 percent. When tax and shelter benefits are considered the borrower's rate of return is much higher.

Now suppose that the actual appreciation is 12 percent. In this case, the lump-sum payment of the mortgage balance and appreciation kicker is $97,266.77 and the net sales price is $163,897.78. The payment is still $817.35. This cash flow implies a return of -1.12 percent which is higher than the return based on a 10 percent appreciation rate. Again, when tax and shelter benefits are included, the rate of return is much higher.

The second variable of importance to the borrower is the appreciation kicker. As mentioned before, as this variable increases, the discount which the lender is willing to offer on the mortgage rate becomes larger. In this light, it is in the borrower's interest to negotiate a higher lender share in the appreciation. However, if the actual appreciation rate greatly exceeds the expected rate, the borrower will give up a windfall gain. Thus, the borrower is confronted with a tradeoff between assuming a low monthly payment and gleaning the most out of the home's appreciation.

The impact of the downpayment size can be determined by comparing the borrower's rate of return under alternative SAM proposals. In an example given earlier, a home valued at $100,000 was financed with a downpayment of $20,000 and a SAM for $80,000. The rate was 11.91 percent as determined from Table 1. The terms called for a 30 percent share of the appreciation at the end of five years. The expected appreciation rate was 10 percent and the lender's expected return was 14.5 percent. The borrower's rate of return was determined to be -6.30 percent.

If the downpayment is increased to $30,000, the breakeven rate (from Table 1) is 11.54 percent. The monthly payment is $695.34 and the lump-sum mortgage balance and appreciation kicker is $83,144.39. The borrower receives 93 percent of the selling price or $149,777.43. This cash flow implies a rate of return of -2.11 percent. Thus, as the downpayment increases, the borrower's rate of return increases.

It is clear that with the implementation of SAMs many current renters will have greater opportunity to purchase their own home. For example, a standard fixed-payment mortgage of $60,000 at 14 percent for 30 years requires a monthly payment of $710.92. If the corresponding SAM is offered with an interest rate of 10.5 percent, the monthly payment would drop to $548.84. Assuming annual property taxes and insurance of $1,000 and a 25 percent payment-to-income rule, the household would need an annual income of $38,124 with the standard mortgage and $30,328 with the SAM. This is a reduction of 20.5 percent. Thus a substantial number of additional households could qualify for homeownership if SAMs were available.

Although the price of this entry is giving a share of the appreciation to the lender, the borrower is still better off because the household can own its own home and benefit from some, but not all, of the appreciation of the property. A SAM is particularly well-suited for first-time homebuyers with relatively short expected housing tenure because it allows these households to buy sooner.

SAMs probably will not be very attractive to repeat homebuyers. These households usually have sufficient housing equity such that a sizable downpayment can be made in order to reduce the monthly payments to a manageable level. Also, to the extent that many households have an investment as well as a consumption motive in purchasing their homes, these households probably will not want to share their appreciation with lenders. On the other hand, SAMs may be attractive to elderly buyers because it allows higher current consumption of nonhousing goods.

Shared appreciation mortgage contracts should include several consumer safeguards. Most important, the contract must include a guarantee that the outstanding balance plus contingent interest will be refinanced at market rates when the loan is due. The borrower should be allowed to select long-term financing from those types of loans the lender offers. In addition, the borrower should be allowed to select the term of the shared appreciation mortgage and the term of the long-term financing. These provisions are necessary in order to prevent a SAM from being a balloon mortgage. Finally, comprehensive disclosures are necessary because of the novelty of the instrument and the long-term financial consequences such loans have for borrowers.

CONCLUDING REMARKS

Shared appreciation financing of residential real estate represents a new and important tool for the homebuyer. The development of this and other new financing mechanisms will be essential if housing is to remain competitive in the nation's capital markets.

Such innovation is a one-way process. While it is true that an unprecedented bout with inflation has accelerated the pace of financial innovation and forced the demise of interest rate ceilings, the return to a more stable economic environment will not provide reason to disregard these new tools. We are thus bearing witness to a benchmark period in the evolution of the nation's capital markets.

Many have suggested that the present evolution signals a convergence of the functions of various types of depository institutions. It is maintained that many thrift institutions will use their new powers to become full-service financial centers. Also, it is expected that many commercial banks will use more flexible mortgage instruments to become more involved in mortgage lending. However, such convergence, the development of financial department stores so to speak, must not mask a trend toward increased specialization in the financing of real estate.

Residential real estate will become increasingly less reliant on an earmarked flow of savings funneled through depositories directly into housing. Thrifts can, if they choose, remain the fulcrum in the process of intermediating funds for real estate investment. An increasing variety of sources of capital will have to be tapped to provide financing for real estate. Stable sources of long-term financing will have to be further developed. Pension funds and life insurance companies will be institutions playing a role in this development. New types of deposits, such as long-term retirement accounts, tax-deferred accounts, and mortgage-backed savings certificates, will provide important new sources of funds for residential real estate investment.

Similarly, more diverse and complex mechanisms will be developed to put this capital in place. Joint ventures, convertible debentures, and a host of other financial mechanisms heretofore commonplace in the commercial real estate sector will be necessary in financing residential real estate. The capability to effectively manage with an increasingly complex set of finan- real estate sector will be necessary in financing residential real estate. The capability to effectively manage with an increasingly complex set of financial tools will require more sophistication and more specialization on the part of the lenders.

This development should come as no surprise. The structure of business enterprise in financial markets is essentially no different than that of any other economic sector. Progress through innovation in information systems, new products, and increased productivity are all associated with increasing specialization in production. The thrift industry can evolve into such a specialized real estate lender.

MORTGAGE-BACKED SECURITIES:The Revolution in Real Estate Finance*

Charles M. Sivesind

20

The rapid development of a variety of mortgage-backed securities has led to a radical transformation in real estate finance in recent years. By integrating the mortgage market into the traditional capital markets, these securities have broadened the financial base for home mortgages. During 1978, the $40 billion of mortgage-backed securities issued in this national market financed nearly one quarter of all home loan originations.

There are two major types of mortgage-backed securities: *bonds* with scheduled principal repayments that are secured by mortgage collateral and *pass-throughs* which provide ownership interest in the monthly payments from a pool of mortgages. Until recently, the market has been dominated by the bonds issued by the Federal National Mortgage Association (FNMA or "Fannie Mae") and the pass-through securities guaranteed by the Government National Mortgage Association (GNMA or "Ginnie Mae"), both backed by Government-insured mortgages. However, a variety of mortgage-backed securities are now financing conventional mortgage lending as well. Building on the success of pass-through securities issued by the Federal Home Loan

The author gratefully acknowledges the assistance of numerous market experts: Phil Cockerill, Arnold Diamond, Marcos Jones, Lee Kendall, Warren Lasko, Dan Laufenberg, Ken Rilander, Dave Seiders, Eric Sheetz, and Steve Shepherd.

*Reprinted from the *Quarterly Review*, Autumn 1979, pp. 1-10, with permission from the Federal Reserve Bank of New York.

Mortgage Corporation (FHLMC or "Freddie Mac"), pass-throughs backed by conventional loans are now being issued publicly by banks, savings and loan associations, and mortgage companies. Mortgage-related bonds are being used to finance mortgage loan portfolios of thrift institutions and various government-sponsored housing programs.

Mortgage-backed securities allow firms dealing in real estate finance either to specialize in originating and servicing mortgage loans (seller/servicing) or to focus on providing the long-term capital investment funds to finance lending activities (investment). Traditionally, commercial banks, savings and loan associations, and mutual savings banks performed both of these functions. Mortgage companies, on the other hand, mainly originated and serviced mortgage loans which they packaged for sale to such permanent investors as insurance companies and pension funds.

The widespread acceptance of mortgage-backed securities has encouraged a broad variety of institutional investors to invest in the mortgage market, once dominated by individuals and thrift institutions. This new market for mortgage-backed securities has reduced geographic and institutional barriers to mortgage lending by distant investors. By attracting a variety of new types of investors to the mortgage market and by integrating the mortgage market into the broader, more highly developed capital markets, mortgage-backed securities promise to stabilize the supply of funds to the housing sector of the economy—once an early casualty in any period of credit stringency.

THE CHANGING HOME MORTGAGE MARKET

The unique financing requirements brought about by widespread home-ownership have caused a continuing evolution in mortgage lending practices. But until recently the housing sector has been plagued by an insecure financial base. The real estate collapse of the 1930's led to a reorganization of mortgage lending practices, sparked by the creation of the mortgage guarantee program of the Federal Housing Administration (FHA) in 1934 and later by the Veterans Administration (VA) mortgage insurance program in 1944. The programs encouraged underwriting of mortgages with standardized terms, relatively low downpayments, and long maturities on properties meeting high-quality standards. Since low-risk FHA-VA loans could be sold to investors across the country, the programs facilitated the early development of an integrated, national mortgage market at little direct cost to the Government.

By encouraging the widespread adoption of the long-term, fully amortized, fixed-payment mortgage as the standard lending agreement, the FHA-VA programs also contributed to an increased role for institutional investors in home loans. The long-term nature of the contract lowered monthly payments, making homeownership affordable for a larger segment of the population, while monthly amortization of principal resulted in a gradual buildup of each homeowner's equity, reducing default risk. For investors, however, this type of contract presented several difficulties. The long maturity made evaluation of the future collateral value of the property particularly difficult, required the loans to be serviced over a long period, and emphasized the need for escrow of taxes and insurance. Liberal prepayment clauses, which were desired by borrowers to facilitate future real estate sales, created uncertainty of investment maturity. In addition, amortization resulted in relatively small but continuous principal repayments, complicating reinvestment options. These factors made mortgage investment attractive primarily to savings institutions and life insurance companies with larger portfolios than most individual investors.

The growth of institutional dominance in the mortgage market continued from the postwar housing boom into the mid-1960's. In 1946, households held over one quarter of the outstanding home mortgage debt (Chart 1). Commercial banks held about one fifth of the total, while thrift institutions and insurance companies held nearly half.

During the next twenty years, savings and loan associations provided most of the conventional financing in the rapidly growing sections of the country while households' relative mortgage holdings shrank. Over this period, strong housing demand made mortgage yields attractive relative to the returns available to institutional investors on many other long-term investments. Banks and thrift institutions, closely tied to their local markets, saw little need for FHA-VA insurance and tended to concentrate on conventional home loans. Life insurance companies, on the other hand, saw these Government-insured loans as a new type of high-yield, low-risk, long-term investment. Mainly to meet the needs of insurance companies for seller/servicing of FHA-VA loans in local communities, many mortgage companies were created during the postwar housing boom. These mortgage companies originated loans, nearly at cost, and sold them to final investors, continuing to earn servicing income over the life of the loan. Home mortgage investments of thrift institutions and insurance companies reached nearly three quarters of the outstanding total by the mid-1960's.

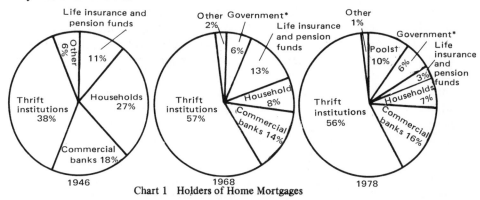

Chart 1   Holders of Home Mortgages

*Federal, state and local, including directly held mortgages and holdings of sponsored credit agencies.
†Pass-through securities backed by these pools are ultimately held by a variety of investor groups, including those listed here, but are carried on the books separately from direct mortgage holdings.
Source: Board of Governors of the Federal Reserve System, *Flow of Funds.*

The activities of mortgage companies began to change in the mid-1960's, when general increases in interest rates (in the face of FHA-VA ceilings which were held below market levels) encouraged life insurance companies to shift their lending focus away from one- to four-family houses toward multifamily dwellings and commercial buildings. Mortgage companies responded by becoming more active in multifamily and commercial lending, but they also were forced to seek new investors for home loans. At first the slack in the home loan market was taken up by the various Federally sponsored credit agencies (mainly FNMA) whose holdings of mortgages on one- to four-family dwellings increased from $2.5 billion in 1965 to $15.5 billion in 1970. Most of the loans sold to these agencies were originated and serviced by mortgage companies and consisted mainly of FHA-VA mortgages.

The search by mortgage companies for new investors took a new turn in the late 1960's with the creation of the first publicly traded pass-through securities backed by pools of mortgages. These new securities—mostly GNMA pass-throughs (see below)—in effect allowed mortgage companies to sell mortgages to investors who were located in other sections of the country and to institutions which had not invested in real estate loans in the past. By 1978, 15 percent of all newly originated home loans was placed in pass-through pools. These pools contained 10 percent of total home mortgage debt by the year-end. Meanwhile, as home mortgage rates declined relative to corporate bond yields, insurance companies and pension funds all but stopped buying home mortgages directly, although they continued to invest in pass-through securities and mortgage backed bonds.

THE INVENTION OF MORTGAGE-BACKED SECURITIES

The Government-related agencies—FNMA, GNMA, and FHLMC—may be credited with the development and widespread adoption of mortgage-backed securities as a means of financing home loans. Each agency fulfills a variety of roles, servicing one or more sectors of the mortgage market.[1] Some agencies subsidize certain types of housing. Some provide securities guarantees. Others purchase mortgages from originators and either package these loans into participation pools for resale to final investors or hold them in portfolio, financing the acquisitions by issuing notes and bonds. Some deal mainly in conventional loans, while others specialize in FHA-VA loans, which typically are made in connection with lower priced or older homes.

The FNMA was organized as a Government agency in 1938 to purchase

---

[1] The twelve Federal Home Loan Banks (FHLBs), while not usually treated as credit agencies, issue debt and lend the proceeds primarily to savings and loan associations on mortgage collateral. FHLB advances, which totaled $30 billion at the end of 1978, effectively increase the liquidity of mortgages held in savings and loan association portfolios but do not directly contribute to the marketability of mortgages.

Government-guaranteed mortgages. After its reorganization as a privately owned corporation in 1968, it began in 1971 to buy conventional mortgages. FNMA programs have been popular with mortgage bankers, who originate most of the loans it purchases, but it also buys from other approved FHA-VA lenders. In 1978, it purchased over $12 billion in mortgages, about half of which were conventional loans. At the end of 1978 it held mortgages with an unpaid principal balance of over $43 billion, one quarter of which were conventional loans. To finance its portfolio, FNMA issues short-term discount notes and intermediate-term debentures, effectively transforming mortgages into securities with a fixed maturity and a single principal repayment at the end.[2] Its short-term debt rose by $2.5 billion in 1978, and it issued debentures totaling $9.3 billion (Chart 2). FNMA purchases facilitate the separation of the seller/servicing and investment aspects of real estate finance, allowing local real estate markets to attract funds indirectly from distant geographic regions and from investors who do not wish to originate, service, or hold mortgage loans.

When FNMA was rechartered as a private corporation in 1968, programs requiring Government subsidies or other direct Federal support were assumed by GNMA, a newly organized Government corporation within the Department of Housing and Urban Development. There are now two major GNMA programs. One is the purchase of mortgages to support housing for low-income families for which private financing is not readily available. These special assistance programs provide mortgage funds at below market rates of

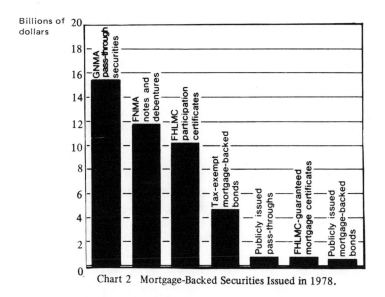

Chart 2   Mortgage-Backed Securities Issued in 1978.

[2] In the past, FNMA issued a few bonds explicitly collateralized by designated mortgages—the forerunner of mortgage-backed bonds now being used by savings and loan associations—but most of its debentures are not explicity collateralized. All FNMA debt is treated as mortgage backed in this discussion. FNMA currently is considering the feasibility of marketing pass-through securities for conventional mortgages.

interest. In its "tandem plan" operations, GNMA issues commitments to purchase certain types of loans with interest rates below prevailing market levels and simultaneously sells these mortgages to FNMA or to private investors at prices resulting in market yields, absorbing as subsidy the difference between the prices paid and received.

The second major GNMA activity is its mortgage-backed securities program, which has revolutionized the secondary mortgage market. Under GNMA sponsorship beginning in 1970, the Government guarantees the timely payment of principal and interest on securities issued by private mortgage institutions and backed by pools of Government-insured or -guaranteed mortgages. These pass-through securities are designed to appeal to pension funds and other institutional investors not wishing to originate and service mortgage loans themselves. Pass-throughs are considered eligible real estate investments by most agencies that regulate commercial banks and thrift institutions, and for purposes of determining the tax status of thrift institutions. The securities provide a safe, easily marketable investment with an attractive long-term yield and a high cash flow each month resulting from interest and principal repayment.

GNMA pass-through securities provide for monthly installments of interest on the unpaid balance at the securities' stated certificate rate plus payment of scheduled principal amortization, whether or not collected by the servicer, together with any prepayment of other recoveries of principal. All mortgages placed in a pool must be issued at the same interest rate and cannot be more than one-year old. The GNMA certificate rate is 50 basis points below the contract rate of the underlying mortgages, 44 basis points going to the originator for servicing and 6 basis points to GNMA for providing its guarantee. Pass-throughs are issued in registered form with coupons. The issuer mails checks for interest and principal repayments to holders of record as of the end of each month to reach the recipient by the fifteenth.

Mortgage pools backing GNMA securities most frequently contain FHA-VA single-family mortgages, although pools may also be formed from other types of FHA-insured or VA- and Farmers Home Administration-guaranteed mortgages, subject to somewhat different terms than those described above. Single-family pools are formed in $1 million minimum amounts (pools for other mortgage types may be half that size), but many pools are substantially larger, containing $25 million or more in mortgages. Pass-through securities are issued in $25,000 minimum denominations with $5,000 increments, although in the national market a round-lot transaction is $1 million.

GNMA pass-through securities are issued by mortgage bankers (who account for three fourths of the annual total) as well as by thrift institutions and commercial banks that originate FHA-VA mortgages. Instead of selling the mortgages outright or financing them through deposits or other debt, the issuer forms a pool, sells pass-through securities, and continues to earn servicing income on the loans. Newly issued securities are marketed for immediate or forward delivery either directly by the issuer or, more typically, a securities dealer. There is a sizable annual volume of trading in seasoned issues, a direct result of the large volume of outstanding securities and their widespread distribution among all types of investors. In addition, there is an active futures market for the securities on the major commodities exchanges.

Until recently, GNMA pass-throughs have dominated the mortgage-backed securities market. There are over 800 active issuers of GNMA pass-throughs and over 33,000 pools. New issues in 1978 totaled $15 billion, financing over half of all new FHA-VA home loans and raising the outstanding unpaid principal balance of GNMA pass-throughs to $52 billion. In the first nine months of 1979, GNMA issues totaled over $16 billion.

FNMA and GNMA securities backed mainly by Government-guaranteed mortgages have dominated the mortgage-backed securities market during the past decade. Now, over 90 percent of all newly originated FHA-VA mortgages on single-family homes is placed in pass-throughs or sold to FNMA, but FHA-VA fixed-payment mortgages represent a declining fraction of total home loans. In May 1979, GNMA began to guarantee pass-through securities backed by graduated payment mortgages[3] insured by FHA, a potential fast-growth area for GNMA securities. However, the key to continued rapid growth of mortgage-backed securities lies in the conventional loan market and the housing bonds of state and local governments.

Mortgage-backed securities have been used only recently to finance conventional loans, which account for four-fifths of all home mortgages. The FHLMC, created by the Congress in 1970 and wholly owned by the Federal Home Loan Banks (FHLBs), has as its primary goal the development of a national secondary market in conventional mortgages. As a general rule, the FHLMC purchases conventional mortgage loans from savings and loan associations (four-fifths of its total purchases), mutual savings banks, commercial banks, and mortgage banks. At first the FHLMC purchased mainly participations and whole loans for its own portfolio, financing the acquisitions by borrowing from the Treasury and the FHLBs and by issuing its own mortgage-backed bonds. In 1974, however, the focus of its operations was shifted toward the sale of mortgage participation certificates (PCs) and guaranteed mortgage certificates (GMCs).

In many respects, PCs are similar to GNMA pass-through securities, although they are not backed by the full faith and credit of either the United States Government or the FHLBs. These certificates represent ownership interest in pools of conventional mortgages purchased by the FHLMC, which guarantees the monthly pass-through of interest, scheduled amortization of principal, and ultimate repayment of principal. Like GNMA pass-throughs, PCs are considered direct mortgage investments for most tax and regulatory purposes. PCs are marketed directly by the FHLMC and through a group of securities dealers who also maintain a secondary market in seasoned issues. The originator retains the obligation to service the loans for a fee of 3/8 percent and the spread between the price paid and received by the FHLMC, usually 30 to 50 basis points, provides a return to cover FHLMC insurance and administration costs.

---

[3] Graduated payment mortgages are a new and rapidly growing type of instrument having a lower monthly payment in the first few years than standard fixed-payment home loans.

PCs differ from GNMA pass-throughs in several respects because they are issued by the FHLMC rather than by individual mortgage lenders throughout the country. The mortgage pool underlying a typical PC comprises about 5,000 mortgage loans with a total value of about $100 million to $300 million. A given pool may contain mortgages issued at several rates, allowing PCs to contain loans issued in different sections of the country. Although the minimum PC denomination is $100,000, $5 million denominations are particularly popular since the unpaid principal balance will remain comfortably above the $1 million round-lot trading size for many years. In 1978, $5.6 billion in PCs was issued, bringing the outstanding unpaid balance to $10.2 billion at the year-end.

In 1974 the FHLMC created a new type of instrument, the GMC, to provide a mortgage investment instrument with much of the convenience of a bond. Like a GNMA pass-through, a GMC represents ownership interest in a pool of mortgages, but the interest on a GMC is paid semiannually and principal repayments are made annually, like some sinking fund bonds. The FHLMC guarantees timely payment on interest, full payment of principal, and promises to repurchase any principal that remains unretired after fifteen years. At irregular intervals, GMCs backed by mortgage pools totaling $200 million-$300 million are issued in minimum denominations of $100,000. In 1978 new issues totaled $700 million, bringing the outstanding unpaid balance to about $1.9 billion by the year-end.

NEW TYPES OF MORTGAGE-BACKED SECURITIES

The success of mortgage-backed securities guaranteed by the Federally related credit agencies has encouraged private mortgage originators to issue both mortgage-backed bonds and pass-through securities without Government involvement. Since 1975, thrift institutions have issued mortgage-backed bonds patterned after bonds issued by various Government-related credit agencies. The securities are similar in most respects to other corporate bonds. They are general obligations of the issuer with a stated maturity and fixed semi-annual interest payments. The bonds are collateralized by pools of mortgages, with a covenant obligating the issuer to maintain a stated level of collateral even when discounted to market value and adjusted for amortization and prepayments. Collateral maintenance levels are normally so high (usually 150 percent or more) that mortgage-backed bonds receive highest ratings.

Mortgage-backed bonds allow thrift institutions to borrow against their mortgage assets to obtain funds for new loans during periods of slow deposit growth, instead of borrowing from commercial banks or the FHLBs. These bonds are particularly attractive when the cost of alternative financing is above the bond rate, provided mortgage yields are higher than bond yields. Moreover, since the thrift institutions do not sell the mortgages outright, they may pledge old, relatively low-yielding loans as collateral without showing capital losses on their books. Most mortgage-backed bonds are issued with original maturities of five to ten years, roughly comparable to the expected average maturity of new mortgages. On the whole, these bonds allow thrift institutions to match more closely their asset and liability maturities and to broaden their funding base. Mortgage-backed bonds issued publicly in 1978 totaled $465 million, bringing the amount outstanding to $1.7 billion. In 1979, bonds totaling $1.0 billion were issued publicly in the first nine months.

Mortgage-related bonds have also become a prominent feature in the tax-exempt sector of the capital markets. State governments have supported single-family housing through general obligation bonds for a number of years (usually associated with veterans' benefit programs) and since 1970 through revenue bonds issued by housing finance agencies.[4] Housing-related revenue bonds were first issued by municipalities in 1978. These three types of bonds, designed to appeal to individuals and institutions who purchase other types of tax-exempt municipal securities, are used mainly to finance loans for low- and middle-income housing at below-market rates. New issues supporting single-family housing totaled $4.7 billion in 1978 and $5.5 billion in the first nine months of 1979.

The use of tax-exempt securities to finance mortgage lending has sparked considerable public debate. Proponents assert that the tax-exempt mortgage bond programs benefit the home buyer, the locality, and the housing industry by making homeownership affordable to more people. As a result, local neighborhoods are stabilized and, with demand pushing house prices higher, the tax base of the locality is enhanced. Critics charge that the use of tax-exempt bonds to finance housing increases borrowing costs to state and local governments for other purposes and reduces Treasury tax revenues and that mortgage funds generated in some programs are not channeled to those most in need of government subsidies. In response to these objections, Congressional legislation, H.R. 3712 and related bills, was introduced in April 1979 to restrict the use of tax-exempt revenue bonds to finance homeownership. The uncertainty about the outcome of this pending legislation has raised questions about the tax status of forthcoming issues.

In a promising application of mortgage-backed securities to the conventional loan market, banks, savings and loan associations, and subsidiaries of private mortgage insurance companies have placed a number of publicly issued pass-through securities (PIPs)[5] without any form of Government guarantee. PIPs provide a means for market pricing and public distribution of mortgage loans, substituting for private placement of whole loans and participations, or sale to a Government-related agency. The issuer forms a mortgage pool or trust, obtains private mortgage and hazard insurance and secures a rating, and sells the securities through an underwriting group—often to customers who regularly buy corporate bonds.

---

[4] Although six states formed housing finance agencies before 1970, only the New York housing finance agency issued bonds prior to that date. Such agencies are now found in forty states.

[5] A number of issuers have coined names for their securities—Connie Mac (Ticor), Pennie Mae (PMI), Maggie Mae (MGIC).

The first PIP was sold by Bank of America in September 1977, followed quickly by an offering of the First Federal Savings and Loan Association of Chicago in October. Securities totaling $728 million were sold in 1978 by four issuers and an additional $445 million was publicly placed in the first nine months of 1979. In a major extension of this market, "conduit" companies recently have begun to issue pass-through securities backed by conventional mortgages and serviced by thirty to forty lenders. This allows smaller originators access to the market, creating pools with broad geographic diversity.

PIPs offer several advantages over other loan sale alternatives. Public distribution provides a broader and deeper investment base than private placements, allowing large amounts of loans to be sold quickly at relatively attractive rates. In addition, details of the offering can be tailored to match the needs of the issuer rather than those of the Government-related credit agencies. For example, some agencies currently place limits on the maximum size of individual home loans that may be pooled as well as limit the amount of commitments accepted from any one seller. The agencies purchase loans in quantities determined by their own investment goals and require sellers to contract for delivery well in advance. Finally, many issuers feel they can provide insurance and administration at lower cost than the spread retained by the FHLMC when it issues PCs.

FORWARD COMMITMENTS

PCs and GNMA securities are sold mainly for forward delivery and settlement. These forward commitment procedures present a variety of new portfolio management options to investors more familiar with the immediate delivery conventions of the bond and equity markets. The necessity for a forward market arises from the special problems of originating home loans and packaging them for sale to final investors. Mortgage companies, thrift institutions, and other mortgage originators make commitments to lend funds in the future to builders and developers and to home buyers, although the borrowers are not obligated to take down the loans. Since home loans have long maturities and are often large relative to the borrowers' net worth, the time-consuming process of checking collateral and creditworthiness is particularly important.

It may take three to six months to accumulate a bundle of completed mortgage loans and process the necessary paperwork before selling the loans to a final investor. During this time, a mortgage originator bears the risk of capital loss if interest rates rise. For highly levered mortgage companies, even a small rate increase could be disastrous, making a purchase commitment from a future buyer desirable in many cases. "Firm" commitments require the loan seller to deliver mortgages at the commitment price; under a "standby" commitment, delivery is optional at the seller's discretion. Standby commitments are usually associated with more distant delivery horizons (often twelve months) and are accompanied by a nonrefundable fee of about 1 percent. To meet the demand for purchase commitments, particularly for twelve-month horizons or during tight money periods, standby commitments are often issued by banks and thrift institutions that may not desire delivery of the underlying mortgages but are willing to bear some price risk in return for the commitment fee. This can be done by fixing the strike price—the price at which delivery is made—at such a low level that the delivery option will not be exercised unless rates increase sharply.

In 1968 FNMA instituted a program for market determination of strike prices on its firm and standby forward commitments. FNMA now holds bi-weekly auctions in which lenders specify the rate at which they will offer various dollar amounts of mortgages. The volume of accepted offers is based on FNMA's cost of funds and the general tone of the mortgage market. Commitments are issued to successful bidders offering mortgages to FNMA at the highest yields (lowest strike prices). Since October 1971 four-month firm commitments have been auctioned biweekly, and since October 1972 twelve-month convertible standby commitments have been available as well. At the loan seller's option, these standby commitments may be converted to firm four-month commitments at the average price established in the most recent auction. These auction-market commitment procedures have not been imitated by other government or private loan purchasers, but an active over-the-counter forward market for pass-through securities serves much the same purpose.

This over-the-counter forward market—often called the "cash" market to differentiate it from the GNMA futures market on the commodities exchanges—is most active for GNMA securities, but similar procedures are followed in all pass-through markets. Dealers issue firm commitments to purchase or sell securities with stated certificate rates for delivery one to six months or more in the future.[6] The bid-asked spread is normally 1/8 percent for recently issued securities and somewhat higher for seasoned issues. Dealers may hedge their commitments with each other, with final investors, or in the futures market.

Some dealers also offer standby commitments that are essentially "put" options traded over the counter.[7] A potential seller of GNMA securities obtains a standby purchase commitment from the dealer for a negotiated fee, about 1 percent for the popular twelve-month contract. The strike price is

---

[6] These forward interest rates must be adjusted to get an unbiased estimate of future mortgage rates. As in any forward market for a durable commodity, forward prices tend to be lower than the cash prices expected to prevail on the delivery date when the cost of carry—anticipated capital gains plus any accrued interest less short-term interest rates and storage costs—is positive. With the usual upward-sloping yield curve and an unchanged interest rate forecast, forward commitment prices would normally be below prices quoted for immediate delivery.

[7] Although there is still some confusion on this point, the Commodity Futures Trading Commission is not expected to treat GNMA forwards as leverage instruments falling under its regulation. However, most regulations of financial institutions treat forward commitments as "puts" that may be questioned by examiners.

usually negotiated at a spread below the firm forward commitment price. The dealer may offset such a commitment by obtaining a standby commitment from a potential buyer, passing along most or all of the commitment fee.

Futures contracts—similar in many ways to firm GNMA forward commitments—may be arranged on the Chicago Board of Trade (CBT) and the Amex Commodities Exchange (ACE). At each exchange, contracts are available for delivery at three-month intervals going forward about two and one-half years. Delivery is guaranteed by the exchange, reducing the risk of delivery failures, and investors are required to post margin in the form of cash, securities, or a letter of credit. Contracts are evaluated at current market prices—marked to market—each day, and a maintenance margin is required to cover accumulated losses.

The contracts are issued in terms of a standard 8 percent GNMA certificate rate, but pass-throughs bearing other rates are deliverable according to an established price adjustment schedule. Because this schedule does not preserve equality of true yield to maturity for securities with different certificate rates, market participants generally find it advantageous to deliver a security with the highest allowable certificate rate. Under the new CBT contract and the ACE contract, only securities selling at or below par are deliverable, so that the "8 percent future", in fact, trades as if it were a contract for a GNMA issued at the current certificate rate.[8]

Because GNMA securities are Government backed, the forward market is exempt from most SEC (Securities and Exchange Commission) regulations. Unfortunately, it also has been associated with several well-publicized financial failures, leading to moves toward a restructuring of market practices.[9] Some dealers now request initial margin and mark outstanding contracts to market, requiring maintenance margins to cover accumulated losses.[10] Dealers also attempt to monitor the credit risk of customers, but a dealer generally has no means to determine a customer's total market exposure on a timely basis.

The risks inherent in issuing forward commitments for the purchase of pass-through securities (or taking the long side of a forward or futures contract) have caused regulators to question whether such activities are consistent with the fiduciary responsibilities of banks and thrift institutions. Firms

---

[8] Under the original CBT contract there was no "par cap", so that market participants tended to deliver securities with the highest available certificate rates.

[9] The three most widely publicized problems in GNMA trading have centered on forward commitment speculation resulting in delivery failures: The Winters Government Securities case involved questionable sales practices by a dealer. The University of Houston case resulted from overzealous investment plans of an investment officer. Most recently, the Reliance case involved massive failures by a mortgage banker to meet purchase commitments.

[10] The Justice Department has said that mandatory margin requirements proposed by the Mortgage-Backed Securities Dealers Association could constitute restraint of trade. Various forms of Government- and self-regulation are pending. These issues are discussed at length in *Analysis and Report on Alternative Approaches to Regulating the Trading of GNMA Securities* (November 7, 1978), prepared for GNMA by R. Shriver Associates.

may issue firm commitments with the hope of selling them prior to delivery at a speculative profit and may issue standby contracts for the fee income. Since delayed delivery contracts are an integral part of mortgage lending, the goal of regulation is to prevent abuses, while allowing financial intermediaries to perform this necessary role. To prevent portfolio managers from accumulating larger losses than can be accommodated at the time of settlement, most regulators and market participants support rules requiring all over-the-counter forward contracts to be marked to market and obligating buyers and sellers to post maintenance margins in the form of cash, securities, or letters of credit to cover any accumulated losses.[11] This would reduce the potential for the failure of one firm to create a chain reaction in the market but does little to insure that forward positions taken by individual investors are authorized by top management and are appropriate to the investment goals of the firm. Most market participants agree that, since little cash changes hands immediately, relative to the price exposure that is assumed in entering into a forward contract, operations of financial firms in either the forward or futures markets should be supervised at the highest management level.

OUTLOOK

The mortgage-backed securities market is coming of age. Up to this point, the market has been dominated by bonds issued by FNMA and by GNMA pass-through securities—both backed by FHA-VA loans. However, the relative importance of most types of Government-insured mortgages in the housing market is declining. Future growth of the pass-through market depends on the popularity of pass-through securities sold by the FHLMC and publicly issued by banks, savings and loan associations, and mortgage companies that are financing conventional mortgage loans. A second type of instrument, the mortgage-backed bond, is being used by thrift institutions to gain access to the capital markets, and tax-exempt bonds are being sold by state and local governments to support housing.

Mortgage-backed securities have important implications for economic efficiency and policy. By reducing geographic and institutional barriers to the movement of funds, the market facilitates a more efficient distribution of available financing to areas where housing demand is strongest. By allowing home buyers to compete for funds on favorable terms with corporate and governmental borrowers, the market contributes to general economic efficiency. Both of these effects increase the ability of the capital markets to generate mortgage funds by reducing the dependence of housing finance on interest-sensitive deposit flows. Thus, mortgage-backed securities help moderate the traditional "boom and bust" cycles in the housing sector by spreading the burden of high interest rates more evenly across all sectors of the economy.

[11] There is some feeling that contracts made by an approved mortgage issuer to sell any loans generated within the normal "production cycle" could be exempt from mark-to-market rules without undue risk of speculative abuse.

APPENDIX: ESTIMATING PASS-THROUGH YIELDS AND MATURITIES

The likelihood that many mortgages placed in a pass-through pool will be prepaid sometime before maturity creates uncertainty about the yield and average maturity of such an investment. Yields commonly quoted for pass-through securities are computed assuming there will be no prepayments until the twelfth year, at which time the entire remaining principal balance will be paid off. Monthly payments are assumed to be reinvested at the average yield, compounded monthly, until the end of the twelve-year horizon. This yield calculation probably does not give the best estimate of the rate of return, and a security's average maturity may differ significantly from twelve years.

To obtain a better estimate of the true yield of a pass-through security, a more realistic prepayment assumption must be employed. But, since pass-through securities are a relatively recent innovation, there is little direct prepayment evidence available. One strategy is to use the prepayment history of Federal Housing Administration (FHA) loans as a bench mark against which other mortgage pools may be measured.

Although few pools are likely to pay down precisely at the historical FHA rate, one plausible assumption is that the pattern of prepayments will be the same but will come in proportionately faster or slower. A "100 percent FHA" pool pays down at the historical FHA rate; a "200 percent FHA" pool pays down twice as fast (percentage of remaining balance that is prepaid each month, not dollar amount); a "0 percent FHA" pool has no prepayments (Chart 3).

Existing GNMA pools show a wide variation in prepayment experience. For example, 8 percent GNMA pass-throughs issued on December 1, 1970 had unpaid principal balances after eight and one-half years ranging from 70 to 29 percent of the original investment, corresponding to FHA paydown rates ranging from 50 to 200 percent. As the various types of pass-through securities have time to establish prepayment track records, it should be possible to determine more precisely which geographic, demographic, and financial factors affect the prepayment profile. Until such fac-

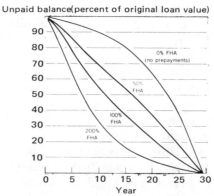

Chart 3 Unpaid balance at different paydown rates
10 percent GNMA certificate rate.

tors are analyzed more fully, buyers of newly issued pass-throughs will be unable to compute expected yields and average maturities with much precision. Similarly, the prepayment rate over the early years of the life of a pool need not give a good estimate of the subsequent prepayment rate.

Some prepayment assumption must be employed to produce a yield estimate well suited for comparison with returns on other types of instruments. If pass-through yields are to be compared with bonds, an adjustment must also be made for semiannual compounding. For example, a 9½ percent GNMA security priced at 96 has a quoted yield of 10.04 percent with the twelve-year paydown calculation. On a "true yield" basis, this security would yield 10.08 percent with a 100 percent FHA paydown or 10.21 percent with a 200 percent paydown. For securities such as this one, selling at prices close to par because they have certificate rates close to current market yields, the assumed prepayment rate does not have a large effect on yield. For securities selling at a deep discount (or premium), however, the prepayment assumption is a critical determinant of yield because the cash flow is assumed to be reinvested at the average yield rather than the certificate rate. As a result, an investor buying a deep discount GNMA pass-through would be willing to pay a premium price for a security backed by a "fast pay" pool expected to prepay at, say, a 400 percent FHA rate.

Because the cash flow from a pass-through security is concentrated in the early years, comparing pass-through yields with returns available in the bond market is not a straightforward exercise. The average maturity of a pass-through security—the proportion of the loan repaid each month times the number of months since the loan was originated—is sensitive to the prepayment assumption. A 9½ percent GNMA pool with no prepayments has an average life of 21.6 years. The average life under a standard twelve-year prepayment assumption is about 11.2 years, two years shorter than the 13.1-year average with a 100 percent FHA paydown. For a 200 percent FHA paydown, the average life drops to 8.9 years. These calculations suggest that most pass-through yields are roughly comparable to returns available on intermediate-term bonds.*

However, since pass-throughs return both principal and interest throughout their lives, reinvestment options must be considered carefully in light of interest rate expectations. When short-term interest rates are higher than the certificate rates on pass-throughs, fast pay pools appear attractive but, if short-term rates are expected to fall, investors would value such pools less highly. Rather than comparing pass-through yields with returns on bonds of similar average maturity, analysts can provide more useful information for investment decisions by comparing pass-through yields with returns on strips of bonds of various maturities weighted to produce a similar expected cash flow. This information may then be combined with estimates of possible reinvestment options, to decide whether the cash flow and yield characteristics of a particular pass-through are superior to the alternative presented by a given bond or combination of bonds.

---

*The calculation of average maturity and yield was recently discussed by Dexter Senft in "The 'True Yield' of a Pass-Through Security", *The Mortgage Banker* (September 1979).

Part II

D. INTEREST RATE FUTURES

This section contains four articles dealing with interest rate futures contracts. The first article, by Marcelle Arak and Christopher J. McCurdy, provides a comprehensive overview of the workings and structure of the futures market. The remaining articles are applications-oriented and show how interest rate futures may be used to achieve certain objectives. The article by George M. McCabe and James M. Blackwell shows how futures contracts can be used by banks to *hedge* the interest rate risk associated with funding loans that have a longer maturity than the under-lying source of funds. In the article by John A. Boquist and John M. Finkelstein, a variety of examples and applications are demonstrated. These include activities related to *hedging, speculation*, and *arbitrage*. In the last article in this section, James Kurt Dew and Terrence F. Martell show how the futures market can be used by a bank (or other lender) to create a *synthetic fixed rate loan*. Such an arrangement may be used to satisfy the needs of borrowers for a fixed rate, while providing the bank (or other lender) with a variable return that satisfies its needs.

INTEREST RATE FUTURES*

*Marcelle Arak and
Christopher J. McCurdy†*

21

On a typical day in 1979, futures contracts representing about $7½ billion in three-month Treasury bills changed hands in the International Monetary Market (IMM) of the Chicago Mercantile Exchange in Chicago. This market and several other new markets for interest rate futures have very quickly become active trading arenas. For example, at the Chicago Board of Trade (CBT), futures contracts representing $820 million of long-term Treasury bonds were traded on a typical day; also, at the CBT, futures contracts representing $540 million of GNMAs (Government National Mortgage Association securities) changed hands on an average day.

Besides these three well-established interest rate futures contracts several new financial futures contracts have recently received the approval of the Commodity Futures Trading Commission (CFTC) and have begun trading. Futures contracts for intermediate-term Treasury notes commenced trading in the summer of 1979; in the fall, the Comex (Commodity Exchange, Inc.), which had traded many metals contracts, inaugurated a three-month bill futures contract, and the ACE (Amex Commodities Exchange, Inc., an affiliate of the American Stock Exchange) introduced a bond futures contract;

*Reprinted from the *Quarterly Review*, Winter 1979-80, pp. 33-46, with permission from the Federal Reserve Bank of New York.

†The authors wish to thank James Kurt Dew, Ronald Hobson, and Anthony Vignola for information and helpful comments. The foregoing do not necessarily agree with the views expressed herein, nor do they bear responsibility for any errors.

in addition, the New York Stock Exchange is intending to start a financial futures unit.

What accounts for the rapid growth of interest rate futures? Who are the most active participants in these markets? Some businesses such as financial institutions and securities dealers use it to hedge or manage interest rate risk. By and large, however, participants are involved for other reasons and help provide much of the markets' liquidity. A large portion of the activity in these markets is speculative—people and institutions betting on which way interest rates will move and how the interest rate in one month will move relative to another. Others are involved in these interest rate futures markets for tax reasons.

Both the enormous size of these futures markets and the nature of the participants are a matter of concern for the regulatory authorities. The Treasury and the Federal Reserve System have become aware of potential problems for the functioning of markets in Government securities; these problems include the possibility of corners or squeezes on certain Treasury issues and the disruption of orderly cash markets for Treasury securities. In addition, the regulatory authorities have become concerned that the substantial numbers of small investors participating in the markets may not be fully aware of the risks involved.

WHAT IS A FUTURES MARKET?

For as long as mankind has traded goods and services, people have made contracts which specify that commodities and money will change hands at some future date, at a price stated in the contract. Such contracts are called "forward" contracts. A forward contract tailored to one's needs offers obvious advantages—one can pick the exact date and the precise commodity desired. On the other hand, there are disadvantages. It may be difficult to locate a buyer or seller with exactly opposite needs. In addition, there is a risk that the other party to the transaction will default.

A *futures* contract is a standardized forward contract that is traded on an exchange. Usually the type and grade of commodity is specified as well as the date for delivery. Once a bargain is struck, the clearinghouse of the futures exchange itself becomes the opposite party to every transaction. Thus, it is the soundness of the exchange's clearinghouse rather than the creditworthiness of the original buyer (or seller) that is of concern to the seller (or buyer) on the other side of the transaction. To ensure its viability, futures exchanges and their clearinghouses set up rules and regulations. These include the requirements that a clearing member firm and its customers put up "margin", that the contracts be marked-to-market daily, and that trading cease if daily price fluctuations move outside certain limits.

Among the oldest futures markets in the United States are those for wheat and corn which date back to the middle of the nineteenth century. Thereafter, futures markets for other farm products and raw materials gradually developed. One of the major purposes was to provide producers and processors with price insurance. Suppose a farmer expects to harvest wheat in July. Nobody knows with certainty what the price will be then; it depends upon the size of the harvest and conditions elsewhere in the world. However, by selling a futures contract for July wheat, the farmer can indirectly guarantee receiving a particular price. This is illustrated in Box 1.

Futures markets for commodities not only provide a forum for hedgers, but they also provide information. This information—about prices expected to prevail on future dates—is printed in the financial section of many daily newspapers. The farmer, for example, can use these futures prices to decide whether to plant corn or wheat. The food processor can gear up to can corn or beans depending upon the expected prices and the prospective consumer demand at those prices.

Interest rate futures are a relatively new development. In the fall of 1975, the CBT inaugurated a GNMA contract. Shortly thereafter, in early 1976, the IMM introduced a contract for ninety-day Treasury bills, and this was followed in 1977 by the CBT's Treasury bond futures contract. These three contracts—the CBT's original GNMA, the CBT's Treasury bond, and the IMM's three-month Treasury bill contract—have proved to be the most popular and heavily traded financial futures contracts. The amount of contracts outstanding, or open interest, in these markets has expanded significantly since their inception (Chart 1). Moreover, trading volume has also become quite large in relation to the underlying cash market securities. In 1979, daily average trading in the eight ninety-day Treasury bill contracts on the IMM was equivalent to about $7½ billion (at $1 million per contract), not much different from the daily volume of Treasury bills traded in the dealer market for United States Government securities.[1] Some interest rate futures contracts, however, have failed to attract much trading activity. For example, activity in the ninety-day commercial paper contract has remained quite light.[2]

HOW FINANCIAL FUTURES MARKETS OPERATE

The financial futures markets operate in the same manner as other futures markets. Their terms and methods are very different from those used in the money and bond markets. One of the most active financial futures markets

[1] The market is described in "The Dealer Market for United States Government Securities", Christopher McCurdy in this bank's *Quarterly Review* (Winter 1977-78), pages 35-47.

[2] One of the problems with this contract has been that commercial paper issuers have at times tended to sell paper with maturities much shorter than ninety days. Also, because the paper of a large number of companies is deliverable against the contract, this generates substantial uncertainty about which paper will be delivered. In addition, the original technical specifications of the contract engendered some confusion.

Box 1

Hedge in Wheat Futures

A farmer planning to harvest wheat in July sells a July wheat futures contract at $2.98 in March.

(1)	Suppose the price in July turns out to be.	$2.50	$3.00	$3.50
(2)	Gain or loss from offsetting futures contract [$2.98 − row (1)] . . .	.48	−.02	−.52
(3)	Sales price of wheat in cash market [same as row (1)]	2.50	3.00	3.50
(4)	Total earnings per bushel [row (2) + row (3)]	2.98	2.98	2.98

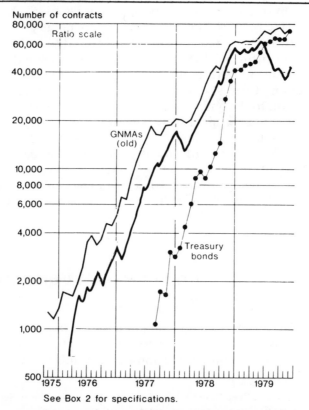

See Box 2 for specifications.

Sources: International Monetary Market and Chicago Board of Trade.

Source: International Monetary Market and Chicago Board of Trade.
See Box 2 for specifications.

is that for three-month Treasury bills at the IMM. Through this exchange, a customer could, for example, buy a contract to take delivery of (and pay for) $1 million of three-month Treasury bills on March 20, 1980. In all, there are eight contract delivery months on the IMM, extending at quarterly intervals for about two years into the future.

A customer places his order with a futures commission merchant—a firm registered with the CFTC and permitted to accept orders from the public—which sends the order to the trading floor of the exchange. There, a member of the exchange enters the trading pit and announces his intention to purchase the March 1980 contract. Another member who has an order to sell that contract shouts out his offer and, if the two can agree on a price, the trade is consummated. The trading in the pit is by *open outcry*, which is typical of futures exchanges and very unlike the over-the-telephone negotiations in the cash market for Treasury Securities.

The contract's price is quoted as the difference between 100 and the discount rate on the bill in question. Thus, a contract fixing a bill rate of 8.50 percent would be quoted at 91.50. This index preserves the normal futures market relationship in which the party obligated to take (make) delivery profits when the price rises (falls). The contract quote is not the price that would actually be paid for the bill at delivery. That price is computed by using the rate of discount in the standard bill price formula.

The clearinghouse interposes itself between the buyer and the seller, so that the buyer's contract is not with the seller but with the clearinghouse. (In the same fashion, the seller's contract is with the clearinghouse and not with the original buyer.)

A key ingredient in the financial viability of the clearinghouse is the margin that the clearing member firms must post on their contracts. For each outright purchase or sale of a three-month Treasury bill contract on the IMM, the firm must post margin of $1,200 per contract, which can be in the form of cash or bank letter of credit. The clearing member firm must, in turn, impose an initial margin of at least $1,500 on the customer. This may be posted in the form of cash, selected securities, or bank letters of credit. Futures firms can and often do require higher than the minimum margins of their customers. Margins formerly were more lenient, at one point down to $800 initial margin, but were raised following the greater volatility that emerged in the financial markets in the wake of the Federal Reserve System's policy actions in October 1979.

For as long as the position is outstanding, the contract will be *marked-to-market* by the clearinghouse at the end of each business day. For example a clearing member with a long position in the March contract would have its margin account credited with a profit if the price rises, or debited with a loss if it declines. The prices used in the calculations are the *final settlement prices*, which are determined by the exchange by examining the prices attached to the trades transacted at the end of trading each day.

Profits in the margin account may be withdrawn immediately. When losses occur and reduce the firm's margin below $1,200, the firm must pay the difference to the clearinghouse in cash before trading opens the next day. It is permissible for the value of a customer's margin account to fall below the initial $1,500 but, once the margin account falls below the $1,200 mainten-ance margin, the account must be replenished in full—brought back up to $1,500. Since the value of a 1 basis point change in the futures bill rate is $25 per contract, relatively small changes in interest rates can result in large changes in the value of a margin account.

The exchanges impose rules that prices may not change by more than a certain maximum amount from one day to the next. At the IMM, for exam-ple, no bill futures trades may be cleared if the price is more than 50 basis points above or below the final settlement price on the previous day although, if the *daily limit* restricts trading for a few days, then wider limits may be imposed on subsequent days. Margins are often temporarily increased during such periods.

When the customer wishes to get out of his contract before maturity, he must take an offsetting position. To cancel the contract he bought, he must sell another contract. His order is forwarded to the pit and a sales contract is executed, but not necessarily with the party who sold it to him in the first place. Once again, the clearinghouse interposes itself between the two parties and the latest sale will be offset against the original purchase. The customer's overall position will be canceled, and the funds in the margin account will be returned to him.

The lion's share of all contracts traded are terminated before maturity in this fashion. Only a very small percentage of contracts traded is delivered. In the case of Treasury bills, delivery takes place on the day after trading stops. The customer who has sold the contract (the short) delivers $1 million (par value) of Treasury bills that have ninety, ninety-one, or ninety-two days to maturity, and the customer who bought the contract (the long) pays for the bills with immediately available funds. The price paid for the bills is the set-tlement price on the last day of trading. (With the daily marking-to-market, almost all losses and gains have been realized before the final delivery takes place.)

Variations in procedures exist on different contracts and exchanges, but they generally adhere to the same principles: open outcry trading, interposi-tion of the clearinghouse, posting of margin, and daily marking-to-market. Box 2 delineates the key specifications on financial futures contracts. Prob-ably the most important difference among contracts is that some allow de-livery of a variety of securities. The active Treasury bond contract, for ex-ample, permits delivery of bonds from a "market basket" of different bonds, all with maturity (or first call) beyond fifteen years. This has the effect of substantially increasing the deliverable supply of securities but generates some uncertainty among those taking delivery as to which bonds they might receive.

The formal organizational structure of futures trading stands in contrast to the informal nature of forward trading. Dealers in the market for United States Government securities often agree to transact trades that call for for-ward delivery of Treasury issues. These trades are negotiated in the same fashion as trades for immediate delivery. There is no standardized contract as in the futures market: the two parties must agree to the specific security involved, the exact delivery date, the size of trade, and the price. These terms are set according to the mutual convenience of the two parties. Often, there is no initial margin and no marking-to-market to account for gains and losses. Thus, each participant must size up the creditworthiness of the other. Finally, these agreements, for the most part, are designed to result in delivery. (Some GNMA forward trades among a few firms can be offset through a clearinghouse arrangement.) If either side wishes to cancel the trade, it must go back to the other side and negotiate a termination.

PARTICIPANTS IN THE INTEREST RATE FUTURES MARKET

Many types of financial institutions participate in the markets for interest rate futures, but private individuals not acting in a business capacity account for the major part of interest rate futures positions in the three most active contracts (Chart 2).

According to a survey by the CFTC of positions outstanding on March 30, 1979, businesses other than the futures industry, commonly called "commercial traders", accounted for only about one quarter of open interest held in the most active contracts (ninety-day Treasury bills on the IMM, and Treasury bonds and the original GNMA contract on the CBT). In an earlier survey, such participants had held about three eighths of those contracts outstanding on November 30, 1977 (Table 1). The involvement of commercial traders is important because they are the only group that can use futures

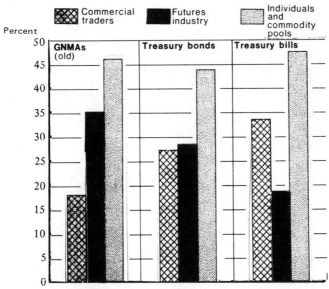

Chart 2   Futures Markets Participants, March 30, 1979. Source: Commodity Futures Trading Commission. Shares of open interest held by various groups.

Box 2

Futures Contracts on Treasury Securities (Currently Trading)

	Treasury bills				Intermediate-term Treasury coupon securities		Treasury bonds	
	ACE	COMEX	IMM	IMM	CBT	IMM	ACE	CBT
Deliverable items . . .	$1 million par value of Treasury bills with 90, 91, or 92 days to maturity	$1 million par value of Treasury bills with 90, 91, or 92 days to maturity	$1 million par value of Treasury bills with 90, 91, or 92 days to maturity	$250,000 par value of Treasury bills due in 52 weeks	$100,000 par value of Treasury notes and noncallable bonds with 4 to 6 years to maturity	$100,000 par value of Treasury notes maturing between 3½ years and 4½ years	$100,000 par value of Treasury bonds with at least 20 years to maturity	$100,000 par value of Treasury bonds with at least 15 years to first call or to maturity
Initial margin* (per contract)	$800	$800	$1,500	$600	$900	$500	$2,000	$2,000[†]
Maintenance margin* (per contract)	$600	$600	$1,200	$400	$600	$300	$1,500	$1,600[†]
Daily limits[‡]	50 basis points	60 basis points	50 basis points	50 basis points	1 point (32/32)	3/4 point (48/64)	1 point (32/32)[§]	2 points (64/32)
Delivery months (each year)	January, April, July, October	February, May, August, November	March, June, September, December	March, June, September, December	March, June, September, December	February, May, August, November	February, May, August, November	March, June, September, December
Total open interest (December 31, 1979) .	106	913	36,495	435	715	265	207	90,676
Date trading began . .	June 26, 1979	October 2, 1979	January 6, 1979	September 11, 1978	June 25, 1979	July 10, 1979	November 14, 1979	August 22, 1977

Non-Treasury Securities Futures

	Government National Mortgage Association (modified pass-through mortgage-backed certificates)				Commercial paper	
	CBT (old)	CBT (new)	ACE	COMEX	CTB (30-day)	CBT (90-day)
Deliverable items .	Collateralized depository receipt covering $100,000 principal balance of GNMA certificates	$100,000 principal balance of GNMA certificates	$100,000 principal balance of GNMA certificates	$100,000 principal balance of GNMA certificates	$3 million face value of prime commercial paper rated A-1 by Standard & Poor's and P-1 by Moody's	$1 million face value of prime commercial paper rated A-1 by Standard & Poor's and P-1 by Moody's
Initial margin* (per contract) . . .	$2,000	$2,000	$2,000	$1,500	$1,500	$1,500
Maintenance margin* (per contract) . . .	$1,500	$1,500	$1,500	$1,125	$1,200	$1,200
Daily limits‡ . . .	1½ points (48/32)	1½ points (48/32)	3/4 point (24/32) §	1 point (64/64)	50/100 point	50/100 point
Delivery months (each year).	March, June, September, December	March, June, September, December	February, May, August, November	January, April July, October ‖	March, June, September, December	March, June, September, December
Total open interest (December 31 1979).	88,982	4,478	3,248	64	12	533
Date trading began	October 20, 1975	September 12, 1978	September 12, 1978	November 13, 1979	May 14, 1979	September 26, 1977

All specifications are as of year-end 1979.

*The speculative margin is shown where margins vary according to whether the contracts cover speculative, hedged, or spread positions.

†For all contracts but those which mature in current month. Then initial margin is increased to $2,500 and maintenance margin is raised to $2,000.

‡Exchanges frequently have rules allowing expansion of daily limits once they have been in effect for a few days (margins may change also).

§ Limits in suspension as of the year-end.

‖Principal trading months; rules allow trading for current plus two succeeding months.

Table 1

Futures Markets Participants

November 30, 1977 and March 30, 1979
Average open interest; number of contracts

Type of participant	Government National Mortgage Association contract (old)				Treasury bond contract				Three-month Treasury bill contract			
	1977 amount	1977 as percentage of total	1979 amount	1979 as percentage of total	1977 amount	1977 as percentage of total	1979 amount	1979 as percentage of total	1977 amount	1977 as percentage of total	1979 amount	1979 as percentage of total
Commercial traders												
(total)	7,226	36.5	10,899	18.3	2,025	67.2	12,393	27.4	4,950	32.8	14,992	33.6
Securities dealers	3,395	17.1	4,270	7.2	1,534	50.9	8,226	18.2	2,758	18.3	5,596	12.5
Commercial banks	263	1.3	655	1.1	99	3.3	1,472	3.3	326	2.2	1,581	3.5
Savings and loan associations	494	2.5	2,500	4.2	–	–	394	0.9	56	0.4	136	0.3
Mortgage bankers	1,198	6.1	1,472	2.5	154	5.1	330	0.7	44	0.3	974	2.2
Other	1,875	9.5	2,003	3.4	238	7.9	1,971	4.4	1,767	11.7	6,706	15.0
Noncommercial traders *(total)*	12,588	63.5	48,705	81.7	989	32.8	32,826	72.6	10,154	67.2	29,661	66.4
Futures industry	7,353	37.1	21,113	35.4	477	15.8	12,924	28.6	2,765	18.3	8,434	18.9
Commodity pools	2,862	14.4	11,097	18.6	254	8.4	9,484	21.0	1,520	10.1	5,640	12.6
Individual traders	2,373	12.0	16,495	27.7	258	8.6	10,481	23.0	5,868	38.8	15,586	34.9
Total	19,814	100	59,604	100	3,014	100	45,219	100	15,104	100	44,654	100

Because of rounding, amounts and percentages may not add to totals.

Source: Commodity Futures Trading Commission Surveys. The 1977 survey covered all positions, but the 1979 survey excluded positions of fewer than five contracts.

contracts for hedging cash market positions to any meaningful extent. (See next section.)

Moreover, some of the businesses who participate in these futures markets are probably not trying to eliminate risk completely. Consider securities dealers, for example, who have been very active in interest rate futures markets—they held about 7 percent of total GNMA positions and about 18 percent of total bond positions in March 1979. Securities dealers are generally risk takers, trying to benefit from interest rate change, or arbitrageurs, trying to benefit from interest rate disparities, rather than hedgers. But, in meeting customers' needs and making a market in Government securities, they do make use of interest rate futures markets to manage their risk exposure.

Among other business participants, mortgage bankers and savings and loan associations combined held about 7 percent of total positions in GNMAs. Their participation in GNMAs is to be expected in view of their involvement in generating and investing in mortgages. A total of sixty-eight of these firms held positions on March 30, 1979, not much above the number reported in the earlier survey. Few commercial banks have been active in interest rate futures—twenty-four had open positions in bill futures, and fourteen in bond futures on March 30, 1979—accounting for a small fraction of total positions in these markets. Their relatively low level of participation may have reflected regulatory restrictions on their involvement in the futures market or some confusion about the regulators' policies.

Futures industry personnel and firms held a significant fraction of the open positions. This group includes many who are speculating on rate movements in general or on the spread relations between rates on successive contracts. Or they might be operating in both the cash and futures markets, arbitraging differences between the two markets.

Individuals and commodity pools—funds which purchase futures contracts—are very important participants in financial futures markets. They held almost half of the open positions in 1979, a substantial increase from their already significant participation in the earlier survey. Indeed, the 1979 share of total positions in financial contracts was certainly higher than that because positions of less than five contracts were not included in the second survey and individuals tend to hold the vast majority of such small positions.[3]

SERVICES PROVIDED BY INTEREST
RATES FUTURES MARKETS

It is commonly believed that futures markets provide certain benefits—in the main, an inexpensive way to hedge risk and generate information on ex-

---

[3]Small positions in the bill futures contracts amounted to about 8,000 contracts at the end of March 1979 and thus would raise the combined share of individuals and commodity pools to a bit more than half of the bill futures market. Comparable calculations cannot be made for the CBT's bond and GMNA contracts because some small positions are posted on a net basis (*i.e.,* long positions are offset against short positions), compared with a gross basis as in the bill contracts.

pected prices. Interest rate futures markets also provide these benefits.

Several observers have noted that interest rate futures markets are not necessary to provide information on future interest rates or as a hedging mechanism. They point out that one can obtain information on future interest rates by comparing yields on outstanding securities which have different maturities. However, the interest rate futures markets do provide future interest rate information in a more convenient form.

It is also true that outstanding securities could be used to hedge market risk. Again, however, the futures market can provide a less cumbersome and expensive hedge. Suppose, for example, that a firm is planning to issue short-term securities three months in the future and is worried about the prospective short-term interest rate. The short sale of a Treasury bill with more than three months to maturity is one way to hedge the risk.[4] In the futures market, the interest rate risk on this prospective issue could be hedged by selling the Treasury bill contract for the month closest to the prospective issue date. If all short rates moved up, the hedger would make a gain on the futures market transaction which would offset the loss on the higher interest rate he would have to offer.

Banks, dealers, and other such financial institutions may find futures markets helpful in achieving a particular maturity structure for their portfolios while having adequate supplies of cash securities on hand. For example, a dealer may need to hold supplies of a six-month bill to be ready for customer orders. However, he may not want the risk exposure on this particular maturity because he thinks its rate is likely to rise. Or, a mortgage banker may wish to hedge the risk on rates between the time of the mortgage loan and the time of its sale as part of a large package of loans. By selling a GNMA futures contract while assembling the mortgage package, the banker can be insured against rate changes. If rates rise, the value of the mortgage portfolio will fall, but that will be offset by the profits on the short sale of the GNMA contract. If, on the other hand, rates fall, the gain on the mortgage portfolio is offset by the loss on the sale of GNMA futures. In this hedge, the banker foregoes the possibility of additional profit (or loss) and is content to profit from the origination and servicing fees associated with assembling the mortgages.

Not every financial transaction has an exact hedge in the futures market. When the cash asset is different from the security specified in the futures contract, the transaction is called a "cross hedge" and provides much less protection than an exact hedge. For example, a securities dealer might find it profitable to buy some certificates of deposit (CDs) and finance them for one month. To protect against a decline (increase) in the price (rates) of CDs over the interval, the dealer might sell Treasury bill futures contracts, assuming the movements in bill rates and CD rates will be similar over the interval.

---

[4]The prospective issuer could borrow a six-month Treasury bill and sell it immediately; three months hence he would buy a bill with the same maturity date to return. If interest rates for that future time interval rise, the security would be purchased more cheaply three months hence than is currently expected. The gain on this transaction would then offset the loss connected with issuing securities at the higher interest rate.

So long as the rates move in the same *direction* the dealer will be protected at least to some degree against adverse price movements. It is conceivable, however, that the rates could move in opposite directions. Thus, a cross hedge is really a speculation on the relationship between the particular cash market security held in position and the particular futures contract involved. In a cross hedge, the participants cannot deliver the cash security against the contract, so there is no threat of delivery that can be used to drive the prices on the two securities back into line as the expiration date approaches.

In contrast to financial businesses, nonfinancial businesses and private individuals are less likely to find a useful hedge in the interest rate futures market. Consider the typical nonfinancial business which is planning to issue securities to finance some capital purchase or inventory. If the rate of inflation accelerates, the firm will typically be able to sell its output at higher prices. Thus, its nominal profit and return from the investment will typically also rise.[5] This means that a rise in inflationary expectations, which is reflected in the nominal rate of interest, will tend to affect profits in the same direction as it does financing costs. Thus, to some extent, the firm is automatically hedged against inflation-induced changes in the interest rate.

A similar intrinsic hedge may be available to investors on any new funds they plan to invest. Presumably they want to be sure that their investment produces a certain real income or purchasing power in the future. If interest rates move down because anticipated inflation has fallen, then the return on any funds invested at the lower rate will be able to buy the same quantity of goods and services that they would have in the circumstances where inflation and interest rates were higher. (The real return on *past* savings, however will move in the opposite direction as inflation.)

Thus, to the extent that interest rate changes reflect revisions in inflationary expectations, many businesses and persons will not be in a very risky position with regard to saving or investment plans. If, as some contend, the variation in interest rates is largely connected with inflationary expectations, these groups would typically not obtain a very useful hedge in the interest rate futures market.

SPECULATION

While some participants use futures markets to hedge risk, others use them to speculate on price movements. Speculators like the high leverage obtainable and the low capital required for trades in futures markets relative to trades in cash markets. Speculation on interest rates could be accomplished in the cash markets but would typically involve greater costs than in futures

---

[5]The firm does not, however, tend to earn nominal profits in proportion to prices because the tax structure collects more in real terms during inflation. See M. Arak, "Can the Performance of the Stock Market Be Explained by Inflation Coupled with our Tax System?" (Federal Reserve Bank of New York Research Paper).

markets. For example, suppose one thinks that the three-month interest rate in the June-September period will be higher than the implicit forward rate for that time interval. The short sale of a September bill in March and its repurchase in June can produce a profit if those high rates materialize. The costs involved in these transactions include the dollar value of the bid-ask spread as well as the charges for borrowing a security. In addition, one must have sufficient capital to put up collateral equivalent in value to the securities borrowed or the credit standing to borrow the securities under a reverse repurchase agreement.

In futures markets, one does not pay for or receive money for the commodity in advance. The cost of trading in the futures market is the foregone interest on the margin deposit (if in the form of cash) plus the commission fees. Assuming a $70 commission, this would amount to about $125 on a three-month bill futures contract at current interest rates, if the contract were held for three months. A change in the discount rate on the futures contract of 5 basis points would therefore recompense the speculator for his costs (Table 2).

Besides speculating on the level of rates, some futures market participants may be speculating on the relationship among interest rates. Such speculation can take the form of a "spread" trade whereby the participant buys one contract and sells another, hoping that the rate on the contract bought will fall by more than (or rise by less than) the rate on the contract sold. Also, if participants believe that the slope of the yield curve will change in a predictable way when the level of the yield curve changes, a spread transaction (which involves a lower margin) can be a less expensive way to speculate on the level of rates.

Frequently, traders will take positions in futures contracts that are related to positions in cash market securities. A trader might think that the rate in the futures market is out of line with cash Treasury bills. If he feels the futures rate is low relative to the rates on outstanding bills, he might sell the

Table 2 **Change in Discount Rate on a Three-Month Treasury Bill Futures Contract Necessary to Cover Cost of a Futures Market Transaction**

In basis points

Holding period	Commission (in dollars)		
	$30	$50	$70
One month.	2.0	2.8	3.6
Three months	3.4	4.2	5.0
Six months.	5.7	6.5	7.3
Twelve months	10.2	11.0	11.8

$$\text{Basis point change} = \frac{C + \dfrac{h(.01i)m}{12}}{25}$$

where h is the number of months the contract is held, i is the rate of interest obtainable over the period h, m is the cash margin, and C is the commission on the futures trade. The numbers shown are based upon i = 15 percent and m = $1,500.

futures contract and buy the bills in the cash market. He could then carry the bill in position until the two rates move back to their more normal relationship. Then the bills would be sold and the short bill futures contract offset. These types of trades are often called "arbitrages" by participants in the cash market although they are not arbitrages in the strict sense in which a security is bought in one market and at the same time sold in another, thereby locking in an assured return. In fact, most arbitraging activity generally reflects speculation on the relationship between cash and futures rates.

USE OF FUTURES MARKETS TO
REDUCE TAX LIABILITY

Individuals and institutions have also used interest rate futures markets to reduce their taxes. One means was through spread transactions.

Until November 1978, spread transactions in the Treasury bill futures market were a popular means of postponing taxes. An individual would buy one contract and sell another, both for the next calendar year. For example, in 1976, the participant might have bought the March 1977 contract and sold the September 1977 contract. An important assumption was that interest rates on all contracts would tend to move together so that the net risk was relatively small. At some point before the end of 1976, whichever position had produced a loss would be closed out. (In the above example, the short position or the sale of the September 1977 contract was the item that showed a loss during the latter part of 1976.) That loss could then be deducted from other income for 1976, reducing the 1976 tax bill. The contract for March 1977, on which the gain had accrued, was not closed out until 1977 when it no longer affected the 1976 tax liability.[6]

What made Treasury bill futures particularly attractive for such spreads was the belief of many taxpayers that, just like actual Treasury bills, they were not capital assets. In contrast, it was clear that other types of futures contracts, not held exclusively for business purposes, were capital assets.[7] If Treasury bill futures were not capital assets, then losses on them could be fully subtracted from other ordinary income (providing that *net* ordinary income did not become negative). Capital losses, in contrast, could be subtracted from ordinary income to a very limited extent.[8]

This attraction of the Treasury bill futures market for tax postponement

[6] After the September 1977 contract was offset, another contract for 1977 would be sold to maintain a balanced position. In our example, the June 1977 contract would be sold to counterbalance the March 1977 contract that was still being held. Then sometime in early 1977, these two contracts would be closed out.

[7] *E.g.*, Faroll v. Jarecki, 231 F.2d 281 (7th Cir. 1956).

[8] Capital losses can be offset against capital gains with no limitation, but the excess of loss over gains that may be deducted from ordinary income in a single year is currently limited to $3,000.

[9] Rev. Rul. 78-414, 1978-2 C.B. 213.

[10] Rev. Rul. 77-185, 1977-1 C.B. 48.

was eliminated in November 1978 when the IRS declared that a futures contract for Treasury bills is a capital asset if neither held primarily for sale to customers in the ordinary course of business nor purchased as a hedge.[9] Further, the IRS, amplifying on an earlier ruling,[10] stated that the maintenance of a "spread" position, in transactions involving futures contracts for Treasury bills, may not result in allowance of deductions where no real economic loss is incurred.

A way that individuals can reduce taxes through the futures market is by indirectly converting part of the interest income on Treasury bills into long-term capital gains. Suppose that the discount rate on a bill is expected to fall as it matures. Since the market usually regards longer dated bills as less liquid (or as having more interest rate risk), an investor would typically expect that a bill maturing in, say, March 1981 would offer a higher annual discount rate in June 1980 than it would in February 1981. Similarly, the interest rate on futures contracts would tend to fall as they approach expiration (their price would rise). Pursuant to the November 1978 IRS ruling, the price increase in a Treasury bill futures contract should, in nonbusiness circumstances, be treated as a capital gain for an investor. In contrast, since a Treasury bill itself is not a capital asset, all the price appreciation on it—from date of purchase to date of sale—would be treated as ordinary income for tax purposes.

An investor would clearly prefer to have the price appreciation treated as a long-term gain rather than as ordinary income, since the long-term capital gains tax rate is only 40 percent of that for ordinary income. If a long position in a bill futures contract were held for more than six months, the profit would be a long-term capital gain. (Gains and losses on short positions in futures are always treated as short-term regardless of the holding period.) Consequently, some investors who might normally purchase 52-week bills would have an incentive to purchase distant futures contracts and, as those contracts matured, sell them off to take their capital gains. They could then invest their funds in three-month bills. These activities would tend to raise the discount rate on the 52-week bill. It would also tend to reduce the required discount rate on distant futures contracts. Thus, the discount rates on futures contracts would be pushed below the implicit forward discount rate on cash bills.

There are, of course, limits on the size of the wedge that can be driven between the forward rate on cash securities and the rate on futures contracts. Financial businesses cannot treat profits in bill futures as capital gains. For them, the futures contract has no tax advantage over a cash bill. When the wedge produced by investors exceeds the cost of arbitrage, these financial businesses will buy long-term bills and sell futures contracts to profit from disparities in rates.

RELATIONSHIP BETWEEN THE CASH AND FUTURES MARKETS

For many commodities, the spot price and the futures price are very closely related. Part of the explanation is that, if a commodity is storable, it can be bought today, stored, and sold at a future date. If the futures price were to exceed the spot price by more than the costs involved, arbitrageurs would buy the commodity in the spot market—raising the spot price—and would sell it in the futures market, lowering the futures price. These activities would reduce the disparity between the future price and the current price.

The relationship between cash and futures markets for bills is somewhat different from that for other commodities. A three-month Treasury bill cannot be stored for more than three months; it matures. However, a longer term bill could be "stored" until it has three months left to run. It is the cash market for that *longer term bill* which bears a relationship to the futures market that is typical of agricultural and industrial commodities. In the case of note and bond contracts, the deliverable item exists throughout the life of the contract.

For example, consider what cash market securities correspond to the IMM's June 1980 three-month Treasury bill contract. This contract calls for delivery of bills which have ninety-one days to run on June 19, 1980. Treasury bills having this maturity date will be sold by the Treasury in two auctions—as six-month bills on March 17, 1980 and as three-month bills on June 16, 1980. During the first three months of its life, the six-month bill issued on March 20, 1980 is the commodity that could be "stored" for delivery on the futures contract.

The funds used to purchase the six-month bill when it is initially issued could have been invested in three-month bills which mature on the contract expiration date. One measure of the interest cost involved in storage is therefore the foregone interest on the shorter bill—this is the "opportunity cost" of the decision to invest in the longer bill which is deliverable on the futures contract. It is common to subtract that opportunity cost from the bill price to get the "forward" price and the corresponding "forward" rate; this rate can then be compared with the discount rate on the futures contract.

Because in the past only three-month and six-month bills matured on Thursdays, only bills originally issued as three-month or six-month bills could be delivered on a ninety-day bill futures contract.[11] In fact, at any date, there was only one bill issue in existence that could be delivered on an IMM bill futures contract. That particular bill had between three and six months to maturity and could be delivered on the closest three-month bill futures contract. For longer bill futures contracts, there was usually no exact correspondence. There is no cash bill in existence today that could be delivered on the September 1980, December 1980, March 1981, and subsequent contracts traded on the IMM. However, there are bills which have a maturity date that may be quite close. For example, the 52-week bill maturing on September 16, 1980 will have eighty-nine days to run on June 19, 1980, while the June futures contract calls for bills which have ninety to ninety-two days to run on that date. By comparing the rate on this 52-week bill with the rate on the 52-week bill which matures twelve weeks earlier, a forward rate which covers

---

[11] Now that the Treasury has begun to issue 52-week bills maturing on Thursdays, there will be some occasions on which bills issued as 52-week bills will be deliverable against the three-month bill contracts.

an interval close to that of the futures contract bill can be calculated. Through
this method, a rough forward rate in the period nine months prior to the
contract's expiration can be obtained.

How does the rate on a three-month Treasury bill futures contract compare with the implicit forward rate in the cash market? The futures rate on
the June 1979 contract and the "forward" rate on the corresponding cash
bill (which matured September 21, 1979) moved very similarly in the last
ninety-one days before the futures contract expired (Chart 3). Typically, the
spread between the two rates was less than 25 basis points, with the forward
rate somewhat higher than the futures rate. On most other futures contracts
for three-month Treasury bills as well, the futures and forward rates were
fairly close in the last ninety-one days or so before expiration.

When the contract's expiration date was far in the future, however, the
link between its rate and the comparable forward rate was much weaker. In
fact, spreads between forward and futures rates have at times been over 100
basis points in the three to nine months before the contract expired. Generally, in recent contracts, futures rates have been substantially below forward
rates, and the spread between the two appears to have been wider than it was
in earlier contracts.

Within three months of the expiration of the futures contract, futures and
forward rates appear to be kept in reasonable alignment by investors and arbitrageurs. An investor, for example, can on the one hand hold a sixth-month
bill, or, on the other hand, hold a three-month bill plus the futures contract

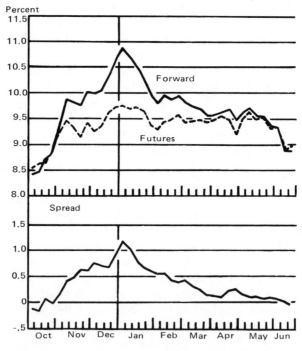

Chart 3 Discount rate on the June 1979 Treasury Bill futures contract (IMM) and the forward
rate in the cash market. Spread equals forward rate minus futures rate.

for the month in which the three-month cash bill matures. If the six-month bill is yielding more than the other combination, investors will tend to prefer six-month bills. And their demand will tend to reduce its discount rate, bringing the forward rate down toward the futures rate. Similarly, if investors find the three-month cash bill plus the futures contract more profitable, their buying pressure on the futures contract will tend to reduce its discount rate, bringing it down closer to the forward rate.

Another group of market participants who help keep rates in line are arbitrageurs. If they observe that the six-month bill provides a forward rate which is high relative to the futures rate, they could buy six-month bills and sell them under a repurchase agreement for three months,[12] at the same time, they would sell a futures contract. They would then have no net investment position: the bill returned to them in three months corresponds to the commitment to sell in the futures market. But they would earn a profit equal to the futures price minus the six-month bill price, the transaction cost, and the financing cost. As arbitrageurs conduct these activities, they put upward pressure on the six-month bill's price by buying it and put downward pressure on the futures price by selling the futures contract. These activities of the arbitrageur usually tend to keep the forward and futures rates within certain bounds.

On contracts other than the nearest, however, there is no deliverable bill as yet outstanding—that is, no security exists that can be purchased, stored, and delivered against the contract. Consequently, arbitrageurs cannot lock in a profit by taking exactly offsetting positions in the two markets. If there is an order flow in the futures market that is persistent, sizable, and at variance with the prevailing view in the cash market, it is possible for speculators to drive a wedge between the rates on futures contracts and the implicit forward rates in the cash market.

One notable example occurred in the spring of 1979. Apparently, many small speculators purchased bill futures contracts due in mid-1980, in the belief that short-term interest rates had reached a cyclical peak and would begin to fall sometime within a year or so. From the end of April to the end of June, their holdings rose from about 25 percent to 35 percent of the total open interest and their net long positions expanded sharply. As a result of this buying pressure and purchases by those trying to get out of large short positions, rates dropped sharply, with the March 1980 and June 1980 contract rates falling by nearly 1¾ percentage points from mid-May to the end of June. Rates also fell on contracts with shorter maturities—those due in the latter half of 1979.

Many other participants were net short, and some of these were firms that felt they were arbitraging between the cash and futures market, holding in this case long positions in the cash bill market against short positions in futures contracts. One of the several cash futures operations they engaged in was a long position in bills in the six-month area (*i.e.,* due in November for the most part) versus a short in the September contract (calling for delivery

[12] A repurchase agreement specifies that the seller will rebuy at a prespecified date and price.

of the bill to mature on December 20 which had not been auctioned yet). As the rates on futures contracts fell, those with short positions faced sizable margin calls. To the extent that they then bought futures contracts to offset their short positions and also sold their cash bills, they greatly enlarged the wedge that was being driven between the rates in these two markets in late May and early June (Chart 4).

The widening wedge between the forward and futures rates made arbitrage involving futures contract sales even more profitable. But, after the shock of seeing large losses mount on short positions and show up in quarterly income statements, financial businesses were reluctant to expand their short positions. The futures and forward rates did not come back into alignment until late in the summer when interest rates started rising again.

PROS AND CONS OF INTEREST
RATE FUTURES MARKETS

Many observers of the new financial futures markets argue that these markets permit investors to obtain flexibility in ownership of securities at a very low cost. Someone who expects to have funds to invest in the period from

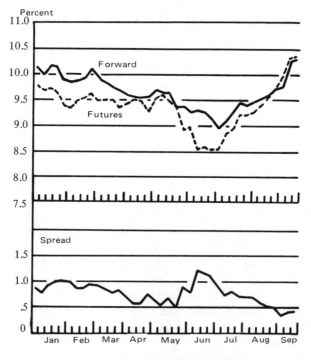

Chart 4 Discount rate on the September 1979 Treasury Bill futures contract (IMM) and the forward rate in the cash market. Spread equals forward rate minus futures rate.

mid-June to mid-September 1980, for example, can lock in an interest rate by purchasing a June Treasury bill futures contract. (For those who plan to purchase or issue other securities such as commercial paper or CDs, the links between the movements of rates in the bill futures market and the rates that obtain on these other instruments can be weak.)

By transferring the interest rate risk to those most willing to assume it, interest rate futures may increase the commitment of funds for some future time intervals. This could reduce the premium attached to funds committed for that future interval relative to funds committed for the nearer term. For example, the yield on 52-week and nine-month bills might fall. The resulting greater liquidity represents a gain to investors, while the lower interest rate on Government debt reduces the taxes necessary to service that debt.

While the provision of hedging facilities is a desirable aspect of interest rate futures markets, much of the activity appears to be speculative, and this has created some concern. One such concern is that speculation in the futures markets might push the prices of certain Treasury bills out of line with the prices of other securities. Because speculation is very inexpensive, entry into the futures market could be much more massive than entry into the cash market. Heavy demand in the futures market could be transmitted to the cash market by arbitrageurs. According to some analysts, the bill deliverable on the June 1979 contract was influenced by activities in the futures market. The June contract specified delivery on the Treasury bill due September 20 and only that bill. While the Treasury had sold $5.9 billion of bills with that maturity date, the Federal Reserve, foreign official accounts, and small investors held about one half. Thus, it appeared likely that the available trading supplies would amount to about $2 billion to $2½ billion.

However, open interest in the June 1979 contract stood at about 4,300 contracts, the equivalent of about $4.3 billion of bills at the end of May (Chart 5). This substantially exceeded the prospective trading supplies. During the spring, dealers reported that trading supplies in the September 20 bill were very thin and that it traded at a rate that was out of line with other bills. For example, it averaged about 4 basis points below the rate on the bill that was due a week earlier. Since investors usually require a higher rate when extending the maturity of their bill holdings, the 4 basis point difference provides a rough lower limit on the pressure that was exerted on the June contract and its spillover on the cash market.

Some observers argued that some investors were desirous of taking delivery because they thought there would be further declines in interest rates. Others pointed out that some people who had booked gains on long positions wanted to qualify for long-term capital gains. In any event, about a week before the contract expiration there was news of large increases in the money supply and industrial production which the market interpreted as indicating that a recession was not imminent and that interest rates would not fall immediately. This view probably contributed toward reducing pressure on the contract, and it was liquidated in an orderly fashion. Deliveries turned out to be a then record high of $706 million of bills due September 20, 1979, about a third of the available trading supplies of that bill. Deliveries on the Septem-

Number of contracts

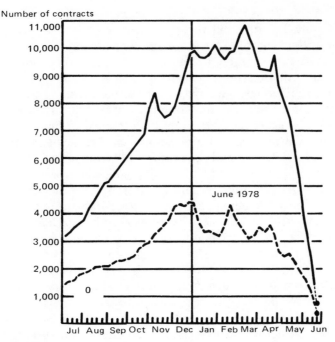

Chart 5 Open interest in Treasury bill futures contracts for June 1978 and June 1979.
Weekly averages, week ending each Wednesday. Total open interest as of last trading day is
indicated by dots. Source: International Monetary Market.

ber contract were somewhat lower, although still sizable (Chart 6), and deliveries on the December contract amounted to $1 billion.[13] Over the last
month before delivery, the rate on the bill deliverable on the December contract averaged 8 basis points below the rate on the bill due one week earlier.
As a result of these events, the question arises whether supplies of the deliverable bill are sufficient to prevent pricing dislocations.

In contrast to bill futures, other future contracts, notably in notes and
bonds, have adopted a market basket approach to deliverable supplies. By
allowing a variety of issues to be delivered, the contracts greatly reduce the
possibility of a squeeze. If, for example, the September 13 bill had also been
deliverable against the June contract, then traders would have had no incentive to deliver the September 20 bill at a rate that was below that on the
September 13 bill. The mere availability of the other bill would therefore
have provided a floor for the rate on the September 20 bill.

This analysis of bill futures has led some to suggest that, instead of a single
deliverable issue, the deliverable security should be any one of a "basket" of
Treasury bills with different maturity dates. However, others see disadvantages with the "basket" approach. In any event, the CFTC has authorized

---

[13] A part of the large amount of deliveries on the three 1979 contracts may reflect investor's preference for ordinary income losses instead of capital losses, a transformation that can be achieved by
taking delivery on a contract on which one has booked a loss. See Arak, "Taxes, Treasury Bills, and
Treasury Bill Futures".

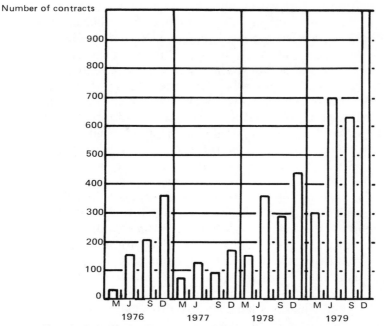

Chart 6   Deliveries on three-month bill futures contracts. Source: International
Monetary Market. where M=March, J=June, S=September, and D=December.

the new exchanges such as the ACE and the Comex to trade futures which involve bills maturing in a different week of the quarter than the IMM bill contracts. If these markets grow and become more active, there should be less likelihood of pressure on the one particular March, June, September, or December bill whose futures contract is traded on the IMM.

Finally, to many of the regulators, the size of the required margin deposit is a key issue. Larger margins would help insure the exchanges against possible defaults as well as discourage excessive speculation with little capital. Moreover, they might make participants more aware of the possibilities of loss inherent in trading in interest rate futures. In early October 1979, the minimum initial margin on Treasury bill futures contracts at the IMM was only $800, and a 32 basis point move in the rate on one of those contracts could have wiped out the entire margin. Now that margin is $1,500, which gives better protection to the exchange and the contract.

CONCLUDING REMARKS

Interest rate futures markets have generated much new activity within a very short time; they have also generated some apprehension on the part of those concerned with orderly marketing and trading of the United States Government debt. Thus far, neither the extreme enthusiasm nor the worst worries appear to be justified.

Interest rate futures markets can provide inexpensive hedging facilities and flexibility in investment. But, to date, participation by financial institutions that might have such a need has not been large. Rather, it appears that participants have so far been primarily interested in either speculating on interest rates or reducing tax liabilities. These participants have been encouraged by fairly low margins. Until recently, the exchanges had shown a penchant for reducing these margins, but in October 1979 when interest rates fluctuated widely following the Federal Reserve System's adoption of new operating procedures, several exchanges raised margins substantially.

Most of the time, the financial futures markets have operated fairly smoothly. In general, there has been no greater volatility in the prices of bills which are deliverable on futures contracts than in the prices of other bills. And despite the huge run-up in open interest in some of the bill futures contracts, actual deliveries have not been large enough to disrupt the operation of the cash market. However, on several bill futures contracts, the price of the deliverable bill was pushed slightly out of line with prices on other issues with adjacent maturities. The CFTC, the Treasury, the Federal Reserve, and market participants themselves will have to continue to observe futures market activities to assure that significant problems are not building up.

Interest rate futures markets have already provided an arena for some institutions to manage interest rate risk. And, as these markets mature, their economic usefulness may come to be more widely appreciated.

THE HEDGING STRATEGY:
A New Approach to Spread Management Banking and Commercial Lending*

*George M. McCabe and
James M. Blackwell*[†]

22

In recent years, large money center banks have increasingly relied on interest-sensitive, short-term purchased money such as large denomination certificates of deposit (CDs) and federal funds as sources of funds for lending. Moreover, there has been a trend toward longer-term loan maturities as banks finance fixed assets as well as the working capital needs of their customers. The profit from this funds brokering, now widely termed "spread management banking," arises from the spread between the interest paid on the funds purchased and the interest received on loans. With the banks borrowing in short-term markets and lending in longer-term markets, this spread is obviously quite volatile. It can result in a high variability of earnings and (when the spread becomes narrow or negative) even in losses.[1]

There are basically two ways that the large banks have attempted to protect themselves from adverse variations in the spread. The first method involves matching maturities or "layering" as it is often called. At each maturity level a bank would try to match the volume of its assets and liabilities. Thus, if a bank has $75 million of CDs coming due in 180 days, it would want to have $75 million of loans or securities maturing in 180 days. This approach

*This paper originally appeared in the *Journal of Bank Research*, Vol. 12, No. 2 (Summer 1981) and is reprinted here with the permission of the Bank Administration Institute.

†The authors are Associate Professor of Finance at the University of Alabama and Credit Analyst, Houston National Bank, respectively.

[1] While this problem is a current one only for banks which obtain a large portion of their assets with purchased money, it will become real for all banks as restrictions on the interest rates banks can pay for deposits are phased out.

not only eliminates the risk of being unable to refund the CDs and having to liquidate long-term assets at fire-sale prices, but it permits the bank to adjust the interest rate on loans in order to maintain the spread. There are several practical problems associated with layering. First, because bank loan departments are oriented toward customer needs, the maturities of many commercial loans are set according to customers' borrowing requirements. Therefore, matching must be accomplished by managing CD maturities as well as attempting to control loan maturities. Matching longer-term maturities is both difficult and expensive due to the thinness of the longer-term CD market. In general, there has not been enough long-term money available at a reasonable price for banks to fund all their longer-term commitments, let alone pick the precise maturity of the sources.

The second method used to protect against adverse variations in the spread involves making floating-rate loans. The interest charge on these loans is not fixed but rather is tied to the prime rate so that when the prime rate changes in response to credit conditions the loan rate changes. While floating-rate loans comprise perhaps 80 percent of the loan portfolio of money center banks, the solution is far from perfect. First, since there is typically a lag between changes in credit conditions and changes in the prime, the spread tends to narrow in periods of rising rates and widen in periods of falling rates. However, these variations are considerably less than if the loan rates were fixed.

The most serious problem with floating-rate loans is that they do not eliminate interest rate risk but merely shift it to the borrower. Thus, the borrower's earnings will fluctuate with interest rates as well as with the many other factors that affect operating results.[2] For this reason, many borrowers do not like floating rates. Indeed, the development of cap-rate loans is evidence of this resistance to floating rates. Money center banks, though, have made fixed-rate and cap-rate loans only reluctantly and then only at substantial premiums over floating-rate loans.

THE HEDGING STRATEGY

A new hedging technique is now available which employs the interest rate futures markets.[3] Using this approach a bank can reduce the risk of fluctua-

---

[2] In some cases where the borrowing customer has a cash flow problem the maturity of the loan may be adjusted to reflect changes in the interest rate, but normal procedure is to adjust the payments. Obviously, this introduces an added element of uncertainty into the firm's cash budgeting.

[3] The legal requirements which national banks must meet to engage in futures trading are spelled out in Banking Circular No. 79, 2nd Revision, dated March 19, 1980 issued by the Comptroller of the Currency. The general thrust of the circular is that the Comptroller must be assured of adequate internal control and monitoring procedures. Also, it limits the use of futures to hedging by requiring that futures transactions be undertaken only to substantially reduce the risk of loss resulting from interest rate fluctuations.

tions in the cost of its purchased funds and make fixed-rate loans without incurring the disadvantages described above. It is not the purpose here to delve into the mechanics and specifics of the interest rate futures market. Rather, this paper focuses on the hedging strategy.

Consider a large money center bank which wishes to make a one-year (360 day) December to November fixed-rate loan and finance it from a series of four 90-day CDs. The bank could employ the hedging strategy. Further assume that 90-day commercial paper futures contracts (CPFC) are trading as follows:[4]

	Index	Discount
March	93.5	6.5
June	93.0	7.0
September	92.5	7.5

and that the bank can sell a 90-day CD today for a 6 percent annualized rate. The 6 percent is the bank's actual cost of funds for the first 90 days of the loan. Assuming for now that CD and commercial paper (CP) rates are identical, the 6.5 percent, 7.0 percent, and 7.5 percent rates are the market's estimates of the cost of funds for future quarters. The bank can then use the futures market to reduce variations in its cost of funds. The average cost of funds will be:

December	–	March	6.0%
March	–	June	6.5
June	–	September	7.0
September	–	December	7.5
			27.0

The average dollar cost of borrowing then should be $1,000,000 × .0675 = $67,500.

Now if the bank makes the loan at a spread of 100 basis points, or 7.75 percent, it should earn $10,000 in net interest margin over the term of the loan. But to lock in this profit, it must simultaneously sell three commercial

---

[4] It will be assumed here that the bank will hedge in the commercial paper futures market. It would be possible, however, for the bank to hedge in the more established and more active Treasury bill futures market. The commercial paper futures market was chosen because it was felt that commercial paper rates are more closely correlated with bank CD rates than are Treasury bill rates. However, both correlations are quite high. Furthermore, it should be noted that there is some confusion as to terminology in these financial futures markets. As matters stand today in the Treasury bill futures market and the new 30-day commercial paper futures market one goes short or sells a contract to deliver the financial instrument (T-bills or commercial paper). In the 90-day commercial paper market one buys a contract or goes long to deliver commercial paper. This quirk in terminology arises because 90-day commercial paper is quoted in terms of its rate of discount while T-bills and 30-day commercial paper are quoted in terms of an index derived by subtracting the rate of discount from 100. This anomaly should be eliminated soon as the Board of Trade has applied to the Commodity Futures Trading Corporation for permission to quote the 90-day contracts in terms of an index. In this paper, 90-day commercial paper futures are treated as if they were already quoted in terms of an index.

paper futures contracts (CPFC) of $1,000,000 each for delivery in March, June and September.[5] If, as we assumed, the CP rate and the bank's CD rate are identical, then the bank is now perfectly hedged and its $10,000 profit assured. We can see this by tracing our hypothetical case through the year.

Suppose that in March the CD is renewed at 8 percent instead of the expected 6.5 percent. The cost of borrowing is .08/4 × $1,000,000 = $20,000 instead of the expected $16,250 or $3,750 more than anticipated when the loan was priced. But the March CPFC will have increased in value by precisely $3,750 (or $25 per change in basis point) and will be closed or offset for a $3,750 profit.[6] The bank's effective cost of funds for March-June is still $20,000 − $3,750 = $16,250 or 6.5 percent.

Now suppose that by June interest rates have risen further so the CD must be renewed at 9 percent instead of the expected 7 percent. The cost of borrowing is $22,500 or $5,000 more than the expected $17,500. But the June CPFC will have increased in value by $5,000 and would be closed out to offset the increased cost of borrowing. By September suppose that interest rates have dropped so the CD is renewed at 6 percent instead of the 7.5 percent expected. The cost of borrowing will be $15,000 or $3,750 less than the expected cost of $18,750. But now the value of the CPFC will have dropped and could only be closed at a $3,750 loss. The hedge cuts both ways.

Table A summarizes the bank's borrowing costs and associated changes in futures position for our example. The effect of the hedge was to protect the bank from unforeseen movements in interest rates and ensure that the bank could raise funds for the $1,000,000 loan at an effective cost of 6.75 percent. The bank has made a fixed-rate loan and avoided the risk of variation in its earnings.

While the discussion above was phrased in terms of floating 90-day CDs

---

[5] We have purposely avoided any discussion of delivery dates. The way the CPFCs are written the seller of the contract (in this case the bank) can deliver the commercial paper on any business day of the delivery month. There is no single maturity date of the contract. The rationale for this arrangement is that by the delivery month, there should be no spread between the cash and futures rates.

This feature does, however, give the sell hedger a slight advantage. The bank can choose the day in the delivery month it wishes to float its CD and deliver or offset its futures contract. Thus, if there is an unusually large positive spread between CDs and CP early in the month the bank may prefer to float the CDs early in the month and close out its futures position.

In the Treasury bill futures market, on the other hand, there is a single delivery date determined in relation to the Treasury's regular Treasury bill auction.

It should also be noted that in the delivery month the cash commercial paper rate and the futures rate will be equal. If this were not true, there would be an opportunity for arbitrage profits. This identity of rates is why the hedge works perfectly.

[6] The rise in value of the futures contract can be understood more clearly by noting that in January the bank sold a contract for delivery of $1,000,000 of 90-day commercial paper in March at 6.5 percent. This means that in March the bank is obligated to deliver $1,000,000 face value of 90-day commercial paper and receive a 6.5 percent discount or $[1 − (.065 \div 4)] \times \$1,000,000 = \$983,750$ in cash. But in March 90-day commercial paper is trading at 8 percent. The bank could close its position if it wished by buying and delivering $1,000,000 of commercial paper at a cost of $[1 − (.08 \div 4)] \times \$1,000,000 = \$980,000$. The difference between the two amounts, $3,750, is the gain on the contract.

Table A
Borrowing Costs for Example

	Expected Interest Rate	Expected Cost of Borrowing	Actual Interest Rate	Actual Cost of Borrowing	Change in Value of Futures Position	Borrowing Cost Plus Change in Futures Position	Hedged Interest Rate
Dec.-Mar.	6.0%	$15,000	6%	$15,000	None	$15,000	6.0%
Mar.-June	6.5	16,250	8%	20,000	+3,750	16,250	6.5
June-Sept.	7.0	17,500	9%	22,500	+5,000	17,500	7.0
Sept.-Dec.	7.5	18,750	6%	15,000	−3,750	18,750	7.5
Avg. or Total for Year	6.75%	$67,500		$72,500	$5,000	$67,500	6.75%

and hedging in the 90-day commercial paper futures market, it should be obvious that 30-day CDs could be floated and hedged in the 30-day commercial paper market just as easily. Indeed, a combination of 30 and 90 days could be hedged.[7]

If we continue to assume equality between the CD and CP rate, the hedge can be kept perfect by matching every CD sold with a sale of a CPFC with the same maturity and delivery date. If the bank plans to fund a 6-month September-March loan with three 30-day CDs coming due in October, November and December and a 90-day CD coming due in March, it can hedge perfectly by selling a 30-day CD now and a November and a December 30-day CPFC and a March 90-day CPFC.[8]

THE COST OF HEDGING

There are some costs associated with hedging but they are negligible. A typical round-trip commission (buying and selling a $1 million dollar futures contract) on the Chicago Board of Trade (CBT) is about $75. However, this is not a minimum fee and transactions can be negotiated, especially by large institutions which trade extensively. An opportunity cost results from posting what is termed a *margin*. The margin is essentially a performance bond. However, since T-bills, other marketable securities, or a bank letter of credit can be posted the effective margin cost may be nominal.

[7] Throughout this discussion it was assumed that all loans and CDs are denominated in multiples of $1,000,000 because this is the denomination of 90-day commercial paper futures contracts. However, 30-day commercial paper futures contracts are in $3,000,000 denominations so the examples would have to be worked out in multiples of $3,000,000. Because of this large denomination, it may be necessary to hedge a *portfolio* of 30-day loans rather than hedging an individual loan.

[8] If the bank wished to sell CDs shorter than 30 days, it could hedge these also albeit not as well. Suppose it wished to sell a 15-day CD maturing in the middle of June. Assuming for expository purposes that the CD and both 30 and 90-day CPFCs are of $1,000,000 denominations, the bank should sell one-half of a June 30-day CPFC. In general, an X-day CD can be hedged by selling X/30 of a 30-day CPFC, or for that matter X/90 of a 90-day CPFC. But because there is no longer a precise matching of maturities and delivery dates the hedge will be less effective.

PREMIUMS FOR FIXED-RATE LOANS

The hedging strategy has not given the bank a method of pricing fixed-rate loans. In our example, with a desired 1 percentage point spread and a current CD rate of 6 percent, the bank might normally charge say 7 percent for a floating-rate loan, ignoring for simplicity the effects of compensating balances. The price of a fixed-rate loan, however, should be based on the expected (and hedged) future cost of funds as given by quotes in the CPFC markets, and the desired spread should be added incrementally to this expected rate. The premium for a fixed-rate loan would then be the difference between the average of the expected rates in the futures market and the current rate, ¾ of one percent in our example.[9] While there might be a slight added premium for the so-called *basis* risk, which is discussed below, and the hedging commissions, the bank's premium on fixed-rate loans under the conditions of the example would not be much more than this ¾ of one percent.

PROBLEMS WITH THE HEDGING STRATEGY

The main problem with hedging is that it involves what is called a *cross-hedge*. This term stems from the fact that the bank is hedging its certificates of deposits in the commercial paper market. In the example above, it was assumed for the purpose of exposition that the two rates were the same when in reality they usually are different. What matters, though, is not that the two rates are identical but the degree of co-movement, or correlation between changes in the two rates. In general, the correlation is not perfect. The problem occurs when the interest rate on the CD rises and that on CP falls. This is known as *basis risk*. In this case, the bank pays more than expected on the CD but instead of having an offsetting gain on the CPFC it has an additional loss. However, this is not a major problem as the correlation between changes in interest rates on CDs and commercial paper is quite high.[10]

Of course, situations where the rate on CDs rise and that on CP falls can occur, but the magnitude of the resulting losses should be quite small. The only case where this type of situation would be a realistic worry would be when the bank was in trouble and there were fears in the marketplace as to its soundness. In cases like that, the bank's CD rate would go up in relation

---

[9] This assumes that commercial paper and CDs have the same interest rate. If this is not the case, the bank would add or subtract the expected difference between the two rates.

[10] This problem of *basis risk* is discussed at some length in: S. Jacobs, "The Short Hedge—Financial Boon for Mortgage Bankers," *Mortgage Banker*, February 1977, p. 44.

to CP rates and CD rates in general. This is an unhedgeable situation. The bank can hedge against unexpected changes in the general level of interest rates but not against a rise in its own cost of funds that is unrelated to money market conditions. Of course, floating-rate loans would not help much in this case either because the bank would be unable to pass on the added cost of its funds without losing customers. In general then, variations in the spread between CD and CP yields are not enough to negate the effectiveness of the hedging strategy for a well-managed bank where there is little prospect of its having to pay substantially more than market rates to obtain funds.

Another problem with this hedging strategy is that once the bank has made a fixed-rate loan and hedged its cost of funds it cannot afford to allow the borrower to prepay the loan without penalty. If the borrower prepays the loan, the bank will have to close out its futures position. If interest rates are above those expected, then the futures position will be closed out at a profit. But, if they are below what was expected, then the futures position must be closed out at a loss. Prepayment penalties are now quite common on fixed-rate loans and the hedging strategy tells the bank exactly how much they should be. Instead of a flat 1 percent, for instance, the prepayment penalty could be equal to the cost of closing out the futures position plus any opportunity cost of reinvesting funds related to the underlying CDs.

At present, futures markets do not exist in commercial paper far enough into the future to allow a bank to hedge all of its loans as described. Commercial paper futures contracts can be bought or sold up to 6 quarters (18 months) in the future. Thus, a bank can hedge a loan of up to 21 months duration (18 months plus the 90-day CD). Beyond 21 months it is necessary to switch the hedge to Treasury bills. Treasury bills are traded up to 8 quarters (24 months) in the future, and by using Treasury bills one could hedge a 27-month loan. This would allow most banks to hedge a very large proportion of their loans. Furthermore as these markets grow, it is likely that additional contracts will be added further and further into the future as the markets gain acceptance.

In the meantime, there are several alternatives. Banks might experiment with a hybrid type loan where the rate is fixed for 27 months, then floats or can be fixed again at rates prevailing in the futures market at the time. Another possibility would be to use a technique employed in other commodities markets called rolling the hedge forward or transferring the hedge. The basic idea would be to hedge portions of the loan beyond nine quarters in the most distant Treasury bill futures contract (8 quarters in the future). These contracts could then be liquidated and new ones established on the relevant months as they become available. If the rates on futures contracts move parallel to each other, this would be the equivalent of placing the hedge on the relevant months initially except for the added commissions.

THE USES OF INTEREST RATE FUTURES CONTRACTS

John A. Boquist and
*John M. Finkelstein**

23

Since the introduction of trading in Government National Mortgage Association (GNMA) interest rate futures contracts on October 20, 1975, the market for trading in interest rate futures has become one of the most successful financial markets ever created. By the end of 1979 there were 14 separate interest rate futures markets dealing in contracts representing a total interest of over $57 billion in the underlying financial instruments. Three markets in GNMA futures, two in commercial paper, two in U. S. Treasury bonds, two in intermediate-term Treasury securities, and four in Treasury bills have been added since the first GNMA market opened.

The deliverable items, margin requirements, delivery months, and daily price fluctuation limits for each of these markets are summarized elsewhere.[1] Because each market, through its exchange, maintains certain detailed rules and procedures, it is suggested that all potential market participants become familiar with them before trading. The most important variation in specifications among the contracts is the acceptable deliverable items under the contract. The publications produced by each exchange are the best source of information for these details and specifications.

There are two primary uses of interest rate futures contracts traded in

---

*The authors are members of the Finance Faculty of Indiana University and the University of Florida, respectively. The article was written specifically for this book.

[1] See Marcelle Arak and Christopher J. McCurdy, "Interest Rate Futures," *Quarterly Review*, Federal Reserve Bank of New York, Winter 1979-80, p. 34. (This article is reprinted elsewhere in this book. Ed. note.)

these markets—hedging and speculation. The markets are effective for these uses because: (1) the hedge can eliminate a substantial degree of interest rate risk provided the contract is closely related to the underlying asset or liability; and (2) the speculative gains can be magnified because of a high degree of leverage. The hedging strategies made available by the markets should be of major interest to those individuals and firms dealing in the underlying securities, e.g., security dealers, commercial banks, savings and loan associations, mutual savings banks, and mortgage bankers. These participants are interested in reducing, or virtually eliminating, the interest rate risk they face in operating their day-to-day business. The interest rate futures markets provide a convenient way to engage in hedging strategies. On the other hand, noncommercial traders are attracted to the market because of speculative opportunities. These participants are willing to accept the interest rate risks shunned by the hedgers in order to have the opportunity for sizable speculative gains.

HEDGING ACTIVITIES

Hedging in interest rate futures markets is undertaken to offset either partially or totally the interest rate risk incurred in lending or borrowing decisions that take place now or in the future. Given that interest rates fluctuate over time, the use of interest rate futures contracts can guarantee or "lock-in" yields as long as a futures market position can be established to remove unfavorable rate movements relative to the decision. It is not necessary to be correct about the direction of rate changes in order to lock-in the yield. Rather, the yield embedded in the borrowing or lending decision must be satisfactory to the hedger in view of current and expected market conditions.

Regardless of the motive, hedging or speculation, all futures transactions can be categorized as either a *long hedge* or a *short hedge. A long hedge* is the purchase of a futures contract to temporarily substitute for the purchase of the underlying security. For example, a hedger may want to take advantage of high yields existing in the current bond market even though investable funds will not be available until later. In order to lock-in an existing yield, a futures contract may be purchased. Later, when the investable funds become available, the contract may be closed out. If rates decrease between the time of the futures purchase and the inflow of investable funds, the profit on the futures contract offsets the higher price on the new bonds. An increase in rates would result in a loss on the futures contract, but this would be offset by the lower price on the new bonds. A *short hedge,* on the other hand, is the sale of a futures contract to temporarily substitute for the sale of the underlying security. For example, a futures contract may be sold by a hedger to protect the value of a portfolio against the loss in value resulting from rising interest rates. If rates rise, the resulting profit on the futures contract offsets the lower value of the portfolio. If rates fall, the loss on the futures contract is offset by the higher value of the portfolio.

It is important to note the differences between hedging in the futures market as described above, and hedging through the use of so-called *forward contracts*. Forward contracts state the price and amount of commodities or securities that will be exchanged at a future date. Since these contracts are negotiated, the exact date, amount of the contract, and specific commodities or securities can be specified by the parties involved. In contrast, futures market contracts are standardized and traded on exchanges. That is, the rules of the various exchanges specify the deliverable items, contract amounts, and delivery dates. While the forward contract offers the clear advantage of tailoring terms to meet a specific situation, there is no guarantee that a buyer or seller could be located for such a contract, especially on short notice. Thus, trading in futures markets can eliminate this uncertainty associated with forward contracts.

The essence of a hedge is that a financial decision entails interest rate risk. In the case of lending in the future or borrowing now, the risk is that the rate will go down in the future, and in the case of lending now or borrowing in the future, the risk is that the rate will go up in the future. To illustrate the nature of long and short hedges, consider the simplified example shown in Table 1 using the Chicago Board of Trade (CBT) GNMA futures market. In the long hedge example, a savings and loan association is located in a capital surplus area such that its savings inflows exceed its local mortgage lending needs. To help meet its commitment to mortgage investments, it is a frequent purchaser of GNMAs in the cash market. The S&L is confident that in the next quarter it will have surplus savings to invest in GNMAs, but it is concerned that the present attractive yields will fall before those inflows are received. To protect itself against such a decline in rates, the S&L creates a long hedge in the GNMA futures market to lock-in the present yield. As shown in the example, the S&L effectively locks in the expected yield of 8.659 percent regardless of the course of interest rates.

In the short hedge example, the S&L has an existing portfolio of GNMA securities and anticipates a rise in interest rates. By establishing a short hedge in the GNMA futures market, the institution protects the value of its portfolio regardless of the direction of changes in interest rates.

An important consideration in these examples is that they are shown to be "perfect" hedges. As such, the examples abstract from transactions costs and changes in the *basis*, which is the difference between the immediate cash price of a security and the price of an interest rate futures contract.

Table 1 Examples of Hedge Transactions

I. Long Hedge—S&L Locks in Yield on Future GNMA Investment

Cash Market	Futures Market	Basis
February 1	February 1	
Decides to lock in 8.659% yield on $2 million principal balance of GNMA 8's at 95-00 ($1.9 million in cash)	Buys 20 May GNMA futures contracts (at $100,000 each) at 92-24[d] (8.992% yield)	+2-08[b]
A. Interest Rates Fall		
May 1	May 1	
Buys $2 million principal balance of GNMA 8's at 98-16 (8.442% yield or $1.97 million in cash)	Sells 20 May GNMA futures contracts at 96-08 (8.478% yield)	+2-08
Higher Purchase Price = $70,000 (3 16/32% of $2 million)	Futures Gain = $70,000 (112 x $31.25 x 20)[c]	
B. Interest Rates Rise		
May 1	May 1	
Buys $2 million principal balance of GNMA 8's at 92-02 (9.096% yield or $1,841,250 in cash)	Sells 20 May GNMA futures contracts at 89-26 (9.444% yield)	+2-08
Lower Purchase Price = $58,750 (2 30/32% of $2 million)	Futures Loss = $58,750 (94 x $31.25 x 20)	

354

II. Short Hedge—S&L Locks in the Value of Existing GNMA Investment

Cash Market	Futures Market	Basis
June 1 Owns $5 million principal of GNMA 8's at 98-00 (8.231% yield)	June 1 Sells 50 November GNMA futures contracts (at $100,000 each) at 97-00 (8.371% yield)	+1-00

A. Interest Rates Rise

Cash Market	Futures Market	Basis
November 1 Sells $5 million principal balance of GNMA 8's at 93-00 (8.954% yield) Loss in Value = $250,000 (5% of $5 million)	November 1 Buys 50 November GNMA futures contracts at 92-00 (9.105% yield) Futures Gain = $250,000 (160 x $31.25 x 50)	+1-00

B. Interest Rates Fall

Cash Market	Futures Market	Basis
November 1 Sells $5 million principal balance of GNMA 8's at 100-02 (7.94% yield) Gain in Value = $103,125 (2 2/32% of $5 million)	November 1 Buys 50 November GNMA contracts at 92-02 (8.983% yield) Futures Loss = $103,125 (66 x $31.25 x 50)	+1-00

[a] Like Treasury notes and bonds, GNMAs are quoted in 32nds. Thus a price of 92-24 means 92 24/32 or 92.75 percent of par.

[b] The *basis* is the difference between the immediate cash price of a security and the price of an interest rate futures contract. Since the prices of GNMAs are quoted in 32nds, the basis is similarly quoted. Thus, the difference between 95-00 and 92-24 is 2-08, or 2 8/32 which is 2.25 percent of par value.

[c] The gain of $70,000 results from the difference between the selling price of 96-08 and the purchase price of 92-24 for the futures contract. This difference is 2 16/32nds or 112/32nds. Since each 32nd is worth $31.25 per $100,000 contract value and this transaction involves 20 contracts, the gain is 112 x $31.25 x 20 = $70,000. The gains or losses in subsequent examples are computed in the same manner.

HEDGE IMPERFECTIONS

A perfect hedge, or complete elimination of interest rate risk, such as those shown in the examples, is not generally possible because of transaction costs and a nonconstant *basis* between the price in the cash market and the futures market. The transaction costs incurred in setting up a hedged position include the brokerage fees charged and the costs related to meeting the margin requirements necessary to maintain a position in the futures contract. The brokerage fee for trading in interest rate futures contracts is very small compared to the value of the contract. For example, the brokerage commission for each $100,000 GNMA futures contract is currently about $75 for a "roundturn." This means that there is no additional charge if a trader makes an offsetting purchase or sale to close out a position, but there is no reduced cost if delivery against the contract is made or accepted.

Another cost of futures market trading results from the requirement that margin be posted by all traders as evidence of financial capability in the event of an unfavorable move in the price of the futures contract bought or sold. Although initial margin requirements are quite low, the total margin commitment to a position over its life could increase if an unfavorable price trend develops. On the CBT, for example, a futures contract for $100,000 requires an initial margin of $2,000. However, a maintenance margin requirement of $1,500 per contract is also imposed. If the margin in an account should fall below the maintenance requirement, it must be brought back to the initial margin requirement or the brokerage firm handling the account will close out the position. Since each GNMA contract is in terms of a principal balance of $100,000, a price movement of 1/32 (or .03125 percent) represents $31.25 per contract. Thus, a price movement of 16/32 would wipe out the margin cushion of $500 between the initial and maintenance margin requirements. In this situation, a long hedger would have to contribute added margin if prices fall by 16/32 and the short hedger would be required to do so if prices rise by the same amount. Any continued unfavorable trend would require added margin until the trend reversed. If the movement in prices results in a gain on the futures contract position, any profits in the margin account above the initial requirement can be immediately withdrawn.

If cash is deposited to satisfy margin requirements, the interest forgone from investing the cash over the period of the futures position is the opportunity cost of such requirements. However, approved securities or bank letters of credit may also be used to satisfy margin requirements. Thus, if suitable interest-bearing securities would normally be held anyway, they could be used as margin and reduce the effective opportunity cost to an amount close to zero. However, the flexibility of selling such securities would be surrendered during the time they are used to satisfy margin requirements. Even if cash is used rather than securities or a letter of credit, the low margin requirements and nominal brokerage commissions represent a relatively minor imperfection in the hedging process.

A more fundamental roadblock in the way of constructing a perfect hedge is a changing basis between the underlying transaction and the futures market contract. In the previous examples of long and short hedges, the basis was assumed to be the same at the time the hedge was created and removed. If the basis did change, however, the effect on the hedge could be either positive or negative depending on the direction of the change. The data in Table 2 shows the effects for both a widening and narrowing of the basis in the long and short hedge examples presented earlier. For simplicity, these calculations again exclude the consideration of transaction costs.

As illustrated in the examples, a narrowing of the basis enhances the value of the long hedge since the gain is increased if interest rates fall and the loss is decreased if rates rise. On the other hand, a widening of the basis favors the short hedge as the interest rate effect is reversed. Thus, a change in the basis alters the results obtained in the case of a perfect hedge with no basis change.

There are a number of factors that may contribute to a changing basis. An obvious case would occur when a *cross-hedge* is established. A *cross-hedge* attempts to hedge a cash market transaction in a financial instrument with a futures contract of a different, although closely related, instrument. For example, S&Ls hedge holdings of conventional mortgages with a GNMA futures market transaction. Such a GNMA futures market hedge for conventional mortgages is the only one possible because a futures market for conventional mortgages does not exist at this time. Even though the forces affecting conventional mortgage yields would be expected to exert similar pressures on GNMA yields, historical evidence indicates that there are times when the two yields move in opposite directions because of temporary market factors.

Even if the same type of instrument is used to hedge a cash transaction with a futures market contract, it is unlikely that the basis will be constant. A changing basis could result from changing supply and demand conditions for the security or close substitutes, altered expectations for future interest rates, or shifts in monetary and fiscal policy. These factors increase the risk associated with a changing basis between cash market and future market prices.

Despite these roadblocks in the way of creating a perfect hedge, a well-designed hedging program to at least partially offset interest rate risk is both desirable and achievable in the interest rate futures markets. Clearly, banks, S&Ls, mortgage bankers, and securities dealers may continue to assume interest rate risk and accept the corresponding speculative gains and losses. However, in a volatile interest rate environment, the impact of these gains and losses on operating results can be significant, to say the least.

Table 2
Effects of a Changing Basis

I. Long Hedge

A. Interest Rates Fall

1. Cash Market–Higher Purchase Price (Loss) = ...	$ 70,000
2. Futures Market Gain Assuming	
a. Constant basis of 2-08, the gain =........................	$ 70,000
b. Widening basis of 2-31 when price = 95-17, the gain is	
89 × $31.25 × 20 = ...	$ 55,625
c. Narrowing basis of 1-16 when price = 97-00, the gain is	
136 × $31.25 × 20 =............................	$ 85,000

B. Interest Rates Rise

1. Cash Market–Lower Purchase Price (Gain)	$ 58,750
2. Futures Market Loss Assuming:	
a. Constant basis of 2-08, the loss = ...	$ 58,750
b. Widening basis of 2-31 when price = 89-03, the loss is	
117 × $31.25 × 20 =............................	$ 73,125
c. Narrowing basis of 1-16 when price = 90-18, the loss is	
70 × $31.25 × 20 = ...	$ 47,750

II. Short Hedge

A. Interest Rates Rise

1. Cash Market–Loss in value	$250,000
2. Futures Market Gain Assuming:	
a. Constant basis of 1-00, the gain =......................	$250,000
b. Widening basis of 1-15 when price = 91-17, the gain is	
175 × $31.25 × 50 =............................	$275,437.50
c. Narrowing basis of 0-15 when price = 92-17, the gain is	
143 × $31.25 × 50 =............................	$223,437.50

B. Interest Rates Fall

1. Cash Market–Gain in Value	$103,125
2. Futures Market Loss Assuming:	
a. Constant basis of 1-00, the gain =......................	$103,125
b. Widening basis of 1-15 when price = 98-19, the loss is	
51 × $31.25 × 50 = ...	$ 79,687.50
c. Narrowing basis of 0-15 when price = 99-19, the loss =	
83 × $31.25 × 50 = ...	$129,687.50

SPECULATION IN INTEREST RATE FUTURES MARKETS

Speculation in the interest rate futures markets consists of establishing a position in futures contracts without an actual or expected offsetting transaction in the cash market. Although such an unhedged position is exceedingly risky, it does offer exceptional rewards if interest rates move as anticipated by the speculator. The magnitude of possible gains, and losses, from outright speculation in the futures market can be observed from the

"Futures Market" column in Table 1. In the long hedge example, a speculator would put up $40,000 ($2,000 for each of the 20 contracts) in margin on February 1 and gain $70,000 or lose $58,750 by May 1. For the short hedge, the speculator would deposit $100,000 of cash or securities in a margin account on June 1 and gain $250,000 or lose $103,125 by November 1. These huge gains and losses for relatively small changes in interest rates are the result of the leverage available in futures market trading. For the long position, $40,000 of margin controls a principal balance of $2 million in GNMA securities, whereas $100,000 controls $5 million in the short position. Clearly, the rewards and risks associated with this trading appeal to speculators.

Needless to say, financial institutions should not engage in the type of outright speculation noted above. However, it is important that the managers of these institutions understand the nature of the speculative motive and process because the speculators make the market work for the hedgers. The interest rate risk that is hedged must be accepted by speculators in order for the market to function. Otherwise it would be exceedingly unlikely that an equilibrium number of short and long hedge positions could clear the market.

There are occasions which favor speculative trading in the futures markets without the acceptance of large risks or the possession of superior forecasting ability. For example, the typical yield curve for government securities is upward-sloping, with lower rates for short maturities. Since this typical curve gradually flattens for the long maturities, one would expect greater spreads between the shorter-term interest rates than between the longer-term rates. An interest rate futures market spread may be used to exploit the yield differentials among these securities.

The *spread trade*, which might also be called a *hedge speculation*, consists of a simultaneous transaction in a long and a short position of different maturities traded in the futures market. If the yield curve is upward-sloping, then the spread in rates between the long and short maturities will widen as the futures contracts approach maturity. A speculative profit is earned if the spread widens as expected. If the spread narrows, a loss results. The absolute level of interest rates does not matter since it is only the yield differential that controls the gain or loss on the position. To see the nature of such a trade, assume that on January 1 the following yields are quoted on the International Monetary Market (IMM) for three-month Treasury bill futures:

	Total Price	Discount	Yield Differential
March '80	$977,750	8.90%	—
June '80	$976,250	9.50%	0.60%
September '80	$975,250	9.90%	0.40%
December '80	$974,500	10.20%	0.30%
March '81	$973,875	10.45%	0.25%

Each of these futures contracts represents $1 million par value of U. S. Treasury bills with a 90-day maturity. The yields quoted are on the usual T-bill discount basis rather than their bond yield equivalents.

A trader who thinks the yield differentials shown will continue in the future can profit by establishing a spread through the sale of a long-term contract and the purchase of a short-term contract. For example, the September contract would be sold against the purchase of a June contract at the existing yield differential of 40 basis points. As long as the differential widens as expected, the trade will be profitable regardless of the level of rates. If in March 1980 the yield level remains the same, then the June contracts should sell as a contract for delivery in 3 months at a price of $977,750 and the September contract for 6 months at a price of $976,250. The yield differential would be the expected 60 basis points. The net profit on the trade of $500 is calculated as follows:

January 1		*March 1*	
Sell September '80 . . .	$975,250	Buy September '80 . . .	($976,250)
Buy June '80	($976,250)	Sell June '80.	$977,750
	($1,000)		+1,500

Even if rates rise or fall, the profit of $500 remains as long as the yield differential widens to 60 basis points by March 1. This result is confirmed below.

Interest Rates Fall

Buy September '80 at 7.7%	$980,750
Sell June '80 at 8.3%	979,250
	+ $1,500

Interest Rates Rise

Buy September '80 at 10.2%	$974,500
Sell June '80 at 10.8%	973,000
	+ $1,500

The transaction would break-even if the yield differential remained at 40 basis points and would show a loss if it narrowed to less than 40 basis points. If a narrowing of the spread were anticipated, the correct strategy would be the exact opposite of that above—the near term futures contract would be sold and the longer one purchased. This type of transaction does not depend critically on the shape of the term structure other than the requirement that it not be flat. Rather, the profitability depends on the widening or narrowing of the yield differential as the underlying securities approach maturity.

HEDGED ARBITRAGES

In contrast to the spread strategy, *hedged arbitrage* techniques, which completely eliminate interest rate risk, critically depend on the shape of the yield curve. As an example of a hedged arbitrage technique, consider a financial institution which has funds available for a three-month investment. The portfolio manager observes that the 90-day T-bill rate is 9 percent. Clearly, the portfolio manager would prefer the higher return on the six-month T-bill but the longer maturity poses a problem. However, by using a hedged arbitrage the portfolio manager can obtain the higher yield on a 90-day investment. This is accomplished by purchasing the 180-day T-bill yielding 9.2 percent and selling the 90-day futures contract priced to yield 9.2 percent and maturing in 90 days. Regardless of what happens to interest rates during the next three months, the change in the price of the T-bill will be exactly offset by the change in the futures contract price. The offset must occur because after three months the original six-month bill is a 90-day bill, which is the same as that specified in the futures contract that was sold. At the end of three months, the T-bill could be delivered against the contract or sold in the cash market with a simultaneous purchase of the futures contract which was sold previously. Thus, the original positions are cleared and the manager was able to earn 9.2 percent on the three-month investment.

Alternatively, suppose that the T-bill futures contract maturing three months hence was trading at 9.80 percent, the rate on the three-month cash bill was 9.40 percent and the six-month cash bill rate was 9.60 percent. The portfolio manager could effect a hedged arbitrage by purchasing T-bill futures maturing in three months and selling the six-month cash bill. In three months the rates must be identical because the instruments have identical specifications.

A different hedged arbitrage technique involves the creation of a "synthetic" security. The logic behind such a security is that if the investor has nine-month money to invest, a comparison of returns should be made between, for example, a nine-month cash bill and the combination of a three-month cash bill, a futures bill maturing three months hence, plus a futures bill maturing six months hence. There is no reason to limit an investment only to the purchase of a nine-month bill. In fact, in many cases, the yield on a synthetic security, which is comprised of the shorter-term security and a series of futures contracts, is greater than that available on an outright purchase of the longer term security in the cash market. For example, consider the situation shown in Table 3. The synthetic security in this example yields approximately 9.37 percent with the 9.3 percent yield available in the nine-month cash market. Note that the acutal yield earned on the synthetic security is not close to the "average" yield of 9.6 percent shown

Table 3
The Advantage of Creating A Synthetic Security

I. Alternative 1—purchase a 9-month T-bill

Cash market quote = 93.025
Cash market yield = 9.3%

Thus $930,250 yields $1,000,000 9 months hence.

II. Alternative 2—create a 9 month synthetic bill

	Price	Yield
Cash market 3 month T-bill	$977,000	9.20%
Futures market 3 months maturity	975,750	9.70%
Futures market 6 months maturity	975,250	9.90%

Thus the average yield on the synthetic 9-month security is (9.20 + 9.70 + 9.90)/3 = 9.6% which is preferable to the 9.3% available in the cash market.

III. Mechanics of synthetic security trade

 A. Now
  1. Allocate $930,250 to purchase 3-month T-bill. Since price is $977,000, the investor can buy $952,150 of principal balance T-bills to be paid in 3 months.
  2. Buy futures contract expiring in 3 months for $1 million principal balance of 90-day T-bills. Quoted price is 97.575, implying a yield of 9.70%.
  3. Buy futures contract expiring in 6 months for $1 million principal balance of 90-day T-bills. Quoted price is 97.525, implying a yield of 9.90%.

 B. Three months later
  1. Collect $952,150 from maturing T-bill
  2. Reinvest proceeds in another 3-month T-bill in cash market. Rise or fall in yields is offset by loss or gain on expiring 3-month futures market contract.

	Yields Fall	Yields Rise
3-month yield	9.1%	9.8%
Implied price	$ 977,250	$ 975,500
Futures market gain (loss)	1500	(250)
Maturing principal	$ 952,150	$ 952,150
Amount to reinvest	953,650	951,900
Principal balance purchased	975,850	975,807

 C. Six months later
  1. Collect principal balance from maturing T-bill.
  2. Reinvest proceeds in another 3-month T-bill in cash market. Gain or loss offset is provided by expiring 6-month futures market contract.

	Yields Fall	Yields Rise
3-month yield	9.0%	10.0%
Implied price	$ 977,500	$ 975,000
Futures market gain (loss)	2,250	(250)
Maturing principal	$ 975,850	$ 975,807
Amount to reinvest	978,100	975,557
Principal balance purchased	$1,000,614	$1,000,571

 D. Nine months later
  1. Collect the principal balance from maturing T-bill

	Yields Fall	Yields Rise
Principal balance	$1,000,614	$1,000,571
9-month return	9.376%	9.371%

in Section II of the table because the futures market hedges are not perfect given the disparity between the amount of funds invested and the $1 million principal balance of the standardized futures market contract. Although the ability to earn higher returns on liquid investments through the use of synthetic securities should be of interest to portfolio managers, the example in Table 3 clearly points out that careful analysis is needed before using such a strategy. Unless the average yield of the synthetic security is sufficiently greater than the cash market yield to compensate for the less-than-perfect hedges involved, a lower actual return could be earned.

If the yield on a synthetic security is less than that of a comparable security in the cash market, an arbitrageur would initiate a hedged arbitrage under the expectation that the yield differential would change to the usual condition of the former yielding more than the latter. For example, suppose the nine-month cash bill is priced to yield 9.5 percent while the synthetic security described above yields 9.35 percent. This unusual rate relationship suggests that a profitable arbitrage opportunity exists for the following transactions:

(1) Buy the nine-month bill in the cash market;
(2) Arrange a repurchase agreement for the bill on a date three months hence; and
(3) Sell a series, or strip, of two futures contracts maturing in 3 and 6 months.

If in three months, the spread moves from the cash bill yielding 15 basis points more than the synthetic security to a less positive or negative differential, there would be a pure arbitrage profit—the basis point change for a 180-day period, which would be the remaining life of the position. On the other hand, a constant or more positive spread would offer no return, or cost, to the arbitrageur since gains or losses on the cash bill would be offset against those on the futures contracts. This neutral result would, of course, be affected by the margin and commission costs plus any carry gains or costs on the cash bill arising from the difference between the cash bill rate and the rate on the repurchase agreement.

The transaction costs associated with establishing a hedged arbitrage, particularly a short position, must be carefully considered relative to the potential gain. The yield differentials likely to exist in the market are probably less remunerative than those in the examples discussed above. On the other hand, there are myriad maturities in both the cash and futures markets to be considered for profitable hedge combinations. The important point, however, is that any time the yield curve is not flat, hedged arbitrages warrant the attention of portfolio managers.

REGULATORY REQUIREMENTS AND CONCLUSION

Speculation with futures contracts can, because of greater leverage relative to other investments, be highly profitable. On the other hand, losses can also be larger. The hedged arbitrages are impressive, but these are principally of concern to sophisticated traders who trade often. Such methods and techniques, however, are at present only of academic interest to most intermediary managers since they are banned by current regulations. What remains for practical concern are the pure long and short hedges.

Certainly all financial managers should analyze their portfolios and commitments with a desire to reduce the adverse effects of interest rate risk. In many ways, it could be argued that not hedging such risk is a form of speculation when interest rates are highly volatile and difficult to forecast. Even pure hedges are circumscribed by various regulations. For example, federally chartered S&Ls may only engage in mortgage futures transactions to hedge against interest rate risk related to mortgage loans or mortgage-related securities. Similarly, federally chartered Credit Unions may only hedge against interest rate risk while assembling a pool of mortgages for sale in the secondary market, while national banks may use futures as a general hedge against the interest rate exposure associated with undesired mismatches in interest-sensitive assets and liabilities.

It is logically inconsistent to permit intermediaries great latitude in any cash asset or liability market while, at the same time, disallowing hedges with some futures contracts in connection with any component of the balance sheet. However, even without an expansion of authority to trade in all markets, it is likely that the proportion of trading by financial institutions in the interest rate futures markets will expand rapidly as portfolio managers become more familiar with their operations and benefits.

TREASURY BILL FUTURES, COMMERCIAL LENDING, AND THE SYNTHETIC FIXED-RATE LOAN*

*James Kurt Dew and
Terrence F. Martell* †

24

Presently, banks use interest rate futures primarily in their dealer operations and in the management of non-loan assets. These areas of banking are the most obvious for futures use since the cash items traded by these parts of a bank are Treasury securities, and the most successful interest rate futures contracts, the 90-day Treasury bill futures traded on the International Monetary Market (IMM) and the 20-year Treasury bond futures traded on the Chicago Board of Trade, are contracts for future delivery of Treasury securities as well. This article, however, considers the possibility of using futures in commercial lending applications. In particular, this article will describe a vehicle for reducing the two key risks the commercial loan officer must consider—credit risk of the borrower and the interest rate risk assumed by the bank.

In the past, the bank could write fixed-rate loans, and thus ease the borrower's burden of repayment in an environment of rising rates. However, at the same time the bank's cost of funds would rise above the earnings on the loan. In other words, the banker reduced the borrower's credit risk by extending a fixed-rate loan, but at the expense of a higher level of interest rate risk for the bank.

In the past several years, circumstances have forced banks to focus more attention on the interest rate risk problem. They have matched their increasingly interest-sensitive liabilities with their assets by offering variable rate

*A version of this article appeared in the June, 1981 issue of the *Journal of Commercial Bank Lending*. Copyright 1981 by Robert Morris Associates. Reprinted with permission.

†The authors are Manager of Financial Research, Chicago Mercantile Exchange, and Associate Professor of Finance, University of Alabama, respectively.

loans. These loans have reduced the risk of a declining spread in the face of rising interest rates. However, a perhaps unanticipated result of this change has been to increase the credit risk of the bank's loan portfolio.

This article will offer commercial banks a practical alternative to the variable rate loan. It will be shown how a bank, using the futures market, can issue loans with the best features of both fixed and variable rate instruments.

The remainder of this paper is comprised of four sections. The next section discusses how variable rate loans can increase the borrower's credit risk. This risk is, of course, assumed by the bank when making the loan. Then, it is shown how the futures market can be used to create a *synthetic fixed-rate loan* that reduces the borrower's credit risk without increasing the bank's interest rate risk. The procedures needed to implement the new loan are then discussed. The final section summarizes the issues surrounding futures-assisted lending programs.

RELATIONSHIP BETWEEN INTEREST RATE RISK AND CREDIT RISK

The 1970s and early 1980s were characterized by a significant increase in both the level and variability of interest rates. The effect of this changing environment was to make bankers far more conscious of the risk inherent in mismatched maturities of bank assets and liabilities. One of the reactions of banks to the changing interest rate environment has been to increase the interest rate sensitivity of assets by writing variable-rate commercial loan contracts. These loans are tied to the bank's prime rate and thus their yields increase as the prime rate rises.

Variable rate loans tied to the prime have considerably reduced the extent of a bank's spread management problem.[1] Yet, in reducing interest rate risk, banks have exposed themselves to increased credit risk. The reduction or abandonment of fixed-rate lending has caused banks to lose some of their most creditworthy customers and has increased the default risk of those loan customers that remain. The reason is that the most creditworthy customers no longer perceive bank loans as the primary type of short-term debt financing. These customers have increased their offerings of commercial paper, availing themselves of a competitive alternative to bank lending.[2]

---

[1] However, variable rate loans have some interest rate risk because changes in the prime do not perfectly match changes in the bank's cost of funds, as demonstrated later in the paper.

[2] There is some indirect evidence that floating rate loans have driven loan customers away in a recent study of the lending behavior of major regional and money center banks during 1977. In a paper discussing loan terms of banks, Boltz and Campbell [1] found that while much of the lending behavior of the major regionals and money center banks was very similar, there was one significant difference. The money center banks had a category of loans not present in the loan portfolio of their regional

Since commercial paper is usually issued with standby lines of credit from a bank, a customer relationship is still in place. However, the bank has substituted standby fees on a credit line for interest on a low credit risk loan. Moreover, the bank retains potentially significant risk exposure from these lines of credit. The lines would be exercised only if some event prevents the company from rolling over its paper. Typically, this would be a result of an increase in the market's perception of the credit risk of the borrower. Thus, one effect of variable rate loan pricing has been to encourage the larger and most creditworthy customers of banks to use the commercial paper market. This in turn reduces the overall credit quality of the loan portfolio.

The vast majority of business borrowers do not have the credit rating required to issue commercial paper. These borrowers continue to accept the variable rate loan package offered by a commercial bank. According to a study by Boltz and Campbell, somewhat more than 50 percent of the loans made during 1977 at major regional banks were floating rate while about two-thirds of the money center banks' loans were floating. They concluded that "the large banks examined here have become proficient at shifting interest rate risk to the borrowers." [1, p. 35.]

By shifting the interest rate risk to their loan customers, commercial banks have introduced another element of uncertainty into the borrower's earning power and cash flow. In an interest rate environment in which the prime rate can move 800 basis points in a quarter, as occurred in the early 1980s, a variable rate loan can cause significant month-to-month variability in the earnings and cash flow of a business. This increase in financial risk, coupled with normal business risk, means that it will be more difficult for borrowers to meet their interest obligations. This increased probability of insolvency increases the credit risk of the loans in the bank's portfolio.

Thus while variable rate loans have reduced bank spread management problems, the loans have also increased the credit risk assumed by banks in their commercial lending operations. This increased risk occurred for two reasons: 1) some of the most creditworthy customers have ceased borrowing from banks; and 2) the remaining customers are greater credit risks due to the effects of the variable rate loan on their costs. The next section will discuss how banks can use the T-bill futures market to reduce the credit risk of customers without increasing the interest rate risk of the bank. This is accomplished by creating a new type of financing arrangement—the *synthetic fixed-rate loan.*

counterparts. These loans were relatively large and long-term, fixed-rate and below prime. Boltz and Campbell explain this unexpected finding by arguing: "Major regional banks (who do not grant loans of this sort) are limited in their capacity to make very large loans by the requirement that lending to an individual borrower not exceed 10 percent of capital; thus the market for the loans of the largest national companies is closed to them. For many large prime and below-prime loans, money center banks compete with each other and with alternative sources such as the commercial paper market." [1, p. 33.]

THE SYNTHETIC FIXED-RATE LOAN

Treasury Bill Futures Market

Before discussing the specifics of this new genre of loan, the pertinent details of the 90-day Treasury bill futures contract will be reviewed. The 90-day Treasury bill contract on the International Monetary Market (IMM) Division of the Chicago Mercantile Exchange is an agreement to exchange a Treasury bill with 13 weeks to maturity for cash at some later date. The contract calls for delivery of a 90-day Treasury bill with a maturity value of $1,000,000. With the purchase of one contract, the buyer commits to accept delivery of $1,000,000 of 90-day Treasury bills at the expiration of the contract.

If a 90-day Treasury bill futures contract is sold, the seller is committed to deliver $1 million of 90-day Treasury bills. If rates rise, the seller, who is in a *short position*, profits, while if rates fall, the buyer, who is in a *long position*, profits. The "price" of the futures contract is quoted in terms of the *IMM Index*. This Index is constructed beginning with the bill's discount yield on a 360-day basis and deducting this yield from 100. For example, a T-bill priced to yield 5.5 percent on a discount basis would be quoted on the IMM at 94.5. The reason for this procedure is that when the Index declines the contract loses value and the short makes a profit, as is the case with all other types of commodity futures contracts. The opposite would be true if trades were quoted in terms of the yield. Newspapers carrying T-bill futures quotes usually carry both the IMM Index and the implied interest yield. However, orders must be given to floor brokers in terms of the Index itself. The minimum price fluctuation in Treasury bill futures, as in the cash market for Treasury bills, is one basis point and each Index point represents 100 basis points. The dollar value of a one-basis-point change in the Index is $25, and thus a change of one Index point (or 100 basis points) is worth $2,500. For example, suppose that the IMM Index for the March contract at the opening of the trading day is at 90. Traders taking a position at that time have committed to buy or sell a 90-day Treasury bill in March to yield 10 percent on a discount basis. The price of the contract is $1 million × [1 − (90×.10)/360] = $975,000. If at the end of the day, the IMM Index closes at 89.00, the buyer must pay the amount of the decline in value of the March bill, or $1 million × [(90×.01)/360] = $2,500, on the following morning. This amount will also represent the seller's gain, and will be deposited in the seller's account on the same day.

The IMM currently trades futures contracts on the December cycle (delivery in March, June, September and December) and the January cycle (delivery in January, April, July and October) although currently only the December cycle has any liquidity. In all cases, the contract expires on the delivery date which is the Thursday after the third Monday of the month.

The use of the futures markets in conjunction with bank lending has traditionally been limited to agricultural lending. That is, the bank would extend production credit to a feedlot operator if all or part of the inventory was hedged in the futures market. By selling a futures contract for live cattle, the feedlot operator locked-in the value of collateral and thus substantially reduced the credit risk assumed by the bank. Note that in this use of futures, it is the *borrower* and *not the bank* that maintains the position in the futures market. By transferring the risk of price fluctuations using the futures market, both the bank and the borrower benefit.

The extension of this principle to the risk of changes in interest rates results in a new type of loan that is similar to a traditional, hedged agricultural loan. The borrower shorts a futures contract to lock in a price; the borrower carries the futures position; and the credit risk assumed by the bank is reduced. However, where a hedged agricultural loan is useful to a small percentage of bank customers, the *synthetic fixed-rate loan* will benefit far more borrowers.

Constructing the Loan

This new loan also allows the bank to have the best of both worlds—a reduction in interest rate risk *and* a reduction in the borrower's credit risk. Thus, the principal advantage of a synthetic fixed-rate loan is that it reduces the interest rate risk now facing a corporate treasurer with a prime-related loan without increasing the exposure of the bank to an adverse movement in interest rates.[3] Moreover, since the bank will be able to issue *de facto* fixed-rate loans, the competitive position of the banks vis-à-vis the commercial paper market will improve.

The synthetic fixed-rate loan is easy to create. From the standpoint of the bank, only one change occurs—the day-to-day changes in earnings on bank loans will now be determined by the marketplace rather than by the loan policy committee. The loan customer must short futures contracts to fix the loan rate. The bank may be willing to offer such a borrower an additional incentive in the form of a lower basic lending rate since the credit risk of the borrowing firm has been reduced.

The elements of a synthetic fixed-rate loan are made up of two parts: 1) the terms of the synthetic fixed-rate loan itself which includes the yield, maturity, prepayment penalties, fees, and compensating balances, and 2) the arrangement for booking and carrying the futures hedge. With respect to the terms, our main concern is with the yield and maturity. To see how these

---

[3] Banks presently determine their loan rates using many different procedures. For example, Citibank for several years has based its prime rate on a formula designed to track the bank's cost of funds. Originally banks based their loan rates on commercial paper rates. However, over time other rates such as domestic and Eurodollar CD rates have become more important. For further discussion of this point, see Merris [4] or Jessup [3, pp. 245-46].

elements fit together, two cases are considered. The first loan is assumed to be negotiated in September 1978, and is a one-year loan funded with three-month CDs rolled over three times. Thus, from the bank's standpoint the interest rate risk is the possibility that the rate on the three-month CDs will rise above the earnings on the loan and result in a loss. In addition to the one-year maturity, the terms call for a principal amount of $10 million with interest payments made quarterly. The loan rate is set at 200 basis points above the settlement yield on the June 1979 contract month of the 90-day Treasury bill futures contract on the day of delivery.[4] Thus, the loan is a floating-rate agreement with the bank's yield tied to the settlement price in the June, 1979 90-day Treasury bill futures market. The example described in Tables 1 and 2 demonstrates how this procedure would work. Table 1 shows the quarterly loan yield, the CD interest expense, and the interest spread for the synthetic fixed-rate loan.

The hedge is initially 30 contracts. These are rolled off ten at a time as the interest rate on the loan for the following quarter is set. For example, the yield on the loan for the quarter from March 15, 1979 to June 15 is determined by the changes in the futures price between September 15 and March 15, or 1.36 percentage points. Thus the loan rate is 10.14 + 1.36 = 11.50%. As the quarter begins, the futures hedge for this particular quarter is rolled off, reducing the futures position from 20 to 10 contracts.

As Table 1 indicates, from the point of view of the bank, this is a floating rate loan funded by quarterly borrowings. As interest rates change, so does the yield on the loan. However, as Table 2 shows this is a fixed-rate loan from the borrower's standpoint. The table illustrates that when the borrowing rate to the corporation rises due to increases in market yields, the increased cost is exactly offset by margin payments so that the borrower basically "passes through" the margin payments and calls to the bank.

The advantages to the bank of this strategy are threefold: 1) reduction in credit risk of the borrower; 2) an increase in the competitive position of the

Table 1
Bank Net Income From a Synthetic Fixed Rate Loan

	Loan Yield	CD Interest Expense	Interest Spread
Dec. 15, 1978	10.14%	7.95%	2.19%
Mar. 15, 1979	11.50	10.16	1.44
June 15, 1979	11.50	9.96	1.54
Sept. 17, 1979	11.15	9.97	1.18

Terms: $10 million synthetic fixed-rate loan, beginning September 1978, one-year maturity with interest paid quarterly at a rate that is 200 basis points above the June, 1979 90-day T-bill futures yield.

[4] The June, 1979 contract month was chosen primarily because it makes the exposition simple since this contract month expires after the loan matures. There are a variety of possible ways to choose the hedge. Typically, there would be lower risk alternatives to this particular choice.

Table 2
Costs to the Borrower for a Synthetic Fixed-Rate Loan

	Futures Positions	Futures Gain on Contracts Closed (in % Points)	Loan Rate	Net Interest Cost to Firm
Sept. 15, 1978	30	–	10.14%	10.14%
Dec. 15, 1978	20	1.36%	11.50	10.14
Mar. 15, 1979	10	1.36	11.50	10.14
June 15, 1979	–	1.01	11.15	10.14

Terms: $10 million synthetic fixed-rate loan, beginning September 1978, one-year maturity, with interest paid quarterly at a rate that is 200 basis points above the June 1979, 90-day T-bill futures yield.

bank vis-à-vis the commercial paper market; and 3) a reduction in what is known as *basis risk*. This third advantage requires elaboration. Basis risk in this case is the risk that the spread between the lending and borrowing rates will decline. This basis risk arises because three-month CD rates are not perfectly correlated with the settlement yields on the T-bill futures contracts. The bank will always face some basis risk regardless of the variable rate pricing procedure used, as long as changes in the bank's cost of funds do not perfectly match changes in the loan yield.

The question then is which variable loan rate pricing procedure, the synthetic loan or the prime rate loan, has less basis risk for the bank. This issue is addressed in Table 3. As the table indicates, the degree of correlation, or co-movement, between CD rates and T-bill futures rates is considerably higher than the corresponding relationship between the CD rate and the prime rate. Thus, by using the futures market both the borrower and the bank are better hedged. The borrower is hedged because it has a fixed-rate loan and thus can invest in longer-lived projects with known costs. The bank is hedged because if its cost of funds rises, the interest rate on the loan tied to the T-bill futures market yields tends to rise as well.

Suppose that instead of floating the loan on a quarterly basis, the bank decided to revise the loan rate on a monthly basis, using month-end settlement prices for T-Bill futures. This would provide a better hedge for the

Table 3
Correlation Coefficients Between Monthly Changes in Large Bank
CD Rates, 90-Day Treasury Bill Futures Rates, and the Prime Rate

	Correlation Coefficient
CD Rate and 90-Day T-Bill Futures Rate	.91
CD Rate and Prime Rate	.72

Data Source: DRI-BMACS, month-end data. January 1979 to October 1980.

bank if the average maturity of the money purchased by the bank to fund the loan was one month. The bank could then set the loan rate 200 basis points above the T-bill futures price as before, but adjust it on a monthly basis. However, since the last payment occurs on August 15, the September contract month, not the June, would be used. The bank's results for the same one-year period are shown in Table 4. The cost of the loan to the borrower is shown in Table 5.

As the example indicates, the length of the period over which the loan may float is flexible, since the corporation will pay the same fixed rate regardless of the length of the float. Hence the length of time between rate changes should depend on other issues, such as the bank's average maturity of borrowed funds.

Table 4
Bank Net Income with Monthly Revision of Interest

	Loan Yield	CD Interest Expense	Interest Spread
Sept. 15	10.22%	8.37%	1.85%
Oct. 13	10.67	8.62	2.05
Nov. 15	11.07	9.02	2.05
Dec. 15	11.49	9.75	1.74
Jan. 15	11.72	9.50	2.22
Feb. 15	11.51	9.65	1.86
Mar. 15	11.56	9.25	2.31
Apr. 16	11.62	9.25	2.37
May 15	11.48	9.12	2.36
June 15	10.71	9.12	1.59
July 13	10.91	9.12	1.79
Aug. 15	11.54	10.12	1.42

Table 5
Borrower Costs with Monthly Interest

	Futures Position	Futures Gain (Loss)	Loan Rate	Net Interest Cost
Sept. 15	44	–	10.22%	10.22%
Oct. 13	40	.45%	10.67	10.22
Nov. 15	36	.85	11.07	10.22
Dec. 15	32	1.27	11.49	10.22
Jan. 15	28	1.50	11.72	10.22
Feb. 15	24	1.29	11.51	10.22
Mar. 15	20	1.34	11.56	10.22
Apr. 16	16	1.40	11.62	10.22
May 15	12	1.26	11.48	10.22
June 15	8	.49	10.71	10.22
July 13	4	.69	10.91	10.22
Aug. 15	–	1.32	11.54	10.22

TERMS AND CONDITIONS OF THE LOAN

As indicated in the previous discussion, the bank does not participate in the futures market for its own account. The involvement with futures is strictly indirect—the market provides the bank with a method for determining interest yield on the loan. The borrower carries the futures hedge on its books. In arranging the terms of this loan, the bank may consider two possible arrangements. The first is for a borrower with relatively good credit and a sophisticated funding operation. This borrower may be interested in retaining the discretion to hedge or not depending on its view of interest rates. In this case, the loan term tying interest payment to the futures contract will be the end of the bank's involvement with futures. The borrower would then sell June '79 futures contracts or not, depending on its view of interest rates. This gives the borrower maximum flexibility.

A second possible arrangement is to require the customer to hedge as part of the loan agreement. This is appropriate for a borrower who has greater credit risk. For a borrower that is required to hedge, analysis of the borrower's assets is necessary. If the value of these assets are related to short-term interest rates, this loan would increase the risk exposure of the borrower and the hedge should *not* be required. In this case, the synthetic fixed rate loan agreement is arranged with the cooperation of a third party, a Futures Commission Merchant (FCM). An FCM is an individual who has been authorized by the Commodity Futures Trading Commission (CFTC) to act as an agent in the entry of futures contracts.[5]

In our example, on September 15, 1978 a one-year synthetic fixed rate loan is being arranged at a rate 2 percentage points above the current rate on domestic CDs, say at 10.14 percent. The terms are for a $10 million principal amount, at a rate of 10.14 percent plus any change in the yield on the 90-day bill futures between the date of initiation and the date of the interest payment. Simultaneously, the borrower places an order with the FCM to short 30 90-day T-bill futures contracts, for June, 1979 delivery. At the first quarterly payment date, the borrower buys back ten of the futures contracts that were sold. If the futures yield has risen during the quarter, there will be accrued margin payments on the account, which the borrower passes through, along with the quarterly fixed-rate payment, as part of the interest accrued to the bank during the second quarter. If the futures yield has declined during the period, then the interest payment to the bank is reduced in the amount of margin payments that had been made on the ten contracts being offset. In either case, from the borrower's point of view, quarterly payments are made on a 10.14 percent fixed-rate loan. From the lender's point of view,

---

[5] The short position should be carried on the books of the firm since accrued interest paid by the borrower is accounted for by banks differently than futures puts and calls. The problems created by this accounting treatment of futures positions are described in a paper by Dew [2].

yield is being adjusted according to changes in the yield on the 90-day Treasury bill futures.

To enter the futures position with the FCM, the borrower must open an account by posting initial margin of $1,500 per contract, in this instance $45,000. Such margin is usually deposited in the form of cash, or in the case of large accounts, Treasury bills. As the price changes on a day-to-day basis, the borrower will be required to make good any losses, and may collect any gains, on the day it is realized. The bank may or may not take a role in the day-to-day transfer of funds between the FCM and the borrower.[6]

SUMMARY

The volatile short-term interest rates of the 1980s have created a need for more effective ways to limit the interest rate risk faced by banks. Although the floating rate loan tied to the prime rate shifts this risk from the bank to the borrower, such an arrangement may be undesirable from the borrower's standpoint because of the need for fixed-rate funds. As a result, floating rate loans often alienate the bank's most creditworthy borrowers and make the least creditworthy borrowers even riskier. These problems may be overcome through the use of the synthetic fixed-rate loan. Such an arrangement has the added advantage of providing a better matching of loan yields with the cost of funds.

Depending on the credit risk of the borrower, and the interest sensitivity of the borrower's assets, hedging may be either optional or compulsory. The interest payments may be made over any period as frequently as daily or as infrequently as quarterly. The frequency of payment should depend at least in part on the maturity of the bank liabilities used to fund the loan. This loan pricing technique is extremely flexible, and does not require direct involvement of the bank in the futures market. Furthermore, it may be helpful in providing improved loan service to existing customers as well as aid in the development of new loan markets.

REFERENCES

1. Boltz, Paul and Tim S. Campbell, "Innovation in Bank Loan Contracting; Recent Evidence," Board of Governors of the Federal Reserve System, Staff Study #104.

[6] In agricultural lending there are three-party agreements of this sort, known as "Assignment of Hedging Account," that have been used for several years.

2. Dew, James Kurt, "Bank Regulations for Futures Accounting," *Issues in Bank Regulation*, Spring, 1981.

3. Jessup, Paul F., *Modern Bank Management*, St. Paul, Minnesota: West Publishing Company, 1980.

4. Merris, Randall C., "Prime Rate Update," *Economic Perspectives*, Federal Reserve Bank of Chicago, May-June, 1978.

Part III

Market Relationships
and Concepts

Part III is made up of seven articles that deal with market relationships and conceptual issues. In the first article, the *term structure* is examined by Kelly Price and John R. Brick. The term structure, which is a graphic portrayal of the relationship between yields and maturities, conveys information regarding both present and expected interest rate conditions. Accordingly, the term structure has forecasting implications. For analytical and decision-making purposes, the interest rate on a class of securities is often evaluated both in terms of an absolute level and relative to other classes of securities. For example, the *yield spread*, or difference, between taxable bonds and tax-exempt bonds has important pricing implications in that one bond may be overpriced relative to another. However, these spreads and thus *relative prices*, changed dramatically over the course of an interest rate cycle. The various spread rela-

tionships and the reasons for these changes are examined in Timothy Q. Cook's comprehensive article.

In recent years, the financial markets have been characterized by a high degree of volatility. A concept known as *duration* enables us to analyze the relative price volatility of different market instruments. This concept and its many other applications is covered in the article by Frank K. Reilly and Rupinder S. Sidhu. The article on *immunization* by Martin L. Leibowitz shows how duration can be used in a portfolio context to ensure target levels of return and minimize the potentially adverse effects of changing interest rates. Many of the financial innovations that have occurred in recent years and covered in this book are a result of the *relationship between interest rates and inflation*. In fact, it could be argued that inflation has brought about a partial destruction of the long-term debt market as it was once known.

In the article by John M. Finkel-stein and John R. Brick, the rationale for inflation-induced innovations in the financial markets is presented within the *Fisher equilibrium framework*.

Although it is well-recognized that an interest rate is simply the price of money, the price may be applied in a variety of ways. In the article by Anne Marie L. Gonczy, examples of alternative *computational procedures* are presented. In the last article, Richard R. Simonds reviews *modern financial theory* with emphasis on the capital asset pricing model and its application to real-world problems.

THE TERM STRUCTURE:
Forecasting Implications

Kelly Price and
*John R. Brick**

25

When a corporate treasurer is faced with a financing decision or a bond portfolio manager must allocate funds to the bond market, each must address similar issues. What is the present state of the bond market? Are interest rates high or low? Should long-term bonds be issued or should short-term bonds be issued in anticipation of falling rates? Are long-term bonds more attractive from an investment standpoint than short-term bonds? What is the most likely direction of future interest rates? These are the types of questions market participants such as the corporate treasurer or the bond portfolio manager must answer on a day-to-day basis. When addressing these and related questions, many market participants rely heavily on their judgment. However, the value of such judgmental analysis may be enhanced if certain aspects of the bond market are understood. Unlike the stock and commodities markets, for example, the bond market conveys considerable information about both present and expected future conditions. The purpose of this article is to provide an overview of a conceptual framework known as the *term structure*, which enables such information to be derived by market participants. An understanding of the various shapes of the term structure and their forecasting implications provide a basis for answering the kinds of market-related questions raised above.

In the next section, an overview of the theory and rationale underlying the term structure is presented. This is followed by a section that describes

*The authors are on the faculties of Wayne State University and Michigan State University, respectively. The article was written specifically for this book.

how so-called *consensus forecasts* can be derived for both interest rates and bond prices. Then the managerial implications of the term structure are examined with particular emphasis on the problem facing the bond portfolio manager of a commercial bank. This is followed by a brief conclusion in which several caveats are discussed.

TERM STRUCTURE THEORY

The *term structure* of interest rates is described as the pattern of yields on a specific date for bonds that are identical in all respects except their terms to maturity. As such, the term structure characterizes the relationships among rates on short-, intermediate-, and long-term bonds. Graphically, it is represented by a plot of the yield-to-maturity (or internal rate of return) of the bonds on the vertical axis and the time remaining until maturity on the horizontal axis. Four typical term structures are shown in Panels A through D in Figure 1.

As a practical matter, few bonds exist that are identical in all respects except for their maturity dates. Most bonds differ in their quality, call provisions, coupon level or some other factor such as marketability. Thus, even if maturities are identical, such differences can result in different yields. As a result, some compromises must be made to empirically observe the term structure. The best set of bond yields for this purpose are the U.S. Treasury note and bond series. These instruments are riskless with respect to default, highly marketable, and available with similar coupons over a wide range of maturities. Their yield quotations are available daily in the financial press. Although Treasury bills may be used in conjunction with notes and bonds, their yields are quoted on a discounted basis using a 360-day year. Thus, if bills are to be included when constructing a term structure, their bond-yield equivalents should be used rather than the quoted yields.[1] Furthermore, since the coupon rate of bonds introduces subtle yield differences because of tax and call effects, a wide range of coupons for a given maturity should be avoided, especially at longer maturities. By minimizing such differences within a set of riskless bonds, a reasonably accurate description of yield-maturity relationships can be developed.

Generally, the shape of yield curves for other debt instruments, such as

---

[1] The bond-yield equivalent for a Treasury bill is given by

$$r = \frac{365}{n} \left[\frac{1 - P}{P} \right]$$

where r = the bond-yield equivalent, n = the number of days to maturity, and P = the price of the bill in decimal form.

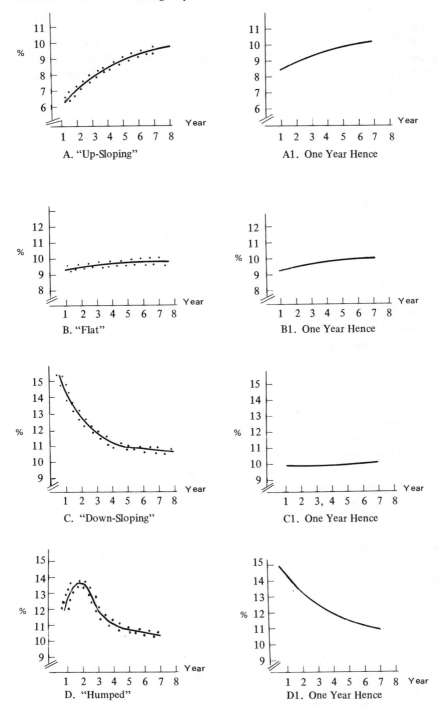

Figure 1   Term Structure and Implied Forecasts

corporate and public utility bonds, are similar to the prevailing term structure for Treasury securities. This, coupled with a high degree of comovement among the different classes of interest rates, means that the term structure for Treasury securities characterizes the general relationship between most short-term and long-term rates.[2]

Shape of the Term Structure

The four graphs on the left side of Figure 1 show different term structures, referred to as *up-sloping, flat, down-sloping*, and *humped*. At one time, these four shapes were strongly associated with particular phases of the business cycle. The *up-sloping* structure was associated with the cyclical trough when loan demand was slack and the Federal Reserve was following a policy of monetary ease. The *flat* structure was usually short-lived and observed during a period of transition from a cyclical trough to a cyclical peak, or vice-versa. The *down-sloping* and *humped* curves, sometimes referred to as *inverted* yield curves, were usually associated with a cyclical peak in the business cycle. Such a period was characterized by strong loan demand and tight credit conditions.

In recent years, inflationary expectations have exerted a strong influence on the term structure.[3] As a result, the traditional relationships between the various shapes of the term structure and the business cycle have become blurred. For example, during a recession, the slack loan demand that has historically characterized such a period would ordinarily result in an upward-sloping yield curve. However, because inflation has persisted during economic recessions in recent years, the effects of slack loan demand have tended to be offset by the combination of continued tight credit and investor expectations of continued inflation. The result has often been a downward-sloping or humped yield curve during the early stages of such periods. It is nevertheless important to bear in mind that the shape of the yield curve continues to characterize conditions in the credit markets and, as will be shown, conveys vital information about expected future interest rates.

The corporate treasurer and the bond portfolio manager must contend

---

[2] Two exceptions to this statement should be noted. When the term structure for Treasury bonds is inverted, or downward-sloping, i.e., long-term bonds yield less than shorter-term bonds, the municipal bond term structure tends to be flat or slightly upward-sloping [2]. Also, Johnson [5] noted that extremely risky corporate debt can have a down-sloping yield curve when the riskless yield curve is up-sloping.

[3] A well-known theory of the impact of inflation on interest rates, attributed to Irving Fisher [3], holds that inflation acts like negative interest. According to this view, the yield on a bond is comprised of a "real rate" and a premium equal to the inflation rate expected to prevail over the life of the bond. The theory holds that the real rate is positive. Therefore, if the economy is experiencing both a business slowdown and high inflation expectations, interest rates can still be high, reflecting a positive real rate and the inflation premium. Expectations of a sharply higher inflation rate are transmitted into correspondingly higher interest rates.

with uncertainty that stems from the joint interaction of business cycle effects, monetary policy, and inflationary expectations. This interaction has been a major factor underlying the volatility of interest rates in recent years. In a volatile interest rate environment, the shape of the term structure can change dramatically in a short period. In 1980, for example, each of the different shapes shown in Figure 1 (A-D) were observed in the bond market. Thus, it is inappropriate to view the term structure shape observed on a particular day as long-lasting.

Behavior of the Bond Portfolio Manager

For the moment, assume that all bond managers have a desired holding period for interest-bearing assets. Given this holding period constraint, there are two ways to characterize portfolio managers' participation in bond markets. One way is to think of managers as being extremely risk averse, and thus unwilling to buy bonds of any maturity except those very close to their desired holding period. Purchase of a longer maturity exposes the portfolio to the risk that interest rates may rise causing the value of the longer-term bonds to be less than desired at the end of the holding period. On the other hand, an investment in shorter-term bonds carries the risk that interest rates may fall and the reinvestment of funds from maturing securities would be at a rate lower than desired. Thus, buying bonds with maturities that are too long or too short exposes the portfolio to risk. This rationale leads to the *segmented markets theory* of the term structure which hypothesizes that bond markets are segmented by maturity, and each maturity segment is independent of each other. The unique supply and demand characteristics of each market determine the yields prevailing in each. If the segmented markets theory is correct, the shape of the yield curve represents nothing more than the prevailing supply and demand characteristics in the various term-to-maturity markets. Furthermore, the theory implies no linkage among term-to-maturity segments represented by the term structure.

The second way to characterize the behavior of market participants is to view bond managers as willing to buy bonds with maturities other than their desired holding periods if they perceive an advantage in doing so. For example, a longer-term bond may be bought and then sold at the end of the holding period, or a series of shorter-term bonds could be linked together. This willingness to shift maturities in response to a perceived yield advantage underlies the *expectations theory* of the term structure. Under this rationale, the various term-to-maturity segments of the term structure are no longer independent markets. Rather, the market segments are linked together because of the participants' willingness to shift maturity preferences in response to yield opportunities. The significance of this theory is that, as will be shown shortly, the actions of bond managers who shift to a maturity other than their desired holding periods reflect an implicit interest rate forecast. From these forecasts, expected bond prices can be calculated. This will be clarified through the use of numerical examples.

Examples of Implicit Interest Rate Forecasts

In order to see how interest rate forecasts are embedded in the term structure, assume a bond manager has three bonds available at this time, as shown below. All bonds have identical characteristics except maturity.

Years to Maturity	Yield to Maturity
1	9.000%
2	9.312
3	9.520

If the desired holding period is two years, the portfolio manager has three options: 1) buy the two-year bond; 2) buy the three-year bond with the intention of selling it at the end of two years; or 3) buy the one-year bond, and at the end of one year, buy another one-year bond.

Suppose the manager takes the option of buying the one-year bond, with the intent of reinvesting the proceeds at the end of one year. The question arises—what yield must be obtained on the subsequent one-year bond in order to be just as well off as if the two-year bond had been purchased? The solution to this problem is to find the *forward rate*. The procedure for finding the forward rate is fairly simple. We know that a 9 percent yield can be obtained for a one-year period. When the bond matures the proceeds will be reinvested at some expected rate r for the second period. This expected rate must be sufficient to cause the wealth at the end of the second year to accumulate to the known ending wealth that would be generated by an initial investment in the two-year bond yielding 9.312 percent. That is,

$$\$1 (1 + .09)(1 + r) = \$1 (1 + .09312)^2$$

$$1 + r = \frac{(1 + .09312)^2}{(1 + .09)}$$

$$r = \frac{1.19491}{1.09} - 1$$

$$r = .09625 \text{ or } 9.625\%.$$

Similarly, assume a three-year bond is acquired with the intention of selling the bond in two years. Then the question is—What rate must the bond be yielding at the end of two years in order for its value to exactly equal the wealth achieved by investing in the two-year bond? This problem may be formulated in the following way. We know that an investment in the two-year bond will result in an ending wealth factor of $(1 + .09312)^2 = 1.19491$. This factor must further accumulate at some rate r in order to have the accumulated three-year wealth be equal to the wealth generated by an initial investment in a three-year bond at a yield of 9.52 percent. That is,

$$(1 + .09312)^2 (1 + r) = (1 + .0952)^3 .$$

Solving for r results in

$$(1 + r) = \frac{(1 + .0952)^3}{(1 + .09312)^2}$$

$$r = \frac{1.31365}{1.19491} - 1$$

$$r = .09937 \text{ or } 9.937\%.$$

The value of r is the one-year forward rate beginning two years hence. This means that after two years, the three-year bond, which will have a remaining maturity of one year, must sell in the market at an expected yield of 9.937 percent.

If investors did not expect the subsequent yields in the above example to occur, the present yield relationships among the three bonds would not persist. That is, the yield curve would shift in response to investor expectations. To see this, assume that the two year rate of 9.312 percent is unsustainably high and likely to fall. Furthermore, they feel that the one-year rate is relatively low. They would tend to sell the one-year bond in anticipation of a price decrease as its yield rises. The proceeds would be used to purchase two-year bonds in anticipation of a rising price. The selling pressure on one-year bonds raises one-year yields, and the buying pressure on two-year bonds decreases those yields. Equilibrium is reached when these bond managers no longer perceive an advantage in switching maturities. A term structure, therefore, implies a *consensus forecast* of future interest rates. Before examining the manner in which forecasts may be derived, it is important to understand a major variation of the expectations theory discussed above.

The Liquidity Preference Theory

Hicks [4] noted a systematic tendency for long-term rates to be higher than short-term rates. This suggests that the forward rate should be adjusted before it is used as an estimate of the *expected* future short-term rate. The reason for this is easy to understand; most borrowers have a strong preference for longer-term funds while most lenders have strong preference to lend in the more liquid short-term sector of the market. This means that lenders must be paid a premium to lend in the longer-term market. Because of their preference, long-term borrowers are willing to pay such a premium. Thus, the predominant shape of the yield curve is upward sloping with long rates exceeding short rates. The version of the expectations theory that takes this bias into account is called the *liquidity preference theory*. It is important to note that under the liquidity preference theory, the willingness of bond managers to switch maturities remains a key underlying assumption. Now, however, portfolio managers take into account the ordinarily higher rates on longer-term bonds. The increment by which the forward rate (as calculated in the numerical examples above) differs from the expected short-term rate is called the liquidity premium. The theory holds that this liquidity premium becomes larger as the maturity increases but its rate of increase diminishes as the maturity lengthens. The liquidity preference theory underlies the remainder of this paper.

FORECASTING INTEREST RATES AND BOND PRICES

In this section, the procedure for deriving interest rate forecasts from a term structure is developed in the context of the liquidity preference theory. Once the interest rate forecasts are derived, their implications for future bond prices (and expected bond price changes) may be examined.

Even in periods of stable interest rates, it is a difficult econometric problem to measure the liquidity premium structure. In the recent high and volatile interest rate environment, this measurement problem has been made even more difficult because the volatility of recent interest rates obscures the subtle effects of the liquidity premium. Therefore, the numerical examples developed in this section and shown in Table 1 use a contrived liquidity premium structure rather than one that has been observed.[4] This assumed liquidity premium structure is consistent with theory in that it increases at a decreasing rate for longer maturity bonds.

A "flat" term structure, as shown in Panel B of Table 1, and Panel B of

---

[4] The term structure literature indicates that the liquidity premium structure is not constant over time, but is related to the general level of interest rates. If interest rates are high according to the general perception of the market, then the liquidity premium is relatively low. This is because the prices of bonds during such a time are low, and expected to rise. The person buying a long-term bond in such a high rate period does not feel that this investment is illiquid, because as rates are expected to fall, the value of the bond is expected to rise. Similarly, when interest rates are low according to general market perceptions, longer term bond prices are high and expected to fall. Hence, buyers demand a greater premium during these times as compensation for this greater expected illiquidity. See Van Horne [8,9] for a discussion of this point. In the examples in this paper, a constant liquidity premium structure has been assumed for expository purposes.

Table 1
Derivation of Implied Forecasts

	1	2	3	4	5	6	7	8
Year	Current Term Structure ($_0R_n$)	Derived One Year Forward Rates ($_nr_1$)	One Year Liquidity Premiums ($_nL_1$)	One Year Expected Rates (w/o Liq. Prem.) ($_n\rho_1$)	Current Bond Prices ($_0V_n$)	One Year Forward Rates Exp. One Year Hence ($_{n+1}r_1$)	Int. Rates Expected One Year Hence (Exp. Term Structure) ($_1\rho_n$)	Bond Prices Expected One Year Hence ($_1V_n$)

A. "Up-sloping" Yield Curve

Year	1	2	3	4	5	6	7	8
1	6.500%				$1000.00	8.499%	8.499%	$993.47
2	7.804	9.124%	.625%	8.499%	1000.00	9.624	9.060	990.14
3	8.510	9.936	.937	8.999	1000.00	9.939	9.352	988.51
4	8.904	10.095	1.093	9.002	1000.00	10.094	9.537	987.57
5	9.156	10.170	1.169	9.001	1000.00	10.170	9.663	987.08
6	9.331	10.210	1.209	9.001	1000.00	10.208	9.754	986.84
7	9.459	10.230	1.231	8.999	1000.00	10.228	9.822	986.76
8	9.556	10.237	1.240	8.997	1000.00	10.238	9.874	986.83
9	9.632	10.242	1.244	8.998	1000.00	10.242	9.915	986.98
10	9.693	10.244	1.246	8.998	1000.00			

B. "Flat" Yield Curve

Year	1	2	3	4	5	6	7	8
1	9.000%				$1000.00	9.000%	9.000%	$1002.92
2	9.312	9.625%	.625%	9.000%	1000.00	9.625	9.312	1003.72
3	9.520	9.937	.937	9.000	1000.00	9.937	9.520	1003.66
4	9.663	10.093	1.093	9.000	1000.00	10.093	9.663	1003.29
5	9.764	10.169	1.169	9.000	1000.00	10.169	9.764	1002.87
6	9.838	10.209	1.209	9.000	1000.00	10.209	9.838	1002.49
7	9.894	10.231	1.231	9.000	1000.00	10.229	9.894	1002.14
8	9.937	10.238	1.240	8.998	1000.00	10.239	9.937	1001.85
9	9.971	10.243	1.244	8.999	1000.00	10.239	9.971	1001.58
10	9.998	10.241	1.246	8.995	1000.00			

Table 1 (continued)

	1	2	3	4	5	6	7	8
Year	Current Term Structure ($_0R_n$)	Derived One Year Forward Rates ($_{n-1}r_1$)	One Year Liquidity Premiums ($_nL_1$)	One Year Expected Rates (w/o Liq. Prem.) ($_n\rho_1$)	Current Bond Prices ($_0V_n$)	One Year Forward Rates Exp. One Year Hence ($_{n+1}r_1$)	Int. Rates Expected One Year Hence (Exp. Term Structure) ($_1\rho_n$)	Bond Prices Expected One Year Hence ($_1V_n$)

C. *"Down-sloping" Yield Curve*

Year	1	2	3	4	5	6	7	8
1	16.000%	10.624%	.625%	9.999%	$1000.00	9.999%	9.999%	$1030.50
2	13.280	9.938	.937	9.001	1000.00	9.626	9.812	1041.63
3	12.155	10.093	1.093	9.000	1000.00	9.937	9.854	1045.33
4	11.636	10.169	1.169	9.000	1000.00	10.093	9.914	1046.20
5	11.341	10.211	1.209	9.002	1000.00	10.171	9.965	1045.87
6	11.152	10.231	1.231	9.000	1000.00	10.209	10.006	1044.93
7	11.020	10.238	1.240	8.998	1000.00	10.229	10.038	1043.70
8	10.922	10.240	1.244	8.996	1000.00	10.236	10.063	1042.33
9	10.846	10.247	1.246	9.001	1000.00	10.245	10.083	1040.96
10	10.786				1000.00			

D. *"Humped" Yield Curve*

Year	1	2	3	4	5	6	7	8
1	12.000%	15.625%	.625%	15.000%	$1000.00	15.000%	15.000%	$989.21
2	13.798	12.936	.937	11.999	1000.00	12.624	13.806	994.98
3	13.510	10.595	1.093	9.502	1000.00	10.439	12.672	1002.48
4	12.774	10.168	1.169	8.999	1000.00	10.092	12.021	1007.05
5	12.248	10.211	1.209	9.002	1000.00	10.171	11.649	1009.54
6	11.906	10.230	1.231	8.999	1000.00	10.208	11.408	1010.95
7	11.665	10.241	1.240	9.001	1000.00	10.232	11.239	1011.75
8	11.486	10.241	1.244	8.997	1000.00	10.237	11.113	1012.19
9	11.347	10.242	1.246	8.996	1000.00	10.240	11.016	1012.36
10	11.236				1000.00			

Figure 1, is defined as the term structure that predicts the same interest rate structure for future periods. If there were no liquidity premiums, this term structure would be perfectly flat, or horizontal. Reflecting the liquidity premium structure, the "flat" term structure shown here has a slight positive slope. The same liquidity premium structure that causes the "flat" term structure to have a slight upward curvature has been used in the other numerical examples shown in Panels A, C, and D of Table 1.

The calculations shown in Panel B of Table 1 demonstrate the development of interest rate forecasts and bond price forecasts from the existing term structure shown in column 1 and the liquidity premium structure shown in column 3. Given the term structure, each one-year forward rate is derived in the same manner as discussed earlier, and placed in column 2. (A generalization of this approach is presented in the Appendix.) For example, the forward rate $_4r_1$ is given by

$$_4r_1 = \frac{(1.09663)^4}{(1.09520)^3} - 1$$

$$_4r_1 = .10093 \text{ or } 10.093\%.[5]$$

In order to derive the one-year *expected* rate for each one-year period in the future, each one-year liquidity premium is subtracted from its corresponding forward rate. The expected rates are placed in column 4. At this point, the reason why the flat term structure predicts the same term structure is revealed—each one-year expected rate is equal to the current one-year interest rate, and the only thing differentiating a one-year forward rate from the current one-year rate is the liquidity premium! Using the notation from Table 1 we have, for example,

$$_4\rho_1 = _4r_1 - _4L_1$$

$$9.000\% = 10.093\% - 1.093\%.$$

The next step in interest rate forecasting is to construct the one-year forward rate structure that we expect to observe one year hence. Recall that column 4 contains all the one-year rates we expect to prevail. Recall also that the difference between an expected rate and a forward rate is an appropriate liquidity premium. One year from now, our expected one-year rate that now begins at time 4 will begin at time 3, but the liquidity premium appropriate for a three-year forward rate stays the same. Therefore, adding the three-year liquidity premium to the four-year expected rate results in the ex-

---

[5] The reader should not be misled by the implied accuracy of calculations carried out to several decimal places. This was done to minimize the errors that result from cumulative rounding when working through term structure calculations.

pected forward rate for three years from *then*, spanning one year. Following our example, we have

$$_{3+1}r_1 = {}_3L_1 + {}_4\rho_1$$

$$9.937\% = .937 + 9.000\%.$$

These rates are carried in column 6. Note that there are only nine of these (and ten rates presently) because the present one-year bond will have matured in one year.

The next step is to construct the expected term structure, as shown in column 7, from the expected forward rates. This is accomplished by adding 1.0 to each expected forward rate (in decimal form) multiplying them together, taking the "kth" root and then subtracting 1.0. In our example,

$$_1\rho_3 = \sqrt[3]{(1 + {}_{1+1}r_1)(1 + {}_{1+2}r_1)(1 + {}_{1+3}r_1)} - 1$$

$$9.520\% = \sqrt[3]{(1.09)(1.09625)(1.09937)} - 1.$$

In this manner, the expected term structure one year hence (or, by appropriately "shifting" the liquidity premium structure, any number of years hence) is derived.

The last step is to analyze the expected price changes of bonds that make up the term structure. For simplicity, all bonds are assumed to be currently selling at par, as shown in column 5, and to have coupon rates equal to the yields shown in the term structure column. Recall that one year from now, a six-year bond will be a five-year bond. Even if the term structure remains constant, the yield of a bond one year from now will be shown in a different location on the term structure because of the passage of time. In our example, the six-year bond is assumed to have a coupon rate of 9.838 percent. One year from now, as a five-year bond, it is expected to yield 9.764 percent, and therefore has an expected price of $1002.87. In this manner, the set of expected bond prices is constructed and shown in column 8.

Reference to column 8 of Panel B reveals that bond prices are expected to rise slightly when the term structure is "flat," regardless of the term to maturity of the bond chosen. The same is true of Panel C, which shows the calculations related to the "down-sloping" yield curve. Similarly, reference to column 8 of Panel A, which shows the calculations underlying the "up-sloping" yield curve, indicates that all bond prices are expected to fall, regardless of the maturity chosen. The "humped" yield that is characterized by the calculations shown in Panel D is noteworthy because short-term bonds are expected to fall in price whereas longer-term bonds are expected to rise in price.

Analysis of the expected prices of bonds need not be limited to one year. The expected price of a bond can be projected in this manner throughout its life, indicating to a bond manager the times during the life of a bond when (or if) it is expected to sell for more than its current market price. This can have profound implications for a bond manager contemplating the tradeoff between risk and return.

THE BANKER'S DILEMMA

The "Low" Interest Rate Scenario

Over the course of a business cycle, commercial banks and other depository-type institutions face an on-going dilemma that is related directly to the term structure. To see this, consider the up-sloping term structure shown in Panel A of Figure 1. Such a term structure is usually associated with lower interest rates and excess bank liquidity stemming from deposit inflows, slack demand for new loans, run-off of old loans, and a general policy of monetary ease on the part of the Federal Reserve Board. Furthermore, bond prices tend to be high relative to prices prevailing under other shapes of the term structure. Because of the declining proportion of loans, the highest yielding and riskiest class of assets held by banks, both the risk level and gross earnings will tend to decline. Thus, it might be argued that in order to maintain the risk level and minimize the deterioration in gross earnings, investments in longer-term bonds are justified. Such a strategy is quite tempting because the current income advantage of long-term bonds relative to short-term bonds is substantial during periods when there is an up-sloping yield curve. For example, in Panel A of Table 1, we see that ten-year bonds provide a current yield (and coupon rate) of 9.67 percent which is 317 basis points higher than the 6.5 percent yield on one-year bonds. Furthermore, management may decide to extend the same strategy to the lending area by offering longer-term, fixed-rate loans in an attempt to stimulate loan demand and obtain higher current income.

If interest rates increase moderately as expected by the market and as shown in Panel A of Figure 1, the policy described above may be effective. The reason is that after one year the higher income of 317 basis points on the ten-year bonds would more than offset the expected loss resulting from the bond's decline in price to \$986.98, as shown in Panel A of Table 1. But one year later, what if interest rates increased such that a down-sloping or humped yield curve prevailed as shown in Panels C or D of Figure 1? If the market rate is 12 percent, the bond, with its coupon rate of 9.67 percent and remaining maturity of 9 years, would sell at a price of \$873.85. This represents a loss of 12.6 percent which far offsets the initial income advantage of the longer-term bond.

The main problem with this strategy is that the loss occurs at a most inappropriate time. During periods characterized by a down-sloping or humped yield curve, most banks also face serious liquidity problems stemming from deposit outflows, strong demand for new loans, renewal requests on old loans, and a policy of monetary restraint on the part of the Federal Reserve Board. It is during just such a period that the bank should be able to sell bonds to help meet these cash needs. If the value of the bond portfolio is depressed, however, most banks become "locked in" because the loss on the sale of the bonds would substantially reduce earnings.[6] Thus, the funds may be unavailable to help meet the stresses that cause an inversion of the yield curve. Had the bank stayed in the short-term sector of the bond market and not succumbed to the temptation of a higher level of current income, the bank would have additional "shock absorbing" capability. Such capability is essential in a volatile interest rate environment.

The "High" Interest Rate Scenario

In a high interest rate scenario, the same temptation exists for bankers to make the wrong portfolio choices. To the extent that a bank has investable funds when the yield curve is inverted, the temptation would be to stay short in order to obtain the higher yields. In Panel C of Figure 1, for example, we see that one-year bonds yield 16 percent versus 11 percent on the longer-term bonds. However, *if* the bank is going to invest in longer-term bonds, this would be the most appropriate time to do so despite the lower current income on the longer-term bonds. The reason, of course, is that the *most likely* change in interest rates is downward. As a practical matter, few banks acquire long-term bonds when the yield curve is inverted because of a lack of liquidity resulting from past investment decisions, or simply a desire to be as liquid as possible.

The key point here is that failure to understand the implications of the term structure coupled with a desire for a higher level of current income leads some bankers into the revolving trap of going long when they should be going short and vice-versa. Often the same myopic policies are extended to the loan portfolio with matching results.

CONCLUSION

The shape of the term structure provides market participants with considerable information regarding present market conditions and the most likely

---

[6] Some bankers would argue that earnings are only affected if the bonds are sold. However, even if the bonds are held, earnings are adversely affected because the return on the bonds is fixed while the cost of funds used to acquire the bonds increases rapidly as the yield curve becomes inverted.

direction of future interest rate changes. However, like any other forecasting technique, caution should be used. Market expectations are formed on the basis of available information at a point in time. As new information becomes available, usually in a random fashion and with varying degrees of significance, market expectations are revised. This means that there is uncertainty associated with the forecasts implied by a term structure. Also, the fact that rates are expected to decline, for example, does not necessarily mean that rates are at a peak. Rates may increase further before receding. Thus, the estimates should be used in a probabilistic or "most likely" context. Despite these caveats, term structure analysis is a useful tool for assessing present market conditions and obtaining an "acted-upon" consensus forecast.

The shape of a term structure and the conditions that give rise to a particular shape have important implications for commercial banks and other depository institutions. Failure to recognize the linkage between the various shapes of the term structure and overall operations of these institutions can lead to a sequence of inappropriate and costly decisions. For this reason, an understanding of the term structure is a prerequisite for the sound management of banks and other types of depository institutions, especially in a volatile interest rate environment.

APPENDIX

A GENERAL MODEL FOR FORWARD RATES

Term structure nomenclature designates known, observable interest rates as $_0R_n$ where the pre-subscript zero refers to the *point in time* that the rate begins and the post-subscript n refers to the number of periods until maturity which is an *interval of time*. For example, $_0R_4$ is the prevailing rate on four-year bonds. Since n is greater than one, this is a multi-period rate. In contrast to the upper-case symbols for known rates, the derived forward rates are denoted by lower-case symbols with the subscripts having the same meaning. For example, $_3r_2$ refers to the forward rate expected to prevail three years hence and span two periods.

According to the expectations theory, the multi-period rate $_0R_n$ is linked to the current single-period rate $_0R_1$, and a set of forward rates, through the formula

$$(1 + {_0R_n})^n = (1 + {_0R_1})(1 + {_1r_1})(1 + {_2r_1}) \ldots (1 + {_{n-1}r_1}). \qquad [1]$$

Note that each side of equation [1] yields the same amount of terminal wealth. Each one-period forward rate on the right hand side of [1] begins at the end of the preceding period. The multi-period rate $_0R_n$ can be thought of as the geometric mean return of all the single-period rates over the period zero through n.

Given an existing term structure, equation [1] may be used to derive forward rates. To see this, equation [1] may be expanded for an n + 1 period bond and written as

$$(1 + _0R_{n+1})^{n+1} = (1 + _0R_1)(1 + _1r_1)(1 + _2r_1)\ldots(1 + _{n-1}r_1)(1 + _nr_1). \quad [2]$$

In expressions [1] and [2] the actual rates $_0R_n$ and $_0R_{n+1}$ are used to derive the forward rate we seek, $_nr_1$, which begins n periods from now and spans one period. Dividing [2] by [1] and cancelling terms, we have

$$\frac{(1 + _0R_{n+1})^{n+1}}{(1 + _0R_n)^n} = \frac{(1 + _0R_1)(1 + _1r_1)(1 + _2r_1)\ldots(1 + _{n-1}r_1)(1 + _nr_1)}{(1 + _0R_1)(1 + _1r_1)(1 + _2r_1)\ldots(1 + _{n-1}r_1)}$$

$$\frac{(1 + _0R_{n+1})^{n+1}}{(1 + _0R_n)^n} = 1 + _nr_1$$

therefore,

$$_nr_1 = \frac{(1 + _0R_{n+1})^{n+1}}{(1 + _0R_n)^n} - 1. \quad [3]$$

Thus, if we have two observed interest rates which differ in their terms to maturity by one period, we can use [3] to calculate the forward rate spanning their interval. For example, referring to Panel A of Table 1 in the text, the four-year observed rate is 8.904 percent and the observed three-year rate is 8.51 percent. The implied one-year forward rate beginning three years hence is found by substituting these rates into equation [3],

$$_3r_1 = \frac{(1 + .08904)^4}{(1 + .0851)^3} - 1 = .10095 \text{ or } 10.095\%.$$

In a similar manner, a multi-period forward rate can be derived from the relationship

$$\frac{(1 + _0R_{n+k})^{n+k}}{(1 + _0R_n)^n} = \frac{(1 + _0R_1)(1 + _1r_1)\ldots(1 + _{n+k}r_1)}{(1 + _0R_1)(1 + _1r_1)\ldots(1 + _{n-1}r_1)}.$$

Cancelling terms results in

$$\frac{(1 + _0R_{n+k})^{n+k}}{(1 + _0R_n)^n} = (1 + _nr_k)^k.$$

Taking the kth root of both sides and subtracting one from each side, the multiperiod forward rate ${}_n r_k$ may be found. That is,

$$
{}_n r_k = \sqrt[k]{\frac{(1 + {}_o R_{n+k})^{n+k}}{(1 + {}_o R_n)^n}} - 1 \qquad [4]
$$

The term ${}_n r_k$ represents the k-period forward rate beginning n periods hence. Referring once again to Panel A of Table 1, to obtain the four-period forward rate beginning one year hence, we have

$$
{}_1 r_4 = \sqrt[4]{\frac{(1 + .09156)^5}{(1 + .065)}} - 1
$$

$$
{}_1 r_4 = .0983 \text{ or } 9.83\%.
$$

As can be observed from these numerical examples, implementation of these formulas is not difficult. Although cumbersome, the subscripting is necessary to position the various rates in time. Once the user is familiar with the procedure, the calculations are relatively simple. Also, recall that in the absence of a liquidity premium, a forward rate is equal to the expected rate. According to the liquidity preference theory, however, the forward rate calculated in this manner is a biased estimate of the expected rate and must be adjusted downward to reflect the presence of any liquidity premium. Such adjustments were made in the body of the text.

REFERENCES

1. Bensten, George, "Interest Rates are a Random Walk Too," *Fortune*, August 1976.

2. Cook, Timothy Q. and Jeremy G. Duffield, "Short-Term Investment Pools," *Economic Review*, Federal Reserve Bank of Richmond, September/October 1980.

3. Fisher, Irving, "Appreciation and Interest," *Publications of the American Economic Association*, XI (August 1896).

4. Hicks, J. R., *Value and Capital*, 2nd edition London: Oxford University Press, 1946.

5. Johnson, Ramon E., "Term Structures of Corporate Bond Yields as a Function of Risk of Default," *Journal of Finance*, 22 (May 1967).

6. Price, Kelly and John R. Brick, "Daily Interest Rate Relationships," *Journal of Money, Credit and Banking*, XII (May 1980).

7. Van Horne, James, "The Expectations Hypothesis, the Yield Curve, and Monetary Policy: Comment," *Quarterly Journal of Economics*, LXXIX (November 1965).

8. Van Horne, James, "Interest Rate Risk and the Term Structure of Interest Rates," *Journal of Political Economy*, 73 (August 1965).

9. Van Horne, James, *Financial Market Rates and Flows*, Englewood Cliffs, N.J.: Prentice Hall 1978, Chapters 3-5.

SOME FACTORS AFFECTING LONG-TERM YIELD SPREADS IN RECENT YEARS*

Timothy Q. Cook

26

The past decade has been a period of unprecedented movement in interest rates. Chart 1 shows the movement over this period in five commonly cited interest rates series. Two observations can be made from Chart 1 about the behavior of the interest rate series in the period shown. The first is that the rates generally move in the same direction over time. All five of the series shown rose greatly in the late 1960s, and all reached a peak in the first half of 1970. The second observation is that the differentials among the interest rate series changed substantially over the 10-year period. This observation is true not only for long-term rates relative to the short-term rate, but it is also true of the long-term rates relative to each other. To take one example, at the beginning of the period in February 1964, the corporate bond rate was only 25 basis points higher than the long-term United States government bond rate. The differential or spread between the two rates rose to 135 basis points in September 1966, fell to 88 basis points in February 1967, increased to 273 basis points in November 1970, and fell to 153 basis points in February 1973.

The lack of stability that characterizes the spread between the corporate bond and U. S. government bond interest rate series extends to the other interest rates as well, as shown in Table I, where all four of the other rates are compared to the corporate bond rate. The spreads between the corporate bond rate and the other rates varied 180 basis points or more in all four cases. In the most extreme case, the spread between the corporate bond rate and the short-term Treasury bill rate moved from a low of 24 basis points in January 1966 to a high of 401 basis points in March 1971.

This characterization of interest rate movement differs substantially from the standard macroeconomic textbook treatment in which "the" interest rate is determined by an appropriately specified model. If the relationships

*Reprinted, with deletions, from the *Economic Review*, September 1973, pp. 2-14, with permission from the Federal Reserve Bank of Richmond.

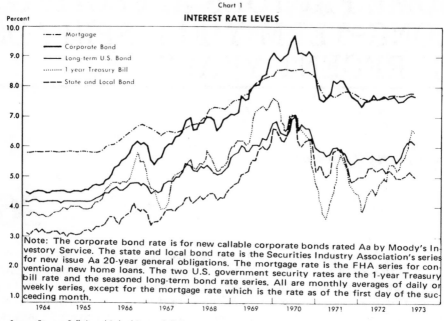

Chart 1

INTEREST RATE LEVELS

Note: The corporate bond rate is for new callable corporate bonds rated Aa by Moody's Investory Service. The state and local bond rate is the Securities Industry Association's series for new issue Aa 20-year general obligations. The mortgage rate is the FHA series for conventional new home loans. The two U.S. government security rates are the 1-year Treasury bill rate and the seasoned long-term bond rate series. All are monthly averages of daily or weekly series, except for the mortgage rate which is the rate as of the first day of the succeeding month.

Sources: Treasury Bulletin and Federal Reserve Bulletin.

among the interest rates were fairly constant over time—that is, if interest rate spreads displayed little variation—then it would be of little concern that there are many interest rates, since an appropriate explanation of the movement in any one of the interest rates would suffice as an explanation for the movement in all other rates. Unfortunately, as shown in Chart 1, the relationships among the various levels show substantial variation over time, particularly in a period of large interest rate movements, such as the late 1960s.

Table I

INTEREST RATE SPREADS

1964-73

	High	Date	Low	Date
Corporate Bond Rate Minus U.S. Bond Rate	2.73	Nov. 1970	.25	Feb. 1964
Corporate Bond Rate Minus Treasury Bill Rate	4.01	March 1971	.24	Jan. 1966
Corporate Bond Rate Minus Mortgage Rate	1.15	June 1970	−1.41	Feb. 1964
Corporate Bond Rate Minus State and Local Bond Rate	3.08	Aug. 1970	1.28	Jan. 1966

SECURITY CHARACTERISTICS

The size and variability of spreads among interest rates raise two important questions. First, of what concern is it that the spreads vary substantially over time? Second, what causes this variation? The answer to the first question is related to the fact that securities are issued to finance a variety of activities. In particular, different long-term securities are issued to finance different types of real investment. State and local bonds finance state and local construction, home mortgages finance residential construction, corporate bonds primarily finance the construction of plant and equipment, and long-term U. S. bonds finance part of the Federal deficit. When an interest rate series for one of these securities rises relative to the interest rate series for another of the securities, the cost of the activity the former finances becomes relatively more expensive, at least at first glance. To the extent that the various economic sectors respond to changing interest rates when making decisions on real investment activity, a rise in one interest rate relative to another can thereby affect the pattern of capital allocation in the economy. Therefore, a change in a particular spread is a matter of concern not only for the sectors supplying the securities but also for policymakers whose decisions can influence interest rate relationships.

The second question—what causes movement in the spreads—is extremely complex.[1] The five interest rate series shown in Chart 1 represent only a small fraction of the total number of available interest rate series. Salomon Brothers' invaluable publication, *An Analytical Record of Yields and Yield Spreads,* alone contains 111 different interest rate or yield series, which implies the existence of literally thousands of spreads.[2] These yield series can best be classified according to the characteristics of the security or securities they represent. For the purposes of this article, these characteristics will be classified into three groups.

The first relevant characteristic of the security is the length of its term to maturity. The *Federal Reserve Bulletin,* for example, provides yield series for U. S. government securities maturing in three months, six months, one year, three to five years, and over ten years. The spread between any pair of these series changes dramatically over time, as can be seen in Chart 1.

Securities can also be characterized by the particular sectors of the economy that issue and purchase them. Underlying the supply of and demand for securities by the sectors is a whole set of factors, sometimes called "fundamental" influences on interest rate movements. They include the savings behavior of the various sectors and the real investment expenditures of these sectors. Also included are certain policy variables of the Federal Government

---

[1] For an excellent discussion of many of these causes, see James C. Van Horne, *Function and Analysis of Capital Market Rates* (Englewood Cliffs, New Jersey: Prentice-Hall, Inc. 1970).

[2] The terms "interest rate" and "yield" will be used interchangeably in the remainder of the article.

that influence economic activity by directly affecting security supply or demand in a particular market. Attempts to determine the effects of these factors on interest rate spreads are greatly complicated because a given factor, such as household saving, has simultaneous effects in many security markets.

The third characteristic, or group of characteristics, of a security relevant to a discussion of yield series is the special features it has with respect to the taxability, timing, and certainty of the returns associated with holding it. There are four such features that vary among securities.[3] The first is whether the interest earned on the security is subject to Federal income tax. The second is whether the security earns income in the form of capital gains (or capital losses), which are subject to lower tax rates than interest income. The third feature is whether the issuer of the security has the option of repaying the principal ("calling" the security) at a time before it matures. And the fourth feature is the degree to which the income promised on a security is subject to uncertainty or risk of default on the part of the borrower.

Each of the three security characteristics mentioned is related to both the level and movement of interest rate spreads over time. The ideal procedure to use in attempting to explain the movement in spreads is to isolate one security characteristic at a time and study yield series for securities that are alike in all respects but that one characteristic. The problem then is to determine the factors underlying the spreads associated with that one characteristic (e.g. maturity). Unfortunately, finding interest rate series that isolate a given security characteristic is sometimes difficult, if not impossible. Nevertheless, this article will attempt to use that procedure in illustrating the effects that the four special features indicated above have had on observed yield spreads in the past ten years. The article will not attempt to explain the elements of observed yield spreads related to differences in maturity or to the behavior of the various economic sectors, but it will be argued that any attempt to explain those spreads requires an understanding of the impact on yield spreads of the special features.

ASSUMPTIONS UNDERLYING THE COMPUTATION OF YIELD SERIES

Observed spreads between interest rate series, such as those in Chart 1, contain an important element that results from inherent shortcomings in the formula employed in calculating yields. Spreads between yield series for securities that differ only with respect to one of the four special features discussed above are related in that they all result from these shortcomings.

---

[3] The feature of convertibility of a bond into a common stock is not considered, since the article is concerned exclusively with bond yield spreads.

The yield of a security is the discount rate, r, which equates the price, P, of a security to the present value of the future cash flows associated with holding it:

$$(1) \quad P = \frac{C_1}{(1+r)} + \frac{C_2}{(1+r)^2} + \cdots + \frac{C_N}{(1+r)^N}$$

where C_i is the promised return in the ith time period.[4] In computing the yield, the assumption is usually made that the security is held to maturity, so that r becomes the "yield to maturity." For simplicity, the remainder of the article will assume that we are dealing with a bond that pays a constant return, C, each year until it matures in period N, at which time it pays the holder of the security its face value of $1000. The yield to maturity is then computed by finding the value of r that satisfies the equation:

$$(1') \quad P = \sum_{n=1}^{N} \frac{C}{(1+r)^n} + \frac{1000}{(1+r)^N} \ .$$

On new issue securities, bonds typically sell at (or near) par, which in this case is $1000. Adjustments in yield are brought about by changes in C, the coupon. For securities that are not new, but "seasoned," P will deviate from $1000 in order to keep the yield of the security in line with current market interest rates. For example, suppose a new 20-year security is issued at a yield to maturity of 5 percent, with P = $1000 and C = $50. Five years later, the security, now seasoned, is resold when the yield to maturity on comparable new securities has risen to 7 percent. Because the $50 annual coupon on the seasoned security is lower than the $70 annual coupon on the new security, investors will only purchase the seasoned security at a reduced price. Assuming the absence of all taxes, the price of the security (where N now equals 15) would have to drop to $817 in order for the yield to maturity to equal 7 percent. The buyer of the security would realize a capital gain at the end of 15 years of $183.

There are two features of the yield formula that, when combined with the four special features, account for a large part of the variation in the yield spreads in Chart 1 and Table I. First, it should be noted that the formula computes the *before-tax* yield to maturity, when clearly the after-tax yield is the relevant consideration for the buyer of a security. Therefore, the yield formula (which is used to compute the interest rate series in Chart 1) cannot differentiate between securities that provide interest income that is or is not subject to personal and corporate income tax. Nor does it differentiate between securities that yield or do not yield a return in the form of capital gains that are taxed at a lower rate than interest income.

In the second place, implicit in the formula is the assumption that the timing and amounts of the returns associated with holding a security are known with *certainty*. Therefore, the formula cannot be used to calculate,

---

[4] An explanation of this formula can be found in any introductory finance book.

with precision, the yield on securities that are callable, either immediately or after a deferred period. Moreover, it cannot take into account the varying degrees of certainty felt by investors that the issuer of the security will not default.

The rest of this article will look at and attempt to explain spreads among long-term interest rates arising primarily out of the failure of the yield to maturity formula to take account of the effects on computed interest rate series of income tax rates, capital gains tax rates, call provisions, and default risk.

INCOME TAX RATES AND YIELD SPREADS

The after-tax yield to maturity of a security for a particular investor is the discount rate, r*, which equates the price of the security to the present value of the future after-tax promised returns:

$$(2) \quad P = \sum_{n=1}^{N} \frac{C(1-t)}{(1+r^*)^n} + \frac{(1000 - P)(1 - cg)}{(1+r^*)^N} + \frac{P}{(1+r^*)^N},$$

where t is the marginal income tax bracket of the investor and cg is the tax rate on long-term capital gains. The interest income, C, is taxed at the relevant personal or corporate income tax rate, while the capital gains ($1000 - P$) are taxed at the capital gains tax rate. Over much of the past 10 years, cg was equal to one-half of t, up to a maximum tax of 25 percent of total capital gains.[5]

By using Formulas (1) and (2) and by specifying an income tax rate, a capital gains tax rate, a maturity date, and a coupon value, it is possible to determine, for any security, a before-tax yield that is consistent with any after-tax yield.[6] The effects of varying income tax rates, capital gains tax rates, maturities, and coupons on the relationship between before-and after-tax yields to maturity, and consequently on yield spreads, can then be isolated.

An example of this procedure is reported in Table II. The relevant marginal income tax rate is shown for values of 30 percent and 40 percent, and the capital gains tax rate is assumed to be one-half the income tax rate. The hypothetical securities are new issues sold at par. It is assumed that one security yields interest income that is tax-free, while the other yields interest income taxable at the indicated marginal tax rates. It is also assumed that

[5] The relationship of t to cg became somewhat more complex in 1970 after maximum capital gains tax rates were increased.

[6] This fact was pointed out in an article by J. W. Colin and Richard S. Bayer, "Calculation of Tax Effective Yields for Discount Instruments," *Journal of Financial and Quantitative Analysis*, 5 (June 1970), 265-73.

Table II

EFFECT OF INCOME TAX ON
BEFORE-TAX YIELD SPREADS

Spread Between Before-tax Yield of a New Issue Security
Providing Taxable Interest Income (r_1) and Before-tax Yield
of a New Issue Security Providing Non-taxable Interest
Income (r_2) Assuming Equal After-tax Yields

t=40%			t=30%		
r_2	r_1	Spread	r_2	r_1	Spread
3.00	5.00	2.00	3.00	4.29	1.29
3.50	5.83	2.33	3.50	5.00	1.50
4.00	6.67	2.67	4.00	5.71	1.71
4.50	7.50	3.00	4.50	6.43	1.93
5.00	8.33	3.33	5.00	7.14	2.14
5.50	9.17	3.67	5.50	7.86	2.36
6.00	10.00	4.00	6.00	8.57	2.57

investors demand equal after-tax rates. Two points, which are evident from examination of the table, are relevant to the discussion of the relationship between the yield to maturity formula and yield spreads. First, in a period of rising interest rates, spreads between yield series for securities that yield taxable interest versus those that yield tax-free interest should rise. And second, increases in income tax rates should also increase those spreads.

As is well known, interest income on state and local securities is generally tax-free. Chart 2 compares the movement of the corporate bond rate with the movement of the spread between the corporate bond rate and the state and local bond rate. Both rates are for new issues.[7] There is clear evidence that the spread rises as interest rates rise, as was predicted in Table II, although it should be clear from the preceding discussion that all the change in the spread cannot be attributed to the tax factor, since the effects of the tax factor have not been isolated from those of the other factors discussed. For the period 1966-1968, it appears that a major part of the movement in the spread can be explained by the differential tax status. In that period, the spread rose and fell with interest rate levels, keeping the relationship between the after-tax yields on the two securities relatively constant. In 1969, however, interest rates rose sharply, while the spread opened only moderately.

It should be noted that since the yield series in Chart 2 are for new securities selling at par, the equal-after-tax relationship between the state and local rate (r_{sl}) and the corporate bond rate (r_{cor}) series can be expressed simply as

$$(3) \quad r_{sl} = (1 - t)r_{cor} .$$

[7] Unless otherwise stated, the interest rate series referred to are those in Chart 1.

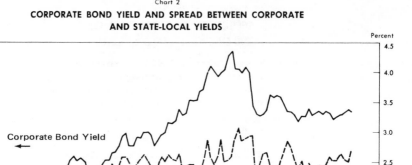

Chart 2
**CORPORATE BOND YIELD AND SPREAD BETWEEN CORPORATE
AND STATE-LOCAL YIELDS**

Although t varies among individuals, it has been fairly constant for corporations, about 50 percent, over the period shown in Chart 2. Formula (3) can be used to determine a marginal tax rate at which investors would be indifferent in choosing between new state and local bonds and new corporate bonds of the same quality. That tax rate would be

$$(3') \quad t^* = 1 - \frac{r_{sl}}{r_{cor}} \ .$$

An investor in a marginal tax bracket greater than t* would prefer state and local bonds to corporates. The t* series is shown in Chart 3. The series averages about 32 percent over the period and never reaches 40 percent. As would be expected, these values of t* lead to a situation in which the market for state and local securities is completely dominated by financial institutions subject to corporate income tax rates—commercial banks and casualty insurance companies—and by high income individuals.

CAPITAL GAINS TAX RATES AND YIELD SPREADS

Chart 4 compares the movement of the corporate bond yield series with the spread between the corporate bond yield series and the long-term U. S. government bond yield series. The yield series and the spread move very closely together indicating that, during the years shown, the spread increased when interest rates rose and decreased when interest rates fell. This section and the following will deal with two of the major factors causing this relationship.

The corporate bond yield series in Chart 1 is for new issue bonds selling

Chart 3

**MARGINAL TAX RATE AT WHICH AN INVESTOR WOULD BE INDIFFERENT
BETWEEN CORPORATE AND STATE-LOCAL BONDS**

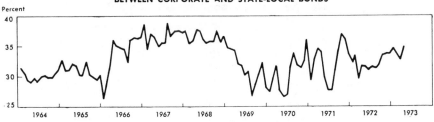

Chart 4

**CORPORATE BOND YIELD AND SPREAD BETWEEN CORPORATE
AND LONG-TERM U. S. YIELDS**

Note: Yield series are those described in Chart 1.

at or near par, while the long-term U. S. government bond yield series is for seasoned bonds. There is no yield series for new issue long-term U. S. bonds since none were issued over most of the period under consideration because the maximum legal coupon was 4.25 percent until 1971. Thus, the long-term U. S. bond yield series over most of the period is for a group of securities having coupons of 4.25 percent or less. The average coupon rate on the bonds making up the yield series in June 1970, when interest rates were at their peak, was only 3.64 percent.

Table III shows the spreads between the before-tax yields on a new security selling at par and a seasoned security with a $40 coupon, for equal-after-tax yields. The income tax rate of the investor is assumed to be 40 percent, the capital gains tax rate, 20 percent, and N, 20 years. As interest rates

Table III

BEFORE-TAX YIELD SPREAD

New vs. $40 Coupon Seasoned Security

Spread Between Before-tax Yield of New Security (r_1) and
Before-tax Yield of $40 Coupon Seasoned Security (r_2)
Assuming Equal After-tax Yields (r^*)
$N=20$ $t=40\%$ $cg=20\%$

r^*	r_2	P_2	r_1	P_1	Spread
2.40	4.00	$1,000.00	4.00	$1,000	.00
3.00	4.79	899.62	5.00	1,000	.21
4.00	6.10	760.72	6.67	1,000	.57
5.00	7.41	649.57	8.33	1,000	.92
6.00	8.73	559.62	10.00	1,000	1.27

rise, the price of the seasoned bond falls, increasing the amount of income that is received in the form of capital gains. Since capital gains are subject to a substantially lower tax rate than interest income, a lower before-tax yield on the seasoned bond is required to provide an after-tax return equal to that of the new bond. Under the assumptions made in Table III, this "capital gains" effect on the seasoned long-term U. S. bond yield series would explain almost one-half the movement of the spread in Chart 4.[8]

Table IV recomputes the spreads with a coupon of $30, and the other assumptions unchanged. As the table indicates, the lower the coupon on the seasoned security, the greater the discount and, consequently, the greater the amount of the return of the security in the form of capital gains. This results in an increase in the spread for any specific after-tax yield.

Table IV

BEFORE-TAX YIELD SPREAD

New vs. $30 Coupon Seasoned Security

Spread Between Before-tax Yield of a New Security (r_1) and
Before-tax Yield of a $30 Coupon Seasoned Security (r_2)
Assuming Equal After-tax Yields (r^*)
$N=20$ $t=40\%$ $cg=20\%$

r^*	r_2	P_2	r_1	P_1	Spread
1.80	3.00	$1,000.00	3.00	$1,000	.00
2.50	3.91	875.71	4.17	1,000	.26
3.00	4.55	799.24	5.00	1,000	.45
4.00	5.83	670.98	6.67	1,000	.84
5.00	7.10	568.70	8.33	1,000	1.23
6.00	8.38	486.23	10.00	1,000	1.62

[8] Of course, over the period, the average term to maturity of the $40 coupon securities would decline; however, at large values of N, this would have a very small effect on the spreads in Table III.

Chart 5 compares two yield series from Salomon Brothers that are for two sets of securities which are ostensibly alike in all respects except that one is new and the other is seasoned with a 4 1/8-4 3/8 percent coupon. The yield series are both for deferred callable Aa public utility bonds.[9] The spread between the two yield series is similar to that indicated under the assumptions made in Table III and corroborates the capital gains tax effect on yield series between yields for new and seasoned discount bonds. Chart 5 indicates an apparent change in the relationship between the spread and interest rate levels beginning in 1970. One explanation for this change is that the Tax Reform Act of 1969 increased maximum capital gains tax rates from 25 percent to 32.5 percent for individuals and to 30 percent for corporations. Assuming an equal-after-tax yield of 4 percent and a marginal income tax bracket of 50 percent, the effect of an increase in the capital gains tax from 25 percent to 30 percent would be to decrease the spread between the before-tax yields of a new security selling at par and a seasoned one bearing a $40 coupon from 114 to 104 basis points. Thus, the increase in capital gains tax rates would explain some, but apparently not all, of the change in the relationship in 1970 between the two curves shown in Chart 5.

When interest rates have fallen from past levels, seasoned securities with coupons higher than prevailing market interest rates will sell at a premium (P > $1000) and, consequently, will yield a capital loss at maturity. Under these circumstances, investors would be expected to demand a higher before-

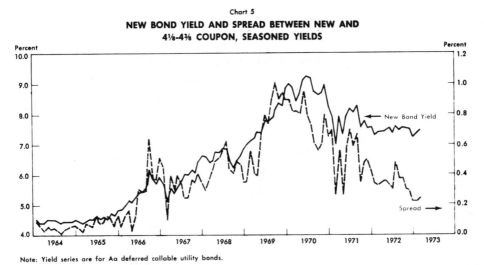

Chart 5
**NEW BOND YIELD AND SPREAD BETWEEN NEW AND
4⅛-4⅜ COUPON, SEASONED YIELDS**

Note: Yield series are for Aa deferred callable utility bonds.

Source: Salomon Brothers, **An Analytical Record of Yields and Yield Spreads.**

[9] The word "ostensibly" is used because a high coupon deferred callable bond is more likely to be called than a low coupon deferred callable bond.

tax yield to maturity on the seasoned bond. Chart 6 demonstrates this effect by comparing the yield of the Aa deferred callable, new, utility bond yield series with the spread between it and the yield series for a similar bond that differs only in that it is seasoned with an 8-8 3/8 percent coupon. The chart clearly indicates that when market rates fell below the coupon (8 percent), the observed yield on the seasoned bond became larger than the new issue bond yield. Table V shows the before-tax yields on a hypothetical premium seasoned bond with an $80 coupon necessary to give after-tax yields equal to those on new issues in a period when interest rates are below 8 percent. The results are similar to the actual spread in Chart 6.

Recently, new long-term U. S. bonds at current coupons have been issued. At the present time, three of the ten bonds in the sample used to compute the long-term U. S. bond series are high coupon (over 6 percent) bonds. The presence of the high coupon bonds in the sample should affect the relationship between the U. S. government bond yield series and the other series. Chart 4 provides some support for this expectation in that it appears that in 1973 the spread between the corporate and U. S. bond rates is smaller than it has been at similar interest rate levels in the past.

CALL PROVISIONS AND YIELD SPREADS

A third element entering into observed yield spreads results from the inability of the yield to maturity formula to account for differences in call provisions. Call provisions give the issuer of the security the option of pre-

Chart 6

NEW BOND YIELD AND SPREAD BETWEEN NEW AND 8-8⅜ COUPON, SEASONED YIELDS

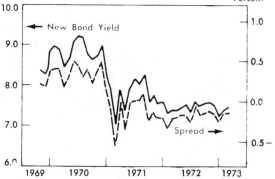

Note: Yield series are for Aa deferred callable utility bonds.

Source: Salomon Brothers, **An Analytical Record of Yields and Yield Spreads.**

paying the face value before the stated time of maturity. Virtually all corporate bonds and mortgages have some kind of call provision, as do most state and local bonds. Some U. S. government bonds are callable, but the long-term U. S. bond yield series shown in Chart 1 excludes bonds callable in less than 10 years. Call provisions for corporate bonds for which yield series are available specify that the bond is callable either immediately or after a deferred period of five years. Typically, if the bond is called, a penalty is paid by the issuer, which varies directly with the remaining years to maturity. A common penalty for a corporate bond called after five years would be one year's coupon.

Yields on bonds with call features are calculated, like yields on bonds without call features, by the yield to maturity formula (1). The resulting effects on observed yield spreads can be seen by considering the case of an investor with money to invest for N years who buys a N-year bond subject to call anytime after it is issued. If the bond is called, the investor reinvests the call price (the face value plus the call penalty), CP, immediately at the current market rate of interest, i, until the end of the original N years. The expected (holding period) yield over the N years is the discount rate, r', which equates the price of the security with the discounted value of the *expected* future income flows.[10]

$$(4) \quad P = \sum_{n=1}^{m} \frac{C}{(1+r')^n} + \sum_{n=m+1}^{N} \frac{(i)CP}{(1+r')^n} + \frac{CP}{(1+r')^N} .$$

The call date, m, and the market interest rate at the date of call, i, are clearly matters of uncertainty, unless there is a deferred call provision, in which case it is at least known that the bond cannot be prepaid before the end of the period of deferment. The attitude of the investor towards the price he is willing to pay for the security will clearly be influenced by the amount of call protection he gets—in terms of the period of deferment and the call price—and by his expectations of the degree and timing of future interest rate movements. A reasonable behavioral assumption is that a price will be determined at which the marginal investor will be indifferent between purchasing the security with a call provision versus one that is noncallable. That is, a price (or coupon) will be determined such that r', the expected holding period yield (which depends on m, CP, and i), will equal r, the yield to maturity of a noncallable bond with a maturity of N years computed by formula (1).[11]

The general implications for yield spreads of the difference between formulas (1) and (4) are fairly straightforward. First, if interest rates are not

---

[10] In order to keep the discussion manageable, taxes will be ignored in both this section and the next. Doing so does not affect any of the basic conclusions.

[11] This assumption implies, contrary to currently accepted theory, that investors do not demand a higher expected return in exchange for the uncertainty associated with buying the security with the call provision. The same simplifying assumption is made in the next section with respect to another type of uncertainty. The assumption does not affect any of the general conclusions.

expected to drop enough to justify the issuer of the security to prepay the face value of the security (given the presence of the call penalty and refinancing costs), then expectations will be that the security will not be called. Investors will not be willing to pay a premium (accept a lower yield) for deferment provisions, and the yield to maturity formula (1) will give comparable yields for securities with different call provisions. If interest rates are expected to fall enough that the security will be called *and* if the subsequent expected holding period yield, as indicated by formula (4), becomes smaller than r, the yield to maturity of a noncallable security, then the coupons on the callable security will have to rise (or in the case of a seasoned security, the price will have to fall) in order to equate r and r´. Under these circumstances spreads will be created between *calculated* yield series for securities with different periods of call deferment.[12]

Salomon Brothers has calculated yield to maturity series up to 1969 for

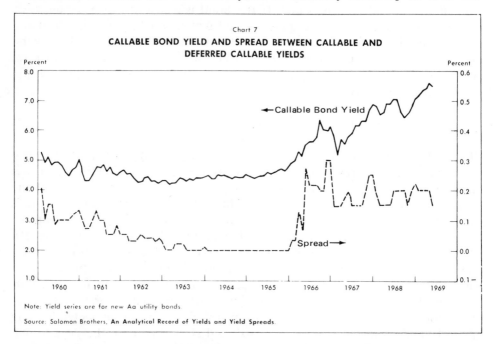

Chart 7

CALLABLE BOND YIELD AND SPREAD BETWEEN CALLABLE AND DEFERRED CALLABLE YIELDS

Note: Yield series are for new Aa utility bonds

Source: Salomon Brothers, An Analytical Record of Yields and Yield Spreads

[12] By imposing the condition that r in formula (1) equals r´ in formula (4), and by specifying values for CP, i, m, and N, specific spreads between calculated values to maturity on bonds with different call provisions are implied. For instance, suppose a noncallable 20-year bond, selling at par, has a $60 coupon and, consequently, a yield to maturity of 6 percent. Let CP = $1000 + C and assume that interest rates are expected to fall to a "normal" level, i, in three years and remain at that level. If i equals 5.50 percent, then no premium will be demanded on bonds with less than 20 years call protection. However, if i is equal to 5.25 percent, the coupon on an immediately callable security with five years of call protection will be $62.61. The calculated yields to maturity will be 6.57 percent and 6.26 percent, respectively, implying that investors demand a premium of 57 basis points to buy the immediately callable security and 26 basis points to buy the deferred callable security. The value of five years call protection would be 31 basis points.

securities that are identical in all respects except that one set is immediately callable, while the other has a deferred call period of five years.[13] Therefore, the spread between these two series, shown in Chart 7, isolates the effect of five years call deferment. Given the above discussion, investor expectation has to be that interest rates will fall in the five years following any period when the immediately callable rate rises above the deferred callable rate. Otherwise, investors would not be willing to accept a lower yield in return for five years of call deferment. The chart shows positive values both in the early and late 1960s. The chart also demonstrates that, over the period shown, expectations of future interest rate changes moved inversely with respect to interest rate levels.

An alternative way of illustrating the effect of the call feature in yields is to compute the yield to call (by assuming the call price is paid at the end of the period of deferment) and compare it to the yield to maturity for a given security. As indicated by formula (4), a low value of expected future interest rates compared to current interest rates will raise coupons (or lower prices) on securities with a call provision, so that the higher yield on the security for the period until it is called will compensate for the lower expected yield thereafter. Chart 8 shows the spread between the yield to call and yield to maturity of 8 1/2-9 1/8 percent coupon Aa utility bonds with a five-year

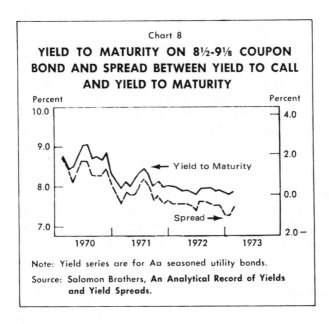

Chart 8

YIELD TO MATURITY ON 8½-9⅛ COUPON BOND AND SPREAD BETWEEN YIELD TO CALL AND YIELD TO MATURITY

Note: Yield series are for Aa seasoned utility bonds.

Source: Salomon Brothers, *An Analytical Record of Yields and Yield Spreads.*

---

[13] The series for immediately callable issues was discontinued in 1969 because of the absence of any new callable issues.

deferment period issued in 1970, at a time when long-term interest rates were at a record high. The chart supports the evidence from Chart 7 that when interest rates are high, purchasers of securities with call provisions demand to be compensated for the expected lower yields following the end of the deferment period. The differential in the two yields was wiped out before the end of the deferment period, however, when long-term rates fell at the end of 1970 and the beginning of 1971.[14]

Chart 7 shows the value of five years call deferment at different points in time arrived at by isolating that particular special feature. An important question posed by Chart 7 is what is the value and what is the effect on yield spreads of longer periods of call deferment? In particular, what is the value of call deferment until maturity (for 20 or 30 years) that characterizes state and local and most U. S. government bonds? The specific answer to that question is unknown, since there are no yield series that isolate longer periods of call deferment. One can only speculate that in periods of high interest rates, such as 1969-1970, calculated yield series for securities with call provisions would rise significantly relative to long-term yield series for securities with complete call protection. It seems likely, for example, that part of the unexplained increase in the spread between the corporate bond and U. S. government bond rates in the late 1960s resulted because the latter series excluded bonds callable in less than 10 years. In any case, the point is that call provisions will not only affect the spreads between various corporate bond rates, but they will also affect spreads between yield series for corporate bonds and other types of long-term securities with longer periods of call deferment.

Yield series for mortgages, unlike those for the other long-term securities, are computed by assuming that the mortgage is called ("prepaid") at a date before maturity. Although there are often "prepayment penalties," they do not enter into the computation of commonly used yield series. For the yield series on conventional mortgages shown in Chart 1, the prepayment date assumption has little effect on the calculated yield series. For yield series on FHA-insured mortgages, however, the prepayment assumption can substantially affect the yield series, because FHA-insured mortgages sell at a discount when market yields are greater than the maximum permissible "interest rate"on the mortgages. In order to raise the effective yield of the mortgage, the purchaser adjusts the actual amount of the loan rather than the monthly payments. In the context of formula (1), when C is at the legal maximum, the yield, r, is adjusted by changes in P, the price of the mort-

---

[14] After setting values for CP, i, m, and N, and imposing the condition that r in formula (1) equals r' in formula (4), the yield to maturity and yield to call on a deferred callable security can be calculated and compared. Because of the call penalty, a yield to call greater than yield to maturity *does not* necessarily imply an expectation of falling interest rates. However, given fixed interest rate expectations, a fall in interest rates from a level at which a deferred callable security has a higher yield to maturity than a noncallable security will decrease the spread between the yield to call and the yield to maturity of the deferred callable security.

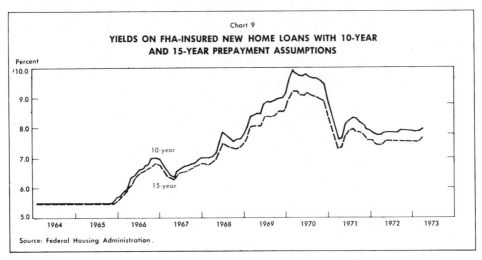

Chart 9

**YIELDS ON FHA-INSURED NEW HOME LOANS WITH 10-YEAR
AND 15-YEAR PREPAYMENT ASSUMPTIONS**

Source: Federal Housing Administration.

gage. When the assumed prepayment date is changed for such discount mortgages, it can have a substantial effect on the calculated yield series. Chart 9 shows the usual FHA-insured yield series compared to a recomputed one in which the call date assumption is changed from 15 to 10 years. The latter rate shows almost as much movement in the last 10 years as the corporate bond yield series in Chart 1. The spread between the conventional mortgage rate, shown in Chart 1, and the corporate bond rate, however, fell considerably during the same period.

DEFAULT RISK AND YIELD SPREADS

The fourth and last element in yield spreads to be considered results from the fact that the yield to maturity formula implicitly assumes that the promised returns associated with holding a particular security are known with certainty and that there is no risk of delay or failure in making those returns. In fact, there is default risk associated with holding most securities, and the amount of this risk as perceived by investors varies from security to security.

Consider, as an example, the situation of an investor faced with the option of buying one of two securities. The first one is, say, a United States government bond, which is assumed to be completely free of default risk. The yield to maturity, r_1, will be accurately determined by the formula (1) and will be known with certainty. The second security is a corporate bond for which the investor definitely feels there is some possibility that the issuing corporation will default, either by nonpayment or delayed payment of the coupons or face value of the bond. He will foresee a number of possible streams of returns associated with holding the bond, only one of which corresponds to the full promised amounts at the promised time periods.

Table V

BEFORE—TAX YIELD SPREAD

New vs. $80 Coupon Seasoned Security

Spread Between Before-Tax Yield of a New Security (r_1) and
Before-Tax Yield of an $80 coupon Seasoned Security (r_2)
Assuming Equal After-Tax Yields (r^*) and No Tax Break
On Capital Losses N = 20, t = 40%

r^*	r_2	P_2	r_1	P_1	Spread
4.80	8.00	$1,000.00	8.00	$1,000	.00
4.50	7.61	1,039.02	7.50	1,000	−.11
4.00	6.98	1,108.72	6.67	1,000	−.31
3.50	6.35	1,184.76	5.83	1,000	−.52
3.00	5.72	1,267.79	5.00	1,000	−.72

By employing formula (1) each possible stream of returns implies a different yield to maturity for the bond. The investor's *expected* yield to maturity on the second bond, r_2^e, can be thought of as the average of all the possible yields to maturity computed in this fashion. Clearly, if r_1, the *promised* yield to maturity on the risk-free bond, is equal to r_2, the *promised* yield to maturity on the bond subject to default risk, then r_1 will be greater than r_2^e, the expected yield to maturity on the risky bond. The investor, that is to say the market, will prefer the default-free bond to the one perceived to have default risk. This preference will drive up the price of the default-free security relative to the price of the risky security to the point where $r_1 = r_2^e$. Hence r_2, the *calculated* yield series on the risky security, will be greater than r_1. The difference between r_2 and r_1 is generally called the "market risk premium" for the risky security. In the world described above, it would equal $r_2 - r_2^e$, the "expected default loss" (difference be-

Table VI

EFFECT OF TAXES ON TERM STRUCTURE
OF BEFORE-TAX YIELDS

Effect of Taxes On The Term Structure of Before-tax Seasoned
Security Yields (r) Assuming Equal After-tax Yields (r*)
C = 40 cg = ½t

r^*	N	t = 40%		t = 50%	
		r	P	r	P
5.5	20	8.07	602.28	9.01	542.54
5.5	15	7.99	658.22	8.86	604.39
5.5	10	7.93	735.35	8.76	690.96
5.5	5	7.90	843.71	8.71	815.19
5.5	1	7.91	963.77	8.73	956.50

tween the promised and expected yields to maturity) on the risky security.

In the real world the perceived quality, or relative lack of default risk, on state and local and corporate securities is apparently determined largely by quality ratings made by investment agencies such as Moody's Investors Service. The market risk premium of a security with a given rating is the spread between the yield series for that rating and that of a U. S. government security of comparable maturity.

Chart 10 shows yield series for four categories of corporate bonds rated by Moody's. The highest, Aaa, is for "bonds with the smallest degree of investment risk; interest payments are protected by a large or by an exceptionally stable margin and principal is secure." The lowest rating shown, Baa, is for bonds whose "interest payments and principal appear adequate for the present but certain protective elements may be lacking or may be characteristically unreliable over any great length of time." Since none of the four yield series ever intersects, the opinions of investors, in general, correspond with those of Moody's.

A commonly asked question is what determines the quality rating of a particular security? Variables that have been cited in response to that question fall into two predictable classes. The first set of variables is related to the balance sheet of the issuer of the security, and the second set to the size and stability of the issuer's net income flows. For example, balance sheet variables that have been determined to be related to the quality ratings of corporate bonds are (1) the ratio of long-term debt to total capitalization, a measure of leverage, and (2) the market value of all publicly traded bonds of the company, a measure of marketability. Income variables that have been related to corporate bond ratings are the earnings variability of the company and the ratio of after-tax net income plus interest charges to interest charges, a measure of earnings coverage.

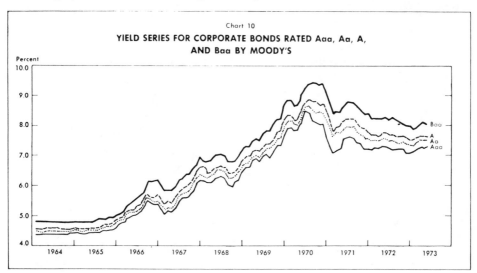

Chart 10

YIELD SERIES FOR CORPORATE BONDS RATED Aaa, Aa, A, AND Baa BY MOODY'S

A second question is whether the yield spreads embodied in market risk premiums respond inversely to cyclical movement in economic activity. The spread between Moody's Baa and Aaa corporate bond yield series is shown in Chart 11. Clearly, the spread rose substantially in the recession of 1970, particularly in the fourth quarter, which was the worst. During the rest of the period, however, the spread did not move closely with changes in real GNP. The same general observation may be made for state and local rates over the period.

Table I shows that the spread between the corporate bond rate series and the long-term U. S. government bond rate series shown in Chart 1 reached its peak in the fourth quarter of 1970. In view of the previous discussion and Chart 11, it appears likely that the movement in the spread between the two interest rate series was affected not only by the capital gains tax effect and call risk but also by a cyclical movement in default risk premiums.

THE RELATIONSHIP OF THE SPECIAL FEATURES
TO THE OTHER SECURITY CHARACTERISTICS

The discussion at the beginning of this article centered around the notion that yield spreads could be neatly divided into three classes related to characteristics of marketable securities. The three classes of spreads were: (1) those associated with differences in maturity, (2) those associated with differences in economic sectors that issue and purchase various securities, and (3) those associated with differences in the four special features discussed in this article.

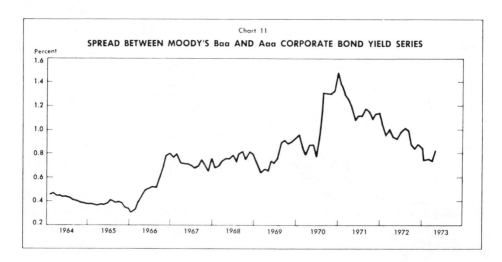

Chart 11

SPREAD BETWEEN MOODY'S Baa AND Aaa CORPORATE BOND YIELD SERIES

In reality, however, it is extremely difficult to isolate the part of an observed yield spread related to each of these characteristics, as has been shown with respect to the special features. It is useful to consider briefly the difficulties the presence of the special features can pose in attempting to isolate and explain the amount of an observed spread between security yields that is related to differences in maturity or to the behavior of the particular economic sectors that participate in the market for the securities. Two examples should suffice.

First, in discussing the movement in yield spreads over time related to different maturities (the term structure), U. S. securities are generally used. The implicit assumption is that these securities are alike in all respects except maturity. Table VI shows, however, that this was not the case in the period under consideration, since the long-term U. S. security yield series was for discount bonds. As the table indicates, a situation was created in which the securities also differed with respect to their tax treatment, implying upward bias, albeit small, in the U. S. security yield curve for maturities greater than five years. This bias increases as the difference between the coupon and current market rates increase and as taxes increase.

Attempts to isolate movements in yield spreads associated with the activity of different economic sectors are also difficult. For example, consider the case of an increase in U. S. government debt financed by long-term bonds. An interesting question is how will this action affect the long-term U. S. bond interest rate relative to other rates, such as the corporate bond rate. To attempt to answer this question, it is clearly desirable to have a corporate bond rate and a long-term U. S. bond rate for securities that are identical in all respects, in order to isolate the movement (if any) in the spread associated with the government debt financing operation. The relationship between the two interest rates in Chart 1, however, is also affected by capital gains tax treatment, by call risk, and by default risk. Furthermore, in the period under consideration, there is no pair of long-term corporate and U. S. bond rates series that is not influenced by these factors.

CONCLUSION

By focusing on the movement of interest rate series over the past 10 years, this article has attempted to demonstrate how the inability of the yield to maturity formula to deal with taxes and uncertainty in calculating yield series contributes to the creation and movement of observed spreads among various long-term interest rates. In particular, the article has shown that both income tax and capital gains tax rates have effects on observed yield spreads that vary with interest rate movements. The article also has illustrated the effect of call provisions on observed yield spreads and has shown how default risk influences yield spreads.

The article has made no attempt to explain elements of observed yield spreads associated with differences in maturity or associated with the behavior of different economic sectors. The article has pointed out, however, that these questions, particularly the latter, are greatly complicated by the effect on the level and movement of yield spreads of the four special features discussed.

THE MANY USES OF BOND DURATION *

Frank K. Reilly and
Rupinder S. Sidhu †

27

The burgeoning interest in bond analysis over the past five to 10 years has led to a rediscovery of a concept originally developed in 1938—Professor Frederick Macauley's measure of bond term known as "duration." This article explains the basic concept of duration and discusses in detail how duration is computed and how it is affected by maturity, coupon and market yield. In addition, we consider the main uses of duration in bond analysis (i.e., its relation to bond price volatility) and bond portfolio management (i.e., how it can be used to "immunize" a bond portfolio). Finally, we consider the application of duration to common stock analysis, including the computation of common stock duration and its implications for risk analysis and equity portfolio management.

AN OVERVIEW

Professor Frederick Macauley derived the basic concept of bond duration in 1938 and disseminated it in a book written for the National Bureau of Economic Research.[1] Originally, duration was conceived as a better way to

*Reprinted from the *Financial Analysts Journal*, July-August 1980, pp. 58-72. Copyright by the Financial Analysts Federation, 1980. Reprinted with permission.

†The authors are Professor of Finance at the University of Illinois at Urbana-Champaign and Investment Analyst with the Prudential Insurance Company, respectively.

[1] Frederick R. Macauley, *Some Theoretical Problems Suggested by the Movements of Interest Rates, Bond Yields, and Stock Prices in the United States since 1865* (New York: National Bureau of Economic Research, 1938).

summarize the timing of bond flows than maturity. Although conceded to be a better measure, duration was generally ignored for about 30 years. Duration was rediscovered in the late 1960s when academicians derived other uses for it. Specifically, Fisher and Hopewell and Kaufman discovered a direct relationship between the duration of a bond and its price sensitivity to changes in market interest rates.[2] Other authors have since demonstrated the usefulness of this relation to the active bond portfolio manager who attempts to derive superior returns by adjusting a portfolio composition to take advantage of major swings in market interest rates.[3] And Fisher and Weil have shown how the relation can be used to immunize a bond portfolio.[4]

Because of the direct relation between bond price volatility and duration, and because volatility is considered a measure of risk, some authors have attempted to use duration as a proxy for risk and to derive capital market lines that relate returns to duration.[5] (Some question remains, however, whether duration is an all-encompassing measure of risk.) Finally, since duration is basically a summary measure of the timing of an asset's cash flows, there is no reason for confining its use to bonds; an article by Boquist, Racette and Schlarbaum examines the concepts as it applies to bonds *and* common stock.[6]

ALTERNATIVE MEASURES

To understand the concept of duration properly, it is useful to place it in the perspective of other summary measures of the timing of an asset's cash

[2] Lawrence Fisher, "An Algorithm for Finding Exact Rates of Return," *Journal of Business*, January 1966, pp. 111-118 and Michael H. Hopewell and George C. Kaufman, "Bond Price Volatility and Term to Maturity: A Generalized Respecification," *American Economic Review*, September 1973, pp. 749-753.

[3] See, for example, Edward Blocher and Clyde Stickney, "Duration and Risk Assessments in Capital Budgeting," *The Accounting Review*, January 1979, pp. 180-188; John Caks, "The Coupon Effect on Yield to Maturity," *Journal of Finance*, March 1977, pp. 103-116; Stanley Diller, "A Three Part Series on the Use of Duration in Bond Analysis and Portfolio Management," *Money Manager*, January 29, 1979, February 5, 1979 and February 13, 1979; David Durand, "Growth Stocks and the Petersburg Paradox," *Journal of Finance*, September 1957, pp. 348-363; Robert A. Haugen and Dean W. Wichern, "The Elasticity of Financial Assets," *Journal of Finance*, September 1974, pp. 1229-1240; J. R. Hicks, *Value and Capital*, 2nd ed. (Oxford: The Claredon Press, 1946), p. 186; Burton G. Malkiel, "Equity Yields, Growth, and the Structure of Share Prices," *American Economic Review*, December 1963, pp. 1004-1031; Richard W. McEnally, "Duration as a Practical Tool in Bond Management," *Journal of Portfolio Management*, Summer 1977, pp. 53-57; and Jess Yawitz, "The Relative Importance of Duration and Yield Volatility on Bond Price Volatility," *Journal of Money, Credit and Banking*, February 1977, pp. 97-102.

[4] Lawrence Fisher and Roman L. Weil, "Coping With the Risk of Interest-Rate Fluctuations: Returns to Bondholders from Naive and Optimal Strategies," *Journal of Business*, October 1971, pp. 408-431.

[5] James C. Van Horne, *Financial Market Rates and Flows* (Englewood Cliffs, NJ: Prentice-Hall, Inc., 1978), Chapter 5.

[6] John A. Boquist, George A. Racette and Gary G. Schlarbaum, "Duration and Risk Assessment for Bonds and Common Stock," *Journal of Finance*, December 1975, pp. 1360-1365.

Table I Specification of Sample Bonds

	Bond A	*Bond B*
Face Value	$1,000	$1,000
Maturity	10 years	10 years
Coupon	4%	8%
Sinking Fund	10% a year of face value starting at end of year 5	15% a year of face value starting at end of year 5

flows. While measurement of the timing of cash flows is important to the analysis of all investments, the ability to measure it precisely is typically limited because the analyst is not certain of the timing and size of the flows. Because the cash flows from bonds are specified both as to timing and amount, however, analysts have derived a precise measure of the timing for bonds. We discuss below the principal measures and demonstrate their application for the two bonds described in Table I.

Term to Maturity

The most popular timing measure is *term to maturity (TM)—the number of years prior to the final payment on the bond.* Our two sample bonds have identical terms to maturity—10 years. Term to maturity has the advantage of being easily identified and measured, since bonds are always specified in terms of the final maturity date, and it is easy to compute the time from the present to that final year. The obvious disadvantage of term to maturity is that it ignores the amount and timing of all cash flows except the final payment. In the case of the sample bonds, term to maturity ignores the substantial difference in coupon rates and the difference in the sinking funds.

A number of years ago some bond analysts and portfolio managers attempted to rectify this deficiency by computing a measure that considered the interest payments and the final principal payment. *The weighted average term to maturity (WATM)* computes the proportion of each individual payment as a percentage of all payments and makes this proportion the weight for the year (one through 10) the payment is made.[7] It equals:

$$\text{WATM} = \frac{CF_1(1)}{TCF} + \frac{CF_2(2)}{TCF} + \ldots \frac{CF_n(n)}{TCF} \,,$$

where

CF_t = the cash flow in year t,
(t) = the year when cash flow is received,
n = maturity and
TCF = the total cash flow from the bond.

[7] Although it is recognized that interest payments are typically made at six-month intervals, we assume annual payments at year-end to simplify the computations.

For example, Bond A (the four per cent coupon, 10-year bond) will have total cash flow payments (TCF) of $1,400 ($40 a year for 10 years plus $1,000 at maturity). Thus the $40 payment in year one ($CF_1$) will have a weight of 0.02857 ($40/1,400), each subsequent interest payment will have the same weight, and the principal payment in year 10 will have a weight of 0.74286 ($1,000/1,400). Table II demonstrates the specific computation of the weighted average term to maturity for each sample bond.

It is apparent from Table II that the weighted average term to maturity is definitely less than the term to maturity because it takes account of all interim cash flows in addition to the final principal payment. Furthermore, the bond with the larger coupon has a shorter weighted average term to maturity because a larger proportion of its total cash flows is derived from the coupon payments that come prior to maturity. Specifically, the interest payments constitute 28.6 percent ($400/1,400) of the total returns on Bond A, but 44.4 percent ($800/1,800) of the total flow of Bond B. Obviously, if one were to compute a measure that included sinking fund payments, the weighted average term to maturity would be even lower.

A major advantage of the weighted average term to maturity is that it considers the timing of all flows from the bond, rather than only the final payment. One drawback is that it does not consider the time value of the flows. The interest payment in the first year has the same weight as the interest payment in the tenth year, although the present value of the payment in the tenth year is substantially less. Also, the weighted average term to maturity would give the $1,000 principal the same weight whether payment was made in year 10 or year 20.

Table II Weighted Average Term to Maturity
              (assuming annual interest payments)

Bond A

(1) Year	(2) Cash Flow	(3) Cash Flow/TCF	(4) (1)×(3)
1	$ 40	0.02857	0.02857
2	40	0.02857	0.05714
3	40	0.02857	0.08571
4	40	0.02857	0.11428
5	40	0.02857	0.14285
6	40	0.02857	0.17142
7	40	0.02857	0.19999
8	40	0.02857	0.22856
9	40	0.02857	0.25713
10	1,040	0.74286	7.42860
Sum	$1,400	1.00000	8.71425

Weighted Average Term to Maturity = 8.71 Years

Bond B

1	$ 80	0.04444	0.04444
2	80	0.04444	0.08888
3	80	0.04444	0.13332
4	80	0.04444	0.17776
5	80	0.04444	0.22220
6	80	0.04444	0.26664
7	80	0.04444	0.31108
8	80	0.04444	0.35552
9	80	0.04444	0.39996
10	1,080	0.60000	6.00000
Sum	$1,800	1.00000	7.99980

Weighted Average Term to Maturity = 8.00 Years

Duration

The duration measure is similar to the weighted average term to maturity, with the exception that *all flows are in terms of present value.* Duration equals:

$$D = \frac{\displaystyle\sum_{t=1}^{n} \frac{C_t(t)}{(1+r)^t}}{\displaystyle\sum_{t=1}^{n} \frac{C_t}{(1+r)^t}}$$

where

C_t = the interest and/or principal payment in year t,

(t) = the length of time to the interest and/or principal payment,

n = the length of time to final maturity and

r = the yield to maturity.

In the style of our equation for weighted average term to maturity, duration is:

$$D = \frac{PVCF_1(1)}{PVTCF} + \frac{PVCF_2(2)}{PVTCF} + \cdots + \frac{PVCF_n(n)}{PVTCF}$$

where

$PVCF_t$ = the present value of the cash flow in year t discounted at current yield to maturity,

(t) = the year when cash flow is received and

$PVTCF$ = the present value of total cash flow from the bond discounted at current yield to maturity—obviously, the prevailing market price for the bond.

Table III shows the computations of duration for the two sample bonds. *Duration is simply a weighted average maturity, where the weights are stated in present value terms.* Specifically, the time in the future a cash flow is received is weighted by the proportion that the present value of that cash flow contributes to the total present value or price of the bond. (We assume that interest payments are made annually; use of the more realistic semiannual payments would result in a shorter duration—7.99 years versus 8.12 years and 7.07 years compared with 7.25 years.)

Table III   Duration *(assuming eight per cent market yield)*

			Bond A		
(1) Year	*(2)* Cash Flow	*(3)* PV at 8%	*(4)* PV of Flow	*(5)* PV as % of Price	*(6)* *(1)×(5)*
1	$ 40	0.9259	$ 37.04	0.0506	0.0506
2	40	0.8573	34.29	0.0469	0.0938
3	40	0.7938	31.75	0.0434	0.1302
4	40	0.7350	29.40	0.0402	0.1608
5	40	0.6806	27.22	0.0372	0.1860
6	40	0.6302	25.21	0.0345	0.2070
7	40	0.5835	23.34	0.0319	0.2233
8	40	0.5403	21.61	0.0295	0.2360
9	40	0.5002	20.01	0.0274	0.2466
10	1,040	0.4632	481.73	0.6585	6.5850
Sum			$731.58	1.0000	8.1193

Duration = 8.12 Years

			Bond B		
1	$ 80	0.9259	$ 74.07	0.0741	0.0741
2	80	0.8573	68.59	0.0686	0.1372
3	80	0.7938	63.50	0.0635	0.1906
4	80	0.7350	58.80	0.0588	0.1906
5	80	0.6806	54.44	0.0544	0.2720
6	80	0.6302	50.42	0.0504	0.3024
7	80	0.5835	46.68	0.0467	0.3269
8	80	0.5403	43.22	0.0432	0.3456
9	80	0.5002	40.02	0.0400	0.3600
10	1,080	0.4632	500.26	0.5003	5.0030
Sum			$1000.00	1.0000	7.2470

Duration = 7.25 Years

As with weighted average term to maturity, the duration of a bond is shorter than its term to maturity because of the interim interest payments. Obviously, a zero coupon bond yielding no interim payments would have the same duration, weighted average term to maturity and term to maturity, since 100 percent of the total cash flow, and 100 percent of total present value, would come at maturity. Also, like weighted average term to maturity, *duration is inversely related to the coupon for the bond*–i.e., the larger the coupon, the greater the proportion of total returns received in the interim, and the shorter the duration. Figure A graphs the relation between duration and maturity for a range of coupon rates.

One variable that does not influence weighted average term to maturity but can affect duration is the prevailing market yield (r). Market yield does not influence weighted average term to maturity because this measure does not consider the present value of flows. Market yield affects both the numerator and denominator of the duration computation, but it affects the numerator more. As a result, *there is an inverse relation between a change in the market yield and a bond's duration*. That is, an increase in the market yield will cause a decline in duration, other things being equal.

Figure A   Relation Between Duration and Term
To Maturity for Alternative Coupons

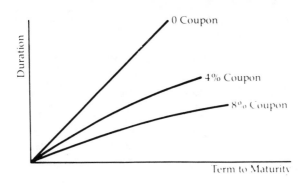

Table IV   How Duration Is Affected by Alternative Market
Yields *(assuming semiannual interest payments)*

	Market Yields			
	0%	*4%*	*8%*	*12%*
Bond A	8.60*	8.34	7.99*	7.59
Bond B	7.87*	7.50	7.07*	6.61

*The durations differ from those in Tables II and
III because of the use of semiannual interest payments.

Table IV demonstrates how different market yields will affect the duration of our sample bonds. The results for the case of zero market yield indicate that duration is the same as weighted average term to maturity when there is no discounting.

EFFECT OF SINKING FUNDS

The discussion thus far has ignored the effects of sinking funds. But a large proportion of current bond issues do have sinking funds, and these can definitely affect a bond's duration. Table V shows the computations of duration for the sample bonds with sinking funds. Inclusion of the sinking funds causes the computed durations to decline by approximately one year in both cases (i.e., from 8.12 to 7.10 for Bond A and from 7.25 to 6.21 for Bond B).

The effect of a sinking fund on the time structure of cash flows for a bond is certain to the issuer of the bond, since the firm must make the payments; they represent a legal cash flow requirement that will affect the firm's cash

Table V Impact of Sinking Fund on Duration *(assuming eight per cent market yield)*

			Bond A		
(1) Year	*(2)* Cash Flow	*(3)* PV at 8%	*(4)* PV of Flow	*(5)* PV/Total CF	*(6)* (1)×(5)
1	$ 40	0.9259	$ 37.04	0.04668	0.04668
2	40	0.8573	34.29	0.04321	0.08642
3	40	0.7938	31.75	0.04001	0.12003
4	40	0.7350	29.40	0.03705	0.14820
5	140	0.6806	95.28	0.12010	0.60050
6	140	0.6302	88.23	0.11119	0.66714
7	140	0.5835	81.69	0.10295	0.72065
8	140	0.5403	75.64	0.09533	0.76264
9	140	0.5002	70.03	0.08826	0.79434
10	540	0.4632	250.13	0.31523	3.15230
Sum			$793.48	1.00000	7.09890

Duration = 7.10 Years

			Bond B		
1	$ 80	0.9259	$ 74.07	0.06778	0.06778
2	80	0.8573	68.59	0.06276	0.12552
3	80	0.7938	63.50	0.05811	0.17433
4	80	0.7350	58.80	0.05380	0.21520
5	230	0.6806	156.54	0.14324	0.71620
6	230	0.6302	144.95	0.13264	0.79584
7	230	0.5835	134.21	0.12281	0.85967
8	230	0.5403	124.27	0.11371	0.90968
9	230	0.5002	115.05	0.10528	0.94752
10	330	0.4632	152.86	0.13987	1.39870
Sum			$1,092.84	1.00000	6.21044

Duration = 6.21 Years

flow. In contrast, the sinking fund may not affect the investor. The money put into the sinking fund may not necessarily be used to retire outstanding bonds; even if it is, it is not certain that a given investor's bonds will be called for retirement.

EFFECT OF CALL

In contrast to a sinking fund, which reduces duration by only one year and may affect only a few investors, all bondholders will be affected if a bond is called, and the call feature can influence duration substantially. For example, consider a 30-year bond of eight percent coupon, selling at par and callable after 10 years at 108. First, compute a cross-over yield.[8] At yields above the cross-over yield, the yield to maturity is the minimum yield. When

[8] This discussion of cross-over yield and its computation is drawn from Sidney Homer and Martin L. Leibowitz, *Inside the Yield Book* (Englewood Cliffs, NJ: Prentice-Hall, Inc., 1972).

the price of the bond rises to some value above the call price, and the market yield declines to a value below the cross-over yield, however, the yield to call becomes the minimum yield. At this price and yield, the firm will probably exercise a call option when it is available.

As Homer and Leibowitz have demonstrated, it is possible to calculate the cross-over yield by deriving the yield to maturity for a bond selling at the call price for the original maturity minus the years of call protection.[9] For the above example, this would involve deriving the yield to maturity for an eight percent coupon bond selling at $1,080 and maturing in 30 years; the implied cross-over yield is 7.24 percent. In one year's time, the bond's maturity will be 29 years, with nine years to call. Assume the market rate has declined to the point where the yield to maturity for the bond is seven percent (below the cross-over yield of 7.24 percent). At this price ($1,123.43), the bond's yield to call will be 6.2 percent.

If a bond portfolio manager ignored the call option and computed the duration of this bond to maturity (29 years) assuming a market yield of seven percent, the duration would work out to be 12.49 years. Recognizing the call option would mean computing the duration for a bond to be called in nine years at a price of $1,080 and using the yield to call of 6.2 percent, for a duration of 6.83 years. Table VI summarizes this example.

The existence of a call option, which is almost universal on corporate bonds, can have a dramatic impact on the computed duration for a bond. The above example assumed a deferred call of 10 years, which is currently the maximum period; five years is more typical.

Duration of GNMA Bonds

During the past several years there has been a substantial increase in investor interest in GNMA pass-through bonds because of the inherent safety of

Table VI   Impact of Call Options on Duration

Original Bond:	8% coupon bond sold at par with 30 years to maturity. Callable in 10 years at 108 of par. (Computed cross-over yield is 7.24%.)
One Year Later:	Market yields on bond decline from 8 to 7%.
	Current market price: $1,123.43
	Yield to maturity (29 years): 7%
	Yield to call (9 years): 6.2%
	Call price: 108
Duration:	At 7% yield and 29 years maturity—12.49 years At 6.2% yield, 9 years to call at 108—6.83 years

[9] Ibid., pp. 58-63.

the bonds and their higher yields relative to other government securities. Without detracting from the safety and yield characteristics of these securities, a portfolio manager should recognize the extreme difference between the initial promised term to maturity, the empirical maturity and the probable duration, taking into account the form of cash flow and the empirical maturity.

An investor in a GNMA pass-through is basically purchasing a share of a pool of mortgages. The investor receives each month a payment from the mortgages that includes not only interest, but also partial repayment of the principal. Of course, homeowners may decide to pay off their mortgages in order to buy other houses (in which case prepayment penalties are usually waived). As a result, mortgage contracts are like bonds with sinking funds because they pay interest and principal over time and they are also like bonds that are freely callable because they can be paid off when the house is sold. *The empirical duration of a GNMA pass-through will thus be substantially less than the stated maturity.*

The stated maturity of most home mortgages is 25 years. Given the nature of the payment stream including principal and interest, the duration of a mortgage without prepayment is substantially less than the stated maturity. For example, assuming a 10 percent market rate and annual payments at the end of the year, a 30-year mortgage has a duration of 9.18 years, a 25-year mortgage has a duration of 8.46 years, and a 20-year mortgage has a duration of 7.51 years. (The consideration of realistic monthly payments would reduce these durations further.)

In addition, because of numerous prepayments, the empirical maturity of most mortgage pools is actually only about 12 years, rather than the stated 25. If one assumes principal and interest payments for 12 years and a prepayment at the end of 12 years (with no call premium), the computed durations would decline further. Under these assumptions, the mortgages have the following durations—30 years, 7.22 years; 25 years, 7.04 years; 20 years, 6.71 years. Bond portfolio managers should recognize that they are acquiring relatively short duration bonds when they invest in GNMAs.

Duration Properties

Except for very long maturity bonds selling at a discount, duration is positively related to the maturity of the bond.[10] It is inverseley related to the coupon on a bond and to the market yield for the bond. Furthermore, durations can be reduced by sinking fund or call provisions.

Weighted average term to maturity and duration will be equal to a bond's

---

[10] For a discussion of this point, see Van Horne, *Financial Market rates and Flows*, p. 120.

term to maturity when the coupon rate is zero—that is, when there are no interim cash flows prior to maturity. But weighted average term to maturity and duration will never exceed a bond's term to maturity. In fact, Fisher and Weil suggest that insurance companies encourage some issuers (including the government) to sell long-term, zero-coupon discount bonds that would have maturities and durations of 30 or 40 years; in this way, they could match their long-term liabilities with long-duration assets.[11] Regardless of coupon size, it is nearly impossible to find bonds that have durations in excess of 20 years; most bonds have a limit of about 15 years.

As Tables II and III show, weighted average term to maturity is always longer than the duration of a bond, and the difference increases with the market rate used in the duration formula. This is consistent with the observation that there is an inverse relation between duration and the market rate. Further, this relation confirms our earlier observation that weighted average term to maturity and duration are equal when the market rate is zero.

DURATION AND BOND PRICE VOLATILITY

Hopewell and Kaufman set forth the specific form of the relation between the duration of a bond and its price volatility:[12]

$$\%\Delta\text{Bond Price} = -D^*(\Delta r),$$

where

$\%\Delta$Price = the percentage change in price for the bond,

D^* = the adjusted duration of the bond in years, which is equal to $D/(1 + r)$, and

Δr = the change in the market yield in basis points divided by 100 (e.g., a 50 basis point decline would be -0.5).

Consider a bond that has a duration of 10 years and an adjusted duration of 9.259 years (10/1.08). If interest rates go from eight to nine percent, then:

$$\%\Delta\text{Bond Price} = -9.259\ (100/100)$$
$$= -9.259\ (1)$$
$$= -9.259\%.$$

---

[11] Fisher and Weil, "Coping With the Risk of Interest-Rate Fluctuations."

[12] Hopewell and Kaufman, "Bond Price Volatility and Term to Maturity."

The price of the bond should decline by about 9.3 percent for every one percent (100 basis point) increase in market rates.

In practice, most investors use the unadjusted duration figure when computing the impact of market rate changes. At high duration figures and reasonable market prices, the difference is relatively minor.

Implications for Portfolio Management

The direct relation between duration and interest rate sensitivity is important to an active bond portfolio manager who attempts to derive superior returns by adjusting the composition of his portfolio to benefit from swings in market rates of interest. Given this portfolio philosophy, the manager should attempt to maximize the portfolio's interest rate sensitivity prior to an expected decline in interest rates, and to minimize it when rising rates are expected. In doing so, duration rather than term to maturity must be considered because duration is a better measure of the interest sensitivity of the portfolio. The manager will take into account coupon, call features and sinking fund provisions in addition to maturity in determining shifts in the portfolio composition.[13]

DURATION AND IMMUNIZATION

A major problem encountered in bond portfolio management is deriving a given rate of return to satisfy an ending wealth requirement for a specific future date—i.e., the investment horizon. If the term structure of interest rates were flat and the level of market rates never changed, the manager of a bond portfolio could deliver a known amount of wealth at the client's horizon by buying a bond maturing at the horizon. Specifically, the ending wealth position would be the beginning wealth times the compound value of a dollar at the promised yield to maturity.

Unfortunately, in the real world the term structure of interest rates is not typically flat and the level of interest rates is constantly changing. Because of the shape of the term structure and changes in the level of interest rates, the bond portfolio manager faces what is referred to as "interest rate risk" between the time of investment and the future target date. Interest rate risk can be defined as the uncertainty regarding the ending wealth position due to changes in market interest rates between the time of purchase and the target date.

Interest rate risk comprises two risks—a price risk and a coupon reinvest-

---

[13] For a discussion of some of the practical aspects of implementing this use of duration, see Diller, "A Three Part Series on the Use of Duration in Bond Analysis and Portfolio Management."

ment risk. *Price risk* represents the chance that interest rates will differ from the rates the manager expects to prevail between purchase and target date, causing the market price for the bond (i.e., the "realized" price) to differ from his assumption. Obviously, if interest rates increase, the realized price for the bond in the secondary market will be below expectations, while if interest rates decline, the realized price will exceed expectations.

Reinvestment risk arises because interest rates at which coupon payments can be reinvested are unknown.[14] If interest rates decline after the bond is purchased, coupon payments will be reinvested at lower rates, and their contribution to ending wealth will be below expectations.

Immunization and Interest Rate Risk

Price risk and reinvestment risk have opposite effects on the investor's ending wealth position. Specifically, with an increase in market interest rates, the bond's realized price will fall below expectations, but the income from reinvesting interim cash flows will exceed expectations. A decline in market interest rates will provide a higher than expected ending price, but lower than expected ending wealth from reinvested interim cash flows.

A bond portfolio manager with a specific investment horizon will want to eliminate these two risks—i.e., to "immunize" the portfolio. According to Fisher and Weil:

> "A portfolio of investments in bonds is *immunized* for a holding period if its value at the end of the holding period, regardless of the course of interest rates during the holding period, must be at least as large as it would have been had the interest rate function been constant throughout the holding period.
>
> "If the realized return on an investment in bonds is sure to be at least as large as the appropriately computed yield to the horizon, then that investment is immunized."[15]

Fisher and Weil's comparison of promised yields on bonds for the period 1925-68 with realized returns on bonds demonstrates the difference between promised yield and realized yield and indicates the importance of being able to immunize a bond portfolio.

Fisher and Weil based their portfolio immunization theory on the assumption that, if the yield curve shifts, the change in interest rates will be the same for all future rates; that is, if forward interest rates change, all rates change by the same amount. Under this assumption *a portfolio of bonds is immunized from interest rate risk if the duration of the portfolio equals the desired investment horizon.* For example, if the investment horizon of a bond portfolio is eight years, the duration of the portfolio should equal eight

[14] For a detailed elaboration of this point, see Homer and Leibowitz, *Inside the Yield Book.*
[15] Fisher and Weil, "Coping With the Risk of Interest-Rate Fluctuations," p. 415.

years. To construct a portfolio with a given duration, the manager should set the (value) weighted average duration at the desired length.

The whole point of the proof of the immunization theorem by Fisher and Weil is that a change in market rates will have opposite effects on price risk and reinvestment risk. That is, when the price change is positive the reinvestment change will be negative, and vice versa. Fisher and Weil proved that *duration is the investment horizon for which the price risk and the coupon reinvestment risk of a bond portfolio have equal magnitudes but opposite directions.*

Application of the Immunization Principle

Fisher and Weil carried out a simulation to compare the effects of applying their portfolio immunization strategy with the results for a naive strategy that set the portfolio's maturity equal to the investment horizon. This simulation computed the ending wealth ratios for the alternative portfolio strategies over five, 10 and 20-year investment horizons and compared them with the ending wealth ratios assuming the expected yield was realized. If a portfolio were perfectly immunized, the actual ending wealth would equal the expected ending wealth implied by the promised yield. Therefore, the comparison should indicate which portfolio strategy offered better immunization.

The duration strategy results were consistently closer to the promised yield, although the results were not perfect (i.e., the duration portfolio was not perfectly immunized). The imperfections could be traced to real-world departures from Fisher and Weil's basic assumption that, when interest rates change, all interest rates change by the same amount. The authors concluded that the naive maturity strategy removes most of the uncertainty of the expected wealth ratio from a long-term bond portfolio, and the duration strategy most of the remaining uncertainty. The authors contend that matching duration to the investment horizon reduces the standard deviation of a bond portfolio so dramatically that the result is essentially riskless.

Alternative Definitions and Duration

Bierwag and Kaufman have pointed out that there are several specifications of the duration measure.[16] The measure derived by Macauley (the one used throughout this article) discounts all flows by the prevailing average yield to maturity on the bond being measured. Fisher and Weil use future one-period discount rates (forward rates) to discount the future flows. Depending upon the shape of the yield curve, these two definitions could give

[16] G. O. Bierwag and George C. Kaufman, "Coping With the Risk of Interest Rate Fluctuations: A Note," *Journal of Business*, July 1977, pp. 364-370.

different results. Only if all forward rates are equal (so that the yield curve is flat) will the two definitions result in equal estimates and duration.

Bierwag and Kaufman note that the definition of duration used for bond portfolio immunization should be a function of the nature of the shock to the interest rate structure. It is possible to conceive of an additive shock to interest rates, where all interest rates are changed by the same nominal amount (e.g., 50 basis points), or a multiplicative shock, where all interest rates change by the same percentage (e.g., all rates decline by 10 percent). Bierwag contends that the optimal definition of duration for perfect immunization of a portfolio will depend upon the nature of the shock to the interest rate structure.[17] In the case of an additive shock, the Fisher-Weil definition is best, but a multiplicative shock requires a third measure of duration. Bierwag and Kaufman computed the duration for a set of bonds using the three definitions of duration and concluded:

> "Except at high coupons and long maturities, the values of the three definitions do not vary greatly. Thus, D_1 [Macauley] may be used as a first approximation for D_2 and D_3 [Fisher-Weil and Bierwag-Kaufman, respectively]. The expression for D_1 has the additional advantage of being a function of the yield to maturity of the bond. As a result, neither a forecast of the stream of one-period forward rates over maturity of the bond nor a specific assumption about the nature of the random shocks is required."[18]

Example of Immunization

Table VII demonstrates the effect of immunizing a portfolio by matching the duration of a single-bond portfolio to the investment horizon. The table assumes that the portfolio manager's investment horizon is eight years and the current yield to maturity for eight-year bonds is eight percent. The ending wealth ratio for a completely immunized portfolio should therefore be $(1.08)^8 = 1.8509$.

Table VII considers two portfolio strategies, one setting the term to maturity at eight years and the other setting the duration at eight years. The maturity strategy assumes that the portfolio manager acquires an eight-year, eight percent bond. In contrast, the duration strategy assumes that the portfolio manager acquires a 10-year, eight percent bond that has approximately an eight-year duration (8.12 years) assuming an eight percent yield to maturity (see Table III). It is further assumed that a single shock to the interest rate structure at the end of year four causes the market yield to go from eight to six percent, where it remains through year eight.

---

[17] G. O. Bierwag, "Immunization, Duration, and the Term Structure of Interest Rates," *Journal of Financial and Quantitative Analysis*, December 1977, pp. 725-742.

[18] Bierwag and Kaufman, "Coping With the Risk of Interest Rate Fluctuations: A Note," p. 367.

Table VII Effect of a Change in Market Rates on a Bond (Portfolio) that Uses the Maturity Strategy versus the Horizon Strategy

Expected Wealth Ratio = 1.8509

	Results with Maturity Strategy			Results with Horizon Strategy		
Year	Cash Flow	Reinv. Rate	End Value	Cash Flow	Reinv. Rate	End Value
1	$ 80	0.08	$ 80.00	$ 80	0.08	$ 80.00
2	80	0.08	166.40	80	0.08	166 40
3	80	0.08	259.71	80	0.08	259.71
4	80	0.08	360.49	80	0.08	360.49
5	80	0.06	462.12	80	0.06	462.12
6	80	0.06	596.85	80	0.06	596.85
7	80	0.06	684.04	80	0.06	684.04
8	1,080	0.06	1,805.08	1120.684*	0.06	1,845.72

*The bond could be sold at its market value of $1,040.64, which is the value for an eight per cent bond with two years to maturity priced to yield six per cent.

Because of the interest rate change in year four, the wealth ratio for the maturity strategy is below the desired wealth ratio, the interim coupon cash flow being reinvested at six rather than eight percent. But the maturity strategy eliminates the price risk associated with interest rate volatility because the bond matures at the end of year eight. The duration strategy portfolio also suffers a shortfall in reinvestment cash flow because of the change in market rates. But this shortfall is offset by the increase in the ending value for the bond arising from the decline in market rates. That is, the bond is worth $104.06 at the end of year eight because it is an eight percent coupon bond with two years to maturity selling to yield six percent.

If market interest rates had increased during this period, the maturity strategy portfolio would have experienced an excess of reinvestment income compared to the expected cash flow, and its ending wealth ratio would have exceeded expectations. In contrast, the duration portfolio would have experienced a decline in ending price that would have offset the excess cash flow from reinvestment. While the maturity strategy would have provided a higher than expected ending value under these assumptions, the whole purpose of immunization is to eliminate uncertainty (i.e., have the realized wealth position equal the expected wealth position); the duration strategy accomplishes this purpose.

The concept of duration is important to the bond portfolio manager with a specified investment horizon who wants to reduce the interest rate risk from his long-term bond portfolio. He does not want to predict future market rates, but simply to achieve a specified result irrespective of future rates.

YIELD CURVES AND BOND MARKET LINES

The typical yield curve is derived by plotting the yield to maturity (on the vertical axis) against the term to maturity (on the horizontal axis) for bonds of equal risk. Hopewell and Kaufman contend that this practice can result in abnormal curves if the bonds used have significantly different coupons.[19] The point is, of two bonds with different terms to maturity and different coupons, the longer maturity bond may have the shorter duration. For example, a 20-year bond with a large coupon could have a shorter duration than an 18-year bond with a small coupon.

Carr, Halpern and McCallum suggest that yield curves should be constructed with yield to maturity on the vertical axis and duration on the horizontal axis.[20] They further contend that forward rates (implied future short-term rates) should be computed on the basis of the duration yield curve. (Of course, the yield curves must still be derived using bonds of equal risk—e.g., all government bonds or all AAA-rated bonds).

Table VIII gives the durations and terms to maturity for a sample of gov-

Table VIII Government Bonds Used to Construct Maturity Yield Curve and Duration Yield Curve
(as of November 1978)

| Bond Description | | Yield to | | |
Coupon	Maturity	Maturity	Maturity	Duration
7⅞ %	5/79	9.41%	0.5	0.500
7⅛	11/79	9.68	1	0.982
8	5/80	9.30	1.5	1.443
7⅛	11/80	9.18	2	1.897
7½	5/81	9.03	2.5	2.322
7¾	11/81	8.89	3	2.729
9¼	5/82	8.76	3.5	3.072
7⅞	11/82	8.76	4	3.499
7⅞	5/83	8.62	4.5	3.865
7	11/83	8.71	5	4.274
7⅞	5/86	8.63	7.5	5.762
7⅝	11/87	8.64	9	6.585
8¼	5/88	8.67	10	6.724
8¾	11/88	8.71	11.5	7.586
8⅝	11/93	8.71	15	8.664
7	5/98	8.41	19.5	10.278
8½	5/99	8.66	20.5	9.963
8¼	5/05	8.62	26.5	10.771
7⅞	11/07	8.80	29.0	11.061
8¾	11/08	8.97	30.0	10.845

[19] Hopewell and Kaufman, "Bond Price Volatility and Term to Maturity."
[20] J. L. Carr, P. J. Halpern and J. S. McCallum, "Correcting the Yield Curve: A Reinterpretation of the Duration Problem," *Journal of Finance*, September 1974, pp. 1287-1294.

Figure B Maturity Yield Curve—Government Bonds (as of November 1978)

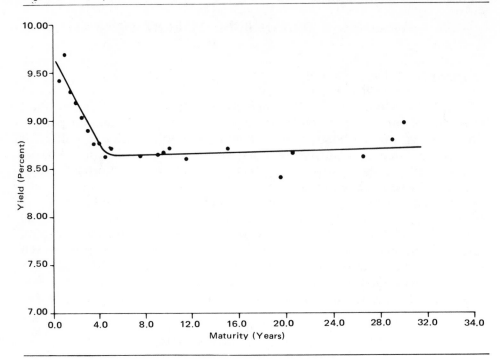

Figure C Duration Yield Curve—Government Bonds (as of November 1978)

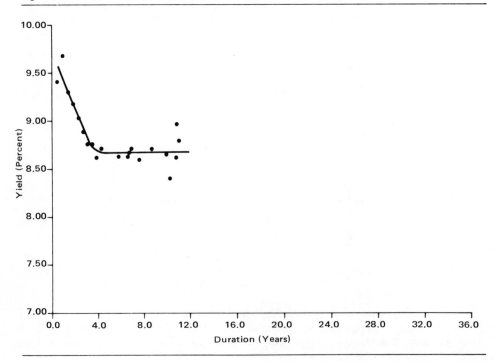

ernment bonds. Figures B and C plot the yield curves using maturity and duration, respectively. The duration yield curve is clearly shorter than the maturity yield curve; any slope in the former (up or down) will be much sharper.

Duration and Bond Market Line

Because bond duration indicates interest rate sensitivity, one can conceive of duration as a useful risk proxy for bonds. Specifically, an increase in duration will make a bond more sensitive to a given change in market interest rates, all else being equal. If one were to consider the computation of a "beta" for a bond (or a bond portfolio) that would indicate the percentage change in price for the bond (or portfolio) for a one percent change in price for a bond market series, one would expect a very high correlation between the beta for the bond (or portfolio) and the bond's (or portfolio's) duration.

Some investigators have suggested that investors should consider constructing a bond market line using duration as the measure of risk.[21] . The vertical axis would represent the realized rate of return on bond portfolios, while the horizontal axis would specify the average duration of the portfolios being examined. The market portfolio used would be some aggregate market series like the Salomon Brothers High Grade Bond Series or the Kuhn Loeb Bond Index. Figure D displays such a market line.

While the concept of a bond market line is appealing, the specification suggested has one major drawback—it does not allow for differences in the risk of default. Because duration indicates bond price volatility caused by changes in market interest rates, duration is a good proxy for interest rate

Figure D A Bond Market Line

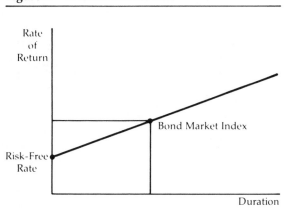

[21] Wayne H. Wagner and Dennis A. Tito, "Definitive New Measures of Bond Performance and Risk," *Pension World*, May 1977 and June 1977.

risk. Unfortunately, the bond market line constructed to take account of interest rate risk does not consider differences in default risk. Because one would expect a difference in the level of yield due to differences in default risk, one would expect a series of bond market lines—a different line for every default class (e.g., one for government bonds, another for AAA-rated bonds, a third for AAA-bonds, etc.). Figure E displays an ideal example of such a multiple set of bond market lines (although the alternative market lines would not necessarily have to be completely parallel as shown), with differences between the bond market lines reflecting the default risk premium.

Figures F, G and H display a set of actual bond yield curves using rated public utility bonds. Note that the AAA-rated duration yield curve in Figure F slopes downward, as does the government bond curve. In contrast, the AA-rated and A-rated yield curves in Figures G and H have small positive slopes.[22] These differences, along with the differences in the general level of yields for the differently rated bonds, mean that attempts to evaluate the performance of portfolios with different average ratings by using one bond market line that considers only interest rate risk is very questionable.

DURATION AND COMMON STOCKS

Although the bulk of the literature on duration has applied the concept to bonds, duration can be used for any investment flow, including common

Figure E   Multiple Bond Market Lines for Bonds with Different Default Risks

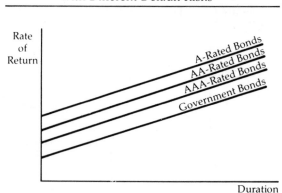

[22] Space does not permit a discussion of the reason for the differing slopes. But see Van Horne, *Financial Market Rates and Flows* and Burton G. Malkiel, *The Term Structure of Interest Rates* (Princeton, NJ: Princeton University Press, 1966).

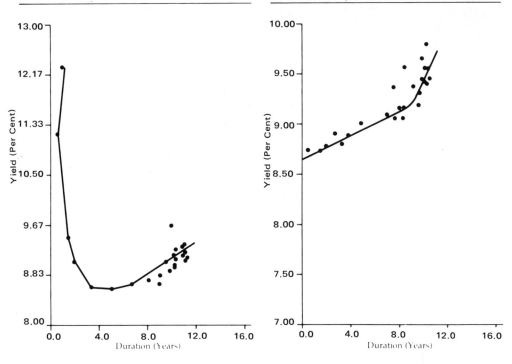

Figure F Duration Yield Curve — AAA Public Utility Bonds (as of November 1978)

Figure G Duration Yield Curve — AA Public Utility Bonds (as of November 1978)

stocks. Once it is acknowledged that duration can be computed for common stocks, its properties can be applied to the valuation of common stocks and the management of stock portfolios.

Computation of Common Stock Duration

The difficulties in computing the duration for a given common stock arise because of the several unknowns involved in the cash flows and discount rate. In the case of high-grade bonds, the analyst knows the timing and amount of interim cash flows based upon the coupon rate and the final cash flow from the principal at maturity. Also, the discount rate (using the Macauley definition) is the prevailing yield to maturity for the bond. In the case of common stocks, the interim cash flow will be the expected future dividend payments, which are uncertain in amount. The timing and amount of the final cash flow are likewise uncertain, since common stock is considered to have perpetual life. Finally, the discount rate used should be the prevailing required rate of return on the security, which in the case of stocks is

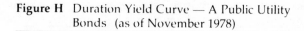

Figure H   Duration Yield Curve — A Public Utility
Bonds   (as of November 1978)

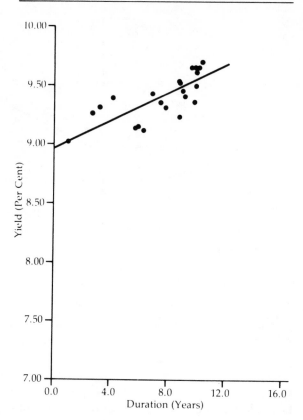

an estimate based on other estimates in the stock valuation model. In the standard dividend valuation model:

$$V = \frac{d_1}{K_i - g_i} ,$$

where
  V = the total value of the common stock,
  d_1 = the next period's dividend,
  K_i = the required rate of return on the stock
        and
  g_i = the expected growth rate of dividends,
so that

$$K_i = \frac{d_1}{V} + g_i .$$

Clearly, the duration for alternative stocks can differ substantially, depending on on the estimates of cash flows and their timing. Still, assuming that the analyst is willing to make the necessary estimates, it is possible to compute the duration for alternative common stocks.

To gain an appreciation of the problems and effects of different characteristics on the stock's duration, consider the examples detailed in Table IX, which progress from short-term, stable payment investments to long-run growth investments. For simplicity, the table assumes that all dividends are paid once a year at the end of the year. The computed durations for these sample stock investments are specific to the estimates of the amount and timing of cash flows and the required rates of return. Obviously, the duration of the same investment could vary substantially between investors holding differing estimates.

The first sample stock indicates the effect on duration of a short time horizon, a reasonable dividend and a small price increase. The second has an extended horizon and some growth in dividend stream and price. The third and fourth examples both assume a 20-year holding period but differ in terms of growth in the dividend stream and ending price; the third stock has a stable dividend throughout and little price change, while the fourth has a great deal of growth in the dividend stream and price. Although both examples assume the same holding period (term to maturity), the duration of the growth stock is 23 percent longer than the stable income stock at eight percent and 36 percent longer at 16 percent. The obvious implication is that *growth stocks have longer durations* than stable, high dividend paying securities. The longest duration stock would be a high growth, zero dividend stock that was acquired on the expectation of large future capital gains.

Because growth stocks have longer durations than other common stocks, growth stocks will be more volatile. In terms of modern portfolio theory,

Table IX Duration for Alternative Common Stocks *(assuming all currently sell at $20/share)*

	K_t		
	0.08	0.12	0.16
Example 1—Expected Dividend = $1.00/year; Expected Holding Period = 5 years; Expected Price = $25/share.			
Duration	4.591	4.549	4.505
Example 2—Expected Dividend = $1.00/year for first five years, $1.20/year for next five years; Expected Holding Period = 10 years; Expected Price = $30/share.			
Duration	8.318	7.996	7.641
Example 3—Expected Dividend = $1.00/year; Expected Holding Period = 20 years; Expected Price = $25/share.			
Duration	12.263	10.364	8.630
Example 4—Expected Dividend = $0.50/year for three years, $0.70/year for three years, $0.90/year for four years, $1.20/year for four years, $1.50/year for four years, $1.75/year for two years; Expected Holding Period = 20 years; Expected Price = $40/share.			
Duration	15.023	13.432	11.717

growth stocks should on average have higher betas.[23] Boquist, Racette and Schlarbaum derived the specific relation between the duration of a security and its beta and also the formula to compute the duration for common stocks.[24] The latter employs the basic dividend valuation model to show that duration (D_i) equals:

$$D_i = \frac{1+K_i}{K_i-g_i}$$

for discrete compounding and

$$D_i = \frac{1}{K_i-g_i}$$

for continuous compounding. Table X shows the effects on duration of differing combinations of K and g, given the continuous compounding formula.

Duration is determined by the spread between K and g. The larger the spread, the lower the duration. Therefore an increase in the growth rate, absent other changes, will increase the duration of a stock. In contrast, an increase in K (due, for example, to inflation) without a commensurate increase in the firm's growth rate will decrease duration.[25]

Table X   Estimated Duration for Common Stocks under Alternative K and g Assumptions

K	g	D*	K	g	D*
0.10	0.04	16.7	0.14	0.06	12.5
0.10	0.06	25.0	0.14	0.08	16.7
0.10	0.08	50.5	0.14	0.10	25.0
0.12	0.04	12.5	0.16	0.06	10.0
0.12	0.06	16.7	0.16	0.08	12.5
0.12	0.08	25.0	0.16	0.10	16.7
0.12	0.10	50.0	0.16	0.12	25.0

*All computations use the continuous compounding formula:
$$D_i = \frac{1}{K_i-g_i}$$

[23] One of the first authors to consider the duration of common stock was Durand ("Growth Stocks and the Petersburg Paradox"), who emphasized the long duration possibilities of growth stocks. Subsequently Malkiel ("Equity Yields, Growth, and the Structure of Share Prices") likewise discussed the long duration of growth stocks and specifically noted the effect this longer duration would have on their relative price volatility. Haugen and Wichern ("The Elasticity of Financial Assets") discuss the interest rate sensitivity of numerous financial assets including common stocks.

[24] Boquist, Racette and Schlarbaum, "Duration and Risk Assessment for Bonds and Common Stocks."

[25] A note by Miles Livingston ("Duration and Risk Assessment for Bonds and Common Stock: A Comment," *Journal of Finance*, March 1978, pp. 293-295) extended the Boquist results by introducing the duration of the market portfolio. The extension indicated that the risk for a stock depended, not only on the rate of growth (i.e., high growth rate, high risk), but also on the covariance between changes in the firm's growth and the market's growth (i.e., high covariance of growth, high risk).

BOND IMMUNIZATION:
A Procedure for Realizing Target Levels of Return[*]

28

Martin L. Leibowitz [†]

"Immunization" is the term coined to describe the design of bond portfolios that can achieve a target level of return in the face of changing reinvestment rates and price levels. Immunization techniques are relevant for many fixed income funds that must address the need to achieve a well-defined level of realized return over a specified investment period.

This need may arise from a variety of motivations. For example, one fund might have a lump-sum liability payment coming due at the end of the period. Another fund may need a relatively assured return for actuarial or accounting purposes. Another may have a simple desire to lock up what is thought to be a sufficiently high level of rates. Or, in yet another instance, the fund sponsor may simply wish to reduce the overall portfolio uncertainty by devoting a portion of the assets to achieving a specified return over a given period. Evidence of the growth in interest in this general form of investment can be seen in the proliferating role of the Guaranteed Investment Contract.

THE REINVESTMENT PROBLEM

When asked to secure such a target return over a given period such as 5 years, a bond portfolio manager might at first respond by selecting a portfo-

*This article is reprinted from memoranda dated October 10, 1979 and November 27, 1979, Salomon Brothers. Copyright 1979, by Salomon Brothers. Reprinted with permission.

†The author is a General Partner of Salomon Brothers and Manager of the Bond Portfolio Analysis Group.

lio of bonds having a maturity of 5 years. If these bonds were of sufficiently high grade, then the portfolio would indeed be assured of receiving all the coupon income due during the 5 years and of then receiving the redemption payments in the fifth year. However, coupon income and principal payments only constitute two of the three sources of return from a bond portfolio. The third source of return is the "interest-on-interest" derived from the reinvestment of coupon income (and/or the rollover of the maturing principal). Since this reinvestment will take place in the interest rate environments that exist at the time of the coupon receipts, there is no way to insure that one will obtain the amount of interest-on-interest required to achieve the target return.

Table 1 illustrates this point. A 5-year 9% par bond will provide $450 of coupon income and $1,000 of maturing principal over its 5-year life. This would amount to an added return of $450 beyond the original $1,000 investment. However, in order to achieve a 9% compound growth rate in asset value over the 5-year period, the original $1,000 would have to reach a cumulative value of $1,553, i.e., an incremental dollar return of $553. This $103 gap in return has to be overcome through the accumulation of interest-on-interest. As Table 1 shows, this amount of interest-on-interest will be achieved when coupon reinvestment occurs at the same 9% rate as the bond's original yield-to-maturity. At lower reinvestment rates, the interest-on-interest will be less than the amount required and the growth in asset value will fall somewhat short of the required target value of $1,553.

This reinvestment problem becomes even more severe over longer investment periods. Table 2 shows the total dollar amount and the percentage of the target return that must be achieved through interest-on-interest for various investment periods ranging from 1 to 30 years.

This "reinvestment risk" constitutes a major problem in closely achieving any assured level of target return. However, there are ways of limiting this reinvestment risk. For example, Table 3 shows the total return and cumulative asset value for a 5-year bond over investment horizons ranging from 1 to 5 years. For the periods shorter than 5 years, the bond's price in Table 3 has been determined by the simplistic assumption that the yield-to-maturity coincides with the indicated reinvestment rate. This set of assumptions cor-

Table 1
Realized Return From A 5-Year 9% Par Bond Over a 5-Year Horizon

Reinvestment Rate	Coupon Income	Capital Gain	Interest On Interest	Total $ Return	Realized Compound Yield
0%	$450	$0	$ 0	$450	7.57%
7	450	0	78	528	8.66
8	450	0	90	540	8.83
9	450	0	103	553	9.00
10	450	0	116	566	9.17
11	450	0	129	579	9.35

Table 2
Magnitude of Interest-On-Interest to Achieve 9% Realized Compound Yield
From 9% Par Bonds of Various Maturities

Maturity In Years	Total Dollar Return	Interest-On-Interest At 9% Reinvestment Rate	Interest-On-Interest As Percentage of Total Return
1	$ 92	$ 2	2.2%
2	193	13	6.5
3	302	32	10.7
4	422	62	14.7
5	553	103	18.6
7	852	222	26.1
10	1,412	512	36.2
20	4,816	3,016	62.6
30	13,027	10,327	79.3

responds to a scenario where interest rates immediately move to a flat yield curve at the level of the indicated reinvestment rate, and then remain there throughout the entire investment period.

Table 3 illustrates a striking compensation effect for investment periods of less than 5 years. For the 3-year period, at the 7% reinvestment rate assumption, the interest-on-interest naturally falls short of the amount required to support a target return of 9%. However, if the bond could be sold at the price corresponding to the assumed 7% yield-to-maturity rate, then a capital gain would be realized which would more than compensate for the lower value of interest-on-interest. Table 3 illustrates the well-known facts that over

Table 3
Realized Return From A 5-Year 9% Par Bond Over Various Horizon Periods

Reinvestment Rate and Yield-to-Maturity At Horizon		Horizon Period			
		1 Year	3 Years	4.13 Years	5 Years
	Coupon Income	$90	$270	$372	$450
7%	Capital Gain	$68	$37	$16	$0
	Interest-On-Interest	$2	$25	$51	$78
	Total Dollar Return	$160	$331	$439	$528
	Realized Compound Yield	*15.43%*	*9.77%*	*9.00%*	*8.66%*
9%	Capital Gain	$0	$0	$0	$0
	Interest-On-Interest	$2	$32	$67	$103
	Total Dollar Return	$92	$302	$439	$553
	Realized Compound Yield	*9.00%*	*9.00%*	*9.00%*	*9.00%*
11%	Capital Gain	−$63	−$35	−$16	$0
	Interest-On-Interest	$2	$40	$83	$129
	Total Dollar Return	$29	$275	$439	$579
	Realized Compound Yield	*2.89%*	*8.26%*	*9.00%*	*9.36%*

the short term, lower interest rates lead to increased returns through price appreciation while, over the longer term, lower interest rates lead to reduced returns through reduced interest-on-interest. For periods lying between the short term and the longer term, it is not surprising to find these two effects providing some compensation for each other.

This leads to the intriguing question as to whether there might be some intermediate point during a bond's life when these compensating effects precisely offset one another. Again, from Table 3, we can see that for a 7% reinvestment rate this offset does exist and occurs at 4.13 years. That such an offset point should exist is not, of course, surprising in a situation where there are two conflicting forces—reinvestment and capital gains—with one force growing stronger and the other force growing weaker with time. What may be somewhat more surprising is that when we look at reinvestment rates of 7, 9, and 11%, we find that this offset point occurs at the same 4.13 years!

THE CONCEPT OF DURATION

In the context of the fund seeking an assured level of return, this finding has great significance. If we were seeking to achieve the guaranteed 9% return over 4.13 years, Table 3 tells us that we would have no problem doing so with the 5-year bond, no matter what reinvestment rates existed (as long as they followed the simplistic "flat yield curve pattern" assumed in the construction of Table 3).

This offset effect occurs because the *duration* of a 5-year 9% par bond is 4.13. The duration of a bond is a concept first introduced by Frederick Macaulay in 1938.[1] Essentially, it is an average life calculation based upon the *present value* of each of the bond's cash flow payments, including coupons as well as principal. For the theoretical case of a pure discount zero-coupon bond, the duration will coincide with its maturity. Since zero-coupon bonds have no cash flows prior to maturity, they are free from the problem of coupon reinvestment. A 4.13-year zero-coupon bond priced to yield 9% would always provide the target 9% return over its maturity period—no matter what interest rates may occur over its life. Hence, the zero-coupon bond would be the ideal vehicle for the problem of achieving a target return except for one obstacle—beyond the 1-year maturity range of Treasury Bills, very few such investments exist.

---

[1] *The Movement of Interest Rates, Bond Yields and Stock Prices in the United States Since 1856*, Frederick R. Macaulay, NBER, 1938. (For a comprehensive discussion of *duration* see: Frank K. Reilly and Rupinder S. Sidhu, "The Many Uses of Duration," *Financial Analysts Journal*, July-August 1980, pp. 58-72, reprinted elsewhere in this book. Ed. note.)

It would obviously be desirable if we could somehow use real coupon bonds to obtain some of the characteristics of zero-coupon bonds. Fortunately, it turns out that this can be done and that the bond's duration is the key link. A coupon bond with a given duration is similar mathematically to a zero-coupon bond having a maturity equal to that duration. For example, as shown in Table 3, a 9% target return over a 4.13-year period could be achieved by either a 4.13-year maturity zero-coupon discount bond at a 9% yield rate or a 5-year 9% par bond. Both these bonds have the same duration of 4.13 years. In fact, for the assumptions underlying Table 3, any other bond yielding 9% and having a duration of 4.13 years will achieve the 9% target return. Although far from obvious, this fact can be demonstrated using the mathematical analysis underlying Table 3. Another feature of the duration concept is that bonds having the same duration will undergo the same percentage price change for small movements in yield-to-maturity.

Table 4 shows the duration of various bonds. Returning to the original objective of providing an assured 9% target return over a 5-year period, we can see that one should choose a bond having a duration of 5 years (as opposed to a maturity of 5 years).

To obtain a duration of 5-years in a 9% par bond, it turns out that one would need a maturity of around 6.3 years. Table 5 shows how such a bond will indeed achieve the required growth in asset value to provide the 9% guaranteed return compounded semi-annually.

Using duration to select bonds would solve the problem of achieving assured returns over specified periods except for one small point: movements in the interest rate structure are not so accommodating as to provide us with permanent shifts to a flat yield curve, as assumed in Tables 1, 2, and 3. Different patterns of rate movement can completely unwind these carefully contrived results. For example, in Table 5, suppose the reinvestment rate indeed moved to 7% and stayed there for most of the 5-year period, but then jumped up to 11% just before the fifth year when we had to sell the bond.

Table 4
Duration of Various Bonds All Priced to Yield 9%

Maturity in Years	Coupon			
	0%	7.5%	9.0%	10.50%
1	1.00	0.98	0.98	0.98
2	2.00	1.89	1.87	1.86
3	3.00	2.74	2.70	2.66
4	4.00	3.51	3.45	3.38
5	5.00	4.23	4.13	4.05
7	7.00	5.50	5.34	5.20
10	10.00	7.04	6.80	6.59
20	20.00	9.96	9.61	9.35
30	30.00	11.05	10.78	10.59
100	100.00	11.61	11.61	11.61

Table 5
Realized Return from 6-Year, 4-Month 9% Par Bond Over A 5-Year Horizon*

Reinvestment Rate and Yield-to-Maturity At Horizon	Coupon Income	Capital Gain	Interest on Interest	Total $ Return	Realized Compound Yield
7%	$450	$25	$ 78	$553	9.00%
8	450	13	90	553	9.00
9	450	0	103	553	9.00
10	450	−13	116	553	9.00
11	450	−26	129	553	9.00

*The computations are based on a bond purchased free of accrued interest in order to obtain a categorization of the sources of return that is consistent with the preceding tables. Semi-annual compounding is assumed.

This scenario would mean that we would achieve the reduced level of interest-on-interest associated with the 7% rate together with the capital *loss* associated with the 11% rate. This combination would provide a total accumulated return of only $502 which is less than the $553 required to achieve the target 9% return.

This immediately raises the following question: is there any way for the portfolio manager to go about achieving the assured return in a way that will succeed in the face of the far wilder interest rate movements that occur in the real world? One can never achieve this growth in an absolute and precise sense. However, there are techniques for periodic "rebalancing" of the portfolio that will minimize the vulnerability of the achieved return across a wide range of interest rate movements. These techniques are generally referred to as "immunization strategies" since they attempt to "immunize" the portfolio's return against the "disease" of fluctuating reinvestment rates and changing pricing yields.

There is an extensive theoretical literature in this field of "immunization strategies." Most of this research work has focused on the more academically convenient case of portfolios consisting of investments along an idealized Treasury yield curve. These portfolios are then periodically rebalanced so as to keep the portfolio's duration equal to the remaining length of the investment period.

MULTIPLE CHANGES IN RATES

In the preceding sections it was shown that it was possible to overcome the reinvestment problem and match the promised yield to maturity—*if* certain rather stringent conditions were satisfied. The key assumption was that interest rates immediately moved from their current level to some given level and remained there for the entire planning period. Under this assumption of a single move to a "flat" yield curve, the new level determines the reinvestment rate for coupon income as well as the final price of the portfolio. For an initial bond investment whose duration corresponded to the length of the planning period, these conditions would result in a realized compound yield that closely matched the promised yield-to-maturity. However, this finding would be of only theoretical interest unless one could find ways to deal with more general and realistic conditions. In particular, before the immunization procedure can really be put into practice, one must come to grips with the assured fact that there will be *multiple* changes in rates during the course of the planning period. In this section, we will explore how rebalancing procedures can be used to accommodate such multiple changes in rates.

It is easy to demonstrate the problems that arise when one drops the "single-move" assumption and allows for multiple movements. In the preceding sections, we set out to achieve a 9% target return over a five-year planning period. To obtain a 9% par bond having this duration, we would need a maturity of 6.7 years.[2] If rates remained at 9% throughout the five-year period, a $1,000 investment in this bond would compound to $1,552.97, thereby providing the 9% return that one would expect in the "no move" case. This scenario is shown in Figure 1A. To illustrate the effects of a "single move" in rates, suppose that rates immediately jumped to 12% and then stayed there for the remaining five-year period. This bond would then generate a coupon income of $436.67, interest-on-interest of $162.49, and a capital loss of $42.91. As shown in Figure 1B, this amounts to a total future value of $1,556.25, which produces a yield that is slightly higher than the 9% target return.

There is another way of viewing the events in Figure 1B. The sudden rate move generates an immediate capital loss of $131.00. In order for the remaining asset value of $869.00 to grow to the target level, a compound growth rate of 12% must be achieved throughout the next five years, e.g.:

$$\$869.00 \times (1.06)^{10} = \$1,556.25.$$

In this sense, the five-year return of 12% is needed to compensate for the immediate price loss incurred as rates jumped from 9% to 12%. In any case, the example in Figure 1B illustrates that, under the "single-move" assumption, even when the move is as large as 400 basis points, we still manage to realize the required target return.

Now let us examine what happens under a simple case involving a "multiple move" in rates. Suppose, as before, that the first move in rates happens immediately after purchase and changes the yield curve to 12%. This rate persists for the next five years. But then, just before the bond is sold at the

---

[2] This example is based on a normal bond structure with accrued interest attached to the bond at the outset. It is in contrast to the bond purchased free of accrued interest that constituted the model for the calculations in Table 5.

Figure 1.   Portfolio Values Developed Under Various Interest Rate Patterns.
Initial Portfolio: $1,000 Investment in 6.7-Year, 9% Par Bond;
Initial Duration: 5.00 Years

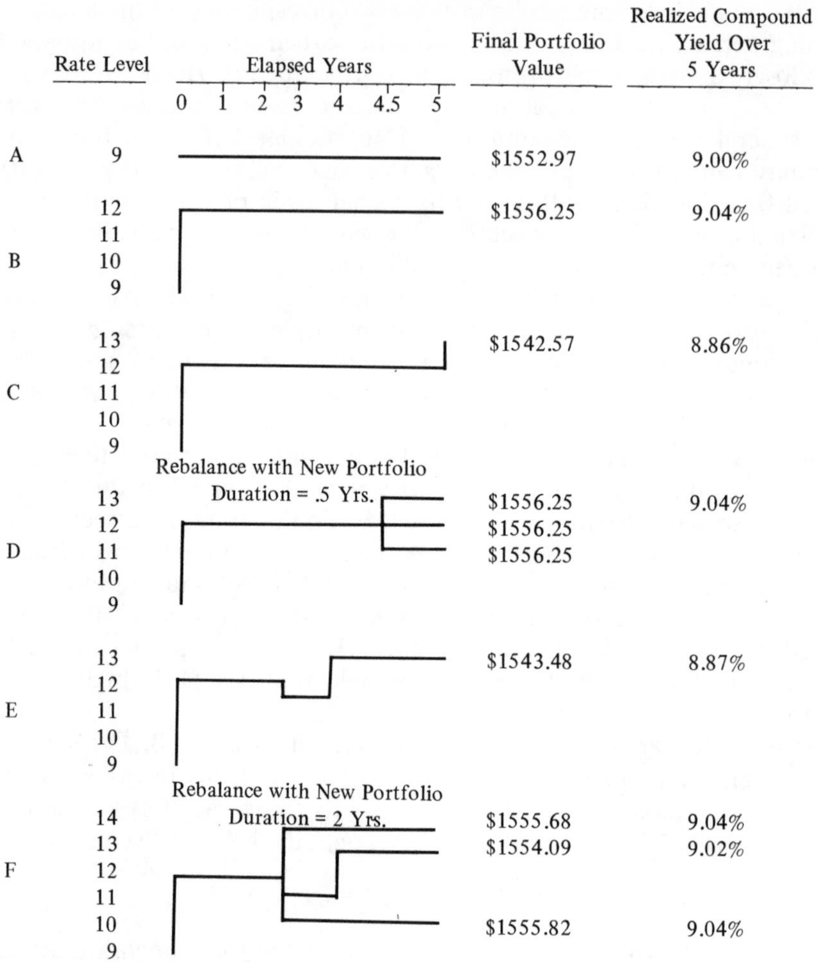

	Rate Level	Elapsed Years	Final Portfolio Value	Realized Compound Yield Over 5 Years
		0 1 2 3 4 4.5 5		
A	9		$1552.97	9.00%
	12		$1556.25	9.04%
	11			
B	10			
	9			
	13		$1542.57	8.86%
	12			
C	11			
	10			
	9	Rebalance with New Portfolio		
	13	Duration = .5 Yrs.	$1556.25	9.04%
	12		$1556.25	
D	11		$1556.25	
	10			
	9			
	13		$1543.48	8.87%
	12			
E	11			
	10			
	9	Rebalance with New Portfolio		
	14	Duration = 2 Yrs.	$1555.68	9.04%
	13		$1554.09	9.02%
F	12			
	11			
	10		$1555.82	9.04%
	9			

fifth year, there is a second jump in interest rates to 13% (Figure 1C). All numbers are then the same as in the earlier example, with the exception of the capital loss which now amounts to $56.58. This greater capital loss brings the total future value down to $1,542.57, for a total realized compound yield of 8.86%. Thus, under this simple two-move assumption, the portfolio falls short of its target by more than 14 basis points.

If immunization procedures could not deal with such simple "multiple movements" in rates, there would clearly be a problem in achieving any sort of application in real life. Fortunately, techniques exist involving portfolio rebalancing that can overcome this difficulty.

REBALANCING USING DURATION

The problem arising from multiple rate movements can be traced to the way that a bond ages over time. Table 6 illustrates how our theoretical bond, having a starting duration of 5 years, ages on a year-by-year basis. With each passing year, the maturity obviously gets shorter by one year, but the duration becomes shorter by less than a year. For example, over the first year, the bond's duration "ages" from 5.0 to 4.4, a drop of only .6 for the year. At the end of the fifth year, when we would clearly like to have a duration of zero, the original bond has a duration of 1.5 years. (Even when combined with the cash flow generated by coupon reinvestment, the blended duration of the portfolio becomes seriously mismatched with the passage of time.)

This "duration drift" can be overcome by periodic rebalancing of the portfolio. For example, suppose that at the end of 4.5 years, the portfolio had been "rebalanced" in the following fashion. The bond was sold at a yield-to-maturity of 12%, leading to a capital loss of $54.22 and a total future value of $1,468.16 (Figure 1D). The entire proceeds were then invested in a 12% par bond, having a duration of precisely .5. Clearly, this instrument would assure us of achieving a 12% rate of return over the final .5-year period. In turn, this would provide a 12% return over the entire five years and therefore bring the total value of the portfolio up to $1,556.25. In other words, by rebalancing prior to the second movement in interest rates, we would have immunized ourselves against the effects of that movement.

As a further example, suppose that a second move to 11% occurred at the end of the third year, and was followed by a third move to 13%. Coupons from the original 9% bond would have been reinvested for three years at 12%, for one year at 11%, and for the remaining year at 13%. At the end of the fifth year, the bond would have been sold on 13% yield-to-maturity, engendering a sizable capital loss. This would lead to a total future value of $1,543.48, well below our target level (Figure 1E). However, suppose the portfolio had been rebalanced at the end of the third year, just before the interest rate jump, so as to have a duration of exactly 2.0 years. This reset in

Table 6
Changes in a Bond's Duration with the Passage of Time
9% 6.7-Year Par Bond

Elapsed Time	Maturity	Bond's Duration	Target Duration	Mismatch
0 yrs.	6.66 yrs.	5.00 yrs.	5.00 yrs.	0 yrs.
1	5.66	4.42	4.00	.42
2	4.66	3.79	3.00	.79
3	3.66	3.11	2.00	1.11
4	2.66	2.35	1.00	1.35
5	1.66	1.53	0.00	1.53

duration will help ensure that the final two years realize a 12% return. This lockup of the 12% rate over the final two years is just what is needed, together with the return achieved over the first three years, to ensure realizing the original target return of 9% (Figure 1F).

The preceding example illustrates the key idea underlying the immunization process. By rebalancing so as to continually maintain a duration matching the remaining life of the planning period, the bond portfolio is kept in an immunized state throughout the period. This guarantees that the portfolio will achieve the target return promised at the outset of every sub-period. By working backwards, this implies that the original target return of 9% can be met in the face of multiple movements in interest rates.

This rebalancing procedure has a dramatic immunizing power even in the face of radical changes in interest rates. This is illustrated in Table 7 where interest rates increase by 100 basis points at the end of each year. Through annual rebalancing (based upon duration), the total portfolio value grows to within four basis points of the original 9% target.

REBALANCING AS PROXY FOR A ZERO-COUPON BOND OVER TIME

At first glance, the success of this rebalancing procedure in keeping the portfolio on target may seem to be somewhat magical. An insight into the rebalancing principle can be provided by thinking in terms of our old friend, the zero-coupon bond. For any change in yield level, the zero-coupon bond automatically retains sufficient asset value to provide the original return over its life. For example, in Figure 1B, when interest rates jump from 9% to 12%, a $1,000 investment in a five-year zero-coupon bond would decline from $1,000 to $867.17. Suppose one were to sell the zero-coupon bond immediately after this jump in rates, realize the $867.17 proceeds, and then hypothetically invest these funds into another five-year zero-coupon bond at its market yield of 12%. Over the remaining five years, the assured 12% compounding would enable the original $867.17 to grow to $1,552.97, i.e., satisfying the original 9% return goal.

The rebalancing process just described is, of course, equivalent to continued holding of the zero-coupon bond. The five-year zero-coupon bond purchased at 9% has truly locked-in the target 9% return over the five-year planning period. Regardless of the magnitude or frequency of subsequent rate movements, the zero-coupon bond always remains "on target.". Moreover, the zero-coupon bond obviously remains *continually* "on target" even with the passage of time. In other words, it always retains the precise amount of asset value needed to realize the original target when compounded at the then yield rate for the remainder of the period.

Table 7
Portfolio Growth with Duration-Based Rebalancing
Initial Investment = $1,000

Period Ending Date	Rebalanced Portfolio at Start of Period			Results Over Year			Realized Coupon Yield		
	New Rate Level	Duration	Maturity	Coupon Flow and Interest-on-Interest	Capital Gain	Total Proceeds	Over Year	Cumulative	Blended*
1 Year	9%	5.00	6.66 yrs.	$ 92.02	$41.18	$1050.84	5.02%	5.02%	8.99%
2	10	4.00	5.14	107.72	−33.03	1125.52	6.98	6.00	8.99
3	11	3.00	3.66	127.22	−24.12	1228.61	8.96	6.98	8.97
4	12	2.00	2.27	151.86	−13.61	1366.87	10.95	7.97	8.97
5	13	1.00	1.00	183.47	0	1550.34	13.00	8.96	8.96

*The 5-year return that would result if the portfolio value at that date were to be compounded at the existing new rate level for all remaining periods.

The key idea here is that the price of the zero-coupon bond moves in lock-step with the change in the required dollar investment at the new interest rate level. Another way of saying this is that, with respect to interest rate movements, the volatility of the zero-coupon bond coincides with the volatility of the assets required to provide the promised payment in the fifth year. Thus, for a bond portfolio to retain the assets needed to stay "on target," it must have the same volatility as the five-year zero-coupon bond. Moreover, it must maintain this volatility equivalence as time passes. As noted earlier, a bond's volatility is related to its duration. In particular, the duration of a zero-coupon bond coincides with its remaining life. Thus, in order to stay "on target" with time—as the zero-coupon bond does automatically—an "immunizing bond portfolio" must maintain the same duration as the zero-coupon bond. An "immunizing" bond portfolio can maintain this equivalence through duration-based rebalancing. Thus, duration-based rebalancing can provide a bond portfolio which mimics the automatic "immunizing" behavior of the zero-coupon bond in the face of multiple interest rate movements over time.

INTEREST RATES, INFLATION, AND THE FISHER EQUILIBRIUM

John M. Finkelstein and
John R. Brick †

29

In recent years, inflation and inflationary expectations have dominated the decision-making process of many participants in the financial markets. This has manifested itself in a variety of ways, most notably in the level and volatility of interest rates. However, other changes have occurred. For example, pension funds and life insurance companies traditionally provided borrowers with funds on a long-term, fixed-rate basis. Recently, many of these institutions have demanded an adjustable interest rate, shorter maturities, substantial equity "kickers," or some other form of contractual protection against erosion of the purchasing power of the funds loaned. In an attempt to hold down the explicit interest cost, some borrowers in the natural resources field have offered debt securities payable at maturity in gold, silver, or dollars at the discretion of the lender. At the consumer level, the *variable rate mortgage*, and so-called *shared appreciation mortgage* in which the borrower shares any gains with the mortgage lender in return for a lower interest rate, are other examples of inflation-induced changes. The point here is that the inflation has brought about what some perceive as a partial destruction of the long-term debt market as it was once known.

The most visible effect of inflation on the financial markets is its impact on the rate of interest. In fact, the contractual changes mentioned above are simply ways of extracting a higher market rate in the event the rate of inflation exceeds the lender's expectations. It is well-recognized that there is a

†The authors are on the finance faculties of the University of Florida and Michigan State University, respectively.

linkage between interest rates and inflation. That is, as inflationary expectations worsen, interest rates tend to increase. However, the relationship is more complex than is generally thought. The purpose of this paper is to examine this linkage using a framework known as the *Fisher equilibrium*. In order to place this framework in perspective, the following section briefly examines the nature of interest rate risk and some of the issues underlying the forecasting process.

INTEREST RATE RISK—AN OVERVIEW

Interest rate risk consists of two elements: 1) the risk associated with price changes resulting from a change in the level of interest rates; and 2) the risk associated with the reinvestment of the principal and/or the interest income at unknown rates. To see the nature of these risks, assume a 10-year, $1,000 par value, 12 percent bond is bought at par to yield 12 percent. After one year, if the market interest rate is 14 percent, the value of the (9-year) bond would then be $899. Similarly, if the market rate drops to 10 percent, the value of the bond would be $1,117. In addition to this price risk, the changing market yields mean that the yield to maturity will be something other than 12 percent because the reinvestment of interest income will be at rates higher or lower than 12 percent. If the market rate remains at 14 percent, for example, the actual yield to maturity will be higher than 12 percent. This partially offsets the corresponding lower bond price. If the market rate remains at 10 percent, the yield to maturity will be less than 12 percent but this is partially offset by a higher bond price. The 10-year bond, therefore, has both price risk and reinvestment risk.

The price risk could be minimized by staying in the short-term sector of the market. For example, a three-month bond would have very little price risk because of the short maturity even though the short-term rates are highly volatile. However, the reinvestment risk would then be much greater because *both* the income and principal would have to be reinvested at unknown and highly volatile rates. The key point here is that all bonds contain some combination of price risk and reinvestment risk. These risks may be shifted or minimized by hedging with interest rate futures contracts or using a duration-based immunization strategy.[1] However, not everyone is content to hedge or immunize and for this reason considerable effort is expended by market participants to forecast interest rates.

---

[1] See, for example, Marcelle Arak and Christopher J. McCurdy, "Interest Rate Futures," *Quarterly Review*, Federal Reserve Bank of New York, Winter 1979-80, pp. 33-46; and Frank K. Reilly and Rupinder S. Sidhu, "The Many Uses of Bond Duration," *Financial Analysts Journal*, July-August 1980, pp. 58-72. (Both of these articles are reproduced elsewhere in this book. Ed. note.)

The methods used to forecast interest rates may be categorized as *excogitation*, the *flow-of-funds approach, term structure analysis*, and *econometric modeling*. The first of these, *excogitation*, is largely a judgmental analysis of the various factors affecting interest rates or an extrapolation of perceived "trends" in interest rates. This approach is exemplified by the writings of columnists in the financial press, as well as "arm-chair" economists. The *flow-of-funds approach* is more sophisticated in that it involves estimating the sources and magnitude of funds flowing through the economy on the one hand and the demands for funds by users on the other.[2] The purpose of such an analysis is to determine potential supply/demand imbalances which will require changes in the level of interest rates to bring about equilibrium in the financial markets. The *term structure* approach involves the analysis of bond yields in relation to maturities. When bond yields are plotted against their corresponding maturities, the resulting term structure contains an implied "consensus forecast" of interest rates by market participants. *Econometric modeling*, on the other hand, attempts to relate interest rates, or changes therein, to other economic variables such as steel production, boxcar loadings, retail sales, and unemployment, to name a few. The objective of this approach is to develop an economically meaningful cause and effect relationship between the variables. Such models are often quite complex in that they can involve a system of equations, rather than a single equation, and reflect the lagged impact of the economic variables.

It is important to note that in addition to predicting the direction of changes in interest rates, the forecasting approach used should specify the timing and magnitude of the projected changes if interest rate risk is to be avoided or capitalized upon. Regardless of the technique used, forecasts that are consistently accurate with respect to the direction, timing, and magnitude of interest rate changes are difficult to find. Such forecasts were especially elusive during the late 1970s and early 1980s, a period characterized by extremely high interest rates and unparalleled volatility. In retrospect, many forecasters would agree that the problem during this period stemmed from a rapid escalation in the rate of inflation. Equally important, however, was that the dramatic increase in the variability of interest rates was a result of market participants more quickly forming and reacting to inflationary expectations. This reaction was predicated on the widespread belief that *ex ante,* or before the fact, lenders generally underestimated the inflation rate. This was recognized by lenders *ex post*, or after the fact. The result, of course, was that the contractual rate on the loan agreements was insufficient to compensate lenders for the erosion of purchasing power of the funds loaned. Borrowers, on the other hand, possessing no greater forecasting ability than lenders, were more fortuitous in that they reaped the benefits of incorrect inflationary expectations on the part of the lenders.

[2] For a discussion of this approach, see: Roland I. Robinson and Dwayne Wrightsman, *Financial Markets: The Accumulation and Allocation of Wealth*, 2nd ed., New York: McGraw-Hill Book Company, 1980, Chapter 5.

As pointed out earlier, the most serious manifestation of this inability to correctly anticipate inflation, and thus interest rates, has been a partial deterioration of the long-term bond market. This has important implications. Such a deterioration means fewer longer-term investments in productive facilities and potentially a slowing in the growth rate of the economy. The latter effect is based on the fact that most corporations are unwilling to incur the interest rate risks that result from funding long-lived projects with short-term funds. It follows, therefore, that a more thorough understanding of the relationship between interest rates and inflation is essential if the dramatic changes in the financial markets in recent years are to be fully understood.

THE FISHER EQUILIBRIUM

The equilibrium framework suggested by Irving Fisher[3] provides both an explanation of market behavior in recent years and insight regarding the process of forecasting interest rates. Stated another way, the Fisher equilibrium both explains market behavior *ex post* and provides an *ex ante* or predictive framework. The Fisher equilibrium may be written as

$$E(i) = E(r) + E(\dot{p}) + E(r)E(\dot{p}) \qquad [1]$$

where $E(\cdot)$ denotes an expectation or prediction, i is the market or *nominal interest rate*, r is the *real rate of interest* determined by the marginal productivity of capital in an inflation-free economy, and $\dot{p}$ is the expected rate of inflation over the life of the bond. The value $E(r)E(\dot{p})$ is a cross-product term. When the rate of inflation is moderate, the cross-product term is small and therefore it is usually ignored for expository purposes. Thus, the model simply states that lenders will require a nominal or market rate i that is equal to the sum of the real rate of return plus an inflation premium. It is important to note that equation [1] is an *ex ante* relationship. As such, the model hypothesizes an equilibrium in which the variables $E(i)$, $E(r)$, and $E(\dot{p})$ will either move in a set relationship with one another, or maintain such a relationship.

The *ex post* counterpart of equation [1] may be developed by assuming a one-period loan of $1. At the end of the period the following definition would hold:

$$\$1(1 + i) \equiv \$1(1 + r)(1 + \dot{p}). \qquad [2]$$

[3] Irving Fisher, "Appreciation and Interest," *Publications of the American Economic Association*, XI (August 1896), pp. 1-100.

Expanding the right hand side of [2] and considering only rates of return results in

$$i \equiv r + \dot{p} + (r)(\dot{p}) \tag{3}$$

which is the *ex post* counterpart of [1]. Again, the cross-product term may be ignored and we have

$$i \equiv r + \dot{p}. \tag{4}$$

In order to see how unanticipated inflation affects the *ex post* real return r, equation [4] may be rewritten as

$$r \equiv i - \dot{p}. \tag{5}$$

Now assume that the expected real rate is 3 percent and the expected inflation rate is 6 percent for an *ex ante* return of 9 percent on a one-year bond. If these expectations are realized the *ex ante* real return of 3 percent equals the *ex post* real return as given by [5]. That is,

$$3\% \equiv 9\% - 6\%.$$

However, if the inflation rate turns out to be 10 percent, the *ex post* real return r is not only less than the *ex ante* return of 3 percent, it is negative, that is,

$$r \equiv 9\% - 10\%$$
$$r \equiv -1\%.$$

In other words, in order to obtain the desired real return and be compensated for the effect of inflation on the principal, the lender should have locked in a rate of 13 percent rather than 9 percent.

Forecasting Implications

While the *ex post* explanatory capability of the Fisher equilibrium is useful, the *ex ante* forecasting implications are more important for decision-making purposes. In order to see these implications, the equilibrium process may be trichotomized as consisting of: 1) the basic equilibrium relationship among the nominal rate i, the real rate r and the inflation rate $\dot{p}$; 2) the short-run departures from the presumed equilibrium due to supply and demand factors; and 3) the rational expectations extension of the basic equilibrium relationship.

The Basic Equilibrium.   The Basic equilibrium relationship was formulated as

$$E(i) = E(r) + E(\dot{p}).$$

Underlying this equation is the hypothesis that enough people will switch between real and financial goods, for example, between houses and bonds, so that the relative prices of the two types of goods will be maintained in an equilibrium which will preclude arbitrage or riskless opportunities for profit. Thus, if houses or other forms of real estate are earning a real return greater than that for bonds, then bonds would be sold and houses bought. The effect would be to decrease the price of bonds and increase the price of houses until their real rates were equal. Even if the hypothesis is accepted, however, there remain various technical problems. These include, for example, the selection of an appropriate inflation rate for use in the Fisher equilibrium. The problem arises because major components of the Consumer Price Index are not storeable and/or tradeable. Furthermore, inflation affects different individuals in different ways, such as homeowners versus renters. Another type of problem arises if money is added to the analysis. Some economists would argue that since there are three classes of assets—money, real goods, and financial goods—inflationary expectations are less important for interest rates since

$$i \cong r \text{ or } E(i) \cong E(r),$$

because the money/bond division is largely a function of the disutility of holding illiquid assets, while the prices for commodities are what adjust to reflect expected changes.

Disequilibrium.   Abstracting from such technical issues and accepting the proposition that the Fisher equilibrium holds in the long run, it may still be readily seen why supply and demand forces lead to a departure from equilibrium in the short run. Disequilibrium, in the context of the Fisher model, means the variables ($E(i)$, $E(r)$, and $E(\dot{p})$ at least in the short run fail to move in a set relationship with one another, or maintain such a relationship. The implication is that additional explanatory variables are necessary for short-run forecasting accuracy. The crux of the disequilibrium is that certain economic agents cannot participate in the interconnection between the prices of real and financial assets. For example, because of balance sheet regulations, commercial banks, savings and loan associations, credit unions, and other types of financial institutions are restricted in their ability to substitute between real and financial assets even if profitable opportunities exist. While balance sheet restrictions, such as the prohibition on the ownership of real estate other than for offices in the case of commercial banks, may be modified by such innovations as the shared appreciation mortgage mentioned earlier, currently it is only the individual sector which is unconstrained. For example, individuals may borrow against insurance contracts to invest in real estate, a substitution between financial and real assets limited only by borrowing capacity. As opposed to demand factors, the supply side may be represented by open market actions of the Federal Reserve System in expanding or contracting the money supply. Thus, uncertain and difficult-to-estimate supply and demand forces may well determine rates at any point in time, while the equilibrium effect dominates on average over the long run.

These same supply and demand factors suggest that, unlike many econometricians' simplifying assumptions for the purpose of forecasting, the *real rate* r is neither constant nor fixed in a set pattern with the inflation rate $\dot{p}$. Depending on the magnitude and nature of the economic shock, such as a change in the demand for real property by commercial banks or in the supply of money due to open market operations of the Federal Reserve System, inflationary expectations need not have an exactly proportional effect on nominal interest rates. The nominal interest rate may increase more or less than the change in the rate of inflation. In some cases, the real rate r would decline *ex ante* and possibly become negative *ex post*, as was often the case during the 1970s and early 1980s. The problem stems from the unobservable nature of r, thus requiring it to be estimated, for example, as the difference between an asset whose return tends to be expressed in real terms such as real estate, and an asset whose returns tend to be in nominal terms such as bonds. This assumes that real goods' reproduction values change directly with the general price level, whereas nominal goods have an inverse relationship. The equilibrium r is obtained, if only in the long run, by switching between financial and real goods, e.g., selling bonds and buying an apartment complex.

Rational Expectations. The rational expectations extension of the Fisher equilibrium posits that the no-arbitrage condition holds not only in the long run but the short run as well, and in the extreme the equilibrium is maintained instantaneously. The underlying hypothesis is that market participants use all available information in an optimal fashion such that excess returns, that is, returns greater than those commensurate with the risk accepted, are unobtainable. This has important implications for a commonly used type of forecasting model based on the Fisher equilibrium. The model is of the form,

$$E(i_{t+1}) = \hat{r} + \sum_{t=o}^{t-n} \beta_t (\dot{p}_t), \qquad [6]$$

which states that the expected nominal rate i is a function of a constant real rate $\hat{r}$ and a weighted average of past inflation rates. The problem with such an approach under the rational expectations extension of the Fisher equilibrium is that it is logically inconsistent to posit an efficient market, or no-arbitrage situation, and yet believe E(i) is predictable using past inflation rates that are presumed to possess informational content.

Empirical Problems

Many econometric forecasting models use some variation of the model exemplified by [6]. However, the results generated by such models are suspect because of a number of serious empirical problems. These are summarized in this section.

Non-Negativity. The Fisher equilibrium may not be operative in deflationary periods. That is, E(i) cannot be negative *ex ante*, for lenders would hold money if, for example, E(r) was a positive constant and E($\dot{p}$) negative and greater in value.

Use of Proxies. During periods of rapidly changing economic conditions, proxies for expectations may be unreliable. The problem may be particularly acute when weighted averages reflecting only past data are used.

Non-Testable Aspect. Inflationary expectations are non-testable in a controlled, laboratory sense. Even if individual economic agents were scientifically asked about their expectations, these do not necessarily lead to action in the controlled sense, such as running mice through a maze.

A Joint Test. Most models assume the real rate E(r) is either constant or moves in a set pattern with inflation rates, and that E($\dot{p}$) is a weighted average of past inflation rates. Thus, the model is a joint test and may fail to predict accurately: a) the relationship between i and $\dot{p}$ which depends upon whether r is constant, moves in a set pattern with $\dot{p}$, or is a variable; and/or b) the true values of the weights.

Rational Expectations. The rational expectations extension implies $i - \hat{r} = E(\dot{p})$ is the best forecast, although it will not generate excess returns. This conclusion must be evaluated relative to other forecasts. However, r is an unknown, and there are few alternative examples of forecasting ability for long-term interest rates that may be used for comparison purposes.

The Adjustment Process. To obtain the correct weights, it is necessary to know how many past periods' inflation rates affect the next period's inflation rate. Equivalently, when $\sum_{t=0}^{t-n} \beta_t = 1$, all past effects have been incorporated. This speed of adjustment conclusion presumes that the relationship between r and $\dot{p}$ are known. If, however, r is an unknown variable, it may interact with $\dot{p}$ such that $\sum_{t=0}^{t-n} \beta_t = 1$ has no economic meaning. While the problem of determining correct weights is not peculiar to the Fisher equilibrium, it arises specifically because of the unclear relationship between r and $\dot{p}$. Thus, consistently accurate weights may be unobtainable due to the possible invalidity of the speed of adjustment rule.

CONCLUSION

It is irrational to consistently find that the realized rate of return is less than the anticipated real rate of return, and often negative. One response to this problem has been to experiment with different forecasting methods. For example, Bomberger and Frazer[4] report improved forecasting results using the variance of difference between business economists' past expectations of the inflation rate.

It should be understood that the mere introduction of more sophisticated methodology does not ensure excess returns from forecasting. In addition, an equality between realized and anticipated real rates of return may well prove to be a self-fulfilling prophecy due to the structural changes occurring within the financial system. These include the dramatic changes in the long-term lending/borrowing markets, hedging with interest rate futures, duration-based immunization strategies, and alternative mortgage instruments such as the variable rate and shared appreciation mortgages.

[4] William A. Bomberger and William J. Frazer, Jr., "Interest Rates, Uncertainty, and the Livingston Data," *Journal of Finance*, 36, (June 1981).

ABCs OF FIGURING INTEREST*

Anne Marie L. Gonczy

30

Although Shakespeare cautioned "neither a borrower nor a lender be," using and providing credit has become a way of life for many individuals in today's economy. Examples of borrowing by individuals are numerous— home mortgages, car loans, credit cards, etc. While perhaps more commonly thought of as investing, many examples of lending by individuals can be identified. By opening a savings account, an individual makes a loan to the bank; by purchasing a Treasury bill, an individual makes a loan to the government.

As with goods and services that an individual might buy or sell, the use or extension of credit has a price attached to it, namely the interest paid or earned. And, just as consumers shop for the best price on a particular item of merchandise, so too should consumers "comparison shop" for credit—whether borrowing or lending.

But comparing prices for credit can, at times, be confusing. Although the price of credit is generally stated as a rate of interest, the amount of interest paid or earned depends on a number of other factors, including the method used to calculate interest.

To an extent, the Truth-in-Lending law passed in 1968 has eliminated some of the confusion concerning what it costs a consumer to borrow. Rules

*This is a revised edition of an earlier article originally published by the Federal Reserve Bank of Chicago in the September 1973 issue of *Business Conditions*. The original article and the revision were written by Anne Marie L. Gonczy. Reprinted with permission from the Federal Reserve Bank of Chicago. The article is presently a part of the Bank's *Readings in Economics and Finance*.

defining creditor responsibilities under Truth-in-Lending are covered in the Federal Reserve's Regulation Z. Most importantly, creditors are required to disclose both the Annual Percentage Rate (APR) and the total dollar Finance Charge to the borrowing consumer. Simply put, the APR is the relative cost of credit expressed in percentage terms on the basis of one year. Just as "unit pricing" gives the consumer a basis for comparing prices of different-sized packages of the same product, the APR enables the consumer to compare the prices of different loans regardless of the amount, maturity, or other terms.

Even with Truth-in-Lending, various interest calculation methods continue to be used. And no similar laws apply to help the consumer who is "lending" rather than borrowing. While Truth-in-Savings legislation, aimed at clarifying how much a consumer earns on savings accounts, has been introduced in Congress a number of times, it has not yet passed. Thus, confusion concerning the amount of interest paid or earned by a consumer persists. The confusion can be lessened, however, if the relationships between the different methods used to calculate interest are understood.

INTEREST CALCULATIONS

Interest represents the price borrowers pay to lenders for credit over specified periods of time. The amount of interest paid depends on a number of factors; the dollar amount lent or borrowed, the length of time involved in the transaction, the stated (or nominal) annual rate of interest, the repayment schedule, and the method used to calculate interest.

If, for example, an individual deposits $1,000 for one year in a bank paying 5 percent interest on savings, then at the end of the year the depositor may receive interest of $50, or he may receive some other amount, depending on the way interest is calculated. Alternatively, an individual who borrows $1,000 for one year at 5 percent and repays the loan in one payment at the end of a year may pay $50 in interest, or he may pay some other amount, again depending on the calculation method used.

SIMPLE INTEREST

The various methods used to calculate interest are basically variations of the simple interest calculation method.

The basic concept underlying simple interest is that interest is paid only on the original amount borrowed for the length of time the borrower has use of the credit. The amount borrowed is referred to as the principal. In the simple interest calculation, interest is computed only on that portion of the original principal still owed.

Example 1: Suppose $1,000 is borrowed at 5 percent and repaid in one payment at the end of one year. Using the simple interest calculation, the interest amount would be 5 percent of $1,000 for one year or $50 since the borrower had use of $1,000 for the entire year.

When more than one payment is made on a simple interest loan, the method of computing interest is referred to as "interest on the declining balance." Since the borrower only pays interest on that amount of original principal which has not yet been repaid, interest paid will be smaller the more frequent the payments. At the same time, of course, the amount of credit the borrower has at his disposal is also smaller.

Example 2: Using simple interest on the declining balance to compute interest charges, a 5 percent, $1,000 loan repaid in two payments—one at the end of the first half-year and another at the end of the second half-year—would accumulate total interest charges of $37.50. The first payment would be $500 plus $25 (5 percent of $1,000 for one-half year), or $525; the second payment would be $500 plus $12.50 (5 percent of $500 for one-half year), or $512.50. The total amount paid would be $525 plus $512.50, or $1,037.50. Interest equals the difference between the amount repaid and the amount borrowed, or $37.50. If four quarterly payments of $250 plus interest were made, the interest amount would be $31.25; if 12 monthly payments of $83.33 plus interest were made, the interest amount would be $27.08.

Example 3: When interest on the declining balance method is applied to a 5 percent, $1,000 loan that is to be repaid in two equal payments, payments of $518.83 would be made at the end of the first half-year and at the end of the second half-year. Interest due at the end of the first half-year remains $25; therefore, with the first payment the balance is reduced by $493.83 ($518.83 less $25), leaving the borrower $506.17 to use during the second half-year. The interest for the second half-year is 5 percent of $506.17 for one-half year, or $12.66. The final $518.83 payment, then, covers interest of $12.66 plus the outstanding balance of $506.17. Total interest paid is $25 plus $12.66, or $37.66, slightly more than in Example 2.

This equal payment variation is commonly used with mortgage payment schedules. Each payment over the duration of the loan is split into two parts. Part one is the interest due at the time the payment is made, and part two— the remainder—is applied to the balance or amount still owed. In addition to mortgage lenders, credit unions typically use the simple interest/declining balance calculation method for computing interest on loans. In recent years, a number of banks have also offered personal loans using this method.

OTHER CALCULATION METHODS

Add-on interest, bank discount, and compound interest calculation methods differ from the simple interest method as to when, how, and on what balance interest is paid. The "effective annual rate," or the Annual Percentage Rate (APR), for these methods is that annual rate of interest which when used in the simple interest rate formula equals the amount of interest payable in these other calculation methods. For the declining balance method, the effective annual rate of interest is the stated or nominal annual rate of interest. For the methods to be described below, the effective annual rate of interest differs from the nominal rate.

Add-on Interest. When the add-on interest method is used, interest is calculated on the full amount of the original principal. The interest amount is immediately added to the original principal, and payments are determined by dividing principal plus interest by the number of payments to be made. When only one payment is involved, this method produces the same effective interest rate as the simple interest method. When two or more payments are to be made, however, use of the add-on interest method results in an effective rate of interest that is greater than the nominal rate. True, the interest amount is calculated by applying the nominal rate to the total amount borrowed, but the borrower does not have use of the total amount for the entire time period if two or more payments are made.

Example 4: Consider, again, the two-payment loan in Example 3. Using the add-on interest method, interest of $50 (5 percent of $1,000 for one year) is added to the $1,000 borrowed, giving $1,050 to be repaid; half (or $525) at the end of the first half-year and the other half at the end of the second half-year.

Recall that in Example 3, where the declining balance method was used, an effective rate of 5 percent meant two equal payments of $518.83 were to be made. Now with the add-on interest method each payment is $525. The effective rate of this 5 percent add-on rate loan, then, is greater than 5 percent. In fact, the corresponding effective rate is 6.631 percent. This rate takes into account the fact that the borrower does not have use of $1,000 for the entire year, but rather use of $1,000 for the first half-year and use of about $500 for the second half-year.

To see that a one-year, two equal-payment, 5 percent add-on rate loan is equivalent to a one-year, two equal-payment, 6.631 percent declining balance loan, consider the following. When the first $525 payment is made, $33.15 in interest is due (6.631 percent of $1,000 for one-half year). Deducting the $33.15 from $525 leaves $491.85 to be applied to the outstanding balance of $1,000, leaving the borrower with $508.15 to use during the second half-year. The second $525 payment covers $16.85 in interest (6.631 percent of $508.15 for one-half year) and the $508.15 balance due.

In this particular example, using the add-on interest method means that no matter how many payments are to be made, the interest will always be $50. As the number of payments increases, the borrower has use of less and less credit over the year. For example, if four quarterly payments of $262.50 are made, the borrower has the use of $1,000 during the first quarter, around

Add-on interest: the more frequent the payments, the higher the effective rate

effective annual rate*
(percent)

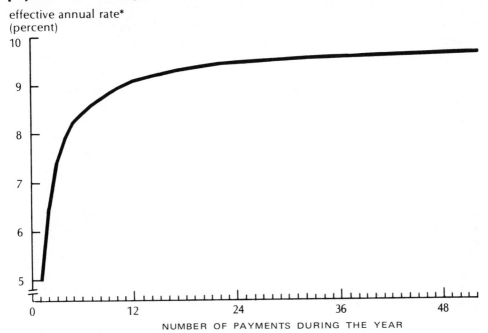

NUMBER OF PAYMENTS DURING THE YEAR

*Based on 5 percent add-on, one-year loan.

$750 during the second quarter, around $500 during the third quarter, and around $250 during the fourth and final quarter. Therefore, as the number of payments increases, the effective rate of interest also increases. For instance, in the current example, if four quarterly payments are made, the effective rate of interest would be 7.922 percent; if 12 monthly payments are made, the effective interest rates would be 9.105 percent. The add-on interest method is commonly used by finance companies and some banks in determining interest on consumer loans.

Bank Discount. When the bank discount rate calculation method is used, interest is calculated on the amount to be paid back and the borrower receives the difference between the amount to be paid back and the interest amount. In Example 1, a 5 percent, $1,000 loan is to be paid back at the end of one year. Using the bank discount rate method, two approaches are possible.

Example 5: The first approach would be to deduct the interest amount of $50 from the $1,000, leaving the borrower with $950 to use over the year. At the end of the year, he pays $1,000. The interest amount of $50 is the same as in Example 1. The borrower in Example 1, however, had the use of $1,000 over the year. Thus, the effective rate of interest using the bank discount rate method is greater than that for the simple interest rate calculation. The effective rate of interest here would be 5.263 percent—i.e., $50 ÷ $950 —compared to 5 percent in Example 1.

Example 6: The second approach would be to determine the amount that would have to be paid back so that once the interest amount was deducted, the borrower would have the use of $1,000 over the year. This amount is $1,052.63, and this becomes the face value of the note on which interest is calculated. The interest amount (5 percent of $1,052.63 for one year) is $52.63, and this is deducted, leaving the borrower with $1,000 to use over the year. The effective rate of interest, again, is 5.263 percent. The bank discount method is commonly used with short-term business loans. Generally, there are no intermediate payments and the duration of the loan is one year or less.

Compound Interest. When the compound interest calculation is used, interest is calculated on the original principal plus all interest accrued to that point in time. Since interest is paid on interest as well as on the amount borrowed, the effective interest rate is greater than the nominal interest rate. The compound interest rate method is often used by banks and savings institutions in determining interest they pay on savings deposits "loaned" to the institutions by the depositors.

Example 7: Suppose $1,000 is deposited in a bank that pays a 5 percent nominal annual rate of interest, compounded semiannually (i.e., twice a year). At the end of the first half-year, $25 in interest (5 percent of $1,000 for one-half year) is payable. At the end of the year, the interest amount is calculated on the $1,000 plus the $25 in interest already paid, so that the second interest payment is $25.63 (5 percent of $1,025 for one-half year). The interest amount payable for the year, then, is $25 plus $25.63, or $50.63. The effective rate of interest is 5.063 percent, which is greater than the nominal 5 percent rate.

The more often interest is compounded within a particular time period, the greater will be the effective rate of interest. In a year, a 5 percent nominal annual rate of interest compounded four times (quarterly) results in an effective annual rate of 5.0945 percent; compounded 12 times (monthly), 5.1162 percent; and compounded 365 times (daily), 5.1267 percent. When the interval of time between compoundings approaches zero (even shorter than a second), then the method is known as continuous compounding. Five percent continuously compounded for one year will result in an effective annual rate of 5.1271 percent.

HOW LONG IS A YEAR?

In the above examples, a year is assumed to be 365 days long. Historically, in order to simplify interest calculations, financial institutions have often

Compound interest: over time, compounding increases the amount of interest paid

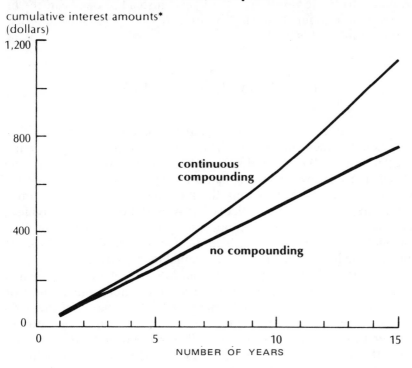

cumulative interest amounts*
(dollars)

continuous compounding

no compounding

NUMBER OF YEARS

*Amount paid on $1000 at 5 percent annual interest rate.

used twelve 30-day months, yielding a 360-day year. If a 360-day year is assumed in the calculation and the amount borrowed is actually used by the borrower for one full year (365 or 366 days), then interest is paid for an additional 5/360 or 6/360 of a "year." For any given nominal rate of interest, the effective rate of interest will be greater when a 360-day year is used in the interest rate calculation than when a 365-day year is used. This has come to be known as the 365-360 method.

Example 8: Suppose $1,000 is deposited in a bank paying a 5 percent nominal annual rate of interest, compounded daily. As pointed out earlier, the effective annual rate of interest for one year, based on a 365-day year, is 5.1267 percent. The interest payable on the 365th day would be $51.27. Daily compounding means that each day the daily rate of 0.0137 percent (5 percent divided by 365 days) was paid on the $1,000 deposit plus all interest payable up to that day. Now suppose a 360-day year is used in the calculation. The daily rate paid becomes 0.0139 percent (5 percent divided by 360 days) so that on the 365th day the interest amount payable would be $52. The effective annual rate of interest, based on a 360-day year would be 5.1997 percent.

Example 9: Suppose that a $1,000 note is discounted at 5 percent and payable in 365 days. This is the situation discussed in Example 5 where, based on a 365-day year, the effective rate of interest was 5.263 percent. If the bank discount rate calculation assumes a 360-day year, then the length of time is computed to be 365/360 or 1-1/72 years instead of one year, the interest deducted (the discount) equals $50.69 instead of $50, and the effective annual rate of interest is 5.34 percent.

WHEN REPAYMENT IS EARLY

In the above examples, it was assumed that periodic loan payments were always made exactly when due. Often, however, a loan may be completely repaid before it is due. When the declining balance method for calculating interest is used, the borrower is not penalized for prepayment since interest is paid only on the balance outstanding for the length of time that amount is owed. When the add-on interest calculation is used, however, prepayment implies that the lender obtains some interest which is unearned. The borrower then is actually paying an even higher effective rate since he does not use the funds for the length of time of the original loan contract.

Some loan contracts make provisions for an interest rebate if the loan is prepaid. One of the common methods used in determining the amount of the interest rebate is referred to as the "Rule of 78." Application of the Rule of 78 yields the percentage of the total interest amount that is to be returned to the borrower in the event of prepayment. The percentage figure is arrived at by dividing the sum of the integer numbers (digits) from one to the number of payments remaining by the sum of the digits from one to the total number of payments specified in the original loan contract. For example, if a five-month loan is paid off by the end of the second month (i.e., there are three payments remaining), the percentage of the interest that the lender would rebate is $(1+2+3) \div (1+2+3+4+5) = (6 \div 15)$, or 40 percent. The name derives from the fact that 78 is the sum of the digits from one to 12 and, therefore, is the denominator in calculating interest rebate percentages for all 12-period loans.

Application of the Rule of 78 results in the borrower paying somewhat more interest than he would have paid with a comparable declining balance loan. How much more depends on the effective rate of interest charged and the total number of payments specified in the original loan contract. The higher the effective rate of interest charged and the greater the specified total number of payments, the greater the amount of interest figured under the Rule of 78 exceeds that under the declining balance method. (See chart on page 477).

The difference between the Rule of 78 interest and the declining balance interest also varies depending upon when the prepayment occurs. This difference over the term of the loan tends to increase up to about the one-third point of the term and then decrease after this point. For example, with a 12-month term, the difference with prepayment occurring in the second month would be greater than the difference that would occur with prepayment in the first month; the third-month difference would be greater than the second-month difference; the fourth month (being the one-third point) would be greater than both the third-month difference and the fifth-month difference. After the fifth month, each succeeding month's difference would be less than the previous month's difference.

Example 10: Suppose that there are two $1,000 loans that are to be repaid over 12 months. Interest on the first loans is calculated using a 5 percent add-on method which results in equal payments of $87.50 due at the end of each month ($1,000 plus $50 interest divided by 12 months). The effective annual rate of interest for this loan is 9.105 percent. Any interest rebate due because of prepayment is to be determined by the Rule of 78.

Interest on the second loan is calculated using a declining balance method where the annual rate of interest is the effective annual rate of interest from the first loan, or 9.105 percent. Equal payments of $87.50 are also due at the end of each month for the second loan.

Suppose that repayment on both loans occurs after one-sixth of the term of the loan has passed, i.e., at the end of the second month, with the regular

Interest paid under the Rule of 78 is always more than under the declining balance—

but how much more depends on:

The term of the original loan contract

The effective annual rate of interest

difference in interest paid (dollars per $100 of interest)

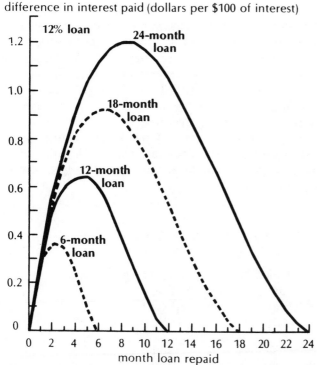

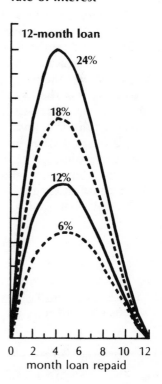

first month's payment being made for both loans. The interest paid on the first loan will be $14.74, while the interest paid on the second loan will be $14.57, a difference of 17 cents. If the prepayment occurs at the one-third point, i.e., at the end of the fourth month (regular payments having been made at the end of the first, second, and third months), interest of $26.92 is paid on the first loan and interest of $26.69 on the second loan, a difference of 23 cents. If the prepayment occurs later, say at the three-fourths point, i.e., at the end of the ninth month (regular payments having been made at the end of the first through eighth months), $46.16 in interest is paid on the first loan and $46.07 in interest paid on the second loan, a difference of but 9 cents.

BONUS INTEREST

Savings institutions are permitted to pay interest from the first calendar day of the month on deposits received by the tenth calendar day of the month, and also on deposits withdrawn during the last three business days of a month ending a regular quarterly or semiannual interest period. If a savings institution chooses to do this, then it is paying for the use of the depositor's money for some period of time during which the savings institution does not have the use of the money. The effective rate of interest is, therefore, greater than it would be otherwise.

Example 11: Suppose that on January 10, $1,000 is deposited in a bank paying 5 percent interest compounded daily based on a 365-day year and that funds deposited by the tenth of any month earn interest from the first of that month. On the following December 31, 355 days after the deposit is made, interest for 365 days is payable on the deposit, or $51.27. The bank, however, had the use of the funds for only 355 days. The effective rate of interest, or that rate which when compounded daily for 355 days would yield the interest amount $51.27, is 5.1408 percent.

Although savings institutions choosing to pay interest for these grace periods are prohibited from advertising an effective yield which takes this into account, depositors should be aware of the effect such practice has on the price paid for the use of their money.

CHARGES OTHER THAN INTEREST

In addition to the interest which must be paid, loan agreements often will include other provisions that must be satisfied. Two of these provisions are mortgage points and required (compensating) deposit balances.

Mortgage Points. Mortgage lenders will sometimes require the borrower to pay a charge in addition to the interest. This extra charge is calculated as a certain percentage of the mortgage amount and is referred to as mortgage points. For example, if 2 points are charged on a $50,000 mortgage, then 2 percent of $50,000, or $1,000, must be paid in addition to the stated interest. The borrower, therefore, is paying a higher price than if points were not charged—i.e., the effective rate of interest is increased. In order to determine what the effective rate of interest is when points are charged, it is necessary to deduct the dollar amount resulting from the point calculation from the mortgage amount and add it to the interest amount to be paid. The borrower is viewed as having the mortgage amount less the point charge amount rather than the entire mortgage amount.

Example 12: Suppose that 2 points are charged on a 25-year, $50,000 mortgage where the rate of interest (declining balance calculation) is 12 percent. The payments are to be $526.61 per month. Once the borrower pays the $1,000 point charge, he starts out with $49,000 to use. With payments of $526.61 a month over 25 years, the result of the 2 point charge is an effective rate of 12.29 percent.

The longer the time period of the mortgage, the lower will be the effective rate of interest when points are charged because the point charge is spread out over more payments. In the above example, if the mortgage had been for 30 years instead of 25 years, the effective rate of interest would have been 12.27 percent.

Required (Compensating) Deposit Balances. A bank may require that a borrower maintain a certain percentage of the loan amount on deposit as a condition for obtaining the loan. The borrower, then, does not have the use of the entire loan amount but rather the use of the loan amount less the amount that must be kept on deposit. The effective rate of interest is greater than it would be if no compensating deposit balance were required.

Example 13: Suppose that $1,000 is borrowed at 5 percent from a bank to be paid back at the end of one year. Suppose, further, that the lending bank requires that 10 percent of the loan amount be kept on deposit. The borrower, therefore, has the use of only $900 ($1,000 less 10 percent) on which he pays an interest amount of $50 (5 percent of $1,000 for one year). The effective rate of interest is therefore, 5.556 percent as opposed to 5 percent when no compensating balance is required.

SUMMARY

Although not an exhaustive list, the methods of calculating interest described here are some of the more common methods in use. They serve to indicate that the method of interest calculation can substantially affect the amount of interest paid, and that savers and borrowers should be aware not only of nominal interest rates but also of how nominal rates are used in calculating total interest charges.

MODERN FINANCIAL THEORY*

Richard R. Simonds †

31

   The most significant academic developments in finance in the past twenty-five years have been portfolio theory, capital market theory, and efficient market theory. Portfolio theory is concerned with how a risk-averse investor should go about selecting an optimal portfolio of investment assets. Capital market theory extends portfolio theory and attempts to describe the way in which the equilibrium market price or expected return of an individual investment asset is related to the asset's risk of return. Efficient market theory deals with the relationship between information and security prices and the resulting implications for investors.

   This article attempts to present the major theoretical concepts in these areas in as nontechnical a manner as possible. Several statistical terms are used along the way but only after the meaning of each is sufficiently developed. Second, empirical support for these theories is briefly summarized. Third, three applications of these theories are illustrated. Although the applications presented are by no means exhaustive, they indicate the scope of the impact of recent academic developments on financial analysis.

   *Reprinted from *MSU Business Topics*, Winter 1978, No. 1, Vol. 26, pp. 54-63, by permission of the publisher, Division of Research, Graduate School of Business Administration, Michigan State University.

   †Richard R. Simonds is a member of the faculty of the Graduate School of Business Administration at Michigan State University.

PORTFOLIO THEORY

The one-period return on an individual investment asset during a specified time is equal to the change in the market value of the asset plus any cash distributions received divided by the initial market value.[1] The return for the ith asset, $\tilde{R}_i$, is given by

$$\tilde{R}_i = \frac{\tilde{V}_{i1} - V_{i0} + \tilde{D}_{i1}}{V_{i0}}, \tag{1}$$

where

$$\begin{aligned}
\tilde{V}_{i1} &= i^{th} \text{ asset market value at the end of} \\
&\quad \text{the period;} \\
V_{i0} &= i^{th} \text{ asset market value at the begin-} \\
&\quad \text{ning of the period; and} \\
\tilde{D}_{i1} &= i^{th} \text{ asset cash distribution during the} \\
&\quad \text{period.[2]}
\end{aligned}$$

The return on a portfolio, $\tilde{R}_p$, is a weighted average of the returns on the individual assets in the portfolio. That is, for n assets,

$$\tilde{R}_p = A_1\tilde{R}_1 + A_2\tilde{R}_2 + \ldots + A_n\tilde{R}_n, \tag{2}$$

where A_i equals the proportion of the initial investment commited to the ith asset, and the sum of the A_i's is one.

Expected Return

Each return, $\tilde{R}_i$, is uncertain at the beginning of the period. A useful way to deal with this uncertainty is to assign subjective probabilities to possible return outcomes. Having done so, the expected return may be computed. The expected return is the weighted average of all possible returns where the weights are equal to the probabilities or relative chances of each level of return occurring. The probability of R_{ij}, where R_{ij} represents the jth level of return for the ith asset, is designated P_{ij}, and the sum of the probabilities, $P_{i1}, P_{i2}, \ldots, P_{im}$, for m possible return levels must equal one. The expected value of $\tilde{R}_i$, $E(\tilde{R}_i)$, given the m possible outcomes shown in Exhibit 1, is

---

[1] Although the theory is properly presented in terms of all investment assets, most applications have focused on financial assets.

[2] The tilde, ~, on $\tilde{R}_i$, $\tilde{V}_{i1}$, and $\tilde{D}_{i1}$ indicates that these quantities are uncertain at the beginning of the period and hence are random variables.

$$E(\tilde{R}_i) = \sum_{j=1}^{m} R_{ij}P_{ij} \tag{3}$$

$$= .1(.05) + .2(.06) + .4(.07) + .2(.08) + .1(.09)$$

$$= .07 \text{ or } 7\%.$$

In accordance with expression (2), the expected value of the portfolio return, $E(\tilde{R}_p)$, is equal to a weighted average of the n individual assets' expected returns,

$$E(\tilde{R}_p) = A_1 E(\tilde{R}_1) + A_2 E(\tilde{R}_2) + \ldots + A_n E(\tilde{R}_n),$$

$$= \sum_{i=1}^{n} A_i E(\tilde{R}_i). \tag{4}$$

Therefore, the contribution of each asset to the expected portfolio return is its own expected return.

Risk of Return

The risk of the portfolio return might be stated in terms of a dispersion measure which takes into account both the likelihood of $\tilde{R}_p$ being less than $E(\tilde{R}_p)$ and the size of the downside deviations. However, if the distribution for $\tilde{R}_p$ is symmetric, a measure of dispersion based on both the upside and downside deviations from the expected return level may be used even

EXHIBIT 1

SYMMETRIC PROBABILITY DISTRIBUTION OF RETURN
FOR THE ith ASSET IN PORTFOLIO p

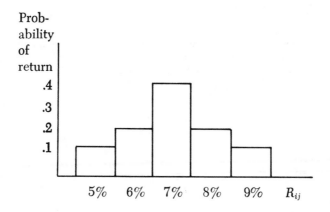

though it is only the downside deviations which leave the investor less well off than if the outcome had been the expected value. Since security returns and hence portfolio returns appear to be approximately symmetric, it is this two-sided measure of dispersion that is generally used.[3] The variance of return is just such a two-sided measure and is defined as the weighted average of squared deviations from the expected return. The variance of the portfolio single-period return, designated $\sigma^2(\tilde{R}_p)$, is given by

$$\sigma^2(\tilde{R}_p) = \sum_{j=1}^{m} [R_{pj} - E(\tilde{R}_p)]^2 P_{pj}. \tag{5}$$

Correspondingly, for a single asset the variance is

$$\sigma^2(\tilde{R}_i) = \sum_{j=1}^{m} [R_{ij} - E(\tilde{R}_i)]^2 P_{ij}, \tag{6}$$

and for the security depicted in Exhibit 1

$$\sigma^2(\tilde{R}_i) = (-.02)^2 \,(.1) + (-.01)^2 \,(.2) + (0)^2 \,(.4) + (.01)^2 \,(.2) + (.02)^2 \,(.1)$$
$$= .00012.$$

The variance of the return on an n-asset portfolio with asset weights A_i, $i = 1, \ldots, n$, is also expressible as

$$\sigma^2(\tilde{R}_p) = \sum_{i=1}^{n} A_i \text{ covariance } (\tilde{R}_i, \tilde{R}_p), \tag{7}$$

where the covariance $(\tilde{R}_i, \tilde{R}_p)$ measures the magnitude of the comovement of the returns on the ith asset and the returns on the portfolio, p, of which asset i is a member.[4] The covariance $(\tilde{R}_i, \tilde{R}_p)$ is expressible as

$$\text{covariance } (\tilde{R}_i, \tilde{R}_p) = (\text{correlation between } \tilde{R}_i \text{ and } \tilde{R}_p) \times \sqrt{\sigma^2(\tilde{R}_i)\, \sigma^2(\tilde{R}_p)}. \tag{8}$$

Expression (7) is significant because it indicates that the contribution of the ith asset to the risk of portfolio p is the covariance $(\tilde{R}_i, \tilde{R}_p)$, and the relative risk of security i in portfolio p is

---

[3] In fact, return distributions on individual securities and portfolios are approximately normal, with monthly returns better described by the normal distribution than daily returns. See Eugene Fama, *Foundations of Finance* (New York: Basic Books, 1976), chapter. 1.

[4]
$$\sigma^2(\tilde{R}_p) = \sum_{i=1}^{n} \sum_{k=1}^{n} A_i A_k \text{ covariance } (\tilde{R}_i, \tilde{R}_k),$$

therefore,
$$\sigma^2(\tilde{R}_p) = \sum_{i=1}^{n} A_i \left[\sum_{k=1}^{n} \text{ covariance } (\tilde{R}_i, A_k \tilde{R}_k) \right],$$

and since
$$\tilde{R}_p = \sum_{k=1}^{n} A_k \tilde{R}_k, \text{ and } \sum_{k=1}^{n} A_i = 1,$$

$$\sigma^2(\tilde{R}_p) = \sum_{i=1}^{n} A_i \text{ covariance } (\tilde{R}_i, \tilde{R}_p).$$

$$\frac{\text{covariance } (\tilde{R}_i, \tilde{R}_p)}{\sigma^2(\tilde{R}_p)} = \beta_{ip}. \tag{9}$$

Alternatively, if one considers a portfolio of n assets in which $A_i = 1/n$, $i = 1, \ldots$, then $\sigma^2(\tilde{R}_p)$ may be expressed as[5]

$$\sigma^2(\tilde{R}_p) = \frac{\substack{\text{average security} \\ \text{return variance}}}{n} + \left(\frac{n-1}{n}\right) \times \left(\substack{\text{average covariance between} \\ \text{returns for pairs of securities} \\ \text{comprising portfolio } p}\right) \tag{10}$$

Two of the most important results of portfolio theory are presented in expressions (7) and (10). Expression (7) shows that the risk contribution of asset i to portfolio p is measured by the covariance $(\tilde{R}_i, \tilde{R}_p)$ and *not* the variance of its own return, $\sigma^2(\tilde{R}_i)$. Expression (10) shows that as a portfolio is expanded to include large numbers of assets, the portfolio variance may not be reduced beyond the average covariance of returns for pairs of securities comprising the portfolio.[6] Consequently, simple diversification in risky assets can be only partially effective in reducing risk.

Two-Parameter Model

Employing expressions (4) and (7), one may calculate $E(\tilde{R}_p)$ and $\sigma^2(\tilde{R}_p)$ for an n-asset portfolio with given weights, A_i. Specifically, if $n = 2$, the possible combinations of expected return and risk for different levels of A_1 and A_2, with the restriction that $A_1 + A_2 = 1$, are indicated by the curved line in Exhibit 2.

Note that it is customary to represent the risk of the portfolio as the standard deviation of the return, which is the square-root of the return variance. The less the returns for assets 1 and 2 are positively correlated, the greater is the curvature of the line representing the locations attainable by combining the two assets.

---

[5] See Fama, *Foundations of Finance*, p. 252. It should be emphasized that the notion that the effects of single-period risk of return tend to cancel out in the longer run is incorrect. The relationship between the future value of a security and the sequence of its n single-period return is

$$\text{Future Value} = [(1 + \tilde{R}_1)(1 + \tilde{R}_2)(1 + \tilde{R}_3) \ldots (1 + \tilde{R}_n)] \text{ (Current Value)},$$

where the subscript refers to the time period. For commonly encountered levels of security returns,

$$\text{Future Value} \simeq [1 + \tilde{R}_1 + \tilde{R}_2 + \tilde{R}_3 + \ldots + \tilde{R}_n] \text{ (Current Value)}.$$

If the returns, $\tilde{R}_i$, are independent and of constant variance, σ^2, then the variance of the future security value after n periods is equal to $\sigma^2 \times$ (current value) $\times$ (n), or n times the variance of the security value one period hence. Single-period risk effects do not cancel out in the longer run.

[6] Almost all security returns appear to be positively correlated with one another, implying positive covariances between asset returns. The average covariance of returns discussed here can therefore be presumed to be positive. See Fama, *Foundations of Finance*, pp. 251-54.

EXHIBIT 2

TWO-PARAMETER PORTFOLIO MODEL
WITH TWO ASSETS

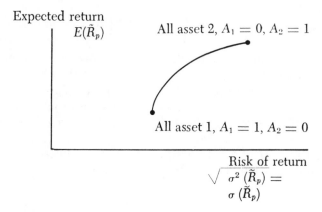

Next assume that the investor has assigned subjective probability distributions to the returns for all risky investment assets. The set of possible portfolio risk-return pairs resulting from different combinations of these assets would appear as the shaded area shown in Exhibit 3. (Momentarily disregard the straight line shown.) Only the darkened border of this set will be of in-

EXHIBIT 3

TWO-PARAMETER PORTFOLIO
MODEL WITH *n* ASSETS

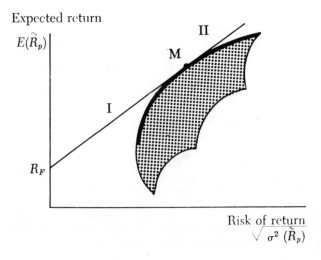

terest to an investor, however. This so-called efficient set offers the highest expected return for a given risk level.[7] Which point on the efficient set of risky assets is best depends on the investor's willingness to accept additional risk in order to increase the level of expected portfolio returns.

CAPITAL MARKET THEORY

Equilibrium Models

Capital market theory seeks to explain the relationship between the expected equilibrium returns on investment assets and their risk of return. Although several slightly different capital market equilibrium models are derivable from two-parameter portfolio theory, depending on the assumptions imposed, only the best-known model, the Sharpe-Lintner Capital Asset Pricing Model, is discussed here.[8]

If a risk-free asset is available with a return R_F, where R_F is a certain rate at which investors may borrow or lend, the new efficient set becomes the straight line emanating from R_F tangent to the original efficient set of risky assets at point M. Anywhere along the straight line is attainable given the proper allocation of funds to the portfolio M and the risk-free asset. If the investor desires to be in region I, funds are invested in the riskless asset, whereas in region II funds are borrowed at the riskless rate and invested in the portfolio M. The combination of riskless asset and portfolio M selected depends on the investor's level of desired risk exposure. Furthermore, all locations along the straight line offer returns that are perfectly positively correlated with the returns on portfolio M since R_F is a certain rate of return.

If investors' expectations regarding uncertain future returns for investment assets are homogeneous, that is, all investors perceive the same set of risk-return pairs, all investors will choose to hold the portfolio M in combination with the riskless asset.[9] Consequently, M is the market portfolio itself, which is the portfolio of all investment assets.

By referring back to expression (7) and replacing portfolio p with the market portfolio M the variance of the return on the market portfolio is seen to be

$$\sigma^2 (\tilde{R}_m) = \sum_{i=1}^{n} A_i \text{ covariance } (\tilde{R}_i, \tilde{R}_m). \qquad (11)$$

[7] The use of the word *efficient* here is not to be confused with its usage in describing capital markets.

[8] See Michael Jensen, "Capital Markets: Theory and Evidence," *Bell Journal of Economics and Management Science* 3 (Autumn 1972):357-98, for an excellent presentation of other models.

[9] This result is frequently referred to as the separation theorem.

The relative risk of the ith asset in the market portfolio, which is referred to as the ith asset's beta coefficient is, from expression (9), seen to be equal to

$$\beta_{im} = \frac{\text{covariance } (\tilde{R}_i, \tilde{R}_m)}{\sigma^2 (\tilde{R}_m)} . \tag{12}$$

Next consider a fractional investment of A_1 in the market portfolio and $(1 - A_1)$ in the riskless asset; then the portfolio return, $\tilde{R}_p$, is

$$\tilde{R}_p = A_1 \tilde{R}_m + (1 - A_1)\tilde{R}_F, \tag{13}$$

and the expected portfolio return is

$$E(\tilde{R}_p) = A_1 E(\tilde{R}_m) + (1 - A_1)R_F. \tag{14}$$

Beta for the portfolio is

$$\beta_{pm} = \frac{\text{covariance } (\tilde{R}_p, \tilde{R}_m)}{\sigma^2 (\tilde{R}_m)}, \tag{15}$$

which, using equation (13), may be expressed as

$$\beta_{pm} = \frac{\text{covariance } (A_1 \tilde{R}_m + (1 - A_1)R_F, \tilde{R}_m)}{\sigma^2(\tilde{R}_m)}$$

or

$$= A_1 \text{ covariance } (\tilde{R}_m, \tilde{R}_m) + \frac{(1 - A_1) \text{ covariance } (R_F, \tilde{R}_m)}{\sigma^2 (\tilde{R}_m)}. \tag{16}$$

Since R_F is a certain rate of return, then expression (16) for β_{pm} reduces to

$$\beta_{pm} = \frac{A_1 \sigma^2 (\tilde{R}_m) + (1 - A_1) (0)}{\sigma^2 (\tilde{R}_m)} = A_1. \tag{17}$$

Using this result for β_{pm} in expression (14) we arrive at

$$E(\tilde{R}_p) = \beta_{pm} E(\tilde{R}_m) + (1 - \beta_{pm})R_F. \tag{18}$$

Equation (18) is the Capital Asset Pricing Model (CAPM) developed simultaneously by William F. Sharpe and John Lintner. Although it was developed here for portfolios on the efficient set, it can be shown to hold for *each* risky asset in the market portfolio.[10] For each risky asset the relationship between expected return and risk is

$$E(\tilde{R}_i) = R_F(1 - \beta_{im}) + \beta_{im}E(\tilde{R}_m),$$

or

$$E(\tilde{R}_i) = R_F + [E(\tilde{R}_m) - R_F]\beta_{im}. \tag{19}$$

---

[10] The best presentation of the complete derivation of the Sharpe-Lintner CAPM is found in Fama, *Foundation of Finance*, chapter 8.

Note that it is the relative risk contribution, β_{im}, of the security to the market portfolio risk that establishes the expected return on the asset and not the total variability of asset return, $\sigma^2(\tilde{R}_i)$. This perspective of risk has dramatic consequences, as will be seen when applications of the CAPM are discussed below.

Beta Coefficients

It is common practice to use past realized data for security and market returns to estimate beta coefficients for individual securities or portfolios.[11] Employing the market-model regression equation

$$\tilde{R}_i = a_i + b_i\tilde{R}_m + \tilde{e}_i, \tag{20}$$

estimates are obtained for b_i using standard statistical techniques. Exhibit 4 shows a regression line fitted to monthly observations on $\tilde{R}_i$ and $\tilde{R}_m$.

When the error term $\tilde{e}_i$ is assumed independent of $\tilde{R}_m$, the b_i term is equal to covariance $(\tilde{R}_i,\tilde{R}_m)/\sigma^2(\tilde{R}_m)$, which is β_{im}. Therefore the estimates of b_i, denoted $\hat{b}_i$, are used as estimates of β_{im}.[12] Equation (20) also provides another description of beta. Beta reflects the sensitivity of the ith asset's re-

EXHIBIT 4

MARKET-MODEL REGRESSION EQUATION

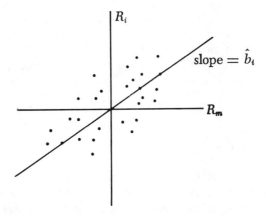

---

[11] A surrogate for the market return, such as the return on the Standard & Poor's 500 index, is usually employed in this process.

[12] An alternative market model specification is stated in terms of excess returns, namely,

$$\tilde{R}_i - R_F = a_i + b_i(\tilde{R}_m - R_F) + \tilde{e}_i.$$

This form is also used by some investigators to obtain estimates of β_{im}.

turns to the returns on the market as a whole. Beta coefficients over one are deemed more risky than the market, and beta coefficients under one less risky than the market, since the market portfolio itself must have a beta coefficient of one.

If one were to consider equation (20) written separately for many individual securities it becomes clear that the return on a portfolio of n equally weighted securities may be expressed as

$$\tilde{R}_p = \frac{1}{n} \sum_{i=1}^{n} a_i + \frac{1}{n} \sum_{i=1}^{n} b_i(\tilde{R}_m) + \frac{1}{n} \sum_{i=1}^{n} \tilde{e}_i. \quad (21)$$

Alternatively, equation (21) may be expressed as

$$\tilde{R}_p = \bar{a}_i + \bar{b}_i(R_m) + \frac{1}{n} \sum_{i=1}^{n} \tilde{e}_i, \quad\quad\quad (22)$$

or using notation to reflect that R_p is the return on a portfolio,

$$\tilde{R}_p = a_p + b_p(\tilde{R}_m) + \tilde{e}_p, \quad\quad\quad (23)$$

where $\bar{a}_i = a_p$ and $\bar{b}_i = b_p$ are averages for the n securities. If the $\tilde{e}_i$ terms are independent of each other then

$$\sigma^2(\tilde{R}_p) = (b_p)^2 \sigma^2(\tilde{R}_m) + \frac{1}{n} \text{ (average variance of the } \tilde{e}_i\text{'s)}. \quad (24)$$

Consequently, as n gets very large the risk of the portfolio can be reduced to that resulting from the comovement of the portfolio returns with the market returns. Variations independent of general market returns can be diversified away, but risk cannot be completely eliminated through diversification. This is the same conclusion we arrive at in expression (10). The standard deviation of the $\tilde{e}_p$ term has come to be called the unsystematic risk and the standard deviation of the $b_p\tilde{R}_m$ term the systematic risk. Diversification can effectively eliminate the unsystematic risk but has no such effect on the systematic risk.

Empirical Evidence

The Sharpe-Lintner CAPM was developed based on the normative idea that risk-averse investors should make portfolio choices based on the expected level and standard deviation of portfolio returns, assumed homogeneous expectations, and on the assumed presence of a risk-free rate of borrowing and lending.[13] Therefore, the model is referred to as a two-parameter market equilibrium model. Since expression (19) is stated in terms of expect-

---

[13] It is also assumed that investors do not incur transaction costs and are indifferent to capital gains or dividends.

ed returns which are unobservable, it may not be tested directly. Various researchers have, however, conducted indirect tests by using data on realized returns for New York Stock Exchange securities. Most notable of these tests are the studies by Eugene Fama and James MacBeth and by Fischer Black, Michael Jensen, and Myron Scholes.[14] Their empirical evidence suggests that the relationship between expected security returns and betas, β_{im}'s, is linear and that beta is the only required factor to explain the differences in levels of expected returns among securities. These findings are consistent with the Sharpe-Lintner CAPM.[15] Furthermore, these findings support the proposition that securities are priced consistent with a two-parameter portfolio model used to describe how investors should select investment portfolios.

EFFICIENT CAPITAL MARKET THEORY

In an efficient capital market, individual security prices fully reflect all available information. Prices adjust completely and instantaneously to new information. Current security prices represent "correct" or unbiased assessments of all information available at the moment.

Academic researchers have attempted to test the extent to which security markets appear to behave as efficient markets.[16] Three classes of testable propositions derivable from the efficient market theory have been examined.[17] First, do current security prices fully reflect all information available in the sequences of past security prices and return data? This proposition is often referred to as the random walk hypothesis, which implies that successive security returns are not statistically associated. To examine this proposition, researchers have tested complicated buying and selling rules based on securities' past price performances. Such rules have not generated returns suffi-

[14] Eugene Fama and James MacBeth, "Risk, Return and Equilibrium: Empirical Tests," *Journal of Political Economy* 71 (May-June 1971): 607-36, and Fischer Black, Michael Jensen, and Myron Scholes, "The Capital Asset Pricing Model: Some Empirical Tests," in Michael Jensen, ed., *Studies in the Theory of Capital Markets* (New York: Praeger, 1972), pp. 79-121.

[15] It must be stated that although these findings are consistent with the Sharpe-Lintner CAPM other evidence suggests that a slightly different version of a two-parameter capital market equilibrium model which does not presume the presence of a risk-free asset is superior. Black has presented such a model in which the expected return on a riskless portfolio ($\beta_{pm} = 0$) replaces the risk-free rate in equation (19). The linearity of the relationship between $E(R_i)$ and β_{im} and the singular importance of β_{im} is not altered in any way, however. See Fama, *Foundations of Finance*, chapter 8, for an excellent discussion of the differences between the various two-parameter capital market equilibrium models which have been developed.

[16] Most of this testing has been conducted using securities traded on the New York Stock Exchange. Caution should be exercised in generalizing these test results to all security markets.

[17] Most of the studies of market efficiency are also implicitly testing a market equilibrium model. See Fama, *Foundations of Finance*, chapter 5, for a discussion of this point.

ciently greater than those available through buy-and-hold strategies to warrant investors behaving in a manner not consistent with the notion that this first efficient market proposition is correct.

A second testable proposition is that security prices adjust fully and instantaneously to *new* publicly available information. The empirical research regarding this proposition is preponderantly supportive. Studies conducted concerning earnings announcements, announced changes in accounting practices, mergers, stock splits, newly filed SEC documents, and so forth, have all supported this second proposition. It should be kept in mind, however, that even though the evidence reported would not lead one to reject this second proposition, any real market is surely not completely consistent with it either. The important point is that the evidence suggests that individual investors are best off conducting their affairs as if the proposition were correct. Finally, if this second proposition concerning publicly available information is correct, it is only because individual investors are trying to identify securities whose current prices do not reflect their intrinsic values and are making investment decisions based on these assessments. This activity is the driving force behind market efficiency. By so behaving, investors are causing the market to behave in accordance with this second proposition.

A third testable proposition is that no sector can, through superior analysis of publicly available information or through access to nonpublicly available information, realize superior investment performance. Research by Michael Jensen in which he examined mutual fund performance strongly suggests that once returns are adjusted for risk these managers have been unable to outperform other investors.[18] On the other hand, evidence from other studies of stock trading by insiders (managers and directors) and New York Stock Exchange specialists suggests that these individuals are privy to information not reflected in current stock prices which may be used to achieve superior returns.[19] This last bit of evidence against the idea of complete market efficiency does not appear to affect the general conclusion that if investors only have access to publicly available information they are wise to act as if the market were efficient.

APPLICATIONS

Almost every facet of financial analysis has been affected by the theories described above. This pervasiveness is illustrated here by examining the impact of modern financial theory on public utility regulation, investor port-

[18] Michael Jensen, "The Performance of Mutual Funds in the Period 1945-1964," *Journal of Finance* 23 (May 1968: 389-416).

[19] Jeffrey Jaffe, "Special Information and Insider Trading," *Journal of Business* 47 (July 1974): 410-28.

folio selection, and corporate capital budgeting. Although this examination must necessarily be brief, an effort has been made to point out several practical problems encountered when trying to apply these theories. This effort is important lest the reader get the false impression that modern financial theory has reduced many areas of financial analysis to mechanical formula manipulation.

Public Utility Regulation

Public utility rate of return regulation is based on the legal principle that "the return to the equity owner should be commensurate with returns on investments in other enterprises having corresponding risk."[20] One concept of commensurate return is the market rate of return which investors expect when they purchase other equity shares of comparable risk. If estimates of the risk and associated expected rate of return alluded to in the legal principle above can be obtained for a utility's stock, these estimates may be used along with debt costs to determine a "fair" company rate of return on assets. This company rate of return may be applied to a rate base such as the book value of capital investment to determine utility service rates.

Portfolio theory and capital market theory may be used to estimate both the risk of the equity and the level of expected equity return. As seen in expression (12), for a well-diversified investor the relevant risk measure of a security is its beta coefficient. Expression (19) specifies the level of expected return for a security with known beta, and it also shows all securities with the same beta have the same expected return. Modern financial theory offers a conceptually sound approach to the implementation of the legal principle of "fair" return in regulatory cases and in fact has been used for this purpose.

Testimony has been offered in regulatory cases such as those involving Communications Satellite Corporation, in which experts were requested to prepare an analysis of Comsat's risk in a portfolio context and to estimate Comsat's expected return on equity capital.[21] Two major problems arise in such an analysis. First, a firm's true equity beta coefficient can only be estimated (see expression [20] for the standard statistical approach), and therefore a firm's inherent risk level may not be known exactly. Furthermore, since the "real" or inherent beta coefficient is determined by a firm's operating and financial characteristics, only if these remain constant over time will the theoretical beta remain constant. Consequently, errors may arise from two sources in predicting the future riskiness of a utility's equity shares.

Second, a major problem arises in using expression (19) to estimate the

---

[20] Supreme Court Decision in *Federal Power Commission* et al. v. *Hope Natural Gas Company*, 320 U.S. 591 (1949) at 603.

[21] Federal Communications Commission, Communications Satellite Corporation. Prepared Testimony, S. J. Meyers. F.C.C. Docket 16070; 1972.

expected return on the utility's equity since values for the expected market return, $E(\widetilde{R}_m)$, and risk-free rate, R_F, must be specified. These can only be specified subjectively, which, of course, means that $E(\widetilde{R}_i)$, the expected equity return, is a subjective estimate. One meaningful way to proceed, however, is not to generate one estimate but to explore the range of estimates that result when different combinations of $E(\widetilde{R}_m)$ and R_F are inserted. Given the limitations cited here it would not appear sensible to consider the CAPM alone a sufficient basis for regulatory decisions but rather one approach to determining the utility's required equity return which should be considered in regulatory proceedings.

Index Funds

An index fund is an investment fund constructed so that its rate of return behavior is approximately the same as that of a major index, such as the Standard & Poor's 500. Therefore, except for transaction costs and compositional differences, these funds offer the same return as the indices they attempt to imitate. The motivation for such funds arises from efficient market theory and portfolio theory.[22]

First, in an efficient market, investors are not able to use publicly available information to identify undervalued or overvalued securities; therefore, market prices reflect intrinsic values. Second, we have shown that the efficient set of portfolios (greatest expected return for a given risk level) is the locus of points on the straight line extending from the risk-free rate through and beyond the market portfolio. All investors should be somewhere on the straight line of efficient portfolios. By combining an investment in the market portfolio with an investment in the risk-free asset one may obtain efficient portfolios less risky than the market portfolio. An efficient portfolio riskier than the market portfolio is achieved by borrowing at the risk-free rate and investing in the market portfolio.

If the Standard & Poor's 500 index is a good surrogate for the market portfolio, investors may approximate the market portfolio by holding the index fund. If less risk is desired part of the investor's wealth can be diverted to short-term Treasury Bills, which serve as a substitute for a risk-free asset. Positions riskier than the market may also be achievable by buying on margin.[23] However, since actual margin loan rates are greater than the risk-free rate, the leveraging process is not as effective as that shown for region II in Exhibit 3. The slope of the efficient set is diminished for points past the market portfolio M.

---

[22] The appeal of index funds stems from efficient market and efficient portfolio considerations. However, if a majority of investors were to invest in a few index funds the market would no longer be efficient. This would destroy the underlying basis for index funds.

[23] Most institutions are legally precluded from buying on margin, however.

Capital Budgeting

The two-parameter portfolio model has been applied in the capital budgeting area to develop a new market portfolio concept of project risk. This perspective suggests that the management of a publicly held firm should not be concerned with the impact a project has on the firm's total variability of return but rather with the project's relative risk. The relative risk is the incremental effect of the project on the variability of returns on a portfolio of investment assets held by a well-diversified investor holding the firm's stock. This is the same concept of risk we developed earlier for investment assets held in a portfolio and was represented by the asset's beta coefficient. It follows that product diversification by a firm for the sole purpose of reducing the variability of the firm's return is not beneficial to investors since they can achieve the same or better diversification within their own investment portfolio. The market portfolio concept of project risk shifts the emphasis away from measuring risk in the narrow context of the firm to measuring it in the context of the entire market of investment assets.

Associated with a project's relative risk measure is a required rate of return on the investment project. This rate of return is estimable using expression (19) for the Sharpe-Lintner CAPM. If the predicted internal rate of return (IRR) on the equity financed portion of a capital investment project does not exceed the project's required rate of return, the project is not acceptable. This required return is represented by the straight line of slope $E(\tilde{R}_m) - R_F$ in Exhibit 5 for a firm with a fixed capital structure.[24]

The project's expected rate of return is interpreted to be the expected return on the equity financed portion of the project. Or, stated differently, we now wish to consider the return of the project based on the generated cash flows adjusted for debt charges and the amount of the investment in the project reduced by the portion financed through debt. The project beta is considered to be the covariance between the return on the equity financed portion and the market return. Projects are positioned in Exhibit 5 by their estimated internal rates of return on the equity financed portion and their estimated betas. If a project lies above the CAPM line of slope $E(\tilde{R}_m) - R_F$ it is acceptable; otherwise it is not. Consequently, projects A and D are acceptable while C and B are not. Note that project A is acceptable even though its expected equity return is below the firm's average cost of equity capital. Apparently project A is sufficiently less risky than the firm's average project to warrant its acceptance.

Estimating betas for capital investment projects is especially difficult, much more so than for publicly traded securities. Several approaches are

---

[24]Questions concerning the optimal capital structure are not considered here. See Mark Rubinstein, "Mean-Variance Synthesis," *Journal of Finance* 28 (March 1973): 167-81, and Robert Hamada, "The Effect of the Firm's Capital Structure on the Systematic Rick of Common Stocks," *Journal of Finance* 27 (May 1972): 435-52, for applications of the CAPM model to questions relating to capital structure.

EXHIBIT 5

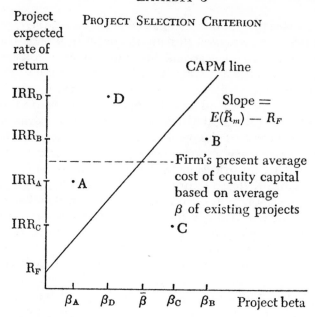

PROJECT SELECTION CRITERION

available, however. First, it may be possible to identify an existing firm, whose stock is publicly traded, which is involved in activities that approximate the project the firm is considering.[25] If such is the case, statistically estimated betas using historical stock return data for this firm may provide an adequate estimate of the project's beta.

Second, if the project is similar to one with which the firm has had prior experience, it may be possible to construct historical rates of return on the equity financed portion for different time periods and combine these with the corresponding market returns (actually a surrogate such as the Standard & Poor's 500) to estimate a beta coefficient using expression (20).[26] Third, the firm might resort to constructing a simulation model of the project under consideration to help in estimating its beta.

SUMMARY

Modern financial theory and empirical evidence suggest that investors are well advised to make investment decisions assuming that security prices

[25] One should in this process adjust the beta coefficient for differences in capital structure that may exist. See Rubinstein, "Mean-Variance Synthesis."

[26] See James Van Horne, *Financial Management and Policy*, 4th ed. (Englewood Cliffs: Prentice-Hall, 1977), pp. 175-78.

fully and instantaneously reflect all publicly available information. Furthermore, investors should hold efficient portfolios. Efficient portfolios offer the highest possible level of expected return for a given level of risk and represent combinations of a risk-free asset and the market portfolio.

When investors hold efficient portfolios, the risk of an individual asset is measured in terms of how much it contributes to the efficient portfolio's risk of return. This contribution is not adequately represented by the individual asset's total variability of return since a portion of this variation may be diversified away. The proper measure of the asset's risk contribution is its beta coefficient, which is based on the covariation between the asset's returns and returns on the market portfolio. The higher this covariation, the more the asset contributes to the risk of an efficient portfolio.

The Sharpe-Lintner capital asset pricing model (CAPM) expresses the equilibrium relationship between the expected return on an individual investment asset and its risk stated as a beta coefficient. The CAPM has been used extensively to analyze theoretical and practical problems in finance. Applications of the model in public utility regulation and corporate capital budgeting were illustrated here. A particularly striking conclusion is that the risk of a capital investment project and its associated required level of return should not be judged on the basis of the project's total variability of returns. The proper basis of evaluation is to examine how the project's returns are estimated to covary with the returns on the market portfolio.

Part IV

Regulation and Financial Innovations

Most states have usury laws that limit the interest rates that may be charged on certain types of consumer-related loans. When interest rates are high and such ceilings are binding, lenders divert funds to investments in unregulated markets or they impose stringent non-price terms in order to ration their funds. As a result, serious market distortions arise as discussed in the *credit rationing* article by Paul S. Anderson and James R. Ostas. In the article by Marvin Goodfriend, James Parthemos, and Bruce Summers, the authors present a summary of the *financial innovations that relate to the nation's payments system*. The combined effects of inflation, high interest rates, regulatory restrictions, advanced technology, and greater competition have all contributed to a dramatic revision of this system.

In the article by Timothy Q. Cook and Jeremy G. Duffield, the *money market mutual fund* phenomenon is examined in detail. The authors conclude that the growth of these funds has been a result of Government regulations as well as a fundamental change in the way individuals and institutions handle their short-term financial assets. Money market funds, therefore, are a permanent fixture in the financial markets regardless of the future course of Government regulations. In the final article, also by Cook and Duffield, the entire range of so-called *short-term investment pools* is surveyed. The most familiar of these is the money market fund. However, there are a number of other specialized types of funds that meet the needs of certain groups or investors. Credit unions, trust departments of banks, and local governments are among the groups served by these specialized short-term investment pools, or *STIPs*, as they are called.

PRIVATE CREDIT RATIONING [†]

Paul S. Anderson and
James R. Ostas [*]

32

It is fall, 1974 in Boston. Savings banks have very little money to lend on home mortgages because depositors have been withdrawing substantial amounts from their savings to invest in securities paying much higher rates than banks pay on savings. What loanable funds a certain savings bank has can be:

(a) used to buy corporate bonds yielding almost 11 percent, and having no servicing expenses, or
(b) lent out at 9½ percent to a long-standing depositor on a mortgage loan which has servicing costs of just under ½ of 1 percent.

Question: Does the savings bank choose (a) or (b)? Most students of economics, as well as most of the public, would choose answer (a). But savings bankers, the people who count usually choose (b). Instead of lending funds to the highest bidders, savings bankers and other institutional lenders choose to charge less and then to distribute, or *ration*, their credit on some basis other than rate paid.

At the present time, funds for lending are plentiful and the question of credit rationing a remote one. However, periods of monetary restraint have been a recurring phenomenon in our economy, and problems of credit ra-

†Reprinted from the *New England Economic Review*, May/June 1977, pp. 24-37, with permission from the Federal Reserve Bank of Boston.

*Paul S. Anderson is an Assistant Vice President and Financial Economist at the Federal Reserve Bank of Boston and James R. Ostas is an Associate Professor of Economics at Bowling Green University.

tioning may return at some future time. The very concept of private credit rationing remains controversial, and its importance in implementing monetary policy is still questioned by many.[1] However, particularly during periods of credit restraint, the allocation of available funds among borrowers clearly is not based entirely upon the interest rate paid.

The impact of direct rationing of some prospective borrowers out of the market necessarily differs from the effect of an increase in interest rates. Specific attempts to measure these factors have been far less frequent than the development of theories to explain credit rationing, however. This article will be confined to a description of some of the lending practices related to credit rationing in the commercial, consumer, and mortgage loan fields.

I. THE RATIONING PHENOMENON

For most people, rationing refers to the procedure used primarily during wartime to allocate goods in short supply. Ration coupons that permitted the purchase of a set amount of the rationed item per time period were parceled out on a per capita basis. Economists call this nonprice rationing, as opposed to the common way of allocating goods by price rationing, which is charging a price that equalizes supply and demand. In price rationing, each dollar bill is, in effect, a ration coupon.

Rationing is defined in this article as the way goods or credit are allocated when their price is set at so low a level that more is demanded than is available. The rationing phenomenon has two aspects, the setting of a below-market or "too-low" price and the method of allocation at this price. Three combinations can be distinguished according to who sets the price and who determines the allocation scheme:

1. Price and rationing method both determined by government. This is the World War II type of rationing where the government controlled the price of goods in short supply and specified, by the use of ration coupons, how the short supply was to be distributed.
2. Price determined by government but rationing carried out by private sector. This type occurred at the time of the 1974 gasoline shortage. The government set the price at a level where more was demanded than was available. The short supply of gasoline was distributed privately, generally on the basis of first come, first served.
3. Both price and rationing determined in private sector. A striking example of this type of rationing occurred in the post World War II years after price controls were abolished in 1946. Auto manufacturers did

---

[1] For a review of the continuing debate in the literature about credit rationing, see Benjamin M. Friedman, "Credit Rationing: A Review," Board of Governors of the Federal Reserve System, *Staff Economic Studies*, 72, 1972, 27 pp. One of the more recent attempts to measure credit rationing used the Federal Reserve System's Quarterly Survey of Changes in Bank Lending Practices. See Duane G. Harris, "Credit Rationing at Commercial Banks: Some Empirical Evidence," *Journal of Money Credit and Banking*, Vol VI, No. 2 (May 1974), pp. 227-240.

not set prices at a level which would equalize demands with supplies, but at a lower level. More cars were demanded at these prices than were available and the automobile manufacturers permitted their dealers to distribute cars according to their best judgment.

All these examples were drawn from the markets for goods, but the rationing phenomenon also occurs in the credit markets. Most credit rationing falls into the second and third types. Examples of the first type, where the government sets both price and the rationing scheme, are rare in this country but have been common in some other countries, such as France.[2] The concept of rationing used here is the process by which lenders allocate their loanable funds when they do not (or cannot) charge a high enough interest rate to balance demands for loans with supplies of funds.

II. USURY LAWS

The most obvious example of "too low" interest rates occurs where usury laws set low ceilings on interest rates that can be charged on loans. Forty-eight states have usury laws which vary in coverage and the level of the ceiling, but most apply only to loans to individuals and noncorporate businesses.[3] Usually small consumer instalment loans are exempt from these general usury ceilings but are covered by special, higher ceilings. Loans to corporations most often are exempted entirely or covered by higher ceilings. As a result, usury ceilings primarily affect personal loans to consumers, mortgage loans to home buyers, and business loans to unincorporated firms.

The intent of usury laws is to protect "unsophisticated" borrowers against "exorbitant" interest rates. While such an intent can be applauded, usury laws really cannot do the job. The basic difficulty is that usury ceilings conflict with the law of supply and demand which sets prices in the market place. If the usury ceiling is below the market interest rate which lenders can get, lenders will tend not to lend to those borrowers, who are "protected" by the ceiling. For example, if conditions are such that the interest rate on mortgage loans should be 9 percent in order to balance demands for loans with supplies of funds but the ceiling on loans is 7½ percent (as it was in Vermont until April 1974), then more funds are demanded at 7½ percent than are available and credit rationing results. What funds banks do lend at the ceiling, they will lend to long-standing customers. Thus those borrowers that do benefit from usury ceilings generally would get favored treatment anyway because they are known to the lender or can provide good security.

---

[2] Donald R. Hodgman, "The French System of Monetary and Credit Controls" Banca Nazionale del Lavoro, *Quarterly Review*, No. 99 (December 1971), pp. 324-353; Donald R. Hodgman, "Credit Controls in Western Europe: An Evaluation Review," and Jacques H. David and Marcus H. Miller, "Discussion," in *Credit Allocation Techniques and Monetary Policy*, Federal Reserve Bank of Boston, Conference Series No. 11, September 1973, pp. 137-177.

[3] Norman W. Bowsher, "Usury Laws: Harmful When Effective," *Federal Reserve Bank of St. Louis Review*, Vol. 56, No. 8 (August 1974), pp. 16-23.

Available evidence suggests that in those states with usury ceilings below the market interest rate, thrift institutions increase their lending on out-of-state mortgages and other credit instruments.[4] As a result, funds lent on local conventional mortgages are reduced, as are new housing starts.[5] While FHA and VA mortgages are exempt from usury laws in several states, they do not serve to fill the "financing gap" that results from usury ceilings on conventional mortgages. FHA and VA mortgages involve a lot of "red tape." Their rates are set in Washington, and while the effective rate can be raised by discounting, many borrowers, and even lenders, object to this practice.

Of the 48 states with usury laws, a large number have raised the ceilings or relaxed the provisions of the law in the last ten years. They recognized that the net effect of usury ceilings substantially below market rates was on balance more injurious than helpful.

III. EVIDENCE OF PRIVATE CREDIT RATIONING ACTIVITY

It is obvious why interest rates on loans can become "too low" when usury ceilings are in force. But even where usury ceilings do not apply, loan rates are often "too low" during periods when funds are in short supply. At such times lenders do not raise rates to levels which would reduce demand to the volume of funds available, but hold rates at a lower level. At this lower level, the demand for funds exceeds the supply and lenders allocate or ration available funds to borrowers on some basis other than willingness to pay.

Borrowers become aware of the rationing phenomenon when they apply for loans. Normally lenders inquire about the applicant's credit rating and then state the terms of the loan. But when funds are in short supply, the lender will first determine whether the applicant is entitled to credit on the basis of his past relationship with the lender. If the applicant is not, he will probably be turned down with no discussion of what rates would be charged and whether the applicant would be willing to pay these rates.

Shown in the chart are comparisons of interest rates which indicate periods when rates charged for loans were lower than rates paid on comparable investments, which is a standard symptom that credit rationing is occurring. In the top panel are rates charged on conventional mortgage loans and the rate prevailing in the secondary or wholesale market for government-insured (FHA) mortgage loans. During periods when supplies of mortgage funds were

[4] Suzanne Cutler, "The Public Policy Objectives of the Regulation of Depository Institutions," in Leonard Lapidus et al., *Public Policy Toward Mutual Savings Banks in New York State: Proposals for Change*, Federal Reserve Bank of New York and New York State Banking Department, June 1974, p. 111.

[5] James R. Ostas, "Effects of Usury Ceilings in the Mortgage Market," *Journal of Finance*, Vol. XXXI (June, 1976), pp. 821-834; Arthur J. Rolnick, Stanley L. Graham, and David S. Dahl, "Minnesota's Usury Law: An Evaluation," *Ninth District Quarterly*, Federal Reserve Bank of Minneapolis, April 1975, pp. 16-25; Norman W. Bowsher, *op. cit.*, p. 19, and Robins, Philip K., "The Effects of State Usury Ceilings on Single Family Homebuilding," *Journal of Finance*, Vol. XXIX, (March 1974), pp. 227-235.

LOAN RATES, MARKET RATES AND INTEREST COSTS
(1965-1976)

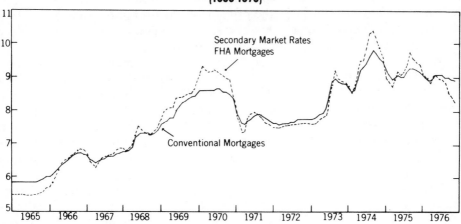

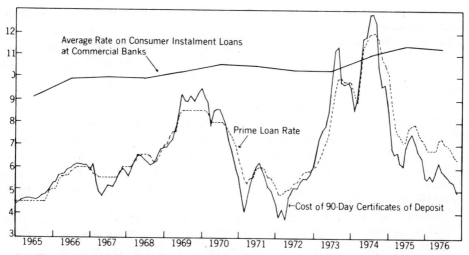

Note-The mortgage rate series are those compiled by the Department of Housing and Urban Development. The cost of 90 day CDs includes the cost of carrying reserves against these time deposits. The consumer loan rate is an estimate based on the Functional Cost survey of the Federal Reserve prior to 1971 and on a sample survey since then.

short, particularly in 1969-70 and 1974, rates in the secondary market rose 50 basis points or more above rates charged conventional borrowers. Not only does this indicate that rates charged for conventional mortgages were relatively low, but that lenders accepted these lower rates when they could have bought insured mortgage loans in the secondary market at a higher rate of return.

The lower panel in the chart compares the prime business loan rate with the cost of 90-day certificates of deposit (CDs) adjusted for reserve requirements. This adjusted CD rate is a measure of a bank's marginal cost of funds. Normally the prime loan rate approximates or slightly exceeds the CD cost, but in 1973 and again in 1974 the prime loan rate did not even keep up with the adjusted CD cost.[6] Again, banks were charging less for these loans than they were paying for their marginal source of funds.

Also shown in the lower panel are rates for consumer loans, which have been relatively stable. From a level of about 9 percent in 1963, rates on consumer loans by banks rose slowly to about 10½ percent in 1970-72 and then more rapidly to 11½ percent in 1974. Since the servicing expenses of these loans amount to around 3 percent per year, the net return on these loans did not cover the marginal cost of funds as represented by the CD rate. Obviously the rate on consumer loans was also below what might be expected during tight money periods.[7]

Why are lenders reluctant to charge what the market will bear? Several factors influence lenders to act circumspectly. They involve the image lenders want to gain and maintain before both governmental bodies and customers. Federal and state governments are quick to express concern if they believe that lenders are raising loan rates to unwarranted levels. In the past, some state governments have imposed restrictive usury ceilings, which can severely limit the operations of lenders.

Possible reactions of borrowers and the public generally also make lenders hesitant about raising loan rates rapidly. Maintaining good relationships with existing customers is important for long-run profit maximization. This is especially the case where the "products" are loans and deposits and one lender's products are practically identical to another's. Lending institutions strive to develop good relations with their customers and rapid and aggressive raising of loan rates can easily alienate them. Thus, lenders tend to delay raising loan rates until most comparable money market rates have risen and even then to raise their loan rates a little less than these other rates. In essence, lenders sacrifice short-run profits because they think that course is more profitable in the long run.

It should be noted that, as contrasted with credit rationing caused by low usury ceilings, voluntary credit rationing diminishes with the passage of time. Lenders do gradually raise their lending rates, and if tight conditions persist long enough, rates may eventually reach the "correct" level so rationing is

---

[6] A special factor serving to hold down the prime loan rate in 1973 and 1974 was the Federal Government's Committee on Interest and Dividends which monitored interest rate and dividend payment developments during this period.

[7] Construction lending provides an interesting contrast to the lending areas discussed in this article because it has little rationing—lenders generally charge the going market rate. The chief construction lenders are commercial banks, savings and loan associations, and real estate investment trusts. The characteristics of construction lending probably explain why credit is allocated on the basis of rate rather than being rationed when credit is tight. Construction lending is risky and the failure rate among builders and developers is much higher than the average among borrowers in general. The soundness of a loan depends on both the competence of the builder and the profitability of the completed project. Builders generally do not have substantial assets of their own, so they cannot provide much additional security. In addition, the construction industry is fairly small so little public attention is paid to its credit costs.

not needed. Also, as tight credit conditions become more common, as has happended since 1966, lenders adjust their interest rates more quickly. This can be seen in the chart; rates on all three types of loans shown were raised more quickly and to a greater extent in 1973-74 than in the two preceding restraint periods. Thus voluntary credit rationing is really a temporary phenomenon and may well become less important in the future as the country becomes more accustomed to large fluctuations in interest rates.

Mortgage Loans

The chief home mortgage lenders are thrift institutions—savings and loan associations and savings banks. These lenders present themselves as "people's institutions" and in the past Congress has granted them various types of favored treatment such as somewhat higher interest rate ceilings than commercial banks. Thrift institutions have also been successful in gaining a favorable and sympathetic attitude from the public. Residential mortgage borrowers have usually obtained more attractive terms than offered by other lenders. This favorable public attitude would be jeopardized if thrift institutions began raising mortgage rates as rapidly as competitive conditions allowed during periods of credit restraint.

Business Loans

Most business borrowers are much more interested in the availability of bank loans than in the current rate of interest. So long as they believe they are not paying more than other business borrowers in the same situation, they will accept higher rates, even though reluctantly. But elected officials express a great deal of concern about rapid rises in business loan rates. If Congress becomes sufficiently antagonistic to banks, it can pass penalizing legislation restricting bank operations and profits. Commercial banks have been quite successful in the postwar years in obtaining greater "tax equality," and they could jeopardize this trend by too aggressive rate-setting. A clear example of banks bowing to governmental pressure occurred in 1973 when the Government Committee on Interest and Dividends requested banks to raise the prime rate slowly and banks complied, even though they were under no legal requirement to do so.

Furthermore, banks do not have to raise the prime rate to the highest point possible in order to make good profits during a period of restraint. This is the case even though the cost of funds rises so rapidly during periods of restraint that for a time the *marginal* cost of funds borrowed by a bank exceeds the interest received from many, if not most, of its borrowers. However, the *average* cost of bank funds does not rise as quickly as do yields on earning assets because about one-third of bank funds on average are obtained from demand deposits which pay no interest. The net result is that although the costs of *additional* funds (those obtained through CDs, for example) rise above the yield on business loans, average costs of funds are low enough to provide a very profitable spread. Moreover, loan rates usually decline more slowly than CD rates when credit conditions ease. As the chart shows, a profitable spread opened up between the prime rate and the net cost of CDs in the easy credit periods of 1971-72 and 1975-76. Thus, when the credit cycle is viewed as a whole, bank profits suffer little, if at all, as a consequence of charging lower-than-market rates on business loans during a tight period.

Banks can also make up a part of the undercharges on business loans by other adjustments. The most common of these is to increase the compensating balances the borrower must hold. For example, if this balance is increased from 10 to 20 percent of the loan or the line of credit, the borrower really gets 10 percent less from his loan, yet his interest payment is the same as before, so his actual cost per $1 used is about 10 percent higher. Banks can also make up for "too-low" interest rates on business loans by adjusting commitment fees, fees for handling trust and pension accounts, and other charges. Still another adjustment is to add a premium to the prime rate, often done with new customers. Even though the new borrower may be as creditworthy as existing prime borrowers, the bank may charge him, say, prime plus 1 percent. This premium charge is continued until a regular customer relationship is established. Thus, for all these reasons the actual level of the prime rate on business loans may not accurately reflect the real cost of lending to any given borrower or its overall profitability to the bank.

These adjustments in the terms of the customer relationship are, at best, only a partial substitute for raising the business loan rate. Like the below-market level of the loan rate, they are symptoms of the fact that an imbalance, or disequilibrium, exists in the supply and demand for funds which requires rationing. If banks felt they could raise rates rapidly enough to balance supplies and demands, they would undoubtedly do so rather than adjusting these other lending terms because interest rate changes are much simpler than the other adjustments which usually involve individual negotiations with borrowers.

But it is not practical for banks (or other lenders) to change loan rates whenever market conditions change, even if they felt they could. Market interest rates, such as on Treasury bills or commercial paper, change continuously. Lenders prefer to delay changing their rates until they are fairly certain that the change will not have to be reversed soon.

Also, business demands for funds are so intense, or inelastic, at times that even fairly substantial rises in the lending rate do little to dampen these demands. For example, a lending officer of a large midwestern bank that was especially short of loanable funds stated that his bank raised the rate for some prime customers by three percentage points above the prevailing prime rate but that resulted in no withdrawals of loan requests.

In sum, there are frictions in rate setting on loans that make it practically impossible for lenders to allocate credit on the basis of rate alone. Thus, whenever credit conditions tighten rapidly, some rationing is inevitable.

Consumer Loans

Rates on consumer loans of banks are by far the most stable of the three types discussed in this article. The explanation involves the marketing strategies of banks adopted as a response to the history of consumer credit. In the 1920s, when consumer loans were first extended in any significant amount, they were considered risky and the rates charged were high. But these loans proved surprisingly sound in the depression of the 1930s. Their loss ratio was small; in fact, the percentage of failures among banks was much higher than the loss percentage on consumer loans. The relatively high interest yield combined with low losses made these loans very profitable during the 1930s, 1940s, and early 1950s when other yields were historically low.

Successful consumer lending requires sufficient volume so that processing costs per loan are moderate. At best, processing costs tend to run over 3 percent, and if not well controlled can easily rise to more than twice that level. But it is difficult to develop consumer loan business "off the street." It takes persistent advertising to gain recognition and habitual acceptance as a low-cost consumer lender with "low bank rates." Such advertising is aimed at influencing the habits of the borrowing public rather than convincing the public the institution merits special treatment.

This marketing effort is a long-term operation—it cannot be turned off when interest rates rise and then resumed with any success when rates decline. Because of this, banks believe it is good marketing policy to hold consumer loan rates as stable as possible during tight money in order to maintain the bank's reputation as a comparatively low cost lender. Thus banks are willing to charge less than is warranted during high rate periods in order to preserve their public acceptance and to profit by it when rates decline.

The other major consumer lenders, sales and consumer finance companies, dominated this market until commercial banks entered on a wide scale in the late 1930s. Since then, the finance companies have gradually lost market shares to commercial banks. Their cost of funds averages higher than that of banks and they typically charge higher rates—about 13 percent on new car loans, for example, as compared to about 11 percent by banks. But they cannot set their rates too far above bank rates or they will lose their market share even faster. Thus their rates tend to be determined by the level of bank rates. On small personal loans, which generally have the highest rates of the various types of consumer loans, usury ceilings often determine the level of interest rates.

IV. HOW LOANS ARE RATIONED

Rationing Mortgage Funds

During tight money periods, the inflow of funds to mortgage lenders declines substantially. Since lenders generally chose not to raise lending rates enough to reduce applications to the volume of available funds, they have a large gap between supplies of funds and demands for them. Their problem is how to parcel out the limited supply.

First, of course, lenders must honor prior loan commitments. Then their first general rationing action is to turn down all out-of-area applicants. According to all mortgage lenders who were interviewed, they want to satisfy borrowers in their main market area first. They also generally refuse all applications for credit for purchases of vacation homes. They believe primary home purchasers deserve priority.

Beyond these criteria, they rank borrowers by group. The following order is fairly typical of the priorities of thrift institutions:

1) Long-established depositors.
2) Buyers of houses on which lenders already have mortgages (refinancing loans).
3) Borrowers referred by brokers and builders who have a long-established association with lender.
4) Commercial mortgage borrowers.
5) Applicants "off the street" with no ties to lender.

Some institutions may tend to have somewhat different rankings and vary in their lending policies. Some lenders, attracted by the high rates paid, will rank large commercial mortgage borrowers second or third in their priority of applicants. Lenders who prize their broker and builder contacts might rank this group second.

Borrowers are further ranked by their relative safety. Those receive preference who can provide a high downpayment, 30 percent or even more, and can pay off the loan within 20 years. Not only do such terms make the loan less risky but they help the liquidity position of the lender by reducing the funds loaned out and increasing the rate of repayment.

A refinancing loan (giving a new loan on the same house on which the bank already held a mortgage) has been attractive in recent years because it allows the lender to obtain a higher rate of interest on what is essentially an old loan and on which the interest rate is usually lower than the prevailing rate. Such loans combined with a high downpayment are particularly attractive since the lender needs to advance less additional cash than for an original mortgage. Lenders will often grant a rate somewhat lower than the prevailing rate on such refinancing loans, in order to expedite the home sale and enable the lender to turn over the loan and get a higher rate than on the original mortgage.

A few mortgage lenders, however, may rely entirely on price to determine their lending policies. For example, one New England savings bank in a predominantly retirement and resort area, finding itself with a large inflow of savings during a period of general restraint, nevertheless charged all applicants a mortgage rate in line with corporate bond rates and higher than the prevailing mortgage rate charged by other thrift institutions. Similarly, a large commercial bank made a substantial short-term profit during a tight money period by lending for home mortgages at a high rate of interest and realizing a capital gain by selling the mortgage loans to a Federal agency at a lower rate of interest.

Normally, most new borrowers are referred by brokers and builders or come to the bank "off the street." Therefore when these two groups are rationed out, the lender has voluntarily cut out most of its new mortgage market. Unless disintermediation is severe, he will still be able to satisfy long-established depositors and the demand for refinancing loans, and occasionally, commercial mortgage borrowers as well. Of course, the lender is not strictly bound by any ranking and he will accommodate new applicants who seem to have an especially urgent need or who appear especially likely to become long-run customers.

Rationing Business Loans

Most business borrowers are long-time depositors of commercial banks, so a close relationship exists between the bank and the business borrower. These long-time depositors traditionally are entitled to a certain quota or line of credit and they generally are more interested in its availability than its cost during a period of restraint, because many profitable business opportunities are usually available at such times. The difficulty is that demands for business loans substantially exceed the volume of funds available then. In fact, a tight money period is generally characterized by rapid increases in business demands for funds which are not accommodated by monetary policy.

During such a period of credit restraint, the first priority of commercial banks is to grant all loan requests that fall within established credit lines. These are considered binding obligations by most banks whether or not a formal commitment fee has been paid. Beyond this, banks provide additional credit on a selective basis using such criteria as credit-worthiness, length or permanence of the customer relationship, profitability of the account over time in relation to bank services provided, proposed use of funds, including analysis of the feasibility of the project, degree of need, and availability of alternative sources of funds. Of course, banks run the risk of alienating customers by unfavorable loan decisions but they also know that applicants will have difficulty obtaining a loan at another bank as well.

Since in rationing business loans, banks first limit their lending to regular customers and to the accommodation of their usual needs, the new venture, the unusual or the risky project, the acquisition loan and the unexpectedly large demand for funds becomes casualties during a tight money period. Thus previous commitments tend to limit the supply of funds available for innovation and expansion. This must be counted an important cost of monetary restraint.

Shown in the accompanying table is a comparison of business lending practices of large commercial banks during easy and tight credit periods. While changes in the interest rate are the most common reaction to ease or tightness, many other reinforcing changes are made in loan terms and in

Changes in Bank Lending Practices at
Selected Large Commercial Banks
on Loans to Nonfinancial Businesses

	Easy credit period: three months to Feb. 1971		Tight credit period: three months to Aug. 1974	
	Firmer	**Easier**	**Firmer**	**Easier**
	(percentages of reporting banks)			
Loan terms:				
Interest rate	0	85	77	0
Compensating balances	2	25	68	0
Credit standards	5	5	60	0
Maturity of term loans	1	26	55	0
Value of applicant as depositor or source of other business	5	19	69	0
Intended use of loan	2	27	64	0

Source: Federal Reserve System Quarterly Survey of Bank Lending Practices.

lending attitudes. This listing of lending adjustments demonstrates that the bank-business borrower relationship includes many facets in addition to the rate charged. A small percentage of banks tightened various noninterest terms in early 1971 even though that was an easing period and no banks raised rates. Presumably this represents a completion of tightening actions these banks had begun during the preceding tight money period of 1969-70 and is further evidence that the loan rate itself does not fully reflect the costs of borrowing.

It is a common assumption that small business gets rationed out of the business loan market at such times. It is a fact that bank lending to large business generally does increase greatly as a proportion of total business lending during a tight money period. For example, between 1972 and 1974, the dollar amount of total new short-term business loans of $1 million and over nearly doubled, according to the Quarterly Survey of Interest Rates conducted by the Federal Reserve System, while the total of similar loans of under $1 million grew less than 10 percent.

However, the substantial increase in bank lending to large business during credit tightness probably reflects cyclically greater use of credit lines by large borrowers rather than changing credit standards. In most cases the bank is the small firm's only source of credit, and the small firm uses this source almost continuously. While large firms maintain compensating balances and lines of credit during times of ease, large firms also use stock issues, commercial paper, loans from insurance companies, and other sources to obtain their funds, and not just bank loans as in the case of small firms. When credit is restricted and other sources of funds such as commercial paper become too expensive or are unavailable, the large firm then relies more heavily on its bank lines of credit, and bank lending to large businesses increases.

Rationing Consumer Loans

The two main lenders of consumer credit, commercial banks and finance companies, are in somewhat different situations with regard to making consumer loans when money is tight. According to the bankers interviewed, the primary goal of most commercial banks is to provide the maximum amount of funds to their priority customers, businesses, and to limit other uses of funds including consumer lending as much as possible. But in trying to limit consumer lending, they must be careful not to tarnish their image as "the bank that likes to say yes." They raise credit standards, but this does not eliminate many applicants because banks typically get the better risks anyway. They discontinue advertising consumer lending, but this has little impact on their established clientele. Banks can do especially little about limiting credit card lending. Once cards have been issued and contracts made with stores to honor them, the volume of credit extended is essentially in the hands of the consumers. Thus, in the final analysis, commercial banks do little effective rationing of consumer credit.

Consumer lending is the priority operation of finance companies, both sales finance and consumer finance. They encounter a severe profits squeeze during a tight credit period because interest costs on their borrowerd funds, of which short-term bank loans and commercial paper are a large share, rise rapidly while their interest income rises little since consumer lending rates are so sluggish. Some finance companies also face a reduction in the availability of funds during such periods because banks that are short of loanable funds often single out finance company credit lines as the area to be cut back. In addition, commercial paper tends to become difficult to market unless the seller maintains an excellent credit standing.

Because of lowered profitability and the reduced availability of funds, finance companies ration credit mainly by raising credit standards. This is quite effective in limiting their lending because their applicants span a wide range of creditworthiness. The result is that the higher-risk, and usually lower-income, consumers get rationed out. Thus charging relatively low rates and rationing loans have the same impact as usury ceilings on consumer loans. Low-risk, high-income consumers pay relatively low rates for their loans, while higher-risk, low-income consumers have difficulty gaining access to conventional sources of credit.

Sales finance companies, which do most of their consumer lending indirectly by purchasing consumer loans from auto and appliance dealers, could conceivably reduce their lending by dropping some of these dealers during tight money periods. But if they were to do so, they would lose the business from those dealers permanently because the disappointed dealers would turn to another source of funds. Therefore, if a sales finance company intends to retain its share of the market during times when lending is profitable, it must do its best to serve its dealers when money is tight. Dealers must then, in turn, limit their credit sales to the better credit risks. Some finance companies did discontinue purchasing mobile home "paper" entirely during the 1973-

74 tight money period even though this meant that they would have difficulty reentering that market if they decided to do so in the future. Mobile home paper had become less profitable than other consumer lending lines and it also absorbed a larger amount of funds per loan.

Other consumer lenders have also had diverse experiences in recent years. Savings banks and savings and loan associations in some states have been empowered to make consumer loans, and some of them aggressively competed with the commercial banks for better-risk loans. But they have been thwarted by their funds shortages during the recent periods of credit restraint. As a result some of them had to stop practically all such lending, and this made it difficult for them to regain a share of the market when fund supplies became more plentiful after 1974. Credit unions, however, have had substantial inflows of funds even in the tight money periods, because they paid somewhat higher rates on their savings than other institutions and they usually had the advantage of convenience as well. As a result, they did not have to ration their loans and they increased their share of the market substantially so that they are now approaching commercial banks in the growth of consumer loans.

V. IMPACT ON LENDERS

Discussions of credit rationing usually focus on the impact on borrowers— who gets credit under rationing and who does not. Often overlooked is the impact on lenders. Since rationing entails a lower interest rate than could be charged, it results in at least a short-term loss to lenders.

The chief lenders to business, commercial banks, probably suffer least among lenders who ration credit. They can generally recoup any loss of income resulting from low rates by making adjustments in other facets of customer service. In any case, during periods of tight credit yields on commercial bank assets, which are almost entirely short-term, rise rapidly (even though less rapidly than they could), while their average costs rise more slowly because a good share of their funds comes from demand deposits on which no interest is paid. As a result, their earnings increase; from 1972 to 1974, for example, the net earnings spread (gross income minus total expenses) of commercial banks rose from 0.66 percent of total assets to 0.81 percent.

Among consumer lenders, sales and consumer finance companies tend to have reductions in net income during periods of credit rationing. For example, net income of these companies declined from a base of 100 in 1972 to 85 in 1973 and 89 in 1974, according to data compiled by the Citibank of New York, while net income of commercial banks rose from 100 in 1972 to 118 in 1973 and 127 in 1974. Rates on consumer loans rise very sluggishly at such times but interest costs of finance companies rise rapidly because they rely heavily on short-term debt, both commercial paper and bank loans, on which rates rise substantially. With respect to their consumer loans, commercial banks are in somewhat the same situation, but consumer loans are a relatively small portion of their assets, just over 10 percent, while these loans are well over 50 percent of the assets of most sales and consumer finance companies.

The chief mortgage lenders, thrift institutions, are affected most severely during tight money periods. Their earning assets are mostly long-term mortgages on which the returns do not rise, of course, when current market rates rise. Therefore they cannot afford to raise rates paid on savings (and are in fact prevented from doing so by Regulation Q requirements). At such times depositors tend to withdraw their funds to invest in higher-yielding assets such as U.S. Treasury bills and notes.

As a result of such savings withdrawals, thrift institutions have few funds to invest. They parcel or ration their funds primarily into mortgages at lower rates than it would be possible to obtain from other investments. This limits their earnings growth, but only slightly because the amount of funds involved is usually very small at such times.

Although savings banks do not sacrifice much income by charging below market rates for home mortgages when their funds are short, they do forego a substantial amount of extra income in years when funds are plentiful by not investing in the highest-yielding assets. For example, since 1967, home mortgage rates have usually been below corporate bond rates on a net yield basis after mortgage servicing expenses. These servicing expenses amount to around ½ of 1 percent, so corporate bonds are more profitable than mortgages if their market yields are within ½ of 1 percent of mortgage yields. Bond yields since late 1967 have usually been within that range of home mortgage yields and, in fact, exceeded mortgage yields in 1969, 1970, 1971, 1974, and 1975. Therefore, for maximum income, savings banks should have invested only in corporate bonds over this period or raised their mortgage lending rate to an equivalent net yield level. In some of these years, notably 1970 through 1972, savings banks had substantial amounts of deposit inflows to invest, so they sacrificed a good deal of income by placing the major part of their available funds into mortgages. This form of rationing is explained by the same factors that lay behind rationing of mortgage loans to customers —savings banks had to maintain their image as "people's institutions."

Another current influence which compounds the earnings problem of thrift institutions is the array of governmental restrictions and programs which are aimed at holding down mortgage rates. Usury ceilings, discussed earlier, are one example. Other rate-depressing actions include the activities of various government and government-sponsored agencies such as the Federal National Mortgage Association, the Government National Mortgage Association, and the Federal Home Loan Mortgage Corporation. These agencies obtain funds from the U.S. Treasury or by borrowing in the credit market and they then channel these funds into the single-family home mortgage market with the express purpose of holding down mortgage rates. This results, of course, in reduced earnings of thrift institutions and serves to weaken their financial positions, particularly in the case of federally chartered savings and loan institutions which do not have the power to invest in corporate bonds as well. While these government efforts to hold down mortgage rates are not directly connected with rationing, the same concept lies behind them, namely, that high mortgage rates should be opposed, whatever the general level or trend of interest rates. Such a public policy attitude must be altered if thrift institutions are to continue to be healthy and viable institutions.

Thrift institutions are, however, modifying their lending behavior as a result of these experiences. Savings banks, which are not restricted to mortgage lending to the same extent as savings and loan associations, have been investing about three-quarters of their net funds inflows since 1974 in bonds. Also, since 1973 both types of thrift institutions have raised their mortgage lending rates somewhat more rapidly when credit markets showed signs of tightening, as seen in the chart. Finally, many thrift institutions are actively selling off the mortgage loans they originate to the government-sponsored agencies. As thrifts do this, they will be forced to raise their rates to keep up with rates in this resale market to avoid a capital loss. As seen in the chart, rates in the secondary market fluctuate more widely than primary rates for conventional loans.

SUMMARY

Credit rationing occurs during tight money periods in mortgage, business, and consumer loan markets because lenders are reluctant to raise interest rates as rapidly as market conditions might indicate, and so must use non-price criteria to distribute scarce funds. Credit rationing is a phenomenon understood by lenders and borrowers alike, despite the nontangible aspects of some of its operations. It may be characterized as one of the costs of contracyclical monetary policy, with the highest price paid by new and high-risk ventures. But credit rationing may also be described as a sound business practice, operating in the best long-run interest of lenders and borrowers who have long-standing relationships.

The most pronounced form of credit rationing now takes place in the home mortgage loan market, where supplies of funds decrease sharply during a period of restraint due to disintermediation at thrift institutions. Funds shortages are not nearly as acute in the business and consumer loan markets, so that rationing is not as severe.

Methods of rationing differ among lenders, but the general pattern at thrift institutions has been to grant first priority to long-established depositors. Since they account for only a small fraction of mortgage loan applicants, this shuts out most would-be borrowers. Second priority is usually given to refinancing loans, while third are applicants referred by realtors and builders with whom the lender has a long-standing relationship. The business loan market differs from the mortgage loan market, in that most large commercial banks in periods of restraint do have access to additional funds to try to satisfy increased demands for business loans. However, commercial banks do not raise rates on business loans enough to reduce demand to the level of available funds, and they also do some rationing.

Rates in the consumer loan market are the most sluggish of the three loan areas. Because demands for such loans generally do not rise much and because severe funds shortages do not occur, drastic rationing is not necessary despite the rate sluggishness. Whatever rationing is needed is achieved by raising credit standards.

Generally lenders are affected only slightly by credit rationing because tight money periods tend to be relatively brief. But in recent years mortgage lenders, and in particular thrift institutions, have been burdened by a rationing effect even when credit was relatively plentiful; home mortgage rates have been kept below competitive levels by a variety of governmental programs, yet thrift institutions are pressured into channeling the bulk of their funds into this market. This has had a long-run unfavorable impact in their earnings, and has weakened their financial position and ability to attract savings.

RECENT FINANCIAL INNOVATIONS: Causes, Consequences for the Payments System, and Implications for Monetary Control

Marvin Goodfriend, James Parthemos, and Bruce J. Summers

33

The past two decades have been characterized by a number of significant innovations in the U. S. financial system, which today differs greatly from the system existing at the beginning of the 1960's. Today's financial intermediaries, including commercial banks, handle a much larger volume of business and generally serve broader geographic markets than their counterparts of two decades ago. They are also more competitive and more inclined to offer a greater variety of services in an effort to maintain or expand market shares. Moreover, some intermediaries, such as credit unions, now play a more important role in the nation's financial system, and entirely new types of intermediaries, such as money market funds, have emerged. Generally speaking, both the variety of institutions offering financial services and the array of such services have increased significantly, especially in recent years.

The expanding variety of services offered by financial intermediaries has been paralleled by an increased diversity of the liabilities of these institutions. Twenty years ago, for example, the liabilities side of a typical commercial bank's balance sheet was heavily weighted with demand deposits and regular savings deposits. Today's typical bank balance sheet shows a sizable reduction in the relative importance of such deposits and a sharp increase in so-called "purchased funds," i.e., negotiable certificates of deposit, nonnegotiable certificates of deposit, repurchase agreements, Federal funds purchased, and in the case of very large banks, perhaps Eurodollar borrowings as well. Likewise, regular savings deposits (deposit shares) typified the liabilities of

*Reprinted, with deletions, from the *Economic Review*, March/April 1980, pp. 14-27, with permission from the Federal Reserve Bank of Richmond.

515

savings and loan associations in the 1950's but today have given way in large measure to time certificates of deposit. Much the same can be said for credit unions and mutual savings banks.

The liabilities of financial intermediaries represent indebtedness to their customers—to households, business, and governmental units for the most part. Collectively, claims on these institutions make up the predominant fraction of the public's holdings of liquid assets. Of the several types of these liquid assets, the public's holdings of demand deposit claims at commercial banks have commanded particular attention because they have traditionally been the principal means of making payment. Until recently, demand deposits possessed an advantage in that they were immediately available for spending while other liquid claims could be spent only after being converted into coin, currency, or demand deposits. For this reason, demand deposits along with coin and currency have been traditionally defined as "money" while other liquid claims at financial intermediaries have been considered to be money substitutes or "near money."

The outstanding volume of monetary assets at a given time and its rate of growth over time are important determinants of aggregate spending and inflation. Two statistical measures of the monetary aggregates, M_1 and M_2, have played an important role in the implementation of monetary policy since 1970. M_1, the measure of money narrowly defined, includes coin and currency in circulation outside the banking system and private demand deposits adjusted.[1] A broader measure, M_2, includes with M_1 time and savings deposits at commercial banks except for large denomination negotiable certificates of deposit.

FINANCIAL INNOVATION AND THE PAYMENTS SYSTEM

Recent innovations have had a direct impact on the payments system, i.e., on the types of assets and institutions involved in the consummation of payments between individual economic units. The payments system has historically comprised the nation's 14,500 commercial banks, a system of correspondent relations between individual banks, local clearing houses, and the Federal Reserve System. This network provides the machinery for transferring demand deposit claims between individual economic units. As mentioned above, until recently payments have been made almost exclusively with demand deposits or currency and coin.

As a result of recent innovations, claims on financial institutions other

---

[1] The demand deposit component of M_1 consists of (1) demand deposits at commercial banks other than domestic interbank and U. S. government demand deposits, less cash items in process of collection and Federal Reserve float and (2) foreign demand balances at Federal Reserve Banks.

than commercial banks are being used to make payments. For several years it has been possible to transfer funds from savings accounts in thrifts to bank checking accounts by telephone, or to use these funds to make prearranged third-party payments. Effective in 1981, commercial banks and thrift institutions will offer Negotiable Order of Withdrawal (NOW) accounts. NOW accounts are a readily transferable means of payment. Share drafts at credit unions have also become a means of payment. NOW accounts and share drafts, however, differ from demand deposits at commercial banks in that they bear interest. Hence, for the first time since 1933, when interest on demand deposits was prohibited by law, what amounts to interest-bearing demand deposits comprises part of the nation's payments medium. Moreover, since November 1, 1978, commercial banks have been allowed to cover their customers' overdrafts by automatically transferring funds from savings to checking accounts. This too allows the use of interest-bearing deposits for making payments.

The emergence of new types of assets that mediate transactions—that is, serve as money—pose special monetary control problems for the Federal Reserve System. A broadened spectrum of money and near money assets complicates the problem of determining an appropriate working statistical definition of money. Moreover, growth of monetary assets issued by institutions beyond the control of the central bank can significantly weaken the Federal Reserve's ability to control the monetary aggregates. The sections that follow contain detailed discussions of major factors promoting innovation, the innovations themselves, and their implications for monetary control.

SOME FACTORS PROMOTING INNOVATION

The rapid pace of financial innovation of recent years is due largely to three major factors. The first of these is the serious inflation the economy has suffered since 1965 and especially since 1973. The second is the rapid development of computer and communications technology. The third is a change in the regulatory environment dating from the early 1960's.

Inflation has accelerated the pace of financial innovation through its impact on interest rates. Inflation is an important determinant of the level of interest rates because the level of interest rates reflects anticipations of future inflation and anticipations roughly follow recent experience with inflation. When inflation has been high anticipations of inflation are also high; and when inflation has been low so are inflationary anticipations. Inflation has continually risen in recent years, so inflationary anticipations have risen as well. In this environment lenders have sought higher interest rates as compensation for the depreciating purchasing power of their savings. Borrowers competing for funds have been willing to pay higher interest rates because they can expect corresponding increases in income from investments financed through borrowings. Consequently, rising rates of inflation have led to higher interest rates.

High interest rates increase the opportunity cost of holding noninterest-bearing assets and encourage the economizing of such assets. An example of how this leads to innovation is seen in the case of commercial banks, which are required by law to hold reserves in the form of noninterest-bearing assets.[2] The interest foregone on these reserves, and hence the cost of holding them, rises with the level of market interest rates. In a period of high rates, banks try harder to reduce the amount of reserves required by law. Banks can do this by encouraging shifts in liabilities from categories like demand deposits, which have a relatively high reserve requirement, to categories for which lower, or even no, reserves are required. For example, they might offer to enter repurchase agreements with customers holding demand deposits. This involves selling the customer government securities under agreement to buy the securities back at a somewhat higher price (determined by prevailing market interest rates on such contracts) after a stipulated period, usually one to seven days. Such repurchase agreements (RP's) are liabilities of the bank to its customers, as are demand deposits. The difference is that unlike demand deposits, there are usually no reserve requirements imposed on RP's. Consequently, the bank in effect pays interest to the customer and simultaneously reduces its required reserves.

Commercial banks can achieve these results in a variety of other ways as well. Their efforts to do so have resulted in a significant diversification of bank liabilities, hence in the claims on banks held by bank customers. As mentioned above, the liabilities side of bank balance sheets now include, in much larger proportion than in the 1960's, RP's, Federal funds purchases, negotiable and nonnegotiable CD's, consumer type CD's, and in the case of large banks, Eurodollar borrowings and other liabilities to foreign branches. These liabilities all involve lower legal reserve requirements than demand deposits. To the extent that banks can find ways to convert demand deposit liabilities into these other forms, required reserves are reduced, allowing a given reserve to support a higher volume of both earning assets and liabilities.

High interest rates provide incentives for individuals and businesses to shift out of demand deposits and into these new types of bank liabilities. Hence, commercial banks and other financial institutions find a ready, indeed eager, market for new interest-bearing liquid substitutes for demand deposits that their ingenuity can devise. As a matter of fact, sharp-penciled corporate treasurers have been known to insist that their bankers stand ready to enter overnight repurchase agreements with them so that they can earn interest on balances that can be used rather promptly for making payments.

---

[2] Reserve balances of member banks held with the Federal Reserve are noninterest bearing. Nonmember banks hold reserves as specified by the individual states. A number of states allow various types of earning assets to satisfy their reserve requirements. However, during the 1980's, a uniform reserve system will be imposed on all depository institutions.

Arrangements allowing banks to reduce required reserves and the public to reduce its holdings of demand deposits are motivated simply by a desire to minimize individual costs of doing business. Unfortunately, however, the aggregate effect of these arrangements is the creation and rapid growth of highly liquid assets used by the public in place of demand deposits. As explained, this complicates monetary control.

The rapid development of computer and communications technology has given individual institutions the capacity to process massive amounts of data and to make transfers rapidly and efficiently. In many instances, sophisticated new equipment has resulted in sizable amounts of excess capacity, thereby creating incentives for expanding existing services and offering new kinds of services. In short, the revolution in computer and communications technology has played an important role in recent financial innovation.

Between the early 1930's and the 1960's, bank regulatory philosophy was dominated by a preoccupation with the soundness of individual institutions. Competition in banking was viewed as a double-edged sword, incorporating notable disadvantages as well as some generally accepted advantages in improving the quality of banking services to the public. Indeed, some bank regulations, such as the prohibition of the payment of interest on demand deposits and the limitation on interest payable on savings deposits, were designed explicitly to discourage competition.

In the early and middle 1960's major changes were made in Federal and state banking laws and regulations, most tending to encourage competition not only among banks but also between commercial banks and other financial institutions. With the introduction of the negotiable certificate of deposit in 1961, large commercial banks found a way to compete for short-term funds. Shortly afterwards, both large and small banks, which up to the 1960's had shown relatively little interest in consumer type savings deposits, began moving vigorously into this market. These moves ushered in an era of ever sharpening competition within the commercial banking community and between commercial banks and other financial intermediaries. Subsequent changes in bank holding company law, liberalization of regulations for thrift institutions, and a more competitive international banking climate reinforced this move to more intensive competition. In any case, there has been in the period after 1961 a more or less steady relaxation of regulatory constraints and a significant increase in competition among all types of financial institutions.[3]

The steady relaxation of regulatory constraints, however, has not always proceeded on the initiative of the regulators themselves. The NOW account case provides a simple illustration of this. The secular rise in interest rates

---

[3] An exception to this steady relaxation of regulatory constraints is the *Interest Adjustment Act* of 1966, which extended coverage of deposit rate ceilings to the thrift industry and established a differential between maximum rates that banks and thrifts could pay on deposits. This action was a direct result of the heightened competition for consumer deposits occurring in the early-and mid-1960's, which had resulted in a decline in thrift institution deposit growth relative to bank deposit growth.

in the late 1960's was especially troublesome for mutual savings banks. As legal ceilings on the interest they could pay became increasingly restrictive, their ability to compete for funds deteriorated and their deposit growth slowed. Federal law prohibited payment of interest on checking accounts, but the prohibition did not extend to mutual savings banks that were not insured by the FDIC. In 1970 a state-insured Massachusetts mutual savings bank, looking for a way to attract deposits, petitioned the state commissioner of banking for authority to offer NOW accounts. The petition was denied but, on appeal, the state supreme court overturned the denial on grounds that state law provided no restrictions on the form in which deposits could be withdrawn. With the public becoming increasingly aware of losses suffered by earning no interest on checking balances, Federal law authorized the issue of NOW accounts by commercial banks and thrift institutions first in the New England states, and later in all states effective in January 1981.

A REVIEW OF SPECIFIC DEVELOPMENTS

Table I is a roughly chronological listing of innovations that have permitted the public to reduce its reliance on demand deposits. The influence of each of these developments on the management of payments balances by businesses and households is described below.

Corporate Cash Management

Like other economic units, businesses have an incentive to minimize cash held for payments purposes. Doing so is a complex task, however, especially for large corporations whose operations are widely diversified geographically and by product line. A number of specialized cash management techniques have been developed to improve the efficiency with which money positions are managed. Some of these techniques, e.g., cash flow forecasting and internal accounting control systems, are available in-house or through nonbank vendors. Because of their central role in the payments process, however, commercial banks are the most important suppliers of corporate cash management services. Bank sponsored cash management systems are designed to accelerate collections into a large firm's regional checking accounts and then to further concentrate demand deposits into one account used to pay bills and fund short-term investments. The key elements in such a system include cash concentration, disbursement, and investment management.

The first step in cash concentration is development of a collection system for funds based on a group of local and regional banking organizations selected for their proximity either to the firm's field operations or to its customers.

Table I

SUMMARY OF REGULATORY, LEGISLATIVE, AND TECHNICAL DEVELOPMENTS ENABLING THE PUBLIC TO REDUCE ITS RELIANCE ON NONINTEREST-BEARING DEMAND DEPOSITS

Development	Date or Period	Description
(1) Corporate cash management services	post-World War II	Corporate cash management services, for example, lockboxes, cash-concentration accounts, and information-retrieval systems, are technical innovations permitting more efficient management of cash balances. Their introduction by commercial banks goes back many years, although such services came to be used much more widely after World War II.
(2) Negotiable certificates of deposit (CD's)	1961	Negotiable CD's are marketable receipts for funds deposited in a bank for a specified period at a specified rate of interest. This instrument was originated in 1961 by a large money center bank.
(3) Savings accounts for state and local governments and businesses	1960's, 11/74, 11/75	Federally chartered savings and loan associations have been authorized to offer local governments and businesses savings accounts since the 1960's. Commercial banks were authorized to accept savings deposits from local governments starting November 1974 and from businesses (up to $150,000) starting November 1975.
(4) Telephone transfers from savings accounts	1960's, 4/75	Telephone transfers allow savings account customers to transfer funds either to checking accounts or to third parties by phone. Federal savings and loan associations have had this authority since the 1960's, whereas banks were granted it in April 1975.
(5) Repurchase agreements (RP's)	1969	Repurchase agreements are primarily short-term contracts for the purchase of immediately available funds collateralized by securities. RP's grew rapidly beginning in 1969 after Regulation D was amended to explicitly exempt from reserve requirements RP's backed by the sale of U. S. Government or Federal agency securities.
(6) Preauthorized third-party transfers	9/70, 4/75, 9/75	Preauthorized transfers are payments made from savings accounts for recurring transactions. Savings and loan associations were permitted to make preauthorized nonnegotiable transfers from savings accounts to third parties for household-related expenditures in September 1970 and for any purpose beginning in April 1975. Commercial banks were permitted to make preauthorized nonnegotiable transfers from savings accounts to third parties for any purpose in September 1975.
(7) Negotiable Order of Withdrawal (NOW) accounts	5/72, 9/72, 1/74 3/76, 10/78, 12/79	NOW accounts are savings accounts from which payments can be made by draft. State-chartered mutual savings banks began offering NOW accounts in Massachusetts after a May 1972 state court ruling authorizing such deposits. NOW's were offered by state-chartered mutual savings banks in New Hampshire in September 1972 with the approval of the state bank commissioner. Beginning January 1974 Congress authorized all depository institutions in the two above mentioned states to offer NOW's. Beginning March 1976, Congress authorized NOW's at all depository institutions in Connecticut, Maine, Rhode Island, and Vermont, authority that was extended to New York in November 1978 and nationwide effective January 1981.
(8) Savings and loan remote service units (RSU's)	1/74	RSU's are machines that allow a customer to make deposits to, and withdrawals from, his savings account at stores and other places away from the institution maintaining the account. The Federal Home Loan Bank Board authorized RSU's in January 1974. Although ruled illegal in April 1979, Congress subsequently passed legislation legalizing the service until April 1, 1980.
(9) Money market funds (MMF's)	early 1974	Money market funds are mutual funds specializing in short-term investments from which shares can be redeemed by checks drawn on designated commercial banks, or by wire transfer, telephone, or mail. Use of MMF's became widespread beginning in early 1974.
(10) Credit union share drafts	10/74, 3/78	Credit union share drafts are payments made directly from share accounts. An experimental share draft program was approved for Federal credit unions in October 1974 and made permanent in March 1978. Although ruled illegal in April 1979, Congress subsequently passed legislation legalizing the service
(11) Preauthorized savings to checking transfers	11/78	Commercial banks were allowed to offer customers automatic savings to checking transfers starting November 1978. This led to the widespread offering of automatic transfer services (ATS), which are essentially zero-balance checking accounts fed from savings accounts. Although ruled illegal in April 1979, Congress subsequently passed legislation legalizing the service

Customers are instructed to mail their payments to a lockbox under the control of a local bank, which collects remittances and credits the firm's checking account. Information on the amount of collected balances in these local depositories is gathered by telephone, and then a depository transfer check (DTC) is written payable to an account in a regional "concentration" bank and drawn on the various local banks. The DTC, which is a nonnegotiable check that requires no signature, is commonly used to transfer funds between a corporation's accounts held in different banks. Since the DTC can be deposited in the regional concentration bank immediately after account balances are ascertained by phone, overnight credit is available as long as the regional bank and local depositories are all located in the same Federal Reserve regional check processing area. The regional bank can then wire the collected funds to the corporation's master checking account held at a bank in the home office city.

Disbursement of corporate funds can be centralized, all checks being written from the master account, or decentralized, with separate divisions of the company making payments in their respective localities. Centralized cash control can be maintained even in a decentralized check-writing environment using zero-balance accounts. Under this system, a company's disbursing agents write checks on designated disbursing accounts maintained at regional banks and having zero balances. Debit balances accumulate in these zero-balance disbursing accounts as checks are written and are offset by charges made on the corporation's master account.

Integral to the concept of corporate cash management is a prompt reporting system that monitors, and perhaps even forecasts, cash flow. Information contained in a reporting system would consist of detailed transactions data, including transfer activity between accounts and daily bank balances. The ultimate objective of such a reporting system is to provide information on the amount of money available for short-term investment.

Negotiable CD's

As corporations became more adept at cash management during the 1950's, their investable bank balances increased significantly. Rather than holding idle demand deposits, short-term investments offering high liquidity and low risk were sought. Since few banks offered corporations interest-bearing deposits as alternatives to checking balances, businesses turned to other investment sources, particularly commercial paper, Treasury bills, and repurchase agreements with securities dealers. Consequently, there was a sharp decline in the importance of corporate deposits on the banking system's balance sheet. Large money center banks especially felt this loss of funds since they relied on corporate demand deposits to a greater extent than other, smaller banks. This situation prompted First National City Bank of New York to introduce in February 1961 the large negotiable certificate of deposit (negotiable CD), a new liability specifically designed to attract corporate funds.

Regulations limit negotiable CD's to a minimum maturity of 14 days. Although relatively short, this maturity is still unattractive to businesses seeking an investment outlet that allows quick conversion back to demand deposits. When first introduced in 1961, therefore, it was also announced that a major government securities dealer had agreed to make a secondary market in negotiable CD's. This secondary market makes negotiable CD's an attractive substitute for demand deposits. Corporations holding CD's can sell these in the secondary market at any time to raise cash, while firms desiring investments with maturities shorter than 14 days can acquire CD's with remaining terms to maturity that fit their liquidity needs. The marketability of prime CD's issued by large well known banks is generally greater than that for those issued by lesser known regional institutions. For this reason, investment in money center bank CD's is favored by corporations.

Negotiable CD's possess some characteristics that limit their attractiveness to corporate money managers. In particular, CD's are not nearly as homogeneous (in terms of rates, denominations, and other contractual features) as are, say, Treasury bills. Also, dealers mainly trade prime CD's in denominations of $1 million and will rarely split or consolidate certificates to facilitate a secondary market transaction. For these reasons, negotiable CD's may not always exactly fit the short-term investment needs of corporations. These limitations notwithstanding, negotiable CD's have become a major source of bank funds.

Repurchase Agreements

Repurchase agreements (RP's) represent a particularly useful instrument for cash management that has become widely used only in the last few years. RP's are income-generating assets having a very low credit risk that are available in maturities as short as one day. Commercial banks became active suppliers of RP's after 1969 and now offer them as part of the cash management systems marketed to corporations.

Businesses having cash concentration systems are able to determine the amount of investable balances available in their checking accounts each morning. If funds are available to invest for only a very short period, they can be placed in the overnight or one-day RP market. To facilitate placement of idle checking balances in the RP market, an investment technique known as the continuing contract has been developed. Under this type of arrangement, a corporation agrees to provide its bank with a specific volume of funds to be automatically reinvested each day for a specified period. Continuing contracts in RP's reduce transactions costs since funds are exchanged only at the beginning and end of the contract period. Liquidity is preserved, however, since either the corporation or the bank can cancel the contract before maturity. Similar to the continuing contract is the preauthorized transfer arrangement. Under the latter arrangement, banks automatically invest a corporation's master checking account funds above a specified minimum in RP's.

The RP market has grown dramatically in recent years, especially the market for very short-term RP's. A special survey of 46 money center banks conducted in December 1977 showed RP's outstanding to nonfinancial businesses of $10.5 billion—31 percent under one-day contract, 11 percent under continuing contract, 22 percent under two- to seven-day contract, and 28 percent under eight- to thirty-day contract. Another $3.8 billion was outstanding to state and local governments, which, like corporations, are active cash managers. The majority of state and local government RP's are either one-day or continuing contracts. Banks indicate that activity in the RP market has increased greatly since 1977.

Savings Accounts for Business

Since a fairly large minimum investment is necessary in negotiable CD's and RP's, these instruments are not generally suited to the requirements of smaller businesses. An amendment to Regulation Q, effective November 10, 1975, has permitted businesses to hold savings accounts at commercial banks, subject to a ceiling limit of $150,000. This change was made to provide an investment outlet to small businesses holding temporarily idle funds. Such balances reached $10.5 billion by June 1979.

Savings and loan associations have been able to offer savings accounts to businesses for many years. Although data on the size of such balances are not available, indications are that they do not make up a large share of savings and loan liabilities.

Telephone and Preauthorized Third-Party Transfers
From Savings Accounts

Use of bank savings accounts by individuals has had the disadvantage in the past of necessitating personal trips to the bank in order to transfer funds to and from checking accounts. This inconvenience was at least partly reduced by 1975 changes in Regulation Q, allowing banks to transfer funds from savings accounts directly to checking or to third parties on the telephone-originated order of a customer, and also to pay recurring bills directly from savings accounts on a preauthorized basis. Telephone transfers to third parties have been authorized at savings and loan associations since the 1960's, while preauthorized third-party transfers for general purposes have been allowed since 1975.

The effect of these regulatory changes has probably been to increase the substitutability between checking and savings accounts. There is no way to measure directly the impact of telephone and preauthorized transfer services on cash management policies of households or businesses. Savings deposit turnover data do show signs of increasing since 1977, the first year they were collected; and it may be that telephone and preauthorized transfer services have encouraged greater use of savings accounts as payments balances.

There are two features of savings accounts that may discourage their use as demand deposit substitutes. First, in the case of direct bill paying from savings, the customer does not have a cancelled check as a record of payments. This is significant because studies of consumer attitudes toward electronic fund transfer (EFT) services have found a deep-seated reluctance to give up the record-keeping services that cancelled checks provide. Second, banks and thrift institutions typically levy charges on savings account withdrawals above some monthly or quarterly minimum. These charges can be fairly substantial, running sometimes 25 to 50 cents per transfer, thereby raising a cost barrier to heavy use of savings transfers.

NOW Accounts and Share Drafts

NOW's are negotiable drafts written on savings accounts at banks, mutual savings banks, and savings and loan associations. Share drafts are written on accounts at credit unions. The use of both NOW's and share drafts is limited by law to individuals only. While both are in practice honored as demand drafts, they are legally time drafts on which financial institutions have the right to delay payment for up to 30 days. NOW's offered by thrift institutions and share drafts are "payable through" instruments, i.e., they are cleared through normal check-clearing channels and are paid by a commercial bank with which the issuing thrift institution maintains a correspondent relationship. Federal law limits interest payments to NOW accounts to 5.25 percent for banks and 5.50 percent for thrifts with the exception of credit unions. The latter are permitted to pay the regular share account rate on balances subject to draft, currently 7 percent.

NOW accounts have been an important catalytic force causing changes in public attitudes toward cash management. This financial innovation, however, has by no means completely altered the public's money management habits. When it passed legislation in 1974 allowing NOW's throughout New England, Congress in a sense created a test of interest-bearing payment accounts. The results of this test show that the public is receptive to interest-bearing payments balances; and also that pricing policies as well as the degree of competition between financial institutions influence the spread of the new service.

Savings and Loan Remote Service Units

A remote service unit (RSU) is defined by the Federal Home Loan Bank Board as an information-processing device, and an RSU account is a savings account accessible through such a device. RSU's can be located directly on sites where frequent payments occur, e.g., the supermarket. Since RSU's are not considered branches, there are few administrative barriers to their establishment by savings and loans.

Money Market Funds

Money market funds (MMF's) were first offered to the public in 1972; but their importance, as measured by growth in number of shareholders and balances in shareholder accounts, increased rapidly only after 1974, and especially in the late 1970s and early 1980s.[4] MMF's offer individuals and businesses having relatively small amounts of funds access to open market investments that in the past were available only to large corporations.

It is reasonable to think of MMF's as being at least partial substitutes for demand deposits. Like savings accounts, they offer high liquidity, since fund shares can be purchased or sold on any business day without a sales charge. Moreover, some MMF's offer a checking option that enables shareholders to write checks in minimum amounts of $500. MMF's, however, appear to have more in common with savings than with demand deposit accounts. Evidence of this is the similarity of turnover rates in MMF accounts and bank savings accounts, both of which are very low compared to turnover rates for checking deposits.

Automatic Transfer Services

Automatic transfer services (ATS) allow depositors to arrange with their banks the automatic transfer of funds from an interest-bearing savings account to a checking account and are the functional equivalent of NOW accounts and share drafts. ATS is a direct substitute for traditional checking balances and has been authorized on a nationwide basis for all commercial banks.

A Summary Overview

Although the developments reviewed above take various forms, there are some general patterns underlying the changes in the payments system during

---

[4] The assets of money market funds increased from about $4 billion in 1974 to over $115 billion in early 1981. (Ed. footnote)

the past several decades. As noted earlier, many changes in the payments system have resulted from a combination of regulatory and legal actions, but it appears that private initiative has been the primary force leading to financial innovation. A number of these innovations, including corporate cash management services, negotiable CD's, repurchase agreements, NOW accounts, and money market funds, came into existence without any prerequisite changes in banking regulations or law. Subsequent regulatory or legal action has been important in encouraging the development of some of the newly introduced services, but it is not clear that such official action would have occurred without the impetus provided by private initiative.

Competition in the financial markets explains a large part of the private initiative in the payments system. Given a competitive environment for financial services, financial innovations that are demand deposit substitutes and pay interest, or that pay interest and can be quickly converted to cash, offer opportunities to aggressive banks and thrifts seeking to increase their shares of the deposit market.

The earliest innovations primarily benefited businesses, since businesses generally operate on a larger scale than do individuals and consequently maintain larger average transactions balances with a significantly greater potential gain from efficient management. Also, in the period following World War II, businesses operated with much higher ratios of transaction balances to total financial assets than did individuals. In 1950, for example, the ratio of currency plus demand deposits to total financial assets was about 60 percent for nonfinancial businesses compared to about 25 percent for households. Having a relatively large share of financial assets tied up in noninterest-earning form, businesses had the greater incentive to find ways of improving cash management procedures. Threatened with the loss of corporate deposits to open market debt instruments, the banking industry responded to these improved cash management practices by providing short-term investment opportunities. Thus, the 1960's witnessed the introduction of two new bank liabilities that provide businesses a positive interest return as well as high liquidity, namely negotiable CD's and RP's.

If the 1960's was the decade of business insofar as cash management is concerned, then the 1970's may have been the decade of the consumer. A number of services designed to facilitate efficient management of liquid balances by households were introduced at banks and thrift institutions in the 1970's. First in this group were telephone and preauthorized third-party transfer services from savings accounts. These were followed by NOW accounts, share drafts, ATS, and money market funds. With the exception of money market funds, all of these services rely on the use of interest-bearing savings accounts for direct third-party payments.

On the whole, the innovations which have been described here, taken both individually and collectively, are needlessly complex. For instance, RP's used by businesses and ATS accounts used by consumers entail constant switching of funds between interest-bearing accounts and noninterest-bearing demand deposit accounts. These two services facilitate the circumvention of the prohibition of interest on demand deposits, but they require a greater investment in management time and data processing than do checking accounts. The ingenuity of the financial markets in developing alternatives to demand deposits has resulted in a bewildering array of new monetary assets.

CHANGES IN BANK LIABILITIES AND THE PUBLIC'S LIQUID ASSETS

To what degree has payments system innovation affected the balance sheets of the banking system and the nonbank public? The paragraphs below present some statistical evidence indicating the extent of change in the nonbank public's total holdings of financial assets and in the composition of bank liabilities.

Changes in the Public's Financial Assets

There has been a significant reduction in the relative importance of traditional money balances in the public's holdings of liquid assets. The ratio of demand deposits plus currency and coin to this total plus time deposits and credit market instruments is shown for the household and the nonfinancial business sectors in Chart 1. The chart indicates a more or less steady decline in the relative importance of traditional money balances for both sectors since 1950. For the nonfinancial business sector the decline has been especially sharp since 1970, with traditional money balances falling from 56 percent of the total in that year to 39 percent in 1978.

For the household sector (including personal trusts and nonprofit organizations) the decline has been considerably less sharp. As a matter of fact, the fraction of the total in traditional money declined more sharply between 1950 and 1965 than in the period since the latter year and remained fairly stable until 1974. Since that time, however, a noticeable downtrend appears to have developed. For households, the fraction of financial assets held in traditional money form fell from 25 percent in 1950 to 15 percent in 1965 and 12 percent in 1978. For the period since 1970, it appears that financial innovations have had a greater effect on the composition of the liquid holdings of businesses than on those of households.

Changes in Bank Liabilities

The liabilities structure of the commercial banking system has been significantly altered as a result of the public's efforts to economize on noninter-

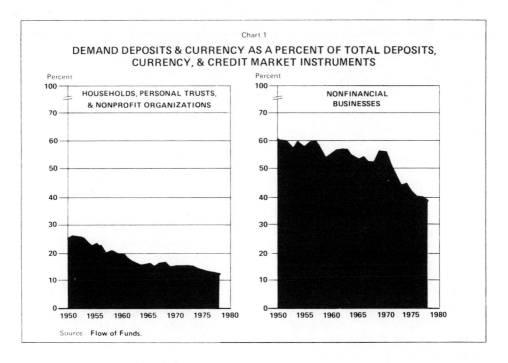

Chart 1

DEMAND DEPOSITS & CURRENCY AS A PERCENT OF TOTAL DEPOSITS,
CURRENCY, & CREDIT MARKET INSTRUMENTS

Source. Flow of Funds.

est-earning cash balances. The major change has been a decline in the relative importance of demand deposits compared with net total bank liabilities.[5] For example, private demand deposits declined from 63 percent of net total liabilities in 1960 to just over 31 percent in 1978. This large drop in the ratio of private demand deposits to net total liabilities, which is shown in Chart 2, reflects a major shift in public preferences from noninterest-earning demand balances to time balances and other short-term liabilities such as CD's and RP's. Recalling Chart 1, it appears that since 1970 businesses have economized on money balances more than households. This conclusion is also supported by a comparison of the growth rates in demand deposits held by these two groups. The compound annual rate of growth of household demand deposits over the eight-year period 1970-1978 was 8.3 percent, about a third greater than the 6.2 percent rate for business deposits.

Chart 2 shows that, as the share of demand deposits to net total liabilities has declined, the shares of time deposits other than negotiable CD's, nonnegotiable CD's, and purchased funds have all increased. From their inception in 1961, negotiable CD's have grown to nearly 10 percent of net total liabilities. Purchased funds, defined to include Federal funds and repurchase agreements, have in only ten years grown to such an extent that they equaled nearly 9 percent of the commercial banking system's liabilities in 1978.

[5] Net total liabilities are defined as total liabilities exclusive of deposits due to other commercial banks.

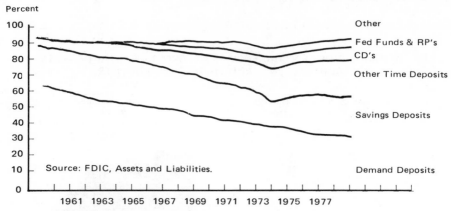

Chart 2

SELECTED SOURCES OF FUNDS AS A PERCENT OF THE COMMERCIAL
BANKING SYSTEM'S NET TOTAL LIABILITIES*

Savings deposits declined in importance as a source of funds until 1974, falling from 25 to 18 percent of net total liabilities. After the 1975 regulatory change which allowed businesses to hold savings accounts, however, savings balances gained moderately in importance, reaching 22 percent of net total liabilities in 1978.

The chart shows a steadily increasing concentration of bank liabilities in those forms not subject to Regulation Q interest rate ceilings. Negotiable CD's and purchased funds are largely free of deposit rate regulation and, therefore, offer the public particularly attractive alternatives to holding sterile demand deposit or low-earning savings deposit balances. Demand and savings deposits combined, which at one time dominated the liabilities side of bank balance sheets, have fallen in relative importance from 90 percent of total liabilities in 1960 to only 53 percent in 1978.

FINANCIAL INNOVATION AND MONETARY CONTROL

Roughly speaking, monetary control means management of the supply of money balances held by the public at depository institutions. The Federal Reserve is concerned with the management of aggregate money balances because these balances are a major determinant of aggregate spending. Aggregate expenditure by the public is, in turn, a key determinant of employment and the rate of inflation. The financial innovations described earlier appear to have interfered with the Federal Reserve's ability to control money growth. A simple view of monetary control is set out below to illustrate the channels through which this interference has been felt.

Control Problems Due to Financial Innovation

The Federal Reserve controls the money supply primarily by buying and selling Treasury securities. Payments made by the Federal Reserve when it purchases securities contribute to what is known as the monetary base. The monetary base consists of currency plus the reserves of the banking system. Since banks hold reserves that are only a fraction of their deposits, each dollar of reserves in the banking system supports several dollars' worth of deposits.

The stock of demand deposits in the banking system constitutes the bulk of what is called the basic money supply or M_1. M_1 has historically served as the nation's payments medium or transactions balances, i.e., money held for the purpose of making payments. Because of its relation to expenditure, M_1 is an important monetary aggregate for the Federal Reserve to control.

To provide a framework for analysis of monetary control, M_1 may be thought of as the product of the stock of base money times a coefficient, m, called the money multiplier, i.e., M_1 = m × [base money]. The Federal Reserve cannot control M_1 directly. Instead, it must do so indirectly by buying or selling Treasury securities to manipulate the stock of base money. For example, if the Federal Reserve wants to raise M_1 by $100 and the money multiplier, m, is 10, it would need to buy $10 worth of Treasury securities to bring about the desired $100 increase.

The Federal Reserve can exercise reasonably close control over the supply of transactions balances by operating on the stock of base money, relying on a relatively predictable money multiplier to achieve the desired results on M_1. However, the rapid pace of financial innovation has made the task more difficult. First, growth of interest-bearing substitutes for demand deposits and currency has made M_1 a less accurate measure of total transactions balances; and second, growth of these substitutes is difficult to predict. Moreover, good data coverage is not yet available because not all financial institutions offering transactions balances are required to report to the Federal Reserve. Therefore, the Federal Reserve does not know whether to interpret a change in M_1 as a change in total transactions balances or simply a substitution by the public of some newly created short-term asset for demand deposits. This means that even if the money multiplier were to remain relatively stable, it would be difficult for the Federal Reserve to know how the stock of base money should be manipulated to affect total transactions balances because M_1 has become a less reliable measure of such balances.

Unfortunately, the money multiplier is not even invariant with respect to substitutions from demand deposits into other types of liquid assets. The reason is that current law requires banks to hold reserves against demand deposits (at graduated rates of 7 to 16¼ percent) that are higher than reserve requirements on demand deposit substitutes. Reserve requirements on NOW accounts, for example, are only 3 percent. This means that if depositors shift from demand deposits to NOW accounts or RP's, excess reserves are created which enable the financial system to expand loans and increase its deposit liabilities. In other words, the money multiplier (for an appropriate measure of transactions balances) can rise with a shift from demand deposits to NOW accounts or RP's because of the different reserve requirements on these liabilities. If reserve requirements on the substituted liabilities remain low, the money multiplier will become very large. A larger multiplier is likely to have greater prediction error, and therefore is likely to make controlling money growth more difficult.

Even changes in the level of interest rates can induce changes in the money multiplier. Higher interest rates, for example, provide additional incentive for individuals and corporations to take advantage of interest-bearing substitutes for demand deposits. Compounding the problem is the fact that the short-run willingness of the public to substitute into interest-earning assets or alternative transactions balances is uncertain. The speed of substitution most likely depends, for example, on the time horizon over which individuals anticipate interest rates to remain high. Because average required reserves are decreased or increased as a result of these substitutions, the M_1 money multiplier can rise and fall with interest rates. However, because the degree of substitution is uncertain, so is the relationship between interest rates and the multiplier. Greater uncertainty about the multiplier makes it more difficult for the Federal Reserve to control M_1 through control of the monetary base.

The apparent weakening of Federal Reserve control over the volume of transactions balances has spawned a number of proposals for basic reform to improve the quality of the System's money control mechanism. A brief critique of those proposals designed to improve monetary control is presented in the sections that follow.

Extending the Coverage of Legal Reserve Requirements[6]

Shifts between deposit instruments with different reserve requirements account for much of the unpredictability in the money multiplier. Extending uniform reserve requirements to all transactions balances at commercial banks would therefore be useful in improving monetary control. However, if regulators continued to impose significantly lower reserve requirements on deposits held outside commercial banks, it would be of only limited value. Deposit institutions whose transactions-type accounts are nonreservable will be able to offer interest rates above those of institutions that must hold a larger portion of their funds in noninterest-earning required reserves. Non-

---

[6] Subsequent to the publication of this article, the proposals discussed in this section were enacted. Under the provisions of the Depository Institutions Deregulation and Monetary Control Act of 1980, uniform reserve requirements will be imposed on transaction accounts offered by *all* depository institutions. The requirements will be phased in during the 1980's. The Act also requires that interest rate ceilings be phased out by 1986. (Ed. footnote)

reservable balances would therefore tend to drive reservable balances out of use. The resulting money multiplier between the stock of transactions balances and the monetary base would consequently be much higher. Controlling the stock of transactions balances with the monetary base would be more difficult, because each dollar error in controlling the base would then have a greater effect on the stock of transactions balances.

Radical expansion in the usual coverage of reserve requirements would appear to be necessary to eliminate different reserve requirements among potential transactions balances while at the same time preventing the money multiplier from increasing. The problem is to devise a law that would allow only those deposits not used as transactions balances to qualify as nonreservable. For example, the law might state that customer orders to transfer funds be delayed at least a week for an account to qualify as nonreservable. But this rule might be circumvented by setting up revolving certificates maturing every eight days, so that one-eighth of the account could be transferred on any business day. This simple example illustrates the potential difficulty in enforcing a law requiring all balances used for transactions purposes to have the same reserve requirements as demand deposits.

Removal of Regulatory Ceilings on Interest Rates

If prohibitions against offering competitive rates of interest at depository institutions were eliminated, then interest rates on deposits at these institutions would tend to move more closely with the general level of interest rates. For example, interest differentials between deposits and other liquid assets such as money market mutual funds would become more stable. This would greatly reduce the incentive to switch from transactions type deposits to higher yielding liquid assets when interest rates rise.

Monetary control would be improved for two reasons as a result of this regulatory reform. First, because there would be less switching among liquid assets with changes in the level of interest rates, a given stock of bank reserves would produce a more stable basic money supply, M_1. Second, because the incentive for use of alternative types of transactions balances would be reduced, M_1, would become a more comprehensive measure of transactions balances. The Federal Reserve's data on transactions balances would become more reliable since it would not, as it currently does, depend on an estimate of the extent to which newly created liquid assets such as RP's or MMF's are being used as transactions balances.

Financial intermediation for banks involves longer maturities on assets than liabilities. Consequently, average returns on bank assets that provide income to pay interest on demand deposits change more slowly than short-term interest rates. Therefore, even if deposits were to pay interest, deposit rates may not move perfectly together with other short-term rates. However, the level of interest rates over longer periods of time varies largely because of changes in inflationary anticipations. The effect of anticipated inflation is reflected in all interest rates. Therefore, rates paid on demand deposits would move in line with other rates on a secular basis. As a result, paying interest on demand deposits would greatly improve the secular stability of the money multiplier and facilitate long-run monetary control.

Lowering the Long-run Rate of Money Growth

Since the rate of money growth is a major determinant of the long-run rate of inflation, the secular rate of inflation can be lowered if reasonably low secular money growth is maintained. A lower rate of inflation would reduce interest rates. As a result, incentives to substitute new forms of interest-bearing transactions balances for traditional demand deposits would be reduced, even if interest payments on the latter continue to be prohibited. The consequent reduction in financial innovation would greatly facilitate monetary control.

CONCLUSION

This article has highlighted some important causes and consequences of the rapid pace of financial innovation of recent years, especially as it relates to the nation's payments system. First, high market interest rates, different reserve requirements on various types of deposits, and legal restrictions on the payment of interest on demand deposits have together provided increased incentive for the market to create and use new kinds of deposit liabilities. Second, rapid development of computer and communications technology has contributed to this outcome. Third, regulators have allowed greater competition among financial institutions, thereby promoting more rapid innovation.

Because financial innovation involves creation of money substitutes, it causes problems for monetary control. In particular, difficulty in forecasting growth of demand deposit substitutes reduces the predictability of the money multiplier. In addition, since data on demand deposit substitutes are limited, it is hard to know the extent of their use, and consequently, it is hard to estimate the total stock of money.

Fortunately, reforms can ease this monetary control problem. The most important of these include extending the coverage of legal reserve requirements to all deposits used as payments balances and removing restrictions on interest payable on deposits. Adoption of these reforms should go a long way toward improving monetary control.

REFERENCES

1. "A Proposal for Redefining the Monetary Aggregates." Study by the staff of the Board of Governors of the Federal Reserve System. *Federal Reserve Bulletin* (January 1979) pp. 13-42.

2. Cagan, Phillip. "Financial Developments and the Erosion of Monetary Controls." Reprint from American Enterprise Institute, *Contemporary Economic Problems*, 1979.

3. Cook, Timothy Q., and Duffield, Jeremy G. "Money Market Mutual Funds: A Reaction to Government Regulation or a Lasting Financial Innovation?" *Economic Review*, Federal Reserve Bank of Richmond (July/August 1979), pp. 15-31.

4. Kimball, Ralph C. "The Maturing of the NOW Account in New England," *New England Economic Review*, Federal Reserve Bank of Boston (July/August 1978), pp. 27-42.

5. Summers, Bruce J. "Demand Deposits: A Comparison of the Behavior of Household and Business Balances." *Economic Review*, Federal Reserve Bank of Richmond (July/August 1979), pp. 2-14.

MONEY MARKET MUTUAL FUNDS: A Reaction to Government Regulations or A Lasting Financial Innovation?*

Timothy Q. Cook and
Jeremy G. Duffield

34

One of the most remarkable changes in the nation's financial system in recent years has been the rapid growth of money market mutual funds (MMFs).[1] These funds are open-end investment companies that invest only in short-term money market instruments.

The general operating characteristics of MMFs are fairly standard, although there are some differences. Investors purchase and redeem MMF shares without paying a sales charge. Expenses of the funds are deducted daily from gross income. Minimum initial investments for most funds vary from $500 to $5,000, although a very small number of funds require no minimum and others, designed for institutional investors only, require minimums of $50,000 or more. The yield paid to the shareholder of a MMF depends primarily on the yields of the securities held by the fund but is also dependent on the expenses of the fund and its accounting policies. Most funds have a checking option that enables shareholders to write checks of $500 or more. Shares can also be redeemed at most MMFs by telephone or wire request, in which case payment by the MMF is either mailed to the investor or remitted by wire to the investor's bank account.

The purpose of this article is to examine the reasons underlying the explosive growth of MMFs. There are two explanations for this growth, both stressing a different broad function served by MMFs. The first explana-

*Reprinted, with deletions, from the *Economic Review,* July/August 1979, pp. 15-31, with permission from the Federal Reserve Bank of Richmond.

[1] In 1974, the assets of MMFs were about $4 billion. In early 1981, MMF assets exceeded $115 billion. (Ed. footnote.)

tion is that MMFs are primarily a means for providing *access* to money market yields. According to this view, government regulations and minimum purchase requirements in the money market have significantly limited the ability of some investors to realize market yields on short-term investments. MMFs provide such investors an opportunity to bypass these obstacles and earn a rate of return close to the yield of money market instruments. To the extent that this explanation is valid, one can argue that changes in certain government regulations would largely eliminate the appeal of MMFs.

The second explanation for the growth of MMFs is that they fill a vacuum in the financial system, which previously lacked an intermediary specializing exclusively in short-term assets and liabilities. According to this view, the growth in MMFs represents a permanent change in the way many institutional and individual investors manage their liquid assets. This change has occurred because MMFs offer these investors the advantages that result from the pooling of large amounts of short-term funds.[2] Briefly the possible advantages are:

Economies of Scale. By pooling the funds of many investors, the MMF may experience lower administrative and operating costs per dollar of assets than the investors themselves could achieve. Consequently, a MMF may be able to offer some investors a higher rate of return *net* of expenses than is available to them through direct investment in money market instruments.

Liquidity and Divisibility. Money fund shares can be purchased and sold on any business day without a sales charge. Also, because of the short-term nature of the money market instruments purchased by MMFs, the investor faces a relatively small probability of loss of principal due to interest rate fluctuations. Consequently, a purchase of money fund shares represents a highly liquid investment. The checking option offered by most MMFs further enhances the liquidity of this investment. MMFs are able to offer such liquidity because of the relatively large size of their portfolios, which allows them to schedule maturities so that they usually can meet redemption requests without selling securities prior to maturity. In addition, after satisfying the initial minimum investment requirement, additions to and withdrawals from MMFs can generally be made in very small amounts. By contrast, a direct investment in money market instruments lacks this divisibility.

Diversification. The MMF diversifies its portfolio by purchasing instruments of a wide variety of issuers. This might expose investors in the fund to lower levels of risk than if they invested their funds directly in the money market.

---

[2] The functions of financial intermediaries are discussed in Van Horne [6].

Of course, these two explanations for the growth of MMFs are not mutually exclusive. In fact, the central conclusion of this article is that the growth of MMFs has been due to both (1) their ability to provide access to the money market to those previously excluded and (2) the advantages they offer some investors as an alternative to direct investment in the money market.

MONEY MARKET FUND INVESTORS

This section discusses the factors contributing to the attractiveness of MMFs for the three major categories of MMF investors. The sectors are discussed in the order of their importance as MMF investors as of the end of 1978. The two major categories of MMF investors are individuals and bank trust departments. The third most important investor category is corporations, although this sector holds a much smaller proportion of total MMF shares than individuals and bank trust departments. This ordering—(1) individuals, (2) bank trust departments, and (3) corporations—is also the order of the relative importance of access to money market yields as an explanation for the use of MMFs by these investors. That is, this explanation appears to be an important one underlying the use of MMFs by individuals. The access explanation applies to a lesser extent to bank trust departments and appears to be of negligible importance as an explanation for corporate use of MMFs. For these investors, and also for those individuals who do have access to the money market, the other advantages offered by the MMF as a financial intermediary for short-term funds appear to provide the primary explanation for the use of MMFs.

Individuals

The role of MMFs in providing access to money market yields is the most prevalent explanation for the use of MMFs by individuals. According to this explanation, the small individual investor has been unable to earn market yields because of minimum purchase requirements in the money market and because regulations limit the rate that can be paid on time and savings deposits at depository institutions. MMFs are attractive to small savers because they provide a means to circumvent these obstacles.

Purchases of money market instruments other than Treasury bills usually require investments of at least $25,000 and more often $100,000 or more. Furthermore, since 1969, purchases of Treasury bills have required a minimum investment of $10,000. In June 1978 banks and thrift institutions were authorized to issue 6-month "money market certificates" with maximum issuing rates tied to the average 6-month Treasury bill discount rate established at the weekly Treasury bill auctions. These certificates, however, carry the same minimum investment of $10,000 as Treasury bills. Consequently, the only short-term investment option facing the investor with less than $10,000 has been to deposit funds in small time and savings deposits at the deposit institutions. The rates paid on these deposits are subject to ceilings established under Reg. Q of the Federal Reserve Act.[3]

For much of the past decade money market interest rates have been significantly higher than the savings deposit ceiling rate. Even for individuals possessing the $10,000 needed to invest in Treasury bills or money market certificates, there may be circumstances under which limited access to the yields of other types of money market instruments influences their decision to use MMFs. In past periods of high interest rates, Treasury bill rates have often been well below other money market rates. For instance, the spread between the quarterly average 3-month CD and Treasury bill rates reached levels of 350 basis points in mid-1974 and in 1978 was as high as 150 basis points. In periods of rising spreads between the rates of other money market instruments such as CDs and commercial paper and the rate on Treasury bills, the yields paid by many money market funds will rise relative to the yield on bills. In these circumstances individuals holding bills or money market certificates may use MMFs to gain access to yields on money market instruments other than bills.[4]

While the role of MMFs in providing small savers access to money market yields has undoubtedly been an important factor contributing to the use of MMFs by individuals, evidence on average size of individual MMF accounts, presented later in the paper, indicates that many individuals who have sufficient funds to invest directly in money market instruments, or at least in Treasury bills, are also using MMFs. For these individuals the benefits of financial intermediation, not access, provide the key attraction of MMFs. This is an important distinction because it implies that even in the absence of Regulation Q ceilings at the deposit institutions, individual use of MMFs would continue.

Two uses of MMFs by individuals deserve special attention because they represent innovations in the management of liquid assets. The first innovation is the large-scale use of MMFs by stockbrokers for the purposes of investing their clients' balances. Many large brokerage firms have established their own MMFs. Most of these are open to the general public but are used mainly by the brokers of the firm as a liquid parking place for investors'

---

[3] In March 1980, subsequent to the publication of this article, the *Depository Institutions Deregulation and Monetary Control Act* was passed. Under provisions of this Act, the interest rate ceilings on deposits will be phased out by 1986. (Ed. footnote.)

[4] This assumes that the rise in the spread between CD and Treasury bill yields was not solely due to an increase in default risk.

funds that become available after a sale of stock shares, bonds, etc. Many brokers unaffiliated with a MMF use MMFs for the same purpose. Previously after a sale of securities, an investor's funds would either have remained uninvested, been placed in a savings account or a relatively low-yielding account offered by the broker, or been invested directly in a money market instrument if the amount of funds made this possible. The increased liquidity and divisibility MMFs provide relative to direct money market investment are probably especially important to this type of investor. Consequently, as a competitive measure, many brokers are using MMFs to ensure that their investors remain fully invested at market rates.

The second innovation is the use of exchange privileges between MMFs and other funds in a mutual fund group. These arrangements allow MMF investors to exchange their MMF shares for shares in any of the other mutual funds in the group, at that fund's share price, plus a sales charge if it is a load fund. Also, shareholders in any of the other funds can exchange their shares for the MMF shares. The exchange privilege offers individual investors the benefit of added flexibility in their investment decisions, allowing them to move in and out of differing types of mutual funds with little or no transactions costs. Just under half of the mutual fund groups whose share prices are listed in the *Wall Street Journal* have established MMFs.

Bank Trust Departments

The second important user of money market funds is bank trust departments. Trust departments serve as fiduciaries for numerous types of accounts which can broadly be divided into two groups: (1) personal trusts and estates and (2) employee benefit accounts. If funds from these accounts were invested separately, many of the potential advantages of intermediation, such as diversification and reduced administrative costs, would be lacking. Furthermore, individual accounts of the bank trust department can have the same kind of limited access problem faced by individual investors. Some of these accounts have less than $10,000 in short-term assets. Consequently, the only available short-term investment is time and savings deposits which, as shown above, has frequently paid rates well below money market rates.

In order to gain the advantages of intermediation, trust departments can establish "collective investment funds" under Regulation 9 of the Comptroller of the Currency. Collective investment funds for accounts of personal trusts and estates are called "common trust funds." Collective investment funds pool monies from different accounts of the trust department and invest them collectively . Two types of collective investment funds have developed for the investment of short-term funds. The first type to evolve was the "variable amount note" (also called a "master note"), which is a revolving loan agreement, generally without a specified maturity, negotiated with a business borrower.[5] Monies from various accounts in the trust department can be put into the variable amount note and withdrawn from it without fees as the need arises. The rate paid by the borrower of the variable amount note is most commonly the "180-day commercial paper rate placed directly by major finance companies" posted in the *Wall Street Journal.*

While the variable amount note is widely used by bank trust departments, it has some limitations. First, the participating accounts gain little in the way of diversification. Second, the agreement with the borrower typically specifies maximum and minimum limits between which the size of the variable amount note must vary. These limitations reduce the liquidity of a variable amount note investment and may necessitate agreements with several borrowers, each of which requires a separate plan, thereby increasing administrative expenses.

As a result of the weaknesses of the variable amount note, a second type of collective investment funds for short-term investments, called a "short-term investment fund (STIF)," has grown in usage by bank trust departments for their own accounts. The STIF pools funds from individual accounts of the trust department and invests those funds in a variety of short-term money market instruments.

Almost all STIFs fall into two broad categories. The first group is for accounts of personal trusts and estates. These STIFs, operated under Regulation 9.18 (a) (1) of the Comptroller of the Currency, receive tax-exempt status under the condition that income earned by the fund is distributed to participating accounts. These STIFs are also limited by the requirement that no participant can have an interest exceeding 10 percent of the value of the fund. The second type of STIF, operated under Regulation 9.18 (a) (2) of the Comptroller of the Currency, is for the accounts of pension, profit sharing, stock bonus, thrift and self-employed retirement plans that are exempt from taxation under the Internal Revenue Code. Because the contributing accounts are themselves tax exempt, the second type of STIF does not have to distribute income to the participating accounts in order to acquire tax-exempt status. In addition, this type of STIF is not subject to the requirement that no participant's interest exceeds 10 percent. Under IRS regulations, monies of personal trust and estate accounts and "tax-exempt" accounts cannot be mixed. Hence, if a bank trust department wishes to provide STIF services to both types of accounts, it must establish both a 9.18 (a) (1) STIF and a 9.18 (a) (2) STIF.

Unlike all other types of collective investment funds, which have to value their assets on a current market basis, STIFs are permitted to value their assets on a cost basis and use the "straight-line accrual" method for calculating income of the trust. Under this method the difference between cost and anticipated redemption value at maturity is accrued in a straight-line

---

[5] The variable amount note is a type of collective investment fund established under Regulation 9.18(c)(2)(ii) of the Comptroller of the Currency.

basis. This accounting procedure is generally preferred by trust departments because it smooths out the flow of income to participating accounts.[6] In granting this exemption to STIFs, the Comptroller of the Currency has imposed fairly strict restrictions on the portfolios of STIFS. They are:

1. 80 percent of investments must be payable on demand or have a maturity not exceeding 91 days,
2. assets of the fund must be held to maturity under usual circumstances,
3. not less than 40 percent of the value of assets of the fund must be composed of cash, demand obligations, and assets that mature on the fund's next business day.

If bank trust departments have the option of operating a STIF, why do so many use money market funds? There are two possible answers to this question. The first is that restrictive regulations on STIFs induce some bank trust departments to use MMFs, at least for some of their accounts. STIFs are affected by both Comptroller of the Currency regulations and various state regulations. As explained above, the Comptroller of the Currency's regulations impose fairly stringent conditions on the portfolios of STIFs. In addition, regulations require that separate funds be established for accounts of personal trusts and estates are not permitted to invest in common trust funds. Agency accounts are those for which the owner retains title to the property and only delegates to the bank trust department certain responsibilities.

While the regulations cited above may have had some impact on the decision of bank trust departments to use STIFs, the advantage of size in the operation of short-term financial intermediaries, such as STIFs and MMFs, has probably been a more important determinant. According to this line of reasoning, small- and medium-sized bank trust departments use the MMFs rather than establishing STIFs because the greater size of MMFs enables them to better provide the benefits of intermediation discussed earlier. A potentially key benefit is economies of scale resulting in lower average costs for large MMFs (and large STIFs) than for relatively small STIFs. In the presence of these economies of scale, small- and medium-sized trust departments could earn a higher yield *net* of expenses for their accounts by placing their short-term funds in MMFs than by establishing STIFs.

Corporations

A third category of MMF investors is nonfinancial corporations. While this sector has a very large amount of funds held in short-term financial

---

[6] For an expanded discussion of straight-line accrual versus market valuation accounting methods, see the original article, pp. 20-21. (Ed. footnote.)

assets, its use of MMFs to date has been limited relative to individuals and bank trust departments. In discussing the attractiveness of MMFs as an investment alternative for nonfinancial corporations, it is useful to consider two components of corporate liquid financial holdings: (1) assets held for transactions purposes and (2) assets held for a slightly longer period and usually invested in the money market.

MMFs and Transactions Balances.   As noted, most MMFs offer checking for amounts of $500 or more. The payment of explicit interest on demand deposits at banks is prohibited by the Banking Act of 1933. Since corporations hold a large amount of demand deposits, the opportunity to write large checks on MMF shares would appear to have created a potential role for MMFs in corporate cash management. The comparison of money market fund shares to demand deposits, however, is complicated by the fact that banks do pay an implicit rate of return on demand deposits. This return is paid in the form of lines of credit, use of credit, cash management services and other banking services. Clearly, MMF shares cannot be considered a substitute for demand deposits held to compensate a bank for services it alone provides. To the extent that the checking privilege of most MMFs can be substituted for this service provided by banks, however, MMFs may enable corporations to reduce the amount of compensating balances held.

The regulatory prohibition of payment of interest on demand deposits has encouraged substantial corporate involvement in the repurchase agreement (RP) market. Corporate demand deposits in excess of compensating balances are often invested overnight in RPs arranged through the bank. A comparison of rates offered on RPs by government securities dealers and average MMF yields for 1978 and the first four months of 1979 shows very little difference. As bank fees for investing in overnight RPs are likely to be higher than the cost of investing in MMF shares, which consists only of wire charges, MMFs appear to have offered corporations a competitive alternative to RPs in this period. Also, MMFs appear to provide an overnight investment opportunity for those corporations without sufficient funds to meet the substantial minimum purchase requirements on RPs.

Despite the fact that MMFs appear to represent a partial substitute for conventional means of holding transactions balances, evidence on MMF share turnover rates strongly suggests that neither corporations nor other MMF investors have used MMFs extensively for transactions purposes.[7]

Two reasons can be advanced for the limited corporate use of MMFs for transactions purposes. First, certain features of MMF share purchase and redemption systems lessen the attractiveness of MMFs as a substitute for repurchase agreements. Secondly, MMFs may be unwilling to allow shares to turn over very rapidly.

---

[7] The turnover rate is measured as the total redemptions in a given month times 12 (to annualize the rate) divided by the average level of deposits or shares outstanding. (For a complete discussion of the turnover rates for bank deposits relative to MMFs, see the original article. Ed. note.)

The share purchase and redemption systems of most MMFs prevent these MMFs from being used by corporations as a substitute for overnight RPs because a corporation can not invest in one of these MMFs one day, and receive payment with one day's dividends the following day. An investment in one of these MMFs entails the loss of one day's dividends (unless shares are redeemed by check), which results in a significant reduction in the rate of return of an investment placed for just a couple of days. Thus, these MMFs are not a substitute for overnight RPs, nor do they provide a competitive yield on an investment for just a few days.

The share purchase and redemption policies of some other MMFs potentially allow the investor to avoid uninvested days. Thus, a corporation investing in one of these MMFs on Monday could earn one day's dividends and expect remittance on Tuesday.[8] However, MMF prospectuses rarely provide guarantees as to what day, let alone what time, remittance will be sent. A MMF's delay in remitting payment may mean lost investment opportunities and a lower effective yield for the corporation. Thus, the attractiveness of a very short-term MMF investment to a corporation may be diminished by the uncertainty as to when remittance can be expected, an uncertainty largely absent in repurchase agreements. Nevertheless, if one of the MMFs in this second group provides assurances of prompt remittance for redeemed shares, a MMF could offer corporations a competitive alternative to RPs depending on the relative net yields of the two forms of investment.

The second, and probably more important, reason for the limited use of MMF shares for transactions purposes is a degree of unwillingness on the part of MMFs to serve their shareholders' transactions needs. Rapid turnover of shares involves significant costs arising from bank charges for processing checks and the MMF's expenses when shares are redeemed. MMFs have not developed pricing systems that allocate these costs to individual shareholders who turnover shares rapidly. In the absence of such systems, MMFs sometimes find it necessary to simply restrict the turnover activity of some investors. A dramatic example is provided by one MMF whose turnover rate reached a level of over 100 because one corporation was using this MMF extensively for transaction purposes. Subsequently, the corporation was asked to refrain from doing so and within a month the fund's turnover rate plummeted to 2.

This discussion is not meant to imply that under no circumstances would a MMF tolerate rapid turnover of its shares by an investor. The costs asso-

---

[8] Shares can be purchased and redeemed in most of these MMFs on business days at noon and at 4 p.m. Eastern time. Dividends are credited just prior to the processing of share orders at either noon or 4, depending on the MMF, to shareholders of record. In the case that the MMF declares dividends at noon, for example, a purchase order effected at either noon or 4 p.m. Monday would first receive dividends at noon Tuesday. If the investor's redemption request was received before noon on Tuesday, shares would be redeemed at noon and payment with a day's dividends could be expected that afternoon.

ciated with a redemption of shares are relatively fixed, while the fees earned by the MMF's manager and advisor on an investor's funds are positively related to the size of the shareholder's investment. Hence, the willingness of a MMF to tolerate turnover by a given customer should increase with the average size of the customer's investment. For any share turnover rate there should be an average share level at which the MMF will permit that rate of turnover. If the investor is not maintaining that level then, under current institutional arrangements, the only options available to the MMF are to ask the investor to decrease the turnover rate of his shares or to refuse to accept new share purchase orders from the investor.

MMFs Versus Direct Money Market Investments.   Nonfinancial corporations also have a very large volume of direct investments in money market instruments such as CDs and commercial paper. The decision of a corporation to use an in-house program of direct investment in the money market or to use MMFs is solely dependent on which investment mechanism offers the highest net yield consistent with the desired degree of liquidity and diversification. Corporations do not appear to be significantly affected in this decision by government regulations. It should be noted, however, that small-sized corporations with savings deposits at the depository institutions are, like individuals, affected by Regulation Q ceilings.

Conversations with MMF officials reveal that those corporations that are using MMFs are at the smaller end of the size spectrum, which seems reasonable since corporations with smaller amounts of short-term funds available for investment are more likely to benefit from the advantages a MMF offers as a financial intermediary. The ability to offer these advantages is a corollary of the MMF's portfolio size. The greater size of the MMF's portfolio may enable the small corporation to gain greater liquidity and diversification than it could get by running an in-house money market investment program. Also, if there are economies of scale in the operation of corporate money market investment programs, as there appear to be in the operation of MMFs, the small corporation may gain a higher net yield by investing through a MMF than through an inhouse program.

MONEY MARKET FUND YIELDS

The assumption that MMFs offer rates of return comparable to money market rates underpin the two broad explanations advanced above for the rapid growth of MMF assets. The first emphasized the ability of MMFs to provide money market rates to those previously denied access. The second explanation emphasized the advantages offered to some investors by MMFs which act as an intermediary for short-term funds. One such advantage is that, due especially to economies of scale, some investors can gain a higher net rate of return by investing in a MMF than by investing directly in the money market. As both explanations depend heavily on the assumption that rates of return on MMF investments on other money market instruments are comparable, this section will examine the relationship between MMF and money market yields.

A crucial distinction must be made in comparing MMF rates with money market rates. When purchasing a money market security, the investor is quoted a rate of return that will be earned if that security is held to maturity, assuming the issuer does not default. A purchaser of MMF shares, on the other hand, receives no quotation as to what the return will be if the shares are held for a certain period. Rather, a yield quoted to the investor on the date of purchase indicates the annualized net yield received on an investment in the MMF over the *past* day, week, month, or year. The actual yield received by the MMF investor is determined after the purchase and is influenced by many factors. These factors are (1) the general level of money market yields, (2) the composition of assets of the MMF, (3) the expenses of the fund absorbed by its shareowners, (4) the movement in interest rates over the period shares are held and (5) the accounting procedure used by the fund to calculate share prices and daily dividends.

The MMF investor's yield is fundamentally dependent on the interest accrued daily on the MMF's ever-changing portfolio of securities. The amount of interest accrued depends on the general level of money market yields and on the type and maturity of securities held at a given time. MMFs vary considerably in both the type and average maturity of securities held. A large percentage of most MMFs' holdings are in domestic and Eurodollar CDs, commercial paper and Treasury bills, but various other high grade money market instruments are also commonly purchased. A small number of MMFs have restricted their portfolio investments to purchases of government securities, apparently to attract more risk-averse investors. The aggregate asset composition of MMFs appears to be quite responsive to changes in yield differentials. For instance, a large spread between Treasury bill rates and other money market rates in the latter half of 1978 resulted in a significant movement out of government securities.

Another important determinant of the yield received by an investor in a MMF is the expenses deducted from the income of the fund before dividends are declared each day. The percent of net expenses (total expenses minus expenses absorbed by the fund's administrator) to average assets on an annual basis varies in a range from 0.4 to 1.4, although most funds have net expense ratios of 1.0 percent or less.

The extent of movement in market interest rates over the period shares are held also affects the investor's yield. These movements affect the rate earned on new assets of the MMF and also result in capital gains or losses on the assets already held by the MMF. The magnitude of the gains or losses is inversely related to the average maturity of the MMF's assets. The shorter the average maturity, the less the change in market value of the MMF's portfolio resulting from a given change in market rates.

The influence of capital gains and losses on the MMF's yield depends on the accounting procedures used by the fund. Some funds, using "mark-to-market" accounting procedures pass on these gains or losses (whether realized or not) on a daily basis. Others, using "amortized cost" accounting methods, do not allow unrealized capital gains or losses to affect yield. The yield of an investor in a MMF that uses amortized cost valuation may be affected by net redemptions (sales) of the MMF's shares in the periods of rising (falling) market rates. The accounting methods used by MMFs have been the center of controversy, not yet fully resolved.

GROWTH OF MMFs

The relationship between the rise in the spread between MMF yields, and the Regulation Q ceiling rate and increases in money market fund shares explains the belief that the growth of MMFs was solely a result of funds being withdrawn from the deposit institutions and put into MMFs. According to this view, the only function served by MMFs is to provide access to money market yields to individuals having relatively small amounts of funds to invest. While it is undoubtedly true that a significant part of the growth of MMFs has resulted from the withdrawal of funds by individuals from the deposit institutions, *the position taken in this article is that much of the growth over this period also represented a lasting change in the way some investors manage their short-term assets.* The best example of this fundamental change is the case of small- and medium-sized bank trust departments, which use MMFs to manage their short-term assets in order to take advantage of the economies of scale resulting from the pooling of large amounts of funds.

The answer to the question of whether the growth in MMFs is simply a result of government regulations or whether it also is due to other advantages MMFs offer investors as a financial intermediary would be aided by a breakdown of money market shares by investor category. Such data is unavailable. However, the rapid growth of MMFs servicing institutional investors cannot be attributed to Regulation Q. Since these investors have direct access to the money market, their participation in MMFs must be attributable to the other advantages offered by MMFs.

With regard to investment in MMFs by individuals, it is impossible to estimate how much is coming from individuals seeking access to the money market and how much is from individuals who already had this access but are nevertheless attracted to MMFs for other reasons. It appears, however, that a significant amount of money from this source is coming from individuals who are not using MMFs primarily to gain access to money market yields. This conclusion stems from the rapid growth of stockbroker-sponsored MMFs, which by May 1979 had combined assets of roughly $10 billion. Most of the money in these MMFs comes from individuals through brokers. It seems unlikely that a large part of the growth of these MMFs is due to money being withdrawn by small investors from deposit institutions. Rather it appears that most of the growth in this group of MMFs has resulted from larger investors taking advantage of the opportunity offered by MMFs as an investment vehicle for funds freed by the sale of market securities.

CONCLUSION: THE FUTURE OF MMFs

The central conclusion of this paper is that the rapid growth of MMFs in recent years has been both a reaction to government regulations and a result of fundamental changes in the way some institutional and individual investors manage their short-term financial assets. A corollary of this conclusion is that MMFs will survive as a new intermediary in the financial markets regardless of the future course of government regulations that have contributed to their growth in the past.

REFERENCES

1. Bank Administration Institute. The Trust Administration Investments Task Force. *Trust Investments*. Park Ridge, Illinois: Bank Administration Institute, 1976.

2. Bent, Bruce R. "Sorting Out the Money Market Funds." *Trusts and Estates* (June 1976), pp. 408-15.

3. Cook, Timothy Q. "The Determinants of Spreads Between Treasury Bill and Other Money Market Rates." Working Paper No. 79-4, Federal Reserve Bank of Richmond, August 1979.

4. ——, and Duffield, Jeremy G. "Average Costs of Money and Market Mutual Funds." *Economic Review*, Federal Reserve Bank of Richmond (July/August 1979).

5. Donoghue, William E. *The Cash Management Manual*. Holliston, Mass.: Cash Management Institute, 1977.

6. Van Horne, James C. *Financial Market Rates and Flows*. Englewood Cliffs, New Jersey: Prentice-Hall, Inc., 1978.

SHORT-TERM INVESTMENT POOLS

Timothy Q. Cook and
Jeremy G. Duffield *

35

Over the last decade numerous types of short-term investment pooling arrangements (STIPs) have emerged in the nation's financial system. The most well-known and widely publicized form of STIP is the money market mutual fund (MMF). However, MMFs are only one of at least eight types of STIPs that were operating in the United States at the end of 1979. While the various types of STIPs differ in some respects, such as the kind of asset held or the type of investor, they are all alike in their basic function, which is to purchase large pools of short-term financial instruments and sell shares in these pools to investors. In almost all instances discussed in this article, the pool allows participants to invest a much smaller amount of money than would be necessary to directly purchase the individual securities held by the pool. This paper examines the STIP phenomenon.

SHORT-TERM INVESTMENT POOLS

Characteristics of different STIPs are summarized in Table I. While all STIPs basically function as intermediaries for short-term securities, they can differ in several ways. First, some STIPs are open to a wide variety of investors while others cater only to a narrow group. Second, some STIPs hold

*Reprinted, with deletions, from the *Economic Review*, September/October 1980, pp. 3-23, with permission from the Federal Reserve Bank of Richmond.

Table I

Characteristics of Short-Term Investment Pools

	Year First One Started	Type of Investors	Minimum Investment	Assets	Maturity End of 1979	Type of Pool	Redemption Methods	Annualized Expense Ratio (basis points)
Money Market Funds	1972	anyone	$1,000 to $5,000 is most common; some funds for institutions require $50,000 or more	wide range	weighted average maturity of 34 days	open-end	wire, check-writing, mail	weighted average ratio of .55
Short-Term Tax-Exempt Funds	1977	investors desiring income free of Federal taxes	varies from $1,000 to $25,000	tax-exempt securities	120 to 150 days	open-end	wire, check-writing, mail	similar to MMF expenses
Short-Term Investment Funds	1968(?)	accounts of bank trust department	negligible	wide range; mostly commercial paper	n.a.; by regulation very short	open-end	daily transfer on request	n.a.
Local Government Investment Pools	1973	state and local government bodies	usually none	wide range	varies greatly (see text)	open-end	wire, checks in some cases (usually 24 hours notice needed for withdrawals of greater than $1 million)	n.a.

Credit Union Pools	1968	credit unions	n.a.	mainly Treasury bills and Federal agencies	varies	open-end	wire, draft	n.a.
Short-Term Investment Trusts	1974	anyone	$1,000	primarily Eurodollar CDs	6 months	unit investment trust	funds returned at maturity; can sell prior to maturity subject to a charge	1.40
Shares in Bills	n.a.	anyone	$1,000	Treasury bills	3 or 6 months	similar to unit investment trust	funds returned at end of 3- or 6-month investment; can sell prior to maturity subject to a charge	varies inversely with maturity and with size of investment; expense ratio for a $5,000 investment in 6-month bill would be 90

many different money market instruments while others confine their investment to one type of security. Third, some STIPs are "open-end" arrangements that allow investors to purchase and redeem shares of an everchanging
pool of underlying securities. In other STIPs investors buy shares of a specific pool of securities. Other features that vary among STIPs include minimum
investment size, expense ratios, and methods of investing and withdrawing
funds.

Money Market Mutual Funds

Because MMFs were discussed in great detail in two earlier articles in this
Review [4, 5], the discussion here will be brief.[1] The general operating characteristics of MMFs are fairly standard. Minimum initial investments usually
range from $500 to $5,000, although a very small number of funds require
no minimum and others, designed for institutional investors, require minimums of $50,000 or more. With the exception of the small number of funds
that limit their investors to institutions, MMF shares are available to any
type of investor. Most funds have a checking option that enables shareholders
to write checks of $500 or more. Shares can also be redeemed at most
MMFs by telephone or wire request, in which case payment by the MMF is
either mailed to the investor or remitted by wire to the investor's bank
account.

MMFs are open-end investment companies that vary considerably in both
the type and average maturity of securities they hold. A large percentage of
most MMFs' holdings are in domestic and Eurodollar CDs, commercial paper
and Treasury bills, but various other high grade money market instruments
are also commonly purchased. A small number of MMFs have restricted their
investments to government securities, apparently to attract more risk-averse
investors, and an equally small number have invested very heavily in Eurodollar CDs.

Because MMFs are generally "no-load" mutual funds, investors purchase
and redeem MMF shares without paying a sales charge. Instead, expenses of
the funds are deducted daily from gross income before dividends are declared. The difference between the yield earned on a MMF's assets and the
yield earned by the shareholders is the MMF's expense ratio. (Alternatively,
this can be measured as the ratio of total expenses on an annual basis to average assets.) In 1978 the expense ratio for different MMFs ranged from .4
percent to 1.4 percent [4]. The weighted average expense ratio for the industry as a whole was .55 in 1979.

The first MMF started offering shares to the public in 1972. By the end of
1974 there were 15 MMFs and by the end of 1979, 76 were in operation.
Total MMF assets at the end of 1979 were $45.2 billion.[2]

---

[1] The article cited in reference [5] is reproduced, with deletions, elsewhere in this book.
[2] In early 1981, MMF assets exceeded $115 billion. (Ed. footnote)

Short-Term Tax-Exempt Funds

Short-term tax-exempt funds (STEFs) are the tax-exempt counterpart to MMFs. STEFs invest primarily in securities issued by state and local governments ("municipals"), which pay interest income that is exempt from Federal income taxes. The first short-term tax-exempt fund offered shares to the public in 1977 and several others were formed in 1979. By mid-1980 there were at least 10 STEFs operating with combined assets of over one-and-a-half-billion dollars.

As a result of the type of financial assets they purchase, STEFs appeal to investors in high Federal income tax brackets. More specifically, an investor facing the choice between two investments that are alike in every respect except that one offers a yield that is subject to Federal income taxes, Y_T, while the other's yield is tax-free, Y_{TF}, will choose the alternative that offers the highest after-tax return. That is, the investor will choose the tax-free investment option if $Y_{TF} > Y_T(1-t)$, where t is the investor's marginal Federal income tax rate. Thus, by examining the ratio of short-term tax-exempt yields to short-term taxable yields it is possible to determine at what minimum marginal tax rate an investor would be better off investing in a STEF than in a MMF. While this ratio varies considerably over time, available evidence suggests that an investor probably has to have a marginal Federal tax rate of more than 50 percent to achieve a higher after-tax yield in a STEF than in a MMF.[3]

While after-tax yield comparisons might indicate that an investor with a very high marginal tax rate would be better off in a STEF than in a MMF, one major qualification must be added. Largely because of the small quantity of very short-term municipal securities available for purchase, STEF portfolios have generally been of longer average maturity than MMF portfolios. To the extent that STEF portfolios have longer maturities than MMF portfolios, the variation in the STEF's share price and in the STEF investor's principal will be somewhat greater than for MMF shares. For some investors this may lessen the relative attractiveness of STEFs.

In order to minimize the perceived problem of a varying price share, most STEFs have opted, like most MMFs, to maintain an average maturity of 120 days or less in order to gain exemptive orders from the Securities and Ex-

---

[3] The ratio of short-term tax-exempt to short-term taxable yields varied from .421 to .492 in 1979 [8]. This implies that a marginal tax rate of somewhere between 50.8 percent and 57.9 percent would have been necessary to make an investor indifferent between the choice of taxable and tax-exempt instruments if no costs were associated with investment. If both the MMF and the STEF had the same expense ratio, ER, the true marginal tax rate which leaves the investor indifferent is

$$1 - \frac{Y_{TF} - ER}{Y_T - ER},$$

which implies that an even higher marginal tax bracket is necessary to make the STEF the preferable alternative.

change Commission permitting the use of accounting policies that should enable the maintenance of a constant net asset value.

As a means of achieving shorter average maturities, some STEFs have retained the right to use a "put option" technique. Under this arrangement, the fund would purchase municipal securities, often at a higher price (lower yield) than it would normally pay for these securities, at the same time acquiring the right or option to sell the securities back to the seller at an agreed-upon price on a certain date or within a specified period in the future. The primary advantage of this technique is that it may allow the fund to tailor a shorter-term portfolio. The major disadvantage is that the fund is dependent on the ability and willingness of the seller to buy back the securities. Furthermore, there are also thorny legal issues yet to be resolved, such as the appropriate method of valuing securities purchased under put options and the tax status of securities purchased under put options.

Unlike the yield curve for taxable securities, the yield curve for municipals is almost always upward-sloping throughout the entire range of maturities, i.e., a higher yield is paid for securities of longer maturity. Consequently, the tradeoff encountered in trying to maintain a very short average maturity in a municipal portfolio is generally a lower yield on the portfolio. For this reason some STEFs retain the option of holding an average maturity of one year or over.

Short-Term Investment Funds

Short-term investment funds (STIFs) are collective investment funds operated by bank trust departments. A collective investment fund is an arrangement whereby the monies of different accounts in the trust department are pooled to purchase a certain type of security, such as common stocks, corporate bonds, tax-exempt bonds, or, in the case of STIFs, short-term securities. The first STIF was started no later than 1968.[4] By the end of 1974 there were over 70 STIFs with total assets of $2.7 billion. STIF assets grew rapidly in 1978 and 1979 and by the end of 1979 total STIF assets were over $32 billion.

STIFs function just like MMFs and offer the same advantages to the accounts of the trust department. In particular, the minimum investment is usually a negligible amount and funds can be put in and withdrawn without transaction fees.

That STIFs and MMFs provide virtually the same services to their customers is illustrated by the fact that many trust departments use MMFs rather than establish STIFs. The decision to set up a STIF or to use a MMF for its customers' short-term assets is largely dependent on the size of the

---

[4] This is the earliest date for which the authors are aware of the existence of a STIF. It is possible that other STIFs were formed prior to 1968.

trust department. The larger the trust department, the more likely it is to have a STIF. Most bank trust departments without STIFs use MMFs.[5]

Both the type and maturity of assets held by STIFs reflect the Comptroller of the Currency's Regulations on the portfolios of STIFs. The two key regulations are that:

(1) at least 80 percent of investments must be payable on demand or have a maturity not exceeding 91 days, and
(2) not less than 40 percent of the value of the fund must be cash, demand obligations, and assets that mature on the fund's next business day.

As a result of these regulations, STIFs hold a substantial amount of variable amount notes (also called master notes), which are a type of open-ended commercial paper that allows the investment and withdrawal of funds on a daily basis and pays a daily interest rate tied to the current commercial paper rate. In addition, STIFs hold a large amount of standard commercial paper and a much smaller amount of time and savings deposits and Treasury securities. A very small number of STIFs invest primarily in short-term tax-exempt securities.

Typically, only the audit expenses of STIFs are charged directly against the income earned by the STIFs and it is only this expense that appears in the STIF annual report. Other expenses are covered by fees charged to the accounts of the trust department. Consequently, it is impossible to calculate the expense ratio of STIFs from published reports.

Local Government Investment Pools

Local government investment pools (LGIPs) were in operation in 11 states by the end of 1979.[6] These pools have been set up to enable local government entities (such as counties, cities, school districts, etc., and in all but two states, state agencies) to purchase shares in a large portfolio of money market instruments. The primary purpose of state legislation establishing the pools has been to encourage efficient management of idle funds.

Since many local government bodies have relatively small sums of money

[5] Cook and Duffield [4] argue that the explanation for the use of MMFs by small- and medium-sized bank trust departments is that both MMFs and STIFs are subject to decreasing average costs as assets increase. Consequently, a small- or medium-sized bank trust department can get a higher yield net of expenses for its accounts by investing in a MMF than by setting up a relatively small STIF. It should also be noted that some agency accounts of bank trust departments are not eligible to invest in STIFs but may invest in MMFs.

[6] These states are California, Connecticut, Florida, Illinois, Massachusetts, Montana, New Jersey, Oregon, Utah, West Virginia, and Wisconsin. In addition, legislation was recently passed in Oklahoma providing for the creation of a LGIP.

to invest, they would seem to benefit most from LGIPs. However, in many LGIPs the majority of assets represent state funds. Surprisingly, through 1979 only a small percentage of eligible local government bodies were investing in the pools. Duncan [6] reports that in July 1979 the percentage of eligible participants contributing to LGIPs ranged from less than 1 percent in Illinois to 35 percent in Massachusetts.

Except for the LGIPs of Massachusetts and Illinois, the pools are administered by the state treasurer's office, often in conjunction with the state investment board and a local government advisory council. The Illinois pool is administered by a bank trust department, while the Massachusetts LGIP is run by an investment management firm.

In most respects, the operating characteristics of LGIPs are identical to those of MMFs. Funds may be invested by wire or check and withdrawn either by telephone request, with payment sent by wire, or in some cases by check. Funds may generally be invested and withdrawn on a daily basis, although several LGIPs require 24 hours' notice prior to the withdrawal of $1 million or more. While there are usually no minimum investment or withdrawal constraints, small transactions are often informally discouraged. Interest is earned daily, except in one LGIP which distributes income quarterly.

The pools invest in a broad range of securities many of which would not be legally available to the participants if they invested their funds individually. That is, many LGIP participants are legally prohibited from directly investing in some of the types of securities which the pool is authorized to purchase.

LGIPs in different states have followed widely different maturity strategies. Whereas at the end of December 1979, the longest average maturity of any MMF was less than three months, several LGIP portfolios had average maturities in the 1- to 3-year range. Others maintained average maturities as short as those of MMFs.

Credit Union Pools

Two short-term pools have been established for the investment of surplus funds of credit unions. The government securities pool of the Credit Union National Association (CUNA), a service organization representing more than 90 percent of the 22,000 credit unions in the U. S., represents one of the nation's earliest short-term pooling arrangements, having commenced operations in 1968. This pool had over $1 billion in assets and more than 10,000 participating credit unions at year-end 1979. The other pool was created in 1976 by the National Association of Federal Credit Unions (NAFCU).

Both pools are operated as common trust funds by bank trust departments. In most respects they are identical to other open-end STIPs. Investments and withdrawals may be made daily. Participating credit unions may request withdrawals by telephone with funds remitted by wire or they may write a draft on their pool account and deposit it at their commercial bank. Drafts may not be used for third-party payment.

CUNA's pool invests solely in U. S. Government and Federal agency securities. The average maturity of its portfolio was seven-and-one-half-months at the end of 1979. The NAFCU pool can invest in any type of security eligible for purchase by a Federal credit union. Thus, in addition to U. S. Government securities, the pool may purchase domestic certificates of deposit but is prohibited from investing in Eurodollar CDs, commercial paper and bankers acceptances. The NAFCU pool has maintained a very short average maturity, 30 days at the end of 1979.

Short-Term Investment Trusts

Short-term investment trusts (STITs), or short-term income trusts, are a type of unit investment trust that invests exclusively in short-term financial instruments. These funds are put together by groups of brokers that sell shares in units of $1,000 to their retail customers. Unlike MMF shares, these shares represent a claim to part of a specific set of securities. Hence, when these securities mature, the fund is terminated. The first eight series of STITs were sold in 1974, all by one broker group. No more STITs were sold until September 1978 when the same broker group again began to offer STITs. A second broker group began to market STITs in January 1979. From September 1978 through the end of 1979, 47 separate series of STITs totalling $6.1 billion were sold to the public. At the end of 1979 there were 35 series of STITs outstanding with total assets of $4.6 billion.

The maturity of all but two of the STIT series sold through 1979 was six months. The assets of the STITs put together by the first broker group have been composed of (1) CDs of foreign branches of U. S. Banks, (2) CDs of foreign banks, (3) CDs of U. S. branches of foreign banks, and (4) CDs of domestic banks. Of these, the first two categories, which are "Eurodollar CDs," comprised 72.1 percent of the total assets of the STITs offered by this group in 1979. The second broker group has generally included in their STITs only CDs of foreign branches (specifically, London branches) of domestic banks.

On an annualized basis the expense ratios of the STIT series sold in 1979 generally ranged from 140 to 150 basis points.[7] (This is calculated as the sales charge plus expenses of the Fund divided by the offering price and annualized.) This calculation assumes that the STIT share is held to maturity.

---

[7] The term "expense ratio" is used broadly here to encompass all expenses, including sales charges, that lower the investor's net yield. There are two possible reasons why the STIT expense ratio is higher than the MMF expense ratio. First, the labor expenses of a STIT may be greater because it requires a large network of dealers to actively market the STIT shares. Second, the size of the average STIT, is much smaller than the size of the average MMF, so that MMFs may benefit more from economies of scale.

The share can be sold prior to maturity subject to an additional charge, in which case the investor's effective ratio would be somewhat higher.

Other Types of STIPs

In addition to the six types of STIPs discussed so far, there are a small number of STIPs for which data were not collected for this article. These fall into two categories.

Shares-in-Bills. One organization of brokers and dealers has established a program whereby investors can purchase shares in specific three- and six-month Treasury bills. From the investor's point of view, this program is similar to a unit investment trust that invests exclusively in bills. The minimum purchase requirement is $1,000. According to the program's advertising literature, it has been in operation since 1969. However, only recently has the program been widely advertised, suggesting that it was relatively insignificant prior to 1979.[8]

The annualized expense ratio of a bill purchased through the program is inversely related to the size and maturity of the investment. An investment of $5,000 in a three-month bill has an annualized expense ratio of 120 basis points while a $5,000 investment in a six-month bill has an expense ratio of 90 basis points.

Other Open-End STIPs. Lastly, at least one other type of financial intermediary—life insurance companies—is already operating open-end STIPs and a second—savings and loan associations—will probably begin to do so in the early 1980's. Life insurance companies provide investment services for various types of thrift and pension plans. In the past, insurance companies have offered these plans such alternatives as investing in commingled bond or stock accounts. Recently, some life insurance companies have also begun to offer short-term investment commingled accounts.[9]

The Depository Institutions Deregulation and Monetary Control Act of 1980 gives federal savings and loan associations the authority to provide trust services. As noted above, most small- and moderate-sized bank trust departments use MMFs while large trust departments generally set up their own STIFs. The savings and loan associations who compete in the market for trust services will have these same options. It is probable that some of the larger associations will establish their own short-term investment pooling arrangements.

[8] Interestingly, unlike a STIT, the shares-in-bills program is not organized as an investment company. Hence, no prospectus or annual report is published and no information on the size of the program is readily available. The authors were unable to get this information from the sponsor.

[9] The authors became aware of the existence of life insurance company STIPs late in the preparation of this article. Consequently, no attempt was made to gather data for this type of STIP.

STIP Growth and Percentage Holdings of Various
Money Market Instruments

The growth of assets of each type of short-term investment pool and the growth of aggregate STIP assets from 1974 through 1979 is shown in Table II. Total STIP assets grew rapidly in the high interest rate period of 1974. Asset growth leveled off in 1976, when interest rates reached a cyclical trough, and accelerated sharply from 1977 through 1979, a period of rising interest rates. Almost all types of STIPs participated in this rapid growth. Assets of the six types of STIPs for which data were available totaled $88.5 billion at the end of 1979. MMFs held slightly over half of this total. Table II confirms the fact that STIPs have become a significant intermediary in the financial system.

FINANCIAL MARKET IMPLICATIONS OF STIPS

Before considering the financial market implications of STIPs, it is necessary to review the three short-term investment options available to investors prior to the emergence of STIPs. First, they could hold deposits in a bank or other financial intermediary. These deposits generally required little or no minimum investment, but were subject to Regulation Q interest rate ceilings that were frequently below market interest rates. The second option was purchase of Treasury bills, which has required a minimum of $10,000 since early 1969. The third option was purchase of private sector money market instruments, such as CDs, commercial paper, or bankers acceptances. These securities are generally only available in minimum denominations of $100,000, although a few issuers will sell commercial paper in amounts as small as $25,000 and bankers acceptances less than $100,000 are sometimes issued.

In this environment investors could be divided into three groups by the amount of funds they had to invest in short-term financial instruments. One group with less than $10,000 had access only to small denomination time and savings deposits. A second group with $10,000 but less than $100,000 had the additional option of purchasing Treasury bills. The final group with at least $100,000 could also invest in private sector money market instruments.

The fundamental importance of STIPs is that they have made this distinction among investors largely meaningless. Because all forms of STIPs have minimum purchase requirements as low as $1,000 and sometimes lower, all three investment options are effectively available to all types of investors, regardless of the amount of short-term funds at their disposal. This increased access to the money market throug STIPs has several implications for the financial markets which are discussed below.

Table II
Assets and Numbers of Various Forms of STIPs
(end-of-year)

	Money Market Funds		Short-Term Tax-Exempt Funds		Short-Term Investment Funds[1]		Local Government Investment Pools		Credit Union Pools		Short-Term Investment Trusts		Total Assets
	Assets ($ mil.)	Number (funds)	Assets ($ mil.)	Number (funds)	Assets ($ mil.)	Number (funds)	Assets ($ mil.)	Number (states)	Assets ($ mil.)	Number (pools)	Assets ($ mil.)	Number (sponsors)	($ mil.)
1974	1,715	15			2,660	73	394	4	1,224	1	846	1	6,839
1975	3,696	36			3,986	102	890	4	1,947	1		0	10,519
1976	3,686	48			3,427	92	2,034	6	1,816	2		0	10,963
1977	3,888	50	2	1	8,409	136	3,044	10	1,151	2		0	16,494
1978	10,858	61	30	1	25,125	na	3,845	11	1,074	2	665	1	41,597
1979	45,214	76	350	3	32,277	251[2]	4,779	11	1,237	2	4,614	2	88,471
Sources:	Investment Company Institute		data gathered by authors from funds		Common Trust Fund Surveys; ABA Collective Investment Funds Survey Report (1978)		data gathered by authors from funds		data gathered by authors from funds		prospectuses		

[1] The STIF data for 1978 is year-end data from a special American Bankers Association, Collective Investment Funds Survey Report. The STIF data for 1974-77 is from the Common Trust Fund Survey. Prior to 1979, the Survey was conducted by the Comptroller of the Currency. Banks that were not national banks reported on a voluntary basis and there appear to be a number of large trust departments not reporting in those years. In addition, assets were reported prior to year-end by some banks. Hence, the 1974-77 data should be regarded as estimates which are on the low side. In 1979 the Common Trust Fund Survey was incorporated into the Trust Assets of Insured Commercial Banks survey conducted jointly by the Comptroller of the Currency, the Federal Deposit Insurance Corporation, and the Federal Reserve Board. The 1979 data is year-end and covers all trust departments.

[2] These 251 STIFs were operated by a total of 155 bank trust departments and 5 trust companies owned by bank holding companies.

The Impact of STIPs on the Administration of
Regulation Q Interest Rate Ceilings

Deposit rate ceilings under Regulation Q originated with the Banking Act of 1933 and were initially applied only to rates paid on commercial bank time and savings deposits. The purpose was to prevent "excessive" rate competition for deposits among banks that might encourage risky loan and investment policies, thereby leading to bank failures. The passage of the Interest Adjustment Act in 1966 expanded the coverage of deposit interest rate ceilings to thrift institutions.

The implicit assumptions underlying Regulation Q through the mid-1970's was that most deposit holders were relatively small investors who were locked into deposits as the only available short-term investment option. As a result, if market rates were to rise above fixed Regulation Q ceiling rates, there would not be a massive flight of funds out of the deposit institutions into other financial assets. That this reasoning was largely correct can be seen by examining the behavior of savings deposits at the deposit institutions in 1973 and 1974, when short-term market interest rates rose to levels over twice as high as the Regulation Q ceiling rate on these deposits. While the growth of savings deposits slowed markedly during this period, total savings deposits actually increased despite the huge positive differential between market rates and Regulation Q ceiling rates.

The emergence of STIPs, by providing *access* to money market yields to virtually all investors, severely damaged the ability of the deposit institutions to raise funds at below market interest rates. As a result, after interest rates began to rise above Regulation Q ceiling rates in 1977, regulators fundamentally altered the application of Regulation Q. This alteration came in June 1978 when the Regulation Q ceiling rate on 6-month deposit certificates ("money market certificates") was tied to the 6-month Treasury bill rate. Subsequently, Regulation Q ceiling rates on 4-year and then 2½-year deposit certificates were also tied to market rates of comparable maturity U. S. Government securities.

One suggested response to the emergence of STIPs as a competitor to the deposit institutions was to expand the coverage of Regulation Q ceiling rates to MMFs. That response ignores the many other forms of STIPs that are either perfect or close substitutes to MMFs. If binding Regulation Q ceiling rates were placed on MMFs, the major effect would probably simply be to shift funds from MMFs to other forms of STIPs. For instance, for bank trust departments STIFs are virtually perfect substitutes for MMFs. If Regulation Q were placed on MMFs, many bank trust departments that now use MMFs would start STIFs. Similarly for many individuals STITs are close substitutes for MMFs. If Regulation Q ceilings were imposed on MMFs, many individuals would undoubtedly shift their funds out of MMFs into STITs. As a result STITs would probably develop for additional types of money market instruments, such as commercial paper.

The Depository Institutions Deregulation and Monetary Control Act of 1980 calls for a total phase-out of deposit interest rate ceilings over a 6-year period. Developments other than the growth of STIPs, such as changing regulatory attitudes, may have also played a part in the decision to end fixed deposit interest rate ceilings. However, the view taken here is that even without these other factors, STIPs would have led to the termination of deposit rate ceilings.

The Impact of STIPs on Short-Term Yield Spreads

Figure 1 shows the spread between the three-month prime CD rate and the three-month Treasury bill rate. The figure shows that the spread between the CD rate and the bill rate has risen in periods when market interest rates have been high relative to Regulation Q ceiling rates, such as 1969, 1973, and 1974.

To understand this relationship it is useful to focus on the three investor categories described above, especially the group with sufficient funds to buy bills but not other money market instruments. When interest rates are above Regulation Q ceilings, many deposit holders with sufficient funds withdraw these funds from deposit institutions (i.e., "disintermediate") to invest them directly in higher-yielding money market instruments. Prior to the late 1970's the bulk of such investment was directed towards Treasury bills, because of the much larger minimum amounts of funds required to purchase private-sector money market instruments such as CDs and commercial paper.

The massive purchases of Treasury bills by individuals in periods of disintermediation has driven down bill rates relative to the rates on other mon-

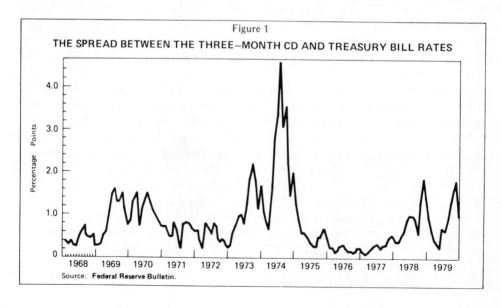

Figure 1

THE SPREAD BETWEEN THE THREE–MONTH CD AND TREASURY BILL RATES

Source: Federal Reserve Bulletin.

ey market instruments. This phenomenon had its peak effect in mid-1974 when the spread between private sector money market rates and bill rates reached a level as high as 400 basis points. The inability of most individuals to meet the minimum purchase requirements necessary to acquire private-sector money market instruments prevented them from reducing this large differential by switching their purchases from bills to these instruments.[10]

The rapid growth of STIPs in the late 1970's (along with the introduction of floating Regulation Q ceiling rates on 6-month money market certificates) has fundamentally changed this situation, because STIPs have effectively broken down the minimum investment barriers that have prevented many individuals from acquiring money market instruments other than Treasury bills. In periods of rising spreads between private sector rates and bill rates, the yields earned by most STIPs will rise relative to the yield on bills. In these circumstances households and all other investors have the option of switching out of bills into STIPs. Furthermore, most STIPs are highly sensitive to yield spreads. Consequently, the aggregate substitution of private-sector money market instruments for bills in periods of rising spreads should be greater than in the past. As a result the presence of STIPs should prevent the spread between bill rates and private sector money market rates from ever again reaching the levels of 1974. The evidence to date provides some support for this view. As shown in Figure 1, in the 1978-79 period of rising interest rates the spread between the CD and Treasury bill rates rose only moderately despite a huge increase in the spread between market rates and the passbook savings ceiling rate.

SUMMARY

Over the last decade numerous types of short-term investment pooling arrangements have emerged in the nation's financial system. These pooling arrangements allow participants to invest a much smaller amount of money than would be necessary to directly purchase the individual securities held by the pool. While the first STIPs were started as early as 1968, rapid growth

---

[10] This explanation for the spread between bill rates and other money market rates prior to the late 1970's along with data on Treasury bill purchases is given in detail in Cook [3]. The explanation rests critically on the fact that sectors other than households—such as commercial banks and state and local governments have been willing to hold bills despite large spreads between bill and other money market rates. This willingness occurs because for numerous reasons other money market instruments are not viewed as perfect substitutes for bills by these sectors. For instance, banks have used bills to (1) satisfy pledging requirements for state and Federal deposits, (2) satisfy reserve requirements in some cases, (3) make repurchase agreements with businesses and state and local governments, and (4) influence the ratio of equity to risky assets, a ratio used by bank regulators to judge a bank's capital adequacy. Private sector money market instruments, such as commercial paper, are not perfect substitutes for bills for any of these purposes.

in STIPs did not occur until 1974. Aggregate assets of STIPs surged from a small amount at the beginning of 1974 to $88 billion by the end of 1979.

Because STIPs generally have minimum purchase requirements of $1,000 or even lower, they provide access to the money market to virtually all investors. This increased access to the money market has had several implications for the financial markets. First, by providing small investors an alternative to deposits, STIPs have played a major role in forcing the termination of Regulation Q deposit rate ceilings. Second, STIPs have increased the liquidity associated with a given volume of outstanding money market instruments. As a result the shares of one type of STIP—MMFs—were included in a redefinition of the monetary aggregates in 1980. For consistency, the shares of other types of STIPs should also be included in the monetary aggregates. Third, the presence of STIPs has increased the aggregate substitution from Treasury bills to other money market instruments in periods of widened differentials between private money market rates and bill rates. This increased substitution should prevent the spread between private money market rates and bill rates from rising to past peak levels.

REFERENCES

1. American Bankers Association. *Trust Software Buyers Guide*, Washington, D. C., 1979.

2. Benston, George J., and Smith, Clifford W., Jr. "A Transactions Cost Approach to the Theory of Financial Intermediation." *Journal of Finance*, XXXI (May 1976): 215-231.

3. Cook, Timothy. "The Determinants of Spreads Between Treasury Bill and Other Money Market Rates." *Journal of Economics and Business*, forthcoming.

4. _____, and Duffield, Jeremy G. "Average Costs of Money Market Mutual Funds." *Economic Review*, Federal Reserve Bank of Richmond (July/August 1979).

5. _____, "Money Market Mutual Funds: A Reaction to Government Regulations or a Lasting Financial Innovation?" *Economic Review*, Federal Reserve Bank of Richmond (July/August 1979).

6. Duncan, Harley T. "Local Government Investment Pools: Potential Benefits for Texas Local Governments." *Public Affairs Comment*, Lyndon B. Johnson School of Public Affairs, The University of Texas at Austin (August 1978).

7. Dunham, Constance. "The Growth of Money Market Funds." *New England Economic Review* (September/October 1980).

8. *Municipal Market Developments*. February 6, 1980. Public Securities Association, New York.